FROM JESUS TO
CHRISTIANITY

FROM JESUS TO
CHRISTIANITY

L. Michael White

HarperSanFrancisco
A Division of HarperCollins*Publishers*

FROM JESUS TO CHRISTIANITY: *How Four Generations of Visionaries & Storytellers Created the New Testament and Christian Faith.* Copyright © 2004 by L. Michael White. All rights reserved. Printed in the United States of America. No part of this book may be used or reproduced in any manner whatsoever without written permission except in the case of brief quotations embodied in critical articles and reviews. For information address HarperCollins Publishers, Inc., 10 East 53rd Street, New York, NY 10022.

HarperCollins books may be purchased for educational, business, or sales promotional use. For information please write: Special Markets Department, HarperCollins Publishers, Inc., 10 East 53rd Street, New York, NY 10022.

HarperCollins Web site: http://www.harpercollins.com

HarperCollins®, ▟ ®, and HarperSanFrancisco™ are trademarks of HarperCollins Publishers, Inc.

FIRST EDITION

Library of Congress Cataloging-in-Publication Data
    White, L. Michael.
        From Jesus to Christianity : how four generations of visionaries & storytellers
    created the New Testament and Christian faith / L. Michael White.
        p.   cm.
    Includes bibliographical references and index.
    ISBN 0–06–052655–6 (cloth)
        1. Church history—Primitive and early church, ca. 30–600.
    2. Bible, N.T.—History of contemporary events.   I. Title.
        BS2410.W47   2004
        270.1—dc22   2004048858

04 05 06 07 08 RRD(H) 10 9 8 7 6 5 4 3 2 1

To

Gwyn W. Shive

. . . for sharing the dream

and

Marilyn H. Mellowes

. . . for the story of the storytellers

CONTENTS

ACKNOWLEDGMENTS

Because this book is the product of many years of research and teaching, many people ought to be thanked, far more, in fact, than space permits. Those few I shall mention here have had a direct impact on the approaches and conclusions reached in this study, even when they might disagree with some of my conclusions.

I begin with those scholars whose work provided foundations for the scope and orientation of this book. A generation of Yale students will quickly recognize that much of this book reflects insights learned from Wayne Meeks both in seminars and in his own teaching. Others will just as quickly recognize Helmut Koester's influence in the geographical and archaeological orientation and in other key details. The result, I hope, is a heightened sense of the social and historical reality of the world out of which the Christian movement arose. As always, a guiding light in my work of examining the Greco-Roman world is my other mentor at Yale, Abe Malherbe.

I also wish to thank my colleagues: first, those with whom I worked so closely in organizing three Society of Biblical Literature research groups: The Social History of Formative Judaism and Christianity, The Archaeology of Religion in the Greco-Roman World, and Hellenistic Moral Philosophy and Early Christianity. Then there are those with whom I have been privileged to serve in the academic trenches, especially at Oberlin and The University of Texas at Austin. I have learned much from all of them and continue to be grateful for the abiding friendships.

Next, I thank my many students at Yale, Indiana, Oberlin, and now at UT Austin, both undergrads and grad students alike, who have been the sounding board in countless ways for these approaches and conclusions. Their questions helped me sharpen not only the "what" but also the "why" and "how" of presenting the history of formative Judaism and Christian origins. Fortunately, the learning never stops.

Finally, I wish to thank several people who have encouraged me to share this story with a broader audience, especially Dr. and Mrs. William Shive, along with their daughters, Dr. Kathy Matthews and Dr. Karen Browning; Rev. and Mrs. Ronald Nelson Smith; Marilyn H. Mellowes of WGBH Boston; David Fanning and Mike Sullivan of *Frontline;* and John Loudon of Harper San Francisco.

As always, I owe an enormous debt of gratitude for their love and support to my family: my parents, Lloyd and Pat White; my wife, Gloria; and my children, Jessica and Travis.

—Austin, Texas
3 May 2004

FROM JESUS TO CHRISTIANITY

CHAPTER ONE

The Story of the Storytellers

Books tell stories. No, that's not quite true. People tell stories and write them down in books. Books record those stories and make them accessible to readers. In that sense they are a medium of communication to a broader audience. Communication is easier when author and audience come from a shared cultural background and time; then it is much like hearing the story told orally. Here the burden is on the storyteller to communicate in words and ideas that the audience will find meaningful.

But books also preserve stories and thus make it possible for later generations of readers to encounter not only a story of a bygone era but also the people who once told *and* heard it. Here the medium of communication is more complex. Now, the reader—not the storyteller—bears the burden. In order to understand the story, the reader must negotiate changes in culture, language, and ideas that come with the passage of time. It is a process of translation from one age to another, from one culture to another, in order to hear the story as once told. At this juncture there are two stories at work. The preservation and subsequent history of the book is its own story, apart from the one on its pages, and the reader must encounter this second story—the story of the book—as well. The reading of any story from the past must respect the different layers of history and story, of *then* and *now*, that make it up.

This book is the story of the origins and development of the Christian movement as told by the people who lived it. It took place roughly two thousand years ago and covers a span of several centuries. It comes out of the history of Israel and the Jewish people but intersects with the histories of Greece and

Rome. The story, at least the best-known version of it, is preserved for us in the book known by Christians as the Bible, and more specifically in the second part, called the New Testament. There are other sources too, but they are not as well known; we shall bring them into the picture as they too begin to reflect the telling and retelling of the story.

Readers of the New Testament today may have a hard time thinking of it as an ancient work. It can be read in English and other languages, and there are numerous "modern" versions that try to make it more intelligible to a contemporary audience. But all of the New Testament was originally written in Greek, the popular form of Greek often called *koine* (meaning "common") that was typical of the Hellenistic age. It was assembled over time, copied and recopied, and passed down through the centuries by Christians. In the Greek Orthodox tradition it remained in Byzantine Greek; in the Roman Catholic tradition it was rendered into Latin; and there were other translations—Coptic, Syriac, Ethiopic, Armenian, Slavonic. Translating the Bible into English came much later and, like German, only became widely used as a result of the Protestant Reformation.

When we encounter the New Testament in English, moreover, we may first perceive it as a single book that traces the story of Jesus, the founder of Christianity, and the lives of his first followers. It begins appropriately enough with the birth of Jesus and continues with his life and death, as reported in the Gospels. Next comes the story of the early church as recorded in Acts, followed by a number of letters written, it would seem, by the same cast of characters— Peter, John, Paul—who show up in the Gospels and Acts as Jesus's followers. On closer reading, however, we quickly realize that this is not just one story; there are in fact four different accounts of Jesus's life—the Gospels of Matthew, Mark, Luke, and John. Nor is it just one book; the New Testament is a collection of books, and a collection of stories. It is more like a library, an ancient library that was intentionally assembled to preserve these stories by and for later generations of readers. Given the more complex and ancient character of its contents, how then shall we go about reading the New Testament?

First, because of its composite nature, it cannot be read like a novel, straight through from beginning to end. The various works represent different genres of literature: biographies, histories, novels, letters, sermons, apocalypses, catechisms, and church-order manuals. They were written at different times by different authors; consequently, there is no cohesive narrative. Even though they were all written in Greek, the language, tone, and style are noticeably different from one author to the next, just as in any library. Hence the various works within the collection must be read first on their own individual terms. Points of connection, comparison, and contrast come later, once we understand something of the origin of each work: where it was written, when, and why.

Second, discovering something about the original author and audience is central to this process. In some cases, knowing who wrote a work and who read it can help us understand the when and why. Conversely, discerning the occasion of a work on the basis of its internal form and language can sometimes help us discover more about the author and audience, especially when those pieces of information are not given, and usually even when they are. The nature of ancient literature requires us to deal with all of these questions in order to make sense out of what is going on in "the story." In other words, we have to employ the tools of history in order to read the story, even when the story is about history or *is* part of the history.

Third, because it is a library and not a single book, we must give some thought to how we ought to "catalog" its contents. On the one hand, we might wish to group the writings by genre—biography on one shelf, letters on another, apocalypses in the back row. Then they can be subgrouped by author. To be sure, this kind of organization would facilitate certain kinds of literary analysis and comparison. In effect, that is the way the New Testament is already laid out. Yet this organization can lead to some problems if we are not also aware of the differences of date and place between the documents. A chronological list yields a different perspective on the writings and how the various parts of the story relate to one another.

In this book, then, we shall attempt to examine the various writings of the New Testament and other pieces of the earliest Christian literature in a more or less chronological progression, from earlier to later. Thus, one of the issues to be discussed at every step is why we should place a particular book of the New Testament at a particular point in time and what other events or writings were happening at that time. For example, although the Gospels come first in the order of New Testament books, they were not the first ones written. Their position comes from the fact that they deal with the life of Jesus, but as we shall see, they were written considerably later. The earliest was at least forty years later, while the last, almost a century. Hence, the way each Gospel tells its story of Jesus may reflect influences and concerns that come from the time of the author and audience rather than from the days of Jesus himself.

That is one of the main problems with this story. We have no writings from the days of Jesus himself. Jesus never wrote anything, nor do we have any contemporary accounts of his life or death. There are no court records, official diaries, or newspaper accounts that might provide firsthand information. Nor are there any eyewitnesses whose reports were preserved unvarnished. Even though they may contain earlier sources or oral traditions, all the Gospels come from later times. Discerning which material is early and which is late becomes an important task. In fact, the earliest writings that survive are the genuine letters of Paul. They were written some twenty to thirty years after the death of Jesus. Yet Paul was not a follower of Jesus during his lifetime; nor does he ever claim to have seen Jesus during his ministry. Moreover, Paul's letters were written not to people who lived in the Jewish homeland or who would have heard reports about Jesus from his own time. Instead, his letters were written to new converts who lived in far-off regions of the Roman Empire, western Turkey, Greece, and even Rome itself. Although they are the earliest version of the story, they nonetheless stand at some distance temporally and culturally from the world of Jesus. Even so, they clearly reflect some information about the life of Jesus based on the stories that circulated orally about him. They are only a portion of the larger story, and yet they each tell their own story.

A Generational Approach

The New Testament preserves a number of these individual stories. It represents layers of material from more than a century of the early Christian movement. It is all the more valuable, therefore, as a historical record, since it preserves the changing story as told over several generations. For this reason, we shall adopt a generational approach to the writings and to the historical development of the early Christian movement. Now the "library" begins to resemble an archaeological excavation, as we dig down through the layers and sift for nuggets of information or buried fragments. We must consider the earlier and later deposits of evidence and how they may relate to one another.

We may think of a generation as roughly forty years, a traditional way of reckoning ancient genealogies. The world into which Jesus was born is, in this sense, the "prior generation" out of which the Jesus movement would emerge. Then come the career and death of Jesus. We shall consider the history, culture, and religion of this period in Part One: The World of the New Testament.

Part Two deals with the first generation. It runs from the death of Jesus, in about 30 CE, to the end of the first Jewish revolt against Rome in 70 CE (for more on dates and chronology, see the last section of this chapter). In this part we shall consider the historical evidence for Jesus's ministry and death, the founding of the Jesus movement and the first oral traditions, and Paul's career. Key elements in this period are the sectarian origins of the movement within Judaism and its first expressions within both Jewish and Greek cultural horizons.

The second generation runs from 70 to about 110 CE and deals with the changes that occurred both within the Jesus movement and outside of it as a result of the failure of the first Jewish revolt and the destruction of the Temple. These "birth pangs and new horizons" are dealt with in Part Three. The earlier Gospels along with some of the other letters belong to this period, as does the book of Revelation. In this period the tensions between the Jesus sect and other Jews were growing stronger, and new questions of self-definition began to emerge, especially in light of increasing contact with Greco-Roman society. The different versions of the story reflect these changing social horizons.

Several writings in the New Testament belong to the third generation, which runs from about 110 to 150. In it we start to see the movement breaking away from its Jewish roots and becoming a separate institutional church, or what we may more properly begin to call "Christianity." We also begin to see other important writings from the generation after the apostles, such as the so-called apostolic fathers, in which issues of church leadership and the relation to the Roman state become important considerations. The other factor that becomes more apparent in this period is regional diversity within the Christian movement.

By the fourth generation, which runs from about 150 to 190, the Christian movement was coming of age socially and intellectually within the Roman world. All the main writings that would eventually make up the New Testament were present; however, there was as yet no New Testament. There were, in fact, many other writings that had come along during the second and especially the third generation, many of them claiming to be from Jesus or the apostles. In light of the spread and regional diversity of Christianity by this time, the question came to be which ones were authentic or authoritative, which ones were to be read or not read. It was this fourth generation that saw the first efforts to shape the New Testament canon and thus produce "the book." Hence, the New Testament is the source for much of our understanding of the development of early Christianity, but it is also a product of that development. That too is part of the story.

Hearing the Storytellers

Over and above how or when these writings came about, we must also consider what was happening to the people who wrote and read them. They are the real-life part of this story; they are the storytellers. So it will become important to discern what they were thinking and saying about Jesus, about their own experience, and in some cases about one another. It is a very human story, after all.

Just as with the documents themselves, we should expect some changes to occur and to be reflected in the writings. For example, the earliest followers of Jesus were all Jewish, just as was Jesus himself. The Jesus movement was initially a sect within Judaism, one of many at that time. Consequently, in order to understand the life and death of Jesus, what really happened and why, we must start with the social and political conditions of Jesus's homeland. Gradually, the Jesus movement began to break away from its Jewish roots, and it eventually became a separate religion of the Roman world. Roughly by the end of the second generation, it had become a movement predominantly of non-Jewish converts. Consequently, there were new social and cultural horizons that came to be part of their understanding of the story. Why did this happen? How did it affect the people who were caught in the middle of this momentous change? Or did they even realize how much they had changed? One of the most dramatic parts of the story is the changing relations between the Jesus movement and its parent religion, Judaism.

As we have already said, the New Testament is not one continuous story, like a novel or a biography; there is no single narrative. Nor is there a single narrator, a single history to be told. Rather, we begin to realize that the dynamism of the Jesus movement and even its complex textures and changes are reflected in its stories. There are many stories and many voices to be heard.

Some basic human traits can be seen in the experience of those earliest followers of the Jesus movement who first told and retold the story. As a first-century Jew experiencing the awesome power of Roman rule, Jesus himself can be seen as narrating a story, or vision if you will, of how God's plan for Israel was to be carried out. But was he an apocalyptic firebrand or a social critic? There were differences of opinion even then. When he was executed by the Romans, however, the story changed. The story was not only the one he told, but the one told about him and what he stood for. Then some began to ask: How? Why? Me too? For us? Even then, the reactions reverberated through centuries of Jewish experience, and the natural recourse was to the Jewish scriptures, especially the Psalms. The vocabulary that grounded their stories came from a stock of songs, symbols, and expressions ingrained through cultural memory: "By the rivers of Babylon, there we sat down and wept . . . ," "The Lord is my shepherd . . . ," "My God, my God, why have you forsaken me?" (Pss. 137:1; 23:1; 22:1). Tradition and experience were mediated by storytelling.

The medium of storytelling was predominantly oral, especially in the earliest days of the Jesus movement. That may be the reason we have no writings from Jesus himself or from any of his followers for at least twenty years. The stories were first passed on by word of mouth. Even when stories were first written down, the mode of expression was essentially oral in character. Ancient letters and books were meant to be read aloud, as if hearing the living voice of the writer. The types of writing reflected these different forms or contexts of expression. Detecting these differences can be very important to our understanding of both what is being said and why. Hence, the social location and cultural horizons of the storyteller and the audience are important clues to meaning, intent, and understanding.

When the social location changes, so do the forms of expression and the cultural resonances. Jesus and his first followers spoke Aramaic, the common Semitic language of the Middle East in that day. Proper Hebrew, the language of most of their scriptures, was largely unknown and certainly unspoken, except by a very few. But apart from meager glimpses of Aramaic, the language of most early Christians, like that of many other Jews, was predominantly Greek. Greek was the primary language of Roman administration and civic life in the eastern part of the empire, especially in the larger cities like Alexandria, Antioch, and Ephesus. All the documents of the New Testament and most of the other early literature were in Greek. Of course, people could still look to the Jewish scriptures, since these too had been translated into Greek, but even so there was a noticeable change in cultural outlook that showed through. What difference did it make when Paul summoned up Stoic maxims alongside Jewish traditions or when Acts recounted Paul's preaching among the Greek philosophers in the Athenian agora? What difference did it make when the stories of Peter and Paul came finally to Rome?

So another factor that affected the way the stories were told is the spread of the Jesus movement into various parts of the Roman world. It produced literary trajectories as older forms of the story were retold in new situations. Sometimes we can even track the pathways of the spread by tracing these literary trajectories. At the same time, retelling the story for new audiences inevitably brought other changes as elements of local culture or native dialects filtered into the telling. Although Roman rule facilitated travel to far-flung regions, Christian communities in some localities developed in marked isolation from other Christian communities. The result was growing diversity from region to region within Christianity. Now there were new voices to be heard: Clement,

Ignatius, Thomas, Hermas, Marcion, and more. As time went on, diversity became more and more of an issue as some Christians, at least, realized they were not all telling the same story. Now new questions began to be asked: about the nature of the scriptures, the sources of authority, and the shape of canon. Even then, they were trying to tell the story. And we are trying to tell theirs.

A Note on Dates and Chronology

Although we focus on the first two centuries of the common era, it is necessary to look at a broader span of time in order to understand the historical backgrounds of the Greco-Roman world and of early Judaism. On the other end, we shall also be drawing from early Christian sources that go beyond the New Testament, and some that even go beyond the year 200 CE. The church historian Eusebius, bishop of Caesarea, who wrote in the early fourth century (ca. 310–24 CE), is an important resource, since he collects and preserves many early Christian writings that are otherwise now lost. Even so, the use of these later writers or fragmentary sources requires that we be careful about matters of historical reliability and chronology. For example, Eusebius frequently retrojects aspects of Christian organization, thought, or tradition that had evolved by his day back onto the early period when such things did not necessarily exist. So these written sources, although valuable, must be used with critical discernment, just like all our ancient sources.

Also, within our overall generational framework, I have attempted to move more or less chronologically while at the same time keeping related materials or regional developments together. At times, mostly in Parts Four and Five, this means that within a particular chapter we will follow a trajectory of development that carries us ahead, in some cases perhaps into the next generation. Then in a subsequent chapter we will retrace our steps a bit to pick up a parallel line of development relating to a different aspect. For this reason, I have generally kept most of the issues relating to the emerging institutional organization of the church in Part Four while treating most issues concerning scriptures and canonization in Part Five, even though both sets of issues bridge the third and fourth generations.

PART ONE

The World of the New Testament

CHAPTER TWO

Entering the World of Jesus

In those days a decree went out from Emperor Augustus that all the world should be registered. This was the first [census] registration and was taken while Quirinius was governor of Syria. All went to their own towns to be registered. Joseph also went from the town of Nazareth in Galilee to Judea, to the city of David called Bethlehem, because he was descended from the house and family of David. He went to be registered with Mary, to whom he was engaged and who was expecting a child. While they were there . . . (Luke 2:1–6)

The story of Jesus and his followers cannot be adequately understood apart from the world in which they lived. It was a world ruled by Rome. Jesus was born during the reign of the emperor Augustus (29 BCE–14 CE) and died under his successor, Tiberius (14–37 CE). He was executed at the hands of a Roman governor named Pontius Pilate, who ruled Judea from 26 to 36 CE. How Rome came to be so central to this story is one of the intriguing aspects of both Roman and biblical history. Indeed, Rome's rise to power and the lives of such greats as Julius Caesar, Cleopatra, Mark Antony, and Augustus all intersect at one time or another with events in the tiny Middle Eastern kingdom of Judea. The architect of these political fortunes was for the most part Herod the Great. Even Shakespeare could not have asked for a juicier plot. By the time Jesus was born, the political intrigue had settled down a bit, at least in Rome; not so, however, in Judea. The transition to Roman rule remained a bitter pill, made more bitter still when Roman governors, accompanied inevitably by Roman legions, first set foot on Judean soil. The year was 6 CE, when Archelaus, the son of Herod the Great, was deposed.

The story of Jesus also starts under Herod the Great. The usual date for Jesus's birth is now typically placed between 7 and 4 BCE. This conclusion is based on the fact that the Gospels of Matthew (2:1) and Luke (1:5) both place the birth of Jesus during the reign of Herod the Great, who died in March of 4 BCE. In addition, Matthew 2:19–22 shows that the birth occurred at least a few years before Herod's death. Joseph and Mary are reported to have taken the infant Jesus away to Egypt, only to return after Herod's death and during the reign of his son Archelaus. That would place their return to Judea and eventual settlement in Galilee between 4 BCE and 6 CE.

Our major source for this period is the Jewish historian Josephus, who tells us that Archelaus was ultimately deposed in 6 CE and Judea was annexed to the province of Syria.[1] Syria was at that point being governed by the proconsul P. Sulpicius Quirinius. This Quirinius was ordered by the emperor to assess and liquidate the estates of Archelaus and to census the people of Judea for tax purposes. Then a lower-ranking procurator, Coponius, was sent to manage Judea while answering directly to Quirinius.[2] Direct Roman rule had come to Judea for the first time.

As long as Herod or one of his heirs was on the throne of Judea, there was no reason to conduct a census. The king alone was responsible for the taxes owed to Rome; how they were collected did not concern the emperor. The census was thus a new imposition in 6 CE, a visible sign that Rome was now directly in charge. Josephus tells us that this census was the spark that set off the first wave of anti-Roman rebellion, led by a famous local chieftain named Judas the Galilean. Josephus also identifies this same Judas as the founder of the Zealot movement, which eventually prompted the outbreak of the first revolt against Rome some sixty years later (66–70 CE).[3] The transition to direct Roman rule that occurred during Jesus's childhood had a far-reaching impact on the politics as well as the religious climate of Judea for years to come. Both rabbinic Judaism and the emergent Jesus movement were products of this turbulent period.

The rebellion led by this Judas the Galilean "in the days of the census" is also mentioned in the New Testament in Acts 5:37. Yet the same author who wrote both Acts and the Gospel of Luke inexplicably places the birth of Jesus at the time of the census of Quirinius (Luke 2:2), and thus *well after* the death of Herod, a discrepancy to which we shall return later in this chapter (see Box 2.5). In fact, Jesus would have been about twelve years old at the time of the census (cf. Luke 2:41–52). Jesus himself would eventually be a victim of the spiral of violence that accompanied direct Roman rule; Pontius Pilate apparently thought he was just another one of those Galilean rebels. There are, therefore, numerous historical wrinkles to this complex and fascinating story.

Pax Romana: The Political Realm

The world into which Jesus was born was complex politically as well as culturally. Jesus was Jewish—as was King Herod—but neither would have been considered in the mainstream of Jewish culture and religion, if it is even possible to speak of a "mainstream." The Jewish homeland was religiously diverse and socially stratified. By birth Herod was Idumean, a descendant of the ancient Edomites who lived around the southern end of the Dead Sea. His grandfather had converted to Judaism after their territory had been annexed to Judea in the first century BCE. Jesus came from the Galilee, a region on the fringes only recently "converted" to Judaism but still with a large population of non-Jews. From Jerusalem, the center of Jewish culture, both would have appeared somewhat marginal, although few would have dared say so to Herod. The dominant political power, however, was Rome, which came with an entirely different set of religious myths and cultural ideals. Rome was entering its heyday of political and cultural domination, under the first emperor, Caesar Augustus. Inscriptions, coins, and popular literature spelled it out: this was the new golden age of Rome, and Augustus was the shining beacon of Rome's power and prestige. The slogan was "Pax Romana" ("Roman Peace") or "Pax Augusta" ("Augustan Peace").

Magicians, Messiahs, and Prophets

In order to understand the life of Jesus and the beginnings of the movement that galvanized around him, we must first understand some of the political, social, and religious conditions that were operating at that time. Jesus did not appear as the founder of a new religion, and what we now know as Christianity did not exist for perhaps two generations after his death. Jesus was a Jew, and the Jesus movement originated as a Jewish sect. Both were products of the historical age and the social environment out of which they came.

During his own lifetime, it seems, Jesus was viewed as some sort of charismatic preacher by some and as a magician or miracle worker by others. They thought of him as an Elijah or one of the prophets of old who performed miracles and spoke in the name of the Lord. Like Martin Luther King Jr., perhaps, or Mohandas Gandhi, prophets can also be thought of as emblematic figures who voice the cries and dreams of a whole generation and are martyred for living out their ideals. Killing the prophet does not kill the dream.

Some thought Jesus was the *messiah*, a king like David of old, reborn to lead the nation of Israel. To others he was perhaps one of several messianic figures, one in the crowd. To others still he was just one in a long line of pretenders. We hear of many charlatans and false prophets from Josephus. All in all, the problem was that no matter how he was perceived at the time, Jesus was not the only one. There were many with competing claims of truth, inspiration, and power in the days of Jesus. The arrival of several such figures who attracted large popular followings around them—and this would include John the Baptist—arose from the same political and religious forces. Those forces gave rise to numerous other religious sects and political parties within first-century Judaism. In this period of dynamic political and cultural upheaval we encounter the context for both the historical Jesus and the way he was perceived and remembered by his followers, the first Christians.

Religion and Culture: Planes of Reference

In order for us to understand how Jesus and the Christian movement arose out of this complex environment, we must be able to examine two intersecting areas of historical development: first, the sociopolitical conditions and, second, the religious thought and institutions. Religious ideas, even those that in retrospect seem to have "changed the world," do not emerge in a vacuum, not in the ancient world and not now. Rather, they are responses to existing conditions and concerns; they are articulated in language that their contemporaries would understand. As we have already begun to glimpse, the religious and social conditions in Jesus's homeland were further complicated by outside political and religious influences coming from the broader Roman Empire. Consequently we should begin to think of the historical development in terms of a complex set of interactions ranging across broader and narrower planes of reference.

The Jesus movement, like other Jewish sects, began strictly within the framework of Palestinian Judaism, which in turn had already been influenced by Greek culture and thought. The eventual growth and success of Christianity, however, depended on its acceptance within the larger Roman Empire. In each one there was a dominant cultural ethos, or what some would call its "moral world,"[4] that informed the thoughts and lives of individuals over many generations. Religious ideas, social values, ethics, and even politics were governed by these basic forces that combine to form what we typically call "culture."

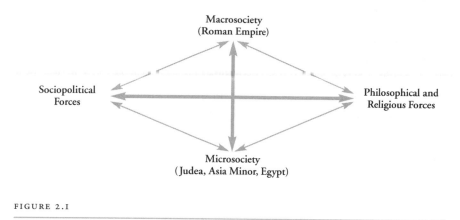

FIGURE 2.1

Religion, society, and culture: planes of reference.

Our planes of reference are represented in Fig. 2.1. On one axis we must consider the broader and narrower planes of society; these range from the macro level, the Roman Empire, to the micro level, the local culture of Judea, Asia Minor, or Egypt. Although Rome's power and influence penetrated throughout, local traditions and religions continued to thrive and to inform the lives and hopes of everyone, villagers and aristocrats alike.

On the other axis the spectrum runs from sociopolitical and legal matters to philosophical and religious ideas. The planes of reference intersect and become mutually interactive. Each node of culture interacts and influences the others. Like a pebble thrown into a pool of water, the ripple effects of one event will be felt elsewhere. Although this is perhaps an overly simplified way of visualizing the dynamics of culture in the Greco-Roman and early Jewish world, it will be helpful to remember that each one of these areas is at work in any given situation or writing, whether it be the execution of Jesus by Roman authorities in Jerusalem or Paul's preaching about the death of Jesus in Athens, the philosophical capital of the ancient world. Gauging the points of interplay will become increasingly important for further study.

Judaism in Transition (300 BCE–200 CE)

One problem that often occurs when people approach the world of Jesus is that they assume the political and religious climate was essentially the same as that of ancient Israel. Nothing could be farther from the truth. The kingdom of David and Solomon had long since passed away, and the "golden age" of Israel, if there really was one, was long gone. Yet romantic ideas of Israel's past glory and future hopes were very much alive. The political changes that occurred after ancient Israel fell to the Babylonians in 586 BCE were far-reaching, but, if anything, the religious changes were even greater. Indeed, the two go together and are mutually reinforcing catalysts to change. From the time that those Babylonian conquerors forced Israel's leading citizens into exile to the age of Rome, the Judean state and Jewish religion were in constant flux due to the external political forces. The responses were as much religious as political, and in the process new religious ideas, groups, and practices resulted within the broad spectrum of what we may call "formative Judaism."

Thus, as a starting point we must be aware of the theological conditioning that is often at work in the way both Jews and Christians have traditionally viewed Jewish history in the first century CE. One of the difficulties is that the emphasis on continuity—on seeing an unbroken line of tradition from ancient Israel to Jesus or the rabbis—tends to gloss over key events or changes in the history. It is as if one could jump directly from the prophets, such as Isaiah, who lived well before the Babylonian exile, to the second century CE without considering any intervening historical developments and influences.

In fact, the entire period from 300 BCE to 200 CE was one of great change and upheaval in the development of Jewish life and culture. New patterns of belief, social organization, and religious practice would emerge during this period. Various terms are used to describe this historical epoch and its significance: Second Temple period, "early" or "middle" Judaism, "postbiblical" Judaism, and the like. Unfortunately, all of these are somewhat inappropriate. Perhaps it is best simply to call it formative Judaism. Indeed, this is the period during which Judaism takes the forms that come down to modern times. Moreover, during this period two new sectarian movements arose within Judaism. One became rabbinic Judaism; the other became Christianity. Thus, the beginnings of the Christian movement, including its founding figure, Jesus, are also a part of the story of formative Judaism, even though they would eventually go their separate ways.

The Dynamics of Change: Crisis and Response

Two points need to be stressed even in a cursory survey of this period of Jewish history. The first is that Jewish religion and culture were extremely diverse; the second, that Jewish religion and culture were undergoing considerable change. Some scholars recently have chosen to speak of the *Judaisms* of this period,[5] so different are some of its groups and forms. But it is precisely this picture of bubbling change, infused with incendiary utopian religious expectations and social upheaval, that is crucial for understanding the world in which the figure of Jesus emerged.

Four Major Crises

Perhaps the best way to encapsulate the complex history of this period is to think of it in terms of a series of political crises that were met with (and sometimes fueled by) religious responses. The four crises are easily identified by outbreaks of war that centered in and around Jerusalem itself. Each one was a monumental event in its own way, but there were also interconnections among them, especially the last three. Of these, one, the first Jewish revolt against Rome, will demand a more detailed discussion later, but for now we may summarize as follows in Box 2.1.

Responses: The Religious and Social Impact

The change and upheaval that accompanied the sequence of crisis events in Box 2.1 cannot be underestimated in giving a new shape and spirit to Jewish culture in the homeland. They also had a marked impact on Jews of the time living in other parts of the Mediterranean and Near Eastern world, or what is called the *Diaspora* (literally meaning "dispersion"). We may summarize some of the major results with regard to their social, political, and religious impact below. (Most aspects that pertain to the situation in Jesus's time will be treated in greater detail in Chapter 4.) They all reflect a gradual and interrelated process in the development of Judaism that must be taken into account. The tendencies sketched out below were dynamic and mutually interactive. Each new crisis was predicated in part on the response to the previous one, so the effects in each of the following areas were cumulative.

Outside Political Domination

From the Babylonian period on, despite a few phases of relative independence, Judah (later called Judea or Palestine) was under the political domination of succeeding world powers out to build empires in the eastern Mediterranean. First came the Persians, then Alexander the Great and his successors (the Ptolemies and Seleucids), and finally the Romans. Changing political and social structures as well as cultural imperialism forced adaptation and response. Yet an ongoing sense of being destined for independent self-rule under a religious hegemony continued to resurface in Jewish expectation.

BOX 2.1
Four Major Crises in Formative Judaism

1. Destruction of the First Temple and Babylonian Exile: 586 BCE

The destruction of the First Temple and the exile to Babylon really spell the end of the ancient nation of Israel. The Kingdom of Judah was dissolved and with it the throne of David and Solomon. The Persians then conquered the Babylonians in 539 BCE, making both the former region of Judah and the captured Israelites (or "Judahites") vassals. Although not all Israelites were taken captive, a core group that had gone to Babylon would return under Persian rule to reestablish the Temple at Jerusalem. This is the beginning of what is called the Second Temple period in Jewish history. During this period of Persian rule a number of reforms and new social organizations were instituted, including a new priestly organization of the Temple and the beginnings of a rift with other indigenous Israelites of the region, notably those later known as the Samaritans.

2. Hellenistic Crisis and Maccabean Revolt: 167–164 BCE

Alexander the Great conquered the last Persian king in 331 BCE, thus bringing the Jewish province of Judah under the control of Greek empires. In 198 BCE, Judea came under control of the Seleucid kingdom, the Hellenistic monarchy of Syria. This shift to Seleucid control produced new social and religious tensions, even though the culture remained Greek. In 167 BCE these tensions erupted in the Maccabean revolt, after the Greek king of Syria, Antiochus IV, desecrated the Jerusalem Temple. What followed were several years of guerrilla warfare until the Jewish partisans, led by Judas the Maccabee ("the Hammer"), managed to recapture and rededicate the Temple. It was commemorated in the books of the Maccabees and by the introduction of Hanukkah to celebrate the rededication of the Temple.

The triumph of the Maccabean forces resulted in the emergence of a new dynastic kingship from the descendants of Judas Maccabeus, called the Hasmoean dynasty from his family name. Hasmonean kings ruled Judea from 143 to 40 BCE, when Herod the Great was named king by Rome.

3. First Jewish Revolt Against Rome and Destruction of the Second Temple: 66–74 CE

Herod ruled Judea as client king to Rome from 40 to 4 BCE. The period of Roman rule was prosperous for Judea, but not without internal upheaval. After Herod's death Judea was partitioned into smaller units and eventually brought under military governorship, beginning in 6 CE; it resulted in new revolutionary groups, many of them with strong religious claims.

Escalating tensions resulted in an outbreak of rebellion against the Romans in 66 CE. The city of Jerusalem was captured in 70 CE after a devastating siege, and the Temple was once again destroyed. This event marks the end of the Second Temple period.

The ensuing political and social reconstruction of Judea would result, by the end of the century, in a marked demographic shift to the northern regions of the country. Out of this reconstruction a new group, the Pharisees, would emerge as the leadership in religious and social as well as political matters. This is the beginning of rabbinic Judaism. It is also the period during which the Christian Gospels were written.

4. Second Jewish Revolt (Bar Kochba) Against Rome: 132–35 CE

Even after the debacle of the first revolt, a resurgence of revolutionary nationalism arose during the reign of Hadrian. A figure by the name of Simeon bar Kosibah, but commonly known as Bar Kochba, announced that he was the new "king messiah" of a free Israel and took control of Jerusalem. Roman armies were sent to quell the disturbance and proved to be particularly devastating in rooting out insurgents in the southern part of Judea.

From the middle to the end of the second century the focus of religious and social reconstruction would shift entirely to the Galilean region and to the leadership of the rabbis. Among the leading rabbis of this period was Judah the Prince. Around 200 CE, Judah oversaw the compilation of a new set of social and religious tractates and codes, the Mishnah, for the governance of Jewish faith and life. It was also during this period that the Christian movement would make its final break with Judaism. The two sects would now go their separate and often inimical ways.

Homeland and Diaspora

An increasing social reality that developed in direct correlation with this dominance by imperial powers was that a growing proportion of the Jewish population lived outside the traditional homeland, in what would become known as the Diaspora. Conversely, there were sizable populations of non-Jews who lived in the homeland. The borders of Judea were expanded and reapportioned, especially under Roman rule. After the revolts against Rome, the majority of Jewish people lived in the Diaspora, primarily in larger cities all the way from the Persian Gulf to Spain. Although Jews maintained ties with the homeland and felt a strong sense of

Jewish identity, the social impact of the Diaspora was significant, especially in language and cultural influences, or what we will call "social location." The Diaspora added yet another dimension to a growing sense of diversity in Jewish culture.

Reforming Movements Undertaken with Religious Motivation

From the time that a small group of exiles returned from Babylon to Jerusalem in the sixth century BCE there was an increasing tendency for religiously motivated reform movements. It began with a reorganization of the priestly leadership and the governance of the Second Temple based on ideals of the Babylonian Jews (as is expressed, for example, in the figures and books of Ezekiel and Ezra) and with calls by self-professed prophets to reform social life (for example, in Malachi, Zechariah, and the so-called Third Isaiah [Isaiah 56–66]).[6]

Increasing Tendencies Toward Sectarianism

New and more radical forms of Jewish piety arose, with the result that there was an increasing polarization along political, socioeconomic, and ethnocultural lines. Yet these differences were often expressed in terms of religious or theological understanding. So, for example, in the eyes of some, the Hasmonean dynasty was an oppressive regime that promoted Hellenistic acculturation rather than resisting it. Thus, by the early Roman period one heard of numerous rival groups—Sadducees, Hasidim, Pharisees, Herodians, Essenes, and others. Some of these (notably the Essenes) are properly thought of as religious sects; others (such as the so-called Herodians) were more like political partisans; and still others were never really organized movements at all. Most Judeans did not belong to any of these groups, even though they considered themselves thoroughly Jewish. In the end, this frenzied diversity and sectarianism gave way to a new sense of uniformity as the rabbinic movement grew out of the post-revolt reconstruction. Sectarians became heretics.[7]

Compilation of Scriptures

The compilation of the Hebrew scriptures into what would become a canonical collection commenced in this period. Almost all of the writings—including the five books of the Torah in their present form, the key historical and poetic works, and the collection of the prophetic writings—were actually completed or reedited during this time. In other words, the Hebrew Bible began to take on its present content and shape—whether Jewish or Christian—precisely during this period of crisis and transition. It is significant, therefore, to note that some of these later developments had a profound and direct influence on the content and shape of those scriptures.[8]

The scriptures were also translated, primarily into Greek, for Jews of the Diaspora. At the same time, new writings were produced in increasing numbers and in several different languages. Many of these writings claimed a "scriptural" authority or legacy by assuming the name of an ancient figure such as Enoch, Daniel, Isaiah, Abraham, or Moses. This proliferation of literature, usually referred to as the Apocrypha and Pseudepigrapha,[9] shows an increasing intellectual vitality in Jewish culture and piety. At the same time these writings reflect other (especially Hellenistic) cultural influences and new modes of literary expression (most notably the rise of the apocalyptic—or revelatory—genre, to be discussed further below).

New Modes of Piety and a Heightened Sense of "Observance"

Closely aligned with reforming tendencies and coming directly from the increased awareness of scripture as a theological warrant for belief and practice was a heightened sense of personal piety. One expression of this tendency can be seen in the rituals and holy days. Some elements of older practice, such as Passover, kashrut (the dietary laws), and even Sabbath observance, were rejuvenated, reinterpreted, or reconfigured. Even circumcision took on a new significance as a mark of Jewish identity after the encounter with Greek culture. Also, new rituals and celebrations—such as Purim and Hanukkah—were introduced during this period. Even so, the Temple at Jerusalem, with its ongoing sacrificial system, remained at the center of Jewish observance and piety. It served as a unifying symbol for both the religious and national identity of the Jewish people. But this very centrality of the Temple meant that its symbolism could produce tensions when one or another of the proliferating groups thought that the direction of the Temple's activities was not in keeping with its sectarian understanding of piety.

A Sense of Destiny and History Revealed

Another unifying element in the vast diversity of Judaism in the formative period was its positive self-consciousness, a sense of election or "chosenness." Of course, this sense was derived in large measure from the national consciousness of ancient Israel, which saw itself as the people of God. But that consciousness had been dealt a severe blow when, contrary to divine promises, both the Davidic throne and Solomon's Temple were destroyed by the Babylonians. The theological response to that event was to reinterpret the promises of God regarding the future of the nation. Thus, one line of interpretation took an introspective turn: Has God abandoned the nation? Or was this outside oppression a punishment for abandoning God's way? This response, known as the

Deuteronomic theology, would become important in later generations and in the interpretation of successive crises.

From this reflection, however, came a note of expectation, for it also suggested that with a return to God's way—through repentance and reformation—the nation would be restored. It is this forward-looking expectation that gradually is translated into a theology of history. It also helped to fuel some of the reforming and sectarian tendencies noted above, as certain groups, thinking of themselves as the "righteous remnant," felt that they held the key to understanding the divine will and thus the correct path of restoration. With such ideas, the sense of urgent expectation was fueled by scrutiny and reinterpretation of the scriptures. The other element that emerged closely from this view of a divinely appointed history or national destiny was the theological outlook known as *apocalyptic*. By the second century BCE, but with an increasing intensity throughout the period of the two revolts against Rome, an apocalyptic worldview dominated much of Jewish thought and historical expectations. We will discuss apocalyptic thought in more detail below (Chapter 4), since it fostered new Jewish expectations regarding messianic deliverers.

The Jews Under Roman Rule

The exploits of Judas Maccabeus and his brothers sounded a triumphant note for many Jews during the early first century BCE. It was a time of prosperity and relative security in an expanding Judean state. This was the tone especially promoted by the partisan chronicle of the period known as 1 Maccabees. Written sometime between 104 and 76 BCE, it recounts the benefits of Hasmonean hegemony, a kind of new golden age for Israel. But apparently not all Jews agreed with this vision of the nation, and new opposition parties, such as the Pharisees and the Essenes, appeared during this period. Two notable elements of Hasmonean policy seem to have prompted the most stringent response. First, Hasmoneans increasingly dominated the political structures of Jerusalem through partisan manipulation of the ruling council, later known as the Sanhedrin. Second, and even more serious, they had claimed the title of high priest for the ruling Hasmonean monarch even though the Hasmoneans were not of a proper Zadokite family.

Roman Rule in Judea: Phase I (63–4 BCE)

By 67 BCE rivalries over the succession to the Hasmonean throne pitched the country into civil war, with each of the factions vying for power and influence using outside intervention from Greeks, Egyptians, Nabateans, Parthians, and eventually Romans. Vying for power were two Hasmonean brothers, Hyrcanus II, who was the king, and Aristobulus II, who was the high priest. Each wanted to claim the title held by the other. Finally, each side appealed to the Roman general Pompey, who was at that time in Damascus completing his conquest of the Seleucid kingdom and turning Syria into a Roman province. So in 63 BCE he intervened in the dispute. But the peace came at a high price, for Rome now began to look on Judea as a protectorate. A chronological chart for this period will be found in Box 2.2.

Herod the Great

Following the arrival of Pompey, the administration of Judea was vested in an Idumean prince named Antipater, who was loyal to Rome. His father, a tribal chieftain from the desert region south of Judea, had served as adviser to the Hasmoneans for some time, after the family had converted to Judaism. Pompey made Antipater the governor of Judea as a kind of second in command to the Hasmonean monarch, Hyrcanus II. Soon the rivalries of the Hasmonean civil war broke out once again. Rome was forced to exert greater force in the region. Ultimately the increased Roman presence worked to the advantage of Antipater. At first he assisted Pompey, but later he befriended Julius Caesar, who passed through Judea en route to Egypt. It was on this trip that Caesar met and fell in love with Cleopatra, the last reigning Ptolemaic monarch. By 48 BCE, therefore, Antipater was effectively the real power, and his two sons had been appointed as regional governors. One of them was named Herod.

Not long thereafter, in 44 BCE, Antipater's political patron, Julius Caesar, was assassinated in Rome; Antipater himself was soon assassinated by Hasmonean partisans. With Cleopatra's help, Herod fled to Rome and asked Mark Antony and the young Octavian for assistance in reclaiming his father's legacy. In the year 40 BCE, then, the Roman Senate proclaimed Herod king of Judea. By 37 Herod had recaptured the province and eradicated, or at least neutralized, most of the remaining elements of Hasmonean opposition. In that year he both oversaw the execution of Antigonus, the son of Aristobulus II, and married the Hasmonean princess Mariamne, granddaughter of Hyrcanus II. During the next two decades he consolidated his power in the region and built a prosperous kingdom with numerous alliances. In some quarters he was viewed as unworthy to be the king of the Jews. Nonetheless, he ruled successfully for over thirty years.

Herod, of course, gets a bad reputation in both Jewish and Christian tradition. In part it may be well deserved, for he is reputed to have been ruthless in

BOX 2.2

Judea Under Roman Domination
Some Important Dates

164–40 BCE	Second Hebrew Commonwealth: Judea/Palestine under Hasmonean dynasty (143–40 BCE)
67–63	Hasmonean civil war (between two heirs, Aristobulus II and Hyrcanus II)
63	Roman general Pompey comes to Jerusalem to settle the dispute; Hasmonean power declines
47–43	Antipater I appointed governor of Judea by Julius Caesar
43–37	Judea under Hasmonean prince Antigonus; civil war resumes (Antipater assassinated)
40	Judea placed under Herod by order of Roman Senate
40–37	Herod "consolidates" power
	Herod the Great marries Hasmonean princess, Mariamne
37–4	Reign of Herod the Great as ethnarch of the Jews
ca. 23	Work begun on Herod's Temple (completed 64 CE)
4	Herod dies; kingdom split among sons (see Fig. 2.2)
4 BCE –6 CE	Archelaus over Judea proper
4 BCE –34 CE	Philip over Iturea, the Golan, and Trachonitis
4 BCE –39 CE	Herod Antipas over Galilee and Perea

removing any potential rivals for the throne, even members of his own family. There is no evidence whatsoever that he actually ordered a mass slaughter of children in order to kill the "messiah" (as reported only in Matt. 2:16). Yet he likely did have a hand in the "mysterious" death of at least one of his wives and several of his own adult children. These stories of Herod's monstrous behavior are probably exaggerated from much later and somewhat legendary sources, beginning with the birth narrative in Matthew. In fact, Herod was in many ways a capable, though tyrannical, administrator. But then ruthless efficiency was not a vice in Roman provincial organization.

Perhaps Herod's most important contribution was the economic prosperity he brought to Judea through territorial expansion (see Fig. 2.2), political alliances, and commercial trade. The middle part of his reign saw an unprecedented build-

6 CE	Archelaus deposed for mismanagement
6–37	Judea placed under Roman procurator (military governor; tax census ordered)
26–36	Pontius Pilate, procurator of Judea
37–41	Herod Agrippa I, king of Galilee and Trachonitis
41–44	Herodian kingdom reconstituted under Agrippa
44–66	Judea returns to procuratorial control
54–66	Galilee and Gaulanitis given to Agrippa II
66–74	First Jewish revolt against Rome
70	Jerusalem falls and Temple destroyed
74	Masada falls
74–130	Judea placed under legionary control; province renamed Palestina
74–ca. 93	Agrippa II client king in north
ca. 90–125	Rabbinic reconstruction 1 (academy at Yavneh)
130	Emperor Hadrian visits Jerusalem (plans to rebuild city as Roman town named Aelia after his family)
132–135	Second Jewish revolt (Bar Kochba) against Rome
ca. 135–190	Rabbinic reconstruction 2 (academy at Usha)
ca. 190–210	Rabbi Judah the Prince codifies the Mishnah

ing boom throughout Judea in public-works projects and in monumental public buildings and royal palaces. Two of his building programs are especially important. He built the city of Caesarea Maritima on the coast into one of the most important shipping and commercial centers in the eastern Mediterranean (see Box 2.3). Eventually it became the Roman provincial capital of Judea. In it he also dedicated a temple to Roma and Augustus. Yet Herod was not completely unsympathetic to the religious sensibilities of his Jewish subjects. In about 20 BCE Herod also embarked on a spectacular building program to refurbish the Temple at Jerusalem (see Box 2.4). When one reads stories of the role of the Temple in the events of the first revolt (as recorded by the Jewish historian Josephus) or in the life of Jesus (e.g., in Mark 11:15–19; 13:1–8), it is this massively rebuilt Herodian complex that must be envisioned.

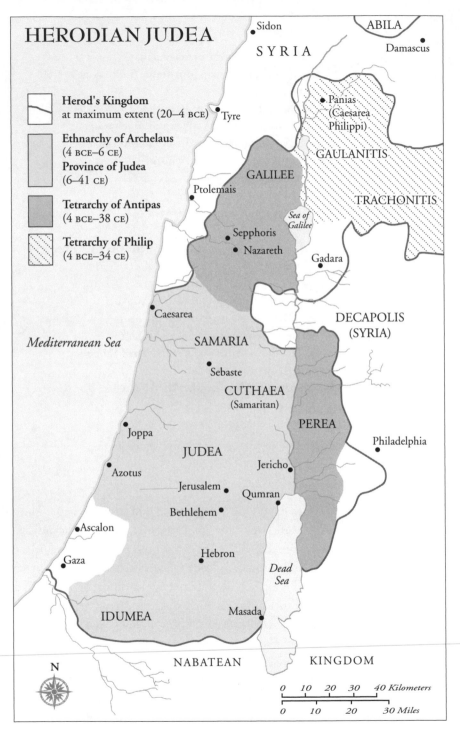

HERODIAN JUDEA

Herod's Kingdom
at maximum extent (20–4 BCE)

Ethnarchy of Archelaus
(4 BCE–6 CE)
Province of Judea
(6–41 CE)

Tetrarchy of Antipas
(4 BCE–38 CE)

Tetrarchy of Philip
(4 BCE–34 CE)

Sidon

ABILA

SYRIA

Damascus

Tyre

Panias
(Caesarea
Philippi)

GAULANITIS

GALILEE

Ptolemais

TRACHONITIS

Sea of
Galilee

Sepphoris

Nazaret

Gadara

Caesarea

Mediterranean Sea

SAMARIA

DECAPOLIS
(SYRIA)

Sebaste

CUTHAEA
(Samaritan)

PEREA

Joppa

Philadelphia

JUDEA

Jericho

Azotus

Jerusalem

Qumran

Bethlehem

Ascalon

Hebron

Gaza

Dead
Sea

IDUMEA

Masada

NABATEAN   KINGDOM

N

0   10   20   30   40 Kilometers

0   10   20   30 Miles

FIGURE 2.2   Map of Judea under Herod and his successors.

BOX 2.3

Herod's Harbor at Caesarea Maritima

During the Persian and Hasmonean periods, Judea was largely landlocked and isolated, since it possessed few or no territories on the Mediterranean coast. In 40 BCE, when Herod was named king by the Roman Senate, he was given a small access to the coast at Joppa. The rest of the coastal plain was

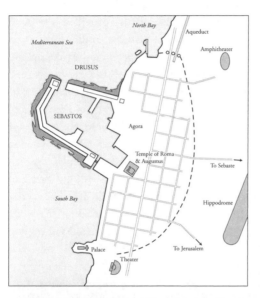

a (left) Caesarea Maritima: Plan of the city and the artificial harbor. (Adapted from Joint Caesarea Expedition by LMW)

b (below) Caesarea Maritima: Reconstruction of Herod's harbor. (Painting by J. R. Terringo; copyright © National Geographic Society)

added to his kingdom in 30 BCE after Augustus defeated Mark Antony and Cleopatra at the battle of Actium.

So in order for Herod to develop Judea into a shipping center for Roman trade, he had to create a new harbor. The cite of Caesarea was a Hellenistic fortress originally known as Straton's Tower. In 22 BCE Herod refounded the city and named it Caesarea after Julius Caesar, Augustus's adopted father. The city contained a Greek-style theater, a hippodrome (or racetrack), an amphitheater, broad colonnaded streets, and a Roman-style central forum (see Fig. a). Caesarea was, in effect, a Roman city. Herod also provided it with an aqueduct to furnish water from the nearby hills of Samaria, and he built a seaside palace for himself. Eventually, this palace would become the praetorium, or government building, of the Roman procurators (cf. Acts 23:35).

The most impressive feat, however, was the construction of the harbor itself, since there was no natural breakwater to protect ships from the waves of the Mediterranean. In order to create the harbor, Herod employed Roman architects and engineers. They used shipwrights to construct huge wooden forms, into which they poured Roman cement made from *pozzolana,* a volcanic pumice imported all the way from the Bay of Naples in Italy. Some of these blocks of concrete weighed up to thirty tons. When finished, these concrete forms were then floated out into position and then sunk some thirty feet to the sea floor until they created the artificial moles that flanked the inner harbor. On top of these moles were then constructed a lighthouse, wharves, and warehouses for the shipping trade.

Finally, Herod crowned his new harbor with a new imperial cult temple dedicated to Roma and Augustus. Josephus describes it as having a golden roof that could be seen from many miles away. It stood in the center of the city overlooking the new harbor, the first thing a newcomer would see upon arriving at Caesarea. The city and harbor were completed in about 12 BCE.

FURTHER READING

Hollum, K. G., et al. *King Herod's Dream: Caesarea on the Sea.* New York: W. W. Norton, 1988.

BOX 2.4

Jerusalem and the Herodian Temple Complex

Among Herod's greatest contributions as king were his extensive building projects throughout Judea, but none were greater than what he did in Jerusalem itself. They began as early as 37 BCE, when he built a new fortress, the Antonia, near the northern perimeter of the Temple. He also rebuilt the Hasmonean palace near the center of the city. At the western gate of the city he added another fortress installation with towers. Herod also added a theater,

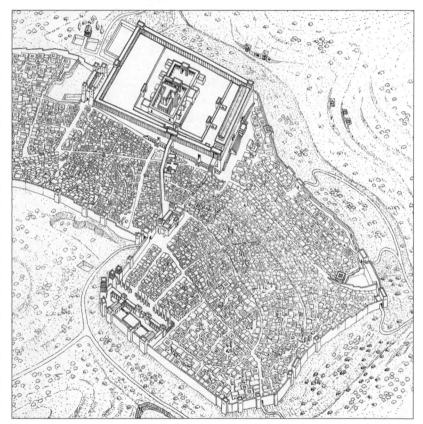

Jerusalem and the Temple after Herod's building program. The Herodian Temple complex is the large rectangular area at the top; the oldest part of Jerusalem is the City of David, which lies on a finger-shaped ridge of land to the south (right) of the Temple complex. Just outside the northwest wall of the city is shown a quarry pit, which was probably the source for some of the stone of the Temple project. Tradition holds that this quarry, with its rugged, "skull-shaped" protrusion, was called Golgotha, the place where Jesus was reportedly crucified by Pontius Pilate. (A reconstruction by Dr. Leen Ritmeyer. Used by permission.)

an amphitheater, and perhaps a hippodrome as well as numerous aqueducts and reservoirs to provide the entire city with water.

His greatest project in Jerusalem, however, was the rebuilding of the Temple complex itself, which began in 23 BCE. So extensive were the plans for the project that they were not completed until nearly eighty-seven years later, in about 64 CE—only six years before the whole complex would be destroyed in the first revolt against Rome.

Herod's Temple project began by improving on some Hasmonean projects around the base of the Temple complex in order to create a large, elevated rectangular platform supported by high retaining walls all around. On top he built forecourts, a basilica, bridges, stairs, ramps for access, decorative gates, and water systems. In the center stood the Temple proper. The outer courtyard was open and accessible to anyone by one of the many ramps and decorated gateways. The Temple proper, however, was surrounded by a barrier wall to prevent entrance by Gentiles into the sacred areas. Herod also paid for renovations and decoration of the sanctuary proper, which were reportedly carried out by priests who were specially trained to do the work. It seems that Herod wanted to make Jerusalem into a showplace of the Roman world to rival other great cities, such as Athens.

For ancient descriptions of the project, see Josephus *Antiquities* 15.380–425; 20.219–222; *Jewish War* 1.401; and Pliny *Natural History* 5.70.

FURTHER READING

Richardson, P. *Herod: King of the Jews and Friend of the Romans.* Minneapolis: Fortress, 1999.

Roman Rule in Judea:
Phase II (4 BCE–74 CE), Herod's Successors

Whatever opposition there might have been to Rome's power in Judea, it remained shadowy throughout most of Herod's reign. It was really only after the death of Herod and with subsequent political reapportionments that a growing unrest can be seen more clearly. When Herod died in 4 BCE, his kingdom was divided among three of his sons (see the map in Fig. 2.2). The region of Iturea, the Golan, and Trachonitis, which extended far to the north and east, was given to Philip, who ruled until 34 CE. The Galilee and Perea went to Herod Antipas, who ruled until 38 CE. Both are mentioned in various connections in the Gospels.[10] The largest and most important region encompassed Judea, Samaria, and Idumea and thus also the two important cities of Jerusalem and Caesarea; it was given to Archelaus, who ruled only until 6 CE. Archelaus is mentioned only in the Gospel of Matthew in the context of Jesus's birth. Matthew explicitly says that Jesus was born while Herod was still alive (Matt. 2:1, 16), and fear of Herod led Jesus's parents to take him away to Egypt (Matt. 2:13–14). Then Matthew says that after Herod died (Matt. 2:19) they prepared to return home but went to live in Nazareth instead because "Archelaus was ruling Judea in place of his father" (Matt. 2:22). All the events in the Matthean birth narrative thus took place before 6 CE.

Apparently Archelaus was inept; he was certainly unpopular in Judea. In 6 CE he was deposed by Augustus at the request of a coalition of the Jewish leaders of Jerusalem.[11] It was the removal of Archelaus, then, that prompted a key shift in the political structures of Judea, since Augustus decided to replace him with a military governor (called a procurator). At this time, then, Judea ceased to be a semi-autonomous client kingdom, or "ethnarchy," and became a province. This first phase of provincial administration of Judea lasted from 6 to 41 CE.

Then there was a brief return to client kingship under a grandson of Herod named Agrippa I. Having grown up in Rome as a childhood friend of the future emperors Caligula and Claudius, Agrippa was eventually given all the territories of Archelaus, Antipas, and Philip, thus reunifying the "kingdom" of Herod. Following his sudden death in 44, however, the entire country returned to provincial status; for the territories of Antipas and Philip, this meant the first time that they had come under direct Roman administration. Later, one of Agrippa's sons, Agrippa II (cf. Acts 25:22; 26:1), was given a small area roughly equivalent to the tetrarchy of Philip, and this was the administrative apportionment that existed down to the beginning of the first revolt.

Despite criticisms of Herod or Archelaus, it was really the shift to procuratorial rule that began to produce greater tensions and social unrest leading up to the outbreak of the first Jewish revolt. Indeed, the reunification of the country under Agrippa I seems to have met with a good deal of popular acclamation, since he could claim direct ancestry from both Herod the Great and the last of the Hasmonean monarchs.[12] Thus, it is after his untimely death that one begins to see increasing political agitation. The two phases of procuratorial rule are distinct both in their effect on the political structures of the Herodian state and in the level of disquiet. The first phase of procurators (6–41) is directly related to the life of Jesus as reported in the Gospels. The second phase (44–66) is directly concerned with events leading up to the first revolt and also with several stories in the latter chapters of Acts.

The Early Procurators and the Gospels (6–44 CE)

There are two key points of connection between the first phase of procuratorial rule and the story of Jesus's life. The first concerns the birth narrative in Luke's Gospel; the second, the event of Jesus's death. The first is more complicated. The key connection lies in the series of events that occurred when Judea was made a province in 6 CE. It was classed as a second-order province under a procurator. The new procurator of Judea was thus answerable to the higher-ranking governor (or "legate") of the province of Syria, since it was considered a senatorial province. As we saw earlier, Josephus says that when Archelaus was deposed, Augustus sent the governor of Syria, P. Sulpicius Quirinius, to liquidate the estates of Archelaus and to conduct a census of Judea.[13] (See Box 2.5.)

Quirinius's census is apparently the event described in Luke 2:1–2, the census that sent Mary and Joseph to Bethlehem. But then these facts produce some problems for two reasons. First, Quirinius would have only been commissioned to census Judea (not the Galilee), since only Judea had been brought under his jurisdiction. Second, it would place the birth of Jesus more than a decade later than the time of Herod the Great.[14] Nor is there any evidence for an earlier census in Judea or for an earlier governorship of Quirinius in Syria. These contradictions in the Gospel narratives are not easily resolved. Even so, the historical significance of this census for life in Judea under Roman rule is telling.

A second result of the shift to procuratorial rule in Judea provides an even more direct connection to the story of Jesus. The key figure from the early phase of procuratorial rule is Pontius Pilate; he was the fifth out of six procurators between 6 and 41 CE and the one to hold the office the longest. He was posted to Judea from 26 to 36 CE and according to all of the traditional accounts was the Roman official who oversaw the execution of Jesus. A recently discovered inscription from Caesarea Maritima (see Fig. 2.3) now gives concrete evidence of Pilate's rule in Judea and even gives his correct military title as "prefect" rather than the more general "procurator."

In addition to their individual connections to the Gospel traditions, these two elements also show the beginnings of political unrest. It is most likely that a Roman procurator would have viewed any political subversion as an immediate threat. This seems to be the grounds for Jesus's arrest and execution. Indeed, Pilate is reputed to have executed Galileans at sacrifice (Luke 13:1). Although this event is not otherwise attested, Pilate's ruthlessness is confirmed by other sources. The Jewish philosopher Philo, a contemporary of Jesus and Paul, specifically says that Pilate frequently executed prisoners without even giving them a trial and was infamous for his general savagery.[15] In one case he was on

BOX 2.5

Quirinius and the Census of 6 CE

Publius Sulpicius Quirinius was from a less than noble family but rose to the ranks of the Roman Senate due to his character, military career, and loyal service to the emperors Augustus and Tiberius. From the perspective of the Roman historian Tacitus, he was a model of duty and honor (*Annals* 3.22–23; 3.48). He was born in the 50s BCE and died in about 22 CE. Aspects of his career are also recorded by the historians Suetonius (*Tiberius* 49) and Strabo (*Geography* 12.6.5).

By 12 BCE he had been named consul of Rome. From 6 to 1 BCE he was governor of the province of Pamphylia-Galatia. He led a successful campaign against the Homanadenses, a tribe from upper Armenia allied with the Parthians, and received a "triumph" at Rome. In 2 CE he was named chief adviser to Augustus's grandson Gaius, who had been appointed commander of the East and governor of Syria.

In 6 CE he was appointed proconsul and legate of Syria and was delegated by Augustus to liquidate the estates of the deposed Archelaus, son of Herod, and census Judea. Judea was annexed to Syria as a second-order province. The account of the census at this time is described explicitly by Josephus in *Jewish War* 2.117–18 and *Antiquities* 17.355; 18.1–4, 23–26; and 20.97, 102.

Josephus's Account of the Census in 6 CE

Now Quirinius, a man of Senatorial rank, when he had progressed through the other magistracies to the consulship, and who was extremely distinguished in other respects, arrived in Syria, dispatched by Caesar to dispense justice to the nation and to make a valuation of their property. And Coponius, a man of equestrian rank, was sent along with him to govern the Jews with all authority. Quirinius also came to Judea, which had been annexed to Syria, to make a census [valuation] of their property and to liquidate the estate of Archelaus. (Antiquities *18.1–2*)

Both Quirinius and the census are mentioned in the epitaph of one of his officers, Q. Aemilius Secundus, who died in about 14 CE (*ILS* 2683). Quirinius's governorship of Syria in 6–7 CE is also documented by coins and other inscriptions.

The Governors of Syria

It has sometimes been argued that there was an earlier census of Judea or that Quirinius might have served as governor of Syria more than once. Neither of these claims has any historical merit. On the first, there was no need for a census of Judea so long as Herod or one of his sons was on the throne. Augustus's census edict only applied to provinces governed directly by Rome, not client kingdoms. On the second, the names of the governors of Roman Syria are now nearly complete between the years 23 BCE and 17 CE. They are as follows:

23–13 BCE	M. Agrippa
13–11	?
ca. 10	M. Titius
9–6	S. Sentius Saturninus
6–4 (? later)	P. Quintilius Varus
4–2	?
2/1 BCE–4 CE	Gaius Caesar
4–5	L. Volusius Saturninus
6/7	P. Sulpicius Quirinius
12–17	Q. Caecilius Creticus Silanus

During this entire period of forty years, the name of the governor is unknown in only two intervals totaling four years. In both cases, however, it is impossible for Quirinius to have been the "unnamed" governor, since his appointments and whereabouts are known to be elsewhere. In the period 13–11 BCE, he was serving as consul in Rome, and in the period 4–2 BCE, he was serving as governor of Pamphylia-Galatia and leading the campaign against the Homanadenses.

FURTHER READING

Brown, R. E. *The Birth of the Messiah*. New York: Doubleday, 1977. Pp. 547–56 (Appendix VII).

Fitzmyer, J. *The Gospel According to Luke*. Anchor Bible. New York: Doubleday, 1981. 1:399–405.

Levick, B. *Roman Colonies in Southern Asia Minor*. Oxford: Clarendon, 1967. Pp. 203–14 (Appendix V).

Potter, D. S. "Quirinius." *Anchor Bible Dictionary*. 5:588–89.

Schmitz, P. C. "Census, Roman." *Anchor Bible Dictionary*. 1:883–85.

Sherwin-White, A. N. *Roman Law and Roman Society in the New Testament*. Oxford: Clarendon, 1963. Pp. 162–71.

the verge of massacring a large group of Jews from Jerusalem who were protesting against him in Caesarea.[16] It seems he was eventually recalled to Rome because of this harsh treatment after slaughtering a number of Samaritans who were on their way to a festival.[17] This event may well be the basis for the passage in Luke 13, perhaps by confusion with another case where the Roman procurator Cumanus (48–52 CE) executed a number of Galileans near Passover time.[18]

FIGURE 2.3

The Pontius Pilate inscription from Caesarea Maritima. The surviving portion of the Latin text reads:

...]S TIBERIEVM
Pon]TIVS PILATVS
Praef]ECTVS IVDEA[e]

It may be translated as follows: "(In honor of ____?), Pontius Pilate, prefect of Judea, (dedicated ____?) the Tiberieum . . ." (Collection of Israel Antiquities Authority; photo © The Israel Museum, Jerusalem)

The further point of connection may be that "Galilean" was at least sometimes associated with rebellion. Again, the story comes back in part to the beginning of procuratorial rule, when Judas the Galilean first began to advocate rebellion against Rome in reaction to the census of Quirinius (cf. Acts 5:37). Josephus calls him the founder of the Zealot movement (the so-called Fourth Philosophy), and his influence and descendants would be heard from throughout the decades and on into the time of the first Jewish revolt against Rome.[19]

The Later Procurators and the Climate of Unrest (44–66 CE)

Although there clearly were tensions earlier, the climate of unrest seems to have been amplified considerably during the second phase of procuratorial rule. Josephus gives a very pointed account of the events of the first revolt. In Josephus's view, the causes of the war were twofold: increasingly corrupt and ruthless procurators and increasingly extreme revolutionary leaders who deceived the populace with prophetic claims while secretly practicing evil. This twin causation is clearer from Josephus's own description. Of the procurators he says:

The administration of Albinus, who followed Festus, was of another order, there was no form of villainy which he omitted to practice. Not only did he in *his official capacity steal and plunder private property and burden the whole nation with extraordinary taxes, but he accepted bribes from relatives of those who had been imprisoned for robbery. . . . Such was the character of Albinus, but his successor, Gessius Florus, by comparison made him appear a paragon of virtue. (*Jewish War 2.272–77)

Similarly, of the rebels Josephus says:

But while the country was thus cleared of these pests [the robbers of an earlier period], a new species of banditti was springing up in Jerusalem, the so-called **sicarii** *[lit., "daggermen"], who committed murders in broad daylight in the heart of the city. . . . Besides these there arose another body of villains, with purer hands but more impious intentions, who no less than the assassins ruined the peace of the city. Deceivers and impostors, under the pretense of divine inspiration fostering revolutionary changes, they persuaded the masses to act like madmen, and led them out into the desert in the belief that God would give them signs of deliverance. Against them Felix, considering this as merely a preliminary to insurrection, sent out a body of cavalry and heavy-armed infantry, and put a large number to the sword. A still worse blow was dealt at the Judeans by the Egyptian false prophet. A charlatan, who had gained for himself the reputation of a prophet, this man appeared in the country, collected a following of 30,000 dupes, and led them . . . to the Mount of Olives. From there he proposed to force an entrance into Jerusalem, and after overpowering the Roman garrison, to rule the people, employing those who poured in with him as his royal honor guard. (*Jewish War 2.254, 58–62)

Now it is true that Josephus had his own ax to grind about the war, since he had been a commander of the Jewish militia but had gone over to the Roman side. Nonetheless, the sheer number of cases he reports shows a steady increase in what some have termed social banditry during the period. A summary of the incidents based on Josephus is found in Box 2.6.

What this survey demonstrates is the diverse but radical array of political and religious activity that proliferated in an increasing spiral in the decades leading up to the first revolt. Clearly Josephus treats most of these as either ruthless brigands or religious deceivers. Yet he shows awareness of claims of miraculous powers, appeals to prophecy, and the ability to persuade a popular following. In recent discussions, there have been attempts to evaluate more carefully some of the lines of this escalating social banditry and to look for both socioeconomic and religious motivations. Under the later Hasmoneans and

Radical Politics in the Time of Jesus
Zealots and Extremists (Based on Passages in the Historical Accounts of Josephus)

1. *Ezekias* (Gk. for Hezekiah): a "robber" chief in Galilee (along the Syrian border); captured and executed by Herod the Great while he was governor of Galilee under the reign of Antipater, ca. 47/46 BCE. (Herod's action brought him favor from the Roman governor of Syria, Sextus Caesar, a kinsman of Julius Caesar.) *Antiquities* 14.158–60; *Jewish War* 1.204–5.

2. *Judas of Galilee* (a.k.a. "Judas the Galilean," or Judas of Gamala): son of Ezekias (no. 1 above); he led revolts in Galilee after the death of Herod and, especially during the unrest arising around the tax census under Quirinius (6 CE), imposed after the ethnarch Archelaus was deposed. He is termed by Josephus the "founder" of the Zealots. *Antiquities* 20.102, 18.4ff.; also referred to in the speech of Gamaliel in Acts 5:37.

3. *Zaddok:* a Pharisee who joined the cause of Judas the Galilean (no. 2 above) in open rebellion against the "slavery" of Roman taxation; he called for a national uprising to achieve independence. *Antiquities* 18.3–10, 23–25.

4. *Theudas:* a self-styled prophet (called an impostor, *goes,* by Josephus) who "persuaded the majority of the masses to take up their possessions and follow him to the Jordan River." Cuspius Fadus, the governor of Judea (44–ca. 46 CE), sent mounted troops to disperse the gathering. Many of the followers were killed; Theudas himself was captured and beheaded. *Antiquities* 20.97f.; also mentioned in the speech of Gamaliel in Acts 5:36.

5. *James and Simon:* sons of Judas the Galilean (no. 2 above) who were tried and executed (by crucifixion, presumably on the charge of insurrection) by the Roman procurator Tiberius Julius Alexander (ca. 46–68 CE). Tiberius Alexander was himself a Jew by birth (the nephew of Philo of Alexandria) who had renounced his faith in order to enter the Roman bureaucracy. *Antiquities* 20.102.

6. *Eleazar Son of Dinaeus:* rebel (or brigand) leader who had been ravaging the Judean countryside for many years; captured by the Roman

governor Antonius Felix (ca. 52–55) and sent to Rome for execution. *Antiquities* 20.160f.; *Jewish War* 2.253.

7. *The Sicarii* (or "Knife-wielders"): a "new" brand of brigand, says Josephus, who became prominent during the administrations of Felix (ca. 52–60) and Festus (60–62). Also, sicarii are credited with the first raid on the fortress of Masada to make it a rebel base. *Antiquities* 20.162ff.; *Jewish War* 2.254–57; 4.400–405.

8. *"The Egyptian":* a self-styled prophet from Egypt (called an impostor, *goes,* by Josephus) who under Felix (in 55 CE) led masses of the common people out to the Mount of Olives, where he promised to show wonders, in particular that he could command the walls of the city to fall down so that they could storm the city (and make him king). Felix dispatched a cavalry unit to attack the mob, and many were killed; however, "the Egyptian" escaped. *Antiquities* 20.168–72; *Jewish War* 2.261–65. Apparently, fears or rumors of his continued activity circulated on occasion thereafter, for (according to Acts 21:38) Paul was mistaken for "the Egyptian" at the time of his arrest in Jerusalem (ca. 58–60) after he stirred up a riot during the reign of Felix.

9. *Eleazar:* son of the high priest Ananias; during the governorship of Gessius Florus (64–66) he set the stage for the revolt of 66 by persuading the priests to refuse all gifts from non-Jews, which meant that the daily sacrifice on behalf of the emperor could no longer be offered. *Jewish War* 2.409ff.

10. *Jesus Son of Ananias:* a peasant who just before the war began to go daily into the Temple and cry out an oracle of doom: "A voice from the East, a voice from the West . . . a voice against Jerusalem and the Temple." He was arrested but released after being severely beaten by the Romans; he was viewed as a maniac, but a loaner and thus no threat. *Jewish War* 6.301–9.

11. *Menahem:* son of Judas the Galilean (no. 2 above) who joined the revolt by leading a band in a raid on Jerusalem after raiding the armory at Masada. Marching on Jerusalem, with Menahem "like a veritable king," the band stormed the palace. After killing some of the Roman soldiers (following their surrender), Menahem became the leader of the insurrection in the city, but he was soon killed by the group led by Eleazar (no. 9 above). *Jewish War* 2.433–40, 442ff.

12. *Eleazar Son of Jairus:* a cousin of Menahem (no. 11 above) who took over the leadership of the rebels during the final siege of Jerusalem and led the survivors to Masada for the last stand (70–74). *Jewish War* 7.253.

13. *John of Gischala:* Galilean rebel leader who came to Jerusalem during the war, creating a second faction. Followers were called the "Galileans." He was captured and executed in 70. *Jewish War* 4.84ff., 538–63.

14. *Simon Bar Giora:* a guerrilla chief who joined the sicarii at Masada and continued to raid in southern Judea and finally marched on Jerusalem. *Jewish War* 4.503ff.

15. *Eleazar:* son of Simon, a Zealot leader during the early stages of the war. Eleazar led the Zealots in a revolt against John of Gischala (no. 13 above), thus creating the third rebel faction in the city. Eleazar led the group occupying the Temple at the final siege but at the last Roman assault he was joined by John of Gischala. *Jewish War* 5.5ff.

even more after Herod, there appears to have been a growing economic rift between the landed aristocracy (including both Jews and non-Jews) and the rural masses (predominantly Jews). There also was a rift between urban centers and rural village life.[20] It was once typical to lump all these rebellious activities together and, based on Josephus, simply to call them all "Zealots." It is the case, rather, that a number of different currents of radical activity are reflected, each with greater or lesser degrees of religious motivation or self-understanding.[21]

Where does Jesus fit in all this? How many messiahs should we expect to find? Some have seen Jesus as a representative of the Zealot movement, while others have seen him as more of a prophet type or a social reformer. Passages in the Gospels themselves can be used to support either view, and it seems that the early Christians often puzzled over the issue of Jesus's own political aims. Although there are distinct beliefs and expectations for the various reformers and rebels, there does appear to have been an underlying urgency for many Jews of that day based on notions that radical changes were about to break into history for the Jewish nation.

CHAPTER THREE

Religion and Society in the Roman World

For a villager from Galilee in the first century CE, Rome's presence loomed large. Even so, it would have been nearly impossible for someone who lived and died in tiny Judea to imagine the sheer magnitude of the Roman Empire. It spanned an area from the Persian Gulf westward to Spain and Britain and from the Rhine frontier in Germany southward to the Sahara Desert. It encompassed the entire perimeter of the Mediterranean basin, while its trade networks extended to Bactria, India, Arabia, and Nubia. Roman expansion began in the third century BCE, but the high-water mark of imperialism was the reign of Augustus (29 BCE–14 CE); nonetheless, the empire continued to expand throughout the first and second centuries CE. The result was a "global economy," or at least the closest to one that can be imagined for the ancient Western world. Indeed, the Greek term often used to refer to the empire was *oikoumene,* often translated as "world" (cf. Luke 2:1). From it we get the English word "economy," but it originally carried the sense of "the managed realm" or, as we might say, "the civilized world." From a Roman perspective it meant "the world we inhabit and control"—our *empire.*

Pax Romana and Empire

Management of so large an empire required an efficient system of travel and communication in order to maintain the flow of goods and services throughout the far-flung provinces. Judea, after all, was one of the farthest. It would have remained a relatively insignificant backwater of the Roman Empire had not

Herod the Great turned it into a gateway to the Middle East for shipping and trade. His new harbor at Caesarea Maritima was a remarkable achievement completed with the aid of Augustus's own architects and engineers. Caesarea was a thoroughly Roman city lying within the borders of the Jewish homeland. That too demonstrates the impact of the Pax Romana.

Roman military conquests and commercial trade helped foster an extensive shipping network throughout the Mediterranean. For overland traffic Rome developed a system of highways that can still be seen crisscrossing desolate stretches of Judea, Syria, Turkey, North Africa, and Spain. Together they fostered an efficient postal system for official and personal correspondence. Along these roads traveled soldiers and merchants to the ends of the empire. With them they carried literature, art, philosophy, and religion. Greek and Roman philosophical ideas mingled with Egyptian, Syrian, Anatolian, Berber, and even Jewish traditions. Egypt was the "breadbasket" of Rome; huge cargo ships annually carried tons of grain from Alexandria to Puteoli and Ostia. Along with them came Egyptian cults as well.

Currents of Cultural Interaction

Two countervailing cultural tendencies accompanied the Pax Romana: as people and ideas spread out from Rome, so also newcomers were drawn to the capital from the conquered territories.[1] Soldiers, merchants, administrative personnel, and bureaucrats (such as Pontius Pilate) went out to manage the far provinces. Educated slaves who belonged to the *familia Caesaris,* or "household of Caesar" (cf. Phil. 4:22), rather than being domestic servants of the palace at Rome, were the civil servants of their age; they served as bookkeepers, scribes, and secretaries in each provincial capital. After their tour of duty was complete, they could retire as free citizens with a pension; many chose to live in the provinces where they had formerly served. Also created were Roman colonies. These included older cities such as Corinth in Greece, which had been refounded by Julius Caesar as a Roman colony; land grants were given to Roman veterans and Italian freedmen to move to Corinth. In turn, the city was to a large extent run on the model of Rome itself. The impulse on the part of these Romans in settling the eastern provinces was to carry with them Roman traditions, ideals, and culture. We may properly call this the *centrifugal* force of Roman rule, as it tended to propel people, ideas, and traditions away from the center—from Rome—toward the periphery. We may also properly call this cultural imperialism.

Traveling in the opposite direction were provincials moving across the empire. The legions often took whole contingents from one province and stationed them in areas far from home. At Newcastle, England, we still find gravestones of Roman soldiers from Palmyra, on the edge of the Arabian desert; following their discharge from the army, some stayed behind to marry and raise families. But Britain was still a Roman province. Yet the biggest draw of all was Rome itself, and the influx of immigrants from all parts of the empire caused more than one old Roman to bemoan the fact that "All roads lead to Rome." Such is the point of a famous barb from the Roman historian Tacitus in reference to Christians. He describes Christianity as a Judean superstition that has even reached Rome, "where all things hideous and shameful from all parts of the world find their center and become popular."[2] We may properly call this the *centripetal* force of Roman rule, as "diasporas" from all over the empire were drawn there, often crowding together in their own neighborhood enclaves.[3] With them they brought their own culture, traditions, and religion, but at the same time they had to find ways to fit in.

From its earliest stages, the Christian movement would also have had to face these same forces. The life of Jesus was set entirely in the region of broader Judea under Herodian and Roman rule. His execution occurred under the provincial authority of a Roman prefect, Pontius Pilate. Jesus was a victim of the centrifugal force of Pax Romana. Paul, in contrast, lived largely in the Diaspora. Although he was also thoroughly Jewish, he spoke and wrote predominantly, if not exclusively, in Greek. The Pauline mission—which would prove so significant to the ultimate shape and success of the Christian movement—relied almost entirely on the mobile population of Greek cities under Roman rule. Paul and Pauline Christianity were products of the centripetal force of Pax Romana.

Pax Romana as Cultural Ideology

Governing both of these currents of interaction was Roman cultural ideology. It is couched in many different terms and symbols of Roman rule, but one stands out above the rest—Pax Romana. Despite their renown as warriors and conquerors, the Romans coveted peace; however, the word "peace" meant far more than just a condition of relative tranquillity or an absence of outright warfare. Instead, it was the code word or symbol for an ideology; it meant bringing Roman culture and administration to all parts of the world. It was a kind of religiously motivated propaganda campaign for Roman life and values.

Yet bringing peace might well mean "keeping the peace" or "pacification," that
is, using military force to put down disturbances or resistance. As a slogan "Pax
Romana" carried many of the same resonances as the American slogan from the
Cold War era: "making the world safe for democracy." It propelled bureaucrats
and traders to extol the virtues of Roman rule in the far-flung provinces. At the
same time it compelled the conquered provincials to accommodate to Roman
rule and mores as well as drawing many of them toward Rome itself.

We get a glimpse of this cultural ideology in the Roman art and literature of
the Augustan age. Augustus stands for peace. So say his public monuments (the
billboards of the time) spread across the empire. Some of this we know from a
series of large inscriptions in both Greek and Latin erected about 13 CE in numerous localities. All of them carried the same basic text, a long official record
of the mighty deeds of Augustus's reign. It is known from its first line as the *Res
Gestae Divi Augusti*, or "The Acts of the Divine Augustus."

> *On land and sea I undertook wars, both civil and foreign, throughout the
> whole world, and when victorious I spared all citizens who sued for pardon.
> Foreign nations that could safely be pardoned I preferred to save rather than
> destroy. (1.3)*

> *When I returned from Spain and Gaul, in the consulship of Tiberius Nero
> and Publius Quintilius, after successful operations in those provinces, the sen-
> ate voted in honor of my return the consecration of an altar to* **Pax Augusta** *in
> the Campus Martius, and on this altar it ordered the magistrates and priests
> and Vestal Virgins to make annual sacrifice. [The temple of] Janus Quirinus,
> which our ancestors ordered to be closed whenever there was peace, secured by
> victory, throughout the whole* **imperium** *[empire] of the Roman people on
> land and sea, and which, before my birth is recorded to have been closed but
> twice since the very foundation of the city, the senate ordered closed three times
> while I was princeps. (2.12–13)*

> *I extended the boundaries of all the provinces that were bordered by races not
> yet subject to our* **imperium***. The provinces of the Gauls, Spain and Germany
> . . . I reduced to a state of peace. The Alps . . . I brought to a state of peace
> without waging unjust war on any tribe. (5.26)*

> *When I had extinguished the flames of civil war, after receiving by universal
> consent the absolute control of public affairs, I transferred the republic from
> my own control to the will of the senate and the Roman people. For this service
> I was given by decree of the senate the title Augustus, and the doorposts of my*

house were covered with laurels by public act, and a civic crown was fixed above my door, and a golden shield was placed in the curia Julia, the inscription on which testified that the senate and Roman people gave me this recognition in honor of my valor, my clemency, my justice, and my piety. (6.34)

The text of the *Res Gestae* reads as though Augustus himself is speaking about his accomplishments, and virtually any citizen of the empire might have been able to imagine him doing so, for images of Augustus were spread far and wide. We find them in Spain, Gaul, North Africa, and far up the Nile, all with the recognizable portrait of Augustus. They were turned out by imperial craftsmen from an official model, but they were paid for and imported by aspiring bureaucrats or admiring provincials aiming to establish themselves as a "friend of Caesar" or "friend of Rome."[4] In Judea, Herod played the same game by establishing temples to Roma and Augustus (see Chapter 2, especially Box 2.3).[5] Some portraits of Augustus were just busts, but many were monumental statues. All were for public display advertising Rome's presence and power. The pose says, "Here stands Augustus—symbol of empire, guarantor of peace." In other cases the pose evoked notions of piety and reverence—Augustus preparing to offer sacrifice, Augustus keeper of the faith and tradition (see Fig. 3.1). His given name, of course, was Octavian Caesar. "Augustus" was his imperial title; it means "revered," "consecrated," or "worshiped," and was translated into Greek as *Sebastos.*

To be sure, much of this sentiment was fostered by and for imperial propaganda. Some old Roman aristocrats might even have sneered in resentment, while quietly longing for the "good old days" before there was a dictator or emperor. Yet even they would have acknowledged the power of such symbols of Augustus for conveying the idea and the ideals of Roman rule.[6] It was, after all, Rome's destiny to rule the world. Rome's sense of imperial destiny carried religious overtones as well. These ideas are well reflected in several pieces of Roman literature from the Augustan era. One of these is Virgil's *Aeneid,* a Latin version of the Trojan War epic. Its hero, Aeneas, escaped the final fall of Troy and, guided by the gods and fortune, finally settled on the shores of Italy. Romulus and Remus, the founders of Rome, were the descendants of Aeneas, and, according to Virgil's epic, Augustus was a direct descendant of Romulus, under the divine guidance of Venus.

Another of Virgil's works also portrays the coming of a Roman "golden age"; this series of shorter poems titled the *Eclogues* has even been called Roman "messianism" for the way it talks about the coming of a golden child to lead the nation:

FIGURE 3.1

Statue of Augustus as priest, with head covered as a sign of reverence. (Rome, Museo Nazionale alle Terme; used by permission of Scala/Art Resource, New York)

The final age of Cumae's song now has come!
The great order of the ages is born anew.
Now even the Virgin returns; the reign of Saturn, too.
Now a new progeny descends from heaven on high.
You alone, chaste Lucina, grant favor at the birth of a boy,
By whom the age of iron shall cease
And a golden race rise upon the whole world.
Now your Apollo reigns.

He shall have the life of a god and see gods and heroes together,
And he shall be seen as one of them,
And he shall rule an earth made peaceful by the virtues of his father.
But to you, O child, shall the earth pour forth its first fruits
Without cultivation; trailing ivy with foxglove everywhere,
The lotus mixed with smiling acanthus.

Take on your great honors—the time is now here—
O dear offspring of the gods, great descendant of Jupiter!
Behold the cosmos bowing with its massive dome—
The earth, the vast sea, and the depths of heaven!
Behold how all things exult in the coming age!
(4.5–10, 15–20, 26–30, 48–52)

Certain references in this poem make it sound like a paean to the birth of Octavian, but that identification of the "golden child" is still debated. It might refer to the empire itself, as the birth of the new "golden age." In any case, as Augustus's empire was solidified, this language came increasingly to be associated with him. The sense of Rome's eternal and divine destiny stands forth; the new age of Rome brings peace and prosperity, at least to those who comply.[7]

Other Religious Implications

Bringing peace and empire, as beneficent overlords, was the Romans' role as well as their right. On the other side, one can imagine that not everyone in the provinces took so positively to Roman rule. The same imperial ideology might easily feel like oppression instead. Such was the case increasingly in Judea, where the memory of self-rule and an equally strong sense of divine destiny fostered revolutionary, apocalyptic sentiments. We shall return to this in the next chapter.

More generally, however, the growth of empire and the movement stimulated by its centrifugal and centripetal forces produced some notable effects in the character of Greco-Roman religion. One of these is *syncretism,* which means a "flowing together" of different currents of thought and practice. But syncretism in no way began with Rome's conquests, at least not where the Middle East was concerned. Syria, Judea, and Egypt had first been dominated by the Babylonians and then by the Persians until Alexander the Great stormed across Turkey and down the Syro-Phoenician coast in 332 BCE. The philosopher Aristotle had already observed the impact on Greek culture, which had previously conceptualized its world on the model of the Greek *polis* ("city-state"). The Hellenistic age produced a new worldview, for both the Greeks and the conquered territories. Following the conquests of Alexander, Aristotle coined a new term: *cosmopolis* ("world city").

After Alexander's death in 323 BCE, his kingdom was divided among three principal successors: the Antigonids in Greece proper, the Ptolemies in Egypt, and the Seleucids in Syria and Anatolia. Especially in the latter two regions "hellenization" was promoted as a way of consolidating Greek rule. Yet in Egypt the Ptolemaic rulers, though ethnically Greek, consciously cultivated elements of Egyptian cultural and religious tradition, which they used to enhance their own prestige. Thus they took on numerous features of the old pharaonic kingship and even co-opted a version of the Isis and Osiris mythology into this new royal ideology. In the Ptolemaic adaptation, Osiris was given a new Hellenistic name, Sarapis, and identified with the Greek god Zeus through a process called *hyphenation.* He was now worshiped as Zeus-Amon-Sarapis. This is the legacy of Hellenistic syncretism, which had already been at work in the eastern Mediterranean for three centuries by the time Augustus was declared emperor in 29 BCE.

The Romans took very naturally to the process and adopted many of the prevailing Hellenistic elements, at least in the East. It is for this reason that we may speak of a "Greco-Roman" world at all, although what this term really signifies is the Hellenistic culture of the East that Rome inherited and further "Romanized." In fact, Greek—not Latin—remained the common language of the eastern Roman Empire down to the time of the Arab conquests in the seventh century CE. Nor was there simply a "melting pot" effect, as some have assumed, whereby local cultures were buried by elements of Greek or Roman culture. Rather, syncretism often took the form of using Greek (or Latin) terms to translate and integrate traditional elements from the local cultures.[8] In Ptolemaic Egypt, local traditions remained strong and substantially influenced both Greek and Roman inhabitants. Likewise, Egyptian religious traditions, such as the cults of Isis and Sarapis, spread first to the Greek world and then to Rome itself. The same may be said for the local cultures and religious traditions of Syria, Turkey, or little Judea, just as Tacitus lamented.[9]

Traditional Religion in the Roman Empire

Naturally, there are differences among the various religious traditions of the Roman world. It has been a commonplace at times to characterize classical Greek religion as more metaphysical and rational, in contrast to archaic Roman religion, which was more practical and legalistic. By the imperial period, however, many of these distinctions disappeared precisely because so much syncretism had already occurred. Roman religion had long since adopted the Olympian gods of Greek mythology by equation with its own deities: Jupiter equals Zeus; Juno equals Hera; and so forth. In traditional Greek and Roman religion, then, the gods were typically associated with governance of particular aspects of the cosmic order: Neptune/Poseidon controlled the seas; Ceres/Demeter controlled crops; and so forth. By specific appellations certain deities were also associated with particular aspects or stages of life: Artemis Lochia helped women in childbirth. Traditional mythology was a means of depicting these functions and inscribing them in the worldview.

BOX 3.1

The Vocabulary of Piety in the Roman World

Greek Term[1]	Latin Equivalent	English Translation	General Usage in Antiquity	Modern Equivalent	New Testament Usage
leitourgia	officia	"service, duty, ministry"	required rituals/ sacrifices performed for civic or sacred duty	liturgy, sacred offices, Mass	Rom. 13:6; 15:16, 22; 2 Cor. 9:12; Phil. 2:17, 25, 30; Heb. 8:2, 6; 9:21; 10:11
pistis	pietas[2]	"faithfulness, loyalty"	sense of duty or devotion to gods, parents, or country	faith, faithfulness	1 Cor. 1:9; Gal. 3:9; Phil. 2:17; 1 Thess. 5:24; 2 Thess. 3:3; 2 Tim. 2:13; Heb. 2:12; 3:2; 10:23; 1 John 1:9
eusebeia	reverentia, religio	"reverence, worship, religion"	sense of awe and respect owed to gods	piety,[3] reverence, worship	1 Tim. 2:2; 3:16; 4:7–8; 5:2; 6:3, 5, 6; 2 Tim. 3:5; Titus 1:1; 2 Pet. 1:3, 6; 2:9; 3:11
philanthropia, philadelphia	humanitas, caritas[4]	"love of humanity," "brotherly love"	sense of civic or social virtue, care for others	philanthropy, charity	Rom. 12:10; 1 Thess. 4:2; Titus 3:4; Heb. 13:1; 1 Pet. 3:4; 2 Pet. 1:7

---

[1] Only the principal noun form of each word is listed here, but in both Greek and Latin there would have been other cognate terms, including verbal, adjectival, and adverbial forms.

[2] Pietas is the Latin word from which we get the modern English "piety" (as shown at note 3); however, the sense of this word in Latin is more that of loyalty and duty rather than a sense of reverence or religious devotion. So, for example, the most frequent epithet used of the hero Aeneas in Virgil's Aeneid is pius, the adjectival form of the word, meaning "loyal" or "faithful." For New Testament usage of this term, listed are examples where the word should properly be translated "faithfulness" and refer to steadfastness, loyalty, or dutifulness.

[3] See note 2.

[4] In the Middle Ages, caritas was the Latin term used to translate the Greek word agape ("love") throughout the New Testament. The usage came into English through the King James Version. See 1 Cor. 13:13.

Piety as Civic Virtue

The other principal function of the gods was as patron deities of the city or the state, and here the traditional myths were closely interwoven with the founda- tion myths of certain cities. Athens had Athena; Ephesus, Artemis. For Rome it was the Capitoline triad, Jupiter, Juno, and Minerva, who were considered the patron deities of the city and the symbol of Rome's identity and destiny. Of course, the other deities of the pantheon were worshiped as well, in their own proper temples and precincts. That was part of keeping the world order. In all cases, then, showing the proper reverence to the gods was required, and this meant the daily rituals of caring for the deities in their temples as well as observ- ing the regular cycle of rituals, sacrifices, and festivals that occurred throughout the year. Extensive regulations prescribed both the timing and the performance of these rituals. Good citizens were expected to show proper faithfulness and piety by carrying out the rituals in a scrupulous manner for the public good. From this practice we derive some key religious terms, such as "piety," "liturgy," and "religion" itself (see Box 3.1). In this sense, a key aspect of traditional Greco-Roman religion—and ancient religion in general—was its civic func- tion. Above all else, *pietas* ("piety") was a civic and social virtue.

The Roman Imperial Cult

The civic function of religion was extended under the influence of the Pax Romana through what is usually called the imperial cult. It took the form of worship or divine honors paid either to the emperor himself or to Roma, the personification of the city of Rome as a deity. It had already begun during the reign of Augustus, especially in the eastern provinces. Remember that Herod the Great built three temples dedicated to Roma and Augustus in his Judean kingdom. Even during Augustus's reign traditional Roman religion would have frowned on declaring a living human to be divine. So at Rome it was more typ- ical to refer to Augustus as *divi filius,* "son of god," with "god" referring to Julius Caesar, who had been deified after his death.

In the eastern provinces, however, this distinction was less an issue for sev- eral reasons. First, in the ancient Near East, notions of divine kingship were more commonplace, as reflected in ancient Egyptian culture, in which the pharaohs were considered to be gods. Second, Greek tradition (in both Greece and Anatolia) also had local "hero cults"; these "heroes" were humans who had been accorded divine or semidivine status for their mighty deeds and great virtue. Third, through syncretism these ideas had already passed into the Hellenistic culture, especially in Ptolemaic Egypt and Seleucid Syria.[10] And last, this Hellenistic appropriation was facilitated by the divine status accorded to Alexander the Great both in stories of his birth and in his status after death.

One of the ways the imperial cult was reflected in Roman religion was in the notion of a divine *apotheosis* of the emperor at death (i.e., deification or, more literally, a "godding away" to heaven). Julius Caesar had been deified in this manner. Imperial art often shows an emperor or empress being carried away to heaven from the funeral pyre on the wings of an angelic figure. Some of the Roman emperors, however, would show even less restraint in accepting or adopting divine status for themselves while still alive. During the first century CE, Caligula (37–41), Nero (54–68), and Domitian (81–96) were criticized for such megalomania, but in later centuries it became more common. In the eastern empire, it was common to incorporate imperial cult processions into local religious festivals and to offer sacrifice and signs of reverence to the statue of the emperor (see Fig. 3.2). In effect, the reverence for the emperor and deified Roma were signs of loyalty (*pietas*) to Rome. Such worship of the emperor, however, would become a scandal to Christians in Ephesus during the reign of Domitian (see Chapter 11).

Personal Aspects of Religion

Jews and Christians were not the only ones to criticize traditional Greco-Roman religion. Beginning with Socrates, Greek philosophers raised questions about the character of traditional piety. Some thought that superstitious appeasement of the gods was irrational. Others frowned on the immoral actions of the gods as depicted in Greek myth, while the authors of Greek tragedy regularly questioned the rule of the gods in human existence. The philosopher Epicurus even denied that the gods of mythology had anything to do with the creation of the world or the governance of human life. For these views Socrates and the Epicureans were often called "atheists"; so were Christians later on. By the Roman period philosophy had become more skeptical regarding traditional Greek mythology and had focused instead on morality and ethics.

Monism and Fickle Fate

Syncretism and the intellectual climate of the Hellenistic and Roman age influenced religion in several key ways. First, there was a growing tendency toward a

FIGURE 3.2

Ephesian coin (early third century CE)
showing an imperial cult temple with a
colossal statue of the emperor inside; before the temple stand worshipers performing a sacrifice while offering a gesture
of obeisance and reverence. (Used by permission of the British Museum)

religious "monism," by which we mean the notion that all supernatural power
comes from a single source. Although none of the philosophers would have denied that the numerous Greek gods existed, some might nonetheless have
claimed that all of them were mere reflections of a single divine nature. Such
was the view advanced by Plato in his late treatise the *Timaeus,* in which he describes a single "mind" that lies behind the created order. Plato even calls it "the
One" or just "God." Similarly, Aristotle referred to "the unmoved prime
mover" as the single divine power originating the universe. Such tendencies toward philosophical monism both facilitated and were reinforced by syncretism
and hyphenation. At the same time, such ideas made it possible for Jews (and,
later, Christians) to accommodate their tradition, with its much stricter view of
monotheism, to the general tenor of Greco-Roman culture. Philo, the Jewish
philosopher from Alexandria, could say, for example, that Platonic philosophy
was entirely consistent with Jewish faith and biblical teaching, at least in part
because of these monistic tendencies (see Chapter 4).

A second tendency influenced by both Hellenistic philosophical ideas and
personal motivations was the concern over Fortune or Fate (Greek *Tyche,* Latin
Fortuna)—what we might call, less grandly, Lady Luck. Tyche was regularly
revered as the patron goddess of cities such as Antioch and Caesarea Maritima.
She was also extolled as the protector and guide of Alexander the Great or
Roman emperors such as Augustus and Trajan. But especially in the view of
Stoicism, which by the early Roman period was the most popular school of Greek

philosophy, Tyche was best treated with caution because of her fickle nature. The Roman geographer and natural historian Pliny the Elder said of her:

> *Throughout the whole world at every hour Fortuna alone is invoked and named by the voices of all. . . . [She is] deemed volatile and indeed blind as well by most people, wayward, inconstant, uncertain, fickle in her favors and showing favor to those not worthy. To her is credited all that is spent and all that is received, and in the whole ledger of mortals she alone fills both pages, and we are so much at the mercy of chance that Chance (sors) herself, by whom even God is proved uncertain, takes the place of God. (*Natural History 2.5.22*)

Tyche was in some ways more powerful than the other gods because she had such a hold on everyday life. She was often depicted as being deaf and blind and teetering on an orb. Although she was able to give gifts—especially wealth and long life—to humans, she did so randomly and blindly. She gave to some and took from others without rhyme or reason, and what she gave she might just as quickly take back again. Of course, this description of the role of fickle Tyche in the human condition went right along with the claim of Stoicism to offer the best antidote by cultivating the proper attitudes toward wealth, possessions, life, death, and ethics.[11] In other words, this characterization of the nature of the problem facing humans was matched by Stoic "preaching": converting to Stoicism is the way to salvation. Epicureans offered a different explanation of why human life was capricious, but the results were similar. Epicureanism itself was the antidote: a mode of living in harmony with nature, yet untroubled by irrational fear of mythical gods.[12]

A Magical Worldview

Most inhabitants of the Greco-Roman world gladly worshiped a wide variety of gods and goddesses. Some were part of civic life and festivals; others were attached to family life and rituals of birth and death; and still others were safeguards against the vagaries of fickle Fate. Temples in the ancient world were places where the gods—or at least local manifestations of them—were thought to dwell. Ordinary worshipers did not venture into a temple proper without a priest or attendant. Nor were the temples used for assembly to worship the god or goddess. Such gatherings, when they occurred at all, took place in the sacred precincts that surrounded the temple. On important festival days, however, the temple staff and worshipers of a particular deity would also take to the streets in a procession—sometimes solemn, sometimes festive—followed by sacrifices, rituals, and even meals back at the temple. It was a grand show, and people might come from far and wide to participate. Of course, the temples benefited too.

Despite the more rationalistic tendencies that one sees among the philosophers, the personal religion of most people, rich and poor alike, was governed by the cycle of observances at local temples dedicated to a plethora of different gods. It was a numinous world with supernatural forces all around, and one dared not show a lack of proper reverence for fear of retribution. Add to that fickle Tyche, and the world became more uncertain and fearful. Thus, the ability to exercise some control over these forces was a major goal of one's personal religious devotion. For this reason, the magical arts—astrology, divination, and magic—were extremely popular in the Greco-Roman world, and we continue to find them in Jewish and, later, Christian practice as well. Each was a specific procedure whereby humans could call upon supernatural forces to help them order life and guard against the vagaries of fickle Tyche. The magical arts were a very prominent part of religion for the people of antiquity. Magical ideas and practices were central to their knowledge and assumptions—combining both empirical science and religious beliefs—of how the cosmos was held together and how it worked. For this reason we may call their perspective a "magical worldview."[13]

Even today, *astrology* refers to the ability to read the stars and planets as signs of what forces might be governing one's life and how one might predict what is to come. Of course, one needed to consult an expert in order to secure the best information. The Magi ("wise men") of the Gospel of Matthew, who followed a star and were warned in a dream (2:2–12), show a positive attitude toward astrology.

Divination refers to consultation of signs in order to interpret current events or predict the future. It took several different forms, and again there were professionals in each of the arts. In general, however, we may break divination into three main types: first, the reading of natural signs such as weather (especially lightning), the flight of birds (called *augury*), or the entrails of sacrificial animals (performed by diviners called *haruspices*).[14] A second type of divination dealt with interpretation of dreams; some dreams were thought to be transmissions or forecasts from the supernatural world. There were even exercises for inducing dreams or visions of the dead in order to achieve certain effects.

The third type of divination was oracles (sometimes called "prophecies"). Oracles were often delivered by professional soothsayers, usually at a particular sanctuary that was thought to have special powers because of its location and its attachment to a deity. Although there were numerous such oracles in antiquity (as seen in Acts 16:16–18), the best known was the Pythian oracle of Apollo at Delphi in Greece. The "oracle" was a priestess who entered a trancelike state during which she received messages from Apollo in response to inquiries made by individuals or delegations from cities or countries. The Roman equivalent was the Sibylline oracle at Cumae (near Naples) in Italy; it was closely linked to the foundation legends and the civic cult of Rome.[15] The Delphic oracle and the Cumaean Sibyl remained extremely popular throughout the Roman period and continued in Jewish and Christian lore, as reflected both in literature[16] and by their representation in Michelangelo's frescoes in the Sistine Chapel.

In the strict sense, *magic* refers to procedures whereby one is able by means of special rites, formulas, or incantations to prompt supernatural forces into action. Ordinary people just called them "miracles" or "wonders." Everyone in the ancient world knew of the many miracle workers and their wondrous feats, for supernatural forces were all around. These supernatural forces were usually called demons (Greek *daimon;* Latin *genius*) and could be good or bad, as with the divine spirit that was said to guide Socrates.[17]

In many respects, demons were to the ancient world what germs are to us today. They were invisible, powerful, necessary, and yet disruptive; when they infected one's body in the wrong way, it caused sickness. So they had to be controlled, or at least managed as much as possible. This is what we call *apotropaic magic;* it used spells and incantations as well as amulets and other devices to ward off demons or, if one was already infected, to expel them. The numerous exorcism miracles found in the Gospels and Acts reflect this type of magic. There was also the healing cult of the god Asclepius, where one could go for medical attention while also making votive offerings in order to be cured of various chronic maladies. Even the Greek word *soteria,* most often translated "salvation," typically referred to such miraculous cures (cf. Matt. 9:22; Mark 5:34; Luke 8:48). It was quite common to seek out special people or places that were reputed to have healing powers in hopes that some might "rub off" (cf. Acts 19:11–12).

On the other side, since demons—not to mention the manifold gods, sprites, nymphs, and other supernatural beings—were so powerful, it was also possible through spells and incantations to employ their powers for one's own benefit or against someone else. This is what we call *aggressive magic;* it often goes under the name "cursing" or "binding spells."[18] It might be used to beat the odds at the racetrack or to attract a lover. It might also be used to sabotage the business of a competitor or to keep a lover from being unfaithful. This was the kind of magic that often gave magicians (*magi*) a bad name in the Roman world, as seen also in the story of Peter and Simon Magus in Acts 8:9–24.[19] Yet Peter's rebuke was a magical curse (Acts 8:20), and even Jesus and Paul employed curse formulas (Mark 11:12–14, 21; Gal. 1:8–9; 1 Cor. 16:21).

Even though ancient magic dabbled in the supernatural realm, it was conceptualized in more or less scientific terms stemming from philosophic naturalism. The Stoics called the mechanism *sympatheia* ("sympathy"), from which we get the designation "sympathetic magic." The theory comes from Stoic physics, in part derived from Aristotle. It argued that the cosmos (i.e., the bounded universe containing the earth, at its center, with the sun, moon, stars, and planets revolving around it) was a giant orb filled with plasma. The cosmos was thus very much like the human body, and as with the body's sensations, whenever a wave was touched off in one part, it would be felt or registered elsewhere. That is *sympatheia*. When projected to the supernatural realm—since it too was contained inside the cosmic orb—*sympatheia* provided an explanation of how prayers, rituals, and incantations could be registered with the appropriate god or demon and cause a superhuman effect. But, of course, it also presupposed that one knew the correct formulas or had access to the secret names and appellations of just the right deity to create the desired outcome. Hence, one of the key elements in all of the magical arts was the knowledge of secret names and formulas. The magician or miracle worker was the one who possessed these secrets and the special powers to make them work.

A good example of the popularity and the practice of this magical worldview can be seen in a document known as the *Paris Magical Papyrus*, which comes from Egypt in about 300 CE. Discovered in the early nineteenth century, it was a kind of magician's recipe book of charms for a wide variety of situations. Some of the charms seem to go back centuries earlier, while others are clearly of Roman date. It thus shows the long history and influence of this magical tradition. Nor is this one book of charms the only such known; the total collection of magical papyri is quite large and ranges over many centuries down to early medieval times.[20] We may look at one particular charm from the *Paris* book; the text reads as follows:

A tested charm of Pibechis, for those possessed by daemons:
    The Preparation: *Take oil of unripe olives with the herb mastigia and the fruit pulp of the lotus, and boil them with colorless marjoram, while saying:*

"IOËL OS SARTHIOMI EMORI THEOCHIPSOITH SITHEMEOCH SOTHE IOE MIMIPSOTHIOOPH PHERSOTHI AEËIOYO IOE EO CHARI PHTHA, come out from NN" (add the usual).

The Phylactery: *On a tin lamella write: "IAËO ABRAOTH IOCH PHTHA AMESENPSIN IAO PHEOCH IAEO CHARSOK," and hang it on the patient. It is terrifying to every daemon, a thing he fears. Then after placing the patient opposite [you], perform the conjure.*

The Conjure: *"I **adjure** [or conjure] **you by the god of the Hebrews, JESUS**, JABA, JAE ABRAOTHO AIA THOTH ELE ELO AEO EOY IIIBAECH ABARMAS IABARAOU ABELBEL LONA ABRA MAROIA BRAKION, who appears in fire, who is in the midst of land, snow, and fog, Tannetis; let your angel, the implacable, descend and let him assign the daemon flying around this form [i.e., the patient's body], which god formed in his holy paradise, because I pray to the holy god, [calling] (more **voces mystici**).*

*I **adjure you** by the one who appeared to Osrael [i.e., Israel] in a shining pillar and a cloud by day, who saved his people from Pharaoh and brought upon Pharaoh the ten plagues because of his disobedience.*

*I **adjure you**, every daemonic spirit, to tell whatever sort you may be, **because I conjure you by the seal which Solomon placed on the tongue of Jeremiah**, and he told. You also must tell whatever sort you may be: heavenly or aerial, whether terrestrial or subterranean, or netherworldly or Ebousacus or Cherseus or Pharisaeus, tell whatever sort you may be, because I conjure you by the light-bearing, unconquerable God, who knows what is in the heart of every living being, the one who formed of dust the race of humans, the one who, after bringing them out of obscurity, packs together the clouds, waters the earth with rain, and blesses its fruit, the one whom every heavenly power of angels and of archangels praises.*

*I **adjure you by the great god SABAOTH**, through whom the Jordan River drew back and the Red Sea, which Israel crossed, became impassable, because I conjure you . . . **by the one who burned up the stubborn giants with lightning**, whom the heaven of heavens praises, whom the wings of the cherubim praise. . . .*

*And I **adjure you**, the one receiving this conjuration, not to eat pork, and every spirit and daemon, whatever sort it may be, will be subject to you.*

The Concluding Gesture: *And while performing this conjure, blow once, blowing air from the tips of the feet up to the face, and it will be assigned. Keep yourself pure [while performing this conjure] for this charm is Hebraic and is preserved among pure men.*[21]

This is a spell for exorcism, the casting out of demons. If a person was thought to have a demon, he or she could go to a magician and purchase this charm, like going to a pharmacist for a prescription. Notice, however, that the instructions are for the "pharmacist" alone; these secrets were not to be given out to the patient.

What is immediately apparent on reading this spell is that it contains both Jewish and Christian language; however, the spell does not appear to be particularly Jewish or Christian in its present form. Rather, it is a spell that calls on the Hebrew God, called variously Jesus, Iaeo, Abraoth, and Sabaoth, whose powers are manifested in biblical stories, as allusions to the Exodus and even pseudepigraphical biblical legends indicate. Here again we find the effects of syncretism. The world of magic was hardly exclusivistic; any source of supernatural power had potential for magical purposes. The name Jesus may appear here because of the Gospel stories of exorcisms or because of the Christian confession that named him son of the Hebrew God. The point is that these stories both function as testimonials to the power of this God and serve as "conjures" to invoke this power.

Note the steps of the procedure. First there is the preparation of a special potion and then a magical amulet to be worn around the patient's neck. Both are given power by the secret magical terms and names that are uttered during the preparation. Then while the patient is wearing the amulet, the magician confronts the demon with the special "conjuring" formulas that are supposed to scare the demon out of the patient's body. Even the words used here are typical of the magical procedure; the word translated "I adjure/conjure" is the Greek *exorkizo* (or simply *orkizo*), from which we get the modern word "exorcism." Again, it is suggestive of the prominence of this tradition that we find the same terms used in stories of Jesus and Paul (Mark 5:7; Acts 19:13; 1 Thess. 5:27).

Gods Old and New: The Mystery Cults

Perhaps one of the most significant aspects of the centripetal force of hellenization and the Pax Romana was the diffusion of "new" religions. As we have already noted, ethnic groups from all parts of the empire carried their native gods with them when they traveled. Official importation of new deities to Rome began as early as 292 BCE, when the Greek healing god Asclepius was introduced. In 203 BCE the Great Mother, Cybele, a very ancient deity native to central

Anatolia, was officially installed in a temple on the Palatine. On the whole Rome was quite tolerant of these "foreign gods," so long as they were the native deities of particular peoples and were not a source of political or social disruption. The Dionysus cult came to Rome in the 190s BCE, and was temporarily suppressed in 186 because of suspicious behavior. Even so, the Dionysus cult continued. Similarly, Judaism was generally tolerated as the ancient national religion of Judea.

Inhabitants of the Roman world were able to tolerate and understand the majority of these new gods through syncretism and hyphenation. Most of these new cults retained largely ethnic constituencies. On the other hand, some of the new cults began to attract more followers from the local population and to become popular across the empire. These are the "mystery cults." Their spread, appeal, and even aspects of their doctrine have been compared to those of the early Christian movement and may help us to understand the religious environment that made Christianity popular.

The Greek Mysteries

The religious tradition associated with the so-called mystery cults actually goes back to early classical Greece. Mystery cults seem to have begun as a local phenomenon, usually attached to a particular site where some important supernatural event occurred and where a local cult sprang up. Several of these were quite prominent from as early as the seventh and sixth centuries BCE. Among the best known are those of Zeus at Andana (near Olympia in Greece) and at Panamara in Asia Minor.

Bacchus, or Dionysus, the god of the vine, had been revered in Anatolia, and later in Greece, since archaic times. Although Dionysiac rituals and mythology were widespread as a civic cult, a form of Dionysiac worship also developed that was particularly practiced among private associations that were still loosely under the control of the city. Eventually this form of the cult began to spread, especially in Hellenistic times, and it came to Rome in 193 BCE. So one might find the official, civic cult of Dionysus operating in close proximity with a more private "mystery" version. The Dionysiac mysteries are also important for their association with some new ideas that emerged in Greek religion beginning in the fifth and fourth centuries BCE. This new tradition is often called Orphism. It used a variant form of the myth of Dionysus's birth to symbolize the human condition and the quest for immortality and afterlife. These ideas were very influential on Plato's thought as well as on other mystery cults.

The Mysteries of Eleusis

Perhaps the best known and most influential of the traditional Greek mysteries were those centered at Eleusis, not far from Athens. They were known far and wide in antiquity as the Eleusinian mysteries of Demeter and Persephone. They were originally a local cult that had been integrated into Athenian civic religion by the sixth century BCE. By the Roman period they were so popular that many notable Roman citizens, and even a few emperors, came to Eleusis to be initiated. When the early Christian missionary Paul traveled from Athens to Corinth in 50 or 51 CE, he almost certainly passed by the Eleusinian sanctuary where the mysteries were conducted, since it was located on the main processional route from Athens. Because of their fame and appeal and because of their initiation rituals, the Eleusinian mysteries became something of a paradigm for a number of the foreign mysteries that arose during the Hellenistic and Roman periods.

The Myth of Demeter and Persephone

At the center of the Eleusinian mysteries stands the traditional Greek myth of Demeter and Persephone known from an archaic collection called the *Homeric Hymns*. Demeter was the goddess of grain, and Persephone (also called Kore, the Greek term for a young maiden) was her daughter.[22] One day while Persephone was out picking flowers in the company of her attendants, the nymphs, she was abducted by Hades (Pluto), god of the underworld, who took her to his realm to be his bride and queen. Demeter, unable to discover what had happened to her, became distraught and wandered endlessly searching for Persephone. She even appealed to the other gods of Olympus to help her, but to no avail.

Finally, traveling in the guise of an old woman, she came to Eleusis, where she was welcomed by the wife and daughters of the local king, Keleus. She soon became the nursemaid to the king's young son. This child she took as a kind of replacement for lost Persephone, and at night she began to make the child immortal by brazing him over a fire. One night, however, she was interrupted by the child's horrified mother; Demeter dropped the child and aborted the process of making him a god. Angry, she then revealed her true, divine nature.

Meanwhile, Demeter's wanderings and her frustration with Zeus and the other gods had caused her to dry up the crops that were her domain. Finally, Zeus relented and convinced Hades to release Persephone so that Demeter could return to Olympus and allow the grain to grow. Before she departed

Hades, however, Persephone was tricked into eating a pomegranate seed, which forced her to spend part of each year in Hades.

In its most archaic form, this myth was primarily etiological; it explained the seasons and the crop cycle. In ancient Greece grain was planted in the autumn and harvested in the spring; the summer months were dry and desolate. Demeter was widely worshiped as both the goddess of grain and a symbol of fertility and motherhood. Sometime in the seventh to sixth century, however, some changes occurred in the myth that reflect a reappropriation of its basic religious ideas. These changes are seen most directly in the episode at Eleusis in which Demeter sought to give the king's son immortality. It has been suggested that this notion was influenced by elements of the Dionysiac/Orphic tradition, and, indeed, Dionysus shows up prominently in Eleusinian ritual and art. The key moment in the new form of the myth is when Demeter revealed herself to the Eleusinians. To appease her, and out of reverence and awe, the king built a temple to her and to Persephone there at Eleusis. In return, she passed along the special knowledge and rites by which at least partial immortality had been given to the child.

By legend, then, this secret information became the source of the Eleusinian mysteries. But there is another connection, for within the large sanctuary at Eleusis is a grotto, where, mythically at least, Persephone ascended from the underworld. Thus the symbolism of Persephone's return to life is matched by the ritual practice of initiation that offers a measure of immortality to the worshiper at Eleusis. Thus the new form of the myth that is directly associated with the sanctuary at Eleusis takes the original vegetative symbolism of Persephone's death and return and transforms it into a symbol of personal immortality for those humans who are initiated into the cult. It is this change that really marks off the Eleusinian mysteries.

The Rituals of Initiation

Two principal rituals were associated with the cult: the Greater Mysteries, which were conducted at Eleusis in September (corresponding to the planting season), and the Lesser Mysteries, conducted at Athens in February/March (corresponding to the grain harvest). Full initiation required both, but the Greater Mysteries at Eleusis were by far the more prominent and better known. The cult was open to all Athenian citizens, but in the Hellenistic period began to be popular for non-Athenians as well. The Greater Mysteries began and ended at Athens; the full cycle of events took ten days to complete. After initial preparations and purifications, the "mysteries" proper began on the sixth day with a sacred procession of all the new initiates from Athens to Eleusis. It took all day for the group to travel the nearly fifteen miles (twenty-five kilometers), as they would pause periodically to offer chants and prayers. The grand entrance to the sanctuary occurred by torchlight, and the initiates spent the rest of the night in singing and dancing. The next day they rested and fasted in preparation for the initiation proper, which was conducted the following night.

That evening everyone entered the great hall, called the Telesterion, which was lined with stepped benches. There were ritual reenactments of the myth of Demeter and Persephone followed by some sacred pronouncements. Then the initiates were escorted one by one into a small central chamber where the sacred objects were revealed to them. This moment of "seeing" (called *epopteia*) was the central act of initiation. What they were shown remains a secret; perhaps it was an ear of grain, symbolizing Demeter's power, or some other representation of Persephone's death and rebirth. The Greek word "mystery" (*musteria*) seems to have originated around this process. It derives from a verb (*muo*) meaning to close the eyes or mouth, hence reflecting the awe of the moment or what cannot be told. From its connection with such rituals, however, the word effectively came to mean "initiation ritual." On the following day, rites were performed on behalf of the dead, and on the last day the initiates returned to Athens.

The Myth-Ritual Complex

Interestingly enough, there was no special religious group to which the initiates now belonged; the word "cult" is often misunderstood to mean some sort of special membership, but there was none at Eleusis. The Eleusinian mysteries remained a part of the Athenian civic religion. For citizens and noncitizens alike, there was a fee for being initiated, and many people commemorated their initiation (or that of their children) with dedicatory inscriptions or other gifts to the sanctuary. Since we know that it was common to have adolescents initiated into the cult, one may infer that initiation performed some sort of moral reinforcement for adult life.

On the other hand, the great popularity of the mysteries in the Hellenistic and Roman periods probably came from the association of the ritual of initiation with the blessings of immortality and afterlife. We may think of this as a *myth-ritual complex,* in which the special powers or benefits that are described in the myth of Demeter and Persephone are thought to be made available through ritual. The participants received these mythic benefits through the rituals of initiation, which in turn both reenacted the myth and employed specific symbols from the myth in what was ritually performed. Thus, the myth, the initiation rituals, and the benefits to initiates were intertwined by story, symbol, and experience, all of which were imbued with sacred power and meaning.

The "Foreign" Mysteries

Beginning in the later third century BCE, several new mystery cults began to emerge. In each case, they developed out of older mythological traditions from the eastern cultures that had come under Greek rule after the conquests of Alexander the Great. For this reason, they are typically associated with the deities of their native cultures; however, the rites and what makes them "mysteries" at all come from some degree of syncretism with Hellenistic culture. More specifically, they all emulate in some fashion the paradigm of myth-ritual complex found in the Eleusinian mysteries. A synopsis of the principal cults of the Roman period is found in Box 3.2. The earliest of these "foreign" mysteries came from Egypt—the cult of Isis and Sarapis. It illustrates both the process of development and the relation to the Greek mystery tradition.

The Egyptian Mysteries of Isis and Sarapis

The myth underlying the Egyptian mysteries goes back to the earliest centuries of Egyptian history, and it continued to be important in later periods of Egyptian religion. Osiris (Sarapis) represents both the Nile itself and the grain that grows along its banks; he was also the god of the dead. His sister and consort was Isis. The myth revolves around Osiris's death and dismemberment; Isis becomes the active figure in the story as she goes searching for Osiris, eventually restores his dismembered body, and is able miraculously to bear a son, a new Osiris named Horus.

At base, one recognizes that the myth is a distinctively Egyptian form of the agrarian cycle, in which Osiris's death and rebirth corresponds to the inundation and harvest seasons along the Nile. Other symbols that are also distinctively Egyptian in character include the concern over keeping the corpse intact as a means of assuring afterlife. Thus, Isis's restoration of the corpse of Osiris is also his mummification. In traditional Egyptian art, Osiris was usually portrayed as a mummy. So symbolic connections between the crop cycle and the cult of the dead were already present from a relatively early stage. We also know that this older Egyptian mythology had already been adapted to political functions in the New Kingdom period of Egypt's history (eighteenth to tenth century BCE) by making Osiris and Horus symbolize the deceased pharaoh and his successor, respectively. Yet none of this was as yet a "mystery cult."

The key change occurred with the arrival of the Greeks and the beginning of Ptolemaic rule in Egypt (332–301 BCE). It was the Greek rulers who co-opted the older political symbolism of Osiris to consolidate their power in the lineage of the pharaohs. In the process, the Ptolemies also changed his name to Sarapis, the form by which he would become known throughout the Greco-Roman world. Then, by the later part of the third century BCE, we begin to find the Egyptian cult in Greece, Turkey, and the Aegean Islands. From there it made its way to Rome and throughout the Mediterranean. When we look at this exported "Hellenistic" form of the cult, we also discover some different versions; some are linked to a civic festival tradition, while others seem to function more as individual rites of initiation. In some cases, both versions operated side by side in Greek and Roman cities.

Our principal source for the myth of Isis and Sarapis comes from the Greek author Plutarch, a younger contemporary of Paul. When Plutarch recounts the story of Isis's wanderings in search of Sarapis, for example, he tells how she came to the home of a king and served as nursemaid to the king's infant son. Then at night she secretly began to braze the child over a fire to give him immortality. Here, of course, we immediately recognize an element from the myth of Demeter and Persephone that has no place in the older Egyptian myth, a point recognized by Plutarch as well.[23] Thus, through syncretism, the Hellenistic form of the cult has taken on elements of both the Eleusinian myth and its myth-ritual pattern. It was this particular version of the Isis-Sarapis cult that functioned as a mystery, and those who participated would have derived the benefits of immortality and blessed afterlife associated with Sarapis through initiation into the cult of Isis. On the other hand, Plutarch was quite willing to give metaphorical meanings to this mythology, showing that there was more than one interpretation of the tradition in its Greco-Roman incarnation.

Why Did These Cults Flourish in the Roman World?

A good example of how these various religious elements came together in popular piety of the Roman world may be seen in a Latin novel or romance of the second century CE titled *Metamorphoses,* but better known as *The Golden Ass.* The author was Apuleius from North Africa, but he studied and traveled extensively in Greece. The hero of the story, Lucius, is a hapless traveler in Greece whose experimentation with magic backfires and transforms him into an ass. Fickle Fate then leads him through many misfortunes until finally he is transformed again by the one deity who is powerful enough to see his plight and

---

BOX 3.2

The "New" Mystery Cults of the Greco-Roman World

The Egyptian Cults of Isis and Osiris (Sarapis)

- Original context: ancient Egypt (from ca. 3500 BCE)
- Principal characters
  Osiris (male): god of Nile river and vegetative cycle, also of under-world/death; killed and dismembered by an enemy (Seth); typically called Sarapis in Greek and Roman usage, and often identified with Zeus
  Isis (female): sister/consort of Osiris, who restored and revived him miraculously in order to sire a son, Horus
- Founded as both public cult and private "mystery"
- Initially outlawed at Rome, but eventually made "official" in mid-first century CE
- One of the most popular in the Roman world

The Great Mother (Magna Mater)

- Original context: Anatolia/Phrygia (central Turkey; from ca. 6000 BCE)
- Principal characters
  Cybele (female): source of fertility in plants and animals
  Attis (male): a shepherd and consort; killed and revived (in some versions he is emasculated)
- Had associations with Mt. Ida, near Troy
- Was accepted at Rome in 203 BCE
- Had both public and private versions of cultic activity
- Major festival day March 25 (the spring equinox and, in later Christian tradition, the feast of the Annunciation to Mary regarding the birth of Jesus), on which there was a public procession

---

save him. Through hyphenation she is identified with many goddesses, but finally her true name is revealed; she is Isis, Queen of Heaven. In the end Lucius becomes an initiate and even advances to become a priest in her cult. This novel is a work of religious propaganda, an advertisement for the power of Isis to save even the most miserable of humans from their predicaments caused by the vagaries of fate and magic in the world. Other cults abound, as the story clearly shows, but none is as powerful and effective as the cult of Isis for securing deliverance and salvation.

- A major ritual for priests, called the *taurobolium,* involved a kind of "baptism" in the blood of a bull

The Syrian Goddess

- Original context: Mesopotamia, Syria, Palestine (from ca. 2000 BCE)
- Principal characters
  Atargattis (female): a combination of Asherah/Astarte and Anat from older Near Eastern myth
  Hadad (male): also known as Ba'al, her consort; killed by evil gods; rescued and revived by Atargattis (Anat)
- Affinities and amalgamation with both Cybele and Isis myths and symbolism
- More popular in eastern Mediterranean

Mithras, "the Persian God"

- Original context: known from older Hindu (Avesta) and Zoroastrian myth; came into Greek world through Persian contacts (sixth–fourth century BCE); however, the "mystery cult" form was a later innovation of Roman period (second century CE)
- Principal character
  Mithras (male): slays cosmic bull and brings life/fertility back to world; consequently deified as "savior" of humanity; later identified with "The Invincible Sun"
- Employed numerous astrological elements
- Birthday of Mithras December 25 (winter solstice and, of course, Christmas in Christian tradition, the celebration of the birth of Jesus)
- Secretive and known for communal dining; especially popular among Roman soldiers

This novel reflects both the common features of religious belief of the period and the competition among the various cults. It may also suggest why people were attracted to many different cults or to one cult over another. Here was a goddess, Isis, who responded directly and personally to the prayers of one humble man. When nothing else availed to overcome magic and fickle Fate, Isis was all-powerful. She brought "salvation" to Lucius by restoring his human form. The novel offered this "demonstration" of her power to provide proof that she could do it for others as well. Yet it shows that knowing her true identity among the myriad of deities was important. Why wander around like Lucius before he came to Isis? Having the correct knowledge and the proper prayers belongs only to those who became devotees of Isis and initiates in her cult.

Because she claimed to encompass all other deities, she was a kind of universal guarantee of divine power. Of course, one could also go to Eleusis in hopes of finding such special powers, but most people were not wealthy enough to make such a trip. In contrast, the new mysteries of the Hellenistic and Roman periods were distinctive for their portability. The Isis cult could be found nearly everywhere. Even a latecomer such as the cult of Mithras rather quickly spread across the Roman Empire from the Persian frontier to Britain. Finally, initiation into Isis's cult brought her followers into a kind of community of experience and belief. In some cases, then, initiation resulted in a kind of special cultic fellowship that included ritual meals and secret handshakes. It would not be too surprising, however, to find other cults making similar claims. Thus, to those at home in the Greco-Roman world, the claims of early Christians may well have sounded very familiar.

CHAPTER FOUR

Judaism at Home and Abroad

By the time Jesus was born, Jewish culture and religion had changed considerably from what it was in the days of David and Solomon or Isaiah and Jeremiah. In Chapter 2 we outlined some of the political factors that contributed to this changing environment. The Babylonian exile, continued domination by one or another world power, hellenization, syncretism, regionalism, Roman rule, and social stratification all had a hand in splintering the fabric of Jewish society in the homeland. Yet there remained a tenacious sense of the "chosenness" of the Jewish people and trust in God's deliverance. Nonetheless, the diverse experiences of various Jewish groups and disagreements over how and when God's deliverance might come resulted in an even more factious religious climate.

The Religious Climate of Judea

The change in character of Judaism began in the period after the Babylonian exile, even though some of its roots came before. The first group of exiles returned home in 538 BCE. By about 520–515 they had set about restoring Solomon's Temple, which had been destroyed in 586 BCE. Some references suggest that this first restoration work was piecemeal at best (Zech. 4:10). Consequently, when other returnees arrived decades later, tensions arose over the state of the Temple and how it was to be run. Still other exiles stayed in Babylon for several more generations before returning to Judea. It seems that many of them were horrified at the state of affairs: the Temple was virtually deserted and the exilic "colony" in Jerusalem was near collapse (Neh. 13:10–22). The result was a more thoroughgoing reform of the Temple and the priesthood along the lines that had developed during the long period in Babylon. Nehemiah, who led the late-fifth-century rebuilding of Jerusalem, was from the fifth generation of his family to live in Babylon. The religious figure most closely associated with this reform was Ezra, who only returned to Judea sometime in the last part of the fifth century or at the beginning of the fourth century BCE, that is, more than a century after the first returnees and nearly two centuries after the destruction.[1]

The Growth of Sectarianism

What resulted was the consolidation of a new priestly order in the Temple; beginning in the early fourth century BCE, it lasted until the Temple was once again destroyed in 70 CE. At the same time, this imposition of a new order also reflects other tensions over religious operations and the beginnings of religious sectarianism in Judaism.[2] Many of these tensions are seen in the later literature of the Hebrew scriptures (Haggai, Zechariah, Ezra, Nehemiah 6–10, and Isaiah 56–66).[3] This is also the period during which the Samaritans emerged as a separate ethnoreligious group. The Samaritans claimed direct ancestry from the ancient Israelites; however, they were not accepted by the new inhabitants of Jerusalem, who referred to themselves as "the congregation of the exile."[4] Each side had a different view of what happened and why, but the religious and ethnic tensions between Jews and Samaritans continued into the Roman period and later history.

At the center of the debates stood the Temple as the symbol of both national and religious identity. At issue was how the Torah (or law of Moses) should be understood in governing the Temple's operations and the daily life of the people. Marriage, Sabbath observance, holy days, purity rules, and social order were now regulated in new ways. New prophets appeared, and new scriptures were produced to reinforce these religious ideas. These same issues would continue to bubble to the surface in all the sectarian debates of later periods.[5] In the meantime, the Judean "colony" continued to grow and expand in the region immediately around Jerusalem.

The Impact of Hellenization

From 538 to 332 BCE, Judea remained a colonial outpost under Persian rule. With the conquest of Alexander the Great, Judea now came under Greek domination. From 323 to 198 BCE it was part of the Ptolemaic kingdom in Egypt. There seem to have been few religious upheavals during this period, since the Ptolemies treated Judea as a Temple state and thus left much of its internal administration to the priestly authorities. Jerusalem continued to grow.

In 198/197 BCE, however, the region of Judea was taken over by the Seleucids, the Greek kingdom of Syria. The Seleucid regime did not give the Temple in Jerusalem as much autonomy; it began to enforce more stringent forms of Hellenistic culture while curtailing certain aspects of Jewish religious practice. The Seleucids were also under pressure from Rome as it began to move into the eastern Mediterranean (especially Greece and Anatolia) in the aftermath of the Second Punic War. By 175 BCE, there were serious debates among the Jews over whether to accommodate to Seleucid cultural impositions or to resist. Politics were involved as the Seleucid authorities interfered in the appointment of first one and then another high priest, seeking one who would support their agenda. The result was a new round of sectarian tensions; the Temple once again became the flash point. Eventually the situation exploded into the Maccabean revolt (167–164 BCE); it resulted in a new era of independent Jewish rule under the Hasmonean monarchy.

When the Maccabean revolt ended, however, sectarian tensions remained. Some groups, notably a conservative faction known as the Hasidim (or "pious ones"), were adamantly opposed to the Seleucid intrusions into Jewish religious practice. Initially they seem to have supported the revolt; however, some, being strictly observant, had refused to fight on the Sabbath (cf. 1 Macc. 2:29–38, 42–48). Later, it appears, they felt that the Hasmonean rulers did more to promote Hellenistic culture than to resist it and disagreed over appointment of the high priest (1 Macc. 7:12–18). The book of Daniel may well be a product of the Hasidic sect penned during the war; it uses the figure of Daniel, a character from the Babylonian exile, to exemplify resistance to outside cultural forces.[6] The book of Daniel also reflects the growth of a new religious outlook that combines resistance to Hellenism with influences from Hellenistic thought and culture to form a new Jewish worldview we call *apocalyptic*.

The Rise of Apocalyptic

The roots of Jewish apocalyptic go back to the Persian period and may be seen in some of the later writings of the Hebrew scriptures, especially Ezekiel and Isaiah 56–66. Among other things these writings look forward to the return of theocratic rule in Judea as a kind of new "golden age." Persian influences may also be seen in the sharpening of lines between good and evil forces. Known as "dualism," this idea has often been traced to Zoroastrianism, the dominant religious tradition of Persia after the sixth century. Even so, none of these elements alone constitutes full-blown apocalyptic as such.

Instead, the rise of apocalyptic thinking in Judaism may be traced to the latter half of the third century BCE, while Judea was still under Ptolemaic control. It combined elements of new astronomical investigations from Greek science, the legacy of Persian and Egyptian influences, and basic Jewish theological convictions about the unity and power of the creator God of Israel. Older forms of Near Eastern and Hebrew creation mythology were reinterpreted. One of these was a combat myth in which the slaying of a cosmic serpent or sea monster resulted in the formation of the earth. Its symbols came to be seen as representing God's eventual deliverance of the chosen people by defeating Israel's enemies.[7] The result was a new kind of cosmological reflection on the nature of the universe that looked back to biblical traditions to understand both present and future conditions. In turn, these new ideas were expressed in a new genre of literature, which came to be known as the *apocalypse*. From about 225 BCE to 200 CE, more than twenty new works of this genre were written by Jews and Christians, although this count does not include the numerous other works among the Pseudepigrapha, the Dead Sea Scrolls, and the New Testament that are apocalyptic in tone but not formally part of the genre.

Apocalypse as Literary Genre

The Greek verb *apocalyptein* means to "uncover" or "reveal"; the derived noun *apocalypsis*—from which we get the English word "apocalypse"—thus means something that is revealed, or "a revelation." Of the many Jewish and Christian works from this genre, the best known is the book of Revelation in the New Testament, which carries the Greek title: the Apocalypse of John. An apocalypse is a type of literature that offers "revelations" about the past and the future. As a literary genre it has several characteristic features.[8]

Usually the revelations come in the form of visions or dreams that are delivered to a righteous person, typically by an angel. The recipient is often one of the patriarchs or heroes of ancient Israel who seems to be recounting what has been revealed about "future events," at least what was "future" at that earlier time. In reality, however, the time of composition of most of these works is much later than the fictional setting of the "visionary"; usually, the end point of the "future" predictions is very close to the present time of the audience. This type of writing in the name of another person from a past time is often called *pseudepigraphy*. It was quite common in antiquity, but was not considered a form of forgery or deception. The visions themselves are full of florid descriptions or mysterious signs that evoke metaphorical interpretation by the angel or revealer. At base they are about understanding the rule of God, the order of the universe, deciphering good and evil, and making the proper choices.

1 Enoch

According to most scholars the first example of the genre of apocalypse in its fully developed form is the Jewish text known as *1 Enoch*. More precisely, the earliest portions of *1 Enoch* (chaps. 1–36, 72–82) probably date to the latter half of the third century BCE.[9] The namesake of the revelation is the patriarch Enoch, father of Methuselah, who lived before Noah's flood. According to Genesis 5:21–24, this Enoch was a righteous man who did not die, for "God took him." This legendary character, therefore, was one of the few mortals who had been transported to the heavenly realm, and his "visions" there constitute the basis for the apocalypse.

Chapters 1–36 are called "The Book of the Watchers" and describe what Enoch saw in heaven, namely, the history of the world, ostensibly before the flood. The core of this section is an imaginative elaboration of a small passage from Genesis 6:1–3. Coming at the beginning of the flood narrative, this passage tells how "sons of God" (i.e., some sort of gods or divine beings) saw "daughters of men" (i.e., human women) and lusted after them; originally, it was meant to show how human life began to deteriorate so that God needed to eradicate it and start over. By extension, then, the drama of *1 Enoch* 6–11 focuses on the actions of the "sons of God"; however, now they are identified as the heavenly luminaries or "stars," also called "angels," who rebelled against God's order and raped human women.

The leader of this rebellion is the angel called either Semyaz or Azaz'el—one of the first forms of the Satan figure. As a result of his actions he was cast out of heaven and bound in a pit under the earth. The illicit union of the rebellious angels with human women produced a race of giants (an elaboration on Gen. 6:4), who proceeded to dominate and harass the humans and to give them tools of war and destruction. One may also recognize here a strong similarity to elements from the Greek myths of the titans and Prometheus. Because of their rebellion, then, God decided to destroy the work of the giants and imprison the evil forces; Enoch was commissioned by God to travel across the world to understand and communicate God's correct plan for the order of the cosmos.

1 Enoch was further elaborated in several stages over the following centuries, finally reaching some 108 chapters in total. Although it was never included in any of the official biblical canon lists, it was clearly one of the most revered and influential texts in all of the early Jewish and Christian traditions. It seems to have been considered "scripture" in Essene theology. Its story of the "fall of the angels" was the source for many of the later apocalyptic legends about Satan as seen in both the New Testament itself (Luke 10:17–18; 2 Pet. 2:4; Jude 5–6, 14–15) and other early Christian literature (see Chapter 15). In other words, by the early Middle Ages it was so deeply ingrained in the fabric of early Christian lore, it held a "quasi-canonical" status by serving as an interpretive filter for Genesis 5–9. What gave the basic story such currency was the way it explained the origins of evil in the world while simultaneously preserving the absolute unity and power of the One God of Israel. As a result of its wide dissemination, therefore, *1 Enoch*—perhaps as much as any other single piece of literature—helped to inscribe the apocalyptic worldview on Jewish and Christian consciousness.

The Apocalyptic Worldview

The main message of *1 Enoch* revolves around understanding the order that God created in the universe and living according to that order. It calls for both deeper commitment to the laws of God and deeper trust that God will prevail over the alien forces of evil. What sets apocalyptic thinking apart is how it casts these theological ideas in the form of a new mythological drama stretching from creation and emphasizing the ultimate power of the One God of Israel. Yet in the process it also creates a new cast of heavenly characters for this cosmic drama. These include angels (as the heavenly luminaries), who then divide into good and bad (in later terms becoming angels and demons), the Satan figure as the rebellious angel who wars against God, and the realms of heaven and hell. All these elements that are so central to the Jewish and Christian tradition in the first centuries CE are innovations of apocalyptic thinking. Apocalyptic defined the universe in ways that were consistent with earlier Jewish theology and at the same time coherent in the light of newer forms of Greek thought. What was created was a new view of reality, or what we may call the apocalyptic worldview.[10]

Some scholars have referred to apocalyptic as literature of the oppressed produced in moments of crisis. Although these aspects may fit certain cases, the phenomenon of apocalyptic is broader.[11] Norman Perrin calls apocalyptic "a child of hope and despair: hope in the invincible power of God in the world he created, despair of the present course of human history in that world."[12] This seems to fit the broader mood. On the one hand, it carries a sense of expectation; on the other, it recognizes a tension arising from opposing forces, usually characterized in dualistic terms: good and evil, God and Satan, angels and demons. Time or history is also conceived in dualistic terms: the present evil age will ultimately give way to a coming good age when God will reign over a pure earthly kingdom.

This sense of history moving according to a divine plan toward its scripted, teleological outcome also produces the Western notion of linear time. It results in another characteristic concept in Jewish and Christian theology, namely, an expectation regarding "end times," called *eschatology*. From the Greek word *eschaton* (meaning "last"), this idea did not originally refer to an "end of the world."[13] Rather, it originated as the "end" of the present evil age, and thus the break in time that inaugurates the coming good age. Harking back to the Near Eastern combat myth (discussed above), this eschatological break was often conceived as a final battle between the forces of God and Satan. From this notion also came the idea that a warrior figure, like David of old, would come to lead the triumph over the forces of evil. Not all forms of apocalyptic include this idea, but for those that do, the figure is quite often given the title *messiah* (or "anointed one"), which also comes from the kingship ideology of the Davidic dynasty. In some forms of Jewish apocalyptic there might be more than one such messiah, while others had none at all.

Apocalyptic Expectation and Sectarian Protest

Although apocalyptic thinking was certainly not restricted to sectarian groups within Judaism, it nonetheless was a tool in galvanizing certain forms of sectarian identity and spirit. One of the best known was the Essene sect, which wrote the Dead Sea Scrolls (see below). So too the Jesus sect seems to have made much of apocalyptic thinking in its own process of self-definition, as we shall see later. By its very nature a sect is a group that feels some sort of tension with the rest of its society. At the very least, a sect feels that somehow the greater part of society has gone wrong, and only a few people—the members of the sect, of course—see the correct way. Sometimes, but not always, this may come from social and economic deprivation or from a sense of political oppression. The sect calls for a cure for these ills through a religious reorientation of the present social order. Far from calling for a radical destruction of its parent religious culture, however, this kind of sectarian rhetoric tends to preserve basic beliefs and practices while calling for a return to "purity" or relief of the oppressed.[14] As a result, the "us versus them" tensions felt by a sect find a natural coherence with the dualistic outlook of apocalyptic.

This outlook likely arose in the Hellenistic period as Jewish culture began to feel threatened by the onslaught of hellenization. This type of dualism pitting Jews against all other nations (or "Gentiles") reflects an early effort to preserve ethnic and religious identity. As Hellenistic influences found greater acceptance within Jewish culture, however, there was an increasing turn toward criticism of other Jews for becoming too "worldly." So long as there is no radical change, sectarianism breeds more sectarianism.

One of the main focal points of sectarian protest was the Temple itself. The Temple was the symbol of God's election of and abiding with Israel. As such it was the most important symbol and rallying point of Jewish ethnic and religious identity. On the other hand, tensions continued to arise over the proper operation of the Temple, and these were usually couched in terms of its "purity." Several pieces of apocalyptic literature from the second and first centuries BCE reflect these ongoing protests. One such text is called the *Testament of the Twelve Patriarchs;* it is a protest against the fact that the Hasmonean kings had also "usurped" the title of high priest. It has strong affinities with the criticisms of the Temple found in the Dead Sea Scrolls. The result is a stringent denunciation not so much of the Temple itself but of those who had "perverted" it.

A different type of criticism of the Hasmonean dynasty comes from a series of poetic oracles ostensibly delivered by King Solomon. Dating to the middle of the first century BCE, the *Psalms of Solomon* views the Hasmonean dynasty and the arrival of the Romans as a time of punishment for Israel's sins. This text looks to a kingly leader, a new Solomon, to deliver Israel from these oppressive powers.

Finally, the *Assumption of Moses,* which dates to the early first century CE, very possibly while Jesus was alive, purports to give Moses's farewell speech to Joshua before he was taken away into heaven.[15] It describes the wrath of God that will be visited on the enemy of Israel (i.e., Rome) when the kingdom is restored and anticipates much of the revolutionary sentiment of the first Jewish revolt against Rome.

Sects, Parties, and Religious Leadership in the Homeland

These diverse examples of sectarian protest help us to understand both the volatility of religious rhetoric and the polarization of Jewish society in the first century CE. Both the Jewish historian Josephus and the Christian Gospels took note of the polarization and the debate. Writing in the late first century CE, Josephus likened the different Jewish factions—Pharisees, Sadducees, Essenes, and Zealots—to the four main "schools" or "sects" (Greek *haireseis*) of classical Greek philosophy.[16] There were others, of course, but Josephus focused on these primarily to soften Roman suspicions regarding the quarrelsome and turbulent nature of Jewish religious debate in the period after the first revolt. Only the Zealots receive significant criticism from Josephus for fomenting sedition against Rome; the wranglings of the others were more in the vein of philosophical dialogue, like that between the Stoics and Epicureans. Or at least that's the way Josephus portrays the situation. The Gospels, on the other hand, stress the theological differences between the Sadducees and the Pharisees as if they were on an even footing and portray them as co-conspirators against Jesus. Other groups are largely ignored, and the Essenes are not mentioned at all. The Gospels have their own agenda (as we shall see later). A careful historical profile of the basic groups is thus in order.

The High Priests and Temple Officials

Prior to the Maccabean revolt the office of high priest was restricted to a member of the Zadokite line that had been reestablished after the priestly reform of the Second Temple. According to 1 Chronicles 6:3–8 and 24:3, Zadok was a descendant of Aaron's son Eleazar. Hence the Zadokite family constituted a select line within the priestly tribe of Levi; they alone could hold the office of high priest.[17] Under the Hasmonean dynasty the office of high priest was combined with that of the king and held by a member of the Hasmonean family (143–40 BCE). This move created a stir among some Jewish groups because the Hasmoneans did not belong to the proper Zadokite family, even though they claimed some priestly descent.

When Herod the Great became king he removed the last Hasmonean high priest (in 34 BCE) and appointed a Zadokite from Babylonian descent instead. This return to Zadokite lineage undoubtedly pleased some conservative Jews (such as the Essenes). A number of the high priests of this period were from

Egypt, such as the family of Boethus, which held the office successively for nearly thirty years until the removal of Archelaus in 6 CE. Soon thereafter Quirinius, the legate of Syria, appointed Annas son of Seth, and his family members would dominate the office during the first period of procuratorial rule and even down to the outbreak of the first revolt. The lineage of Annas is uncertain, but he may have been from an aristocratic Jerusalem family. It appears that he and his descendants were kept in office by the procurators because they were willing to collaborate with Roman rule. Hence, the office of high priest was important religiously but was often used as a political tool. Debates over the worthiness of certain families carried considerable theological and symbolic weight.

The high priest presided over the ceremonial and sacrificial operations of the Temple. These included a regular cycle of daily purifications, sacrifices, and prayers as well as the extensive rituals and sacrifices conducted in the Temple at the major Jewish holy days: Rosh Hashanah, Yom Kippur, and Succoth in the early fall, Hanukkah in December, and Passover and Shavuoth (Pentecost) in the spring. These three main seasons brought the largest number of religious pilgrims to Jerusalem prior to 70 CE, when the Temple ceased operations. The high priest's principal ceremonial function, however, occurred at Yom Kippur. For the rest, he was assisted in the actual performance of the rituals and sacrifices by a consistory of other hereditary priests, who served in Jerusalem on a rotating basis. This group was further subdivided into those actually called "priests," who took care of all duties in the inner precincts of the Temple, and those called "Levites," who served as assistants and handled the outer precincts. At the major festivals, such as Yom Kippur and Passover, there would have been a large number of these priestly functionaries occupied for hours and days at a time with matters of ritual purity and sacrificial preparations.

The Sanhedrin

Contrary to some portrayals, prior to 70 CE the Sanhedrin was, in effect, the city council of Jerusalem; it had judicial as well as legislative authority but was not a "religious" governing body per se. Nor is there any evidence for such a religious council prior to the rabbinic period (after the second century CE). The name *Sanhedrin* is actually from one of the standard Greek terms (*sunedria*) for a council, and it appears that this body was organized only during the later Hasmonean period on the model of Greek city administration. Under the early Romans, the entire country was divided into five administrative districts, each of which had its own *sunedria;* after Herod's reign only the Jerusalem council continued to function. Even so, it is not clear that its authority extended much, if at all, beyond the city of Jerusalem.

The council chambers of the Sanhedrin were located in the center of Jerusalem near the western wall of the Temple. The council's membership was made up of leading citizens, mostly of the aristocratic, landholding class; however, the actual number of members is not known. At times the high priest presided over the council, but that does not seem to be the normal structure. Nor is it the case that particular groups or sects, including priests, were given any representative status in the council on an ex officio basis. As an institution, the Sanhedrin disappeared after the destruction of Jerusalem in 70 CE. Beginning in the second century CE, the titles Sanhedrin and Bet Din (lit., "house of judgment" or "court") were used interchangeably in reference to the leading rabbinic council, which was concerned with both judicial and religious matters for the governance of Jewish life. The terminology causes some confusion in regard to the pre-70 period.

Sadducees

By all ancient accounts the Sadducees were a dominant group, both politically and religiously, in Jerusalem in the period before 70 CE. Yet it is not likely that they constituted a religious sect or even a political party as such. The name probably comes from a Greek rendering of a Hebrew name like Zaddokim, that is, the descendants of the high priest Zadok. It may well be that the name derives from the oligarchic families who inhabited Jerusalem in the period after the postexilic restoration and reforms, many of whom may have originally been of Zadokite descent from Babylon. Or it may be that they supported the priestly reform movement associated with Ezra. The term does not appear before the Hasmonean period (and then only in Josephus's history), and other literary references from the period are rare. By the later Hasmonean period, however, the term ceases to be limited to the priesthood. Instead, the picture suggests the well-entrenched, landholding aristocracy of Jerusalem, some of whom might have been from priestly families. Only one high priest is clearly called a Sadducee by Josephus.

The Sadducees seem to be closely linked to the Sanhedrin and to the Hasmonean dynasty. Herod undercut their influence by disrupting the economic position of the old aristocracy of Jerusalem and Judea, and also by appointing high priests who were not from Jerusalem. The Sadducees' continued domination of the Sanhedrin after Herod's death may account for the political challenges to Archelaus that came from the Jerusalem leadership. Josephus does indicate that the high priest Ananus (ca. 62 CE, a descendant of Annas) was a Sadducee.[18] Hence, tacit support for Roman administration may account for an increased posture for the Sadducees and closer alignment with the high priest during the period of procuratorial rule.

Both Josephus and the Gospels describe the Sadducees as a conservative group that rejected certain "newer" theological and philosophical ideas. Specifically, they are noted for rejecting the role of Fate in human life as well as belief in afterlife and resurrection of the dead. In some respects the ideas they reject are closely associated with Greek thought and influence, and their opposition would be consistent with some of the conservative reactions that surfaced during the Maccabean revolt. More important, perhaps, is the theological basis for rejecting these newer ideas, since Josephus says they only accepted the five books of Torah as authoritative. Both Josephus and the Gospels portray their opposition to the Pharisees on matters of interpretation of the law, but at base this may come down to the fact that they held a strict or minimalist position derived exclusively from the levitical regulations in the Torah for determining ritual purity. Such a view of purity would necessarily have implications for participation in the Temple operations.

Pharisees

Both Josephus and the Gospels portray the Pharisees as the chief opposition group to the Sadducees; however, their connection to the later development of the rabbinic movement has led to many misconceptions regarding their position in the time of Jesus. According to Josephus, the Pharisees originated during the time of the Hasmonean king John Hyrcanus (134–104 BCE), but they only become prominent under later Hasmonean rulers. Their name comes from a Hebrew term (*parash*) meaning "to divide or separate," but in what sense remains unclear. It might refer to their sectarian origins, to their emphasis on purity, or to their interpretation of Torah. Most recent scholars think they originated out of the Hasidim, conservatives protesting against the Hasmonean leadership in the period after the Maccabean revolt. The book of 2 Maccabees also comes from this same critical stance.

In any event, by the time of Herod the Great, they had largely lost their political edge and turned primarily to matters of religious interpretation and fellowship. Within Pharisaism there emerged different schools of interpretation, such as those associated with the teachers Hillel and Shammai, contemporaries of Herod the Great. The most common self-designation for a Pharisee was "associate" (*haber*); they regularly gathered in a small group, called a "fellowship" (*haburah*), where they practiced communal dining and study under the guidance of a teacher. Similarities to the portrayal of Jesus with his disciples are apparent. Because they had no connection to the priestly tradition, their interpretation of Torah was often at odds with that of the Temple authorities or scribes. In this sense, the Pharisees are properly considered a religious sect, and a number of pieces of literature from the period have been linked to their protests.

Three key features of their theology set the Pharisees apart. First, they had a broader view of scripture, as reflected in a characteristic phrase, "the Law and the Prophets" (cf. Matt. 5:17). The Jewish canon that comes down to us today, consisting of the Law, the Prophets, and the Writings, comes from this Pharisaic tradition as developed in later rabbinic Judaism. Thus, their belief in the afterlife and resurrection of the dead (cf. Matt. 22:23–33; Mark 12:18–27) was grounded in the later scriptures, notably Daniel, Ezekiel, and 4 Maccabees.

Second, they accepted a broader mode of interpretation that augmented a limited or literal reading of Torah with oral tradition. This idea has been called "the twofold Torah," that is, the written Torah and the oral Torah. Other writings (such as Daniel) as well as the wise sayings of individual teachers (such as Hillel) constituted oral Torah. What is often called the "Golden Rule" (cf. Matt. 7:12; Luke 6:31) may come from Hillel, and "summing up the whole Torah in two commandments" was a typically Pharisaic way of thinking (cf. Matt. 22:34–40; Mark 12:28–31).

Third, they stressed a broader sense of ritual purity than the one that was traditionally restricted to the Temple cult. This idea was thought of as "making the Torah livable" and was concerned with making purity a practical part of daily life. Many Pharisaic purity regulations thus concerned domestic activity. They "transformed the notion of the sacred," along with the sense of *righteousness* and *purity* required, "by associating it with the group that keeps itself pure and loyal to the commandments—not just in the Temple precincts at festival time, but daily in the home, in the midst of an unclean world."[19]

For this reason, the Pharisees represent a "populist" orientation toward piety, in contrast to the "elitist" orientation associated with the Sadducees and the priests. Their scholastic debates over what seem like legal minutiae are often portrayed as excessive, legalistic, and hypocritical (as seen in some of the Gospels). In reality, however, they come from these broader or liberalizing trends in theology. After all, debating what constitutes "work" on the Sabbath is of far less concern to a wealthy aristocrat than it might be to a subsistence farmer or day laborer, for whom no work meant no food for the family. Pharisaic interpretation thus sought greater flexibility rather than rigidity in matters of Torah observance, and Pharisees criticized the tendency of other Jews (notably the Sadducees and priests) to restrict the sense of religious piety to matters associated only with the Temple and sacrifice. In contrast to the impression given by the Gospels, from the Herodian period down to the first revolt the Pharisees had little or no political power and only a limited popular following. But their emphasis on Torah and tradition and their view of purity and piety not centered solely in the Temple would become most important in the period after 70 CE, when the Temple no longer existed. During the next century, the Pharisaic movement would gradually develop into what we now know as rabbinic Judaism.

Essenes and the Dead Sea Scrolls

Perhaps the best example of the volatile nature of sectarian protest fueled by religious zeal and apocalyptic expectations are the Essenes, whom Josephus describes as a mystical, ascetic, and prophetic "school" analogous to the Pythagoreans in Greek tradition. Since the discovery of the Dead Sea Scrolls (beginning in 1947), the vast majority of scholars identify the Essenes with the settlement known as Khirbet Qumran on the banks of the Dead Sea, approximately thirteen miles from Jerusalem. There may well have been other Essene settlements, but the Dead Sea Scrolls and related documents give the best evidence for their history, beliefs, and practices.

Like the Pharisees, the Essenes originated as a protest against the Hasmonean dynasty, probably in the last part of the second century BCE. The nature of their protest appears to have been a reaction to the Hasmonean monarchs taking over the office of high priest. Indeed, allusions in some of the scrolls indicate that their founder or leader was known as the "righteous teacher"; he was probably a member of the Zadokite priestly line who was disenfranchised by a Hasmonean, who is called "the wicked priest." Other references suggest that the "righteous teacher" was persecuted or even killed for opposing the Hasmoneans. Sometime thereafter, his followers fled Jerusalem and established the settlement at Qumran. Calling themselves the "covenanters," they sought to establish a pure priestly community to carry on the Zadokite traditions and to prepare for their return to Jerusalem to repurify the Temple.

On the basis of archaeological evidence, it appears that the Qumran settlement remained active throughout the Hasmonean period but declined under

Herod. Josephus reports that Herod was very respectful of the Essenes and thought of them as prophets of God. Conversely, the Essenes must have felt that Herod was an ally of sorts, since he removed the last Hasmonean high priests and replaced them with Zadokites from Babylon. An earthquake in 31 BCE severely damaged the Qumran settlement, and it seems to have been abandoned through the remainder of Herod's reign.

With the shift to procuratorial rule in 6 CE, however, it appears that Roman meddling in the appointment of the high priest Annas was viewed as a new crisis. The settlement was rebuilt, and a new phase in the life of the Essene community began (see Fig. 4.1). Its heated attacks on the Temple and priesthood during this period were strongly laced with anti-Roman rhetoric. In 68 CE the Essenes were evidently annihilated and their settlement burned, when they marched out to fight the Roman armies during the first Jewish revolt. They clearly believed that the revolt was the eschatological battle in which God would destroy the enemies of Israel and restore the Temple. One of their documents, called the *War Scroll*, lays out the battle plan for this final confrontation. It opens with these words: "This is the war of the Sons of Light against the Sons of Darkness."

The Dead Sea Scrolls were the library of the Essenes (see Fig. 4.2). They were either deposited or hidden in caves in the cliff face around the settlement.

FIGURE 4.1

The Essene settlement at Khirbet Qumran.

FIGURE 4.2

The Rule of the Community from the Dead Sea Scrolls. (The Shrine of the Book, Israel Museum; photo © Israel Museum)

Some of the documents go back to the earlier phase of the community, while others seem to come from the period of the procurators leading up to the war. All the scrolls were written in Hebrew, some in an intentionally archaic script. Since most Jews could not read or write Hebrew in that day, it further indicates that professional scribal activities were central to their life.

The scrolls comprise three distinct types of material. First, there are copies of the Jewish scriptures. From the many fragments found in the caves scholars have identified copies of every book of the Hebrew Bible (with the exception of the late work known as Esther) plus many of the pseudepigraphical writings, notably *1 Enoch* and *Jubilees*. Second are interpretive commentaries (using the term *pesher*) on many of the biblical books. The prophets Isaiah, Nahum, and Habakkuk seem to have been especially important, along with much of the material dealing with David in 1–2 Samuel and the Psalms. The nature of this interpretation was to explain the "hidden" meaning of key passages, which transformed them into apocalyptical prophecies about coming events. Finally, there are documents that deal with the life and management of the sect. These include a text known as the *Rule of the Community,* a plan for the restoration of the Temple (called the *Temple Scroll*), and the *War Scroll.*

Membership in the sect was controlled through a series of probationary stages; also, the members of the community maintained a very strict disciplinary code. This included regular purifications and washings, careful ordering of congregational assemblies, and judicial procedures if one of the members was detected in sinful or unacceptable behavior. Although it appears that the community was primarily made up of men who practiced an ascetic lifestyle, at least during some phases of its history there are indications that women were also present. The sect also followed the older ritual calendar from the Temple that had been replaced in the Hellenistic period.

Essene theology was heavily apocalyptical. In particular, it expected the imminent arrival of two messiahs. One, called the "Messiah of Israel," was to be from the line of David; he would lead the war against the enemies and restore the kingdom. Having done so, he would then yield to the other, called the "Messiah of Aaron." He was to be a priest from the line of Aaron/Zadok, and he was to oversee the restoration and purification of the Temple. So we begin to see how social location and self-understanding of the sect were expressed through their messianic expectation and strict community life. All Jews who recognized the Essenes' authority and followed their regulations would be admitted into the new kingdom; those who did not would perish along with the forces of Satan and Rome. Apparently, the Essenes had some small local followings in certain cities. There have been numerous attempts to link Jesus and John the Baptist with the Essenes, but there is no evidence of any connection other than a sharing of the broad streams of Jewish apocalyptic thought.

Zealots and Other Groups

These three main groups, Sadducees, Pharisees, and Essenes, show the diversity of religious and political expressions within Judaism in the homeland. But, in fact, all together they were still a small minority of the total Jewish population. Most Jews did not belong to any particular group or sect, and they went about their daily lives and religious observance with little concern for theological wranglings. A number of smaller sects are mentioned in passing, but little is known of most of them. These include groups like the "Morning Dippers" (or Hemerobaptists), who practiced daily ritual washings for purification. The movement that developed around John the Baptist probably belongs in this general category too. His practice of baptizing in the Jordan River carried apocalyptic overtones that symbolically reenacted the entry of the Israelites into the land and the reaffirmation of the covenant with God as a preparation for an eschatological kingdom. He was also known as a vocal critic of the impurity of the Herodian family and others.

Finally, Josephus mentions the Zealots. He calls them a "philosophy" like the Sadducees, Pharisees, and Essenes, but they were not so well organized; nor did they have such clear theological ideas. It is difficult to label them as a religious sect. Instead, they represent a diverse and growing spirit of social banditry and revolutionary sentiment probably coming through very different motivations and types of people.[20] Some of them clearly had genuine religious convictions and apocalyptic expectations about the arrival of a new kingdom; others made explicit messianic claims. But Josephus says some were "false prophets and charlatans," and he says they, not the other Jewish groups, were the real force behind the disastrous first revolt (see Chapter 2 and Box 2.6). In any case, together with the distinct voices of criticism and theological debate already discussed, they reflect the great religious diversity and social turbulence that was characteristic of the Jewish homeland during the life of Jesus and the first generation of the Jesus sect.

Judaism in the Diaspora

The Greek term *diaspora* means "scattering" or "dispersion." It refers to Jews who lived outside the homeland, effectively beginning with those Judeans who were taken away to exile in Babylon. Although many of their descendants eventually returned home, others did not; the Babylonian Jewish community continued to be very important down through the end of late antiquity. The real diffusion of Jewish groups began during the Hellenistic period; by the time of the Roman Empire, there were Jewish enclaves in virtually all parts the Mediterranean world. The most populous were in Egypt, especially Alexandria, which had an estimated Jewish population of nearly a hundred thousand. Rome also was said to have this many Jews in the imperial period. Even if these numbers are rather exaggerated, they point to the fact that increasingly Jewish groups were choosing to live outside the homeland. By the mid-second century CE, after the failure of the two revolts against Rome, it may well be the case that the vast majority of Jews lived in the Diaspora.

Although Rome generally tolerated its Jewish residents and guaranteed their rights, things were not always so serene. In 19 CE, for example, the emperor Tiberius expelled at least some of the Jews from Rome. The case, which is reported in some detail by Josephus, is instructive for understanding both the treatment of Jews and Jewish thought in the Diaspora. According to Josephus, the Jews were expelled at the same time as the cult of Isis and for similar reasons. In the case of the Isis cult, some of its priests had been implicated in helping arrange a scandalous sexual liaison involving the wife of an aristocratic Roman citizen. In the case of the Jews, Josephus claims that the perpetrators were "renegade" Jews who conned a wealthy Roman matron, a recent proselyte (i.e., gentile convert) to Judaism, into giving them money. Ostensibly the money was a contribution toward the Temple in Jerusalem. When it was discovered that they had kept the money for themselves, the emperor expelled the entire Jewish community from the city and conscripted four thousand Jewish men into the army.[21]

In both cases, there seems to have been some concern over proselytizing Roman citizens, particularly women. Even so, it is not likely that all of the Jews actually left greater Rome, and certainly not all of Italy, for only thirty years later, in 49 CE, the emperor Claudius once again expelled from Rome Jews who were creating disturbances "at the instigation of a certain Chrestus."[22] This case has been much discussed because of the name Chrestus, which can easily be understood as a mispronunciation of Christus ("messiah"). Some have suggested that the "disturbances" were debates between Jews and Christians within the Jewish community of Rome. There is no direct evidence to support this idea. According to Acts 18:1–2, when Paul first met the missionary couple Prisca and Aquila in Corinth, they had recently come from Rome because of this expulsion. Again, the expulsion does not appear to have been universal, since Jewish presence in Rome is attested in the mid- to late 50s CE and beyond. There was a synagogue at Ostia, Rome's port city, from at least the end of the first century. By the third century there were at least ten different Jewish congregations in the city of Rome.

Other Jewish enclaves experienced sporadic persecution by their pagan neighbors. One case occurred in Antioch in the mid-40s CE. The most famous case occurred in Alexandria, where lingering ethnic tensions between the large Jewish population and the Greek citizens erupted in 37 CE in anti-Jewish rioting. Flaccus, the Roman governor of Egypt, probably had a hand in fanning the flames, and afterward he charged the Jews with instigating the hostilities and demanded that they pay reparations. The Jewish community responded by sending a delegation to Rome to appeal directly to the emperor Caligula. The delegation was led by Philo, a philosopher from one of the most prominent Jewish families in Alexandria. By the time it arrived in Rome Caligula had been killed and Claudius put on the throne in his place. The delegation was eventually allowed to deliver its petition to Claudius, and he in turn ruled in their favor. The emperor then sent a letter to the governor and citizens of Alexandria reaffirming the rights and status of the Jewish community.

These cases do not suggest that there was a single cause of or form to the outbreaks of anti-Jewish violence. Some were caused by ethnic prejudice; others, by economic competition; others, by concerns over proselytizing or by the unwillingness of at least some Jews to accommodate to Hellenistic culture. The violence tended to be local and sporadic. Jewish enclaves in other localities seem to have fared far better. They were generally accepted into local social life, held prominent positions, and were supported by local non-Jews. Many pagans also found the strong ethical tradition appealing, and pagan "sympathizers" were commonplace even though there does not appear to have been a general Jewish "missionary" effort to convert pagans.

Aspects of Jewish Religion in the Diaspora

Jews living in the Diaspora faced a constant pull between remaining faithful to their ethnic, cultural, and religious identity and acculturating to local society and cultural norms. Jews in the homeland also faced the issue of acculturation, of course, but the experience is quite different for those of the majority group than for those living as a minority in a foreign land. Thus, Jews in the Diaspora walked this line carefully by making some accommodations.

The Septuagint (LXX): The Scriptures in Greek

One accommodation was the translation of the Hebrew scriptures into Greek. This process largely took place in Egypt beginning as early as the third century BCE with the books of Torah. This translation came to be called the Septuagint, after the legend that it was translated by seventy Jewish elders with the aid of divine guidance. The term *septuaginta* means "seventy"; hence the standard abbreviation for this version of the Jewish scriptures is the roman numeral LXX. Eventually it included all the books now considered part of the Jewish canon plus a number of other works that are now part of the Apocrypha. In some cases the translation is more literal; in other cases, the Greek is freer and incorporates Greek ideas. Some books, such as Daniel, Esther, and Jeremiah, have lengthy additions composed in Greek. Other works of the Apocrypha, such as Tobit, Judith, and the Wisdom of Solomon, were Greek compositions from the start.

There were many other Jewish writings in Greek, suggesting that there was a lively and engaged Jewish literary and intellectual tradition in the Diaspora. The dominant language of Jews living in the Diaspora, including Rome itself, remained Greek throughout most of late antiquity.

Modes of Interpretation: The Wisdom Tradition

Translating and writing in Greek required Jews to express themselves in new ways and to accommodate aspects of Greek philosophy and culture. At the same time, it allowed them to express Jewish traditions and ideas to their pagan neighbors in a way that would make their faith and culture more intelligible. In turn, the pagans might have become more sympathetic toward Jewish religion. A good example comes from the Greek text known as the Wisdom of Solomon. It dates to the period either just before Jesus's birth or shortly after he died, and it is another elaboration on a passage from the Hebrew scriptures. This text purports to be Solomon's words in praise of wisdom after he chose it out of all the worldly gifts that God could give (1 Kings 3:6–15). What is striking is the way that God is conceived through this form of the wisdom tradition.

The wisdom tradition goes back to the later literature of the Hebrew Bible, specifically the book of Proverbs, which gives practical advice on daily life. The other main Jewish example of this tradition is a text known as the Wisdom of Jesus Son of Sirach, which dates to the late second century BCE. Its author claims to have gotten the material from his grandfather, a wise man in Jerusalem, and then to have taken it to Alexandria, where he translated the text into Greek. We possess only the Greek version as it was preserved in the Septuagint.

One of the key features of wisdom literature is its tendency to personify "wisdom" (Hebrew *hochmah*, Greek *sophia*) as female based on the gender of the noun in both languages (cf. Prov. 8:2; 9:1; Sir. 24). "She" was God's first creation (Prov. 8:22; Sir. 24:9). The most striking version of this personification comes from the Wisdom of Solomon, which describes "her" in great detail. Solomon says:

> *Therefore I prayed, and understanding was given me; I called on God, and the spirit of Wisdom came to me. I preferred her to scepters and thrones, and I accounted wealth as nothing in comparison with her. Neither did I liken to her any priceless gem, because all gold is but a little sand in her sight, and silver will be accounted as clay before her. I loved her more than health and*

*beauty, and I chose to have her rather than light, because her radiance never ceases. All good things came to me along with her, and in her hands un-counted wealth. I rejoiced in them all, because Wisdom leads them; but I did not know that she was their mother. . . . **I learned both what is secret and what is manifest, for Wisdom, the fashioner of all things, taught me.** There is in her a spirit that is intelligent, holy, **unique**, manifold, subtle, mo-bile, clear, unpolluted, distinct, invulnerable, loving the good, keen, irre-sistible, beneficent, humane, steadfast, sure, free from anxiety, all-powerful, overseeing all, and penetrating through all spirits that are intelligent, pure, and altogether subtle. For Wisdom is more mobile than any motion; because of her pureness she pervades and penetrates all things. For she is a breath of the power of God, and a pure emanation of the glory of the Almighty; therefore nothing defiled gains entrance into her. For she is a reflection of eternal light, a spotless mirror of the working of God, and an image of his goodness. Al-though she is but one, she can do all things, and while remaining in herself, she renews all things; in every generation she passes into holy souls and makes them friends of God, and prophets; for God loves nothing so much as the per-son who lives with Wisdom. (Wis. Sol. 7:7–12, 21–28)[23]*

This description goes well beyond the use of personification as a metaphorical device. It is strongly influenced by ideas from Greek philosophy, seen especially in the divine attributes of Wisdom above.[24] It also contains reverberations of the praises of Isis. Wisdom was both the first act of God's creation and the one who created everything else. Thus, according to this view, when in Genesis 1:26 God says, "Let *us* make humankind in *our* image," it refers to God and Sophia. *She* is called "God's holy Spirit" (Wis. Sol. 9:17), and she is the one who actually interacts with humans in the world. So, when "God" is reported by Torah as performing some action, in this text it is Wisdom who does it. *She* looked after Adam (10:1–2) and punished Cain (10:3). *She* saved the earth during the flood by guiding Noah (10:4), and she directed Abraham's migrations (10:5–6). *She* watched over Jacob (10:10–12) and Joseph (10:13–14). *She* delivered Israel from Egypt and guided Moses to the land of promise (10:15–11:14). *She* gave Moses the Torah.

In the final analysis, however, all these works of divine Wisdom are meant to show thoughtful pagans that all creation and every good thing in the world ac-tually comes from the One God of Israel through Wisdom as a universal philo-sophical ideal. At the same time, the work holds out fearful prospects for anyone who fails to recognize God's power or who persecutes Jews. It may well be that this text was written in Alexandria sometime after Augustus defeated Antony and Cleopatra (31 BCE) or possibly after the anti-Jewish rioting there in 37 CE.

A Jewish Philosopher: Philo of Alexandria

A variation of the interplay between Jewish tradition and Greek philosophy can be seen in the works of another Alexandrian writer of nearly the same time. Philo of Alexandria was born about 25 BCE and lived until the early 40s CE. He was the one who led the Jewish delegation to the emperor after the pogrom of 37 CE. Despite his advanced age, Philo was undoubtedly chosen for this task because he was from one of the most prominent Jewish families of Alexandria and because he was well respected as a philosopher. He was well versed in Greek philosophy and law and could therefore argue persuasively for Jewish rights.

Philo was also a voluminous writer. His literary output included commentaries on biblical books and characters and treatises on philosophical, theological, and ethical topics. He also wrote several apologetic works, "apologetic" used in its traditional Greek sense as a defense speech, here defending Jewish religion and culture. Philo interpreted the scriptures from the Septuagint version and so was working in a Greek intellectual medium. Although he was an observant Jew and held to a rather literal sense of Jewish law, Philo also used allegorical interpretation of the Jewish scriptures as a main vehicle for deriving theological and philosophical meaning acceptable to both Jews and pagans. For example, the story of Abraham's journeys from Mesopotamia to Egypt to Canaan (Gen. 11–25), for Philo (*On the Migration of Abraham*) becomes an allegory for the soul's journey toward union with God. The story of the giants in Genesis 6:1–4 (the passage so central for *1 Enoch*) becomes an allegory for how a divine spark enters the human soul (*On the Giants*). Both allegories are heavily Platonic in their thought, as they stress both immortality of the soul and the soul's yearning to return to its divine source. Both works also have a deeply ethical content, since understanding this nature of the human soul should cause one to seek the truly divine way of life. For Philo, Torah was the repository of divine revelation, and Judaism was a "mystery" by which one could find God (cf. 1 Cor. 2:1; 4:1; 15:51).[25]

One of Philo's most significant lines of allegorical interpretation concerned the creation of humanity in Genesis 1–2. His ideas on this topic were worked out in several distinct treatises (*On Creation, Allegorical Interpretation of Genesis, Questions and Answers on Genesis*) and influenced many others. His interpretation began from a recognition that the act of creating humanity was described using different words in Genesis 1:26 ("create") and Genesis 2:7 ("form"). This contrast allowed him to see two distinct stories of creation: the first was the creation of a "heavenly human" made in the image of God; the second was the construction of Adam out of earthly matter. The first was an ideal type of humanity existing in the realm of God's pure thought; Philo calls this "heavenly human" God's *Logos,* or "Word" (cf. John 1:1–3). The second brought into existence an inferior copy of the ideal as a physical human being. What we quickly recognize in this scheme is that Philo was reading the Genesis creation story through the lens of the Platonic theory of forms. Of course, this makes it much easier for Jews and pagans to find a common ground if Platonic worldview is inscribed in scripture. Yet for Philo the stream of influence ran the other way, since Plato had gotten his philosophical ideas from Moses and the Torah in the first place. Philo makes this point clear in his elaborate *Life of Moses.*

Community and Congregation: The Synagogue

Today most people in the English-speaking world are familiar with the term "synagogue" as the standard designation for a place of Jewish worship. Sometimes it is also called "temple." Generally, these stand in contrast to "church" as a place of Christian worship, although sometimes one hears the word "temple" used this way. This derived sense, however, causes some confusion when we look at the world of the New Testament. First, in formative Judaism, there was only one Temple at Jerusalem. It was the place where God's presence dwelt as a sign of the election of Israel as the people of God. Even the Samaritans, whose temple stood on Mt. Gerazim, would concur that there was only one temple. In contrast, *synagoge* was the Greek word for "a gathering together" or "assembly" and may best be translated as "congregation." Initially it had no reference to a building as such, but rather to the assembly itself. Often the word was used in the Septuagint to render Hebrew phrases such as "the congregation of Israel." Similarly, the word "church" (Greek *ekklesia*) originally meant an assembly or "congregation," and in the Septuagint it was often used synonymously or in conjunction with forms of *synagoge.* Only much later would "synagogue" and "church" come to be used as distinctive or sectarian "signposts" for the two traditions as they began to split apart. Then, gradually, the terms also began to take on the meaning of the "place" or building where the respective congregations regularly met.

When Jews of the Greco-Roman Diaspora spoke of their assembly places, they generally used a Greek term (*proseuche*) roughly meaning "prayer hall." In contrast, "synagogue" was preferred by Jews of the homeland to designate a "meeting place" for various purposes. As long as the Temple at Jerusalem was still standing, it alone remained the center of Jewish worship, even though there were some who criticized those in charge. The synagogue as a formal institution would only assume its full significance in Jewish worship after the Temple was destroyed in 70 CE, and particularly in conjunction with the rabbinic movement of the second century CE. But for Jews of the Diaspora, living far from Jerusalem, the synagogue had already begun to play an important role in communal life alongside devotion to the Temple. For most diaspora Jews it was a goal to go to Jerusalem at least once to observe the major holy days and to offer the appropriate sacrifices in the Temple. Diaspora Jews also supported the upkeep of the Temple. The rest of the time, however, the center of piety came to be the local congregational assembly—the synagogue.

The place of meeting for the synagogue varied greatly in the early Roman period. There was no standard architectural form. Most of the diaspora synagogue edifices seem to have been structures built for other purposes—many of them houses—that were then taken over and gradually renovated for Jewish communal use.[26] Only gradually, by the third and fourth centuries CE, did these buildings begin to take on more of a formal liturgical plan or architectural style (see Fig. c in Box 17.1). Also, the buildings served multiple functions. They generally had a place set aside for the group to assemble; it might be larger or smaller depending on the local Jewish population and its level of wealth. Many of the diaspora synagogues also had clearly defined social functions, including cooking and dining facilities for congregational fellowship.

Finally, the organization of diaspora congregations often was a mix between religious cults and voluntary clubs, burial societies, or professional associations that were common in Greco-Roman cities. Like these associations, usually called *collegia,* the synagogue communities regularly relied on their most prominent and wealthy members to support the life and activities of the group. In many cases, these patrons also supplied the place for meeting or paid for special construction projects to enhance the synagogue facilities. In the earlier Roman period, there was not as yet a highly developed organizational structure; a patron often served as "president" or "ruler" of the congregation. A more formal organization evolved in parallel with the architecture and the liturgy in the third and fourth centuries CE under the influence of the rabbinic movement.

Jewish Identity Between Two Worlds

A sense of community was very important to the diaspora Jewish enclaves. In some ways because diaspora Jews were living in an alien environment in which they were a minority element, they had to band together. In contrast to the vibrant sectarianism that characterized the homeland, the Diaspora does not reflect as much "us versus them" debate directed at other Jews. That is not to say that diaspora Judaism was more homogeneous or that homeland Judaism was less influenced by Greek ideas. Instead, it points to the cultural impact of living in an environment dominated by another cultural idiom. Most diaspora Jews lived in cities or large towns rather than in rural areas. From the perspective of their Greek or Roman neighbors, they were just another "foreign cult." A sense of community helped buffer the tensions arising from minority status and the pressures of urban life. Likewise, intellectual affirmations of the respectability of Jewish tradition or its coherence with Greek philosophy, as seen in Philo, were responses to these same tensions. The dominant culture exerted a subconscious pressure on foreign groups to conform or acculturate to its ideals, practices, and social norms. Many other "diaspora" groups have had similar experiences throughout history.

Jews living in the Roman world felt this pressure in manifold ways, and it was further magnified by the overlay of the Pax Romana on an already pervasive climate of hellenization. They lived in two worlds: the one, Jewish; the other, Greco-Roman. The dilemma for diaspora Jews was that either extreme was potentially threatening at the level of both personal identity and cultural experience. To opt for social isolation as a way of protecting their cultural traditions from the majority culture could only breed further misunderstanding and prejudice. Some diaspora Jews thus faced resentment for their cliquish exclusivity.

On the other hand, to become too acculturated to Greek and Roman ideas and thus to integrate them into their tradition might threaten to dilute or erase their distinctively Jewish identity and heritage. Debates over certain practices, such as circumcision, kosher laws, or dining with pagans, reflect these tensions. It was as if to ask, "How Greek can we become before we cease to be Jewish?" It was part of the intersecting planes of reference that came with living in the Roman world. The Christian movement would face all these same tensions. Jesus and his first followers were products of the apocalyptic and sectarian environment of the Jewish homeland. Very much like Philo, Paul was a product of the acculturated Jewish Diaspora. The differences in cultural experience will become noticeable.

PART TWO

The First Generation

Sectarian Beginnings

CHAPTER FIVE

The Historical Figure
of Jesus

Jesus did not come as the founder of a new religion, and yet a new religion, Christianity, was founded in his name or, more precisely, in his memory. In this section we will look at how it all began. Belief in Jesus was central to the new movement from the very beginning, in the obscure days and years following his death. Ironically, that is where the story commences—with the death of Jesus. Jesus was a Jew born in the last years of Herod's reign, sometime before 4 BCE. He died as a criminal at the hands of the Roman provincial governor of Judea, Pontius Pilate. As with his birth, the date of his death can only be approximated; he probably died in the first few years of Pilate's administration, that is, around 26–29 CE. Ever since, the questions have been: "What happened?" and "Why?" But those are not easy questions.

An Irony at the Eye of a Storm

We may start with some basics. That Jesus was a real figure of first-century Judean history is no longer much questioned, as it once was. Later sources from opposing camps—Romans, Jews, and Christians—show that all sides acknowledged both his life and his death. The Roman historian Tacitus, writing in about 117 CE, clearly outlines some of the raw facts. Speaking of the great fire of 64 CE that ravaged Rome, Tacitus says:

> *Nero fastened the guilt and inflicted the most exquisite tortures on a class*
> *hated for their abominations, called Christians by the populace. Christus,*

from whom the name had its origin, suffered the extreme penalty during the reign of Tiberius at the hands of one of our procurators, Pontius Pilatus, and a most mischievous superstition thus checked for the moment, again broke out not only in Judea, the first source of the evil, but even in Rome, where all things hideous and shameful from every part of the world find their center and become popular. (Annals 15.44)

As this text shows, by Tacitus's day Christians had become a known commodity in Rome; the author was neither impressed nor sympathetic. Nor did he like Jews very much.[1] So there is hardly any reason to think that Tacitus has somehow doctored the facts. Although Tacitus confirms the basic facts regarding Jesus's death under Pilate, he tells us little more and Jesus remains an enigma.

The Ancient Sources About Jesus

The Jewish and Christian sources, on the other hand, are more difficult in this regard. Although they tend to give us considerably more information, they are inherently biased either in favor of or against a religious understanding of Jesus. Neither sort of biased presentation can be taken at face value, especially when it comes to the reporting of past events. And therein lies the difficulty, since none of these sources come from the time of Jesus himself. Nor are there any contemporary court records or even casual reports as to what happened. All accounts are from decades and even centuries later. Jesus himself wrote nothing and left no direct archaeological evidence on the landscape of Judea. It is as if no one really cared to keep a record at the time, but later, after the movement had started to take off, people began to reflect on Jesus's life, what happened to him, and why. But then, as time passed and the Christian movement became more organized, the "why" was increasingly the object of apologetic interests and theological interpretation. Later still, as Jews and Christians came into greater conflict over Jesus's identity, Jewish texts take a polemical stance in order to counter Christian claims. Thus, these later sources—and here we must include the Gospels—reflect ideas and issues that were not at work in Jesus's own day or at the time of his death.

A good example can be seen in some of the later Jewish polemics culled from rabbinic literature. Jesus's life and death were never denied, nor that he had a following. Instead, these sources claimed that he was born out of wedlock; came from Egypt, whence he learned magic; deceived the masses through his magic and false teaching; was tried and executed for heresy and revolutionary acts under Pilate; and had five disciples who continued to practice evil magic in his name.[2] How should one evaluate the historical reliability of these claims? It is rather transparent that each one is a kind of reversal of some of the standard elements found in the Christian Gospels—the "virgin birth" was a cover for an illegitimate child; instead of miracles, Jesus practiced deception and black magic; and so forth.[3] Thus, these claims provide no new or valid historical information, and each one can be accounted for as a secondary reaction rather than a primary "fact."

On the other side, Matthew 28:11–15 clearly reflects a similar effort on the part of Christians. The story concerns the guards stationed at the tomb of Jesus, who were bribed to say that his body was merely stolen. But this account only appears in Matthew and ends with a telling comment: "And this story is *still* told among the Jews *to this day*" (Matt. 28:15). Thus, the author has given us a subconscious clue that reflects an effort to refute later Jewish polemics that had begun to circulate by the time the Gospel came to be written. It too is a secondary reaction, not a primary fact.

Other ancient sources reflect a different problem—later tampering with texts to make them support certain ideas. This problem is seen in an infamous passage from Josephus. Because Josephus is such an important source for Jewish history in the early period and an eyewitness to the first revolt, his possible knowledge of Jesus has received considerable speculation. The passage, known as the *Testimonium Flavianum,* comes from *Antiquities* 18.63–64:

> *About this time came Jesus, a wise man, **if indeed it is appropriate to call him a man.** For he was a performer of paradoxical feats, a teacher of people who accept the unusual with pleasure, and he won over many of the Jews and also many Greeks. **He was the Christ. When Pilate, upon the accusation of the first men amongst us, condemned him to be crucified, those who had formerly loved him did not cease [to follow him], for he appeared to them on the third day, living again, as the divine prophets had foretold, along with a myriad of other marvelous things concerning him.** And the tribe of the Christians, so named after him, has not disappeared to this day.*

Josephus wrote the *Antiquities* in the mid-90s CE; however, the passage above is widely considered to be a Christian forgery, either whole or in part, inserted centuries later.[4] The parts in bold above almost all scholars agree are Christian interpolations; the remainder is doubted by some but accepted by others. There are several reasons. The parallel sections of Josephus's *Jewish War* make no mention of Jesus, and Christian writers as late as the third century CE who made extensive use of Josephus's *Antiquities* show no awareness of it. Had it been there, they would have gladly used it for proof of Christian claims. Instead, these same writers, notably Origen, admit that Josephus did not believe in Jesus.[5]

On the other hand, another passage in the *Antiquities* makes reference to an event in 62 CE under the high priest Ananus. The event was the trial and death of the Christian leader James, whom Josephus describes as "the brother of Jesus, who was called the Christ."[6] Since few scholars doubt that this passage is authentic, it indicates that Josephus knew about Jesus, or had at least heard Christian claims about him. So it appears that the nonboldfaced portions of the *Testamonium Flavianum* may well be genuine. Even so, it may be read as a disparaging statement, especially the second sentence: "For he was a performer of *paradoxical* feats, a teacher of people who accept *the unusual with pleasure,* and he won over many of the Jews and also many Greeks." Each part clearly reflects some of the early traditions about Jesus, yet each one does so in a way that has a negative tone.[7] Although it gives added support to Jesus's existence and awareness of his followers in the late first century, it tells us little more about him.

The Four Gospels as Historical Sources

So where do the Christian Gospels fit in all of this? They are without doubt some of the earliest sources we possess regarding the life and death of Jesus. Some are earlier than, or at least contemporaneous with, Josephus; almost all are earlier than Tacitus. But they still come from a considerably later period than Jesus himself. The earliest is the Gospel of Mark, which was written sometime between 69 and 75 CE. The typical dates suggested by scholars for the four Gospels in the New Testament are shown in Box 5.1. Thus, all of the Gospels come from a period at least forty years—or one full generation—after the death of Jesus. In fact, they all come *after* the first revolt. The latest, the Gospel of John, might be from a full century later, depending on where we finally date it. These questions of dating will be discussed at greater length in later chapters.

The Gospels are not "histories" as such, at least not in any modern sense. Rather, they fall into the ancient literary category known as "lives," such as were written of Alexander the Great and other famous people. It was quite common in such literature to embellish the story with fanciful or romantic details, some of which might or might not be true. Many times the sources were oral traditions, legends, and exaggerations that grew up to fit the fame or *persona* of the character in later times. So, for example, it became common in the later lives of Alexander the Great to attribute his birth to a miraculous concep-

BOX 5.1

Charting the Ancient Sources

Dates	Events	Christian Writings	Non-Christian Writings
Before 4 BCE	Birth of Jesus		
ca. 26–29 CE	Death of Jesus		
ca. 50–60		Letters of Paul	
ca. 60–64	Death of James, Peter, and Paul		
64	Great fire in Rome		
66–74	First Jewish revolt vs. Rome		
ca. 69–75		Gospel of Mark	
ca. 80–90		Gospel of Matthew	Josephus, *Jewish War*
ca. 95			Josephus, *Antiquities*
ca. 96	Death of John		
ca. 90–100		Gospel of Luke, Acts	
ca. 96–?		Gospel of John	
ca. 117			Tacitus, *Annals*

tion, accompanied by a number of signs and omens, all of which were to demonstrate that this was to be a person with divine gifts and powers.[8] A similar story later crept into some versions of Augustus's life.[9] Such hyperbole clearly comes from a time well after Augustus had died, when his accomplishments had become legendary, and when he had become an object of worship in the imperial cult. In like manner, the Gospels were written as "lives" of Jesus as the founder of the Christian movement. They are thus products of later reflection on his life in light of the importance that later believers placed on him. They are, in that sense, expressions of the faith of those early Christians who told and retold the story of Jesus in the later decades of the first century.

From a historical perspective, therefore, we must constantly be aware of several important methodological considerations when looking at the Gospels. In some ways, they apply to any piece of ancient narrative that depicts past events, just as in our discussions of Jewish polemics and Josephus.

1. We must always be aware of when the *account* was written relative to the actual *events* that it purports to describe. Of course, it is much easier when there is a clear date given for a particular writing. Even so, most ancient sources (and modern ones too) give us some clues about the perspective from which they were written, which lead to several other historical questions.

2. What is the stance or perspective from which the author is recounting the events, and is there some indication of later perspectives or new information?

3. What was the situation or purpose of the writing, and what was the *account* doing in its own time and later?

4. What were the sources for the author, and how were they used?

5. From there we can begin to ask whether the *account* is an accurate rendering of the earlier *event* in all respects. Or is there some sort of "spin" being put on the *account* that becomes more intelligible in view of the author's situation or agenda?

In the final analysis, then, we are always asking two equally important historical questions simultaneously: *What really happened?* and *Why did a later writer tell the story of what happened in a particular way?* We cannot hope to answer either question without addressing them both. In both cases, and in all our historical study, the most important issue will be *context*—the original context of an event as well as the context of those who told the story of that event in later generations. Nor is this an effort to deny the faith stance of the Gospels (or any other piece of religious literature) or to discount it in favor of some arbitrary notion of history. Quite the contrary. Only by recognizing the beliefs and goals of both the authors and their audiences can we hope to understand their writings.

The Quest for the Historical Jesus

What is commonly known as the "quest for the historical Jesus" is an ongoing reflection of these historical considerations. As a scholarly enterprise, the quest began in the seventeenth century when early modern scholars began to analyze the Gospel stories in light of both new archaeological discoveries and Enlightenment ideas of history. Thomas Jefferson was one of the early thinkers who engaged these issues, in a book now frequently called *The Jefferson Bible*. Published in 1821, it was originally titled *The Life and Morals of Jesus of Nazareth Extracted Textually from the Gospels in Greek, Latin, French, and English.*[10] The premise behind the work was that, through research and reading, Jefferson had come to believe that the Gospel authors had incorporated both events and teachings that could not be historically accurate to Jesus himself. As early as 1813 he described his project in a letter to John Adams:

> *We must reduce our volume to the simple evangelists, select even from them, the very words only of Jesus paring off the amphiboligisms [sic, ambiguities] into which they [the Evangelists] have been led. . . . I have performed this operation for my own use, by cutting verse by verse out of the printed book, and by arranging the matter which is evidently his, and which is as distinguishable as diamonds in a dunghill.*[11]

Thus, Jefferson set about to identify which events and teachings in the Gospels were authentic and which were not. There were many others who embarked on similar studies, but none commanded complete success in the eyes of all. And yet there was a growing awareness that the Gospels were not just the unvarnished account of Jesus's life, teachings, and death.

Nearly a century after Jefferson, Albert Schweitzer penned a work that both surveyed the twists and turns in biblical research and bequeathed it a name. Published in Germany in 1906, the work was then translated into English with the title *The Quest of the Historical Jesus: A Critical Study of Its Progress from Reimarus to Wrede.*[12] One of the startling results of Schweitzer's review of more than a century of earlier research was that the quest to "discover" the historical Jesus had largely proven inconclusive. Since then, there have been two more recent phases in biblical scholarship in which a focus on recovering the historical Jesus has occupied center stage, and the research continues.

From Jesus to the Gospels

Although this book is not primarily about the quest as such, the historical issues it has raised have been at the center of developments in biblical scholarship and theology for almost 250 years. They have important implications for how we look at the Gospels and the New Testament in general. So we may begin with a resumé of Jesus's life as told by the Gospel authors, while also noting some of the historical questions and issues that have been raised.

Jesus: A Resumé

Birth

Prior to 4 BCE, during the last years of Herod's reign; clearly indicated in Matt. 2:1–23 and also in Luke 1:5. *Historical consideration:* The story of the census under Quirinius in Luke 2:1–2 cannot be reconciled with this date, since it occurred in 6 CE, after the removal of Archelaus.[13]

Location

Both Matthew and Luke place the actual birth in Bethlehem (in Judea), while Jesus grew up living in Nazareth (in the Galilee). *Historical consideration:* Only Luke accounts for this fact by having Joseph and Mary travel from their home in Nazareth to Bethlehem, as a result of the census (see above). Matthew seems to indicate that Joseph and Mary lived in Bethlehem at the time and only moved to Nazareth after returning from Egypt after the death of Herod and while Archelaus was still on the throne (Matt. 2:19–22). In any case, Jesus's "hometown" was understood to be Nazareth.[14]

Upbringing

None of the Gospels say anything about Jesus's childhood or education, with the exception of one story in Luke 2:41–52 (a visit to Jerusalem at age twelve). Mark 6:3 says Jesus was a carpenter, while the parallel passage in Matt. 13:55 calls him the "son of a carpenter." *Historical consideration:* Recent archaeological work has shown that Nazareth was actually a satellite village of a large urban center named Sepphoris, which was less than four miles away and visible from Nazareth. Sepphoris was founded by Herod (ca. 30–15 BCE) and built up by his son, Antipas (4 BCE–38 CE), at one point serving as the capital of the Galilee. This would have occurred while Jesus was growing up. Scholars have recently suggested, therefore, that if Jesus (or his father) was indeed working in the building trade as a carpenter, it most likely would have taken him to Sepphoris on a regular basis. This urban setting for Jesus's early life changes our understanding of his "typical" Galilean background and language. Scholars disagree, however, on whether his status as an artisan or craftsman would have placed him higher or lower on the socioeconomic scale relative to ordinary rural peasants. In the Roman world, an artisan should typically have been of a higher social standing than a peasant farmer.[15]

Language

None of the Gospels explicitly indicate Jesus's spoken language. Very few people in that time other than an educated scribal elite could speak, read, or write biblical Hebrew. There is no indication that Jesus had such an education, even though he is portrayed on occasion as reading from the scriptures (cf. Luke 4:16–20). *Historical consideration:* Luke's account of this event only gives the scripture in Greek following the text of the LXX, and the quotation is a composite of two distinct passages from Isaiah that are several chapters apart. Calculations based on typical ancient manuscripts make it impossible for a standing man to hold a scroll open in such a way as to see these two passages simultaneously. Scholars have long suggested that Jesus's everyday tongue was Aramaic, which had been the predominant Semitic language of the ancient Middle East since the Babylonian and Persian periods. It was the common language for most Jews in Judea and Galilee. The Gospel of Mark notes Jesus using Aramaic phrases on occasion, especially in performing miracles. For example, Josephus says that he wrote his first edition of *The Jewish War* in Aramaic and then had help in translating it into Greek.[16] Thus, he spoke and read Greek but was not initially as fluent as he wished. In light of the recent discoveries at Sepphoris (see above), it has also been suggested that Jesus might have had some facility in Greek, since Sepphoris has clear signs of extensive Greek usage.[17]

John the Baptist

All the Gospels mention that Jesus was baptized by John just at the beginning of his ministry. *Historical consideration:* Josephus's account of John the Baptist, however, suggests that he was the more famous "popular voice" of the period, and some scholars have suggested that Jesus was originally a disciple of John's and only later (perhaps after John was killed by Antipas in ca. 27–28) embarked on his own ministry. There is no certainty either way.[18]

Ministry

Only John's Gospel gives the duration of Jesus's ministry as more than two years, based on the fact that three annual Passover celebrations are reported after Jesus had begun his public ministry (John 2:13; 6:4; 13:1 + 19:31). It is on this basis that the traditional "three-year ministry" developed. *Historical consideration:* None of the other three Gospels say explicitly what the duration was;

however, they only mention the one Passover at which Jesus died. On the basis of the rapid "pace" of events, seen especially in Mark, scholars have suggested that his public ministry might have been well less than one year.

Miracles

By far one of the most common traits reported about Jesus was that he performed miracles, particularly healings. Even the rabbinic polemics "admit" to this fact by trying to explain them away as magical trickery (see the beginning of this chapter). *Historical consideration:* Since the Enlightenment, scientific skepticism has led many people to question the reality of the miracles. On the other hand, in more recent scholarship, it has been recognized that magic and miracles were much more commonly accepted in the ancient world (see Chapter 3). There were other Jewish miracle workers who achieved a similar fame at that time. Consequently, it is historically more responsible to examine the individual miracle stories for how they present Jesus in the light of the ancient culture. Difficulties sometimes arise from the fact that the Gospels differ over what happened in a particular case (cf. Matt. 9:20–22; Mark 5:25–34).[19]

Teachings

All the Gospels make Jesus's teachings, especially the parables, a central feature of his public ministry. *Historical consideration:* The Gospels differ at times over precisely what Jesus said or as to the occasions for his teachings. For example, a major block of his teachings in Matthew's Gospel occurs in what is popularly known as the Sermon on the Mount (Matt. 5:1–7:28). None of the other Gospels mention this sermon (cf. Luke 6:20–29; see also below). Perhaps more than any other single issue in study of the Gospels, scholarly debate has focused on which sayings or which form of a given saying might have been original to Jesus. One example of the difficulty is Jesus's fiery apocalyptic language in Matthew 10:34–35 (cf. Luke 12:49–53) compared to the more familiar beatitude: "Blessed are the peacemakers" (Matt. 5:9).[20]

Death

All the Gospels, and most other ancient notices (e.g., Tacitus), agree that Jesus was executed by Pontius Pilate, who was the Roman governor of Judea from 26 to 36 CE. If he was "about thirty years old" (Luke 3:23) when he began his ministry, then this might place his death as early as 26 or 27 CE. It does not appear that his death occurred later than 29 or 30 CE. All the Gospels place the death near Passover, but with some notable differences. *Historical considerations:*

The Gospels disagree dramatically regarding the cause of the arrest and execution and the role of various Jewish groups. Mark 11 suggests that the "cleansing of the Temple" was the cause and that the priests were behind his demise (cf. Mark 15:11). In John's Gospel, however, the "cleansing" occurs two full years before Jesus's death and has no direct role in his arrest (cf. John 2:13–22). Matthew 21 seems to make the "triumphal entry" the cause and the priests along with the Pharisees the chief instigators (cf. Matt. 21:45–46). There are numerous other differences between the accounts.[21] Scholars, finally, differ over who was actually responsible. Almost all would agree that it was ultimately Pilate; that the main reason was political (rather than "blasphemy" or heresy); and that the majority of the Jewish population had nothing to do with it or say about it. A few scholars would still argue that perhaps the Temple leadership might have had a hand in identifying Jesus to the Roman authorities as a "troublemaker"; however, most of these same scholars would not include the Pharisees in this group. It is also difficult to account for an all-night trial before the Sanhedrin during Passover, while Luke adds an extra trial before Herod Antipas.[22]

Resurrection

All the Gospels agree that Jesus rose from the tomb on the third day and appeared to his disciples. *Historical considerations:* The Gospels differ on numerous details. Only Matthew has the account of guards being placed around the tomb. Mark and Matthew have the postresurrection appearances occur only in Galilee. Luke has the appearances occur only in and around Jerusalem. John has some of both. Luke also adds that Jesus was present for forty more days after the resurrection before he ascended (Acts 1:3–12).[23]

Comparing the Gospels

What emerges from this survey is a realization of both similarities and differences between the four New Testament Gospels. The most noticeable occur between John's Gospel and the other three. For this reason, the first three Gospels (Matthew, Mark, and Luke) have traditionally been called the "synoptic Gospels" (or just the "Synoptics," for short), because they follow a more similar outline. Hence they can be compared side-by-side, or "synoptically." Even so, there are some noticeable difficulties. Only Matthew and Luke contain accounts of Jesus's birth, but with some key differences. In content alone, Luke's complex version is more than ten times longer than the rather brief account in Matthew. Often overlooked, however, are the numerous other minor changes

BOX 5.2

The Day Jesus Died — A Comparison of the Passion Week in the Synoptics and John

	Sunday	Monday	Tuesday	Wednesday	Thursday	Friday	Saturday	Sunday
Synoptics	Triumphal Entry	Cleansing Temple (Matthew/Luke) (Mark)		Anointing at Bethany Mark & Matthew (Luke to Ch. 7)	Trial(s) — Last Supper Passover (1st Seder)	Shabbat — Burial "Day of Preparation" Crucifixion	Guards at Tomb & Bribe (Matthew only)	Road to Emmaus & Dinner (Luke only) — Empty Tomb
John	Anointing at Bethany	to Ch. 2 — Triumphal Entry			Trial(s) — Last Supper (not a Seder)	Passover (1st Seder) Shabbat — Burial "Day of Preparation" Crucifixion		Empty Tomb

Time markers (Synoptics): 6 PM, Noon, 6 AM
Time markers (John): 6 PM, Noon, 6 AM

of specific episodes, such as Jesus's anointing at Bethany, which takes place in Matthew and Mark during the last week of Jesus's life but in Luke much earlier (chap. 7).

To understand the cumulative impact of these differences we must compare the events of "Passion week" on a day-by-day basis, as shown in Box 5.2. John's repositioning of the Temple cleansing also creates John's unique "three-year" ministry for Jesus. As a result, the cleansing occurs two full years before Jesus's death and has no direct connection to either the triumphal entry or his arrest. Other characteristic differences revolve around Jesus's going to Jerusalem earlier and more often than in the Synoptics; the last supper (John 13) is not a Passover meal and contains no institution of the Lord's Supper; and John includes several lengthy "self-disclosure" discourses and some unique miracles (cf. 2:1–11; 4:46–54).

There are also some key differences between the synoptic Gospels, as we already noted in conjunction with individual episodes in the Passion narrative. Box 5.3 shows a parallel chart that illustrates the nature of the problem by tracking six key episodes in the early ministry of Jesus as they appear in each of the three Synoptics. Using the familiar titles by which they are known, these six episodes are:

a. The first miracles and the calling of the disciples (Matt. 8 + 4; Mark 1–3; Luke 4–5)

b. The Sermon on the Mount/Plain (Matt. 5–7; *not in Mark;* Luke 6)

c. The parables of the kingdom (Matt. 13; Mark 4; Luke 8)

d. A group of three miracles (Matt. 8–9; Mark 4–5; Luke 8)

e. The rejection at Nazareth (Matt. 13; Mark 6; Luke 4)

f. The mission of the twelve disciples (Matt. 9–10; Mark 6; Luke 9)

The first thing to notice is that the Sermon on the Mount, one of the best-known events of Jesus's ministry, only occurs as an actual "sermon" delivered on a mountain and containing a specific group of teachings (such as the Beatitudes) in Matthew's Gospel. It is quite lengthy, covering three full chapters (Matt. 5:1–7:28). Mark does not contain it at all, and Luke contains only a few of the same teachings (such as the Beatitudes), but in a different situation. Luke's version is usually called the Sermon on the Plain (Luke 6:20–46), but it is hardly a sermon in the same way as that in Matthew. Another key difference

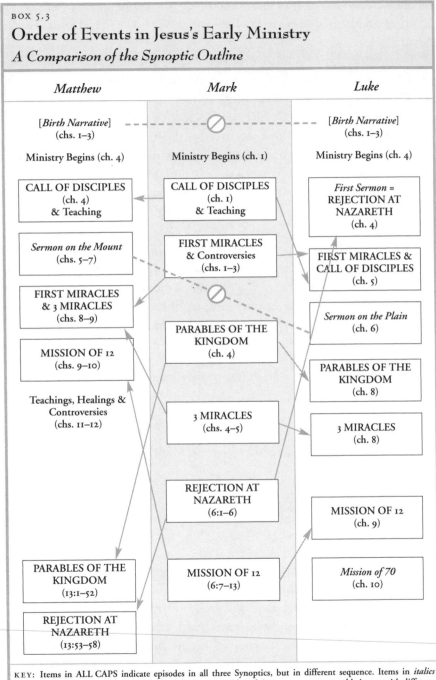

BOX 5.3

Order of Events in Jesus's Early Ministry
A Comparison of the Synoptic Outline

Matthew	Mark	Luke
[Birth Narrative] (chs. 1–3)	⊘	[Birth Narrative] (chs. 1–3)
Ministry Begins (ch. 4)	Ministry Begins (ch. 1)	Ministry Begins (ch. 4)
CALL OF DISCIPLES (ch. 4) & Teaching	CALL OF DISCIPLES (ch. 1) & Teaching	First Sermon = REJECTION AT NAZARETH (ch. 4)
Sermon on the Mount (chs. 5–7)	FIRST MIRACLES & Controversies (chs. 1–3)	FIRST MIRACLES & CALL OF DISCIPLES (ch. 5)
FIRST MIRACLES & 3 MIRACLES (chs. 8–9)	⊘	Sermon on the Plain (ch. 6)
MISSION OF 12 (chs. 9–10)	PARABLES OF THE KINGDOM (ch. 4)	PARABLES OF THE KINGDOM (ch. 8)
Teachings, Healings & Controversies (chs. 11–12)	3 MIRACLES (chs. 4–5)	3 MIRACLES (ch. 8)
	REJECTION AT NAZARETH (6:1–6)	MISSION OF 12 (ch. 9)
PARABLES OF THE KINGDOM (13:1–52)	MISSION OF 12 (6:7–13)	Mission of 70 (ch. 10)
REJECTION AT NAZARETH (13:53–58)		

KEY: Items in ALL CAPS indicate episodes in all three Synoptics, but in different sequence. Items in *italics* indicate episodes that appear in only one of the Synoptics (though in some cases comparable items, with different shape or wording, appear in one of the others, usually Matthew and Luke).

between Matthew and the other two is in the events surrounding Jesus's call of the first disciples and his first preaching in Capernaum and Galilee. In Mark and Luke this first calling is accompanied by the performance of several miracles (Mark 1:16–2:17; Luke 4:31–5:32), whereas in Matthew these same miracles are not recorded until much later (8:14–17). The call of the first disciples occurs in Matthew 4:18–22, just prior to the Sermon on the Mount (5:1–7:28).

Next, we should notice what happens with another very familiar group of Jesus teachings, the parables of the kingdom (c), especially in relation to a group of three miracles (d), the rejection at Nazareth (e), and the mission of the Twelve (f). Mark has the four episodes in the sequence (c)-(d)-(e)-(f). The three miracle stories are a distinctive cluster comprising the stilling of the storm, the Gadarene demoniac, and the unusual double miracle of Jairus's daughter and the hemorrhaging woman. This miracle cluster (d, Mark 4:35–5:43) stands between the parables (c, 4:1–42) and the rejection (e, 6:1–6), which is followed immediately by the mission (f, 6:7–13). The ordering is very tight: the three miracles thus become the immediate cause of the rejection at his hometown (cf. Mark 6:2, 5), and the expanded mission of the Twelve is the direct result.

In Matthew, the mission of the Twelve comes first (9:35–10:42), and contains a unique and lengthy discourse to the disciples. Just before it (8:18–9:26) comes the same cluster of three miracles found in Mark 4:35–5:43; however, in Matthew these three miracles have been supplemented by the other miracles (comparable to the first miracles [a] in Mark 1–3) and some additional episodes. Although the three miracles thus form part of the setting, the primary force of the mission in Matthew is testing the willingness of the disciples to "follow" Jesus (cf. Matt. 8:18–22; 10:17–25) in the face of trial. Then there are two more chapters before we get to the parables of the kingdom (Matt. 13:1–52), followed immediately by the rejection at Nazareth (13:53–58). Thus, Matthew's sequence is (d)-(f) < > (c)-(e). There is a good bit of narrative (and thus time) between f and c; now these two subsections operate in parallel, inasmuch as both relate to the theme of discipleship. In Matthew the parables have likewise been supplemented with additional material to become the immediate cause of Jesus's rejection and come considerably later in the Matthean temporal framework of Jesus's career.

In Luke, on the other hand, the rejection at Nazareth occurs as the very first episode in Jesus's career (4:16–30), comparable in temporal sequence to Mark 1:14–15. It has also been elaborated by additional material. The parables of the kingdom do not occur until Luke 8:4–18, and as in Mark, they are followed by the same three miracles (Luke 8:22–56), which are in turn followed immediately by the mission (Luke 9:1–6). The Lukan sequence is (e) < > (c)-(d)-(f); now the miracles have become the main purpose of the mission. Luke's mission of the Twelve is nearly identical in length and content to that in Mark (thus, much shorter than in Matthew). Luke 10:1–16 then follows with another mission, of seventy disciples, shortly thereafter, where again the main purpose is to perform miracles as an advance team for Jesus's own preaching. In Luke the rejection has been entirely disconnected from this sequence and its new placement creates a different set of expectations from the very beginning of Jesus's career.

The Synoptic Problem

Comparisons such as these between the three synoptic Gospels have led scholars to formulate some theories about literary relationships between Matthew, Mark, and Luke. In turn, these relationships have significant bearing on both when and how the Gospels were composed. Scholars call it the Synoptic Problem.

Taking the examples discussed above, we can see the nature of the problem. On the one hand, several key episodes occur in each of the three Synoptics. Clearly these are meant to be the same "events." The sequence of these events, however, is different from one Gospel to the next. In Matthew the mission is earlier and the rejection is later in comparison to Mark; in Luke the rejection is earlier and the parables and miracles are nearly identical to Mark's. Both Matthew and Luke contain a "sermon" with beatitudes, but they occur in different settings, while Mark does not contain this episode at all. Some versions are longer and more elaborate (the mission in Matthew, the rejection in Luke), while the other two versions of the same episode remain brief and very similar in wording. Then when we look at the narratives that surround these different sequences, we discover that the cause-and-effect relationships for the course of Jesus's career—particularly as they lead up to his death—are changed significantly from Gospel to Gospel.

So, the Synoptic Problem asks the question this way: How can it be that these three Gospels have so much material in common, even verbatim in some instances, but still have episodes moved around and new or distinctive material added? To answer this question, we must conclude that there were some common sources lying behind the written Gospels, but that the various Gospel authors compiled their accounts with some flexibility by stitching these source materials together in different ways. There are then two key components to this process: first, the oral circulation of stories about Jesus as a source prior to any written accounts; second, the literary dependency of one Gospel author on another.

Oral Tradition

The ancient cultures of the Middle East, Egypt, Greece, and Rome have been called "oral cultures." Although all of them had writing systems and developed important pieces of "literature" (such as the biblical narratives, the *Epic of Gilgamesh,* and the *Iliad* and *Odyssey*), they were not primarily "writing cultures" in the same way the modern Western world is. What this means is that these ancient cultures (like some others today) conceived of the transmission of tradition and information primarily through oral storytelling rather than through any written form. Writing was effectively a secondary form of preservation.

Storytelling was an oral performance medium, and storytellers were important to cultural transmission. Often their stories carried a profound sense of national or ethnic identity while also conveying important values and ideals. As a living, performance medium, storytelling remained somewhat more fluid. The stories themselves tended to be shorter, or many short episodes might be linked together into a longer epic. The ability of ancient storytellers to remember these lengthy epics is quite remarkable. Even so, we know that numerous variations tended to arise, just as in the Homeric tradition, where new episodes appear in some versions. Some smaller stories circulated widely and were picked up in different ways by different cultures, as seen in the case of the many ancient versions of a great flood. While retaining some basic similarities, a flood story came to be embedded into very different narrative traditions and resultant forms. Thus, oral storytelling both preserves traditions and allows for fluidity.

Neither Jesus nor his first disciples wrote anything. Even those Gospel materials that clearly profess to come from original disciples, such as John's Gospel claims (John 21:24), were nonetheless written down much, much later. Even then, it must be remembered that John's Gospel was called the "spiritual Gospel" because its account differed so markedly from the others. Hence, prior to the first efforts to write down any aspects of the life, teachings, miracles, and death of Jesus, there were numerous stories that must have circulated orally. The first generation of the Jesus movement seems to have relied predominantly on oral traditions about Jesus. Many of them were likely in Aramaic, the language of both Jesus and his first followers. Only later were they translated into Greek, and later still collected into what we call the Gospels. In Chapter 6 we shall examine some of these oral traditions from the first generation in greater detail.

From Oral to Written Form

At the center of the story of Jesus stands the account of his death. The birth narratives, in contrast, seem to come later. Stories of Jesus's miracles or his teachings circulated somewhat independently at first and slowly coalesced into small collections by virtue of similar types of material. In each case, the particular stories that were told were meant to convey and reinforce the faith of the followers. We know that at times there were differences in the telling. For example, Paul *never* mentions Jesus's miracles, while the synoptic Gospels contain a large number (thirty-two), with special emphasis on storm miracles, healings, and especially exorcisms.[24] John's Gospel mentions that Jesus performed many "signs and wonders" (John 20:31), but it contains only seven actual miracle stories, and none are exorcisms. Of the seven only two are directly comparable to those in the Synoptics (John 6:1–21); the other five are unique to John. So it would appear that when it came to the miracles of Jesus, John and Paul were using two distinct oral traditions quite apart from those used by the Synoptics.

Some of the sayings or teachings of Jesus occur in only one Gospel, others in all three Synoptics, and others in only two of the Synoptics (especially Matthew and Luke). For the most part, all the sayings recorded in Mark occur in one form or another in both Matthew and Luke; however, Matthew and Luke also contain some 250 verses of sayings that are very similar, at times identical, to one another but that do not occur in Mark. These include the Beatitudes and other portions of the Sermon on the Mount/Plain (Matt. 5–7; cf. Luke 6; 9). Also, the general outline of the three Synoptics follows Mark, especially in the final chapters surrounding the death of Jesus. When either Matthew or Luke places an episode in a different location from Mark (such as Matthew's mission of the Twelve or Luke's rejection at Nazareth; see Box 5.3), the other one will remain similar, and in some cases almost identical, to Mark.

Modern Theories of Synoptic Relationships

The patterns of difference and similarity between the three synoptic Gospels have led the majority of New Testament scholars to conclude that there is also an intricate web of literary dependency between them. What that means is this: the similarities between the Synoptics derive from two of them using the other as a common source; the differences derive from their use of other distinctive sources and their ability to weave the stories together in different ways. Modern biblical scholars have proposed three main theories to explain these relationships. These are schematized in Box 5.4.

By far the most widely accepted theory of synoptic relationships is called the Two-Source Hypothesis (no. 1 in Box 5.4). It assumes that Mark was the first of the New Testament Gospels to be written down, sometime between the end of the first Jewish revolt and about 75 CE. Mark's Gospel was composed from a variety of oral traditions that had been transmitted separately. By the time of Mark's composition, they had been rendered into Greek. Sometime later, Matthew and Luke each used Mark as a source, but did so independently of one another. This helps to account for how Matthew and Luke can move materials around in such different ways while still retaining the same basic episodes. It also explains how Matthew and Luke can add some items of unique material by suggesting that each one had its own separate line of oral tradition. These are sometimes called the M source and L source, respectively, and include some materials in their respective birth narratives as well as other unique teachings.

Matthew and Luke also use a second common source apart from Mark. This is reflected in the roughly 250 verses of similar material found in Matthew and Luke but not found anywhere in Mark. It consists almost completely of teachings of Jesus and includes such famous passages as the Beatitudes, the Lord's Prayer, and the parable of the lost sheep. Since this material is often nearly verbatim in Greek in the two Gospels, it suggests that the oral tradition surrounding these teachings had at some earlier stage been translated from Aramaic into Greek. This translation may account for its separate transmission as a "sayings source" for Jesus's teachings. It does not contain miracles or some other common narrative features of Jesus's life. Scholars usually call it Q (from the German word *Quelle*, meaning "source") or the Synoptic Sayings Source. Scholars date this Q material between 50 and 70 CE.[25] It is not clear, however, whether it was already written down in some fixed order, since Matthew and Luke arrange the sayings quite differently. The only form in which it is preserved is that found in Matthew and Luke, and perhaps the *Gospel of Thomas.*

Whether written or oral, the Q tradition seems to reflect an early stage in the transmission of the oral tradition in the life of an early Christian community (or perhaps several). The Two-Source Hypothesis proposes that Matthew and Luke used *two major, earlier sources* (Mark and Q) to compose their respective Gospels. Both Matthew and Luke used Mark as their base outline, but each one modified it by reordering material and inserting the Q material in unique ways.

BOX 5.4

The Synoptic Problem
Some Alternative Solutions

1. The Two-Source Hypothesis

- The majority opinion among biblical scholars; first proposed in 1855. Stresses Markan priority.
- Best discussion of the overall issues: Helmut Koester, *Ancient Christian Gospels* (Philadelphia: Trinity Press Intl., 1990). See also *Anchor Bible Dictionary*, s.v. "Synoptic Problem" and "Two-Source Hypothesis."

SYNOPSIS

Mark was written first, and Matthew and Luke both used it as a source. Matthew and Luke also used a second source, usually called "Q," as well as other unique materials.

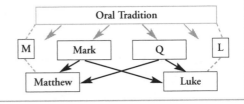

2. The Two-Gospel Hypothesis (The Griesbach Hypothesis)

- Minority opinion today; first suggested in the eighteenth century. Stresses Matthean priority.
- Best discussion: W. R. Farmer, *The Synoptic Problem* (Dillsboro: Western North Carolina Press, 1976). See also *Anchor Bible Dictionary*, s.v. "Two Gospel Hypothesis."

SYNOPSIS

Matthew was written first. Luke came next and modified Matthew. Finally, Mark used both to create a composite.

3. The Farrar-Goulder Hypothesis

- Minority opinion; first suggested 1955. Supports Markan priority.
- Best discussion: E. P. Sanders and Margaret Davies, *Studying the Synoptic Gospels* (Philadelphia: Trinity Press Intl., 1989).

SYNOPSIS

Mark was written first. Then Matthew used Mark, but revised and supplemented it with some unique material (including what would be called the Q material). Last, Luke used both Mark and Matthew to create a composite.

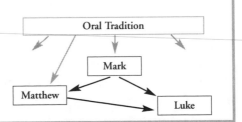

Each of the three synoptic Gospels is thus seen as a distinctive configuration of both oral and written traditions. Each one is an expression of early Christian faith trying to preserve the memory and message of Jesus as taught in different communities in the light of their own experience and tradition.

Not all New Testament scholars have accepted the Two-Source Hypothesis, but those who do not are a small minority and fall into the groups supporting the two other hypotheses (see Box 5.4). Still, their objections are noteworthy for what they also suggest about the process of composition of the Gospels. Both of these alternative theories are skeptical that a separate Q source ever existed or that it exercised such a profound influence. One theory (no. 2 in Box 5.4) proposes that Matthew was written first and that its unique source for the teachings of Jesus (sometimes called M) contained all of the so-called Q materials. It further argues that Luke was based on Matthew, but made some major changes in the order and contents. Finally, Mark was composed as a blending of the other two, sometimes following Matthew and other times, Luke.

The third theory (no. 3 in Box 5.4) is something of a compromise theory. It accepts the view that Mark was written first but denies the existence of Q. It explains the relationships by arguing that Matthew was based on Mark and added the so-called Q material, and then Luke rewrote Mark while using Matthew as a second source, but only for some of its added material, which it then freely modified. A good example is the parable of the marriage feast/banquet (Matt. 22:1–14; Luke 14:16–24; cf. Box 6.4).

One difficulty with each of these alternative theories is the rather sharp differences in order and content between Matthew and Luke, seen especially in their respective birth narratives. In order to argue that Luke used Matthew as a direct source, as they both do, they must assume that the author of Luke was willing to make much more radical changes in the contents of its source Gospels than the Two-Source Hypothesis assumes. For example, using the case of the rejection at Nazareth, discussed above (and see Box 5.3), it would mean that Luke would have had to move the rejection story from Matthew's relatively late position (Matt. 13:53–58) immediately following the parables (13:1–52) to a radically early position (Luke 4:16–30) while also placing the parables, the miracles, and the mission in almost the identical position (and with very similar wording) to that in Mark. This move means that Luke then had to delete several parables contained in Matthew, reorder the miracles back into their Markan form, and delete a large block of so-called Q material from the mission to be inserted elsewhere. In either case, the Gospel authors are making editorial changes in the story; however, the Two-Source Hypothesis calls for a simpler process by having Matthew and Luke independently make changes and additions to Mark and the Q source.

In the final analysis all current scholarly theories assume four major components to the development of the Gospel tradition.

1. That there was a vibrant and influential oral tradition about what Jesus said and did and that the Passion narrative was its earliest core (see Chapter 6).

2. That these independent oral traditions were circulated within and among individual Christian communities, where they were given context and meaning in the worship life of the communities.

3. That transmission of these source traditions, whether in oral or written form, to other communities allowed for retelling and reconfiguration to fit new needs and situations.

4. That the order, themes, and content of the individual Gospels of the New Testament reflect the local context of the respective authors and communities as an expression of their faith in Jesus in the light of their cultural background and social experience.

In other words, the Gospels as we now have them are not direct or firsthand biographies of Jesus. Nor do they operate under modern conceptions of writing history. Instead, they are early attempts to tell the story of Jesus for a particular audience in a particular context or social location. To be sure, the historical figure of Jesus stands behind the stories, but the stories are nonetheless removed from that historical figure in important ways.

Each of the Gospels thus tells the story in a different way. That means more than merely rearranging certain episodes or adding new sayings here and there. The different ordering and the narrative shaping that occur in each Gospel (as illustrated above) give new shades of meaning to the teachings, interpret cause and effect in the death of Jesus, and explore themes about faith, discipleship, and community. Changing the order and wording of such episodes usually reflects a distinctive understanding of Jesus's life, teachings, and death on the part of a Gospel author who was far more interested in the theological significance carried by the story than in historical accuracy. Ultimately, the Gospels are stories about the growth of belief in Jesus. As a result, their differences are historically important, but in a different way, since they may tell us more about the development of the early Jesus movement than about Jesus himself. In later chapters we shall look at each of the Gospels in its own time and context as reflections of the growth and development of the Christian movement. This is the story of the "storytellers."

CHAPTER SIX

Before They Were Christians

The Beginnings of the
Jesus Movement

The historical Jesus did not appear as the founder of a new religion called "Christianity." In fact the name "Christianity" as a designation for the new movement did not even exist until nearly a century after Jesus's death. Jesus himself seems to have been some sort of reforming preacher—some might say a "prophet"—within the complex and contentious religious environment of early-first-century Judaism. The movement that grew up around Jesus—insofar as it may properly be classed as a "movement" prior to his death—probably resembled other Jewish sects of the time, in which there was considerable diversity and, at times, rancor over matters of Jewish observance and piety.

Hence, we must be cautious about assuming that the Christian church erupted onto the scene as a discrete and identifiable religious institution shortly after the death of Jesus or that it began at a single moment or as a single phenomenon. Although the traditional account of the origins of the movement—based almost exclusively on the book of Acts in the New Testament—may reflect some aspects of the early days, it does not likely tell the whole story. More to the point, it tells its story of the rise of the Christian movement from a later perspective, when the church had already begun to develop a more distinctive identity. Consequently, we must be careful of retrojecting conditions or developments that only arose much later onto the period of its origins. To do so is to create a *myth of beginnings* that never actually existed.

Like the quest for the historical Jesus, then, finding the origins of the Christian movement faces problems derived from distilling historical information out of these later sources. As we have already seen, the earliest written accounts of the life of Jesus do not appear for some forty or fifty years after his death. Likewise, the earliest account of the founding of the movement, that in the book of Acts, was written as part of this process by the same author who wrote the Gospel of Luke, and hence some sixty or more years after Jesus's death. Although all these written accounts are considerably later, we do know that they used earlier sources of information. Some may have been written (as suggested by some scholars for the Q source), but the majority were oral traditions repeated and preserved within the congregations themselves. The members of those communities preserved the memory of Jesus and of his first followers by telling and retelling stories about them. In fact, our earliest sources regarding the foundations of the movement occur in situations where they were also reminiscing about Jesus himself.

Rediscovering the Earliest
Oral Traditions

The problem is that oral traditions are often difficult to recognize or isolate when they have been rather thoroughly woven into the fabric of a later narrative, such as in Luke and Acts. Take, for example, the tradition of Jesus's "last supper." All three of the synoptic Gospels report this episode as a celebration of Passover at which Jesus instituted a commemorative Lord's Supper, but there are some differences in the three accounts.[1] John's Gospel, however, clearly states that the last supper was *not* a Passover meal and makes no mention whatsoever of the institution of the Lord's Supper. So it is difficult on the basis of the Gospel accounts alone to discern the earliest tradition. Yet the Lord's Supper was clearly an early practice of Jesus's followers, and this fact is given a clear and very early witness in oral tradition, at least when we are able to identify these early oral tradition materials.

The earliest writings in the New Testament are the genuine letters of Paul, written between 50 and 60 CE. They are, therefore, some twenty to forty years earlier than the Gospels and Acts. Because they are letters written to congregations in specific circumstances, they often tell us much more about early Christian practice and belief. In addition, they tell us how the early oral traditions were used. One of these is Paul's account of the institution of the Lord's Supper found in 1 Corinthians 11:23–26:

*For **I received** from the Lord **what I also handed on to you, that** the Lord Jesus on the night when he was betrayed [lit. "delivered up"][2] took a loaf of bread, and when he had given thanks, he broke it and said, "This is my body that is for you. Do this in remembrance of me." In the same way he took the cup also, after supper, saying, "This cup is the new covenant in my blood. Do this, as often as you drink it, in remembrance of me." For as often as you eat this bread and drink the cup, you proclaim the Lord's death until he comes.*

Clearly this account is very similar to that in the synoptic Gospels, but written down much, much earlier. As we shall see, 1 Corinthians was probably written in about 53–54 CE and was one of Paul's earlier letters.

We are further able to recognize the oral-tradition quality of this material from the way Paul introduces it. He uses a formula: "I received . . . what I also handed on to you, *that*. . . ." Paul uses the identical formula in reverse order in 1 Corinthians 15:3–7 in rehearsing the oral tradition of the Passion and resurrection of Jesus. The first part of this formula—"I received and handed on"—was regularly used for passing on oral tradition and is also found in the rabbinic sources. It is sometimes called the *tradition summary formula*.[3] The word *"that"* functions in Greek like quotation marks, to mark direct discourse or cited material. In other words, this formula tells us that the words immediately following "that" are part of the oral tradition being quoted. We can see this better if we lay out these two key passages graphically (Box 6.1).

The way Paul appeals to the earlier oral tradition assumes that the audience was already very familiar with it, most likely from Paul's own preaching. The use of these units of oral tradition pushes Paul's account to yet an earlier stage—at least into the 40s. Thus, we are much closer to the time of Jesus and within the first decade or so of the movement. It also shows us something about the nature of oral tradition itself. On the one hand, there is certainly a reverence for the tradition and the way it continues in the life of the early churches. We must assume, therefore, that these are the same kinds of sources that also contributed to the compilation of the Gospels and Acts.

On the other hand, there are some noticeable differences. In Paul's recounting of the oral tradition of the "last supper," there is no mention of Passover at all. A careful look at section 4 in the oral materials from 1 Corinthians 15, Jesus's appearances, also reveals a degree of fluidity in the tradition: two of those reported by Paul—the appearance to "five hundred brethren" (4b) and to "James [the brother of Jesus] and all the apostles" (4c)—do not occur in the Gospels or any later Christian sources. They seem to have disappeared from the oral tradition.[4] Even the appearance "to Peter *and the twelve*" is not without problems

BOX 6.1

The Earliest Christian "Texts"

Paul's Oral Tradition

1 Corinthians 11:23–26

For *I received* from the Lord *what I also handed on to you, that* . . .

> the Lord Jesus on the night when he was delivered up took a loaf of bread, and when he had given thanks, he broke it and said, "This is my body that is for you. Do this in remembrance of me."

> In the same way, after the dinner, he took the cup also, saying, "This cup is the new covenant in my blood. Do this, as often as you drink it, in remembrance of me."

For as often as you eat this bread and drink this cup, you proclaim the Lord's death until he comes.

1 Corinthians 15:3–9

For *I handed on to you* as of first importance *what I in turn had received,*

that . . .	(1) **Christ died** *{for our sins}* *{in accordance with the scriptures}*
and *that* . . .	(2) **he was buried,**
and *that* . . .	(3) **he was raised on the third day** *{in accordance with the scriptures}*
and *that* . . .	(4) (a) **he appeared to Cephas, then to the twelve;**
next	(b) **he appeared to more than 500 brethren at one time** *{most of whom are still alive, though some have died};*
next	(c) **he appeared to James, then to all the apostles.**

KEY: Bold type = units of oral tradition
   Regular type = Paul's framing elements
   Italics = tradition summary formula
   {small italics} = Paul's editorial comments

relative to the later Gospel accounts, since the betrayal by Judas and his subsequent death (Matt. 27:3–10; Acts 1:15–26) mean that all the appearances in the Gospels are to only eleven of the original disciples, at most.[5] Although neither Acts nor the Gospels report an appearance to Jesus's brother James, Paul clearly knew him as an early leader of the Jerusalem church alongside Peter and John (see Gal. 1:19; 2:9). In Acts James only appears as leader of the church in Jerusalem after the departure or death of Peter and the other original disciples (Acts 12:17; 15:13; 21:18). Thus, we have a number of glimpses at the earliest stages of the movement, but the picture is far from clear; it remains shrouded in a historical *mist*.

De-*mist*ifying Christian Origins

Even the book of Acts calls attention to the fact that in the earliest stages of the movement certain ideas had not yet developed. For example, in Acts 11:26 we are told: "It was in Antioch that the disciples were first called Christians." In Greek the word is *Christianoi*. Now what does this comment tell us? Well, the most obvious point is that the main term that is now thought of as the name of the movement was not known or used for a number of years after the movement began. And when the term occurred, it was not in Galilee, Jerusalem, or Judea—where Jesus had lived and died and where even Acts says it began. Instead, the term "Christian" was first used in Antioch, the capital of the Roman province of Syria, a thoroughly Greek city. Nor is it clear when this new title arose. It might easily have been forty to fifty years or more after the death of Jesus. The missionary Paul, who lived and worked in Antioch for quite some time (Gal. 1:21–2:14), never uses the term; nor does it appear in any source, Christian or otherwise, prior to the time Acts was written. Finally, the derived name "Christianity" (*Christianismos*), as a designation for the religion itself, does not appear before about 112–15, interestingly enough also with a connection to Antioch.[6]

So what did the followers of Jesus call themselves during those early decades before the term "Christian" was coined? Most likely they just thought of themselves as devout Jews. Other terms used in the early chapters of Acts, such as "the Way" (Acts 9:2; 19:23), are consistent with a Jewish sectarian identity (Acts 24:14); some used "sect of the Nazarenes."[7] Even the term "church" (Greek *ekklesia*, "assembly" or "gathering"; Acts 8:3; 9:11; 11:22, 26), which was used of Greek city councils, was also regularly used by Greek-speaking Jews to refer to the Jewish people as a whole or to individual Jewish congregations. Hence, "church" (Greek *ekklesia*) and "synagogue" (Greek *synagoge*) were originally synonyms.

So when we look again at this distinctive, new term "Christian" (*Christianoi*), what does it mean and where does it come from? The term is clearly derived from *christos,* the ordinary, literal Greek translation for the Hebrew title *messiah*. Already we see that its coinage depends on a cultural shift to a Greek-speaking environment. The ending *-ianos* (plural, *-ianoi*), however, seems to come from Latin (*-ianus,* plural *-iani*). This suffix was commonly used to designate the followers of a particular leader or camp, or what we might call *partisans*. Thus, we hear of *Caesariani* and *Pompeiani,* that is, the partisans of Julius Caesar and Pompey in the civil war. In the eastern part of the Roman Empire, then, this suffix crossed directly into Greek usage; the partisans of Herod were the *Herodianoi* ("Herodians"), as seen in Josephus[8] and the Gospels (Matt. 22:16; Mark 12:13). Hence, the new term *Christianoi* means "partisans or proponents of Christ."

Yet the *-ianus* suffix usually carried political connotations, and scholars now think that this term was coined, not by the Christians themselves, but rather by Roman officials in Greek cities like Antioch, who used it in a derogatory way. It was a slur hurled at the followers of Jesus by outsiders. So it remains unclear whether it initially was meant to label them as "the party of Jesus who is called the Christ" or simply as "the party that espouses messianism." Only much later would this slur be revalorized as a badge of honor and internalized to become the new name of the movement.

This change will mark yet another major shift in cultural location and self-understanding on the part of the followers of Jesus, and we shall return to it in a later chapter. For now, however, we may take these observations as a starting point for looking more closely at the nature and characteristics of the movement in those earliest days before its members knew they were "Christians."

The Jesus Movement: An Aramaic Substratum

The term "Jesus movement" (German *Jesusbewegung*) was popularized by the New Testament scholar Gerd Theissen in an effort to get behind the social and cultural changes associated with the later term "Christianity."[9] Since then it has become a regular part of the scholarly vocabulary. There are a number of clues in the New Testament that the earliest form of the movement was Aramaic in language, culture, and social location. Aramaic is the dialectical cousin of biblical Hebrew (on analogy, like Spanish and Italian). Aramaic had become the common language of the Middle East during the Babylonian and Persian periods (608–332 BCE). By Jesus's day very few Jews could speak, read, or write Hebrew. In larger Jewish cities such as Sepphoris the primary languages were Greek and Aramaic. For this reason, it is usually thought that Jesus's own native tongue was Aramaic, although it is likely that he might also have known a little Greek. Writing in about 130 CE, Papias, the Christian bishop of Hierapolis (in Turkey), seems to affirm this basic idea when he says that Matthew's Gospel preserved "the sayings [of the Lord] in Hebraic dialect."[10]

The Gospel of Mark, although written in Greek, depicts Jesus himself as speaking Aramaic. In several of the miracle stories, Jesus's words are reported in a transliteration of the Aramaic and then translated into Greek for the audience. For example, in Mark 5:41, when Jesus raises the daughter of Jairus, Mark reports as follows: "He said to her, '*Talitha cum*,' which is then translated into Greek as, 'Little girl, I say to you arise.'" Similarly, in Mark 7:34 Jesus's words in healing a blind man are reported as "*Ephphatha*," meaning "Be opened." Here again, we have a subtle clue about the social and cultural development of the movement, for although Mark's Jesus speaks Aramaic, Mark's audience clearly does not.

Even so, there are no written collections of Jesus's teachings in Aramaic. The Gospels of the New Testament were all written in Greek and preserve Jesus's words almost entirely in Greek forms that are difficult to retrace to Aramaic roots. The Gospels also differ on this matter. A clear indication of the actual Aramaic words of Jesus remains elusive, even though many scholars would agree that an Aramaic sayings source stands behind at least some of the teachings of Jesus as preserved in the New Testament Gospels.[11]

Even so, it does appear that there was what we may call an "Aramaic substratum" to the Jesus movement. For example, there are hints of some early tensions between those followers who spoke Greek and those who did not. This idea is reflected in an episode set in the early days of the Jerusalem church (Acts 6:1–6). As the church began to grow numerically "the Hellenists complained against the Hebrews because their widows were being neglected in the daily distribution of food" (Acts 6:1). In response the leaders of the church allowed the Hellenists to appoint seven men of their own, all with Greek names, to see to these needs. The two most famous are Stephen and Philip; one other, Nicolaus, is explicitly identified as a proselyte (i.e., a gentile convert to Judaism) from Antioch. Since it seems clear enough that the "Hellenists" are understood as Greek-speaking Jews, the term "Hebrews" (Greek *Hebraioi*) here must reflect a linguistic distinction, that is, those Jews who do not speak Greek. It is not clear whether this really means Hebrew or Aramaic, even though the latter is the more likely from a historical perspective.

We may get a more direct clue to the existence of an Aramaic substratum, not so much from the words of Jesus, but from the memory of Aramaic terms in later Christian usage. One of the best examples in this regard is the term *abba* (a determinative or vocative form of the Hebrew/Aramaic word for "father," *ab*), used by Jesus in addressing God in his Gethsemane prayer, at least according to Mark 14:36 ("Abba, Father, for you all things are possible").[12] Although both Matthew 26:39 and Luke 22:42 drop the word *abba*, leaving only the Greek word "father" (*pater*), some scholars think that the wording of the Lord's Prayer (Matt. 6:9; Luke 11:2)—which begins with "Our Father" or just "Father" (Greek *pater* in both instances)—depends on an earlier version in Aramaic using *abba* or a similar derivation of "father" as a form of reverent address.

A more telling clue to the significance of the phrase "*Abba*, Father" can be seen in the fact that it was preserved and used even by Greek-speaking gentile converts in the churches of Paul. Two passages in Paul's letters clearly reflect this usage:

> And because you are children, God has sent the Spirit of his Son into our hearts, crying, "**Abba!** Father!" (Gal. 4:6)

> For you did not receive a spirit of slavery to fall back into fear, but you have received a spirit of adoption. When we cry, "**Abba!** Father! . . ." (Rom. 8:15)

In both instances Paul adduces the term in the context of prayers to God in which the Spirit is also mentioned. These letters date between 50 and 60 CE and were written to two entirely different Greek-speaking audiences, one located in the city of Rome and the other located in the hinterlands of Asia Minor (modern Turkey). Hence, the similarity of form and context is all the more striking. That the Aramaic element is retained in both is further testimony to its preservation through oral tradition. It would seem to be a kind of prayer formula used in the churches of Paul that was thought to go back to the words or practice of Jesus and his first followers. Even so, this Aramaic formula seems to have dropped out of usage, for it does not appear in any other writing of the New Testament or of Christians in the early to mid-second century CE, although it continued in formal usage in some later rabbinic Jewish sources.

A final indication of Aramaic terms and ideas is found in Paul's 1 Corinthians. At the end of the letter Paul gives fairly typical greetings and exhortations and then concludes by saying: "I, Paul, write this greeting with my own hand.

Let anyone be accursed who has no love for the Lord. *Our Lord, come!* The grace of the Lord Jesus be with you. My love be with all of you in Christ Jesus" (1 Cor. 16:21–24). The curse formula gives this a harsh tone, but the phrase translated above as "Our Lord, come!" provides an important clue. These words are actually written in Greek as *Marana tha,* another transliterated Aramaic phrase.[13] Also important is the way Paul uses it here, since it stands as a kind of stamp on the preceding curse formula. Since Paul makes no effort to explain the phrase, it must be assumed that the audience recognized it and knew its significance, undoubtedly from Paul's own earlier preaching. So here again we have evidence of an oral tradition that preserves elements of Aramaic language. More to the point is the religious connotation of the phrase, since it conveyed a heavily apocalyptic expectation even as it moved into a predominantly Greek-speaking and increasingly gentile environment.

The Apocalyptic Moorings
of the Jesus Movement

What do these meager elements tell us about the beliefs, practices, and expectations of the earliest followers of Jesus? One later text may provide some additional clues. The *Didache,* or *Teaching of the Lord Through the Twelve Apostles,* comes from Syria sometime in the early second century CE (for fuller discussion see Chapter 13). It also preserves the Aramaic *Marana tha* formula in transliterated form in a Greek text (*Did.* 10.6). The fact that it is used in a eucharistic prayer supports the idea that it had been handed down in a formulaic way since the early days of the movement, just as we saw in Paul. It also makes implicit references to an apocalyptic expectation: the passing away of "this world (*kosmos*)."

Similar apocalyptic ideas are reflected in Paul's own early preaching, as indicated by a summary statement that comes from his very first letter, 1 Thessalonians. Writing in about 51 CE, Paul refers to his experience with the early gentile converts in Macedonia:

> For the people of those regions report about us what kind of welcome we had among you, and how you turned to God from idols, to serve a living and true God, and to wait for his Son from heaven, whom he raised from the dead— Jesus, who rescues us from the wrath that is coming. (1 Thess. 1:9–10)

Here is made explicit the connection between the impending "wrath," an eschatological judgment on those who stand opposed to God, and the imminent return of the risen Jesus from heaven. The idea that Jesus was coming back soon (also called the *parousia*, or "presence") was a prominent element in most forms of early Christian preaching, and most likely is the root meaning underlying the Aramaic phrase *Marana tha*—"Our Lord, come!"

A number of other passages from the Gospels attribute this sense of imminent expectation to Jesus himself. For example, Mark 8:38–9:1 shows Jesus instructing his core group of disciples on the eschaton as follows:

> *"Those who are ashamed of me and of my words in this adulterous and sinful generation, of them the Son of Man will also be ashamed when he comes in the glory of his Father with the holy angels." And he said to them, "Truly I tell you, there are some standing here who will not taste death until they see that the kingdom of God has come with power."*

That this eschatological expectation was to be fulfilled within that first generation of the movement is also found in the Gospel of Matthew, when Jesus instructs his disciples on preaching:

> *These twelve Jesus sent out with the following instructions: "Go nowhere among the Gentiles, and enter no town of the Samaritans, but go rather to the lost sheep of the house of Israel. As you go, proclaim the good news, '**The kingdom of heaven has come near.**' . . . But the one who endures to the end will be saved. When they persecute you in one town, flee to the next; for truly I tell you, you will not have gone through all the towns of Israel before the Son of Man comes." (Matt. 10:5–7, 22–23)*

An imminent expectation of the coming kingdom seems to be the common thread of all these statements. Matthew's instruction adds another element: the message is only for Jews. This idea likely also reflects one early strand of the movement in which non-Jews, and even Samaritans, were excluded. It may well accord with some of the early resonances of the Aramaic language and cultural context we have already seen. That the movement was initially understood this way is further attested by the confrontation between Peter and Paul at Antioch over whether to admit Gentiles into their fellowship (Gal. 2:11–15; see Chapter 8).

Matthew's mission instructions provide some additional clues regarding the self-understanding, or ethos, of at least one strand of the Jesus movement. The middle portion of the passage has Jesus saying:

> *"Cure the sick, raise the dead, cleanse the lepers, cast out demons. You received without payment; give without payment. Take no gold, or silver, or copper in*

your belts, no bag for your journey, or two tunics, or sandals, or a staff; for la-
borers deserve their food. Whatever town or village you enter, find out who in
it is worthy, and stay there until you leave. As you enter the house, greet it. If
the house is worthy, let your peace come upon it; but if it is not worthy, let your
peace return to you. If anyone will not welcome you or listen to your words,
shake off the dust from your feet as you leave that house or town. Truly I tell
you, it will be more tolerable for the land of Sodom and Gomorrah on the day
of judgment than for that town. . . . Do not think that I have come to bring
peace to the earth; I have not come to bring peace, but a sword. For I have
come to set a man against his father, and a daughter against her mother, and
a daughter-in-law against her mother-in-law." (Matt. 10:8–15, 34–35)

Here we see four more elements.

1. The followers of Jesus are to perform miracles, but for free.

2. They are to be itinerants who travel with no food, money, or extra possessions.

3. They are to rely on the hospitality of those who will willingly accept their message about the coming kingdom.

4. They will be hated and rejected by some (who are likened eschatologically to the residents of Sodom and Gomorrah), and their preaching will cause strife and dissension within households.

The last two items are especially characteristic of a sectarian movement that relies on persuading members of its own culture to take on a new and even controversial set of ideas. It has thus rightly been called an apocalyptic revitalization movement. The first two items point to what Gerd Theissen has called an "ethos" of homelessness and itinerant miracle working, patterned in some measure after Jesus himself. This is a quintessentially Jewish sect, and Jesus is both its eschatological prophet and its deliverer. The early chapters of the book of Acts confirm this basic sense when they report that the earliest followers continued to attend the Temple daily and to have dinner fellowship, teaching, and prayers in their homes (Acts 2:42–47; 5:42). Other passages reflect similar adherence to traditional forms of Jewish piety, such as fasting (Matt. 6:17), reverence for Torah (Matt. 5:17–21), study of the scriptures (1 Cor. 15:3–4), and observance of the Sabbath (Acts 9:2; 17:2) and Jewish holy days (Passover: Acts 20:6; Pentecost: Acts 20:16; cf. 1 Cor. 16.8). In many ways they resemble other Jewish sects, but especially Pharisaic home fellowships and study groups (or *haburoth*).

A Jewish Sect and
Its Social Location

Within this picture, however, there are some variations. Matthew 10 points to an exclusively Jewish mission in a semirural village culture. Both Matthew and Mark locate Jesus's postresurrection appearances exclusively in the Galilee, where most of Jesus's ministry had occurred (Mark 16:7; Matt. 28:6, 16). In contrast, Acts focuses on urban centers, beginning at Jerusalem, and all the postresurrection appearances in both Luke and Acts are in or around Jerusalem itself (Luke 24:13, 33, 47, 50–52; Acts 1:4, 8, 12; 2:1–5). It may well be the case that there was more than one early locus where the movement germinated.

The earliest form of the Jesus movement is best understood as an apocalyptic Jewish sect; however, the evidence already discussed points to greater diversity as each local cell experienced success or failure in different ways. A key, then, is what we may call the social location of each group, and this may help to understand why there are subtle differences within the early Christian sources. As long as the emergent Jesus sect remained exclusively within the realm of Jewish culture in the homeland, then its message and appeal were shaped by this cultural horizon, even though it might have been at odds with the religious establishment or with other sectarian groups. Like the Essenes or Pharisees, its members might have debated the proper forms of Jewish piety and goals of social reform, but this would hardly have constituted a denunciation of Judaism.

In a short time the Jesus movement had developed into diverse centers, some of which began to explore external contacts. It may well be the case, as John Gager argues, that this was prompted by a failure to persuade other Jews.[14] Even the Gospel of Matthew, which emphasizes the exclusively Jewish identity (Matt. 10:5, 23), ends by affirming a commission "to make disciples of all nations" (Matt. 28:18–20). The early diffusion of the movement was a by-product of new impulses and experiences arising out of diverse social circumstances.[15] Eventually, we know that some movement members began to work increasingly among Greek-speaking diaspora Jews in cities like Antioch. In the long run, this primarily gentile movement became what we know as Christianity.

Changes in social location will also have affected the ethos and makeup of these groups. Here traditional uses of terms like *sect* and *cult* are often misleading. What we need is a way of describing the early Jesus movement (or movements) that accurately reflects the cultural context in which it arose as well as the cultural context in which it would eventually develop (see Box 6.2).

BOX 6.2

Sect and Cult
Getting the Terminology Straight

Because the terms "sect" and "cult" have such a negative connotation in popular usage, many sociologists and social anthropologists who deal with religious phenomena prefer not to use these terms any longer. They opt instead for neutral categories such as "religious minorities" or "new religious movements," or just the common shorthand "NRMs." Although not inappropriate, there are two problems with this new jargon. The NRM category is so broad it lacks nuance for distinguishing different types of new movements. It does not mesh with much of the traditional vocabulary, especially that found in connection with ancient culture and literary sources.

In fact, both "sect" and "cult" are ancient terms. "Sect" (Latin *secta;* Greek *hairesis*) was typically used of particular schools, religious groups, or factions, and "cult" (Latin *cultus;* Greek *hiera* or *leitourgia*) usually referred to the sacred rites for a particular deity and thus came to be applied to certain types of rituals, especially sacrifices or the "mysteries." By derivation, then, was it applied to "foreign cults," meaning those ethnic groups with different gods and peculiar religious rituals, such as the worship of Isis and Osiris. In that sense too Romans would have called Judaism a "foreign cult."

In contrast, there really was no ancient term in either Greco-Roman or Jewish tradition that corresponds to our use of the word "religion." Latin *religio* was virtually a synonym for *cultus,* meaning the proper festivals, rituals, and observances due to the gods of the city or state. The closest Greek equivalent was *eusebeia,* meaning the proper "reverence" for the gods, again with the sense of proper "observance." Excessive concern over what to believe or how the gods governed one's life was usually called *superstitio,* except perhaps when taken up by philosophers.

Sect and Church

The modern sense of the word "sect" in English comes directly from the Latin but over time became restricted to mean a dissident religious faction that is opposed to the national church (see the *Oxford English Dictionary*). Thus, Roger Bacon's statement (1625) is typical: "When the Religion formerly received is rent by Discords; . . . you may [not] doubt the Springing up of a New Sect." The reference, of course, was to groups like the Puritans, who opposed the Church of England. Thus much of the modern usage comes from the period after the Protestant Reformation, with its "sectarian" attacks on the Catholic Church.

It was Ernst Troeltsch (*The Social Teachings of the Christian Church*, 1911) who provided the first systematic definition from a sociological perspective. To explain pluralism, change, and conflict in Western Christian culture, he used "church-type" to refer to a religious movement that accepts and preserves the existing social order and "sect-type" to reflect hostility toward the social order and a seeking to build an alternative one through small religious groups. H. Richard Niebuhr (*The Social Sources of Denominationalism*, 1929) then applied this basic idea to the proliferation of Christian denominations in the United States, since most began as sects within other denominations. He argued that sects tend to arise out of social discontent but remain unstable forms of religious organization. Consequently they tend to disappear or to develop into more organized "denominational" churches. In turn, this greater degree of organization will produce new discontent, and so the cycle continues.

Rethinking the Issue of Context

Although the definitions of Troeltsch and Niebuhr apply relatively well in postmedieval Christian culture, they do not fit quite so well the first century. The Roman world tolerated considerable religious diversity, and "foreign cults" from the conquered provinces moved freely through the empire. There was no "state church" in early Judaism; even so, there was, as we have already seen, heated sectarian debate within the Jewish homeland over operation of the Temple and proper forms of "observance." For the purposes of this study, we need terminology that is consistent with the ancient cultures under consideration, but also that is sociologically descriptive. In particular we need definitions that will address several issues simultaneously: (1) how a new religious movement arises out of one culture and society and moves into another; (2) how it can feel both connections and tensions with its original parent culture and also with its new host culture; and (3) how it can retain much of its original beliefs and religious rhetoric from the first while transforming it in new contexts. Thus our terminology must be more attuned to the multifaceted relations of the movement to changing cultural contexts.

Definitions

For this reason, I have chosen to retain the traditional terms "sect" and "cult" because they offer additional subtlety and differentiation in thinking about the historical processes of religious development in the Jewish and early Christian world.[1]

*A **sect** is a separatist (or schismatic) revitalization movement that arises out of an established, religiously defined cultural system, with which it shares its symbolic worldview.*

*A **cult** is an integrative, often syncretistic, movement that is effectively imported (by mobilization or mutation) into another religiously defined cultural system, to which it must seek to synthesize its novel symbolic worldview.*

At the point of introduction both sects and cults will appear "deviant" within their respective social contexts; that is to say, they will stand in some sort of tension. This tension will be reflected in both their religious "message" and their social organization, but they will have different vectors of response to these tensions. Because sects arise in a shared worldview, they are constantly threatened with reabsorption; consequently, "sect rhetoric" tends to erect boundaries that stress differences with "the world" (the parent culture). In fact, sect rhetoric by its very nature tends to breed more sectarianism. In contrast, because cults by definition introduce an "alien" worldview, they tend to ameliorate this tension by stressing similarities with their new host culture.

By these definitions, the same religious movement might be a sect and a cult simultaneously if it moves from its original parent culture into a new host culture. It might even reiterate the same basic language and beliefs in both situations, but the religious value of that language will necessarily be transformed to fit each cultural context. Finally, if these different cultural experiences then produce changes from cell to cell within a movement, then these differences will result in the individual cells treating one another as dissident sects.

---

[1] These definitions come from L. M. White, "Shifting Sectarian Boundaries in Early Christianity," in *Sects and New Religious Movements,* Bulletin of the John Rylands Library 70, no. 3 (1988): 7–24, esp. 17, which in turn reflects the recent discussions in sociology of religion, especially Rodney Stark and William Sims Bainbridge, *The Future of Religion: Secularization, Revival, and Cult Formation* (Berkeley: University of California Press, 1985); and their article "Networks of Faith: Interpersonal Bonds and Recruitment to Cults and Sects," *American Journal of Sociology* 85 (1980): 1378–95.

In keeping with this approach, the early Jesus movement is properly understood as a Jewish *sect* when it began as a separatist revitalization movement within the established culture of homeland Judaism. As such, its followers shared a basic set of values, beliefs, and worldview with other Jews, even though they might have argued over key issues. On the other hand, when it moved into predominantly non-Jewish or "pagan" culture, then the Jesus movement appeared to be more of an alien phenomenon, or a *cult.* In this sense, the new *cult* will tend to synthesize itself to the basically foreign worldview of its host culture, while at the same time attempting to convince its new neighbors that the new message it brings is ultimately meaningful and beneficial.

Matthew's Gospel may best be seen as reflecting the ethos of a Palestinian Jesus sect several decades after the first revolt; this group is now beginning to face new tensions with its dominantly Jewish culture (see Chapter 10). Paul, on the other hand, reflects an experience of taking an essentially Jewish message to a non-Jewish culture and at a slightly earlier period before a serious rift with Judaism had begun. Paul can thus be seen as a Jewish sectarian relative to other Jews (and even other followers of Jesus), while simultaneously appearing as the purveyor of a foreign *cult* to non-Jewish audiences in large cities like Ephesus and Corinth. There is considerable evidence, then, for different experiences of the emerging movement, a gradual shift in ethos, social location, and cultural horizons, and different forms of social and organizational development.

Trajectories and New Horizons

From the beginning, then, the Jesus movement seems to have taken slightly different forms based on its cultural locations within Judaism. There must have been several distinct cell groups that grew up in different areas of the Jewish homeland and then spread gradually into neighboring territories. As we have already seen, at least some of these groups were probably located in the Galilee or nearby in southern Syria. These groups seem to have been associated particularly with Matthew's Gospel by the latter part of the first century. Paul shows no apparent knowledge of these groups. It is perhaps significant, therefore, that Acts mentions congregations in the Galilee only once in passing (Acts 9:31). Instead, after the beginnings in Jerusalem (Acts 2–7), the story jumps abruptly from the growth of the church in the southern areas of Samaria (Acts 8:25) and Caesarea (Acts 8:40; 10:1) to Damascus (Acts 9:2, 10, 19), Phoenicia, and Antioch in Syria (Acts 11:19). The turn to Antioch then sets the stage for the disciples "to be called Christians" there (Acts 11:26),[16] and at this juncture the work of Paul becomes the focus of Acts. The Galilean churches are never mentioned again.[17]

The Jerusalem Trajectory

Paul himself certainly knew those congregations of the Jesus movement in Jerusalem (Rom. 15:26; 1 Cor. 16:3; Gal. 1:18; 2:1) and Judea (Gal. 1:22). He tells us that within ten years after the crucifixion, Jesus's brother James was the central figure in Jerusalem along with Peter (Cephas) and John (Gal 1:18–19; 2:9). This James also plays a prominent role in the latter half of Acts (12:17; 15:13), and the Letter of James in the New Testament is usually attributed to him (see Chapter 11). According to Josephus, James continued in Jerusalem until about 62 CE, when the rising tide of revolutionary sentiment contributed to his arrest and death (see Chapter 9).[19] Paul depicts the Judean Jesus movement still very much in Jewish terms, with some apparent division between those who were more hard-line on the matter of strict Jewish observance and those who were less so (Gal. 2:4–7, 12–13). Acts also seems to reflect these tensions (Acts 11:1; 15:1), but shows Peter and James as taking a more moderate position (Acts 15:6, 13). Even so, Paul seems quite clear that the Jerusalem group viewed its primary responsibility as preaching to other Jews, whether in Judea or elsewhere (Gal 2:8, 13).

These cryptic pieces of information from Paul, Acts, and the Gospel of Matthew suggest that there were several distinct branches of the Jewish Jesus sect in the homeland during the period prior to the first revolt (66–74 CE). Yet we have no writings preserved from any of these early groups. From whom did Paul get his knowledge of the oral tradition of the Lord's Supper and the Passion? Peter and James, perhaps. What about Jesus's teachings? Paul seems to know a few "sayings of the Lord," but apparently nothing about Jesus's miracles.[19] The oral traditions about Jesus seem to have circulated rather widely and with some degree of fluidity. They are sometimes referred to as the earliest *kerygma*, meaning the "core proclamation" about Jesus. These materials were preserved by repetition, storytelling, and preaching, but they were shaped and configured in different ways in individual communities, depending on the social location.

The Q Trajectory

It may well be that what we call Q or the Synoptic Sayings Source represents one such localized oral tradition of Jesus's sayings. Because it appears to be a relatively fixed body of material that antedates the writing of Matthew and Luke, scholars usually date it between 50 and 60 CE, and thus roughly contemporary with Paul's Aegean mission. At least some of the Q material may go back to an even earlier period following the death of Jesus.

(X) Like Paul, the Q tradition may well reflect elements of the Aramaic substratum. Apart from Paul, it is the earliest discoverable layer of the Jesus tradition. Nonetheless, it reflects a secondary stage of transmission, since its preserved form comes from a stage of composition in Greek.[20] It has also been argued that the large number of Q sayings in the *Gospel of Thomas* seems to reflect an independent form of this tradition.[21] Scholars generally think that the original wording and order of Q materials is preserved more authentically in Luke than in Matthew. Even so, the author of Luke edited the material, and in a few cases Matthew seems to preserve the more original wording.

What can the form and content of Q tell us about the early Jesus movement that preserved and used this material? It has been proposed that Q fits into the Jewish wisdom tradition and observes the genre of wisdom instruction.[22] This use of the Jewish wisdom tradition and much of the content seems to suggest a setting in the Jewish homeland. The fact that several Galilean cities are named, often in a negative light, may well suggest the early Q collection originated in the Galilee. Saying 23 reads:

> *"Woe to you, Chorazin! Woe to you, Bethsaida! For if the deeds of power done in you had been done in Tyre and Sidon, they would have repented long ago, sitting in sackcloth and ashes. But at the judgment it will be more tolerable for Tyre and Sidon than for you. And you, Capernaum, will you be exalted to heaven? No, you will be brought down to Hades. (Luke 10:13–15; cf. Matt. 11:23–24)*

Since Chorazin, Bethsaida, and Capernaum were part of the Lower Galilee, as was Nazareth, these negative sayings may be taken to reflect either the earlier days of Jesus himself or that the movement had moved somewhat to the north, into the Upper Galilee, where there was more contact with the Syrian border regions and towns such as Tyre and Sidon. Either way, the area of the Galilee would seem to fit well with Q's social location. Based on wording and the use of quotations from the LXX, the movement had already shifted into a Greek-speaking context where contact with Gentiles was possible on a regular basis. Again, these elements fit the region of the Upper Galilee, especially in the period prior to the first revolt. The Gospel of Matthew probably comes from a later phase of this same trajectory, still operating in the predominantly Jewish regions of the Upper Galilee or lower Syria. But this makes the omission of references to Galilean cells of the movement in Acts all the more glaring, since the author clearly knew this same material. Perhaps the Q tradition had already been transported to other regions by then, or there may be a more sinister reason. If so, one must wonder what new experiences and cultural reverberations might have come with these new horizons.

Also, indications within the Q material suggest a layer of material has been overlaid or elaborated with additional comments that come from a later context, but one still before the first revolt. A number of these seem to deal with rejection of the teaching *of* Jesus but in fact hint at rejection of the preaching *about* Jesus. In other words, the community's own experience is being projected onto Jesus himself. (See Box 6.3.)

A good example of how this works out in Q's self-understanding comes in a statement defending Jesus and John against social criticism (S 20):

> *To what then will I compare the people of this generation, and what are they like? They are like children sitting in the marketplace and calling to one another, "We played the flute for you, and you did not dance; we wailed, and you did not weep." For John the Baptist has come eating no bread and drinking no wine, and you say, "He has a demon"; the Son of Man has come eating and drinking, and you say, "Look, a glutton and a drunkard, a friend of tax collectors and sinners!" Nevertheless, Wisdom is vindicated by all her children. (Luke 7:31–35; cf. Matt. 11:16–19)*

Here we clearly see an appeal to the authority of Sophia, Woman Wisdom, who is depicted as the parent of Jesus and John. To be called the child of Sophia was a typical way of referring to the prophets of old or to the righteous person in wisdom literature.[23] Similarly, many of the prophetic sayings of Jesus in Q, which take the form of short pronouncement stories, or *chreiai,* show secondary elaboration to meet the circumstances of the community.[24] It is worth noting that most of the Pauline parallels to the Q material come from this same body of instructions, and Paul likewise employs them in exhortation to his churches (see Box 6.3 for the parallels).

These secondary features in Q seem to cluster around two key issues arising from the experience of those in the movement—sectarian identity and apocalyptic expectations. Many of the sayings in Q are defensive or apologetic; that is, they reflect an experience of resistance or antipathy on the part of others. An appeal to divine authority, as we saw in the appeal to Sophia (S20 = Luke 7:31–35), helps to reinforce the sect's sense of its rightness in the face of human criticism and persecution (S35–39 = Luke 12:2–12). Another indicator of this

BOX 6.3
The Content of Q
Synoptic Sayings Source

Since it is typical in scholarship to reference the Q material using the verse numbering in the Gospel of Luke, we shall follow this convention (column 2); the Q ordinals (or Saying numbers) in column 1 follow Kloppenborg, as do the topical headings (with some modification). Column 3 gives the Matthean parallel; column 4 gives parallels in Paul; and column 5 gives the parallels in the *Gospel of Thomas,* cited by logion number (following Koester). Sources: J. S. Kloppenborg, *Q Parallels* (Sonoma, CA: Polebridge, 1988), xxxi–xxxiii; H. Koester, *Ancient Christian Gospels* (Harrisburg, PA: Trinity Press International, 1990), 53, 87–89.

Q / Luke	Matthew	Paul	*Gospel of Thomas*
The Preaching of John			
S3 3:7–9	3:7–10		
S4 3:16b–17	3:11–12		
The Temptation			
S6 4:1–13	4:1–11		
A Sermon			
S7 6:20a	5:1–2		
S8 6:20b–23	5:3–12		54; 68; 69
S9 6:27–35	5:38–47; 7:12	Rom. 12:14, 17	
		1 Thess. 5:15	95; 6b
S10 6:36–38	5:48; 7:1–2	Rom. 14:10	
S11 6:39b–40	15:13–14; 10:24–25		34
S12 6:41–42	7:3–5		26
S13 6:43–45	7:15–20; 12:33–35		43; 45
S14 6:46–49	7:21–27		
John and Jesus vs.			
Their Generation			
S15 7:1b–10	8:5–13		
S16 7:18–20,			
22–23	11:2–6		
S17 7:24–28	11:7–11		78; 46
S18 16:16	11:12–15		
S20 7:31–35	11:16–19		

Q / Luke	Matthew	Paul	*Gospel of Thomas*
John and Jesus vs Their Generation (continued)			
S21 9:57–62	8:18–22		86
S22 10:2–12	9:36–38; 10:1–16	1 Cor. 9:14	72; 14b
S23 10:13–15	11:20–24		
S24 10:16	10:40		
S25 10:21–22	11:25–27		61b
S26 10:23b–24	13:16–17		17
S27 11:2–4	6:7–13		
S28 11:9–13	7:7–11		92; 94
S29 11:14–18a, 19–23	12:22–30; 9:32–34		
S30 11:24–26	12:43–45		
S31 11:27–28	—		79a
S32 11:16, 29–32	12:38–42		
S33 11:33–36	5:14–16; 6:22–23		33b; 24
S34 11:39b–44, 46–52; 13:34–35	23:1–39; 13:34–35		89
On Anxiety or the Fate of God's Messengers			
S35 12:2–3	10:26–27		5; 6; 33a
S36 12:4–7	10:28–31		
S37 12:8–9	10:32–33		
S38 12:10	12:31–32		
S39 12:11–12	10:17–20, 23		44
S40 12:13–14, 16–21	—		73; 63
S41 12:22–31	6:25–34		36
S42 12:33–34	6:19–21		76
On Judgment			
S43 12:35–38	22:11–14; 25:1–13*		21c; 75
S44 12:39–40	24:42–44	1 Thess. 5:2	21b; 103
S45 12:42b–46	24:45–51		
S46 12:49, 51–53	10:34–36		10; 16
S47 12:54–56	16:2–3		91
S48 12:57–59	5:25–26		
Parables of Growth			
S49 13:18–21	13:31–33		20; 96

Q / Luke	Matthew	Paul	Gospel of Thomas
The Two Ways			
S50 13:24–27	7:13–14, 22–23		
S51 13:28–30	8:11–12; 20:16		
S52 13:34–35	23:37–39		
S54 14:11 / 18:14b	23:6–12		
S55 14:16–24	22:1–10		64
S56 14:26–27; 17:33	10:37–39		55; 101
S57 14:34–35	5:13		
Miscellaneous Sayings			
S58 15:4–7	18:12–14		107
S59 15:8–10 (?)	—		
S60 16:13	6:24		47
S61 16:16–18	11:12–13; 5:18, 32		
S62 17:1b–2	18:6–7		
S63 17:3b–4	18:15–17, 21–22		
S64 17:6b	17:19–20		48
Eschatological Sayings			
S65 17:20b–21 (?)	—		113
S66 17:23–29, 30, 34–35, 37b	24:23–28, 37–42		61a (cf. 3; 51)
S67 19:12–13, 15b–26	25:14–30		41
S68 22:28–30	19:27–29		

tension is found in sayings that deal with social division, as in S46. Here it will be instructive to see both renderings:

Luke 12:49, 51–53	*Matthew 10:34–36*
I came to bring fire to the earth, and how I wish it were already kindled! . . . Do you think that I have come to bring peace to the earth? No, I tell you, but rather division! From now on five in one household will be divided, three against two and two against three; they will be divided: father against son and son against father, mother against daughter and daughter against mother, mother-in-law against her daughter-in-law and daughter-in-law against mother-in-law.	Do not think that I have come to bring peace to the earth; I have not come to bring peace, but a sword. For I have come to set a man against his father, and a daughter against her mother, and a daughter-in-law against her mother-in-law; and one's foes will be members of one's own household.

It may well be that Matthew preserves a more original form here than Luke, but it is worth noting that elements of both versions appear in the *Gospel of Thomas*.[25] The key here is the sense of discord, even within families.[26] Perhaps more than any other element this speaks to the experience of those who have joined a sect, but whose family and friends remain unsympathetic to its beliefs and teachings.

In each case these subtle changes in the use of these Q materials by the later Gospels reflects the changing social location and cultural horizons of the movement, or at least particular communities within the movement. A good example is the parable of the great dinner (S55; see Box 6.4). Careful analysis of this parable shows that there is a common outline and Greek vocabulary to the story underlying the three versions, but that each of the three writers has modified it for a particular audience or situation.

The base parable stresses the unreceptiveness of the originally invited guests and a resultant invitation to new guests. The *Gospel of Thomas* seems to turn this theme in an antimaterialist direction. Matthew has juxtaposed it to the parable of the wicked tenants and even worked features of that story into the dinner parable, most notably when the angry king kills the offending guests and "burns their city" (Matt. 22:6–7). These elements create an intertextual allusion to the destruction of Jerusalem in 70 CE; therefore, by implication Matthew turns the originally invited guests into the people who rejected and killed Jesus. Then he adds another parable to the end, regarding a man who shows up without the proper wedding garment;[27] it continues the theme of eschatological judgment with a strong sectarian tone: not even all the ones who make it to the dinner will be saved. This addition may well suggest a tension between Matthew's later Jewish Christian community and other forms of the Jesus movement, including those with ties to Jerusalem.

Luke is in many ways very close to the original; however, there is an added invitation for new guests inserted into the middle (Luke 14:21b–22). Because these new invitees ("the poor, the crippled, the blind, and the lame") replicate the same terms in the added saying that precedes it (Luke 14:13–14), this too is an intentional intertext on the part of the Lukan author and not part of the original Q parable. This shows that Luke's own interest is in social welfare, and it turns the second invitation—the original in the Q parable—in the direction of the Gentiles.

These secondary features found in Matthew, Luke, and Thomas do not seem to be part of the Q original. So what is the original parable saying? It would seem to be a reflection of the Q community's experience of resistance to and rejection of its basic message about Jesus and its resultant willingness to

BOX 6.4

A Parable from the Q Trajectory
The Great Dinner (S55)

Matthew 22:1–10, 11–14	Luke 14:13–15, 16–24	*Gospel of Thomas 64*

Matthew 22:1–10, 11–14

[Parable of the Wicked Tenants 21:33–46]

1 Once more Jesus spoke to them in parables, saying: **2** *"The kingdom of heaven may be compared* to a **person,** *a king, who* **gave** *a wedding-banquet for his son.* **3 He sent his slaves to call those who had been invited to the** *wedding-banquet,* **but they would not come. 4 Again he sent other slaves, saying, 'Tell those who have been invited:** Look, I have **prepared** my dinner, my oxen and my fat calves have been slaughtered, and **everything is ready;** *come to the wedding banquet.'* **5** But they made light of it and went away, **one to his farm, another to his business, 6** *while the rest seized his slaves, mistreated them, and killed them.* **7** *The* **king** *became angry. He sent his troops, destroyed those murderers, and burned their city.* **8 Then he said to his slaves,** *'The wedding-banquet is ready, but those* invited *were not worthy.* **9 Go therefore into the main streets, and invite everyone you find to** *the wedding-banquet.'* **10** Those

Luke 14:13–15, 16–24

13 *But when you give a banquet, invite the poor, the crippled, the lame, and the blind.* **14** *And you will be blessed, because they cannot repay you, for you will be repaid at the resurrection of the righteous.*

15 *One of the dinner guests, on hearing this, said to him, "Blessed is anyone who will eat bread in the kingdom of God!"*

16 Then he **said to him, "A person gave a great dinner and invited** many. **17** At the time for the dinner **he sent his slave to say to those who had been invited,** 'Come; for **everything is ready** now.' **18** But they all alike began **to make excuses. The first said to** him, 'I have bought a **farm, and I must go out and see it; please excuse me.' 19** Another said, 'I **have bought** five yoke of oxen, **and I am going** to try them out; **please excuse me.' 20** Another said, 'I **have just been married, and therefore I cannot come.' 21** So the slave **returned and reported this to his master.**

Then the owner of the house *became angry and said to his slave, 'Go out at*

Gospel of Thomas 64

Jesus said, "A person was receiving guests. When he had readied the dinner, he sent a servant to invite the guests. The servant went to the first and said to that one, 'My lord invites you.' The guest said, *some merchants owe me money, and they are coming to me tonight.* Please excuse me from the dinner.' The servant went to another and said to that one, 'My lord invites you.' The guest said to the servant, 'I have bought a house, and I have been called away for a day. I shall have no time.' The servant went to another and said to that one, 'My lord invites you.' The guest said to the servant, 'My friend is to be married, and I am to arrange the [wedding] dinner. I shall not be able to come. Please excuse me from the dinner.' The servant went to another and said to that one, 'My lord invites you.' The guest said to the servant, 'I have bought an estate, and I am going to collect the rent. I shall not be able to come. Please excuse me.'

The servant returned and said to the lord, 'Those

Matthew 22:1–10, 11–14	Luke 14:13–15, 16–24	*Gospel of Thomas 64*
slaves went out into the streets and gathered all whom they found, *both good and bad; so the* wedding-hall was filled *with guests.*	*ones into the streets and alleys of the town and bring in the poor, the crippled, the blind, and the lame.* 22 *And the slave said, 'Sir, what you ordered has been done, and there is still room.'*	whom you invited to dinner have asked to be excused.' The lord said to his servant, 'Go out on the streets, and bring back whomever you find to have dinner.'
11 *But when the king came in to see the guests, he noticed a man there who was not wearing a wedding robe,* 12 *and he said to him, 'Friend, how did you get in here without a wedding robe?' And the man was silent.* 13 *Then the king said to the attendants, 'Bind him hand and foot, and throw him into the outer darkness, where there will be weeping and gnashing of teeth.'* 14 *For many are called, but few are chosen.* "	23 **Then the master said to the slave, 'Go out into the roads** *and lanes,* **and compel people to come in, so that my house may be filled.'** 24 *For I tell you, none of those who were invited will taste my dinner.* "	*For buyers and merchants [shall] not enter the places of my Father.* "

KEY: Bold type = similar wording in all three versions that probably reflects the original form of the parable
Regular type = each Gospel author's editorial work in smoothing the narrative
Italics = framing elements and interpretive changes by each Gospel author

turn to new "invitees" who would not have been part of the original audience of the Jesus movement. Many of the members of this group may already be from among these new "invitees." The context of dining seems to connect the parable to the passage seen earlier ostensibly criticizing Jesus for "eating with tax collectors and sinners." The parable serves as a warrant for this change of audience and its social implications regarding group fellowship. It thus reflects a new or changing social location for the group. On the other hand, this does not mean that the Q tradition is abandoning its Jewish roots or that it has become a separate gentile movement; rather, it is beginning to turn outward with an eye toward converting some Gentiles to Judaism and Jesus. This may well be an early form of the gentile mission both *before* and *apart* from Paul; and yet it remains very much within a Jewish sectarian matrix.

Finally, the group's sectarian experience is interpreted apocalyptically. The theme of a great dinner has social implications for the sect's sense of fellowship and solidarity; yet, it also carries the sense of the "eschatological banquet," when the elect will be brought into the kingdom. This kingdom expectation retains much of the traditional Jewish apocalyptic tone. The members of this group are fighting not only human resistance but also demonic forces (S29; Luke 11:14–23). Those who do not follow the way of righteousness, that is, join the Jesus sect, face judgment (S10–14). Jesus is their prophet, the child of Sophia, and will return as eschatological judge. The stakes are high, and the time is short.

CHAPTER SEVEN

Paul

His Life and Significance

Perhaps more than any other figure in the early days of the Jesus movement, Paul stands out as the one who really catapulted the movement to a new level by virtue of his mission to non-Jews. At least that is the traditional picture. He has been called the "first Christian," the "second founder," and the "hellenizer" of Christianity. The actual picture is slightly more complex.

This way of understanding Paul goes back over a century and reflects some important shifts in understanding. For one, it reflects the realization that Jesus himself was Jewish and the additional realization that the earliest movement retained its basic Jewish identity for some time before becoming a separate religion. The "Christian church" did not simply erupt onto the scene as a fully developed and separate religious institution at a single moment fifty days after the death of Jesus. It was still a Jewish sect, as we saw in the last chapter.

Admitting that, however, we are left with the question of how the separation occurred, and to this question the usual answer is Paul. Writing at the turn of the twentieth century, Adolf Harnack reflects a common sentiment:

It was Paul who delivered the Christian religion from Judaism. . . . Without doing violence to the inner and essential features of the Gospel—unconditional trust in God as the Father of Jesus Christ, confidence in the Lord, forgiveness of sins, certainty of eternal life, purity and brotherly fellowship—Paul transformed it into a universal religion and laid the ground for the great church. . . . When the breach with the Jewish national communion had once taken place, there could be no doubt about the necessity for setting up a new community in opposition to it. The self-consciousness and strength of the Christian movement was displayed in the creation of the Church which knew itself to be the true Israel. . . . We have seen that in the course of [the apostolic age] the Gospel was detached from the mother-soil of Judaism and placed upon the broad field of the Graeco-Roman empire. The apostle Paul was the chief agent accomplishing this work, and in thereby giving Christianity its place in the history of the world.[1]

Although this attitude persists in some theological circles, it is not consistent with more recent historical scholarship on the New Testament. There are several reasons:

1. *Paul was not the "hellenizer" of the Jesus movement.* There was already vibrant interaction with both Greek-speaking Jews and non-Jews before and apart from Paul. The Q document already reflects this trend, and there was a substantial Jesus community in Alexandria from an early day. Neither of these branches of the early Jesus movement had any discernible contact with or influence from Paul. In writing his letter to the churches in Rome, Paul makes clear that he had never been to Rome (Rom. 1:9–14; 15:22–24). Hence, he clearly was not responsible for establishing the congregations in Rome, and some of them had been operating for quite some time.

2. *Paul was not the "second founder" of the movement.* This idea is based on the false assumption that, prior to Paul, the Jesus movement was still very monolithic and stuck, as it were, in a kind of theological rut resulting from the Jewish social location of the original teachings of Jesus. Paul is thus viewed as the one who broke out of this rut. As we have already seen, however, there was considerable diversity in the movement from the beginning, and there were already explorations of its ideas in new social and cultural contexts. Greek-speaking followers were already in Antioch well before Paul arrived. Paul himself may have encountered the movement after it had already moved out into Greek-speaking Jewish areas. Nor was the Jewishness of the sect an impediment to diversity and theological exploration. More to the point, Paul did not invent the "church" either as terminology or as a form of Christian worship and organization. Many of these elements, at least in the first generation, derive directly from Jewish practice.

3. *Paul was not the "first Christian."* In fact, Paul never uses the term "Christian." Instead, he clearly saw himself as a pious Jew who had been called on by God, through Jesus, to take this new message to non-Jews. Thus, Paul's self-understanding remained thoroughly Jewish, even when he argued with Peter, James, or other, more stringently Jewish followers of the Jesus movement. Paul, then, must be seen as a part of the sectarian diversity of the movement that gave it vitality and opened new horizons.

We shall examine each of these issues in more detail as we go through our study of Paul's own religious experience, his missionary methods, his relations with other branches of the Jesus movement, and his thought as reflected in his letters.

Paul's Career

We are primarily concerned here with understanding Paul during his own lifetime and his place in the early decades of the Jesus movement. It is also important to recognize Paul's legacy in later generations, when, in fact, he came to be viewed as a key figure in both turning the movement into a predominantly gentile phenomenon and effecting the separation of Christianity from Judaism. We shall return to these issues in later sections of this book, when we deal with stories about Paul and letters written in his name (see Box 7.1). These changing perceptions of Paul from his own day down to his later legendary persona must also be considered in reconstructing Paul's life and career.

There are two main sources of information about Paul's life. The more familiar is the book of Acts. Because Acts provides a flowing narrative for Paul's career, it has been typical to start with its outline of his life and then fit the letters to this outline. We shall discover once again that the real picture is more complex. Even Acts does not tell us what happened to Paul after he traveled to Rome or how he died. Already in the second century there was an impulse among early Christians to finish off the story of their founders and heroes from the beginning of the movement. They did this by creating elaborated versions of the "acts" of each individual apostle (see Chapter 15). There was one for Peter and another for Paul, and they told how the apostles died as glorious martyrs in Rome after the great fire of Nero in 64 CE. Local church tradition in Rome kept these legends alive. Yet the stories themselves have little or no historical basis.

In the final analysis we do not know precisely when or how Paul died. By most estimates, he probably died sometime between 60 and 62 CE, shortly after

BOX 7.1

The Pauline Literary Corpus

The following is a classification of all early Christian writings associated with Paul. They range from those New Testament letters clearly written by Paul to later letters either falsely attributed to Paul or written pseudepigraphically in Paul's name, and to the later novelistic literature about Paul.

"Undisputed" Letters in the New Testament

Romans	Philippians
1 Corinthians	1 Thessalonians
2 Corinthians	Philemon
Galatians	

"Debated" Letters in the New Testament

Ephesians	2 Thessalonians
Colossians	

"Doubtful" Letters in the New Testament

1 Timothy	Titus
2 Timothy	

Falsely Attributed Letter in the New Testament

Hebrews

Later Apocryphal Letters

Letter to the Laodiceans	3 Corinthians
Correspondence of Paul with Seneca	

Literature About Paul

Luke-Acts (New Testament)	*Martyrdom of Paul*
Acts of Paul and Thecla	*Apocalypse of Paul*

he left Corinth for Jerusalem and Rome. Nor do we know precisely when he was born. He once refers to himself as an "old man" (Philem. 9). Thus, he might have been in his fifties or early sixties at this time, and that would place his birth somewhere between 5 BCE and 5 CE. That would make him almost a precise contemporary of Jesus. Acts says that he was a diaspora Jew born in Tarsus, in the Roman province of Cilicia (Acts 21:9), although he was also educated in Jerusalem by the Pharisaic teacher Gamaliel (Acts 22:3). Paul himself does not confirm these facts, although he does clearly say that he had been a devout Pharisee before turning to the Jesus movement (Phil. 3:5).

The account of Paul's life in Acts faces other historical problems when we compare it closely with Paul's own statements in his letters (see Box 7.2). A good example comes from statements about Paul's visits to Jerusalem. According to Acts, Paul made five significant visits to Jerusalem after becoming a follower of Jesus. According to Acts 9:19–30, the first of these occurred almost immediately after his conversion in Damascus, whereupon Barnabas introduced him to the followers in Jerusalem. Paul then stayed for some time preaching. Here is the central portion of the account from Acts 9:

> *When he had come to Jerusalem, he attempted to join the disciples; and they were all afraid of him, for they did not believe that he was a disciple. But Barnabas took him, brought him to the apostles, and described for them how on the road he had seen the Lord, who had spoken to him, and how in Damascus he had spoken boldly in the name of Jesus. So he went in and out among them in Jerusalem, speaking boldly in the name of the Lord. (Acts 9:26–28)*

Paul's own account from his Galatian letter is very different in several respects:

> *But when God, who had set me apart before I was born and called me through his grace, was pleased to reveal his Son to me, so that I might proclaim him among the Gentiles, I did not confer with any human being, **nor did I go up to Jerusalem to those who were already apostles before me,** but I went away at once into Arabia, and afterwards I returned to Damascus.*
>
> *__Then after three years I did go up to Jerusalem to visit Cephas and stayed with him fifteen days;__ but I did not see any other apostle except James the Lord's brother. In what I am writing to you, before God, I do not lie! Then I went into the regions of Syria and Cilicia, and __I was still unknown by sight to the churches of Judea that are in Christ;__ they only heard it said, "The one who formerly was persecuting us is now proclaiming the faith he once tried to destroy." And they glorified God because of me. (Gal. 1:15–24)*

BOX 7.2

Paul's Career
Comparing Acts and the Letters

Acts	The Letters
1. Conversion (9:1–8)	1. Conversion or "Call" (Gal. 1:15–17)
a. "The Damascus road" [cf. 22:6–21 and 26:12–20]	a. *Gal. 1:15, "from my mother's womb"*
b. Into Damascus and escape (9:10–25)	b. At Damascus (1 Cor. 9:1; 15:8; 2 Cor. 11:32)
c. 1ST VISIT TO JERUSALEM (9:26–27)	
d. Preaches openly in Jerusalem, with help of Barnabus (9:28–30)	c. *No visit to Jerusalem (Gal. 1:17–18)*
	2. "3 years" in Syria and Arabia (Gal. 1:18)
2. At Tarsus and Antioch (9:30 ➠ 11:25–26)	
	• 1ST VISIT TO JERUSALEM (Gal. 1:18–20) Sees only Peter and James!
3. 2ND VISIT TO JERUSALEM (11:29–30) for famine relief (cf. 12:25)	
Returns to Antioch	3. "14 years" in Syria and Cilicia (Gal. 1:21 + 2:1, Antioch as base)
4. "First Missionary Journey" (chs. 13–14) (Antioch ➠ Antioch, cf. 5:23)	4. 2ND VISIT TO JERUSALEM (Gal. 2:1–10) "The Jerusalem Conference" (NB: agrees to begin "relief effort" [2:10])
5. 3RD VISIT TO JERUSALEM (15:1–19) "The Jerusalem Conference"	
6. "Second Missionary Journey" (15:36–18:21) (Antioch ➠ Caesarea)	Confrontation with Peter after return to Antioch! (Gal. 2:11–14)
	5. Begins Aegean mission (writes letters)
7. 4TH VISIT TO JERUSALEM (18:22) (Returns to Antioch)	*No visits to Antioch or Jerusalem*
8. "Third Missionary Journey" (18:23–21:14) (Antioch ➠ Caesarea)	6. Plans new mission to Spain (Rom. 15:25ff.)
9. 5TH VISIT TO JERUSALEM (21:17) (Results in Arrest! [21:37])	7. 3RD VISIT TO JERUSALEM: to deliver the "collection for the poor" (Rom. 15:25ff.; 2 Cor. 8–9; 1 Cor. 16:1–3; Gal. 2:10)
10. Trials and Journey to Rome (21:37–28:31) (Caesarea ➠ Rome)	8. Arrest and Death (?)

Even if one were to allow the time frame in Acts, which describes his stay in Damascus as "considerable days" (9:23), to be equivalent to Paul's "three years" (Gal. 1:18), which seems unlikely, one must still account for several other key discrepancies. Acts does not mention his going away into Arabia and then returning to Damascus. Also, Paul quite adamantly says that he did not confer with anyone in Jerusalem until after three years, and then he stayed for only two weeks and only saw Cephas (Peter) and Jesus's brother James. The rest of the churches in Judea only *heard* about him. In fact, Paul's account of his first visit—after three years—accords better in some ways with the "second" visit mentioned in Acts 11:29–30. So it would seem that Acts has added an extra visit at the beginning, perhaps to make Paul appear in closer contact with the Jerusalem church. The same might also be said of the "fourth visit" recorded in Acts 18:22, which is the break between the so-called second and third missionary journeys. It has no correspondence with anything in Paul's letters. Indeed, the situation of the letters seems to preclude any such interlude for a visit to Jerusalem or Antioch.

Two more of Paul's visits to Jerusalem in Acts match up much better with Paul's own account, at least in terms of basic chronology. One is the "conference" concerning gentile converts (Acts 15:1–19; Gal. 2:1–10), the "third" visit according to Acts. Even so, Paul clearly states that this was only his second trip to Jerusalem and that he, not the leaders of the church in Jerusalem or Antioch, initiated the visit. He also says that he met "privately" with the Jerusalem leaders—meaning Peter, James, and John (Gal. 2:2, 9)—while Acts suggests that these same leaders had called "the apostles and elders" together to hear the discussion. The final visit (Acts 21:17–37) is also one that Paul mentions by way of anticipation (Rom. 15:25–33), but we have no account from Paul as to what really happened when he arrived. One difference, however, is that Paul clearly states the purpose of this final visit as bringing a collection for the poor, while Acts only mentions famine relief in conjunction with an earlier visit (Acts 11:30). So in both cases there are differences in the Acts account, even though basic facts are confirmed by Paul's own letters.

As a result of careful study of these considerable differences, New Testament scholars have concluded that one must reconstruct Paul's career by starting with the letters themselves, and then correlate the events described in Acts when and where they seem to fit. On the basis of Paul's own autobiographical statements in the Galatian letter, it is possible to give the following basic chronology for the main phases of his career (see Box 7.3).

BOX 7.3
Phases of Paul's Career

I. "Conversion" and Early Work

DATES: ca. 35 (or 32) to ca. 37 (or 35)
LOCATION: Damascus ➡ Arabia ➡ Damascus
ACTIVITIES: Unspecified
CONCLUSION: First visit to Jerusalem ("after 3 years")
SOURCE: Gal. 1:15–18

II. Antioch Phase

DATES: ca. 37 (or 35) to ca. 48
LOCATION: Syria (capital, Antioch) and Cilicia (capital, Tarsus)
ACTIVITIES: Regional mission among Gentiles; based in Jewish congregations of Antioch (?); initiates second visit to Jerusalem for the "conference"
CONCLUSION: Results in a confrontation with Peter in Antioch, after which Paul decides to leave for a new mission area
SOURCE: Gal. 2:1–14

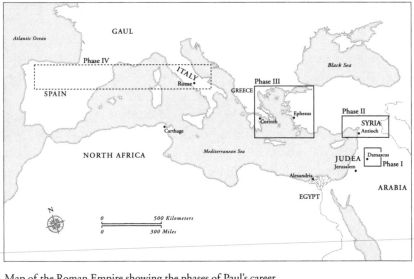

Map of the Roman Empire showing the phases of Paul's career.

III. The Aegean Mission

DATES: ca. 48/49 to ca. 59/60

LOCATION: Cities of western Asia and eastern Greece (the Aegean Rim)

ACTIVITIES: Setting up network of local house churches in major cities; begins writing letters to these churches

(Note: All the genuine letters of Paul belong to this phase.)

CONCLUSION: Faces legal problems and opposition from other Jesus missionaries; decides to make third visit to Jerusalem to deliver the "collection" and plans to go to Rome and Spain.

SOURCE: Rom. 15:22–32; 2 Cor. 1:8–22; 8–9; Philippians; Gal. 5:1–15; cf. Acts 16–20

IV. The Final Mission

DATES: ca. 59/60 to death (ca. 60–62?)

LOCATION: Corinth ➡ Jerusalem ➡ Rome ➡ Spain

ACTIVITIES: Delivers the collection to James in Jerusalem; intends to go to Rome and have the churches in Rome sponsor a new mission to Spain (never completed)

CONCLUSION: Arrest and death (in Rome)

SOURCE: Rom. 15:22–32; cf. 1 Cor. 16:1–4; 2 Cor. 8–9; cf. Acts 21–28

Establishing Dates for Paul's Career

As with most of our ancient sources, we have very few concrete dates that we can use to establish a precise chronology for Paul's life or for his career as a missionary. The dates typically used by New Testament scholars are derived from a system of calculations based on Paul's autobiographical statements in Galatians 1–2.[2] In this passage he gives two relative indications of time for when he visited Jerusalem, thus: "after three years" (Gal. 1:18) and "after fourteen years" (Gal. 2:1). These visits to Jerusalem also help mark off the main phases of Paul's career (as shown in Box 7.3). But this relative sense of time remains useless without some concrete date. Fortunately, Acts 18:12 seems to provide us with just such a key date when it tells us that Paul was brought up on charges before a certain Gallio, the Roman proconsul for the province of Achaia (southern Greece). Since Corinth was the provincial capital of Achaia, this statement fits well with the historical circumstances reflected in both Acts 18 and Paul's Corinthian correspondence, even though he never mentions the episode with Gallio.

An additional piece of corroborating evidence comes from several fragments of an inscription discovered at Delphi between 1895 and 1905; it contains a letter from the emperor Claudius (41–54 CE) to the city of Delphi in which he mentions this same Junius Gallio, "my friend and proconsul of Achaia."[3] The text of the inscription as restored reads as follows:

> *Tiberius [Claudius] **Caesar Augustus Germanicus**, [Pontifex*
>   *maximus, in his tribunician] power*
> *[year 12, acclaimed emperor for] **the 26th time, father of the***
>   ***country**, [consul for the 5th time, censor, sends greeting to*
>   *the city of Delphi].*
> ***I have for long been zealous for the city of Delphi** [and favorable*
>   *toward it from the]*
> ***beginning, and I have always observed the cult of the** [Pythian]*
>   ***Apollo**, [but with regard to]*
> 5   ***the present stories, and those quarrels of the citizens of which** [a*
>   *report has been made by Lucius]*
> ***Junius Gallio my friend, and** [pro]consul [of Achaea] . . .*

This Lucius Junius Gallio Novatianus was the brother of the philosopher Seneca, court adviser to the emperor Nero. Born Lucius Annaeus Novatus, he had been adopted into the senatorial family of Junius Gallio and had embarked on the public career of a Roman aristocrat, as befits the rank of proconsul in a prestigious province. This type of Roman imperial inscription is extremely valuable for historical information, because it gives a rather precise dating formula based on the titles and regnal years of the emperor (line 2). Using this information, the inscription can be securely dated between January 25 and August 1, 52 CE. Since a proconsul normally held office for one year or sometimes two, it is then possible to deduce that Gallio was posted to Corinth in the years 51–52 CE.[4] Acts seems to suggest that this episode occurred after Paul had already been in Corinth for some time and that he spent some eighteen months there altogether (Acts 18:6–11). Hence Paul's time in Corinth may be dated generally between late 50 and 52 CE.

Since this inscription now gives us a firmer date for Paul's first visit to Corinth, say 51 (plus or minus six months) for a convenient number, it now becomes possible to reconstruct the rest of his career, at least in broad lines, by plugging in the other relative values gleaned from Galatians. Of course, some allowances must be made for the imprecise nature of the information; therefore, the usual practice is to allow for a three-year range of dates in the earlier phases of Paul's career.[5] Based on these calculations, we can give the following rough dates for Paul's career:

His "conversion" or "call" (beginning of Phase I)	ca. 35 (or perhaps 32)
First visit to Jerusalem (beginning of Phase II)	ca. 37 (or perhaps 34/35)
Second visit to Jerusalem (the "conference")	ca. 47/48 (the "conference")
Confrontation at Antioch and departure for Aegean mission (beginning of Phase III)	ca. 48/49
Arrival in Corinth	ca. 51

Finally, all of Paul's genuine letters date from the Aegean phase of his career (Phase III), which commences with his departure from Antioch in the aftermath of his confrontation with Peter (Gal. 2:11–14). We can deduce from comments in each of the letters at least some information about where and when it was written. For example, 1 Thessalonians seems to have been his first letter, written while Paul was in Corinth on that initial visit to Greece. Hence we can now begin to date the letters accordingly, as we shall see.

Paul's "Conversion" or "Call"

How Paul came to be a follower of the Jesus movement is a matter of legend that has inspired countless works of art and imitative notions of what a true conversion ought to be like. Acts gives three distinct accounts, adding to its drama and significance. The first and longest of these comes in the form of a narrative of the events in Acts 9.1–31. Then in later chapters Paul is made to re hearse the episode again, once during his arrest in Jerusalem (Acts 22:6–21) and then at Caesarea during his trial before the governor Festus and the Jewish tetrarch Agrippa II (26:12–20). Both of these accounts are given as part of speeches by Paul. Although there are some inexplicable discrepancies even between these three accounts, the basic story goes as follows:

> Paul (then called Saul) had become a ferocious antagonist of the early followers of Jesus in Jerusalem. From the Jewish leaders in Jerusalem he obtained the authority to travel to Damascus in order to arrest followers of Jesus there too. It was while on the road to Damascus that he experienced a blinding light and heard a voice from heaven, which then identified itself as "Jesus, whom you are persecuting" (Acts 9:5; 22:8; 26:15). Left blind and having been led into Damascus by his companions, Paul was then met by a man named Ananias, a follower of Jesus, who had been instructed in a vision to go and minister to Paul. As a result of his care and teaching, Paul then was baptized and became an equally zealous proponent of Jesus.

It is on the basis of this later version of Acts that Paul's experience has been termed a "conversion." He went from being a persecutor of the faith to its most ardent and successful advocate because of his visionary experience of the risen Jesus. In this version, Paul seems very much the "first Christian" or at least the most important "convert," because he then goes on to epitomize the experience of gentile converts while also forging a predominantly non-Jewish form of the movement. He thus becomes the hero of the second half of Acts.

Paul's own account of his experience is far less dramatic and, alas, more sketchy on details. Nonetheless, he gives quite a bit of information both about his Jewish piety prior to becoming a follower of the Jesus movement and about his understanding of what had taken place in the process. Some features of his description bear strong resemblances to the story in Acts; others do not.

Paul's Jewish Background

Paul clearly asserts his Jewish pedigree in several of the letters: "circumcised on the eighth day, a member of the people of Israel, of the tribe of Benjamin, a Hebrew born of Hebrews; as to the law, a Pharisee; as to zeal, a persecutor of the church; as to righteousness under the law, blameless" (Phil. 3:5–6; cf. 2 Cor. 11:22; Rom. 11:1). More than once he refers to his zeal for his Jewish faith, out of which he in good conscience initially persecuted the Jesus movement (cf. Gal. 1:13; 1 Cor. 15:9), and this accords with at least the broad lines of the account in Acts.

Although he once refers to being a Pharisee in regard to the interpretation of Torah (Phil. 3:5), he does not give any indication of having studied with known Pharisaic teachers in Jerusalem, such as Gamaliel (as suggested by Acts 22:3).[6] Paul, however, does not claim any affiliation with the Jewish authorities of Jerusalem in his persecution of the church and only mentions residing in Damascus. He never refers to Tarsus as his hometown (cf. Acts 21:39; 22:3); nor does he mention being a Roman citizen (cf. Acts 16:21, 37–38; 22:25–29; 23:27). The hardships that Paul claims to have faced at the hands of Roman authorities (2 Cor. 11:24–25) are not typical for those possessing Roman citizenship. These glaring differences from the account in Acts have led many scholars to question whether Paul was indeed a full-fledged "citizen" of Rome, although he may well have been a Tarsian citizen.[7]

Paul's Experience of Jesus

For many of these same reasons the account in Acts of a blinding light on the road to Damascus must be viewed as elaboration or legend. Nonetheless, Paul had some sort of visionary experience of the resurrected Jesus, and it was without doubt the event that caused him to become a follower of the movement. Paul alludes to this experience in two of his letters, Galatians and 1 Corinthians.

> *But when God, who had set me apart before I was born and called me through his grace, was pleased **to reveal** his Son to me, so that I might proclaim him among the Gentiles, I did not confer with any human being . . . (Gal. 1:15–16)*

> *He [Jesus] **appeared** to Cephas, then to the twelve. Then he **appeared** to more than five hundred brothers and sisters at one time, most of whom are still alive, though some have died. Then he **appeared** to James, then to all the apostles. Last of all, as to one untimely born, he **appeared** also to me. For I am the least of the apostles, unfit to be called an apostle, because I persecuted the church of God. (1 Cor. 15:5–9)*

The terms that Paul employs here to refer to the nature of his experience are important. In Galatians he uses "to reveal" (Greek *apokalypsai*), the verb form of the word "apocalypse" or "revelation." In light of his adamant claim that he "did not confer with any human being," this can only be taken as an apocalyptic vision of some sort. In 1 Corinthians he uses the word "appeared" (Greek *opthe*), a more general term; however, he uses the identical verb form in the preceding verses to describe the appearances of the risen Jesus to Peter, James, and the five hundred. It will be remembered that this is the same passage discussed previously (Box 6.1), in which Paul rehearses the earliest oral tradition about Jesus. As a result of this context, then, his use of the word "appear" must carry the sense of an "epiphany" or a vision of the risen Jesus.[8]

Unfortunately, he does not tell us more, and some people have resorted to unwarranted psychological explanations. These are not necessary. Paul indicates that he is quite accustomed to having such revelatory visions, in keeping with the apocalyptic and magical religious environment out of which he came. For example, when Paul went to Jerusalem for the second time to consult with Peter and James on the issue of Gentiles, he says that he "went up by revelation" (Gal. 2:1). Elsewhere he refers to having other "visions/appearances and revelations" (2 Cor. 12:1), following which he goes on to describe one such experience where he was "caught up into the third heaven" and saw paradise (2 Cor. 12:2–5). This last description is very much in line with Jewish apocalyptic tradition of heavenly ascents and visions.[9]

A "Conversion" or "Call"?

Paul clearly had a profound experience. He also gives some insights into the way he understood it, when he says, "when God, who had *set me apart before I was born and called me* through his grace" (Gal. 1:15). The terminology he adopts here is remarkably similar to that found in two passages from the Hebrew prophets Jeremiah and Isaiah:

> *Now the word of the Lord came to me saying, "Before I formed you in the womb I knew you, and **before you were born I consecrated you; I appointed you a prophet to the nations [Gentiles].**" (Jer. 1:4–5)*

> *Listen to me, O coastlands, pay attention, you peoples from far away! The Lord **called me before I was born,** while I was in my mother's womb he named me. He made my mouth like a sharp sword, in the shadow of his hand he hid me; he made me a polished arrow, in his quiver he hid me away. And he said to me, "You are my servant, Israel, in whom I will be glorified."*
>
> *But I said, "I have labored in vain, I have spent my strength for nothing and vanity; yet surely my cause is with the Lord, and my reward with my God." And now the Lord says, **who formed me in the womb to be his servant,** to bring Jacob back to him, and that Israel might be gathered to him, for*

I am honored in the sight of the Lord, and my God has become my strength—
he says,

> *"It is too light a thing that you should be my servant*
> *to raise up the tribes of Jacob*
> *and to restore the survivors of Israel;*
> **I will give you as a light to the nations [Gentiles],**
> **that my salvation may reach to the end of the earth."** *(Isa. 49:1–6)*

Both of these passages use the language of being "set apart," "consecrated," or "called" from before birth (or "from my mother's womb") to refer to a prophetic calling by God.[10] In other words, Paul's language still places his outlook on his experience entirely within a Jewish self-understanding.

Paul viewed himself as a special agent called by God to perform a certain task. That task, in keeping with the language of Isaiah and Jeremiah, was to serve as a prophet, or "light," to the nations. But it must also be remembered that the term "nations" in the Greek, as used by both the LXX and Paul, is the same as the word "Gentiles." So Paul seems to have understood his mission as being the divinely appointed messenger to the Gentiles in fulfillment of the prophecies of Isaiah and Jeremiah. This places Paul very much within his Jewish heritage, even when he was preaching to Gentiles. It means also that there was no sense that he had left Judaism behind either by becoming a follower of the Jesus movement or in his reaching out to non-Jews. For this reason, many scholars prefer to define Paul's experience as a "calling" rather than a "conversion."[11] Or if one uses the term "conversion," it must be understood in sectarian terms only; Paul had not "converted" away from Judaism. Rather, he had merely "converted" from one sect of Judaism, the Pharisees, to another, while staying within the same worldview and set of values. In this light, Alan Segal sees Paul as a kind of "religious quester" who gradually came to realize that the very group he had been persecuting as an aberrant form of Judaism was indeed the true way of Judaism after all.[12]

The Elements of Paul's New Faith

Paul, like most others in the first generation of the Jesus movement, did not cease being Jewish when he became a follower of Jesus. Of course, the experience would be quite different for those Gentiles to whom he then preached, for they would indeed have to undergo a more radical form of "conversion" to an entirely different worldview, the worldview of Judaism, in which there is one and only one God. Although none of Paul's actual sermons have been preserved, we can nonetheless see some elements of his preaching and his new faith reflected in the letters. Many scholars think that 1 Thessalonians 1:9–10 represents a kind of capsule summary of Paul's own preaching to his Gentile converts: "For the people of those regions report . . . how you turned to God from idols, to serve a living and true God, and to wait for his Son from heaven, whom he raised from the dead—Jesus, who rescues us from the wrath that is coming."

We see that his message begins by asserting belief in the one, true God in keeping with his strict Jewish monotheism.[13] Next, he had come to believe that Jesus was, in fact, the Jewish messiah after all and that his death could be understood in keeping with the prophetic tradition of Israel (1 Cor. 15:3–4). That Jesus was the crucified messiah (or *christos* in Greek), whom God had vindicated by raising from the dead, was clearly a centerpiece of Paul's message: "For I decided to know nothing among you except Jesus Christ, and him crucified" (1 Cor. 2:2). In addition to his knowledge of the early oral tradition of the death, burial, and resurrection, already discussed, Paul shows awareness of early hymns about Jesus that celebrate his humiliation, death, and glorification:

> *He humbled himself and became obedient to the point of death—even death on a cross. Therefore God also highly exalted him and gave him the name that is above every name, so that at the name of Jesus every knee should bend, in heaven and on earth and under the earth, and every tongue should confess that Jesus Christ is Lord, to the glory of God the Father. (Phil. 2:8–11)*[14]

That Jesus had come as the messiah of Israel meant further, for Paul, that the apocalyptic end times had commenced and would be consummated soon when Jesus came back again (cf. 1 Thess. 4:13; 5:1–11). Finally, he was convinced that he himself had been set apart "from before birth" for a special mission to bring the Gentiles into this new, eschatological kingdom, in keeping with the prophecies of Isaiah and Jeremiah.

Paul the Letter Writer

Paul's indisputable impact in both early and later phases of Christian history derives in large measure from the fact that he wrote letters to his churches. His letters are the earliest Christian writings that have been preserved for us, and the later effort to collect them into a single volume was the beginning of the New Testament canon. Before there were Gospels, there were letters, and letter writing continued to be one of the principal genres of literary activity among

Christians throughout the ancient period. Of the twenty-seven documents that make up the Western New Testament, twenty-two are either wholly or partially letters in form.[15] Some of the later letters of the New Testament and even later ones from the second century were written in conscious imitation of Paul. He has thus been viewed at times as a literary model, even though Paul would not have thought of himself in this way. Instead, he adapted ordinary forms of letter writing to meet his own needs in addressing specific situations within his churches, and in so doing used them to express his creative theological insights in new social and cultural contexts.

Letters in the Greco-Roman World

Letters were a common form of literary expression in the Greco-Roman world. The Roman statesman M. Tullius Cicero (106–43 BCE) was widely known in his own day as a "man of letters"; by Paul's day, volumes of his letters were being published alongside Homer and Virgil as prized literary possessions.[16] The Roman Stoic L. Annaeus Seneca (5/4 BCE–64 CE), a contemporary of Paul,[17] used the genre of letters as a means of philosophical and moral instruction. But then so had the Greek philosopher Epicurus (341–270 BCE) over three centuries earlier. The Roman aristocrat Pliny the Younger (61–113 CE) would eventually collect his own personal and professional correspondence into several books and edit them for publication; one whole volume contained letters to and from the emperor Trajan, one of which includes the earliest Roman reference to the Christians.[18] Later Christians, especially aristocratic bishops and church leaders, including Cyprian of Carthage (ca. 200–258 CE), Athanasius of Alexandria (296–373 CE), Basil of Caesarea (330–379 CE), John Chrysostom (347–407 CE), Jerome (342–420 CE), Augustine (354–430 CE), and many others, continued this tradition of writing and collecting letters, both official and personal, in both Greek and Latin.

Because so many of these letter writers were self-conscious of their literary legacies, comparing their letters to those of Paul has sometimes been considered a waste of time. In later antiquity and the Middle Ages, Paul's letters were viewed as "scripture" and, thus, governed by different literary assumptions. In early modern scholarship, Paul's letters were more properly viewed as ordinary correspondence; however, they were considered to be inferior in form and style to the great literary "epistles" of the classical authors.[19] Although this latter view is not supported by recent scholarly research, it grew up in part out of the vast discoveries of papyrus documents from Roman Egypt beginning in the

later nineteenth century. These discoveries have led to a much greater awareness of the extensive use of the letters in the Roman world at all levels of society
and degrees of sophistication.

The enormous administrative bureaucracy of the Roman Empire made
writing and written documents more of a necessity than perhaps in any period

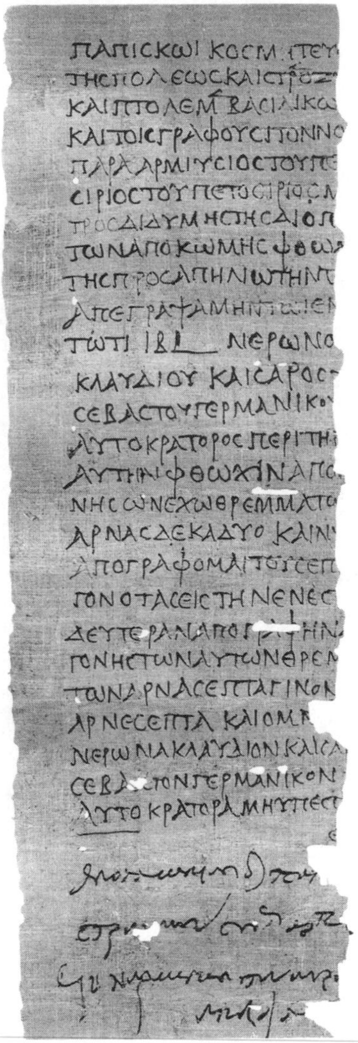

Translation

To Papiscus, ex-kosmetes of the city and strategus
of the Oxyrhynchite nome, and to Ptolemaeus,
royal scribe, and to the scribes of the nome, 5 from
Harmiysis, son of Petosiris, son of Petosiris, his
mother being Didyme, daughter of Diogenes, of
the village of Phthochis in the eastern toparchy.

10 I registered in the present 12th year of Nero
Claudius Caesar Augustus Germanicus, the Emperor,
in the region of the 15 said Phthochis, 12 lambs born
from sheep in my possession, and I now register for
the 20 second *tax registration** a further issue of 7
lambs born from the same sheep. Total, 7 lambs.
And I swear by the Emperor, Nero Claudius Caesar
25 Augustus Germanicus that I have not withheld
anything. Farewell.

Second hand: I Apollonius, agent of Papiscus, the
strategus, sign 7 lambs. 30 Year 12 of our Lord Nero,
11th of Epeiph.

Third hand: I Horion, agent of Ptolemaeus, sign 7
lambs (same date)

Fourth hand: I Zenon, agent of 'the scribes of the
nome' sign 7 lambs (same date)

* The word in line 20 for "tax registration" (*apographe*)
and the related verb "to register" (used in lines 10 and 18)
are the same technical terms used by Luke 2:1–2 and
Josephus (*Antiquities* 18.1–3) in reference to the tax census of Quirinius in 6 CE.

FIGURE 7.1

A property registration on papyrus showing the work of a professional scribe, with signatures by
other hands; from Oxyrhynchus, Egypt (66 CE; P.Oxy 246). (From *The Oxyrhynchus Papyri,* ed.
Grenfell and Hunt, vol. 2, Plate VII; © Egypt Exploration Society, London)

of ancient history down to relatively modern times. As a result, more people could read and write, at least at some minimal level.[20] Greek was still the predominant language in the eastern half of the empire; Latin was used in the western half. Of the large numbers of trained scribes, some served as public notaries to assist those who could not write in Greek or Latin or those who needed more official documents produced (see Fig. 7.1). Other professional scribes worked almost exclusively in the production of literary manuscripts.[21] Still others were employed as private secretaries, trained in the writing of letters for both personal and official occasions.[22]

We know also from several comments that Paul employed such scribes for his letter writing. The most obvious occurs in Romans 16:22, when his scribe Tertius offers his own greetings. So too Paul on several occasions says something like, "See what large letters I make when I am writing in my own hand!" (Gal. 6:11) or "I, Paul, write this greeting with my own hand" (1 Cor. 16:21). In these cases we must imagine him at that point taking the pen from the scribe and writing a personal greeting in his own, distinctive handwriting, similar to what we see very often in the papyri (see Fig. 7.1). It is unfortunate that none of the originals of Paul's letters have survived, for we would be able to get a glimpse of him, at least as the "second hand."

An additional correlative of this extensive writing activity was the industry in writing materials and implements (see Fig. 7.2). These ranged from wax tablets, which could be used for taking notes and then erased and reused, to vellum or parchment made from animal hides (very durable, but much more expensive) to inscriptions on stone (often used to display imperial letters and decrees).[23] By far the most common and affordable writing material in the Roman world was *papyrus,* from which we get the word "paper." Papyrus was a lanky marsh plant that grew natively along the banks of the Nile in Egypt. It was already used as a writing material in earlier Egyptian history (as in the Egyptian *Book of the Dead*), but became even more popular during the Hellenistic and Roman periods, when a major industry grew up around it.

The production of papyrus was extensively described by natural historians in antiquity.[24] It involved slitting the papyrus reed into thin strips and then laying them lengthwise to form a sheet; then another layer of strips was laid across the first layer, and the two were pressed together. Water and plant juices then coated the fibers to form a natural glue. Finally, the sheets were trimmed into somewhat standard sizes. One could go to a local papyrus merchant and purchase a sheet the size one needed or could afford. For longer documents, such as lengthy books, which were usually written on one or more *scrolls* (Latin

FIGURE 7.2

Portrait of Paquius Proculus and his wife from Pompeii (first century CE). He is holding a papyrus scroll with red *index* tag, while she is holding a wax tablet *codex* and a *stilus* for writing on it. (Museo Nazionale, Naples; used by permission of Scala/Art Resource, New York)

volumen; Greek *biblios*), it was typical to glue sheets together to give the length of document needed. Although a typical scroll did not usually exceed about six meters (eighteen feet), we do know of literary scrolls from antiquity that went up to nearly thirteen meters (thirty-nine feet).

Letter Form in the Greek Papyri

Key issues in everyday writing were the cost and availability of papyrus and whether there was someone capable of writing in the manner required by the situation. As a result, many features of writing style in wills, contracts, marriage documents, and ordinary letters derived from formulaic conventions that helped to conserve paper when needed. Many of these features of letter style were actually taught in schools and are preserved in ancient "handbooks" on letter writing.[23] Different types of letters had different formal features as befitted particular social circumstances, relationships, or occasions. A good example is what is known as the letter of recommendation; here is what one of the ancient handbooks gives by way of description followed by a sample letter.

> *Now the recommending type [of letter is] that which we write on behalf of one person to another, weaving together praise at the same time also speaking to those formerly unacquainted as if being known. It goes like this.*
>
> *So-and-so, who is carrying this letter to you, is beloved on account of the faithfulness he possesses; you will do well to deem [him] worthy of a welcome reception both on my account and on his, and so too even on your own account. For you will not regret talking to him on whatever matters you wish, whether a confidential word or deed. Instead, you too will praise him to others once you have perceived what need he is able to fill in every matter.[26]*

Here is a papyrus letter dating to about 25 CE showing how these formal characteristics were actually put into practice:

> *Theon to his most honored Tyrranus, many kind greetings. Heracleides, who is carrying this letter to you, is my brother. Wherefore, I beseech you with all my power to hold him as one who has been highly recommended. I have also asked your brother Hermias to communicate with you in writing concerning this man, Heracleides. You will be doing me a great favor if he should meet with a welcoming gesture from you. Before all else, I pray for your good health with unimpeded prosperity. Farewell.[27]*

The text was written on the inner face of a small single sheet of papyrus measuring 20 by 14.7 centimeters (approximately 8 by 6 inches); the letter was then rolled up and tied or sealed and a simple address—"To Tyrranus, diocesan official"—was written on the outside. This would be typical of an ordinary letter from a local villager to a Roman official. It is short and follows the accepted conventions rather carefully, suggesting both the social deference for the recipient and the work of a trained scribe who was hired to pen the letter for the sender, Theon. Study of the many papyrus letters reveals many aspects, not only of epistolary form and style from the time, but also of the social circumstances. Despite their relative formality, often a great deal of daily life and human pathos comes through (see Fig. 7.3).

Now we may turn to Paul. Paul wrote ordinary letters concerning concrete situations, although he often packed them with religious reflections and ideas. But the formal features and social situation should not be overlooked in favor of the religious content. Instead, these three aspects are almost always intertwined in the way Paul writes. The particular circumstances must be grasped in order to understand how he replies in religious terms. He regularly adopts such common epistolary conventions in his letters to his churches because they are expected in letter writing. For example, near the end of his letter to the Romans, Paul says: "I recommend to you our sister Phoebe, a deacon of the church at Cenchreae, so that you may welcome her in the Lord as is fitting for the saints,

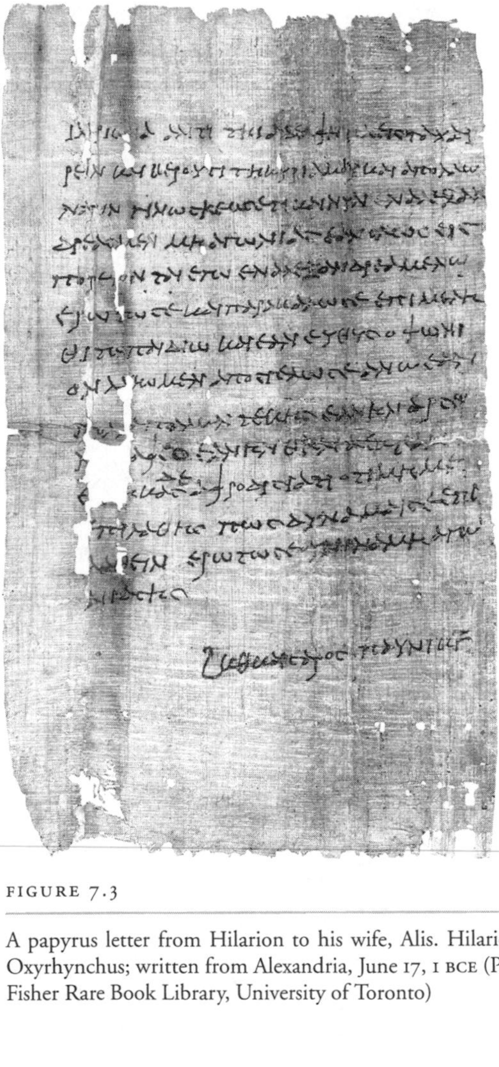

Translation

Hilarion to his sister,* Alis, very many greetings. Also to my lady Berous and to Apollonarion.

Know that we are still in Alexandria. Do not be anxious. If they enter [the service?] altogether, I shall remain in Alexandria. I beg and entreat you, take care of the little one, and as soon as we receive our wages, I will send it up to you. If by some chance you give birth to the child, should it be a boy let it be; should it be a girl, throw it out.† You have said by way of Aphrodisias, "Do not forget me." How can I forget you? I beg you, then, not to be anxious.

The 29th year of Caesar [Augustus], Pauni 23.

On the reverse:

From Hilarion, deliver to Alis

*"Sister" and "Brother" were regularly used as terms of endearment between husband and wife. Berous may be his mother or hers.

†This statement refers to "exposure" as a form of infanticide, commonly practiced in cases of female births in order to control family size.

FIGURE 7.3

A papyrus letter from Hilarion to his wife, Alis. Hilarion seems to be an Egyptian laborer from Oxyrhynchus; written from Alexandria, June 17, 1 BCE (P.Oxy 744). (Photo courtesy of the Thomas Fisher Rare Book Library, University of Toronto)

and help her in whatever she may require from you, for she has been a benefactor of many and of myself as well" (16:1–2). We can now recognize that here Paul has adopted the standard form and terminology for a letter of recommendation. In this case he is introducing the woman Phoebe, from the house church at Cenchreae, one of the suburbs of Corinth, whom he calls "deacon" (or "minister") as well as "benefactor" (or "patroness"). He is asking that she be received with a fitting welcome by the house churches in Rome.

Virtually all of Paul's genuine letters contain some type of letter of recommendation or request for hospitality. We shall return in the next chapter to the implications of the terms used for understanding the social organization of Paul's churches. But for now we may make two final points. First, his use of the letter of recommendation formula here indicates that Phoebe was, in fact, the one who was delegated by Paul to carry the letter to Rome. Second, the letter of recommendation formula was intended to secure hospitality for her from someone in Rome, most likely Prisca and Aquila "and the church in their house," who are mentioned next in the greetings (Rom. 16:3–5). Thus, these formulaic elements of typical Greco-Roman letters are important to our understanding of both the way Paul writes the letter and the historical circumstances and social conditions that lie behind the writing.

Paul's Letter Form

Many of the formulaic elements of Paul's letters come from ordinary epistolary conventions, but Paul also adapted the letter form to suit his needs. A typical papyrus letter would follow a basic outline, although with variations due to the purpose or situation, as we saw above in the case of the letter of recommendation. The basic outline is as follows:

Address	Sender's name "to" recipient's name
Greeting formula	"Kind greetings"
Health petition	"I pray for your health"
Body	Information; purpose of the letter
Final instructions/wishes	"Don't worry"; "take care of so-and-so"; etc.
Closing formulas (may contain a combination)	"Greet so-and-so for me"; "I wish you well"; terms of affection; farewell formula

Paul has his own typical phrases that fit each of these same basic elements. For example, instead of the ordinary formula "Greetings" (Greek *chairein*), Paul always says, "Grace and peace to you." This may be taken as flowery variation, since "grace" (Greek *charis*) is a noun form of the same greeting term, while "peace" (Greek *eirene*) would be the Greek form for the traditional Jewish greeting "shalom." Paul also embellishes the greeting and closing formulas with religiously loaded phrases, such as "from God the Father and our Lord Jesus Christ," which add a doxological tone, perhaps deriving from Jewish prayer formulas.

We see further adaptations in the middle portions of the outline. The petition or prayer formula typically becomes "I give thanks to my God always, when I remember you in my prayers," or similar phrases. Because Paul so frequently opens these petitions with "I/We give thanks" (from the Greek word *eucharisto*), this particular Pauline formula has come to be known as the Thanksgiving or Eucharisto. Analogously, Paul almost always introduces the final instructions section with the formula "I/We beseech you" using the Greek word *parakalo*. Hence this section is typically called the Exhortation or Parakalo.[28] The Thanksgiving, then, often signifies the theme of the letter, which will be taken up in greater detail in the Body, while the Exhortation provides some extended admonitions that derive from his main points. As a result, the typical Pauline letter outline is as follows:

Greeting	"Paul . . . to the church of God that is in Corinth. . . . Grace to you and peace from God our Father and the Lord Jesus Christ" (1 Cor. 1:1–3).
Thanksgiving (Eucharisto)	"I give thanks to God always . . ." (1 Cor. 1:4).
Body	"Now concerning . . ." (1 Cor. 7:1). "You yourselves know . . ." (1 Thess. 2:1).
Exhortation (Parakalo)	"Finally, brothers and sisters, we ask and urge you . . ." (1 Thess. 4:1).
Closing	"Greet every saint in Christ Jesus. The brothers and sisters who are with me greet you. . . . The grace of the Lord Jesus Christ be with your spirit" (Phil. 4:21–23).

A synoptic chart showing these formal elements in all Paul's genuine letters is given in Box 7.4.

Paul's letters are relatively long by comparison to typical papyrus letters. Only the little letter to Philemon, a mere twenty-five verses, is more in keeping

BOX 7.4
Pauline Letter Form — A Synopsis

Section references for the undisputed letters are listed in canon order.

Section / Letter	Romans	1 Corinthians	2 Corinthians	Galatians	Philippians	1 Thessalonians	Philemon
Greeting	1:1–7	1:1–3	1:1–2	1:1–5	1:1–2	1:1	vv. 1–3
Thanksgiving (Eucharisto) or Blessing	1:8–17	1:4–9	1:3–7[1]	1:6–9[2]	1:3–11	1:2–10	vv. 4–7
Body	1:18–11:36	5:1–16:12	1:8–7:15 8:1–9:15 10:1–13:4	1:10–5:12	1:12–2:30 3:1–4:1	2:1–3:13	vv. 8–20
Exhortation (Parakalo)	12:1–15:33	1:10–4:21[3] 16:13–18	13:5–10	5:13–6:10	4:2–20	4:1–5:22	vv. 21–22
Closing	16:1–27	16:19–24	13:11–14	6:11–18	4:21–23	5:23–28	vv. 23–25

[1] 2 Cor. 1:3 has "Blessed be," a fairly typical blessing formula in Jewish tradition.

[2] Gal. 1:6 has "I am astonished" instead of "I give thanks," and this seems to be an intentional or ironic twist on the expected wording.

[3] Notice that the Body and the Exhortation are reversed, even though the formulas are consistent. Again, this appears to be an intentional modification.

with the ordinary one-page letter so commonly seen in papyri from that period. What is perhaps more important is the way that Paul intentionally modifies his own basic outline in order to suit his purpose in writing any particular letter. These modifications can also help us to understand both the situation of the letter and Paul's intentions and ideas in writing. Individual modifications and adaptations of the letter form (as reflected in Box 7.4) will be discussed in greater detail when we look at the situation of each letter in the next chapter.

CHAPTER EIGHT

Paul

The Aegean Mission

About the year 48 CE Paul returned from Jerusalem to Antioch with his traveling companions Barnabas and Titus. Barnabas was Jewish; Titus, gentile. It is Paul himself who gives us the report of what happened at Jerusalem in Galatians 2:1–10: his meeting with the "pillars" of the Jerusalem church—James, Cephas (Peter), and John—had resulted in Paul and Barnabas receiving "the right hand of fellowship" (Gal. 2:9). Perhaps more important for Paul was the fact that, despite vocal opposition, Titus was not required to undergo circumcision (Gal. 2:3). Now they had returned to Antioch to report to Paul's fledgling congregations there. They too were a mixture of Jews (and perhaps some proselytes) and Gentiles, who, like Titus, had not been circumcised when they joined the Jesus movement. Other Jewish congregations at Antioch, including some that followed Jesus, must have looked at Paul's cell groups with misgivings. After all, having fellowship with Gentiles—and especially eating with them on religious occasions—was viewed by many as a breach of Jewish purity laws. This was the issue that had taken Paul to Jerusalem; Paul returned convinced that he had carried the day.

A Fateful Encounter in Antioch

Shortly thereafter Peter came to Antioch, probably to check out the situation there and perhaps to do some follow-up work among the exclusively Jewish congregations of the Jesus movement. That too seems to have been one of the agreements struck in the meeting at Jerusalem (Gal. 2:7–8). Perhaps this was meant to assuage the stricter among them while allowing Paul's mixed cell groups to continue operating within their social orbit. But the results were disastrous:

> But when Cephas came to Antioch, I opposed him to his face, because he stood self-condemned; for until certain people came from James, he used to eat with the Gentiles. But after they came, he drew back and kept himself separate for fear of the circumcision faction. And the other Jews joined him in this hypocrisy, so that even Barnabas was led astray by their hypocrisy. But when I saw that they were not acting consistently with the truth of the gospel, I said to Cephas before them all, "If you, though a Jew, live like a Gentile and not like a Jew, how can you compel the Gentiles to live like Jews?" (Gal. 2:11–14)

Initially, it seems, Peter had moved freely between the different factions, even to the point of joining in the dinners of Paul's mixed groups. Then some other Jewish followers of the movement came from Jerusalem—"from James"—and caused Peter to draw back from fellowship involving uncircumcised Gentiles. It seems that James's emissaries had aligned with stricter Jewish cells at Antioch and intimidated other Jews, including Peter. Much to Paul's chagrin, even Barnabas turned on him.

Paul must have realized the implications quickly. His hard-fought efforts to secure a place for Gentiles in the Jesus fellowship were about to face total rejection even by those Jews who had formerly been sympathetic. Paul lashed out. Whether he first implored Barnabas and others to give it another chance is not reported. Whether he once again passionately defended his own understanding of the commission "revealed by God" (Gal. 1:16; 2:2, 7) is not reported. It came down finally to a confrontation with Peter himself. Paul now erupted. Peter "stood condemned" of hypocrisy, and Paul told him so to his face in front of witnesses (Gal. 2:11, 13–14). What follows in Galatians 2:15–21 may well represent what Paul wished he had said to justify his position. But the reality was far different; nor was it a mere difference of opinion. Paul persuaded no one, not even Barnabas, who, according to later legends, became a protégé of Peter.[1]

The blowup with Peter was a total failure of political bravado, and Paul soon left Antioch as persona non grata, never again to return. It has been suggested that Jerusalem was trying to extend its authority over Antioch, but the attitude of local Jewish followers of the movement must also be taken into account.[2] The picture in Acts shows that the church in Antioch later viewed the relationship in these terms, while consciously playing down the rift between Peter and Paul. What happened to Paul's mixed Jewish and gentile enclaves remains unclear, but one must suspect that the "circumcision party" prevailed.[3] For Paul the immediate result was clear. He had to leave Antioch. He chose to embark on a new mission where there was not such a strong and traditional Jewish community. He would go west, toward Greece and Rome, where he could work independently as "missionary" or "apostle" to the Gentiles.[4] And so begins the most important phase in Paul's career, the Aegean mission.

The Aegean Mission: An Overview

For the next decade Paul traveled extensively and exclusively in the region of the Aegean Rim, meaning the western coast of Asia Minor (modern Turkey) and the eastern coast of Greece (see Fig. 8.1). With him were traveling companions and helpers, such as Timothy and Titus. Together they followed the Roman highways and shipping routes through this region, stopping in major cities, where Paul would try to attract some followers. In contrast to the picture

FIGURE 8.1

Map of the Aegean Rim, showing major Roman roads.

in Acts, Paul seems not to have started within local synagogue congregations, if there were any at this time. Instead, he concentrated on Gentiles. Local cell groups meeting in the homes of converts became his base of missionary work in each city and its surrounding district. Then Paul moved on to the next major city. He began to write letters back to those earlier congregations as a way of supporting and encouraging them or to answer questions. Again he moved on and wrote more letters.

During this period, several large urban centers served as hubs for Paul's mission work: Philippi and Thessalonica in Macedonia, the northern province of Greece; Corinth in Achaia, the southern province of Greece; and Ephesus, in the province of Asia. All were important Roman cities. Both Philippi and Corinth were Roman colonies, while Thessalonica, Corinth, and Ephesus were the capitals of their respective provinces. What we know about these churches and their experiences in the movement comes from Paul's letters. In this chapter, then, we shall take up the letters in their chronological order (see Box. 8.1), and from them discover more about the social and religious dimensions of Paul's Aegean mission. The dating of some of the letters is debated among New Testament scholars, and we shall discuss these matters in each case.

BOX 8.1

Paul's Letters from the Aegean Mission

Letter Name	Date	Written From	Written To	Letter Carrier
1 Thessalonians	50–51	Corinth	Thessalonica	Timothy (1 Thess. 3:2, 6)
1 Corinthians	53–54	Ephesus	Corinth	Stephanas (1 Cor. 16:15–18)
Philippians	55–56	Ephesus	Philippi	Epaphroditus (Phil. 2:25–30)
Philemon	55–56	Ephesus	Colossae	Onesimus (Philem. 12, 17)
Galatians	55/57	Ephesus	Galatia	Not given
2 Corinthians	55/56, 57/58 (2 stages)	Ephesus and Philippi	Corinth	Titus and others (2 Cor. 7:13; 8:17f)
Romans	58–59	Corinth	Rome	Phoebe (Rom. 16:1–2)

The First Circuit (49–51 CE): 1 Thessalonians

We know almost nothing of Paul's movements immediately after leaving Antioch in 48–49 CE until he arrives in Greece and writes his first letter, 1 Thessalonians. He must have traveled across eastern Turkey, perhaps stopping in Tarsus along the way. From there his exact route and his intervening stops are uncertain.[5] He eventually made his way to the western coast of Asia, probably at Alexandria Troas, the Roman port city near ancient Troy. From there he could sail directly to the port at Neapolis in Greece and catch the Via Egnatia. The Via Egnatia was the main Roman highway running across northern Greece from Byzantium to Dyrrachium (Fig. 8.1), and thus the main overland route connecting Anatolia to Italy. Philippi and Thessalonica were important stops along this route.

Because of comments on his itinerary and activities in 1 Thessalonians, we are able to reconstruct the sequence of events in greater detail:

> *You yourselves know, brothers and sisters, that our coming to you was not in vain, but though we had already suffered and been shamefully mistreated at Philippi . . . (1 Thess. 2:1–2)*

> *For we wanted to come to you—certainly I, Paul, wanted to again and again—but Satan blocked our way. (1 Thess. 2:18)*

> *Therefore when we could bear it no longer, we decided to be left alone in Athens; and we sent Timothy, our brother and co-worker for God in proclaiming the gospel of Christ, to strengthen and encourage you . . . (1 Thess. 3:1–2)*

> *But Timothy has just now come to us from you, and has brought us the good news of your faith and love. He has told us also that you always remember us kindly and long to see us—just as we long to see you. (1 Thess. 3:6)*

As we see, Paul came first to Philippi and then, after experiencing some sort of "opposition," moved on to Thessalonica. Paul stayed long enough in both cities to establish some small congregations.[6] His comment in 1 Thessalonians 1:9

("you turned to God from idols") makes it clear that most, if not all, of these new followers were Gentiles. But then Paul was forced to move on again. Why, we are not told (1 Thess. 2:18). He traveled south from Macedonia to Achaia, Rome's southern province in Greece, and paused in Athens, apparently just long enough to dispatch his traveling companion Timothy to go back to Thessalonica and check up on the followers there.[7] Then Paul moved on to Corinth, the provincial capital of Achaia (cf. Acts 18:1, 5). Eventually, Timothy caught up with him in Corinth and reported that the followers in Thessalonica were all right and remembered him kindly.

It was at this point that Paul wrote the letter now known as 1 Thessalonians. From Paul's comments we can see that it was written from Corinth on his first visit there, sometime in late 50 or 51 CE (for this chronology, see Chapter 7). On this basis we can now give a summary profile of the letter (see Box 8.2). First Thessalonians was meant to be a rather intimate letter of exhortation addressed to Paul's recent gentile converts. It is not in any sense a theological treatise, although Paul does appear to respond to some questions that have arisen since his departure. Throughout the letter he expresses his concerns for them over the fact that he had to leave and had been unable to return. He seems to be concerned that they might think he is some sort of fly-by-night preacher. Consequently he stresses his impeccable behavior while with them and his abiding affection and concern for them. In this context, he presents himself using the common model of a "philosophic missionary" whose only goal is their betterment (2:7, 11). The letter is thus suffused with typical philosophic language of exhortation and consolation.[8]

Paul seems to adapt the form of the letter to the situation and his purpose in minor ways. The body of the letter begins formally in 2:1, but the "thanksgiving" language recurs in 2:13 and 3:9. As a result, there is no real content to the body of the letter other than Paul's rehearsal of his itinerary, and it becomes little more than a continuation of the thanksgiving. The exhortation of the letter begins formally in 4:1, using the standard terminology, but in 4:9, 4:12, and 5:1 Paul reverts to formulas that typically introduce topics in the body of a letter. So it appears that Paul has intentionally deferred taking up these questions until the exhortation.

This subtle shift tells us several things about the situation of the letter. First, it is likely that the questions addressed in chapters 4–5 were issues that had cropped up among the Thessalonians since Paul's departure and that Timothy had reported on his return. Second, the chief theological question seems to

BOX 8.2

The First Letter to the Thessalonians

DATE: 50–51 CE

AUTHOR: Paul (Silvanus, Timothy, 1:1)[1]

LETTER CARRIER: Timothy (or Silvanus)[2]

LOCATION: Corinth

AUDIENCE: Paul's recent gentile converts in Thessalonica, the Roman provincial capital of Macedonia (cf. 1:9)

OCCASION AND PURPOSE: The return of Timothy with good news regarding the church in Thessalonica (cf. 3:6–7). Also, the Thessalonians request information regarding issues that have come up since Paul's departure (4:13; 5:1). A letter of exhortation.

OUTLINE

   I. Greeting (1)

   II. Thanksgiving (1:2–10; cf. 2:13; 3:9)

   III. Body (2:1–3:13; cf. 4:9, 12; 5:1)

   IV. Exhortation (4:1–5:22)

   V. Closing (5:23–28)

FURTHER READING

Hendrix, H. L. "Thessalonica." *Anchor Bible Dictionary.* 6:523–27.

Jewett, R. *The Thessalonian Correspondence.* Philadelphia: Fortress, 1986.

Krentz, E. M. "Thessalonians, 1st and 2nd Epistles to the." *Anchor Bible Dictionary.* 6:515–23.

Malherbe, A. J. *The Letters to the Thessalonians.* Anchor Bible. New York: Doubleday, 2000.

———. *Paul and the Popular Philosophers.* Minneapolis: Fortress, 1989.

———. *Paul and the Thessalonians.* Philadelphia: Fortress, 1987.

---

[1] Some scholars have argued that Silvanus (and Timothy) coauthored the letter with Paul, in part to help explain some difficulties of the relationship between 1 and 2 Thessalonians. Despite the fact that Paul uses the first-person plural throughout the letter, this seems unlikely, but see the following note.

[2] Silvanus is also mentioned as Paul's co-worker in 2 Cor. 1:19 and 2 Thess. 1:1, but cf. 1 Pet. 5:12. The name is Latin, but he is supposed to be the same as Silas in Acts, who is Jewish. Silas first appears in Acts as a delegate from Jerusalem to Antioch (15:22, 32), but he then teams up with Paul as a replacement for Barnabas (15:40). On the other hand, Silvanus was a common name in Philippi due to its large population of Italian colonists. So it is possible that he joined Paul there as an early convert and then accompanied Paul to Thessalonica and Corinth. If so, it is also possible that Silvanus was designated to carry the letter rather than Timothy, which would explain why he is so prominently mentioned in the greeting.

concern the recent death of someone in the church at Thessalonica; the members are worried about the eschatological implications: Will that person share in the coming kingdom? It is clear from their concern, as well as his own summary statement in 1:9–10, that in his earlier preaching Paul had stressed apocalyptic themes regarding the messiah, an imminent eschaton, and divine wrath. Paul now has to explain to them that there will indeed be a place for those who have already died, based on the Jewish expectation of resurrection (4:16), when Jesus returns at the eschaton (5:23). By packing these instructions into the exhortation section, he thereby delivers a more comforting and personal reply to their concerns. At the same time, the overall theme and tone of exhortation is entirely consistent with his self-presentation in the first half of the letter: he is a "gentle nurse" (2:7), a caring teacher, a personal guide for their improvement (both individually and communally), and, thereby, the one who brings them to God.

From Corinth to Ephesus (51–54 CE): The Early Letters to Corinth

Paul in Corinth

By the early Roman period Corinth had become one of the most important shipping centers in the eastern Mediterranean (see Box 8.3). Refounded as a Roman colony by Julius Caesar, Corinth became the provincial capital of Achaia. As a result, Corinth developed several large and affluent "suburbs," including Cenchreae (cf. Rom. 16:1).

As we have already seen, Paul arrived in Corinth late in the year 50 or early 51 CE after leaving Athens and passing directly by the sanctuary of the Eleusinian mysteries. According to Acts 18:1–2, when he arrived, Paul met up with a Jewish couple named Prisca (or Priscilla) and Aquila, who were already followers of the Jesus movement and who had recently arrived from Rome. Paul is said to have stayed with them because they were also in the tent-making business. We know from Paul's letters that Prisca and Aquila were indeed important contacts later at Ephesus and eventually at Rome (1 Cor. 16:19; Rom. 16:3–5). In each instance, Paul mentions that they host a "church in their house." According to Acts 18:11 Paul stayed a total of eighteen months, and it was during this period that he was brought up on charges before the Roman proconsul L. Junius Gallio (18:12; see Chapter 7 on the date of this event).

BOX 8.3

Roman Corinth at the Time of Paul

The city of Corinth goes back to archaic Greek times when it was an early rival of Athens. Its fame and prominence continued into the Hellenistic period, and the irascible Cynic philosopher Diogenes was buried there. Then in 196 BCE Greece became a province of Rome's growing empire. In defiance of Rome, however, the Achaian League attempted to reassert the independence of old Greece. The Roman consul Lucius Mummius took command, and his armies defeated the Greeks and destroyed Corinth, the league's principal bastion, in 144 BC. The city was not entirely abandoned, but it remained a mere shell for nearly a century, until it was refounded as a Roman colony (*Colonia Laus Julia Corinthiensis*) by Julius Caesar between 56 and 44 BCE. It was then named the new capital of the southern province of Greece, Achaia.

The status of *colonia*, or colony, was highly prized, since it automatically gave the city special privileges in the Roman administration, and its citizens

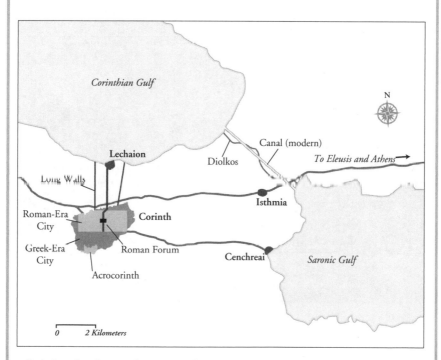

a Corinth and environs under Roman rule.

were considered Romans. Roman veterans and freedmen were allowed to settle the city, and they soon set about turning it into a Roman-style city. Apart from its colonial status and its position as provincial capital, what gave Corinth its signal place in the Roman economy was its unique geographic position sitting astride the isthmus that connected the Peloponnesus to the mainland of Attica. With the help of Roman engineering, the Corinthians were able to exploit this position by building harbors on both the Aegean side (at Isthmia and later Cenchreae) and the Corinthian Gulf (at Lechaion). This meant that cargoes from the eastern Mediterranean could be off-loaded on one side and reloaded on the other for a direct sail to the Adriatic and Italy.

The real growth of the city began under the first emperors, Augustus and Tiberius. Eventually Corinth developed into one of the most prosperous and "Roman" cities in the eastern Mediterranean. As a result, it developed several large and affluent "suburbs" around the central city. Also, due to its trade and political standing, it attracted a diverse array of peoples from across the empire.

b Photo of the Forum of Roman Corinth, looking toward the Temple of Apollo.

The Occasion of Paul's Early Letters to Corinth

Paul apparently departed Corinth by early 52 CE and moved to Ephesus (cf. Acts 18:18). It is clear that he wrote 1 Corinthians from Ephesus (1 Cor. 16:8) and that Prisca and Aquila had accompanied him there (1 Cor. 16:19). It is also clear, however, that the letter now called 1 Corinthians was not Paul's "first" to them, for in 1 Corinthians 5:9 Paul refers to an earlier letter: "I wrote to you in my letter not to associate with sexually immoral persons." We also know that the Corinthians had already written a letter to Paul in Ephesus—1 Corinthians 7:1 says: "Now concerning the matters about which you wrote." So we can see that there had already been two earlier exchanges of correspondence between X Paul and the Corinthians before our 1 Corinthians. For the sake of clarity, then, we shall call the earlier letter by Paul Letter A, and 1 Corinthians Letter B. We might well guess that shortly after Paul arrived in Ephesus he wrote a letter of instruction and exhortation to the Corinthians, much as he had done to the Thessalonians. This sets the stage for understanding the occasion and purpose of the B letter, which was probably written in 53 or 54 CE (see Box 8.4).

Sometime after his earlier letter (Letter A) to Corinth, Paul began to receive disturbing reports regarding the situation in Corinth. These reports came from two distinct sources mentioned in the later letter (Letter B). One of these is mentioned in 1 Corinthians 1:11: "It has been reported to me by Chloe's people that there are quarrels among you." This seems to have been information given to Paul orally by some members of the household of a woman named Chloe. It is the first clue regarding the main problem to be addressed in the letter—division and social strife. But it also appears that Paul had received information by way of a letter written by some other people within the Corinthian congregations (1 Cor. 7:1); it was carried by three men, Stephanas, Fortunatus, and Achaicus (1 Cor. 16:17). This letter apparently asked Paul to address certain questions that had already engendered debate and division among the Corinthian churches.

The Problems of Status and Division

It is not entirely clear how the information from these two reports might have overlapped. It is typically suggested that Paul takes up the issues more or less in serial order in the body of the letter, so that 1 Corinthians 5–6 deals with the "Chloe report," while chapters 7–14 deal with the "Stephanas letter." The actual situation is not likely this simple, since it appears that Paul saw some larger

BOX 8.4
The First Letter to the Corinthians

DATE: 53–54 CE

AUTHOR: Paul

LETTER CARRIER: Stephanas (1 Cor. 16:15–18)

LOCATION: Ephesus

RELATED LETTERS: Letter A (cf. 1 Cor. 5:9), ca. 52 CE; letter from Corinth to Paul (cf. 1 Cor. 7:1). Neither letter is preserved.

AUDIENCE: A circular letter to the several house churches in Corinth

OCCASION AND PURPOSE: Reports of divisions and status conflicts at Corinth from two sources: (1) an oral report given Paul by members of Chloe's household (1 Cor. 1:11); (2) the letter from Corinth to Paul (1 Cor. 7:1) carried by Stephanas, Fortunatus, and Achaicus (1 Cor. 16:17). An appeal for unity (1:10–4:21), followed by advice and correctives on specific issues (5:1–15:58).

OUTLINE

    I.   Greeting (1:1–3)

    II. Thanksgiving (1:4–9)

    III. Exhortation: Paul's Appeal for Unity (1:10–4:21)

    IV. Body: Paul's Response (5:1–15:58)

       A. Problems reported by Chloe's household (5:1–6:20)

problems of theological misunderstanding underlying both reports, and he weaves them together in his response. That Paul viewed the problem of social conflict as a contributing factor in the debates over individual issues is further indicated by the way Paul once again adapts the letter form (see the outline in Box 8.4). After the typical greeting and thanksgiving sections, Paul launches immediately into language typical of the exhortation section (1:10). This extended "appeal for unity" (1:10–4:21) serves as a thematic response to the underlying problems. Then in 5:1 he turns to the individual issues in the body of the letter, which runs through chapter 15.

Many of the conflicts reflected in the letter seem to result from questions of social status. In the thematic appeal Paul says:

> Consider your own call, brothers and sisters: not many of you were wise by human standards, not many were powerful, not many were of noble birth. But God chose what is foolish in the world to shame the wise; God chose what

1. The immoral man (5:1–13)
2. Lawsuits (6:1–20)

B. Questions raised in the letter from Corinth (7:1–14:40)
   1. Marriage and the single life (7:1–40)
   2. On freedom in eating and social life (8:1–11:1)
   3. Gender, head coverings, and worship (11:2–16)
   4. Abuses of fellowship at the Lord's Supper (11:17–34)
   5. Abuses of unity in the exercise of spiritual gifts (12:1–14:40)

C. Questions concerning the resurrection (15:1–58)
D. Final instructions (16:1–12)

V. Final Exhortation (16:13–18)
VI. Closing (16:19–24)

FURTHER READING

Hurd, J. C. *The Origins of 1 Corinthians*. 2d ed. Macon, GA: Mercer University Press, 1983.

Malherbe, A. J. *Social Aspects of Early Christianity*. 2d ed. Philadelphia: Fortress, 1983.

Martin, D. B. *The Corinthian Body*. New Haven, CT: Yale University Press, 1995.

Meeks, W. A. *The First Urban Christians: The Social World of the Apostle Paul*. New Haven, CT: Yale University Press, 1983.

Mitchell, M. M. *Paul and the Rhetoric of Reconciliation*. Tübingen: Mohr-Siebeck, 1991.

Theissen, G. *The Social Setting of Pauline Christianity: Essays on Corinth*. Philadelphia: Fortress, 1982.

Willis, W. L. *Idol Meat at Corinth: The Pauline Argument in 1 Corinthians 8 9*. Chico, CA: Scholars Press, 1985.

Wire, A. C. *The Corinthian Women Prophets: A Reconstruction Through Paul's Rhetoric*. Minneapolis: Fortress, 1990.

is weak in the world to shame the strong; God chose what is low and despised in the world, things that are not, to reduce to nothing things that are, so that no one might boast in the presence of God. He is the source of your life in Christ Jesus, who became for us wisdom from God, and righteousness and sanctification and redemption, in order that, as it is written, "Let the one who boasts, boast in the Lord." (1 Cor. 1:26–31)

Thus, at least some of the Corinthian followers were of higher socioeconomic status, even though most were not. Some key issues later in the letter, particularly conflicts over attending elite pagan dinner parties (chaps. 8–10) and divisions arising in the Lord's Supper (11:17–34), seem to depend on these socioeconomic divisions.

Other questions, however, seem to arise from the fact that some members of the congregations have a sense of "spiritual superiority" that allows them to do things that others find socially offensive or downright immoral. The sexual and gender issues addressed in chapters 5–7 and 11 all revolve around the idea that, for some people, being a follower of the Jesus movement had given them the liberty to do certain things.

Baptism and the Problem of Spiritual Elitism

But where had the members gotten these ideas of "spiritual superiority" reflected in slogans such as "All things are lawful for me" (6:12–13; 10:23–24) and "All of us possess knowledge" (8:1)? Probably from Paul's own preaching, and that is why he was so concerned to disabuse them of their misunderstanding regarding his message and intent. Perhaps the clearest indicator of the underlying problem is the case of the "immoral man":

> It is actually reported that there is sexual immorality [porneia] among you, and of a kind that is not found even among pagans; for a man is living with [lit., having] his father's wife. And you are arrogant! Should you not rather have mourned, so that he who has done this would have been removed from among you? (1 Cor. 5:1–2)

The situation seems to be that a man in one of the Corinthian congregations is known to be in a sexual relationship with his stepmother. For Paul the problem lies not only in the sexual behavior itself, but also in the attitude of the man and of those in the congregation who seem to approve of his behavior: "And you [plural] are arrogant!" (5:2). Apparently they are of the opinion that being "in Christ" now makes such behavior permissible.

What seems to stand behind this problem is the idea that some of the Corinthians think they have transcended the ordinary boundaries of human society by entering into a new realm of existence "in Christ," meaning that because they have become followers of Jesus, they have become spiritually superior. This idea is usually called "realized eschatology." It means that the eschatological transformation is not an imminent future expectation, but a present reality. Paul counters by asserting that the death and resurrection of Jesus (15:3–7) is proof, not only that it can happen, but that it *must* happen in order for mortals to attain immortality (15:20–50). The length and intensity of the argument on the resurrection (15:1–58) suggest that Paul sees it as underlying many of the other issues of spiritual superiority.

It may well be the case that even these concerns over resurrection came from

Paul, or at least from a misunderstanding of Paul's own rhetoric, especially that used in conjunction with baptism. "Baptism" comes from a common Greek word meaning a bath, but carries the sense of a ritual washing for purification. In Paul's theology, however, baptism seems to have taken on new and added significance for his gentile converts, because it was understood as a substitute for circumcision. It is not clear where or when this idea originated, but it may well be one of the points of disagreement between Paul and the "circumcision party" at Antioch.[9] Although this idea is not explicit in 1 Corinthians, it is reflected in some early Pauline rhetoric that links baptism as circumcision with the death and resurrection of Jesus (cf. Col. 2:11–12; 3:9–11).[10]

In other words, as the central ritual of initiation for entrance into Paul's churches, baptism took the place of circumcision—thus bringing the person into the congregation of Israel—by dying and rising with Christ. But notice that gentile converts would have also heard Paul say that in baptism they "*had been* raised from the dead." Here we have another myth-ritual complex (see Chapter 3), as the story of Jesus's death was ritually enacted in baptismal initiation. Elsewhere Paul juxtaposes this "dying and rising" symbolism with the imagery of "putting off and putting on" clothing (Col. 3:9–11; Gal. 3:27).

Baptism was actually performed in the nude: the initiate undressed, went down into the water, came out, and redressed. As Wayne Meeks has shown, the act of disrobing and redressing in the ritual of baptism was seen as symbolic of putting off the old body and putting on a new one in the "image of the creator," a reference to Genesis 1:26.[11] In turn, the actions were accompanied by a ritual pronouncement: "As many of you as were baptized into Christ have *put on* Christ. There is no longer Jew or Greek, there is no longer slave or free, there is no longer male and female; for all of you are one in Christ Jesus" (Gal. 3:27–28).[12]

Now called the *baptismal reunification formula,* it stresses that in baptism one returns to the state of creation, as in Genesis 1:26, when all humanity was unified. That the Corinthians also knew this formula is confirmed by Paul's allusion in 1 Corinthians 12:12–13 in the context of discussing spiritual gifts as signs of superiority. Among other things, this symbolism must have been very appealing to women and slaves. Ultimately Paul argues that discord produced by wrangling over symbolic status markers, as seen in connection with the Lord's Supper (11:23–34) and in other problems in 1 Corinthians, was absolutely contrary to being "one in Christ" (Gal. 3:28; cf. 1 Cor. 12:13), both as present reality and in anticipation of the coming eschatological renewal.

The Social Organization of House Churches

The level of discord at Corinth was probably heightened by the fact that there were several different congregations in the city, due to its size and geographic spread across several extra-urban regions. It is likely that Chloe's household represents one such group, and the household of Stephanas (1:16; 16:15) represents another. This might also help to account for how so many different interpretations of Paul's message could develop simultaneously. Of course, there were no church buildings in Paul's day, nor would a distinctively Christian church architecture evolve for nearly three centuries.[13] Likewise, there was no fixed synagogue architecture at this time, especially in the Diaspora. In fact, most of the Christian and Jewish meeting places from the early centuries that have been discovered by archaeologists were renovated houses. In Paul's day, however, congregations of the Jesus movement were centered in households and met in the homes of individual members. For this reason we call them *house churches*.

A number of references confirm this basic unit of social organization, especially when Paul sends greetings to or from "so and so, and the church in his [or her, your, their] house" (1 Cor. 16:19; Rom. 16:5; Philem. 2; Col. 4:15). Acts supports this picture, for both the earliest meetings in Jerusalem and Paul's missionary activity.[14] During the course of Paul's dealings with Corinth, we hear of at least six distinct house-church groups. They are associated with:

Prisca and Aquila (Acts 18:1; cf. 1 Cor. 16:19)	Stephanas (1 Cor. 1:16; 16:15)
Chloe (1 Cor. 1:11)	Gaius (Rom. 16:23; 1 Cor. 1:14)
Phoebe (Rom. 16:1–2)	Crispus (1 Cor. 1:14; Acts 18:8)

Other references within the letter make it clear that the gatherings for worship took place in these homes, typically in the dining room, where they also celebrated the Lord's Supper (see 1 Cor. 11:17–34; 14:26–27).

These basic facts have some important implications for the social organization and makeup of Paul's churches:[15]

1. The house churches tended to cluster around established households, which included not only the "nuclear family" but also extended family, domestic slaves, and other clients or business associates.

2. Both men and women are known to have headed individual house churches.

3. The owner of the house where the church met on a regular basis was considered its host and patron, and he *or* she also exercised considerable authority within the group. Phoebe (Rom. 16:2) and Gaius (Rom. 16:23) were clearly important benefactors to Paul and their respective churches at Corinth.

4. Paul and his traveling co-workers usually stayed with the house-church patron (Rom. 16:23; Philem. 22).

5. Paul typically baptized the house-church patrons, but they in turn baptized most of the rest (1 Cor. 1:14–16).

6. Paul received financial support from his congregations, but this usually came in the form of hospitality or aid from the patron (Rom. 16:2, 23; Philem. 18, 22; Phil. 4:15–20).

7. When Paul wrote letters to various congregations, they were typically disseminated through the house-church patron (Philem. 2); thus, the letter-of-recommendation form that figures so prominently in Paul's writing was a formal mechanism for accessing hospitality in the house church (Rom. 16:1–2).

8. Hospitality and communal fellowship through dining and worship were important features of congregational solidarity and social life, and thus became important virtues in service to the church community.

As we shall see, a number of these elements of house-church organization will become important in understanding Paul's other letters of the Aegean period.

Ephesus (54–56 CE): Letters from Prison (Philippians and Philemon)

Ephesus became the base for Paul's mission in the Roman province of Asia. It was the provincial capital and chief commercial center (see Box 8.5). It would appear that Paul was based in or near Ephesus for about five or six years, making occasional trips out along important routes to other key cities of the region. New churches were founded at Colossae, and Paul had contact with the interior regions of Phrygia and Galatia. (Galatians will be discussed later in this chapter). At some point, however, it seems that Paul was put in prison. We know little of the details, since Paul only alludes to being "in chains" and Acts never mentions it.

BOX 8.5

The City of Ephesus

Ephesus was the capital of the Roman province of Asia and its leading port city. The ancient city was famed for its monumental Temple of Artemis, an Anatolian fertility goddess who was equated with the Greek goddess of the same name. The temple was known as one of the seven wonders of the ancient world. In 287 BCE the general Lysimachus moved the Hellenistic city to higher ground between the hills Coressos and Pion, and it became the new Roman center beginning under the emperor Augustus (see Fig. b).

Because the city remained sacred to Artemis, a processional way led from the ancient sanctuary through the city, passing along Curetes Street, past the theater, and out again by the northern gate (see Fig. c). A harbor channel was created from the river, thus allowing ships to dock at the western edge of the city, which became its warehouse district. From the theater (Fig. a) the outline of the harbor can still be seen at the end of the marble thoroughfare.

Ephesus was made the provincial capital of Asia under Augustus but also retained its status as a free Greek city. Because Ephesus had supported Marc Antony over Octavian (Augustus), Ephesus was refused the honor of

a The theater at Ephesus, looking toward the ancient harbor.

hosting an imperial cult temple. That honor went instead to Pergamon, one of Ephesus's chief rivals among the cities of Asia. The first imperial cult temple established in Ephesus occurred under the Emperor Domitian in 89 CE and thus becomes important for understanding the book of Revelation (see Box 11.6).

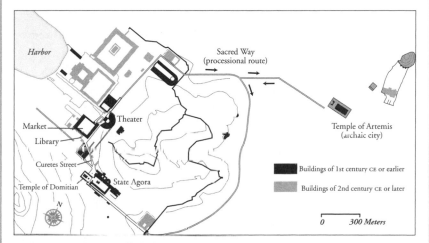

b Map of Ephesus in Roman times.

c Curetes Street, or the Processional Way, leading from the State Agora toward the Library of Celsus.

The Ephesian Imprisonment

In contrast to the story in Acts, Paul clearly states that he experienced several incarcerations during the Aegean phase: "with far greater labors, far more imprisonments, with countless floggings, and often near death" (2 Cor. 11:23). At least one of these seems to have been in Asia and just prior to the writing of his later letter to Corinth: "For we do not want you to be unaware, brothers and sisters, of the affliction we experienced in Asia; for we were so, utterly, unbearably crushed that we despaired of life itself" (2 Cor. 1:8). It is now argued by many New Testament scholars that this "deadly peril" (2 Cor. 1:10) was an imprisonment of some duration in greater Ephesus and that at least two of the so-called prison letters—Philippians and Philemon—come from this situation.

The situation of Philippians requires some special comments in this regard because two passages in the letter have traditionally been associated exclusively with Rome. One is: "I want you to know, beloved, that what has happened to me has helped to spread the gospel, so that it has become known throughout the *whole imperial guard* and to everyone else that my imprisonment is for Christ" (Phil. 1:12–13). The Greek here translated "imperial guard" is *praetorion,* which was traditionally taken to refer to the Praetorian Guard, the emperor's personal bodyguards in Rome. But the more recent translations rightly note that this phrase can also be translated "in the whole *praetorium,*" in which case it would refer to the governor's palace and administrative center for any provincial capital.[16] Ephesus certainly had such a facility.

Then at the end of the letter, Paul sends his usual greetings, but with an added note: "All the saints greet you, especially those of the *emperor's household*" (Phil. 4:21–22). A reference to "Caesar's household," as the Greek puts it, was easily assumed to mean Rome; however, this phrase is now recognized to refer instead to the imperial bureaucracy working in the *praetorium* of each provincial capital.[17] So both comments fit Ephesus, and other aspects of the situation in both letters favor proximity to Ephesus. As we shall see, Paul shows every expectation of being released from prison and visiting his churches again soon (see Phil. 2:23–24; Philem. 22). Such expectations fit neither his later situation in Rome nor his trials in Caesarea as described in Acts.[18]

The Situation of the Philippian Letter

As we saw earlier, Paul had established house churches in Philippi on his very first stop in Greece in 49–50 CE, prior to going to Thessalonica. He also mentions opposition there that forced him to move on (1 Thess. 2:2).[19] It is not until we get to this later letter that we realize that Paul had maintained a solid relationship with them ever since. It is likely that he had written earlier letters to them and visited them again, and Philippi continued to be his Macedonian hub for missionary operations in the later part of his Aegean period.[20] The letter also hints at some of these earlier dealings, first in the thanksgiving section (Phil. 1:3–11), where Paul stresses their "partnership in the gospel from the first day until now" (v. 5). The word "partnership" (Greek *koinonia*), which can also be translated "fellowship," "sharing," or "communion,"[21] sets an important theme for the letter (see Box 8.6).

The letter also refers to the Philippians' ongoing financial support of Paul's mission activity in a note near the end (4:10–20). It is noteworthy that Paul twice uses verb forms of this same word, *koinonia*, translated "share," to refer to their financial gifts to him:

> *I rejoice in the Lord greatly that now at last you have revived your concern for me. . . . In any case, it was kind of you to* **share** *my distress. You Philippians indeed know that in the early days of the gospel, when I left Macedonia, no church* **shared with me in the matter of giving and receiving,** *except you alone. For even when I was in Thessalonica, you sent me help for my needs more than once. Not that I seek the gift, but I seek the profit that accumulates to your account. I have been paid in full and have more than enough; I am fully satisfied, now that I have received from Epaphroditus the gifts you sent, a fragrant offering, a sacrifice acceptable and pleasing to God. (Phil. 4:10–18)*

As this passage shows, at least one main purpose for this letter was to say thank you for the Philippians' gift. The occasion was most likely Paul's imprisonment. Roman imprisonment was usually temporary while the accused awaited a magistrate's hearing or a formal trial and was rarely used as a long-term punishment. Those found guilty of serious crimes or unable to pay fines were sentenced to exile or death. There were no amenities for people placed in prison. If one had means or friends to supply basic necessities, including food, one fared far better. Paul had solicited aid while in prison. His situation must have caused great worry, but friction as well.

The Purpose and Occasion of the Philippian Letter

Despite the prevalent theme of fellowship that runs through the letter, there are notes of discord, especially in the polemical language of 3:2–4:3. For this reason, some scholars have proposed that the present letter is a collection of several fragmentary letters that were put together like a jigsaw puzzle in the second century (see Box 8.7).

BOX 8.6

The Letter to the Philippians

DATE: 55–56 CE

AUTHOR: Paul (with Timothy, 1:1)

LETTER CARRIER: Epaphroditus (2:25)

LOCATION: Ephesus, in prison (1:7, 13)

OTHER LETTERS: Presupposes that Paul had written at least one or two earlier letters, and some scholars have argued that the present letter is a combination of either two or three letters (see Box 8.7).

AUDIENCE: The first missionary congregations in Greece, who had supported Paul financially for several years.

OCCASION AND PURPOSE: A thank-you letter for financial aid while in
prison; a letter of recommendation for Epaphroditus's return; a letter of
exhortation and reconciliation in terms of the Greek ideal of friendship
and partnership or fellowship (*koinonia*).

OUTLINE

    I. Greeting (1:1–2)

    II. Thanksgiving (1:3–11)

    III. Body (1:12–2:30; 3:1–4:1)

    IV. Exhortation (4:2–20)

    V. Closing (4:21–23)

FURTHER READING

Bakirtzis, C., and H. Koester. *Philippi at the Time of Paul and After His Death.* Harrisburg, PA: Trinity,
1998.

Beare, F. W. *The Epistle to the Philippians.* New York: Harper & Row, 1959.

Duncan, G. S. *Paul's Ephesian Ministry: A Reconstruction with Special Reference to the Ephesian Origin
of the Imprisonment Epistles.* New York: Scribner, 1929.

Engberg-Pedersen, T. *Paul and the Stoics.* Louisville, KY: Westminster–John Knox, 2000.

Fee, G. D. *Paul's Letter to the Philippians.* Grand Rapids, MI: Eerdmans, 1995.

Fitzgerald, J. T. "Philippians, Epistle to the." *Anchor Bible Dictionary.* 5:318–26.

———, ed. *Friendship, Flattery, and Frankness of Speech: Studies on Friendship in the New Testament
World.* Leiden: Brill, 1996.

Gnilka, J. *Die Philipperbrief.* Herders Theologischer Kommentar zum Neuen Testament. Freiberg:
Herder, 1987.

Koester, H. "The Purpose of the Polemic of a Pauline Fragment (Phil iii)." *New Testament Studies* 8
(1961/62): 317–32.

Martin, R. P. *Carmen Christi: Philippians 2:5–11 in Recent Interpretation and in the Setting of Early
Christian Worship.* Cambridge: Cambridge University Press, 1967.

———. *Philippians.* Grand Rapids, MI: Eerdmans, 1980.

Sampley, J. P. *Pauline Partnership in Christ: Christian Community and Commitment in the Light of
Roman Law.* Philadelphia: Fortress, 1980.

White, L. M. "Morality Between Two Worlds: A Paradigm of Friendship in Philippians." In *Greeks,
Romans, and Christians.* Edited by D. L. Balch, E. Ferguson, and W. A. Meeks. Minneapolis:
Fortress, 1990. Pp. 201–15.

BOX 8.7

Partition Theories
Were There Multiple Letters to Philippi?

It is without doubt that Paul wrote other letters to Philippi. In the early second century CE, the Christian bishop Polycarp of Smyrna[1] wrote his own letter to the Philippian churches, in which he referred to Paul's "letters" to them. So it appears that they still knew of multiple "Philippian" letters, but only one has been preserved in the New Testament. In this light, some features of the letter have been thought to represent fragments of distinct letters that were only later put together when a collection of Paul's letters was being assembled. This idea of combining several letter fragments into one composite letter is known by scholars as "partition theory" or just "partitioning," and it has been proposed for several other letters, notably 2 Corinthians (see Box 8.10).

One of the key bits of evidence in support of this view occurs in Philippians 3:1–2: "To write the same things to you is not troublesome to me, and for you it is a safeguard. Beware of the dogs, beware of the evil workers, beware of those who mutilate the flesh!" Immediately after this Paul launches into a long tirade against those who demand circumcision for his gentile converts. The topic of this section seems to be disconnected from anything else in the letter, and his comment about writing "the same things to you" seems naturally to reflect the presence of other letters. In the case of Philippians, therefore, it has been proposed that there were two or three short or partial letters later pieced together.

An early form of the two-letter hypothesis argued that section 3:1b–4:20 was written as a letter of thanks after receiving the gift, while 1:1–3:1a + 4:21–23 constituted a later letter sent after Epaphroditus fell ill and in preparation for his return. More recently this view has been revised as follows:[2]

Letter 1 (1:1–3:1a + 4:2–7, 10–23)	The letter of thanks, sent after Epaphroditus had recovered from the illness and was preparing to return
Letter 2 (3:1b–4:1 + 4:8–9)	A later letter sent after Paul was released from prison and was preparing to visit Philippi (cf. 2:23–24)

The three-letter hypothesis, once favored by many scholars,[3] is as follows:

Letter 1 (4:10–20)	A brief but formal thank-you note sent by Paul immediately after receiving the gift brought by Epaphroditus
Letter 2 (1:1–3:1)(? + 4:4–7)	A letter regarding Epaphroditus's illness, with emphasis on encouragement and courage in the face of the trials experienced by Paul and Epaphroditus
Letter 3 (3:2–4:3)	A polemical letter preserved only as a fragment (may also include 4:8–9)

A number of other scholars have argued that there is a more consistent tone and vocabulary to the letter than such partitioning allows and have argued instead that it is a single integral work. This view has become the most popular among scholars of late.

In support of this more unified view of the letter is the fact that the theme of partnership or fellowship (Greek *koinonia*) is found throughout the letter, including the polemical section (3:2–4:1)[4] and the thank-you note (4:10–20). In the final analysis, it seems better to read the letter as a unitary whole, although the portion in 3:2–4:1 might contain a reworking of an older letter.

---

[1]Polycarp, *To the Philippians* 2.3. On Polycarp, see Chapter 13.

[2]This is the view of E. J. Goodspeed and L. E. Keck. The more recent version of the two-letter hypothesis is that of J. Gnilka, *Der Philipperbrief,* Herders Theologischer Kommentar zum Neuen Testament 10 (Freiberg: Herder, 1987), 6–18. See J. T. Fitzgerald, "Philippians, Epistle to the," *Anchor Bible Dictionary,* 5:321.

[3]This is the view espoused by H. Koester, *Introduction to the New Testament,* 2d ed., 2 vols. (Berlin: DeGruyter, 2000), 2:136–38, but also favored by Beare, Bornkamm, Fitzmyer, Barth, Lohse, and others. For references, see J. T. Fitzgerald, "Philippians, Epistle to the," *Anchor Bible Dictionary,* 5:321, and W. G. Kümmel, *Introduction to the New Testament,* rev. ed. (Nashville, TN: Abingdon, 1975), 333.

[4]In addition to the use of *koinonia* itself (3:10), the passage has several compound word forms using a preposition meaning "together" or "with" (*syn-*) that are quite common in discussions of friendship and harmony: thus, "becoming like" (3:10, 21), "join in imitating" (3:17).

More scholars would now agree, however, that the letter is an integral composition, although it might well contain allusions to earlier letters (3:1). The key to understanding the occasion and purpose of the letter is its consistent use of friendship motifs, especially in the language of "having the same mind" (1:7; 2:2, 5; 3:5, 19; 4:1, 10). Friendship and partnership language are used to reflect on Paul's long-standing relationship with the Philippian congregations (1:7); to exhort the Philippians to harmony with one another and to avoid selfish interests (2:1–4, 14–18), modeled after the selfless death of Jesus (2:5–11); to describe the sufferings of Paul and Epaphroditus on behalf of Christ and the Philippians (2:17, 25–30; 3:17–4:1); to encourage the women Euodia and Syntyche to patch up their differences (4:2–3); and to describe the kindly feelings that the Philippians expressed through their financial support of Paul in prison (4:10–20). For this reason, Philippians has been called a "friendly letter of exhortation."

Yet just below the surface of all this friendship language there lurks a problem of division and enmity. It shows up in the polemic against "the enemies of Christ" who refuse to "have the same mind" with Paul (3:15, 18), and it is clearly at issue in the relationship between Euodia and Syntyche. Does this suggest a difference of opinion between two house churches headed by women? Perhaps. In this light we should also notice that, in giving thanks for their gift, Paul adds a telling comment: "I rejoice in the Lord greatly that *now at last you have revived your concern for me;* indeed, you were *concerned* for me, but had no opportunity to show it" (4:10).[22] It seems that there has been some delay in their sending the monetary gift to Paul in prison. If these telltale signs of discord are in any way connected to one another, then it suggests that there may be some disagreement among the Philippian congregations over whether to support Paul any longer. We may suspect that the situation of Epaphroditus, who was delayed by illness in returning home to Philippi (2:25–30), was also a contributing factor. In the end, however, those people who favored Paul won out. Paul is now sending Epaphroditus home carrying the letter both to thank them and to encourage them to see his efforts in a favorable light, as their partner in the cause of spreading the gospel.

We may reconstruct the sequence of exchanges that led up to the present letter as follows:

1. After Paul is imprisoned (in Ephesus), word is sent to Philippi (probably via a letter).[23]

2. The Philippians, longtime financial supporters of Paul, respond to this news by sending a "gift" (of money) along with a letter of encouragement carried by Epaphroditus (Phil. 2:25; 4:18).

3. Epaphroditus becomes critically ill while visiting with Paul in Ephesus, so Paul sends Timothy with a note or letter informing the

Philippians. He also asks for more money, presumably to help take care of Epaphroditus.

4. A dispute arises in Philippi over Paul's request. As a result the Philippians do not immediately send more aid. The dispute must somehow revolve around whether to continue supporting Paul financially in light of his legal problems.

5. The Philippians are finally persuaded by the pro-Paul faction to send more aid/money (Phil. 4:10–20). Timothy finally returns to Ephesus, but with the bad news of the dissension caused by his plight.[24]

6. Paul now writes the Philippian letter (as we know it) as a thank-you note, to bring some reconciliation both for himself and for the conflicting parties at Philippi. Now healthy, Epaphroditus carries the letter (Phil. 2:25–30).

7. Paul himself expects to be released from prison soon (2:23) and plans to visit Philippi again (cf. Philem. 22). He will send Timothy ahead to announce his coming (Phil. 2:24).

Thus, the Philippian letter as we now have it is really the end of a longer process of communication that included two earlier letters by Paul and two earlier letters by the Philippians. It also sheds important light on the financial dealings that Paul maintained with his congregations as patrons and supporters. Indeed, Paul did get out of prison and go to Philippi. His last letter to Corinth was written from there (cf. 2 Cor. 1:8–11; 2:12–13; 8:1–4). So it would seem that his friendly letter of exhortation and reconciliation, as partners in Christ, was successful.

The Letter to Philemon

The Philemon letter was sent to a house church located most likely in Colossae, some 175 miles to the east of Ephesus. The location is not stated in the letter; this guess stems from the similar names that show up in the concluding greetings of the Colossian letter. Though not itself on the main highway, Colossae was one of a triangle of cites including Hierapolis and Laodicea that anchored the rich interior region of the province of Asia. Among the undisputed letters of Paul, Philemon is unique for the fact that it is short—only one page long, much like ordinary papyrus letters of the time—and addressed to an individual rather than to one or more congregations. It was eventually placed last in the Pauline corpus in the New Testament in part because it was traditionally thought of as dealing with practical rather than theological matters. At issue is Paul's advice to a slave owner, Philemon, regarding the treatment of his slave Onesimus, whom Paul is sending back. The traditional assumption has been that Onesimus was a runaway, and thus Paul was intervening on his behalf by writing a kind of "safe conduct" letter for his return.

In more recent New Testament scholarship the proximity of Colossae to Ephesus has been viewed as an important component for understanding the situation of the letter (see Box 8.8). Paul clearly states that he is in prison (Philem. 1), and thus it is more likely that a runaway slave would have encountered him in nearby Ephesus rather than far-off Rome. But many scholars now question whether Onesimus was a runaway after all or that he met up with Paul by accident.[25] Two other scenarios have been proposed.

The first scenario starts from the recognition that Paul already knew Philemon and had personally baptized him; Philemon was the house-church patron (v. 2). Since Paul had visited in Philemon's home and planned to do so again (v. 22), he might well have been known to the domestic slave Onesimus as someone whom his master respected. It is thus proposed that Onesimus had gotten into trouble with Philemon (v. 18) and had intentionally sought out Paul to serve as an intermediary on his behalf. At stake for Onesimus was the fact that domestic slaves might normally expect to gain their freedom in time, unless they angered the master.[26] Thus, Paul is viewed as facilitating Onesimus's return to good standing and his progress toward the legal process of manumission.

According to the second scenario, Onesimus had been sent by the house church to Paul in Ephesus to deliver some financial aid for his imprisonment. While he was there, Paul decided to keep him on for a while as a helper, and this delay was at issue in the relation with Philemon.[27] In favor of this understanding is the way that Paul refers to Onesimus's "service" for Paul on behalf of Philemon: "I wanted to keep him with me, *so that he might be of service to me in your place* [lit., on your behalf] *during my imprisonment for the gospel;* but I preferred to do nothing without your consent, in order that your good deed might be voluntary and not something forced" (Philem. 13–14). In this view, Paul was sending Onesimus back in hopes that Philemon would then free him and send him back as Paul's mission helper.

If in fact the real occasion of Onesimus's visit to Paul was as messenger for the house-church patron, Philemon, as seems most likely, then we may perhaps understand what has happened. Onesimus was performing a "service" for Paul

BOX 8.8

The Letter to Philemon

DATE: 55–56 CE

AUTHOR: Paul (with Timothy, 1)

LETTER CARRIER: Onesimus

LOCATION: Ephesus, in prison (1)

AUDIENCE: Philemon, a house-church patron in Colossae whom Paul had baptized

OCCASION AND PURPOSE: A "letter of recommendation" for the return of Onesimus, Philemon's domestic slave; appeal for Onesimus to be received as "brother." Paul expects to be released from prison and visit again; requests hospitality and a guest room (22).

OUTLINE

   I.   Greeting (1–3)
   II. Thanksgiving (4–7)
   III. Body (8–20)
   IV. Exhortation (21–22)
   V.   Closing (23–25)

FURTHER READING

Bartchy, S. S. "Philemon, Letter to." *Anchor Bible Dictionary.* 5:307–8.

Dunn, J. D. G. *The Epistles to the Colossians and Philemon.* New International Greek Testament Commentary. Grand Rapids, MI: Eerdmans, 1996.

Hock, R. F. "A Support for His Old Age: Paul's Plea on Behalf of Onesimus." In *The Social World of the First Christians.* Edited by L. M. White and O. L. Yarbrough. Minneapolis: Fortress, 1995. Pp. 67–81.

Lampe, P. "Keine 'Sklavenflucht' des Onesimus." *Zeitschrift für die neutestamentliche Wissenschaft* 76 (1985): 135–37.

O'Brien, P. T. *Colossians and Philemon.* Word Biblical Commentary 44. Waco, TX: Word, 1982.

Osiek, C., and D. L. Balch. *Families in the New Testament World: Households and House Churches.* Louisville, KY: Westminster–John Knox, 1997.

Petersen, N. R. *Rediscovering Paul: Philemon and the Sociology of Paul's Narrative World.* Philadelphia: Fortress, 1985.

White, L. M. "Paul and Pater Familias." In *Paul in the Greco-Roman World.* Edited by P. Sampley. Harrisburg, PA: Trinity, 2003. Pp. 736–89.

Winter, S. C. "Methodological Observations on a New Interpretation of Paul's Letter to Philemon." *Union Seminary Quarterly Review* 39 (1984): 203–12.

———. "Paul's Letter to Philemon." *Novum Testamentum Supplement* 33 (1987): 1–15.

very similar to that of Epaphroditus in the Philippian letter.[28] While in Ephesus, Paul had also baptized Onesimus (v. 10) and wanted to "keep him" for some sort of continued service (vv. 11–13).[29] Onesimus's tardiness in returning from his appointed task may well lie behind Paul's concern that Philemon has been "wronged" in the process (v. 18) or was angry.

In calling on Philemon to take Onesimus back with some sort of new status, Paul relies on both the social obligations of patronage and his own rhetorical skills. Even as a friend, he could hardly *command* Philemon in such a matter, much less as a client, and less so still if Philemon had somehow been "wronged" by Onesimus or Paul. Instead, Paul says, "Charge it to my account" (v. 19). Since Paul had accepted hospitality and financial support from Philemon, especially while in prison, he now says, in effect, "Just write off the Onesimus affair to what you would have given me as your client and partner." Next, by calling Philemon to account to the one who baptized him (vv. 19–20), Paul turns the tables on him. This is a rhetorical tour de force, saying, in effect, that Paul is Philemon's "spiritual patron."[30] In so doing he places Philemon and Onesimus on a more equal footing, at least in the house church, because Paul had personally baptized both of them.

Ephesus (55–57 CE): Growing Opposition (Galatians and 2 Corinthians)

Paul's time in Ephesus proved tumultuous in other ways. In particular he began to encounter other missionaries of the Jesus movement who were moving into *his* territory. This growing opposition probably led him finally to decide to leave Asia for good and prepare for a mission in another region.

The Churches of Galatia

Paul had established churches in the region of Galatia sometime earlier in his Aegean mission, but there is considerable debate over which area of Galatia is meant and, by implication, when Paul worked there. The problem is in the name Galatia. Originally it referred to the ethnic or tribal region in upper central Turkey around Ancyra. In 25 BCE this area was joined to the region of Pisidia, in south-central Turkey, and made a Roman province called Galatia. According to Acts 14, Paul worked in this "southern" area in the principal cities of Antioch, Lystra, Derbe, and Iconium prior to the Jerusalem conference; he

stopped by there again afterward (16:1–5). Acts, however, never calls this southern region "Galatia"; it says instead that Paul went through a more northerly
area, which it calls the "Phrygian and Galatian regions," soon after leaving the
southern cities on his way toward Alexandria Troas and Philippi (Acts 16:6; cf.
18:23). So the question is this: Is the letter "to the churches of Galatia" addressed
to the southern cities, described by Acts as an earlier mission of Paul, or to the
old ethnic region of Galatia in the north, described by Acts as an early part of
his trip to the Aegean? The "southern hypothesis" tends to favor an early date,
even before 1 Thessalonians, while the "northern hypothesis," a later one.

The Situation of the Galatian Letter

Scholars have long been divided over the issue of the Galatian setting.[31] At
issue, once again, is how to reconcile Paul's letters with the account in Acts. Any
conclusion is dependent on how one reads the internal evidence of the letter itself, which is highly rhetorical in nature. One fact seems clear. The followers to
whom Paul was writing were gentile converts who were now told by other missionaries of the Jesus movement that they must be circumcised (4:21; 5:2–3;
6:12–15). If anything, this feature of the situation slightly favors the northern
hypothesis, because Paul is clearly reported to have worked primarily with Jewish followers in the southern cities (Acts 14:1, 19; 16:1), and he seems not to have
had any continuing contact with them after moving to the Aegean. The fact
that the Galatian converts had only lately encountered this demand for circumcision does not fit so well with the social setting of the southern cities. For this
reason, we shall here follow the northern hypothesis.

Even so, the date of the letter is unclear. In 1 Corinthians 16:1–4 (dated
ca. 53–54; see Box 8.4), Paul mentions instructions he had already given to the
churches of Galatia concerning a collection for Jerusalem. No reference to the
collection is contained in the Galatian letter, so it must be earlier or later than
these instructions, and this probably means there is a lost Galatian letter. Hence
Galatians might have been written in 50–51 from Achaia (just after 1 Thessalonians) or in 52–53 from Ephesus (just before 1 Corinthians). Of these two dates,
the latter is the most widely accepted by scholars.[32]

Alternatively, it has been suggested that the instructions about the collection
for Jerusalem mentioned in 1 Corinthians 16 represented the earlier stage of
Paul's dealings with the Galatians. The circumcision crisis came later, at about
the same time that Paul was facing opposition in Corinth. In favor of this view
is the fact that there are numerous similarities of language, tone, and argument

between Galatians and 2 Corinthians. The Galatian letter would thus come just before or just after his imprisonment, while he was still in Ephesus.[33] The discussion that follows assumes this later date, ca. 55–57 (see Box 8.9).

Paul's Response to the Galatian Crisis

Galatians is probably Paul's harshest letter. The sharp tone starts from the opening words, when Paul emphatically stakes out the independence of his apostleship: "not *by* human commission, nor from human authorities, but *through* Jesus Christ and God the Father" (1:1). It continues in the thanksgiving section, which has been transformed into an ironic rebuke and compounded by double curse formulas:

> *I am **astonished** that you are so quickly deserting the one who called you in the grace of Christ and are turning to a different gospel **not that there is** another gospel, but there are some who are confusing you and want to pervert the gospel of Christ. But even if we or an angel from heaven should proclaim to you a gospel contrary to what we proclaimed to you, **let that one be accursed!** As we have said before, so now I repeat, if anyone proclaims to you a gospel contrary to what you received, **let that one be accursed!** (Gal. 1:6–9)*

We would do well not to underestimate the raw rhetorical force that these words must have carried, especially given the magical powers implied by curses.

The problem is this. Paul views the fact that his gentile converts are now prepared to undergo circumcision as a denial of his gospel and a betrayal of himself. He took it very personally. He was the one who brought them to God as adopted children; for them now to undertake full Torah observance would be like returning to the shackles of idolatry (Gal. 4:8–10) or throwing away the special grant of adoption that they as Gentiles had received by baptism into Christ (5:2–11). Yet this is not a denunciation of Torah observance, even for Jewish followers of Jesus. Instead, Paul seems to view baptism and adoption as a special dispensation for Gentiles in view of the impending eschaton (see the discussion of Romans below).

For the other missionaries who have "unsettled" the Galatians, Paul has nothing but opprobrium: *"I wish they would castrate themselves!"* (Gal. 5:12). They are sometimes called the "Judaizing teachers," but in all probability they are gentile converts to the Jesus movement who had been circumcised, following Paul's opponents in the blowup at Antioch. For this reason, there is another line of Paul's argument that runs throughout the letter, namely, his defense of

BOX 8.9
The Letter to the Galatians

DATE: 55 or 57 CE

AUTHOR: Paul

LETTER CARRIER: Not given

LOCATION: Ephesus

RELATED LETTERS: A letter advising the Galatians about the Jerusalem collection, ca. 52–53 (cf. 1 Cor. 16:1–4), now lost.

AUDIENCE: Gentile converts in the region of the upper areas of the province of Galatia

OCCASION AND PURPOSE: Gentile converts are being convinced to undergo circumcision by other missionaries of the Jesus movement; a harsh letter of rebuke for hypocrisy and enmity by accepting circumcision and thus abandoning Paul; extended autobiographical defense of Paul's apostolic calling and gospel.

OUTLINE

   I. Greeting (1:1–5)

   II. Thanksgiving (1:6–9)

   III. Body (1:10–5:12)

      A. Defense of his apostleship (1:10–2:21)

      B. Defense of his gospel (3:1–5:12)

   IV. Exhortation (5:13–6:10)

   V. Closing (6:11–18)

FURTHER READING

Betz, H. D. "Galatians, Epistle to the." *Anchor Bible Dictionary.* 5:872–75.

———. *Galatians: A Commentary.* Hermeneia. Philadelphia: Fortress, 1979.

Dunn, J. D. G. *The Epistle to the Galatians.* Black's New Testament Commentary. Peabody, MA: Hendriksen, 1995.

Esler, P. F. *Galatians.* London: Routledge, 1998.

Koester, H. *Introduction to the New Testament.* 2d ed. 2 vols. Berlin: DeGruyter, 2000. 2:123–26.

Kümmel, W. G. *Introduction to the New Testament.* Rev. ed. Nashville, TN: Abingdon, 1975.

Martyn, J. L. *Galatians.* Anchor Bible 33A. New York: Anchor/Doubleday, 1997.

Perrin, N., and D. Duling. *The New Testament: An Introduction.* 2d ed. New York: Harcourt Brace, 1982.

Sampley, J. P. "Paul's Frank Speech in Galatians and Corinthians." In *Philodemus and the New Testament.* Edited by J. T. Fitzgerald, G. Holland, and D. Obbink. Leiden: Brill, 2004. Pp. 295–321.

White, L. M. "Rhetoric and Reality in Galatians: Framing the Social Demands of Friendship." In *Early Christianity and Classical Culture: Comparative Studies.* Edited by J. T. Fitzgerald, T. H. Olbricht, and L. M. White. Leiden: Brill, 2003. Pp. 307–49.

his apostleship. We see it in the greeting, in his autobiographical comments on his apocalyptic calling (1:15–16), in his emphatic assertion that he got nothing from Jerusalem (1:17), and in his replay of the Jerusalem conference when Peter, James, and John accepted his views (2:1–10). But more than anywhere else he stresses his clear and resolute sense of divine calling in his confrontation with Peter (2:11–14). Having shown Peter, of all people, to be a hypocrite, he soundly rebukes the Galatians for teetering on the same precipice. In the final analysis, however, it is not clear that Paul convinced them, and the harshness of his rhetoric may signal growing desperation.

The Later Letters to Corinth

By about 57 or 58, after having gotten out of prison, Paul decided to leave Ephesus for good. Apparently his legal problems combined with growing opposition from other missionaries made him feel there was little promise for him there. This is the situation reflected at the beginning of 2 Corinthians, when he refers to the "affliction we experienced in Asia" (1:8–9). From Ephesus he moved to Troas, where he had hoped to meet up with Titus, who had been off on an errand to one of the other churches (2:12). When Paul did not find him, he moved on to Macedonia, probably back to Philippi (2:13). Still there was no news of Titus, and Paul waited anxiously (7:5). Finally, Titus arrived (7:6). It turns out he had been to Corinth and had returned with some good news for Paul:

> He told us of your longing, your mourning, your zeal for me, so that I rejoiced still more. For even if I made you sorry with my letter, I do not regret it (though I did regret it, for I see that I grieved you with that letter, though only briefly). Now I rejoice, not because you were grieved, but because your grief led to repentance. (2 Cor. 7:7–9)

This sequence of events gives several pieces of information regarding the later stages of Paul's Aegean mission. Earlier, there had been a breakdown of some sort in Paul's relation with the Corinthians. If it had been brewing for very long, it would have been on Paul's mind when he faced his other setbacks in Ephesus—first imprisonment and then the Galatian crisis. Paul had sent the Corinthians a reprimanding letter that caused them grief and mourning, but Titus reported that they were sorry and wanted to see Paul again. Paul was relieved, and he now wrote the letter we call 2 Corinthians to patch things up with them.

But what about this other letter, the one that made them sorry and penitent? What happened to it? Although 1 Corinthians is strong at times, it is not that kind of reprimand. No, it appears that between 1 Corinthians (Letter B; see Box 8.4) and 2 Corinthians, Paul had written another letter. For clarity, we may designate these later letters C (the reprimanding letter) and D (the letter of reconciliation reflected in 2 Cor. 1–7). Paul gives additional clues about the problem and this earlier letter:

> *I wanted to come to you first, so that you might have a double favor; I wanted to visit you on my way to Macedonia, and to come back to you from Macedonia and have you send me on to Judea. Was I vacillating when I wanted to do this? . . . But I call on God as witness against me: it was to spare you that I did not come again to Corinth. I do not mean to imply that we lord it over your faith; rather, we are workers with you for your joy, because you stand firm in the faith. So I made up my mind not to make you another painful visit. For if I cause you pain, who is there to make me glad but the one whom I have pained? And I wrote as I did, so that when I came, I might not suffer pain from those who should have made me rejoice. (2 Cor. 1:15–17; 1:23–2:3)*

Now we can see what happened. Sometime after moving to Ephesus in 52, Paul visited Corinth. He calls it a "painful visit" (2 Cor. 2:1); afterward he wrote the Corinthians a letter that caused them pain (2:2). This is the same as the letter of reprimand (Letter C) mentioned in 2 Corinthians 7:8–9. Paul had planned to make another visit to Corinth and had even mentioned it in Letter C as a kind of warning. But then he backed out; he says it was because he did not want to have another painful experience with them. This aborted visit must have come sometime after Paul's release from prison in Ephesus, since he mentions that he had intended to go to Corinth and then to Macedonia and then back to Corinth on his way to Jerusalem (2 Cor. 1:16; cf. 2 Cor. 8:1–4). Since he had also planned to visit Philippi after his release (Phil. 2:23–24), it may well be that Letter C to Corinth was written just prior to his imprisonment. Now he has begun this final circuit of his churches in Greece, but, because of his uncertainty about the situation in Corinth, he has gone the other way, to Macedonia, first. The full sequence goes like this:

1. Paul first visits Corinth (50–52 CE).

2. Paul travels to Ephesus and writes Letter A to Corinth (52–53).

3. He gets news and a letter from Corinth and writes Letter B (1 Corinthians; 53–54).

4. He makes a second visit to Corinth that turns out to be "painful" (55).

5. After returning to Ephesus, Paul writes the painful letter of reprimand to the Corinthians (Letter C) and warns them that he will deal with them when he visits again; about the same time he is imprisoned in Ephesus (55–56).

6. Paul gets out of prison, hears of the Galatian crisis, and decides to leave Ephesus after writing the harsh letter of rebuke to the Galatians (57); he dispatches Timothy and Titus to prepare for his visits with other churches.

7. He goes to Troas, meets up with Timothy, and then goes to Philippi, where he finally finds Titus; there he writes the letter of reconciliation to the Corinthians (Letter D) in anticipation of going on to Corinth (late 57 or early 58).

8. From there he plans to go to Jerusalem with a relief fund he has been collecting, and from Corinth he writes the letter to the Romans in preparation for a visit after he finishes in Jerusalem (58).

Compositional Issues in 2 Corinthians

This complex set of movements and letters is crucial for understanding the last stages of Paul's Aegean mission as well as 2 Corinthians itself. Most scholars now agree that what we call 2 Corinthians is a actually a combination of several letters, or a "partitioned" letter (see Box 8.7). Central to these discussions is the fact that 2 Corinthians 10–13 have a markedly different and much more hostile tone than do chapters 1–7, where the emphasis is on comfort and reconciliation. In tone, chapters 10–13 fit better as the painful letter of reprimand (Letter C), in which he threatens the Corinthians with punitive action on his upcoming, third visit if they do not mend their ways (2 Cor. 13:1–2, 11). The situation is rather more complicated, however, since some scholars see six (or more) different fragments, which might go back as far as Letter A to Corinth. The different positions regarding the number and order of the fragments are summarized in Box 8.10.

BOX 8.10

The Second Letter to the Corinthians

DATE: 55–57/58 CE

AUTHOR: Paul (with Timothy, 1:1)

LETTER CARRIER: Titus (and possibly Timothy)

LOCATION: Ephesus and Philippi

OUTLINE AND THEMATIC ISSUES: Since 2 Corinthians 2:1–2, 7–9 clearly presuppose an earlier "painful letter" that cannot be 1 Corinthians, there must have been another letter between these two. As early as the second century, there was an effort to supply one in the apocryphal *Acts of Paul.* As early as 1776, J. S. Semmler first argued that small portions of 2 Corinthians seem to be extraneous; since then all modern scholars have had to deal with the marked differences in tone, theme, and subject between the three main sections of the letter as we now have it:

1–7	A letter of reconciliation after a painful visit and a reprimand
8–9	Encouragement regarding the collection for Jerusalem
10–13	The polemic against the "super-apostles" and a self-defense in terms of "weakness"

But the question remains how these sections fit together and how they are to be understood in relation to both 1 Corinthians and the so-called painful letter.

In addition, the section 6:14–7:1 has often been thought to be an interpolation and not even by Paul, since it is so different in tone and language from the surrounding material and more similar to things found at Qumran or in early apocalyptic literature. Others have argued that it is out of place in 2 Corinthians, but may be a fragment of the lost Letter A to Corinth. Consequently, there have been a number of partition theories to explain the relationship of the three main parts. A few commentators have argued for the total integrity of the letter in its present form, while an extreme theory of W. Schmithals partitioned 1 and 2 Corinthians into a total of nine letters. In the main, however, the partition theories regarding 2 Corinthians have proposed one, two, or three main letters with some smaller letters and fragments, but ordered in various ways.

The Principal Partition Theories

1. One main letter (1–13), but with inserted fragments: Espoused by Kümmel and Munck.

In this view, 2 Corinthians was written in 55–56, after Paul got word from Titus that the Corinthians had repented.

Sequence

Letter C: the painful letter (lost)

Letter D: 2 Cor. 1–13, the letter of reconciliation

2 Cor. 6:14–7:1 is likely an insertion, and may not be by Paul (so Kümmel).

Chapters 8–9 seem to have a tone of their own and may reflect an interruption.

II. Two main letters in proper order, but with an inserted fragment:

First proposed in 1776 (Semmler); espoused by Bruce, Barrett, Furnish, Martin.

The order is correct: chapters 1–9 are the earlier letter, and chapters 10–13 later.

Sequence

Letter C: the painful letter (lost)

Letter D: 2 Cor. 1–9, the letter of reconciliation, written after Paul got word from Titus that the Corinthians had repented

Letter E: 2 Cor. 10–13, a polemic, written after the situation had worsened again; therefore, it may recapitulate some of the polemic in the earlier Letter C (so Martin).

Not all agree about 2 Cor. 6:14–7:1, but tend to argue that Paul intentionally inserted it in its present position (so Furnish), even though it may be an older unit of material (so Martin), like that of the lost Letter A.

III. Two main letters not in order, with extraneous fragment(s):

Proposed in 1870 (Hausrath); espoused by Lake, Strachan, Enslin, Filson, Vielhauer.

Sequence

Letter C: 10–13, the painful letter, written after Paul's second visit to Corinth

Letter D: 1–7, the letter of reconciliation, written after Titus reported that the Corinthians had repented

Frag. E/F: 8–9, one or two fragmentary letters concerning the collection

Not all agree about 6:14–7:1; still thought by some to be a non-Pauline interpolation or a fragment of the lost Letter A. Others argue that it is integral to Letter D.

IV. Three main letters not in order, with extraneous fragments:
Proposed in 1904 (Halmel); espoused by Bornkamm, Georgi, Perrin, Koester, Betz.

Sequence

Letter C[1]: 2:14–6:13 + 7:2–4, a letter of defense written shortly after 1 Corinthians, upon hearing that there were other missionaries, after which Paul made his second visit to Corinth to deal with the matter

Letter C[2]: 10–13, the painful letter, written after he was rebuffed in Corinth

Letter D: 1:1–2:13 + 7:5–16 (and perhaps 13:11–13), the letter of reconciliation, after Paul got out of prison

Frag. E: 8, a final note sent with Titus for the completion of the collection

Frag. F: 9, another (earlier) note regarding the collection but sent to other churches of Achaia

Frag. G: 6:14–7:1, a non-Pauline fragment added later by the editor who compiled the rest; Letter D, which is virtually complete, serves as the frame into which the editor inserted the other parts.

FURTHER READING

(The most complete bibliographies are found in the works by Betz and Furnish below.)

Barrett, C. K. *Essays on Paul.* Philadelphia: Fortress, 1982.

———. *A Commentary on the Second Epistle to the Corinthians.* New York: Harper & Row, 1973.

Betz, H. D. "Corinthians, Second Epistle to the." *Anchor Bible Dictionary.* 1:1148–54.

———. *2 Corinthians 8 and 9.* Hermeneia. Philadelphia: Fortress, 1985.

Bornkamm, G. "Die Vorgeschichte des sogenannten zweiten Korintherbriefs." In *Geschichte und Glaube.* 4 vols. Munich: Evangelischer Verlag, 1971. 4:162–94.

Bruce, F. F. *1 and 2 Corinthians.* New Century Bible. Grand Rapids, MI: Eerdmans, 1971.

Enslin, M. S. *Christian Beginnings.* 2 vols. New York: Harper & Row, 1938. 2:254–61.

Filson, F. V. "2 Corinthians." *The Interpreters Bible* (1953). 10:264–425.

Furnish, V. P. *II Corinthians.* Anchor Bible. Garden City, NY: Doubleday, 1984.

Georgi, E. *The Opponents of Paul in Second Corinthians.* Philadelphia: Fortress, 1986.

Koester, H. *Introduction to the New Testament.* 2d ed. 2 vols. Berlin: DeGruyter, 2000. 2:140–42.

Kümmel, W. G. *Introduction to the New Testament.* Rev. ed. Nashville, TN: Abingdon, 1975. Pp. 280–93.

Lake, K. *The Earlier Epistles of Paul.* London: Rivington, 1927.

Martin, R. P. *2 Corinthians.* Word Biblical Commentary. Waco, TX: Word, 1986.

Munck, J. *Paul and the Salvation of Mankind.* Richmond, VA: John Knox, 1959. Pp. 168–71.

Perrin, N., and D. Duling. *The New Testament: An Introduction.* New York: Harcourt Brace, 1982. Pp. 181–82.

Schmithals, W. *Gnosticism at Corinth.* Nashville, TN: Abingdon, 1971.

Strachan, R. H. *The Second Epistle of Paul to the Corinthians.* Moffatt New Testament Commentary. New York: Harper, 1935.

Vielhauer, P. *Geschichte der urchristlichen Literatur.* Berlin: DeGruyter, 1975.

The view taken here (closest to item III in Box 8.10) is as follows:

Letter C	2 Corinthians 10–13: The letter of reprimand to the Corinthians after Paul's "painful" visit; caused by a confrontation with other missionaries, whom Paul disdainfully calls "super-apostles." Written from Ephesus (55–56 CE); letter carrier, unknown.
Letter D	2 Corinthians 1–7: The letter of reconciliation as Paul prepares for his final visit to Corinth, at which time he will complete the collection for Jerusalem.[34] Written from Philippi (57–58 CE); letter carrier, Titus (or possibly Timothy).
Letter E	2 Corinthians 8: An "administrative letter" regarding the collection for Jerusalem. It is possible that a version of this letter was carried by Titus when he was dispatched to check on the Corinthians while Paul prepared to go to Philippi. But it is most likely that Paul attached this copy of the letter to Letter D (assuming that Titus carried both).[35] Written from Philippi (57–58 CE); letter carrier, Titus.
Letter F	2 Corinthians 9: A separate "administrative letter" regarding the collection sent to the churches of Achaia. It is possible that this is the earlier version of the letter carried by Titus, and hence written from Ephesus (57 CE), or it may be a separate letter altogether from an earlier date. Written from Ephesus (57 CE, or earlier); letter carrier, Titus (probable).

The Super-apostles and Paul's Response
(2 Corinthians 10–13)

We do not know exactly what went wrong on Paul's second visit to the Corinthians, but from his perspective it was a disaster. He left hurt, angry, and frustrated, and he wrote a blistering letter back to them. It is only from the clues that we catch in Paul's following letters (C and D) that we are able to discern what might have happened and how Paul responded. What seems clear now is that the problems encountered by Paul on his second visit have little to do with the issues dividing the community in 1 Corinthians. Paul was facing a new problem created by the arrival of some other missionaries of the Jesus movement, to whom he only refers indirectly and rather disdainfully. Once he calls them "false apostles" (11:13); twice he calls them "super-apostles" (11:5; 12:11). The last term seems to be mocking them in particular for their claims to possess special miraculous powers, and Paul is forced to defend himself not so much on theological grounds (as in the slightly later Galatian letter), but rather on the basis of his own charismatic powers (12:12). Apparently, these new missionaries had denigrated Paul's powers and even his personal appearance and speaking ability (10:10–11; cf. 11:12–15). Paul castigates them for unwarranted boasting but then proceeds to do a little boasting of his own (10:12–18; 11:16–21) in order to make his main point: "I think that I am not in the least inferior to these super-apostles" (11:5).

These new missionaries sound very much like the charismatic prophets and miracle workers from the earliest days of the Jesus movement in Judea. If so, they might indeed be able to claim to be closer to Jesus or the first Jewish disciples.[36] In response, Paul boasts of his own Jewish heritage (11:22) and his sufferings in the service of Christ (11:23–33). Finally, he boasts on behalf of "another man" who ascended into heaven and saw an apocalyptic vision of things unutterable (12:1–4). In reality this too is autobiographical, but told in such a way as to turn it into a kind of boasting in weakness, which he likens to the suffering of Jesus (12:5–10). He concludes with a telling statement of the problem:

> *I have been a fool! You forced me to it. Indeed you should have been the ones commending me, for I am not at all inferior to these super-apostles, even though I am nothing. The signs of a true apostle were performed among you with utmost patience, signs and wonders and mighty works. How have you been worse off than the other churches, except that I myself did not burden you? Forgive me this wrong! (2 Cor. 12:11–13)*

The problem, then, is that these charismatic missionaries have snubbed Paul, and at least some of the Corinthian house churches have accepted them and shown them hospitality. The "painful visit" must refer to the fact that Paul came at about the same time and was rebuffed by one or more of the house-church patrons whom he had expected to visit. Paul views this as a betrayal of his friendship, since he is the one who betrothed them to Christ (11:1). He also seems to be on the defensive regarding his financial relationship with the Corinthian house churches. He has to apologize for *not* accepting their money at times in the past. At issue is whether they will continue to support him in other ways if their allegiance and patronage have shifted to the "super-apostles." In Roman society, the giving and receiving of money or hospitality was an important symbol of loyalty and friendship. It was not to be treated lightly.[37]

A Crisis Averted: The Letter of Reconciliation
(2 Corinthians 1–8)

As we have already seen, the comments in 2 Corinthians 1:15–2:3 and 7:5–9 show that Paul's letter of reprimand had done the job, as had Titus in personally mediating the situation. It was probably never the case that all the Corinthian house churches had turned on him, but at least one had—and an important one at that, from Paul's tone (2 Cor. 2:5–7; 7:12). Most likely this means that the *one* who "wronged" Paul was the house-church patron who had welcomed the "super-apostles" and rejected Paul. It might even have been Gaius, who was one of Paul's early converts (1 Cor. 1:14) and who was his host on the last visit to Corinth (Rom. 16:23). Alas, we shall never know for sure. Part of Paul's (or Titus's) strategy, however, seems to have been to galvanize support from other house church patrons to pressure or even ostracize the one who had offended Paul (2 Cor. 2:6–7). Now that he has come around, it is time to mend the fences and rebuild the cohesion of the various congregations. Thus, Paul calls on them "to reaffirm your love for him. . . . Anyone whom you forgive, I also forgive" (2:8, 10). The bulk of Letter D, then, is devoted to appeals for harmony and reconciliation (2 Cor. 5:17–20).

Now too it is time to prepare for Paul's final visit, and the theme of harmony will be important for the next phase of his mission. Paul wants the Corinthians now to serve as his point of departure for his trip to Jerusalem (2 Cor. 8), after which he will go to Rome. He must rely not only on their hospitality and financial support, but also on their influence upon house churches in Rome in order to make it work.

The Collection for Jerusalem and the
Letter to Rome (58–59 CE)

One of the most overlooked aspects of Paul's Aegean mission is the collection for Jerusalem. It is mentioned in 1 Corinthians 16:1–3, Galatians 2:10, 2 Corinthians 8–9, and Romans 15. Apparently, it was a project that Paul had launched from the beginning of his Aegean mission, since it was part of his agreement with Peter and James at the Jerusalem conference (Gal. 2:10). Early on it seems he had expectations that the Galatian churches, and perhaps others in Asia, would participate (1 Cor. 16:1). By the time we get to the reconciliation with Corinth (Letter D), however, it seems that only the churches of Macedonia and Achaia are involved (2 Cor. 8:1; cf. Rom. 15:26). One must guess that his decision to leave Ephesus was precipitated, at least in part, by his frustration over the collection.

Corinth was to be his staging ground for assembling the final collection as well as for his trip to Rome and to Spain. Writing from Corinth in about the year 58, he detailed his plans in his last letter, Romans:

> But now, with no further place for me in these regions, I desire, as I have for many years, to come to you when I go to Spain. For I do hope to see you on my journey and to be sent on by you, once I have enjoyed your company for a little while. At present, however, I am going to Jerusalem in a ministry to the saints; for Macedonia and Achaia have been pleased to share their resources with the poor among the saints at Jerusalem. They were pleased to do this, and indeed they owe it to them; for if the Gentiles have come to share in their spiritual blessings, they ought also to be of service to them in material things. So, when I have completed this, and have delivered to them what has been collected, I will set out by way of you to Spain; and I know that when I come to you, I will come in the fullness of the blessing of Christ. (Rom. 15:23–29)

Paul intended to have representatives from the various cities gather in Corinth, and each one would carry that church's gift to the leaders of the Jesus movement in Jerusalem. Paul must have longed to see the look on James's face when all these gentile congregations presented the money they had collected. Given the symbolic role of money and patronage, as seen elsewhere in Paul's missionary activity, for James to accept the collection constituted a tacit acceptance of Paul's mission and his gentile churches.

The Purpose of Romans

Paul's immediate concern was getting the collection to Jerusalem, but the letter to Rome had another purpose: to prepare for a new mission to Spain, where, once again, he expected to be able to work directly with Gentiles. Since Paul had never been to Rome and had not founded any of the house churches there, the letter was intended to serve as an introduction. In saying he wants "to be sent on" to Spain by the house churches of Rome after "enjoying your company" (15:24), Paul was using the formal language of letters of recommendation. In other words, Paul was saying, "I want you to show me hospitality and to pay for the next leg of my trip to Spain." Undoubtedly some in Rome had heard of his troubles or considered him risky. Hence, by explaining his mission theology, the Roman letter was meant to lay the groundwork for them to be his new missionary patrons, just as the churches at Philippi had been in the Aegean.

Another component to Paul's strategy involved friends in Rome. Notably, Prisca and Aquila had now moved back to Rome, where they hosted another house church (Rom. 16:3–5).[38] Given the number of other people in Rome he calls by name (Rom. 16:6–15), Paul must have had numerous contacts from Antioch or the Aegean now living there; that is, assuming that chapter 16 belongs with the Roman letter.[39] Moreover, the grouping of the names suggests that there were some five to eight house churches about which Paul already knew. Paul thus needed someone to carry the letter around to the different house churches, perhaps accompanied by individuals known among the congregations at Rome, in order to make the introductions. Prisca and Aquila or the "famous" apostolic couple Andronicus and Junia (Rom. 16:7) might have helped in this way.

The emissary delegated to carry the letter, however, and to present it in each church was one of Paul's most trusted co-workers from the Aegean mission. Her name was Phoebe, the house-church patron from Cenchreae, the eastern harbor of Corinth. Romans 16:1–2 is Paul's letter of recommendation for her as the bearer of the letter. Paul calls her a "minister" (Greek *diakonos,* or "deacon") and his patroness: "benefactor of many and of myself as well" (Rom. 16:2). He asks for her to receive hospitality, just as she had given it. Coming from Corinth, she might well have known Prisca and Aquila personally, and so she was likely supposed to stay with them in Rome.

The Argument of Romans: A Place for Gentiles in a Jewish Theology

Because of its length and theological complexity, Romans has often been treated as more of a theological treatise than a letter. The occasion outlined above shows that it was, like all the others, a real letter; however, its purpose included introducing Paul's missionary theology in order to garner support. So the body of the letter (1:16–11:36) was given over to this theological explication, while the exhortation section of the letter (12:1–15:33) was intended to show how this theology helped reinforce basic values and social ethics within the house churches (see Box 8.11).

BOX 8.11
The Letter to the Romans

DATE: 58 CE

AUTHOR: Paul

LETTER CARRIER: Phoebe

LOCATION: Corinth

OTHER LETTERS: Some scholars have argued that chapter 16 does not belong to the original form of the letter as it was sent to Rome, but this now seems unlikely.

AUDIENCE: Several mixed Jewish and gentile house churches in Rome (Rom. 16:3–15)

OCCASION AND PURPOSE: A letter of introduction for Paul and his missionary theology sent to prepare for Paul's visit to Rome and to secure financial support for an intended new mission to Spain. In the meantime, Paul is on his way to Jerusalem with a relief fund collected among his gentile congregations of Macedonia and Achaia. After delivering the collection he plans to travel to Rome.

OUTLINE

    I. Greeting (1:1–7)

    II. Thanksgiving (1:8–17)

    III. Body (1:8–11:36)

    IV. Exhortation (12:1–15:33)

    V. Closing (16:1–27)

FURTHER READING

Bassler, J. M. *Divine Impartiality: Paul and a Theological Axiom*. Chico, CA: Scholars Press, 1982.

Bornkamm, G. *Early Christian Experience*. New York: Harper & Row, 1969.

Dahl, N. A. *Studies in Paul*. Minneapolis: Augsburg, 1977.

Donfried, K. P. *The Romans Debate*. Minneapolis: Augsburg, 1977.

Gager, J. *The Origins of Anti-Semitism: Attitudes Toward Judaism in Pagan and Christian Antiquity*. New York: Oxford University Press, 1993.

Gamble, H. Y. *The Textual History of the Letter to the Romans*. Grand Rapids, MI: Eerdmans, 1977.

Jewett, R. "Paul, Phoebe, and the Spanish Mission." In *The Social World of Formative Christianity and Judaism*. Edited by J. Neusner et al. Philadelphia: Fortress, 1988. Pp. 162–77.

Räisänen, H. "Paul, God, and Israel: Romans 9–11 in Recent Research." In *The Social World of Formative Christianity and Judaism*. Edited by J. Neusner et al. Philadelphia: Fortress, 1988. Pp. 178–206.

Sanders, E. P. *Paul and Palestinian Judaism*. Philadelphia: Fortress, 1977.

———. *Paul, the Law, and the Jewish People*. Philadelphia: Fortress, 1983.

Stendahl, K. *Paul Among Jews and Christians and Other Essays*. Philadelphia: Fortress, 1976.

Stowers, S. K. *The Diatribe and Paul's Letter to the Romans*. Chico, CA: Scholars Press, 1981.

———. *A Rereading of Romans: Justice, Jews, and Gentiles*. New Haven, CT: Yale University Press, 1994.

Tomson, P. J. *Paul and the Jewish Law: Halakha in the Letters of the Apostles to the Gentiles*. Assen: Van Gorcum, 1990.

Watson, F. *Paul, Judaism and the Gentiles: A Sociological Approach*. Cambridge: Cambridge University Press, 1986.

A number of theories have been proposed trying to relate the argument of the letter to a particular situation or problem in the churches at Rome. A major component of the argument is carried in the thematic hinge that opens the body of the letter:

> *For I am not ashamed of the gospel; it is the power of God for salvation to everyone who has faith, to the Jew first and also to the Greek. For in it the righteousness of God is revealed through faith for faith; as it is written, "The one who is righteous will live by faith." (Rom. 1:16–17)*

Throughout, Paul asserts the place of both Jews and Gentiles in the scheme of salvation. Some have seen reverberations of conflict between Jewish and gentile followers of the Jesus movement in Rome, exacerbated perhaps by the fact that the emperor Claudius had expelled most of the Jews in 49 CE. On the other hand, there are no real polemics against opponents as such. So Paul's strenuous efforts to address each side may reflect a simple awareness that he is entering a community where there are both Jews and Gentiles and that questions have arisen over his sometimes strident preaching. Is Paul now calling for the Jesus movement to abandon its Jewish roots altogether? Does he see the movement as somehow different, set apart from Judaism by virtue of its affirmation that Jesus was the messiah? Or is biblical Israel as such no longer God's chosen people? To each question his answer is an emphatic no.

To understand Paul's argument in Romans as a theological reflection, one must see it as taking the basic premise of his gentile mission—"to the Jew first and also to the Greek"—and refining it through a series of rhetorical questions and counterstatements. The argument may be outlined as follows:[40]

I. God's Righteousness for Gentiles Too (1:16–3:31)
   A. "To the Jew first, and also to the Greek": God shows no partiality (1:16–3:20)
      1. God's wrath revealed to Gentiles because of idolatry (1:16–2:16)
      2. Jews who sin are also punished (2:17–29)
      3. Jews have the advantage of Torah, but equal opportunity for sin (3:1–20)
   B. God's righteousness revealed for all through the death of Jesus (3:21–26)
   C. Questions and potential objections (3:27–31)
      1. Has God rejected his people, the Jews? (see chaps. 9–11)
      2. If salvation is a gift, is morality undermined? (see 6:1–7:6)

3. Is the Torah evil, or has it been overthrown? (see 7:7–25)
4. What about the promise to Abraham? (see chap. 4)

II. Abraham's Righteousness as Paradigm (4:1–25)

III. How Righteousness Comes About (5:1–8:39)
    A. The results of being made righteous ("justification"; 5:1–11)
    B. The new Adam (5:12–21)
    C. Answers to objections from chapter 3 (6:1–7:25)
    D. Life in the Spirit and the eschaton (8:1–39)

IV. Has God Thus Rejected Israel? (9:1–11:36)
    A. Opening oath: Paul's concern for Jews (9:1–5)
    B. God's freedom demonstrated in Israel's past (9:6–29)
    C. Israel's errors in the past (9:30–10:21)
    D. But God has not rejected Israel! (11:1–32)
    E. Concluding doxology: the awesome mystery of God (11:33–36)

The gospel to which Paul refers is the death of Jesus as the crucified messiah. He views this death as an expiation that fulfills the promise to Abraham for being willing to sacrifice his son Isaac (Rom. 8:32).[41] For Paul, the *fact* that the Jewish messiah has come means also that Israel's eschatological age has been inaugurated. But in his understanding, the verging of the eschatological age is that time when some Gentiles will finally turn to God. As the "light to the Gentiles," Paul sees his mission as one of announcing this limited opportunity. These underlying assumptions of his theology, hammered out through preaching to Gentiles during his Aegean mission, now summon a more systematic essay regarding the general condition of Gentiles in Jewish thought and how they might now—after centuries of denying the one true God of Israel—be allowed back into the status of righteousness that is required for being part of the congregation of God's elect. Paul's answer: "through faith"—meaning the faithfulness of Jesus in dying on the cross. By this one mechanism, he argues, both the promise for Israel's salvation is fulfilled and the opening to Gentiles to join in that salvation is revealed.[42] Even though his formulation would later prove monumental in the development of a distinctively Christian theology set adrift from Judaism, for Paul there is no such dichotomy because the eschatological time frame is short (cf. Rom. 13:11–14 and Chapter 9).[43]

PART THREE

The Second Generation

Birth Pangs and
New Horizons

CHAPTER NINE

The First Jewish Revolt and Its Aftermath

About the year 59 CE Paul returned to Jerusalem for the first time in more than a decade. His expectations were high. He was bringing a sizable collection of money donated by his gentile congregations of Greece as a gift for the churches of Judea. He planned to lay it at the feet of James. Traveling with him were representatives of the various congregations who had contributed; most, if not all, of them were Gentiles. In Paul's view, he was fulfilling eschatological prophecies by escorting these "gentile brethren" bearing gifts for Zion:

> I am coming [says the Lord] to assemble all nations and tongues; and they shall come and shall see my glory. I will bequeath to them a sign: I will send out from them those **who have been saved** unto the Gentiles—unto Tarshish, Put, Lud, Mosoch, and Iubal, **and to the Greeks, and to far-off islands,** to those who have not heard my name or beheld my glory—and they shall declare my glory among the Gentiles. They shall lead **your brothers** from all the Gentiles as an offering to the Lord with horses and chariots, in mule-drawn covered wagons, to the holy city Jerusalem, says the Lord, **as though the children of Israel were bearing their sacrifices to me with psalms to the house of the Lord.** (Isa. 66:18–20, LXX)[1]

This passage calls those Gentiles who turn to God "your brothers," a phrase that resonates with Paul's usage, and it likens their coming to Jerusalem to an Israelite sacrificial procession. In other words, by bringing their gifts they were becoming part of righteous Israel in the verging eschaton. A few verses earlier, the Isaiah text describes Jerusalem awaiting its day of vindication before the

Lord as an expectant mother about to give birth (Isa. 66:7–11). This highly charged metaphor filled with eschatological implications will ring throughout the period of the first Jewish revolt against Rome.

Jerusalem Expectant

What happened when Paul arrived in Jerusalem is less clear. Acts makes no mention of the collection but reports a meeting with James (21:18–22). According to Acts, Paul went to the Temple and was accused of bringing uncircumcised Gentiles into the area restricted to Jews, thus inciting a riot (21:23–30). Paul was arrested, and the Roman centurion reportedly thought that he was "the Egyptian," an infamous rebel and self-proclaimed prophet-messiah who only a few years before had threatened to storm the Temple.[2] From there Acts follows the story of Paul's trials under Felix and Festus and his journey to Rome, but the ensuing events in Jerusalem are not narrated. We know from other sources, however, that these were tumultuous years in Jerusalem as apocalyptic expectations and revolutionary sentiments mounted, finally catapulting Judea into open rebellion against Rome.

FIGURE 9.1

The Jewish historian Flavius Josephus.
(*HarperCollins Concise Atlas of the Bible*)

The Jewish historian Josephus gives a clearer picture of the conditions and events that led up to the first revolt (see Fig. 9.1). He blames the increasing tensions on two factors: first, increasingly inept and oppressive Roman procurators,[3] and, second, a rising tide of fanatical Jewish revolutionaries: "Deceivers and impostors, under the pretense of divine inspiration, fostering revolutionary changes, they persuaded the masses to act like madmen and led them out into the desert in the belief that God would give them signs of deliverance."[4] (See Chapter 2.)

The period 62–66 CE only saw matters go from bad to worse as increasing mob violence disrupted the city. Josephus reports a band of assassins, the *sicarii,* who murdered people, even a high priest, in broad daylight and kidnapped Jewish officials.[5] Roaming brigands also burned and looted villages.[6] Josephus ultimately blames the rise of the Zealot movement, which he calls the "fourth philosophy," for having sown the political seeds—deeply tinged with apocalyptic sentiments—of rebellion against Rome; it all began, he says, at the time of the census of Quirinius in 6 CE.[7]

Even in more peaceful moments, apocalyptic prophets delivered oracles of doom. One of these, named Jesus son of Ananias, came to the Temple in 62 CE, crying: "A voice from the East, a voice from the West, a voice from the four winds; a voice against Jerusalem and the temple, a voice against the bridegroom and the bride, a voice against all the people."[8] It was a disconcerting scene, for the massive renovation of the Temple, begun over eighty years earlier by Herod the Great, had just been completed. The prophet was arrested and beat senseless but eventually released on the grounds that he was merely crazy and posed no military threat. Yet there were other signs of unrest. Whenever the Roman authorities were absent, fanaticism broke out. Prior to the arrival of the new governor, Albinus, in 62, James the brother of Jesus, leader of the Jerusalem church, had been arrested by the high priest Ananus and executed.[9] In fact, by 62–64 CE it is likely that Peter and Paul had both died as well. A generation of the Jesus movement was passing away, and that too had its eschatological implications: "Truly I tell you, there are some standing here who will not taste death until they see that the kingdom of God has come with power" (Mark 9:1).

The Course of the Revolt (66–74 CE)

Jerusalem was already a tinderbox by the year 66, when the actions of the last procurator, Gessius Florus, set it off. Florus was already antagonistic toward the Jews at Passover in the spring of 66; by May there were outbreaks of hostilities between the Greek and Jewish residents of the provincial capital, Caesarea Maritima.[10] Florus responded by arresting the Jewish leaders of Caesarea, blaming them for instigating a riot. Next, he ordered that seventeen talents be confiscated from the Temple in Jerusalem to pay their fines and damages. The result was a riot in Jerusalem.[11] Florus sent more troops, who then went on what Josephus describes as a bloody rampage through the streets.[12] Despite calls for restraint, the tide of rebellion grew, and by the end of the summer, Jewish insurgents had taken full control of Jerusalem. In the fall, Roman reinforcements under Cestius, the governor of Syria, took Jerusalem again, but then decided to return to Caesarea. On their return march they were ambushed in the narrow pass of Beth-horon, where Judas the Maccabee had also won a major skirmish over two centuries earlier. Cestius fled to Caesarea and sent word to the emperor Nero that the situation was out of control.[13]

Rome Responds: The First Campaigns
(Spring 67–Winter 69 CE)

The triumphant Jewish rebels returned to Jerusalem confident that this was a sign of their imminent victory, that God was on their side. In Jerusalem armies were being formed, and Josephus, who describes himself as an enthusiastic young aristocrat, came to the fore to take charge of the Jewish army of the Galilee. Through the early winter of 67, Jewish forces moved to consolidate their territory. Meanwhile, the emperor Nero summoned a battle-hardened general named Flavius Vespasian, who had recently put down a similar rebellion in Britain, to take charge of the situation. Having massed two full legions at Ptolemais, in the spring of 67 Vespasian began by attacking the Galilee and isolating it from the Jewish forces in the south. Much of the Galilee, especially the larger cities such as Sepphoris, surrendered almost immediately. But Josephus's army fought on until his forces were finally bottled up at Jotapata by the end of that summer. Eventually Josephus surrendered and became an important witness to the rest of the war (see below).

By the end of 67, Vespasian, now joined by his son Titus as vice commander, had returned to Caesarea to begin planning his southern campaigns. Roman forces had already started to attack and encircle the outlying regions. Samaria had fallen after a massacre of Samaritan worshipers at their temple on Mt. Gerazim.[14] Another Roman force was dispatched to the eastern borders of Perea and the plain of Jericho early in 68. It was at this time that the Essenes of Qumran marched out to meet the Roman armies, thinking this was the "War of the Sons of Light Against the Sons of Darkness."[15] They too were massacred, and their settlement burned.

Vespasian now began to plan for the final campaign in Judea, with Jerusalem as his main target. He already knew that it was likely to take a protracted siege. With the Galilee subdued and the noose tightening in the south, many of the remaining rebel groups began streaming into Jerusalem. By June of 68 most of the outlying regions had been pacified except for central Judea. The Zealots were still rampaging at will in both Jerusalem and the Judean desert, where they even captured Masada, the legendary fortress of Herod on the cliffs above the Dead Sea.[16] Vespasian had considered attacking Jerusalem with one force to keep the rebels occupied and contained while allowing the rest of his legions to mop up remaining resistance in the outlying regions of the south. But then he received word of startling developments in Rome: the emperor Nero had been killed and a bloody coup was developing.[17]

Vespasian delayed embarking upon his expedition against Jerusalem. The following year (69) saw three new emperors ascend the throne only to be assassinated. Rome was tense, and other generals began to look toward Vespasian to deal with the ongoing civil crisis. Leaving Titus in command of Judea, Vespasian moved to Alexandria, where he was acclaimed emperor.[18] In December, having restored peace at Rome, Vespasian ordered Titus to resume the war in Judea.[19]

The Siege of Jerusalem (Winter 69–Fall 70 CE)

With the war in Judea effectively on hold, the Jewish rebels were emboldened. The death of Nero and civil war in Rome could be taken as a sign of God's intervention on their behalf. They conducted raids as far south as Idumea, and a new rebel chieftain, Simon bar Giora, added his band to the mix in Jerusalem; however, this only added to the infighting among the different factions. One group of Zealots under Eleazar commanded the inner courts of the Temple, while John of Gischala held the outer courts and the adjacent fortress called the Antonia, and Simon bar Giora occupied the Upper City (southwest Jerusalem; see Box 2.4 for a plan of Jerusalem). Josephus says that they were as often firing arrows at one another as at Romans. Worshipers coming to the Temple were caught in the cross fire and killed. Gradually the city was being overtaken by famine as well.[20]

Titus now marched on Jerusalem with four legions. With camps on the surrounding heights, they began a systematic and withering siege that would last for eight months. They also began to build siege engines to breach the walls and catapults to begin an artillery barrage. By late May of 70 the Roman armies had breached the two outermost walls and taken over those areas of the city. The fighting had been fierce on both sides, and Titus called a temporary halt to offer peace terms.[21] Some of the Jerusalemites wanted to surrender, but the rebel factions refused to let them leave. Meanwhile, Josephus reports that he was called on to make speeches outside the walls imploring the people to give up, saying that God had now sided with the Romans.[22] The famine and the atrocities of the rebels were devastating, and Josephus paints a horrifying picture of the conditions in the city during the last months of the siege.[23]

It was now the summer of 70. By July final preparations were being made to breach the last walls and attack the Temple and the inner city. By the beginning of August, the Antonia fortress had been demolished and the religious operations of the Temple suspended. On August 12 the final assaults began. Jewish rebels had built fire traps in the outer porticoes of the Temple; Romans who made it through began to set fire to the rest.[24] Fighting in the streets and from house to house increased daily until the end of August, when the Temple finally was engulfed in flames, on the same month and day that the Babylonians had burned Solomon's Temple in 586 BCE.[25] Again, Josephus describes the ensuing carnage in gruesome detail.[26] The last of all the Jewish priests were executed, and Roman soldiers offered sacrifices to their legionary standards in the burned out courts of the Temple.[27]

In September the Romans began the systematic destruction of the remaining areas of the city and captured the last rebel bands in the Upper City. On September 29, 70, Titus marched into Jerusalem.[28] In 71 Titus returned to Rome in triumphal procession.[29] The relief sculptures on his arch at the east entrance to the Forum depict the procession of soldiers parading the spoils of the Temple and leading Simon bar Giora to execution (see Fig. 9.2). Meanwhile, the Tenth Roman Legion was stationed in Judea to finish mopping up; some bands of rebels had escaped in the final days of the siege. One of these groups would hold out for nearly four years at the fortress of Masada (see below).

Responses to the Destruction of Jerusalem

It would be hard to overstate the magnitude of the trauma caused by the failure of the first Jewish revolt. It was a huge triumph for Vespasian and ensured the political fortunes of the Flavian dynasty, which would hold the imperial throne for twenty-five years.[30] The event sent shock waves through the Jewish population both in the homeland and in the Diaspora. Josephus reports a total of 1.1

FIGURE 9.2

Side panel of the Arch of Titus in Rome showing the triumphal procession with spoils from the Temple and Jewish captives; at the front is Simon bar Giora in chains.

million casualties, mostly Jewish; another 97,000 Jews were taken prisoner.[31] The loss of life was devastating to be sure, but the destruction of Jerusalem and especially the Temple—symbol of the nation and God's election—was even more devastating politically, economically, and emotionally.

Several other effects were discernible in the period of the postwar reconstruction:

1. Gradually, the Jewish population began to move increasingly to the northern regions of the Galilee, which had not experienced as much fighting and destruction. Over time it became the new center of Jewish culture, and the rise of rabbinic Judaism would take place largely in the new Galilean "homeland."

2. Now too Jews had to face the constant presence of a Roman occupation force whose goal was to keep the peace.

3. The province of Judea was again reorganized and even renamed Palestina (the Latin form of the old regional name Philistia). The name change was another slap in the face to Jewish identity.

4. A new tax was imposed on Jews to pay for the war damages. Called the *fiscus Iudaeus,* it redirected the old Temple tax to Rome. Since census and taxation had long been a source of tension, this penalty could only be viewed as a sad irony.

5. Finally, Roman coinage of the period carried the legend *Judaea Capta* ("Judea Captured"), a clear statement of the subjugation (see Fig. 9.3).

As with previous political crises—the Babylonian exile and the Maccabean revolt (see Chapter 2)—in order to survive the Jews had to produce a religious response that helped them adjust to this new and difficult reality. The Jewish followers of the Jesus movement had to face it too. In this section we shall survey several kinds of religious responses that emerged in the decades immediately following the first revolt.

The Persistence of Apocalyptic: Masada and 4 Ezra

The failure of the revolt would gradually result in a shift in apocalyptic thinking for Jews and Christians alike, but not overnight. Apocalyptic sentiments and expectations like those of the Essenes and Zealots persisted. The most immediate evidence comes from Masada, the legendary "last stand" of the revolt. According to Josephus, our only ancient source for these events, the Zealot leader Eleazar escaped from Jerusalem near the end of the siege and led some six

FIGURE 9.3

Coin issued by the emperor Vespasian; it depicts Judea as a woman in mourning (seated) with a Roman soldier standing over her. It bears the legend *Judaea Capta* ("Judea Captured"). (Photo used by permission of the British Museum)

FIGURE 9.4

Masada, aerial view from the west: (1) Roman military camps encircling the perimeter; (2) earthen ramp built by the Roman army and Jewish prisoners to attack the fortress; (3) the three-tiered palace of Herod. (R. Cleve, ROHR Productions Limited)

hundred followers, including women and children, to the fortified palace of Herod on the banks of the Dead Sea.[32] (See Fig. 9.4.) There they held out for nearly four more years.

Following the final destruction of Jerusalem, Titus dispatched the Roman general Lucilius Bassus to root out any remaining pockets of resistance.[33] He was succeeded by another general, Flavius Silva, who oversaw the siege of Masada, the last of the holdouts. Masada was virtually impregnable because of its sheer escarpments. So the Romans simply encircled it with camps and conscripted Jewish prisoners to build an earthen ramp up one side of the mountain in order to have a means of attack. For months the Zealots watched from atop the mountain as the Roman siege works rose higher, until it was clear that a final assault was near. When the Romans broke through the walls, however, all they found was an eerie silence; the Jewish defenders had all committed suicide. Josephus reports the marvel of the Roman soldiers at the courage of the Zealots.[34]

Some scholars, including archaeologists who excavated at Masada, now doubt that there was a mass suicide.[35] What really happened that day is forever lost. For Josephus, however, the episode is a symbol of remarkable resolve to suffer death rather than endure slavery.[36] On the other hand, Josephus presents the two impassioned speeches that Eleazar supposedly delivered to encourage the suicide, and these suggest another dimension as well. Eleazar's second speech ends with these words:

> I cannot but wish that we had all died before we had seen that holy city de-molished by the hands of our enemies, or the foundations of our Temple dug up in such a profane manner. But since we had an excessive hope that deluded us. . . , though it is now vain and has left us alone in distress, let us make haste to die bravely. . . . This is what our laws command us to do; this is what our wives and children crave at our hands; this is what even God himself has brought upon us as a necessity.[37]

Whether this really represents Eleazar's words or Josephus's own thoughts is de-batable; however, it points a condemning finger at the apocalyptic expectations of the Jewish rebels. It is the ultimate irony that their political hopes, symbol-ized in the Temple itself, should have resulted in the destruction of that most sacred of Jewish symbols.

Although the political situation of Judea was quickly stabilized under the Roman occupation force, apocalyptic expectations did not disappear alto-gether. Roughly twenty years later a flourish of new Jewish apocalypses began to appear. These include 4 Ezra, *2 Baruch, 3 Baruch,* and the *Apocalypse of Abra-ham*.[38] In some ways they reinterpret older apocalyptic expectations. They had to in light of the failure of the first revolt and do so in part for pastoral reasons. On the other hand, they still show a strong expectation that God will finally de-liver Judea from the Romans. The mechanism for providing this new interpre-tation is to look back to important figures from the time of the destruction of Solomon's Temple in 586 BCE. The figures of Baruch and Ezra provide such a fictional setting for reflection on the events of 70 CE.

These new apocalypses generally take the view that the present suffering of Jerusalem is a purging of its past sins to prepare for an eventual deliverance. The eschaton and a messianic age are still to come. There is also a warning that becoming too much like the Romans is not the proper course of action. As in the past, God might use foreign nations to punish Israel, but eventually they will be punished for idolatry and Israel restored. These works also function as a stern call to proper piety. Some of these ideas are also reflected in the Christian

Gospels and in the book of Revelation, which were being written at about the same time.

Within sixty years of the destruction of Jerusalem a new wave of revolutionary sentiment arose, again fueled by apocalyptic expectation. The outbreak of the second Jewish revolt, with its self-proclaimed messianic leader, Bar Kochba, shows how these deeply rooted ideas continued in some quarters (see Box 14.2).

The Failure of Apocalyptic: Josephus

Josephus's account of Masada, as we have seen, takes a rather different view of these traditional apocalyptic expectations. Rather than deliverers, the Jewish rebels were either deluded or deceivers. They were to blame for the destruction of the Temple and the catastrophe that now faced the Jewish people. Of course, Josephus's own role in the revolt must be considered here, and one quickly recognizes that Josephus has some conflicted emotions in his telling of the Masada story, for when Josephus was captured after the battle of Jotapata, he was faced with just such an option.[39]

Josephus ben Mattathias was born in 37 CE to an aristocratic Jerusalem family that claimed Hasmonean descent on his mother's side. He entered the war as a general at age twenty-nine, which may well imply that he outfitted his troops for the campaign in Galilee. According to Josephus, when it became clear that the Romans were about to overrun Jotapata, he and his officers fled the city and hid in caves. But the Romans discovered where they were hiding and prepared to starve them out. Some wanted to commit suicide rather than face capture, but Josephus tried to dissuade them on the grounds that it was against Jewish law. When he failed to do so, he proposed that they draw lots to see who would die first.[40] Thus, it was divinely ordained through the lots that Josephus and one other should be the last to die.[41] The two of them then surrendered to the Romans. When he was finally granted an audience with Vespasian, Josephus offered a prophetic prediction that his captor would be the next emperor. On this basis, says Josephus, he was granted freedom and Roman citizenship, finished out the war as special aide to Titus, and retired to Rome as a retainer of the Flavians. As a Roman citizen, he followed convention by adding the name of his patron to his own and thus became Flavius Josephus.

This is a remarkable story in light of Josephus's attitude toward the Zealots and the war in general. Clearly he had fought the Romans vigorously, so why the change? Josephus gives an interesting answer in his account of the cave, for he claims to have experienced a series of dreams and visions that had made him come to realize that the war, with its apocalyptic hopes, was not only futile but also against the will of God. God was on the side of the Romans. In other words, Josephus had been the recipient of a new apocalyptic revelation and through divine inspiration was being given the proper understanding of biblical prophecies from the past. Now Josephus was to serve as a prophetic messenger for the future of Israel. His revelation regarding Vespasian was just part of the unfolding of this divine plan. His surrender was a divinely appointed ministry for his beloved nation.[42] All this may rightly be seen as utterly self-serving, but it does show how even Josephus's own denunciation of the apocalyptic origins of the war could be turned in another direction. The key is reinterpretation.

The Spiritual Temple: Yohanan ben Zakkai

Josephus was not the only one to turn against the war. Yohanan ben Zakkai was reputed to have been a disciple of Hillel, one of the founders of the Pharisaic school. According to the legend, Yohanan had opposed the war early on and during the siege of Jerusalem was smuggled out of the city in a coffin by his disciples. Once free of the revolutionaries, he was taken to Vespasian's tent, where he prophesied that the general would be the next emperor. As a reward, he was allowed to move to Yavneh (Jamnia) on the coast and there establish an academy to continue the teachings of the Pharisaic masters.[43]

The story of Yohanan ben Zakkai bears some strong similarities to that of Josephus; however, his impact on later Judaism was far greater. Despite the historical problems with the legend of his escape from Jerusalem, it is clear that he represents an important line of development from the early Pharisees in the period before the war to the postwar establishment of the rabbinic tradition. His decision is rightly viewed as a turning point in the history of Judaism.[44] It is an important shift that will have a direct bearing on our reading of the Christian Gospels, for their portrayal of the Pharisees in the time of Jesus is colored by many of these post-70 developments and the growing tension between emergent Christianity and rabbinic Judaism.[45]

Unfortunately, most of the sources and legends about Yohanan are very late and less reliable for historical purposes, but they reflect both the mode and the tenor of Pharisaic reinterpretation coming out of the two revolts against Rome. Typical is this story about Yohanan's response to seeing Jerusalem in ruins:

> *Once as Rabbi Yohanan ben Zakkai was coming from Jerusalem, Rabbi Joshua followed after him and beheld the Temple in ruins.*

> *"Woe unto us," Rabbi Joshua cried, "for the place where the iniquities of Israel were atoned is destroyed!"*
>
> *"My son," Rabbi Yohanan said to him, "do not grieve. We have another atonement as effective as this. And what is it? It is acts of loving-kindness, as it is said: 'I desire mercy and not sacrifice' (Hos. 6:6)."*[46]

What this story reflects is an important mode of reinterpretation. It uses a famous passage of scripture from Hosea, also exploited by Christian interpreters (cf. Matt. 9:13; 12:7), to argue that one can still perform atoning sacrifices even without the Temple. There are two key ideas here: first, that acts of piety, such as prayer, alms, and study of Torah, are equivalent forms of personal sacrifice to God; and, second, that there is another form of God's true Temple in the heart of the believer.

It should be remembered that one of the aims of the early Pharisees was to take aspects of Temple ritual and apply them to daily life in the home (see Chapter 4). In view of the loss of the Temple, this mode of Pharisaic piety offered a natural solution. The development of rabbinic tradition through the period of the second century CE saw the gradual codification of rules for purity and piety in keeping with this theological shift. At the center was the Torah or, in Pharisaic terms, the "twofold Torah"—the written Torah given to Moses and the oral traditions of interpretation carried on from him. In time, this elevated view of Torah merged naturally with the worship of the synagogue and became a kind of spiritual temple that might be carried anywhere. At first transmitted from rabbinic teacher to disciple, by the end of the second century these oral traditions were being compiled in written form. The first of these compilations was the Mishnah, which was assembled by Rabbi Judah the Prince in Sepphoris in about 200 CE.

Apocalyptic Denials: The Pella Legend

Given the overall significance of the first revolt, it seems odd that there is so little direct mention of it in early Christian writings. As we shall see, however, there may be more reflection of the events than has sometimes been recognized. But a factor may well be the decided turn away from apocalyptic thinking that came as a result of the war. Later Christian tradition took the position that the early followers of Jesus had not participated in the war because they had already rejected that kind of Jewish apocalyptic thinking.

In part this notion that the followers of Jesus resisted the war grew out of the legends regarding the death of James, the brother of Jesus. Josephus reports that he was killed during the tumultuous years leading up to the war (see above). A later legend developed that after the death of James, the church in Jerusalem left the city and migrated to Pella, a city of the Decapolis, a region of Hellenistic cities on the other side of the Jordan. Here is the principal account given by Eusebius of Caesarea in the early fourth century:

> *Moreover, the people of the church at Jerusalem, in accordance with a certain* **oracle** *that was vouchsafed by way of revelation to approved men there, had been commanded to depart from the city before the war, and to inhabit a certain city of Perea. They called it Pella. And after those who believed in Christ had left Jerusalem, as if holy men had utterly deserted both the royal metropolis of the Jews and the whole land of Judea, the justice of God then visited upon them all their [the Jews'] acts of violence toward Christ and his apostles, by destroying that generation of* **wicked persons** *root and branch. (Church History 3.5.3)*

According to this account, then, the early Christians of Jerusalem were not led astray by the apocalyptic expectations and revolutionary sentiments of other Jews. Instead, they received divine guidance by revelation ("oracle") to flee before the war broke out. Once again we see apocalyptic ideas being used to reinterpret earlier apocalyptic expectations. This legend further serves to claim a high degree of separation between Christians and Jews before the war. It also provides an alternative way of understanding the destruction by arguing it was God's punishment of the Jews (the "wicked generation") for killing Jesus, James, and others. This line of reinterpretation would later become very significant in Christian anti-Jewish polemics.

In reality, however, there is no evidence whatsoever that the church in Jerusalem fled the war. In fact, as we shall see below, it is likely that many followers of the Jesus movement initially viewed the war as the fulfillment of eschatological promises. The growing rift between Christians and Jews began only after the first revolt and came to a head in the period of the second revolt. We have this report from the second-century Christian Justin Martyr, who had been born in the region of Samaria near the end of the first century:

> *For in the Jewish war which recently raged, Bar Kochba, the leader of the revolt of the Jews, gave orders that Christians alone should be led to cruel punishments, unless they would deny Jesus [as the] messiah and utter blasphemy [by following him as the messiah]. (Apology 1.31)*

This report contradicts that of Eusebius, since it shows that there were still Christians in and around Jerusalem at the time of Bar Kochba (132–35 CE; see

Chapter 14). But it may well provide the source of the later Pella legend coming not out of the experience of the first revolt, but out of the second. By then Christians were becoming more separate from Judaism and would have been more likely to denounce apocalyptic and messianic expectations regarding someone other than Jesus.

The First Gospel:
Mark as Postwar Reinterpretation

What all these responses show is the profound impact of the loss of the Temple, and the role of apocalyptic in both giving rise to the war and reinterpreting the outcome. An additional component is the use of literature as a way of dealing with the trauma and delivering the message of reinterpretation. As in the case of the new Jewish apocalypses mentioned above, even a fictional setting in the distant past might serve this function without ever mentioning the events of 70 directly. So too we see that the disastrous turn of events raised important questions about the previous expectations of the followers of the Jesus movement. One way of addressing these problems was by retelling the story of Jesus in light of the new situation. The first effort to do so was the Gospel of Mark.

Author, Setting, and Date

In contemporary biblical scholarship Mark is overwhelmingly viewed as both the first of the written Gospels and the principal source of Matthew and Luke. An early tradition attributed to Papias (ca. 130 CE) holds that the Gospel of Mark came from John Mark, who traveled with Peter to Rome and there wrote down his reminiscences of Jesus. This tradition would seem to place the writing of Mark sometime before 64 CE, the traditional date of Peter's death.[47]

It does appear that the Gospel was written for a Greek-speaking audience that had little or no knowledge of Judean culture and language. Consequently, a setting in Rome is a distinct possibility, and some have wanted to see the triumphal procession of Titus, returning with the spoils of the Temple, as a possible motivation for the writing. But Antioch might also provide a likely setting for the writing, since it had an established community of the Jesus movement, and John Mark is last reported in Acts as based there (Acts 15:36–39). Antioch also had a clear view of the war, and there were threatened reprisals against Jews in Antioch afterward. Moreover, Titus passed through Caesarea Philippi, Berytus, and Antioch with the Temple spoils and prisoners in tow on his way back to Rome.[48] With its large Jewish community and close ties to Jerusalem, one could imagine that the course of the war was also watched with considerable interest in Alexandria.[49]

Although we cannot be sure in which city Mark was written, the situation is rather clearly dependent on the war. The main question debated by scholars is whether it was written just prior to the destruction of Jerusalem or sometime afterward. Arguments based on internal evidence of the Gospel can be mounted on both sides but tend to favor a date of writing after the destruction had taken place, hence sometime between 70 and 75 CE. In large measure, the dating depends on how one understands references and images in chapters 11–13 in relation to the destruction of Jerusalem. These features will be discussed in the final section below.

The occasion for the writing arises from concerns regarding Jesus's teachings and his messianic identity in light of the failure of the revolt. It appears that some followers of the Jesus movement, like other Jews, viewed the revolt as a sign that the eschatological kingdom was about to arrive. To followers of the Jesus movement, it also meant that Jesus was about to return. When the revolt failed and Jerusalem was destroyed instead, there were questions—the same sort of questions that other Jews were asking. It may well be the case that the failure of their imminent eschatological expectations regarding Jesus's return had also fueled opposition attacks against both the messiahship of Jesus and the beliefs of the followers. Mark's Gospel was not written, however, to address the outsiders directly, but rather to reinforce the beliefs of those within the Jesus community by responding to the implied criticisms or their own misconceptions. For this reason, many of the themes and motifs of the Gospel deal with opposition to Jesus or misunderstanding of Jesus.

Organization and Themes

Mark's Gospel has sometimes been called "a Passion narrative with an extended introduction," since fully a third of the text is devoted to the last week of Jesus's life (see Box 9.1). Even though it is the first-known effort to construct a narrative of the life and death of Jesus, it is not really a "biography" in the strict sense. The story is heavily laced with dramatic irony and with veiled allusions to allegorical images of Jesus's death. In many cases these literary devices are meant to signal issues that relate to the circumstances of the audience, either by way of affirmation or correction. Consequently, due caution is required in taking events or episodes as historical realities of Jesus's own day.

BOX 9.1

The Gospel of Mark

DATE: ca. 70–75 CE

AUTHOR: Unknown

SETTING: Rome, Antioch, or Alexandria?

ATTRIBUTION: John Mark, disciple of Peter

AUDIENCE AND OCCASION: Greek-speaking followers of the Jesus movement in the period following the first revolt. Concerns over how to understand the messiahship and teachings of Jesus in light of the failure of the revolt and the disconfirmation of widely held apocalyptic expectations regarding the war.

OUTLINE

I.   Apocalyptic Announcements: "The Beginning of the Gospel" (1:1–13)

II. Jesus's Ministry in Galilee (1:14–6:6)
     A. Authority displayed in word and deed (1:14–3:6)
     B. Jesus's teachings misunderstood (3:7–4:41)
     C. Jesus's miracles misunderstood—rejection at Nazareth (5:1–6:6)

III. The Ministry Beyond Galilee (6:6–10:52)
     A. Mission of the Twelve (6:6–29)
     B. Miracles misunderstood by the disciples and others (6:30–8:26)
     C. Confession and first Passion prediction (8:27–9:1)
     D. Transfiguration and second Passion prediction—misunderstood by disciples (9:2–50)
     E. Journey toward Jerusalem and third Passion prediction (10:1–52)

IV. The Ministry in Jerusalem and the Passion Narrative (11:1–16:8)
     A. Triumphal entry (11:1–10)
     B. Cleansing the Temple, cursing the fig tree (11:11–25)
     C. Teaching and controversy in the Temple (11:27–12:44)
     D. Apocalyptic discourse regarding the destruction of the Temple (13:1–37)
     E. The Passion narrative (14:1–15:47)
        1. Conspiracy (14:1–2, 10–11)
        2. Anointing at Bethany (14:3–9)

3. Last supper (14:12–25)
4. Mount of Olives, betrayal, and arrest (14:26–52)
5. Trial before the Sanhedrin, Peter's denial (14:53–72)
6. Trial before Pilate (15:1–20)
7. Crucifixion and death (15:21–41)
8. Burial (15:42–47)

F. The empty tomb (16:1–8)

FURTHER READING

Achtemeier, P. J. "Mark, Gospel of." *Anchor Bible Dictionary.* 4:541–57.

————. "Toward the Isolation of Pre-Markan Miracle Catenae." *Journal of Biblical Literature* 89 (1970): 265–91.

Black, C. C. *The Disciples According to Mark: Markan Redaction in Current Debate.* Sheffield: Sheffield Academic Press, 1989.

————. *Mark: Images of an Apostolic Interpreter.* Columbia: University of South Carolina Press, 1994.

Bryan, C. *A Preface to Mark: Notes on the Gospel in Its Literary and Cultural Settings.* New York: Oxford University Press, 1993.

Fowler, R. M. *Let the Reader Understand: Reader-Response Criticism and the Gospel of Mark.* Minneapolis: Fortress, 1991.

Garrett, S. R. *The Temptations of Jesus in Mark's Gospel.* Grand Rapids, MI: Eerdmans, 1998.

Juel, D. H. *A Master of Surprise: Mark Interpreted.* Minneapolis: Fortress, 1994.

————. *Messiah and Temple: The Trial of Jesus in the Gospel of Mark.* Missoula, MT: Scholars Press, 1977.

Kermode, K. *The Genesis of Secrecy: On the Interpretation of Mark.* Cambridge: Cambridge University Press, 1979.

Mack, B. *A Myth of Innocence: Mark and Christian Origins.* Philadelphia: Fortress, 1988.

Myers, C. *Binding the Strong Man: A Political Reading of Mark's Story of Jesus.* Maryknoll, NY: Orbis, 1988.

Robbins, V. K. *Jesus the Teacher: A Socio-Rhetorical Interpretation of Mark.* Rev. ed. Minneapolis: Fortress, 1992.

Tuckett, C. *The Messianic Secret.* Philadelphia: Fortress, 1983.

One such dramatic element is distinctive to Mark. It revolves around a cluster of themes dealing with secrecy and misunderstanding that weave throughout narrative. It has long been noticed, for example, that Mark's Jesus regularly conceals his true identity or the meaning of his teachings from all but his closest disciples (Mark 1:34; 3:12; 4:10–12, 33–34; 5:43). Many people, including his own family, misunderstand his words and miracles (6:14–16; 8:11–13); they think he is either crazy or demon-possessed (3:19–30). Even the disciples, who ought to understand, fail again and again to see things clearly (8:14–33). But the disciples, in turn, are surrogates for the later followers of the Jesus movement who are having trouble understanding things in the aftermath of the war. Thus, one can also imagine how the audience might have heard these tales and reacted to them.

Jesus and the Temple in Mark

Much of the Markan narrative is carried by dramatic irony, but the most important and complex scenes occur when Jesus is in the Temple during the last week of his life. We shall here focus on two of them: the cleansing of the Temple (11:11–25) and the apocalyptic discourse (13:1–37).

A famous episode in all the Gospels is the one in which Jesus casts the money changers out of the Temple. In the Gospel of Mark, however, this episode plays an especially important role, since it is the act that ultimately gets Jesus killed. The scene is also presented in Mark in an unusual way, since Jesus's actions in the Temple are spliced together with an odd miracle story in which Jesus curses a fig tree. This literary construction, known as *intercalation,* is diagrammed in Box 9.2.

The scene follows directly on the triumphal entry (A), but whereas Matthew and Luke have Jesus cleanse the Temple immediately, Mark only has Jesus enter the Temple and leave (B[1]). Then on the way to the Temple the next day Jesus first curses the fig tree (C[1]) and then cleanses the Temple (B[2]). Mark then says explicitly that his action caused the "chief priests and scribes" to plot his death, and through the remainder of Mark's Passion narrative, they, and they alone, are responsible. Finally, the sequence ends with another trip past the fig tree, now withered. Sandwiching the Temple cleansing in between the two encounters with the fig tree forces readers to look at one in the light of the other. In other words, the fig tree becomes an allegorical symbol for the Temple, so that the cleansing is actually a cursing. The withered fig tree represents the destruction of the Temple.

But why a fig tree? The story is odd in another way, since it says that the tree was in leaf but it was not the season for figs; so why should Jesus curse it for not having any? An additional clue to the dramatic play of the story comes when the fig tree shows up again in the apocalyptic discourse of chapter 13:

> *"From the fig tree learn its lesson: as soon as its branch becomes tender and puts forth its leaves, you know that summer is near. So also, when you see these things taking place, you know that he is near, at the very gates. Truly I tell you, this generation will not pass away until all these things have taken place." (Mark 13:28–30)*

Now the fig tree in leaf becomes a symbol of the approaching eschaton, and the destruction of the Temple is understood by Mark as a sign that the eschaton would arrive during that very generation.

BOX 9.2

The Temple Cleansing in Mark (11:11–25)

A *Triumphal Entry*	(Mark 11:1–10)
B¹ *In the Temple*	11 Then he entered Jerusalem and went into the temple; and when he had looked around at everything, as it was already late, he went out to Bethany with the twelve.
C¹ *Curses Fig Tree*	12 On the following day, when they came from Bethany, he was hungry. 13 Seeing in the distance a fig tree in leaf, he went to see whether perhaps he would find anything on it. When he came to it, he found nothing but leaves, for it was not the season for figs. 14 He said to it, "May no one ever eat fruit from you again." And his disciples heard it.
B² *Cleanses Temple*	15 Then they came to Jerusalem. And he entered the temple and began to drive out those who were selling and those who were buying in the temple, and he overturned the tables of the money changers and the seats of those who sold doves; 16 and he would not allow anyone to carry anything through the temple. 17 He was teaching and saying, "Is it not written, 'My house shall be called a house of prayer for all the nations'? But you have made it a den of robbers."
B³ *The Conspiracy*	18 And when the chief priests and the scribes heard it, they kept looking for a way to kill him; for they were afraid of him, because the whole crowd was spellbound by his teaching. 19 And when evening came, Jesus and his disciples went out of the city.
C² *Lesson of Fig Tree*	20 In the morning as they passed by, they saw the fig tree withered away to its roots. 21 Then Peter remembered and said to him, "Rabbi, look! The fig tree that you cursed has withered." 22 Jesus answered them, "Have faith in God. 23 Truly I tell you, if you say to this mountain, 'Be taken up and thrown into the sea,' and if you do not doubt in your heart, but believe that what you say will come to pass, it will be done for you. 24 So I tell you, whatever you ask for in prayer, believe that you have received it, and it will be yours. . . ."

The key to understanding Mark is the apocalyptic discourse, sometimes called the "Little Apocalypse" (Mark 13:1–37). It begins with Jesus and the disciples leaving the Temple for the day and heading back to Bethany, where they were staying. That would take them across the Mount of Olives, and as they go one of the disciples comments on the architectural grandeur of the Temple (13:1), to which Jesus replies: "Not one stone will be left here upon another; all will be thrown down" (13:2). Clearly this is a reference to the destruction of the Temple in 70. Next, the inner circle of disciples asks Jesus, "When will this be?" (13:4), and that prompts the rest of the discourse, given by Mark as a single speech by Jesus (13:5–37). Following a warning about some signs that will foreshadow the events, including false messiahs, famine, and war (13:5–7), comes the powerful apocalyptic image of expectant Jerusalem: "This is but the beginnings of the birth pangs" (13:8). Next comes a warning about persecution for those who proclaim the gospel (13:9–13). Here we see a reference to the experiences of the later followers of the Markan community. Then come the real "signs" of the destruction:

> *"But when you see the **desolating sacrilege** set up where it ought not to be (**let the reader understand**), then those in Judea must flee to the mountains. . . . Woe to those who are pregnant and to those who are nursing infants in those days! Pray that it may not be in winter. For in those days there will be suffering, such as has not been from the beginning of the creation that God created until now, no, and never will be. And if the Lord had not cut short those days, no one would be saved; but for the sake of the elect, whom he chose, he has cut short those days. And if anyone says to you at that time, 'Look! Here is the Messiah!' or 'Look! There he is!'—do not believe it. False messiahs and false prophets will appear and produce signs and omens, to lead astray, if possible, the elect. But be alert; I have already told you everything." (13:14–23)*

Here we see the author of Mark step out from behind the character of Jesus and speak directly to the audience: "let the reader understand" (13:14). The phrase "desolating sacrilege" is one used in writings of the Maccabean revolt period to refer to the desecration of the Temple by Antiochus Epiphanes (1 Macc. 1:54; Dan 9:27; 11:31; 12:11); here it may refer to the confiscation of the Temple treasury, the occupation of the Temple by the Zealots, the cessation of Temple rituals in the last months of the siege, or the final destruction and looting of the Temple by Titus's soldiers. At the very least, the "desecration" is a sign that destruction is nigh. Then the passage warns again of false messiahs who will arise in conjunction with these events.

Mark 13 seems to be an effort to correct a misunderstanding on the part of at least some in the Markan community who had thought that the war really was to be the eschatological return of Jesus. Instead, Mark has Jesus "predict" these events as a way of correcting the apocalyptic expectations by using, as we have seen before, an apocalyptic mode of discourse to deliver the reinterpretation. The point of Mark is twofold. First, the destruction of the Temple was—like the cursing of the fig tree—a punishment because the Temple had not been pure. In this view Mark's reinterpretation is very much in line with other Jewish views of the day. To this Mark adds another dimension, however, by linking the impurity of the Temple with the role of the priests in the death of Jesus. Second, Mark makes the destruction of the Temple not the eschatological event itself, but merely the "birth pangs" for the eschaton. In other words, Mark's readers were being told that the traumatic events that had so recently transpired in Jerusalem were—like the onset of labor—the signal that the eschatological age was now about to dawn, in fact within the lifetime of that very generation (13:32–37). Despite their previous misunderstanding, Jesus would return soon. Thus, by portraying the various *misunderstandings* of those around Jesus— friend and foe alike—the Markan narrative thereby gives shape to *proper* understanding of Jesus's messianic identity and eschatological expectations for its own community of followers. In other words, it too is a mode of reinterpretation in the light of the war.

CHAPTER TEN

Sectarian Tensions and Self-Definition

Gospel Trajectories

As we have already seen, the Gospel of Mark represents the initial efforts of a particular community of the Jesus movement to reinterpret both the messiahship of Jesus and eschatological expectations in light of the destruction of Jerusalem. In fact, each of the Gospels serves a similar purpose within its own community and social context. Many of the differences between the Gospels can be attributed to changes in the social location and the situation being faced by its author and audience. Thus, each Gospel is its own reflective compilation written in and for a particular community of believers. To understand them, one must look for clues to the social context, circumstances, and purpose.

The Gospel of Matthew

Author and Date

The Gospel of Matthew was probably the second of the New Testament Gospels to be written down. Unlike Mark, it was attributed to one of the actual disciples of Jesus. Matthew is described as a Jewish tax collector first encountered by Jesus in Capernaum (Matt. 9:9–13). The narrative emphasizes both his identity and his role in unique ways.[1] The early tradition of Papias (ca. 130 CE) regarding the authorship raises other questions: "Matthew collected the sayings [of the Lord] in Hebraic dialect, and each one interpreted them as he was able."[2] The problem is that this statement does not fit the New Testament Gospel of Matthew very well, since it is far more than a collection of sayings, and it was composed in Greek instead of Hebrew or Aramaic. These elements suggest, therefore, that there might have been an early Hebrew (more likely, Aramaic) tradition of sayings of Jesus associated with the name of Matthew and that later on there was an effort within one particular community to incorporate that tradition into its own self-understanding. Some have even suggested that what we now call the Q source was originally attributed to Matthew. The Gospel of Matthew as we now have it, however, comes from a later author who compiled various sources, including Mark, Q, and other materials, into a new composition, probably between 80 and 90 CE.

Setting and Location

The Gospel of Matthew is by far the most Jewish of the Gospels, and most of the ancient traditions, including that of Papias (noted above), seem to reflect this fact. On the other hand, it was clearly written in Greek. A number of different localities have been proposed for the composition of Matthew, but by far the most common view for many years was that it came from Antioch, the capital of Roman Syria.[3]

In light of recent archaeological work, a growing number of New Testament scholars would now locate the Matthean community somewhere in or near the village culture of Upper Galilee.[4] Even though the author and the audience admit gentile converts into their fellowship, their primary social location and self-understanding are Jewish. Even the polemics against the Pharisees, a distinctive feature of Matthew, arise in this Jewish matrix; they are to be understood in view of the gradual demographic shift to the Galilee in the period after the first revolt, where the Pharisaic movement would emerge as the new voice of Judaism.[5] Thus, it is quite feasible to see the author of Matthew as a Jewish follower of the Jesus movement whose community is facing conflict with other Jews, and especially these latter-day Pharisees.

Organization and Themes

One clue to the situation of the Gospel of Matthew is the way it reorganizes the Markan outline and supplements it with new material. A comparison of the outlines of Matthew and Mark is given in Box 10.1.

BOX 10.1

Comparison of the Outlines of Matthew and Mark

Matthew	*Mark*
Jesus and John the Baptist (3:1–4:11) Baptism Temptation	Jesus and John the Baptist (1:1–13) Baptism Temptation
Ministry Phase I: Galilee (4:12–13:58)	Ministry Phase I: Galilee (1:14–6:6)
I. Sermon on the Mount (5:1–7:28)	Rejection at Nazareth (6:1–6)
II. Mission Sermon (9:35–10:42)	Ministry Phase II: Beyond Galilee (6:7–9:50)
III. Parables Sermon (13:1–52)	Mission of the Twelve (6:7–13) Confession at Caesarea Philippi (8:27–33)
Rejection at Nazareth (13:53–58)	Transfiguration (9:2–8) Passion Prediction (9:31)
Ministry Phase II: Beyond Galilee (14:1–18:35)	Ministry Phase III: Judea (10:1–52)
Confession (16:13–23) Transfiguration (17:1–8) Passion Predictions (16:21; 17:22)	Passion Prediction (10:32–34)
IV. Sermon on Discipline (18:1–35)	Preaching in Jerusalem (11:1–13:37)
Move to Judea (19:1–20:16)	Triumphal Entry (11:1–10) Cleansing of Temple, Curse of Fig Tree (11:11–25)
Preaching in Jerusalem (21:1–25:46)	The Conspiracy (11:18) Teachings in Temple (11:27–12:44)
Triumphal Entry (21:1–9) Cleansing of Temple (21:10–22)	Discourse on the Destruction of the Temple and the Eschaton (13:1–37)
V. Sermon[a] vs. Pharisees (23:1–36) Sermon[b] on Destruction (24:1–51) Sermon[c] on Judgment (25:1–46)	The Passion Narrative (14:1–16:8)
The Passion Narrative (26:1–28:20)	The Conspiracy (14:1–2) Anointing at Bethany (14:3–9) Betrayal Arranged (14:10–11) Last Supper (14:17–31) Prayer and Arrest (14:32–52)
	Trial Before Sanhedrin (14:53–72) Trial Before Pilate (15:1–21)
	Crucifixion and Death (15:22–41) Burial (15:42–47) Empty Tomb (16:1–8)

The Passion narrative in Matthew follows Mark for the most part; however, it organizes the ministry of Jesus around five major discourses of Jesus, the most famous of which is the Sermon on the Mount. In each case these "sermons" are uniquely Matthean compositions with only partial similarities to Mark or Luke. For example, where Matthew has the three-chapter Sermon on the Mount (Matt. 5:1–7:28), Luke gives only a brief part of this same material in a discourse on the plain near the Sea of Galilee (Luke 6:20–49). Comparative analysis shows that Matthew has drawn together material from Mark, Q, and some unknown source to yield the Sermon on the Mount. In addition, Matthew has three such sermon blocks within the first phase of Jesus's ministry, at least according to Mark's geographical outline. Taken together with other episodes that have been repositioned (e.g., the mission of the Twelve, which is now several chapters earlier than the rejection at Nazareth), this means that the bulk of the narrative is devoted to the Galilean ministry of Jesus. The weight thus attached to the Galilee by the narrative seems to correspond with the situation of the Matthean audience, while both the second and third phases of Jesus's ministry as described in Mark are thus relatively later.

Matthew's narrative still follows the broad lines of Mark's geographical outline, but it is governed by the five sermon blocks (see Box 10.2). The structure of the narrative has other thematic implications. Jesus is now portrayed more as a teacher, and the miracle stories are played down. The five sermons have been thought by some scholars to be a conscious allusion to the five books of Moses, the Torah, so that Jesus is a teacher of the law. Matthew also adds a birth narrative (Matt. 1:1–2:23) that opens with these words: "The book of the generations of Jesus, the messiah . . ."[6] For anyone steeped in the tradition of the Jewish scriptures these words would have been immediately recognizable allusions to the language of Genesis.[7] Another important thematic feature of Matthew is its emphasis on the fulfillment of prophecies from the Hebrew scriptures, especially in relation to the person of Jesus or events in his life. Here too one sees elements of a Jewish cultural background, and one can even find similarities in the pattern of scripture citation between Matthew and the rabbinic tradition.[8]

Finally, Matthew's use of scripture stresses not only the Davidic lineage and messiahship of Jesus but also his similarities to Moses. So when Jesus goes up on a mountain and begins to discuss particular commandments from the Mosaic law (e.g., Matt. 5:21, 27), he would appear to readers of that time very much like Moses or one of the rabbis of their own day. Jesus's attitude toward the Torah is overwhelmingly positive:

Do not think that I have come to abolish the law or the prophets; I have come not to abolish but to fulfill. For truly I tell you, until heaven and earth pass away, not one letter, not one stroke of a letter, will pass from the law until all is accomplished. Therefore, whoever breaks one of the least of these command-ments, and teaches others to do the same, will be called least in the kingdom of heaven; but whoever does them and teaches them will be called great in the kingdom of heaven. For I tell you, unless your righteousness exceeds that of the scribes and Pharisees, you will never enter the kingdom of heaven. (Matt. 5:17–20)

Although this passage reflects Matthew's tensions with Pharisees, it is impor-tant to note that referring to the scriptures as "the law and the prophets" is a de-cidedly Pharisaic way of talking.

Our Church and Their Synagogue: Matthew's Jewish Sect

Many of the thematic features of the Gospel of Matthew reflect a tension be-tween Matthew's community and the Jewish culture around it. On the one hand, Jesus is a Jewish teacher of disciples and interpreter of Torah very much like the Pharisees. In the mission instructions he explicitly tells the disciples: "Go nowhere among the Gentiles, and enter no town of the Samaritans, but go rather to the lost sheep of the house of Israel" (Matt. 10:5–6). On the other hand, Matthew's Jesus consistently rails against the Pharisees, especially in the long and bitter tirade of the final sermon (Matt. 23:1–36). Matthew also blames the conspiracy to kill Jesus directly on the Pharisees in collusion with the priests (Matt. 22:15, 34, 41; 26:3–5), even though it is historically unlikely. These ten-sions ultimately say more about the experience of Matthew's community in the period after the first revolt than they do about the days of Jesus.

However, Matthew's congregations have not broken away from Judaism. Quite the contrary. The problem is one of sectarian identity and community boundaries. The Matthean narrative has some subtle changes of language that reflect sectarian tensions. For example, the Gospel of Mark on only one occa-sion makes reference to Jesus preaching in "their synagogues" (Mark 1:39), and in context this reference simply means "the local synagogue of each city" in the Galilee. In contrast Matthew's Gospel seems to take this one case and turn it into a regular pattern, one in which the connotation now is "the synagogues of

BOX 10.2
The Gospel of Matthew

DATE: ca. 80–90 CE

AUTHOR: Unknown

SETTING: The village culture of the Upper Galilee or lower Syria

ATTRIBUTION: Matthew, the tax collector, one of Jesus's disciples

AUDIENCE AND OCCASION: A predominantly Greek-speaking Jewish community of the Jesus movement in a dominantly Jewish cultural context. In the period after the first revolt, the community is being faced with new pressures from the emergence of the Pharisaic movement in the Galilean region, with the result that many Jews are now beginning to side with the Pharisees and the followers of Jesus are being marginalized.

OUTLINE

I. The Book of Generations and the Birth of the Messiah (1:1–2:23)

II. Book 1 (Galilee): Call of the Disciples and First Sermon (3:1–7:29)
Sermon on the Mount (5:1–7:27)

III. Book 2 (Galilee): First Miracles and Mission of the Twelve (8:1–10:42)
Sermon: Mission instructions (10:5–42)

IV. Book 3 (Galilee): Controversies and Rejection at Nazareth (11:1–13:58)
Sermon: Parables of the kingdom (13:1–52)

the Jews."[9] More specifically, in Jesus's final sermon Matthew links "their synagogues" with the Pharisees:

*[The Pharisees] love to have the place of honor at banquets and **the best seats in the synagogues,** and to be greeted with respect in the marketplaces, and to have people call them rabbi. But you are not to be called rabbi, for you have one teacher, and you are all students. . . . "Woe to **you,** scribes and **Pharisees,** hypocrites! . . . Thus you testify against yourselves that you are descendants of those who murdered the prophets. Fill up, then, the measure of your ancestors. You snakes, you brood of vipers! How can you escape being sentenced to hell? Therefore I send you prophets, sages, and scribes, some of whom you will kill and crucify, and some **you will flog in your synagogues** and pursue from town to town, so that upon you may come all the righteous blood shed on*

v. Book 4 (Beyond Galilee): Death of John; Jesus Predicts His Own Death (14:1–18:35)

Sermon: Repentance and forgiveness in the church (18:1–35)

vi. Book 5 (Judea): Triumphal Entry and Conflict with Pharisees (19:1–25:46)

Sermon: Woes vs. Pharisees (23:1–36)

Sermon: Apocalyptic discourse (24:1–51)

Sermon: Eschatological judgment (25:1–46)

vii. The Passion Narrative (26:1–28:20)

FURTHER READING

Balch, D. L. *Social History of the Matthean Community*. Minneapolis: Fortress, 1991.

Bornkamm, G., M. Barth, and H. J. Held. *Tradition and Interpretation in Matthew*. Philadelphia: Fortress, 1963.

Duling, D. C. "Matthew [Disciple]." *Anchor Bible Dictionary*. 4:618–22.

Hare, D. R. A. *The Theme of Jewish Persecution of Christians in the Gospel According to Matthew*. Cambridge: Cambridge University Press, 1967.

Harrington, D. *The Gospel of Matthew*. Sacra Pagina 1. Collegeville, MN: Michael Glazier/Liturgical Press, 1991.

Kingsbury, J. D. *Matthew: Structure, Christology, Kingdom*. Philadelphia: Fortress, 1975.

———. *Matthew as Story*. Philadelphia: Fortress, 1986.

Meier, J. P. "Matthew, Gospel of." *Anchor Bible Dictionary*. 4:622–41.

———. *The Vision of Matthew*. New York: Crossroad, 1979.

Overman, J. A. *Church and Community in Crisis: The Gospel According to Matthew*. Valley Forge, PA: Trinity Press International, 1996.

———. *Matthew's Gospel and Formative Judaism: The Social World of the Matthean Community*. Minneapolis: Fortress, 1990.

Saldarini, A. J. *Matthew's Christian-Jewish Community*. Chicago: University of Chicago Press, 1994.

Stendahl, K. *The School of St. Matthew*. Philadelphia: Fortress, 1968.

earth, from the blood of righteous Abel to the blood of Zechariah son of Barachiah, whom you murdered between the sanctuary and the altar. Truly I tell you, all this will come upon this generation. (Matt. 23:6–8, 29–36)

Again, this is a reflection of emergence of the rabbinic movement in the period after the destruction of Jerusalem.[10] An explicit parallel is found in the mission instructions to the disciples, which predict, "they will flog you in *their* synagogues" (Matt. 10:17).

Standing over against "their synagogues" is "the church" as the marker of the Matthean sect. Matthew is alone among the Gospels in using this term (once in Matt. 16:18 and twice in Matt. 18:17). The second of these passages is very telling, as it comes from Jesus's fourth sermon and concerns discipline and forgiveness within the "church." Jesus is speaking:

If another member [lit., brother] sins against you, go and point out the fault
when the two of you are alone. If the member listens to you, you have regained
that one. But if you are not listened to, take one or two others along with you,
so that every word may be confirmed by the evidence of two or three witnesses.
*If the member refuses to listen to them, tell it to the **church**; and if the offender*
*refuses to listen even to the **church**, let such a one be to you as **a Gentile and a***
***tax collector.** (Matt. 18:15–17)*

Here we have disciplinary regulations for a sectarian community that are
closely paralleled by those in the *Rule of the Community* from the Dead Sea
Scrolls. The sectarian group is thus called the "church," that is "congregation,"
as in traditional Jewish usage synonymous to "synagogue." But now these two
terms for congregations stand in opposition to one another. On the other hand,
a striking feature comes out when an offender is ousted, for then he is to be
shunned as "a Gentile and a tax collector." If being removed from the community's fellowship causes the offender to be labeled as "Gentile," then being *in*
the community can only be understood as being Jewish. Consequently, although Matthew's "church" is clearly at odds with the Pharisaic synagogues, it
still thinks of itself very much as a Jewish sect.

An additional clue to the social as well as geographical location of the
Matthean community comes from the episode that immediately precedes and
introduces this fourth sermon. It is not contained in any of the other Gospels
and thus reflects some distinctive experience of the Matthean community. It
concerns a question about Jesus posed to Peter: "Does your teacher not pay the
Temple tax?" Peter's answer is, "Yes, he does" (Matt. 17:24–25). What follows
then is a discussion between Peter and Jesus on this matter. Jesus first asks a riddle whose point is that the children of the king should *not* have to pay tribute;
that is, they really should not have to pay such a tax. But then Jesus tells Peter:
"However, so that we do not give offense to them, go to the sea and cast a hook;
take the first fish that comes up; and when you open its mouth, you will find a
coin (shekel); take that and give it to them for you and for me" (Matt. 17:27).

This seemingly minor episode is quite telling, for the half-shekel "Temple
tax" was what was appropriated by the Romans after the revolt as the *fiscus*
Iudaeus to pay war reparations to Rome (see Chapter 9). In addition to being a
punishment for the war, it was also, quite literally, a per capita tax on being Jewish. Only Jews had to pay it, and its collection was diligently monitored in the
Jewish homeland as a sign of submission to Rome. Thus, for Matthew's Jesus to

say "pay the tax" in order not to offend is the same as admitting to being Jewish too. It also points strongly at a location in or very near the homeland. On the other hand, the little riddle does hint at a growing rupture. Perhaps those gentile converts in the Matthean community, even if they had been circumcised and were Torah observant, were now beginning to question whether maintaining Jewish identity was really necessary or worth the trouble. Matthew's answer is a solid yes. Despite the tensions with other Jews, they were nonetheless still a Jewish sect.

We must conclude, therefore, that the Gospel of Matthew originated within a rather exclusively Jewish sect of the Jesus movement somewhere in the Upper Galilee or nearby. It had been in existence from before the war but was now beginning to find itself marginalized in the period of postwar reconstruction. The emergence of the Pharisaic movement as a new leadership, along with a large transplanted population from the south, meant that the earlier mission of the Jesus movement was now facing rejection and even persecution by Jewish neighbors. Local synagogues, now dominated by Pharisaic leaders, were becoming both the community centers and worship centers in the village culture of the Galilee. Matthew's response seeks to reinforce the weakened boundaries of his sectarian community by launching a polemic against this new Pharisaic leadership. Thus, for Matthean Jews there are tensions with other Jews, with earlier forms of the Jesus movement, and with their gentile converts. Matthew's "biography" is, in reality, a sectarian battleground in the changing social climate of the Jewish homeland.

The Gospel of Luke and Acts of the Apostles

Author, Date, and Setting

The traditional author of both the Gospel of Luke and Acts is Luke, the physician, a co-worker of Paul's.[11] That these works come from a follower of the Pauline tradition, and probably a gentile convert, is not disputed. Since all references to him in the Pauline corpus occur in so-called prison letters (Philippians and Philemon), the legend grew up that he had accompanied Paul to Rome and there wrote down his account of Paul's career sometime just before or after Paul's death in 64 CE.[12] There are several points in Acts at which the narrative shifts from third to first person, and these "we passages" are assumed by some to reflect the work of an actual traveling companion of Paul (see Acts 16:10–17; 20:5–15; 21:8–18; 27:1–16). As we have shown in the case of Paul's career, however, there are some notable differences between the account in Acts and that in Paul's own letters (see Chapter 7).

There are also problems of dating in light of current theories of Gospel relations, and especially the Two-Source Hypothesis, since the Gospel of Luke must be later than both Mark and Matthew, and thus no earlier than 80–85 CE (see Chapter 5). An earlier generation of scholars argued that Luke and Acts might have been written as late as the mid-second century or after, but this opposite extreme is no more attractive on historical grounds. In current New Testament scholarship, the dates given for Luke-Acts are usually 80–90. Even at this later date, some scholars still assume that the "historical" Luke was the author, but most do not.[13] A recent trend among scholars has seen the date edge slightly later, to about 90–100 CE or even later, and this now seems more likely.[14]

Similar questions surround the author's location. The Greek is of fairly high quality and filled with quotations and allusions to the Septuagint. A setting in Rome is a possibility, but rather unlikely. Because Acts makes quite a lot of the early days of the church in Antioch—where they were first called "Christians" (Acts 11:26; see Chapter 6)—many scholars have located the writing there. But the author shows far more direct awareness of local landmarks and events in the cities of the Aegean, especially Ephesus and Corinth. Given the author's attachment to Pauline tradition and strong sense of gentile mission, one of the cities of Paul, probably Ephesus, is preferable, but certainty is not possible. Ultimately, any conclusion about the authorship, date, or location is dependent on how one understands the genre and composition as well as the occasion and intention of the work.

A Two-Volume Narrative

Even though Luke and Acts are separated from one another in the New Testament canon and all extant manuscripts reflect this fact, scholars are now unanimous in the view that they were originally a single work. This view has given rise to the shorthand designation "Luke-Acts" to refer to the original, unitary form.

Several internal indicators show that the two parts of the work constitute a continuous narrative; they include linguistic and stylistic similarities, thematic continuities, and even parallel episodes or doublets occurring in the Gospel and

Acts. The most important single piece of evidence, however, is the presence in each part of an authorial prologue with important interconnections.

> *Since many have undertaken to set down an orderly account of the events that have been fulfilled among us, just as they were handed on to us by those who from the beginning were eyewitnesses and servants of the word, I too decided, after investigating everything carefully from the very first, to write an orderly account for you,* **most excellent Theophilus,** *so that you may know the truth concerning the things about which you have been instructed. (Luke 1:1–4)*

> *In the first book,* **O Theophilus,** *I wrote about all that Jesus did and taught from the beginning until the day when he was taken up to heaven after giving instructions through the Holy Spirit to the apostles whom he had chosen. (Acts 1:1–2)*

The fact that both prologues address the work to a person named Theophilus and that Acts refers to a "first book" dealing with the deeds and teachings of Jesus make the conclusion of a unitary composition inescapable. Multivolume historical works of this sort were quite common in antiquity, and the type of prologue found in Luke-Acts is quite typical.

The nature of the prologue also says something about the literary level of the work, since it would typically indicate a work that was formally "published." Publication in this sense means that the work was intentionally produced for wider distribution and adhered to certain literary conventions. In this regard the address to Theophilus again becomes important, since it was normal to dedicate such works to the patron who paid for the publication, meaning the costs of papyrus, ink, secretaries, and copyists and in many cases support for the author. For a work of any appreciable length, these costs could be substantial. The two-volume form of Luke-Acts is by far the longest work in the New Testament (by more than double) and one of the longest of any produced during the first two centuries of the Christian movement. Thus, there are much higher literary pretensions and expectations at work in this composition.

This literary self-consciousness brings us to the issue of the genre of Luke-Acts. The Gospels are generally considered to be part of the ancient literary genre known broadly as "lives." Although not governed by the same concerns as modern biography, these ancient "lives" were devoted to the words and deeds of important figures, including philosophers, emperors, rhetoricians, and religious leaders. An important parallel in Jewish tradition is the *Life of Moses,* a two-volume work composed by Philo of Alexandria in the early first century CE. Whereas this genre seems to fit well enough with the Gospel of Luke, Acts lacks the central figure and other features to qualify as a "life." Because it traces the rise of the early Christian movement for some thirty years or more, it has been likened more to the genre of ancient "history." In recent scholarship, however, it has been noted that there are many features of the story and the style, especially in the birth narrative or the travels of Paul, that seem to fit better with the ancient genre of the "novel" or "romance." Each of these genres contributes different features to the work. One must conclude finally that there was a conscious intent to transform the earlier Markan Gospel as a "life" into a "history" that continued through the early decades of the movement, but included were especially strong influences from novelistic literature as well.

Organization and Themes

Whereas Matthew substantially rearranges Mark's outline, the Gospel of Luke generally keeps the running order as it was in Mark and supplements with Q and other materials at various points along the way. There are, nonetheless, three key points at which the Lukan author substantially modifies the basic Markan outline.

The first of these, Luke 4:14–30, occurs at the very beginning of Jesus's public career in the Galilee. It opens with a very brief transitional statement (4:14–15), which is very close to the parallel moment at the beginning of Mark (1:14–15). But then Luke moves the story of Jesus's rejection at Nazareth from its later position in Mark (6:1–6) up to this point in the story and further elaborates the account by describing his reading from the prophet Isaiah followed by a messianic pronouncement: "Today this scripture has been fulfilled in your hearing" (4:16–21). There follows another, more critical statement of Jesus, which prompts his hometown folks to become enraged, run him out of town, and nearly kill him (4:22–30). The importance of this shift is that it allows Luke's Jesus to be open to Gentiles from the very beginning of his ministry. It is also linked thematically to the first sermon of Peter on the Day of Pentecost (Acts 2).

The second substantially reworked portion is Luke 9:51–18:14. This lengthy part of the narrative is sometimes called "Luke's Special Section." It is the parallel to the section in Mark 10:1–52, in which Jesus turns from his "ministry beyond Galilee" toward Jerusalem. Luke now transforms this short transitional section into a major travel narrative, so that Jesus teaches his disciples and others while he is en route to Jerusalem. This is where the Lukan author inserts most of the Q sayings and other uniquely Lukan material, including some of the most famous parables (the good Samaritan and the prodigal son). This section also includes the unique episode of a mission by seventy disciples of Jesus, which again is directed at Gentiles as well as Jews (10:1–20).[15] Another effect of this section is to have Jesus focused on Jerusalem from a much earlier point in his ministry.

Luke 24:1–53 is the third section that represents a striking change. The Passion narrative in Luke again follows Mark very closely until it gets down to the end, specifically in narrating the postresurrection appearances. In sharp contrast to Mark and Matthew, instead of having the disciples "go to Galilee" to witness the resurrected Jesus, Luke has all the appearances in and around Jerusalem (cf. Mark 16:7; Matt. 28:7; Luke 24:6). In fact, the "road to Emmaus" story (24:13–35) has the effect of driving the scattering disciples back to Jerusalem. This sets up two final scenes for the Gospel of Luke. In one Jesus appears to the disciples in the same upper room where they had held the last supper and dines with them (24:36–49); then he instructs them on the proclamation they will soon witness "beginning at Jerusalem" (24:47). In the other, Jesus's ascension, which is only narrated by Luke-Acts, is set on a summit outside Jerusalem (24:50–53; cf. Acts 1:9–12).

The emphasis on Jerusalem created by these last two changes is very important narratively and thematically, since it sets the stage for the opening section of Acts, where Jesus tells the disciples explicitly not to leave Jerusalem (Acts 1:4–5). Consequently, the instructions in Acts 1:8, "But you will receive power when the Holy Spirit has come upon you; and you will be my witnesses in Jerusalem, in all Judea and Samaria, and to the ends of the earth," is the natural continuation of this scene and is generally viewed as the geographical outline for the narrative of Acts. On this basis we can see the continuity of the narrative through the two volumes (see Box 10.3).

An Epochal View of History: Historiography in Luke-Acts

Other thematic interests of Luke-Acts revolve around its use of historical materials and its *historiography*, meaning its thematic and theological views on history. It is ironic that the work is so hard to pin down on date and location, given the fact that the Lukan author is by far the most interested among the Gospel writers in locating the story of Jesus (and similarly the early church in

---

BOX 10.3
The Book of Luke-Acts

DATE: ca. 90–100/110 CE

AUTHOR: Uncertain

ATTRIBUTION: Luke, the physician, a traveling companion of Paul

SETTING: Ephesus, Corinth (or Antioch?)

AUDIENCE AND OCCASION: A predominantly gentile audience in the tradition of the churches of Paul from the Aegean region. As a late expression of the second generation, the work begins to reflect on the history of the movement and how far it has come since the days when the church was founded. This reflection allows for a further apologetic interest in promoting tolerance for the Christians in the larger Roman political arena and a concomitant distancing from Jews.

OUTLINE

Part I: The Gospel of Luke

A. Prologue (1:1–4)

B. Birth Narrative and Ministry of John (1:5–3:22)
   <Interlude: the genealogy (3:23–38)>

C. The Ministry of Jesus in and Around Galilee (4:1–9:50)
   1. Temptation (4:1–13)
   2. Rejection at Nazareth (4:14–30)
   3. Wider Galilean ministry (4:31–9:16)
   4. Confession at Caesarea and Passion predictions (9:17–50)

D. The Journey Toward Jerusalem (9:51–19:27)
   1. Samaria and the mission of the seventy (9:51–10:20)
   2. Instructions to the disciples (10:21–13:35)
   3. Teaching in parables at a dinner (14:1–18:14)
   4. Further teachings on the road to Jerusalem (18:15–19:27)

E. Jesus Enters Jerusalem and Teaches (19:28–21:38)

F. Passion Narrative (22:1–24:6)

G. Postresurrection Appearances in and Around Jerusalem (24:7–53)

Part II: The Acts of the Apostles

A. Prologue (1:1–2)

B. Final Instructions in Jerusalem and Ascension (1:3–11)

C. The Disciples Wait in Jerusalem (1:12–26)

D. Arrival of the Spirit and Peter's Sermon on Pentecost (2:1–42)

E. The Church in Jerusalem (3:1–5:41)

F. Persecution in Jerusalem Scatters the Church (6:1–8:3)

G. The Church in Judea, Samaria, and Beyond (8:4–11:30)

   1. Disciples go out to Judea and Samaria (8:4–40)

   2. The "conversion" of Paul (9:1–31)

   3. The first gentile convert (9:32–11:18)

   4. The church in Antioch (11:19–30)

H. Persecution in Jerusalem (12:1–25)

I. The Missions of Paul: The Church Goes "to the Ends of the Earth" (13:1–28:31)

   1. First journey and Jerusalem conference (13:1–15:35)

   2. Second and third journeys (15:36–19:20)

   3. Arrest in Jerusalem and journey to Rome (19:21–28:31)

FURTHER READING

Barrett, C. K. *Luke the Historian in Recent Study*. London: Epworth, 1962.

Conzelmann, H. *The Theology of St. Luke*. New York: Harper & Row, 1961.

Esler, P. F. *Community and Gospel in Luke-Acts*. Cambridge: Cambridge University Press, 1987.

Fitzmyer, J. A. *The Gospel According to Luke*. Anchor Bible. New York: Doubleday, 1981.

Hengel, M. *Acts and the History of Earliest Christianity*. Philadelphia: Fortress, 1979.

Johnson, L. T. "Luke-Acts, Book of." *Anchor Bible Dictionary*. 4:403–20.

Keck, L. E. *Studies in Luke-Acts*. Nashville, TN: Abingdon, 1966.

Marshall, I. H. *Luke: Historian and Theologian*. 2d ed. Exeter: Exeter University Press, 1979.

Moessner, D. P. *Lord of the Banquet: The Literary and Theological Significance of the Lukan Travel Narrative*. Minneapolis: Fortress, 1989.

Pervo, R. I. *Profit with Delight: The Literary Genre of the Acts of the Apostles*. Philadelphia: Fortress, 1987.

Plümacher, E. "Luke as Historian." *Anchor Bible Dictionary*. 4:397–402.

Talbert, C. H. *Perspectives on Luke-Acts*. Danville, VA: Intervarsity, 1978.

Tannehill, R. C. *The Narrative Unity of Luke-Acts*. 2 vols. Philadelphia: Fortress, 1986, 1990.

Tyson, J. B. *Images of Judaism in Luke-Acts*. Columbia: University of South Carolina Press, 1992.

Wilson, S. G. *The Gentiles and the Gentile Mission in Luke-Acts*. Cambridge: Cambridge University Press, 1973.

Acts) in Roman historical terms. The author's emphasis on recognizable people, places, and events is akin to that of Josephus, who was a contemporary.

Emphasis on history is not the same as saying that the work is historically accurate, however. In fact, most historians of the ancient world were rather loose when it came to historical accuracy. This problem has already been noted in relation to Luke's dating of Jesus's birth at the time of the census in 6 CE (see Chapters 2 and 5, Box 2.5). Even Josephus is notoriously difficult at times for precise historical dates or chronological sequence of events, and he has been shown to color the stories to suit his own personal or religious interests (see Chapter 9). Thus, it becomes very important to identify the author's *historiographical* agenda in order to understand why the story is being told in a certain way.

The changes already noted in the outline of Luke-Acts are but one clue to its historiography. Two themes are at the center of the story: the role of Jerusalem and the role of the Holy Spirit in directing key moments in the narrative. These elements can be seen most clearly by looking at the first sermon of Jesus in Luke and the first sermon of Peter in Acts:

> *When [Jesus] came to Nazareth, where he had been brought up, he went to the synagogue on the sabbath day, as was his custom. He stood up to read, and the scroll of the prophet Isaiah was given to him. He unrolled the scroll and found the place where it was written:* **"The Spirit of the Lord is upon me,** *because he has anointed me to bring good news to the poor. He has sent me to proclaim release to the captives and recovery of sight to the blind, to let the oppressed go free,* **to proclaim the year of the Lord's favor."** *And he rolled up the scroll, gave it back to the attendant, and sat down. The eyes of all in the synagogue were fixed on him. Then he began to say to them,* **"Today this scripture has been fulfilled in your hearing."** *(Luke 4:16–21)*

> *But Peter, standing with the eleven, raised his voice and addressed them, "Men of Judea and all who live in Jerusalem, let this be known to you, and listen to what I say. Indeed, these are not drunk, as you suppose, for it is only nine o'clock in the morning. No, this is what was spoken through the prophet Joel: 'In the* **last days** *it will be, God declares, that* **I will pour out my Spirit** *upon all flesh, and your sons and your daughters shall prophesy, and your young men shall see visions, and your old men shall dream dreams. Even upon my slaves, both men and women, in those days I will pour out my Spirit; and they shall prophesy. And I will show portents in the heaven above and signs on the earth below, blood, and fire, and smoky mist. The sun shall be turned to darkness and the moon to blood, before the coming of the Lord's great and glo-*

rious day. Then everyone who calls on the name of the Lord shall be saved.'"
(Acts 2:14–21)

These two sermons are thematically parallel. In both cases we have a "prophetic" event: in Luke 4 it is the fact that Jesus opens the scroll to find just this passage;[16] in Acts it is the descent of the Spirit and the tongues miracle (Acts 2:1–4). In both cases the speaker points to the event and says, either directly or indirectly, that what has just been witnessed is the fulfillment of apocalyptic expectations. In Luke the fulfillment is the arrival of the anointed one, the messiah, in the person of Jesus and his proclamation of the "acceptable year of the Lord"; in Acts the miracle is explained by Peter as the fulfillment of a group of prophecies concerning the "last days."[17] Thus, both sermons are made to revolve around themes of messianic end times, the pouring out of the Spirit, and the fulfillment of prophecy.

These two scenes are pregnant with theological significance for Lukan historiography. They serve to divide the narrative as well as the framework of eschatological time into three main ages or epochs (see Box 10.4). For this reason it has been called an "epochal view of history" as well as a "history of salvation."[18] Both characterizations accurately reflect the theological dimensions of the way history is reconceptualized around the figure of Jesus and current world events. It will prove to be one of the most important reinterpretations of eschatology for the subsequent development of Christian theology and self-understanding.

Eschatology in Luke-Acts

To understand the import of the Lukan scheme, we must remember that virtually all the apocalyptic understandings of the first and second generation of the Jesus movement were dominated by imminent eschatological expectations very much in line with traditional Jewish apocalyptic thinking. In this context, the character and identity of the messiah figure were inextricably bound to his role in ushering in the eschaton. The stark saying of Mark 9:1 reflects this basic idea, as Jesus predicts that the eschatological kingdom will arrive during that very generation: "Truly I tell you, there are some standing here who will not taste death until they see that the kingdom of God has come with power." Of course, this leaves open to interpretation what is meant by the "kingdom" and how it will come about. Even so, this is a very traditional form of imminent eschatology. Throughout the first generation of the movement, this imminent expectation continued unabated (cf. 1 Thess. 1:9–10; Rom. 13:11–12) and

BOX 10.4
The Epochal View of History in Luke–Acts

1. The Epoch of the Law and Prophets
(from Abraham to John the Baptist)

*"The law and the prophets were in effect until John came;
since then the good news of the kingdom of God is proclaimed,
and everyone tries to enter it by force."*
(Luke 16:16)

Ends with the arrest and death of John the Baptist (Luke 3:19–20).
Note placement of Lukan genealogy as interlude (Luke 3:23–38).

2. The Messianic Epoch of the Proclamation of the Kingdom
(period of Jesus's ministry and death)

*"The Spirit of the Lord is upon me . . . to proclaim
the year of the Lord's favor."*
(Luke 4:18–19)

The beginning of Jesus's ministry with "Sermon and Rejection at Nazareth"
(Luke 4:14–30). Ends with the ascension (Acts 1:9–11).

3. The Epoch of the Kingdom in the Church
(beginning from the Day of Pentecost)

*"So when they had come together, they asked him, 'Lord, is this
the time when you will restore the kingdom to Israel?' He replied,
'It is not for you to know the times or periods that the Father has set
by his own authority. But you will receive power when the Holy
Spirit has come upon you; and you will be my witnesses in Jerusalem,
in all Judea and Samaria, and to the ends of the earth.'"*
(Acts 1:6–8)

The arrival of the Spirit on Pentecost (Acts 2:1–16).
Peter's Pentecost sermon; the prophecy fulfilled (Acts 2:17–47).

REFERENCES: This basic scheme was first proposed by H. Conzelmann in *The Theology of St. Luke* (New York: Harper & Row, 1961), 16–17. It has been revised in more recent works, such as that of J. A. Fitzmyer, *The Gospel According to Luke*, 2 vols. Anchor Bible (New York: Doubleday, 1981, 1985), 2:181–92. More recently, D. Moessner, in *Lord of the Banquet: The Literary and Theological Significance of the Lukan Travel Narrative* (Minneapolis: Fortress, 1989), makes a convincing argument that this scheme must be seen in the light of older theological understandings of Israel's history, notably the so-called Deuteronomistic theology.

undoubtedly contributed to their consternation over the destruction of Jerusalem, as we saw in Chapter 9.

But what happens when the time begins to drag on or the apparent signs of Jesus's return fail to materialize? This crisis of expectation, usually called the "delay of the *parousia*," is most pronounced in the period after the first revolt, when Jews were more generally having to wrestle with what went wrong. They had thought that the war was the sign that the kingdom was about to arrive. This view is precisely what the apocalyptic discourse of the Gospel of Mark was addressing (see Chapter 9). The answer given there was that these purported signs associated with the war were a deception (Mark 13:21–23), but that the whole episode, including the destruction of the Temple, was itself the true "sign" that the return of Jesus was still imminent (Mark 13:24–29). In fact, Mark says it is the "generation" that witnessed the war that will also see the *parousia* (13:30–32). Although this reinterpretation preserves the imminent expectation, it nonetheless allows for the time to be protracted. It is thus called an "imminent delayed eschatology."

Luke-Acts takes a rather different form of reinterpretation by saying, in effect, that the "kingdom" has *already* arrived on the Day of Pentecost. In addition to the sermon of Peter that gives this reading of the events, it is also set up in the thematic statement of Acts 1:6, when the disciples ask, "Lord, is this the time when you will restore the kingdom to Israel?" Jesus's answer is an anticipation of the events of Pentecost and the spread of the church that follow in Acts: "It is not for you to know the times or periods that the Father has set by his own authority. But you will receive power when the Holy Spirit has come upon you; and you will be my witnesses in Jerusalem, in all Judea and Samaria, and to the ends of the earth" (Acts 1:7–8). Thus, the events of Pentecost are explicitly equated with both the arrival of the kingdom (Acts 1:6) and the arrival of the eschaton, or "last days" (Acts 2:17).

Yet, these events are clearly *not* to be equated with the return of Jesus. Luke's version of the apocalyptic discourse excises any such expectation; it refers only to the destruction of Jerusalem (Luke 21:8–36) as a punishment for Israel's sins. As a result, the *parousia*, or return of Jesus, is now pushed off to a more distant and unspecified point in the future in a manner very similar to what one sees in some rabbinic reinterpretations. On the one hand, it is very Pauline, in the sense that it picks up the dual moments of the eschatological "already but not yet." On the other hand, this reinterpretation allows the imminent expectations to be fulfilled, while the final eschatological consummation remains a future expectation. Any time lag in the interim now becomes less problematic, and in later appropriations of the Lukan scheme, this interim period becomes theologically institutionalized in an emerging Christian self-understanding as the age of the church. An additional implication of this shift is that the eventual return of Jesus is now decoupled from the arrival of an earthly kingdom; it will become instead the "last judgment" and the arrival of a heavenly kingdom. This form of eschatology, therefore, has been called either a "present and future eschatology" or "inaugurated eschatology."

Roman Apologetics and Christian Self-Definition

The author of Luke-Acts stands on a new plateau in the development of the Jesus movement. The effort to write a history of the movement is also a new moment of self-definition for those in the movement, or at least those who will read Luke-Acts. The emphatic use of Roman historical persons and events is also part of an emerging self-consciousness to place the Jesus movement on the world stage of the Roman Empire. Still, its epochal view of history and picture of the growth of the church were clearly written for insiders. This would seem only natural in writing to predominantly gentile followers in the last decade of the first century who now have begun to call themselves "Christians."

This new self-consciousness begs other questions for Christians living in Greek and Roman cities: Isn't this a Jewish sect? Wasn't the founder a renegade Jew who was executed by the Roman authorities? Aren't these the same people who only a few years before rebelled against the authority of Rome? In some ways, these are the same kinds of questions that Josephus had to address, and his "histories" likewise function as apologetics. In the case of Josephus, however, the apologetic is for Judaism more generally; in the case of Luke-Acts we have the first apologetic for the Jesus movement as such. This kind of apologetic literature was meant to address the perceptions and prejudices of outsiders, but not directly. It was written primarily for insiders living on the margins of the larger Greco-Roman culture whose neighbors might have had such perceptions and prejudices. Luke-Acts now serves as a kind of apologetic instruction for answering the questions and in so doing also shapes a new sense of Christian self-definition.[19]

CHAPTER ELEVEN

Accommodation and Resistance

A Footing in the Roman World

The two-volume history known as Luke-Acts was written near the end of the first century. Now another generation was drawing to a close. Most if not all of the apostles were now dead. The first Jewish revolt against Rome was a distant, though still painful, memory. Yet the reinterpretation of imminent eschatology that took place in the aftermath of the revolt helped to deal with the trauma. The widening gulf with other forms of Judaism forced much of the Jesus movement to establish a firmer footing in the Greco-Roman world. Christians, as many were now called, were becoming more recognizable in the larger cities from the Greek East to Rome. A growing percentage of these Christians were ethnically gentile rather than Jewish, and they were beginning to see themselves in a new light—as citizens of the Roman Empire. Even so, there was still a strong current of traditional apocalyptic rhetoric about the evils of the world. Like other diaspora Jews, they still faced the dilemma of accommodation or isolation. The loss of the first generation of leaders combined with the challenges posed by these new cultural horizons left a void. Now they began to look to the past, to the leaders of an earlier day, for answers.

In part the synoptic Gospels provided such answers by shaping new understandings of the teachings of Jesus for their respective communities, whether as Jewish sects or Christian cults. For day-to-day guidance on living in the Roman world, however, many looked again to Paul or Peter. The problem was that they were gone, and there were new questions to be answered. Strikingly absent was the living authority of a Peter, who had walked with Jesus, or Paul, who had claimed direct revelation from God. Gradually church offices would evolve to provide such leadership, but that would take more time to be fully realized.

In the interim, the memories of those who knew Peter and Paul would have to do, and beyond them new legends and oral traditions would carry their legacy forward for a new generation of followers. Another response was to collect the individual letters of Paul together to circulate among those churches that did not have their own or to form a kind of guidebook of his writings on different topics. The process had already begun just about the same time that Luke-Acts was being written. Eventually this process would give rise to the formation of the New Testament canon. The stories of Paul in Acts were part of this process too. Luke-Acts was a product of the "Pauline school."

The Pauline School

The *Pauline school* refers to the later phases of development in Paul's churches or among those who continued his theological tradition. It also refers to those writings produced in the name of Paul but not actually written by Paul himself or during his lifetime (see Box 7.1). As noted earlier in Chapter 7, letter writing was a widespread and highly conventionalized practice in the Roman world. Letter writing was taught in the gymnasium, the second level of Greek education. One of the keys, as we saw in each of the letters of Paul, was that the letter should be properly suited to the situation. In addition to handbooks on epistolary style, one common mode of instruction in letter writing was having students imagine situations for which a letter might be written or write in imitation of a famous figure from history in addressing a particular situation. These school exercises, some of which are preserved among the papyri, show that the production of fictitious letters was not uncommon.

At the same time, the generally positive attitude of the ancient world, Jewish and pagan alike, toward writing pseudepigraphically, that is, in the name of some long-dead person, led to the production of collections of fictitious letters. Much like Plato composing fictional dialogues between Socrates and his disciples, other disciples wrote fictional letters in the name of Socrates, Diogenes, Crates, and other famous philosophers of old. The goal seems to have been to express the ideas of a particular school of philosophy by writing letters in the name of one of its famous teachers. This was especially important, it seems, in the case of the Cynics, who were not known for writing systematic philosophical treatises. Their teachings were largely unwritten and preserved in the form of oral reports. Later production of fictional letters was one means of creating a written corpus of their instructions.

Since Paul was known as a writer of letters and not, on the whole, of systematic treatises, the process of writing in his name seems to have grown up by the latter part of the first century. Some of these later letters seem to be much closer to Paul in both spirit and date, while others seem to reflect a greater distance and more manifest differences in situation and tone. Generally the documents of the Pauline school fall into two groups based on scholarly discussion over their authenticity and date. The earlier group, where authenticity is still debated, is discussed here: Colossians, Ephesians, and 2 Thessalonians. The later group, comprising the so-called Pastoral Epistles (1 and 2 Timothy and Titus), for which Pauline authorship is more widely doubted, will be discussed in Chapter 16.

Colossians

Of all the debated letters, Colossians is the closest to Paul, if it is not actually by Paul himself. Like all of the Pauline school documents, it explicitly claims to be by Paul in the opening address, and the form is quite similar to that of the genuine letters, at least at the beginning and end (see Box 11.1). Internal references, especially those to Onesimus and Archippus (4:9, 17), rather clearly link the recipients in Colossae with the letter to Philemon, and this view was affirmed in later tradition.[1] In fact, a number of Paul's co-workers also mentioned in the concluding salutations (Epaphras, Mark, Aristarchus, Demas, and Luke; see Col. 4:10–14) show up in Philemon 23–24. Consequently, it was once thought that the two letters were written simultaneously, with Colossians addressed to the entire church and Philemon addressed to the particular situation of Onesimus. If so, this would place the date of writing in 55–56 and the location in Ephesus.

Yet this very similarity to Philemon begins to raise some questions, since other internal references seem to assume some time has passed. For example, in Colossians the assumed situation of Onesimus, who is called "the faithful and beloved brother, who is one of yourselves" (Col. 4:9), seems to imply that he has been a member of the church for some time but has most recently been

BOX 11.1

The Letter to the Colossians

DATE: ca. 70–80 CE (or ca. 85–95)[1]

AUTHOR: Unknown

LOCATION: Ephesus (probable)

ATTRIBUTION: Paul

AUDIENCE AND OCCASION: A Pauline congregation somewhere in Asia Minor, perhaps Ephesus itself. The "letter" serves primarily as ethical exhortation for living in the Roman world based on baptismal symbols. It was probably written after Paul's death to carry on the Pauline legacy.

OUTLINE

   I. Greeting (1:1–2)

  II. Thanksgiving (1:3–8)

 III. Body (1:9–2:5)

 IV. Exhortation (2:6–4:6)

  V. Closing (4:7–18)

FURTHER READING

Barth, M., and H. Blanke. *Colossians*. Anchor Bible. New York: Doubleday, 1994.

Burgess, J. "Colossians." In *Ephesians, Colossians, 2 Thessalonians, the Pastoral Epistles*. Proclamation Commentaries. Philadelphia: Fortress, 1978. Pp. 41–71.

Dunn, J. D. G. *The Epistles to the Colossians and Philemon*. New International Greek Testament Commentary. Grand Rapids, MI: Eerdmans, 1996.

Furnish, V. P. "Colossians, Epistle to the." *Anchor Bible Dictionary*. 1:1090–96.

Gnilka, J. *Der Kolosserbrief*. Freiburg: Herder, 1980.

Lindemann, A. "Die Gemeinde von 'Kolossä': Erwägungen zum *Sitz im Leben* eines deuteropaulinischen Briefes." *Wort und Dienst* 16 (1981): 111–34.

Lohse, E. *Colossians and Philemon*. Hermeneia. Philadelphia: Fortress, 1971.

Martin, R. P. *Colossians and Philemon*. New Century Bible. Grand Rapids, MI: Eerdmans, 1973.

Meeks, W. A., and F. O. Francis. *Conflict at Colossae*. Missoula, MT: Scholars Press, 1973.

O'Brien, P. T. *Colossians and Philemon*. Word Biblical Commentary 44. Waco, TX: Word, 1982.

Sanders, E. P. "Literary Dependence in Colossians." *Journal of Biblical Literature* 85 (1966): 28–45.

---

[1]See the discussion of Ephesians and Box 11.2.

working with Paul and is just now returning.[2] The situation of others has also changed. In Philemon Epaphras is Paul's "fellow prisoner" and Aristarchus is mentioned as a co-worker. In Colossians, Aristarchus is Paul's "fellow prisoner," while Epaphras is said to be "one of yourselves, a slave of Christ" (4:12) and the one who founded the churches in Colossae (1:7–8) and Laodicea (cf. 4:12, 15). He is now with Paul, but not actually in prison. All of this suggests that, if genuine, Colossians was written from a different imprisonment than the one that produced the letter to Philemon—thus Caesarea or Rome—and yet no reference is made to the intervening events that must have transpired.

Some scholars have proposed scenarios to solve this dilemma and affirm Pauline authorship, but most now take this evidence together with other linguistic, stylistic, and theological differences to show that Colossians was written sometime later, probably after Paul's death. In particular, both the Christ hymn of Colossians 1:15–20 and the errant teachings criticized in Colossians 2:16–18 seem to reflect later theological developments. Even so, the theological foundation affirmed as what was heard from Paul (Col. 2:1–6) does indeed seem to be characteristically Pauline and of a relatively early sort, especially in its use of baptismal terminology and symbolism (2:11–13; 3:1, 5, 9–12). Thus, if the letter was not written by Paul, it may be dated relatively soon after his death, probably in the 70s and from Ephesus or another Pauline congregation in Asia Minor. A relatively early date is favored by most scholars who do not think the letter was written by Paul, based on the fact that the Ephesian letter shows knowledge of Colossians. On the other hand, some scholars see Colossians and Ephesians as coming from a similar time and context somewhat later (a discussion of Ephesians follows below).

But what would be the reason for writing such a letter in Paul's name? Early theories made much of the so-called heresy implied in Colossians 2:8–23. It warns against "philosophy and empty deceit . . . according to the elemental spirits of the universe (*kosmos*)" (2:8) and against some apparent false teacher who claims visionary powers and insists that the Colossians practice "self-abasement and worship of angels" (2:18). Thus, it seems to follow ascetic practices and cosmological or astral symbols. Nonetheless, it is not possible to identify the so-called opponents as either Jewish or some early form of Gnostic heresy. Whatever its source, it is a far different problem from that faced by Paul in Galatians or 2 Corinthians. On the other hand, the amount of space devoted by Colossians to refuting these false teachings is rather small, and they almost all occur in the early part of the letter in the context of affirming the true teaching that had been received "from Paul." This contrast, then, is used to issue an exhortation to walk according to these true teachings (Col. 2:6–7).

Rather than a polemic against heretics, then, the real purpose of Colossians seems to be an extended exhortation based on early Pauline baptismal symbols, such as dying and rising with Christ (2:11–13) and "putting off the old nature" and "putting on the new" (3:9–10). These symbols are punctuated in 3:11 with a recitation of the baptismal reunification formula (see Chapter 8). These basic patterns of early baptismal ritual are then used to inculcate recognizable forms of ethical instruction through lists of vices (3:5–9) and virtues (3:12–17). These lead directly into a series of instructions on household management and duties by addressing relations between husbands and wives, parents and children, and masters and slaves (3:18–4:1). These exhortations are then summed up as follows: "Conduct yourselves wisely toward outsiders, making the most of the time. Let your speech always be gracious, seasoned with salt, so that you may know how you ought to answer everyone" (Col. 4:5–6). In other words, a primary function of this ethical exhortation is to address issues of Christians living in the pagan world. This feature is seen most clearly in the "household duty code" (3:18–4:1), which will be discussed further below since it also figures prominently in Ephesians and 1 Peter.

One other distinctive feature of Colossians is the way it portrays Paul's imprisonment and suffering, even in the closing words of the document: "Remember my chains" (4:18). Of course, the real Paul was not bashful about his sufferings and imprisonment for Christ, but in Colossians they seem to take on an added dimension as somehow vicarious for the church (1:24–27).

These rather un-Pauline affirmations of Paul's role also offer a rationale for following the ethical instructions that dominate Colossians. As a result, the attitude toward Paul sounds much like an early form of veneration after his death. Thus, the occasion and purpose of the document, couched as a letter from Paul himself, function as baptismal catechism and exhortation for Christians living in the Roman world, so that the community might carry on the memory and tradition of Paul. We know, however, that the city of Colossae was virtually destroyed by an earthquake in 60–61 CE. It is likely that the document was produced to serve the needs of a different congregation, perhaps in Laodicea (cf. Col. 4:13, 15–16) or, more likely, in Ephesus itself.

Ephesians

The so-called letter to the Ephesians is neither a real letter, nor was it addressed to Ephesus. Its occasion and composition thus merit close scrutiny, because it represents an important step in the later Pauline tradition with strong similarities to developments in Luke-Acts. Moreover, Ephesians seems to be based in large measure on Colossians.[3] Similarities of phrasing and theological ideas not found in other letters of Paul run throughout. A striking similarity to Colossians occurs in the final reference to Tychicus, who is supposedly carrying the letter:

Ephesians 6:21–22	*Colossians 4:7–8*
So that you also may know about me, *what I am doing,* Tychicus will tell you everything He is a beloved brother and a faithful minister in the Lord.	Tychicus will tell you everything about me. He is a beloved brother, a faithful minister, *and fellow servant* in the Lord.
I am sending him to you for this very purpose, so that you may know how we are, and so that he may encourage your hearts.	I am sending him to you for this very purpose, so that you may know how we are, and so that he may encourage your hearts.

These two statements are nearly verbatim in the Greek.[4] Given the close relationship between the two documents in both style and theology, we must conclude that either both documents are by Paul or both are pseudonymous. The weight of the evidence points to the latter.

Two basic scenarios can explain the many verbal similarities between Colossians and Ephesians. The first is that the author of Ephesians had a copy of Colossians and, thinking it a genuine letter of Paul, used it to give the new work a more Pauline flavor. This is the view taken by most scholars, even those who would not consider Colossians to be authentic. Hence the basis for the earlier dating assigned to Colossians (in the 70s) by these scholars. They date Ephesians to the late 80s or 90s and suggest a probable writing location of Ephesus.[5] That both Clement of Rome and Ignatius of Antioch seem to show knowledge of it would further indicate that it was circulating by the end of the first century.

The second scenario is that Colossians and Ephesians were written at about the same time, and perhaps even by the same person, as part of a larger effort to carry on the legacy of Paul. In this view, the date of Colossians would shift later, to the time of Ephesians, that is, in the 80s or 90s and close in time to the writing of Luke-Acts.[6] It is even possible that what we call "Ephesians" was originally penned as the companion letter to the Laodiceans mentioned in Colossians 4:16: "And when this letter has been read among you, have it read also in the church of the Laodiceans; and see that you read also the letter from Laodicea." In fact, Marcion, who was in Asia in the 130s and compiled an early collection of Paul's letters, identified it as this Laodicean letter.[7]

The problem is that the name Ephesus does not appear in the opening address of the document in the earliest manuscripts (see Fig. 11.1). It reads simply: "To the saints who are also faithful in Christ Jesus" (Eph. 1:1). This fact is confirmed by the arguments of both Marcion and his opponents. The title "To the

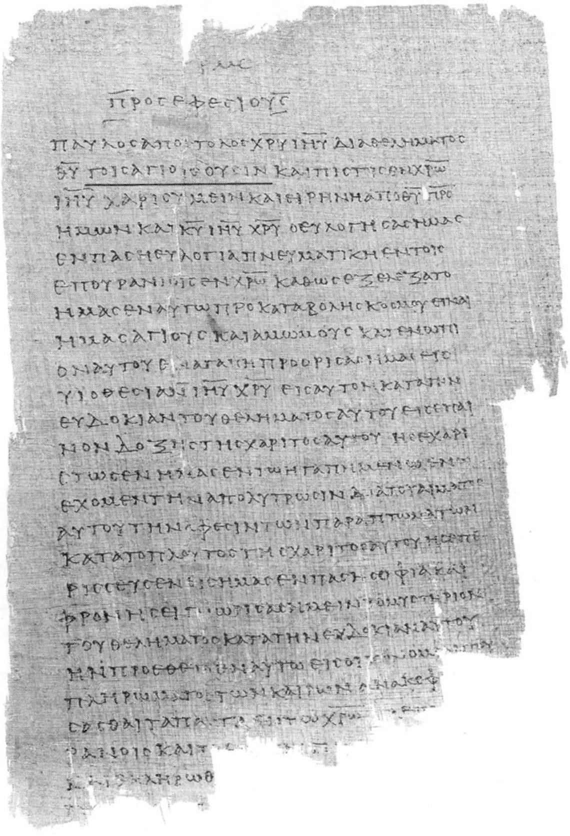

The title: [Page] 146
"To the Ephesians"

The letter address:
*". . . to the saints who are
also faithful in Christ Jesus"*
(Eph. 1:1)

Even though the title shows
that this letter had come to
be associated with Ephesus
by ca. 200 CE, the words *en
Epheso* ("in Ephesus") are
missing from the actual address. In some later manuscripts they will be inserted
following the words "saints
who are" (*tois hagiois ousin*)
in line two, as underlined on
the photo.

FIGURE 11.1

The first page of the letter to the Ephesians from one of the earliest surviving books of the letters of
Paul, 𝔓⁴⁶ (ca. 200 CE; Michigan Papyrus 6238, page 146 [leaf 75 recto]. (Used by permission of the
Papyrology Collection, Graduate Library, The University of Michigan)

Ephesians" was added sometime in the later second century, probably because
it was associated with the collection of Paul's letters assembled in Ephesus
around the end of the first century. Only later still were the words "in Ephesus"
added to the address in Ephesians 1:1. Even so, for the sake of simplicity in our
following discussion, we continue the usual practice of calling it Ephesians.

Ephesians is not typical of Paul's letters in form, style, or theological language.[8] Stylistically, it is characterized by lengthy sentences that pile numerous
synonyms together for ornamental effect and abstract tone in a way uncharac-
teristic of Paul. In the Greek the first sentence alone runs from 1:3 to 1:14, while
the second sentence goes from 1:15 to 1:23. The standard epistolary features and

formal conventions found so consistently in Paul's genuine letters (and retained to a greater extent in Colossians) are only used in limited ways in Ephesians, being restricted to two verses at the beginning (1:1–2) and four verses at the end (6:21–24), which include the reference to Tychicus. The use of the thanksgiving (1:16) and exhortation (4:1) formulas are superficial gestures to emulate Pauline epistolary style, but they introduce more abstract discussions. Instead, Ephesians is an extended treatise or homily on the place of the church in God's cosmic plan of salvation (1:15–3:21) and an ethical exhortation for those in the church (4:1–6:20; see Box 11.2).

The outlook on the church is an important development in the theology of Ephesians. No longer thought of as distinct congregations or house churches of the people of God, "the church" is now an abstract entity that was ordained to come into existence as part of God's plan for the ages. Using language drawn from the hymn of Colossians 1:15–20, Ephesians calls the church the "body of Christ" and Christ its head because of his cosmic act in bringing salvation:

> *God put this power to work in Christ when he raised him from the dead and seated him at his right hand in the heavenly places, far above all rule and authority and power and dominion, and above every name that is named, not only in this age but also in the age to come. And he has put all things under his feet and has made him the head over all things for the church, which is his body, the fullness of him who fills all in all. (Eph. 1:20–23)*

The church now becomes the place of reunion and reconciliation between Jews and Gentiles by breaking down "the dividing wall of hostility" (Eph. 2:14), but this means that the church is also coming to be thought of as something new and distinct from Judaism.

The metaphor of the church as a body, of course, has roots in Paul's thought based on the baptismal reunification formula (1 Cor. 12:12–14); however, Ephesians and Colossians extend this idea into more highly regimented ethical instruction. Again following Colossians, Ephesians begins its ethical exhortation by using baptismal symbols to stress unity, but unity is maintained by understanding one's proper place in the body (Eph. 4:1–16). The ritual symbols of "putting off" and "putting on" are again used to distinguish the vices of the old life from the virtues of the new (Eph. 4:22–26; cf. Col. 3:9–12). Ethics are understood as the "walk of life" that comes with baptism (Eph. 5:2, 15; cf. Col. 2:6). Finally, these ethical instructions lead directly into the idea of proper order in the church as the household of God (Eph. 5:15–21), and this additional metaphor introduces an elaborated form of the "household duty code" (5:22–6:9).

BOX 11.2

The Letter to the Ephesians

DATE: ca. 85–95 CE

AUTHOR: Unknown

ATTRIBUTION: Paul

LOCATION: Ephesus (probable)

AUDIENCE AND OCCASION: A Pauline congregation somewhere in Asia Minor, perhaps Ephesus itself. The "letter" serves primarily as an extended homily on the church and an ethical exhortation for living in the church. Probably written after Paul's death to carry on the Pauline legacy. Either based on Colossians or written as a companion piece to Colossians.

OUTLINE

I. Greeting (1:1–2)

II. Blessing (1:3–14)

III. Body (1:15–3:21)
   A. Thanksgiving (1:15–23)
   B. The mystery of Christ (2:1–22)
   C. The mystery in the church (3:1–21)

IV. Exhortation: Unity in the Church (4:1–6:20)
   A. Exhortation to unity (4:1–16)
   B. Vices and virtues (4:17–24)
   C. Personal ethics (4:25–5:14)
   D. Communal ethics (5:15–6:9)
   E. Concluding appeals (6:10–20)

V. Closing (6:21–24)

FURTHER READING

Barth, M. *Ephesians*. Anchor Bible. New York: Doubleday, 1974.

Best, E. *Ephesians*. New Testament Guides. Sheffield, UK: JSOT Press, 1993.

———. *One Body in Christ*. London: SCM, 1955.

Dahl, N. A. "Ephesians, Letter to the." *Interpreter's Dictionary of the Bible*. Supplement (1976): 268–69.

Furnish, V. P. "Ephesians, Epistle to the." *Anchor Bible Dictionary*. 2:535–42.

Gnilka, J. *Der Epheserbrief*. Freiburg: Herder, 1971.

Käsemann, E. "Ephesians and Acts." *Studies in Luke-Acts*. Edited by L. E. Keck and J. L. Martyn. Nashville, TN: Abingdon, 1966. Pp. 288–97.

Lincoln, A. T. *Ephesians*. Word Biblical Commentary. Waco, TX: Word, 1990.

Meeks, W. A. "The Unity of Humankind in Colossians and Ephesians." In *God's Christ and His People*. Edited by W. A. Meeks and J. Jervell. Oslo: Universitetsforlaget, 1977.

Mitton, C. L. *Ephesians*. New Century Bible. Grand Rapids, MI: Eerdmans, 1973.

Sampley, J. P. "Ephesians." In *Ephesians, Colossians, 2 Thessalonians, the Pastoral Epistles*. Proclamation Commentaries. Philadelphia: Fortress, 1978. Pp. 9–39.

Taylor, W. C. *Ephesians*. Augsburg Commentary. Minneapolis: Augsburg, 1985.

Even its standard formulas (cf. Col. 3:18–4:1 and discussion below) are now infused with new theological significance by the likening relations between husband and wife to Christ and the church as his bride (5:22–33).

Finally, the church is coming to be thought of as neither Jewish nor gentile, but a third ethnicity, a new people:

> *He has abolished the law with its commandments and ordinances, that he might create in himself one new humanity in place of the two, thus making peace, and might reconcile both groups to God in one body through the cross, thus putting to death that hostility through it.* (Eph. 2:15–16)

The understanding of the church explored in Ephesians and Colossians also shows a new self-consciousness. Imminent eschatology is gone. Apocalyptic ideas are reinterpreted through the idea of the church as the army of God on earth waging its war with the devil (Eph. 6:10–20). Although it is not possible to prove that the author of either of these two works (or both) was the same as the author of Luke-Acts, there is a strong correlation between them in the theological understanding of salvation history and the place of the church in that history.[9] These Pauline school documents thus become important filters for the reinterpretation of Paul once the separation from Judaism became complete.

2 Thessalonians

Standing in quite a different relationship to both the genuine letters of Paul and these other documents of the Pauline school is 2 Thessalonians, since it reflects a later controversy over eschatology between two wings of the Pauline tradition. The issue is further complicated by the fact that it so stringently asserts its authenticity (2 Thess. 3:17) in a way that is not found in either the indisputably genuine letters or other letters that are widely accepted as pseudepigraphic. At the same time, the outline, some phrases, the greeting formulas, and the persons named are very similar to those found in 1 Thessalonians. So are these elements to be read as signs of its authenticity or of overzealous attempts to make it sound so? A number of theories have been proposed on both sides.

Among those scholars who have defended the authenticity of 2 Thessalonians, the vast majority have assumed that it must be the later of the two letters based on the travelogue of 1 Thessalonians 2:17–3:6 (see Chapter 8). In this view, it is assumed that Paul's instructions about the eschaton in 1 Thessalonians 4:13–18 later led to some problems when people started watching for signs and prompted the second letter. On the basis of the inconclusive nature of the

evidence against authenticity, a number of recent scholars have taken this position.[10] A few older theories argued that 2 Thessalonians was the earlier of the
two letters and represents the older problem of eschatology that was finally settled only in 1 Thessalonians. Others also argued that 2 Thessalonians was actually
written more or less simultaneously to a different congregation in Thessalonica
or to a different group within the same congregation. Both of these views have
largely been abandoned. The date and situation assumed are thus very cloudy
within the later phases of Paul's Aegean mission.

Those scholars who regard the letter as pseudonymous argue instead that it
consciously used 1 Thessalonians as a model to address a new crisis over eschatology that developed sometime after the death of Paul.[11] (See Box 11.3.) One
important little comment in 2 Thessalonians is a warning against false eschatological teaching "to the effect that the day of the Lord is already here" (2:2). Apparently, this false teaching circulated via a letter purporting to be from Paul
(2:2). That such a letter could have been sent during Paul's Aegean mission, and
especially within months of the writing of 1 Thessalonians, is probably the
strongest single argument against authenticity. On the other hand, it has been
proposed that this "false letter" might actually be 1 Thessalonians itself, but that
its imminent eschatology had later been misinterpreted, so that 2 Thessalonians was a repudiation of this misreading. Attractive as this is in some ways, it is
not provable because we do not have evidence that 1 Thessalonians was actually
misread in this way during or after the first revolt. So the other alternative is
that another, now lost, pseudonymous letter attributed to Paul was sent to
Thessalonica or one of the other congregations. Then 2 Thessalonians was written as "Paul's" authoritative answer on the matter.

The likely situation of the letter comes from after the first revolt when new
apocalypses were being generated in both Judaism and the Jesus movement to
reinterpret the war, and this puts it at a date between 75 and 100. It depends on
the view prevalent at the time, as we have seen, that the war was indeed a sign
that the eschaton was breaking in and the return of Jesus was near. The response offered by 2 Thessalonians, however, shows that some changes were occurring in eschatological views in light of the war and recent persecutions
(2 Thess. 2:14–17). These might even be understood as outbreaks of anti-Jewish
sentiment in light of the war in Judea, as we know happened in Antioch and
elsewhere, and at a time and locality where the Jesus movement was still considered Jewish. These new circumstances cause the author to give warnings to help
the Thessalonians understand why the expectations have dragged on and on.
Notably, 2 Thessalonians warns about a "man of lawlessness," a henchman of

---

BOX 11.3

The Second Letter to the Thessalonians

DATE: ca. 75–100 CE

AUTHOR: Unknown

ATTRIBUTION: Paul

LOCATION: Thessalonica (?)

AUDIENCE AND OCCASION: A Pauline congregation facing new persecutions and an eschatological crisis in the period after the first revolt. Responds to another letter claiming to be from Paul that says the eschaton has already come. Offers encouragement and a call for endurance, but warns about false eschatological teachings and the "signs" that will accompany the actual return of Jesus.

OUTLINE

  I. Greeting (1:1–2)

  II. Thanksgiving (1:3–12)

  III. Body (2:1–17)

  IV. Exhortation (3:1–15)

  V. Closing (3:16–18)

FURTHER READING

Bailey, J. A. "Who Wrote II Thessalonians?" *New Testament Studies* 25 (1978): 131–45.

Best, E. *The First and Second Epistles to the Thessalonians*. New York: Harper & Row, 1972.

Collins, R. F. "The Second Epistle to the Thessalonians." In *The Letters That Paul Did Not Write*. Good News Studies. Wilmington, DE: Michael Glazier, 1988. Pp. 209–41.

Holland, G. S. *The Tradition You Received from Us: 2 Thessalonians in the Pauline Tradition*. Tübingen: Mohr-Siebeck, 1988.

Hughes, F. W. *Early Christian Rhetoric and 2 Thessalonians*. Sheffield: JSOT Press, 1989.

Jewett, R. *The Thessalonian Correspondence*. Philadelphia: Fortress, 1986.

Krentz, E. M. "Thessalonians, Second Epistle to the." *Anchor Bible Dictionary*. 6:517–23.

Krodel, G. "2 Thessalonians." In *Ephesians, Colossians, 2 Thessalonians, the Pastoral Epistles*. Proclamation Commentaries. Philadelphia: Fortress, 1978. Pp. 73–96.

Malherbe, A. J. *The Letters to the Thessalonians*. Anchor Bible. New York: Doubleday, 2000.

Marshall, I. H. *1 and 2 Thessalonians*. New Century Bible. New York: Harper & Row, 1983.

Satan, who must arise before the return of Jesus. Thus, in attempting to allay the crisis of expectation, 2 Thessalonians now adds new "signs" to the eschatological drama. In some ways, these elements seem to reflect a rhetoric similar to that in the book of Revelation, which was written in Asia Minor at about the same time, in the mid-90s.

The Petrine Legacy

As much as any other figure, Peter is associated with the foundations of Christianity. He is the leader and spokesman of Jesus's disciples in all the canonical Gospels and part of the "inner circle" with the brothers James and John. Peter along with John and James the brother of Jesus were the "pillars" of the church in Jerusalem during the early days (Gal. 1:18–19; 2:9), and Luke-Acts makes Peter the hero of the first third of Acts. Paul further cites oral traditions that may come directly from him (1 Cor. 15:5) and calls him the "apostle" (or missionary) to the circumcised (Gal. 2:7–8). According to legend, after leaving Jerusalem in the 40s Peter traveled through Asia Minor and eventually to Rome, where he was martyred under the emperor Nero after the great fire of 64. These legends, however, come from later developments in the Petrine tradition, including the production of an extensive apocryphal literature in his name (to be discussed in Chapters 12 and 15). Two letters in the New Testament are attributed to Peter. The style, theology, and situation of the two letters are quite different, and they have for a long time been recognized to be from different authors. As a result, 2 Peter will be discussed in Chapter 16, while 1 Peter will be discussed here.

1 Peter

Although 1 Peter clearly claims to be by the apostle and was not seriously questioned in the early church, there are numerous reasons why its authenticity is now doubted by almost all modern scholars. Its final greetings include the names Silvanus and Mark (1 Pet. 5:12–13), who show up in several of Paul's letters. The same greetings mention "she who is chosen in Babylon" (5:13), a reference to the church in Rome.[12] Babylon as a cipher for Rome arose in some Jewish apocalyptic works,[13] but only after the destruction of Jerusalem, and thus, *after* the death of Peter. The references to being a "witness [or martyr] of the sufferings of Christ" (4:13; 5:1) may also reflect the tradition of Peter's martyrdom at Rome. On the other hand, references to the life and ministry of Jesus are almost totally lacking. In fact, it may well be the mention of Mark in this letter that led to the legend of Papias (ca. 130 CE) about Peter and Mark in Rome. Polycarp, bishop of Smyrna, writing in about 115–30 CE, seems to allude to several key passages. Both would provide evidence for the letter's existence by the early second century. A better indication of date may come from its reference to Babylon (noted above). It is most likely that it was written during the last decade or so of the first century (see Box 11.4).

The writing has numerous Pauline epistolary and language features, many of them similar to Paul's Roman letter.[14] Hence, 1 Peter may come from someone at Rome adopting the style of Paul but invoking the authority of Peter to address Christians experiencing persecution. In reality, however, 1 Peter, like Ephesians, is more of an exhortation to Christian living than a letter as such (5:12). It is addressed to "exiles of the Dispersion" (1:1) living in the Roman provinces of central and western Anatolia (Turkey). The exhortations begin already in 1:13, but the appeal soon takes an important tone:

> *Beloved, I urge you as aliens and exiles to abstain from the desires of the flesh that wage war against the soul. Conduct yourselves honorably among the Gentiles, so that, though they malign you as evildoers, they may see your honorable deeds and glorify God when he comes to judge.*
>
> *For the Lord's sake accept the authority of every human institution, whether of the emperor as supreme, or of governors, as sent by him to punish those who do wrong and to praise those who do right. For it is God's will that by doing right you should silence the ignorance of the foolish. As servants of God, live as free people, yet do not use your freedom as a pretext for evil. Honor everyone. Love the family of believers. Fear God. Honor the emperor. (1 Pet. 2:11–17)*

We see first that the author addresses the audience as "aliens and exiles," which continues the opening theme "to the exiles of the Dispersion" (1:1; cf. 1:17). This language is drawn from the experience of diaspora Jews and led early readers to assume that it was addressed to Jewish Christians.[15] There may have been some ethnic Jews in these congregations, but other statements make it clear that the primary perspective is that of gentile converts (see 1 Pet. 1:14; 2:9–10; 4:3). Thus, this terminology is being appropriated as a way of defining Christian group identity over against the macrosociety in ethnic terms formerly used to define the minority status of diaspora Jews in relation to Gentiles. Here again we see a distinctive Christian self-definition beginning to emerge; moreover, reflections on this identity are being made in theological terms.

At the same time, Christians' identity as "aliens and exiles" is now used to exhort them to ethical behaviors in accommodation with their alien environment. Specifically they are told to honor the emperor and accept the authority of local Roman officials "for the Lord's sake." Again, there are reverberations of Pauline language from the Roman letter: "Let every person be subject to the governing authorities; for there is no authority except from God, and those authorities that exist have been instituted by God. . . . For rulers are not a terror

BOX 11.4

The First Letter of Peter

DATE: 80–95

AUTHOR: Unknown

ATTRIBUTION: The apostle Peter

LOCATION: Rome

AUDIENCE AND OCCASION: Addressed to Christians in the provinces of western Anatolia (Turkey), where their emerging identity as a distinct religious group is beginning to bring them to the attention of their neighbors
and the Roman authorities. Primarily offers ethical exhortation as a
means of accommodation to living as a religious and cultural minority in
the Roman world.

OUTLINE

I. Epistolary Greetings (1:1–2)

II. Homily: Ethical Obligations for the Household of God (1:3–4:11)

    A. Introduction: Blessings to the God who brings salvation (1:3–12)

    B. The conduct of Christians (1:13–2:10)

        1. Exhortation to obedience and holiness (1:13–21)

        2. Exhortation to love of the community of faith (1:22–25)

        3. Christ as cornerstone of church (2:1–10)

    C. Aliens and exiles in a foreign land (2:11–3:12)

        1. Introductory exhortation (2:11–12)

        2. Subjection to Roman authority (2:13–17)

to good conduct, but to bad" (Rom. 13:1, 3). In 1 Peter, however, similar to
Ephesians and Colossians, this general ethical exhortation to accommodation
with the imperial environment leads directly into the instructions known as the
"household duty code" (2:18–3:7).

The Household Duty Code:
Ethical Instruction and Cultural Accommodation

The *household duty code* was a well-known formula drawn from Greek philosophical discussions on household management. Treatments of this topic appear frequently among Stoics in the Hellenistic and Roman periods and derive

    3. Household duty code (2:18–3:7)

    4. Appeal to unity (3:8–12)

  D. Admonitions regarding suffering and righteousness (3:13–4:11)

    1. Suffering in a hostile world (3:13–17)

    2. Baptism and the death of Christ (3:18–22)

    3. Imitating the suffering of Christ (4:1–6)

  E. Doxological conclusion (4:7–11)

III. Final Admonitions: The Fiery Ordeal to Come (5:1–11)

IV. Epistolary Salutations (5:12–14)

FURTHER READING

Achtemeier, P. J. *1 Peter: A Commentary*. Hermeneia. Minneapolis: Fortress, 1996.

Balch, D. *Let Wives be Submissive: The Domestic Code in 1 Peter*. Chico, CA: Scholars Press, 1981.

Best, E. *1 Peter*. New Century Bible. Grand Rapids, MI: Eerdmans, 1971.

Elliott, J. H. *A Home for the Homeless: A Sociological Exegesis of 1 Peter*. Philadelphia: Fortress, 1981.

———. "Peter, First Epistle of." *Anchor Bible Dictionary*. 5:269–78.

Goppelt, L. *A Commentary on 1 Peter*. Grand Rapids, MI: Eerdmans, 1993.

Kelly, J. N. D. *A Commentary on the Epistles of Peter and Jude*. Harper Commentary. New York: Harper & Row, 1969.

Krodel, G. "The First Letter of Peter." In *Hebrews, James, 1 and 2 Peter, Jude, Revelation*. Proclamation Commentaries. Philadelphia: Fortress, 1977. Pp. 50–80.

Martin, T. W. *Metaphor and Composition in 1 Peter*. Atlanta: Scholars Press, 1992.

Michaels, J. R. *1 Peter*. Word Biblical Commentary. Waco, TX: Word, 1988.

Talbert, C. H. *Perspectives on First Peter*. Macon, GA: Mercer University Press, 1986.

principally from the formulations of Aristotle.[16] From there they also came into Hellenistic Jewish writings, as seen in Philo and Josephus.[17] In both cases, these ethical codes were used for apologetic purposes, especially to defend diaspora Jews, or Judaism more generally, against criticism by pagan neighbors. The use of the formula in Colossians, Ephesians, and 1 Peter similarly shows an apologetic intent relative to the Roman environment. The point is to argue that Jewish or Christian religious teachings promote the highest ethical ideals, to which pagans would also subscribe.[18]

The conventional nature of the code can be seen from the similarities between the three versions: Colossians 3:18–4:1, Ephesians 5:22–6:9, and 1 Peter 2:18–3:7. Of the three, Colossians, with its parallel structure of three reciprocal pairs of admonitions, provides the basic outline:

Wives, *be subject to* your husbands.	Husbands, love your wives.
Children, *obey* your parents.	Fathers, do not provoke your children.
Slaves, *obey/be subject to* your masters.	Masters, treat your slaves justly.

These rules for household order are written, of course, from the perspective of the father (or *pater familias*) as the head of the household and so reinforce the patriarchal household structure that was assumed to be the norm in the Roman world. Since the order of the city or state was also likened to a well-ordered household, it was common among Greco-Roman moralists and politicians to link these rules to civic behavior and responsibilities, just as we see in 1 Peter. Both 1 Peter and Ephesians provide further theological warrant for the subjection of inferiors to the *pater familias* by likening the church to the household and by equating Christ to the head of the church, thus extending the hierarchical structure to the cosmic level.

Finally, the introduction of the household duty code into Christian ethical exhortation stands in some tension with the order seen in the early Pauline house church, where women were patrons and leaders, and "apostolic couples" seemed to share more equal responsibility. It is all the more striking, then, that these later household codes are often linked to baptismal instruction, since the baptismal reunification formula in Paul stressed reunification of slaves and free, male and female. It may well be that the similarities of these pairings and the connection to baptismal exhortation made the substitution seem natural.[19] Although they remain typical of the genre, these Christian versions of the code do give more attention to the reciprocal obligations of the *pater familias* than do some pagan discussions. In the first phase of its introduction, therefore, as seen in Colossians, Ephesians, and 1 Peter, the household duty code primarily served apologetic purposes, as an implicit political and social trade-off for greater acceptance by Roman society. Noticeably lacking are any connections of the code to church order or offices. In later stages, however, as seen in the Pastoral Epistles, other issues regarding the hierarchical structure and offices of the church will come into play.

The James Tradition: The Letter of James

Since several people named James are associated with Jesus and the early movement, there has often been some confusion about them, especially once we get to medieval legend. Of these, the two most central are James son of Zebedee and James the brother of Jesus. James son of Zebedee was the brother of John, and both are mentioned in all the lists of the twelve disciples of Jesus (Mark 6:17; Matt. 10:2; Luke 9:14; Acts 1:13). James, like John, is often placed in the inner circle with Peter (Mark 9:2; Matt. 17:1; Luke 9:28); however, Acts reports that he was killed in Jerusalem by King Agrippa I, the grandson of Herod the Great, in the early 40s CE (Acts 12:2). There are no references to any writings attributed to him.

James the brother of Jesus is never mentioned among the disciples in the Gospels; however, the earliest oral tradition places him among the apostles and witnesses of the resurrected Jesus (1 Cor. 15:7). As we have already seen, Paul certainly knew him firsthand as the leader of the church in Jerusalem (Gal. 1:9; 2:9), a view supported by the story in Acts 15. Josephus confirms both his identity and role in Jerusalem up to his death in 62 CE in the tumultuous period before the first revolt.[20] That he was the sibling of Jesus is a consistent feature of the earliest testimonies about him, but this fact has also stimulated both discussion and other legends.[21] Several pieces of apocryphal literature, including two Gnostic treatises known from Nag Hammadi and the legend regarding the early life of Mary known as the *Protevangelium* (or "proto-Gospel") *of James* were later developed under his name. He is closely associated with the Jewish form of the Jesus movement at Jerusalem, and other legends continue this legacy (see Chapter 9; we will discuss his place in later Jewish Christianity in Chapter 15). It is also this aspect of the traditions about him that probably gave rise to the document known as the letter of James.

The letter of James is not cited by early Christian authors prior to the middle of the third century CE, and it seems to have been associated with Palestine.[22] It was not generally regarded as part of the New Testament until the mid-fourth century and afterward. Although a few contemporary scholars have cautioned against a too hasty dismissal of the work—a corrective to its treatment in the Protestant Reformation—there are no strong arguments for the authenticity of the work in its present form (see Box 11.5.) It may range in date anywhere from 75 to 125 CE. Proposed similarities of language with *1 Clement* and the *Shepherd* of Hermas, both written from Rome, would likely affirm a date at the very end of the first century or early in the second century.[23] If the legacy of "James" has any bearing on the trajectory of the text, it may well reflect the moral instruction of an early Christian group in Syria or Palestine, but one cannot be more precise.

Rather than a true letter, James is really a collection of moral instructions in the form of aphorisms or maxims introduced by a brief epistolary address, "to

BOX 11.5

The Letter of James

DATE: ca. 75–125 CE

AUTHOR: Unknown

ATTRIBUTION: James, brother of Jesus

LOCATION: Uncertain

AUDIENCE AND OCCASION: A little handbook of moral instructions for an established Christian community.

OUTLINE

    I. Epistolary Opening (1:1)

   II. Sayings on Wisdom and Endurance (1:2–18)
     Final maxim: Every good gift from God (1:17)

  III. Sayings on Hearing and Doing What Is Right (1:19–27)
     Final maxim: True religion defined (1:27)

  IV. Sayings on Partiality (2:1–13)
     Final maxim: Judgment under the law of liberty (2:12)

   V. Sayings on Faith and Works (2:14–26)
     Final maxim: Faith apart from works is dead (2:26)

  VI. Sayings on the "Tongue" (Proper Speech) (3:1–12)
     Final maxim: Blessing and cursing should not come from the same mouth (3:10)

 VII. Sayings on Contentiousness and Strife (3:13–4:12)
     Final maxim: Who are you to judge your neighbor? (4:12)

VIII. Sayings on Abuse by the Wealthy and Endurance (4:13–5:11)
     Final maxim: Remember Job; the Lord is compassionate and merciful (5:11)

  IX. Final Exhortations Regarding Church Life (5:12–20)

FURTHER READING

Dibellius, M., and H. Greeven. *James: A Commentary.* Hermeneia. Philadelphia: Fortress, 1975.

Johnson, L. T. *The Letter of James.* Anchor Bible. New York: Doubleday, 1995.

Laws, S. *A Commentary on the Epistle of James.* New York: Harper & Row, 1980.

———. "James, Epistle of." *Anchor Bible Dictionary.* 3:621–28.

Sloyan, G. S. "James." In *Hebrews, James, 1 and 2 Peter, Jude, Revelation.* Proclamation Commentaries. Philadelphia: Fortress, 1977. Pp. 28–50.

Watson, D. F. "James 2 in the Light of Greco-Roman Schemes of Argumentation." *New Testament Studies* 39 (1993): 94–121.

the twelve tribes in the Dispersion" (1:1). As in the case of 1 Peter, this address does not necessarily indicate that the audience was Jewish Christian, but a background in Hellenistic Judaism is quite feasible. The sayings are grouped together by topics, and the letter is thus similar to works in the Jewish wisdom tradition. Most topics are brief and formulaic, and each ends with a pithy final maxim. Much of the work's moral exhortation is quite typical of day-to-day ethical precepts found in Hellenistic philosophers and in Paul (esp. James 4:1–3).

The letter seems to be addressed to an established church with a thoroughly Christian self-understanding. Local authority is vested in "teachers" and "elders" (3:1; 5:14), and they pray over the sick and practice mutual confession of sins (5:15–16). There are also indications of socioeconomic level in its negative statements regarding wealth and visits by rich people (1:9–11; 2:1–3; 5:1–3). On the other hand, there is a strong communal ethic of sharing (1:27; 2:15–16). The ethics are also warranted by appeal to Torah, but as the law of liberty (2:8–13). These elements might suggest a rural or semirural location (cf. 5:4–6), but it is not provable. Nor is it possible to see this work as a direct refutation of Paul. Even so, its rhetoric retains a sectarian polemic against worldliness (4:4–10). There are vague references to eschatology and the return of Jesus, but these do not suggest the heightened apocalyptic milieu of Judea prior to either the first revolt or the second.

A Radical Response: The Revelation of John

As we have seen, the last decade or two of the first century witnessed a proliferation of new literary works to address the changing social location of the Jesus movement. Most of these reflect an emerging Christian identity, a greater sense of separation from Judaism, and a sense of accommodation to Roman culture. Yet different Christian groups in diverse locations seem to have consolidated their new social position in distinctive ways. Luke-Acts, Colossians, and Ephesians represent one such line of accommodation by stressing ethics in the tradition of Paul. Coming from the church in Rome, 1 Peter takes a similar line in ethical exhortation and similarly uses the household duty code as a signal that Christians uphold the social order. Yet it goes even farther by calling for Christians to "honor the emperor" (1 Pet. 2:17). Some Christians must have found such an injunction shocking, especially coming from Peter. At least one found this move toward accommodation with Rome to be abhorrent and said so in vehement terms by appealing to the older tradition of apocalyptic.

Author, Date, and Setting

The book of Revelation was given its traditional title "The Apocalypse of John" in early Greek manuscripts. The opening words of the text probably give its original title: "The Revelation of Jesus Christ, which God gave him to show his servants what must soon take place; he made it known by sending his angel to his servant John" (1:1). The author further claims that the revelation was delivered to him in the form of a vision while he was on the island of Patmos (1:9–10). In genre and tone, therefore, the work is very much in the tradition of Jewish apocalyptic, and it should be remembered that there was a resurgence of new Jewish apocalypses during the 80s and 90s in response to the destruction of Jerusalem.[24] Several of these Jewish apocalypses take as their authorial namesake characters from the Babylonian exile, such as Baruch and Ezra. It also allows them to use the Babylonian destruction of Jerusalem as an interpretive lens through which to understand recent experience. From this literary stance, then, came the symbolic gesture of calling Rome, the new destroyer of Jerusalem, by the name Babylon. Among New Testament and early Christian writings only 1 Peter and Revelation use this cipher, and it may well hint at a source of tension between them.[25]

In the early centuries the book of Revelation was quite controversial and not uniformly considered scripture. It was not received into the Western canon until 393–94 CE, and then only after a symbolic reading became the authoritative interpretation through Augustine.[26] Prior to that there was an ongoing debate in the early church whether the "John" named as author was the apostle John or another person. Irenaeus, bishop of Lyons (ca. 180 CE), thought it was the apostle John who also wrote the Gospel, while Gaius, bishop of Rome, and Dionysius, bishop of Alexandria (both early third century), denounced it as a work of the heretic Cerinthus (a notorious opponent of John in later legends).[27] Ultimately Eusebius, following a tradition from Papias (ca. 130), attributed it to a different John "the Elder" (also from Ephesus) and denied it scriptural status.[28]

In large measure, these ancient debates over authorship were really concerned with the book's canonical status and interpretation of its radical apocalyptic imagery. Several notable Christian writers of the second century (including Papias and Tatian, a disciple of Justin Martyr) took it as a literal prediction that a thousand-year kingdom was coming during their lifetime.[29] Especially after more time passed, these predictions were given up as false. So the early debates do not ultimately solve the question of who actually wrote the book. On the basis of style, vocabulary, and tone, however, it is *most unlikely* that it was written by the same author who wrote the Gospel of John. That it was claiming apostolic authority in the name of John is nonetheless possible, for that is typical in apocalyptic literature.

The location is provided by the address to the "seven churches that are in Asia" (1:4); the author further claims that he received the revelation while he was on the island of Patmos, off the coast of Asia (1:9–10). One later legend held that John (the apostle) had been exiled to Patmos "on account of the word of God and the testimony of Jesus" (1:9), but the precise situation is unclear. It might be part of the literary fiction of the work, again quite consistent with the apocalyptic genre. Two other internal features make it certain that the work was written for Christians in the province of Asia: first, the seven churches, which are enumerated in 1:11,[30] are all important cities in this region; and second, its polemic against the "whore of Babylon" (17:7–18) presupposes the Roman imperial cult in Ephesus.

It was once popular to date Revelation to the period of Nero and thus before the destruction of Jerusalem. The traditional date for the death of the apostle John is about 95–96 CE, near the end of the reign of Domitian. This was the date given by Irenaeus (see above) and remains the date most frequently assigned to the work by scholars. Recent work on the imperial cult at Ephesus makes a date under Nero impossible and confirms a date near the end of the reign of Domitian (81–96) as the most likely.[31] (See Box 11.6.)

The Flavian Imperial Cult at Ephesus

Although Ephesus was the Roman provincial capital of Asia, it had previously had a checkered relationship with Rome. During the civil war between Mark Antony and Octavian, Ephesus had actually sided with Antony. Its rival city Pergamon supported Octavian. After Octavian defeated Antony at the battle of Actium (31 BCE) and took the imperial title Augustus (28 BCE), he then allowed certain cities to establish imperial cult temples in his honor, just as Herod the Great did at Caesarea Maritima (see Box 2.3). Naturally, the honor of hosting the imperial cult temple in Asia fell to Pergamon, not Ephesus; Augustus remained somewhat spiteful toward Ephesus throughout his life. For a century, Pergamon continued as the principal seat of the provincial imperial cult in Asia, and it used the title *neokoros* ("temple warden") to symbolize this singular honor.

BOX 11.6

The Apocalypse (Revelation) of John

DATE: ca. 95–96 CE

AUTHOR: "John"

LOCATION: Ephesus

AUDIENCE AND OCCASION: An apocalypse written in reaction to the growing accommodation of Christians to Rome (cf. Luke-Acts, Ephesians, 1 Peter). It explicitly rejects participation of Christians in any aspect of the public imperial cult, especially as practiced in the city of Ephesus in the last decade of the first century, and calls for Christians to stand against Rome and the emperor as the worldly agents of Satan.

OUTLINE

I. Preface (1:1–3) and "Cover Letter" (1:4–3:22)

   A. John's "Cover Letter" (1:4–11)

   B. The first vision (1:12–20)

   C. The letters to the seven churches of Asia (2:1–3:22)

II. Second Vision: The Throne Room of Heaven (4:1–11:19)

   A. The throne room and its occupants (4:1–11)

   B. The scroll and the Lamb (5:1–14)

   C. The Lamb opens the seven seals (6:1–8:1)

   D. The seventh seal and the seven trumpets (8:2–11:18)

   E. The heavenly temple opened! (11:19)

III. Third Vision: Great Signs in Heaven (12:1–16:21)

   A. Sign 1: The pregnant woman (12:1–2)

   B. Sign 2: The great red dragon (12:3–4)

   C. The war in heaven (12:5–17)

   D. The war descends to earth (12:18–14:20)

      1. The Beast from the Sea (12:18–13:10)

Pergamon is one of the seven cities mentioned in Revelation 1:11 and the letter to Pergamum (2:12–17) calls it "the place where Satan's throne is" (2:13). This may well be a reference to the Augustan imperial cult temple there or perhaps its famous Altar of Zeus (see Fig. 11.2). The other larger cities of Asia, including Ephesus, were allowed to participate only by hosting local cults and festivals or other important events for the provincial assembly. In fact, all seven of the cities mentioned in Revelation were centers for some sort of imperial cult activ-

2. The Beast from the Land (13:11–18)
3. The good army of the Lamb masses on Mt. Zion (Jerusalem; 14:1–20)

E. The battle commences on earth: seven angels, plagues, bowls of wrath (15:1–16:21)

IV. Fourth Vision: The Great Whore, Babylon (= Rome; 17:1–22:5)
   A. The allegory and its explanation (17:1–18)
   B. The fall of Babylon (18:1–8)
   C. Lament over Babylon (18:9–19:10)
   D. Heaven is once again opened to reveal the final resolution (19:11–21:8)
   E. The new Jerusalem (21:9–22:5)

V. Epilogue (22:6–21)

FURTHER READING

Caird, G. B. *The Revelation of St. John.* New York: Harper & Row, 1966.
Collins, A. Y. *Crisis and Catharsis: The Power of the Apocalypse.* Philadelphia: Westminster, 1984.
———. "Revelation, Book of." *Anchor Bible Dictionary.* 5:694–708.
Farrar, A. *A Rebirth of Images: The Making of St. John's Apocalypse.* Boston: Beacon, 1963.
Ford, J. M. *Revelation.* Anchor Bible. New York: Doubleday, 1975.
Friesen, S. J. *Imperial Cults and the Apocalypse of John: Reading Revelation in the Ruins.* New York: Oxford University Press, 2001.
———. *Twice Neokoros Ephesus: Ephesus, Asia, and the Imperial Cult of the Flavian Family.* Leiden: Brill, 1993.
Hellholm, D. *Apocalypticism in the Mediterranean World and the Near East.* Tübingen: Mohr-Siebeck, 1983.
Hemer, C. J. *The Letters to the Seven Churches of Asia in Their Local Setting.* Sheffield: JSOT Press, 1986.
Price, S. *Rituals and Power: The Roman Imperial Cult in Asia Minor.* Cambridge: Cambridge University Press, 1984.
Schüssler Fiorenza, E. *The Book of Revelation.* Philadelphia: Fortress, 1985.
Thompson, L. L. *The Book of Revelation: Apocalypse and Empire.* New York: Oxford University Press, 1990.

ity.[32] Smyrna (Rev. 2:8–11), another of Ephesus's rival cities, had been granted an imperial cult center under Tiberius (14–37 CE).

Ephesus's fortunes in regard to the imperial cult finally changed in 89 CE, when the emperor Domitian allowed it to establish a new imperial cult. Called the Temple of the Flavian Sebastoi in honor of the Flavian dynasty, that is, Vespasian (69–79 CE), Titus (79–81), and Domitian (81–96), the new temple nearly doubled the size of the Roman state agora. It was an architectural marvel as it was

FIGURE II.2

Pergamum, "Where Satan's throne is" (Rev. 2:13); view of the acropolis from the temple of Asclepius: (A) the imperial cult temple of Trajan; (B) the Altar of Zeus; (C) theater.

suspended above the hillside on the western descent from the "upper" city (see Box 8.5). Ephesus was finally able to claim the honorific title *neokoros*.[33] Asia was given a signal place and prestige within the empire, since no other province could claim three imperial cult centers. The colossal statue of Domitian found at Ephesus was the cult statue of this new temple (see Fig. 11.3). This statue is what is being referred to in Revelation 13:14–17 as the "image of the beast" that people are made to worship. Later coins from Ephesus (see Fig. 3.2) show local citizens paying homage to just such a colossal statue of an emperor in a temple.

The Beasts of Revelation and the Flavian Emperors

That "Babylon" is Rome is not difficult to see from the description in Revelation 17; it starts with the "sign" or vision of a woman riding on a scarlet, seven-headed beast, which is then interpreted by one of the angels (17:3, 7–9). The description makes clear that this is the same seven-headed beast described in Revelation 13:1–4, who is said to have been given his power, throne, and authority by the dragon, Satan. The angel says that the beast's seven heads are the "seven hills on which the woman is seated" (17:9), an age-old allusion to Rome even in antiquity. Then it says that the heads are also "seven kings" (17:10).

This complex set of symbolic equations is one of the most important keys to the book, since it is a reference to the description of 13:1–18, capped by the enigmatic "mark of the beast"—666. These seven kings are described as follows:

> *"This calls for a mind that has wisdom: the seven heads are seven mountains on which the woman is seated; also, they are seven kings, of whom five have fallen, one is living, and the other has not yet come; and when he comes, he must remain only a little while. As for the beast that was and is not, it is an eighth but it belongs to the seven, and it goes to destruction." (Rev. 17:9–11)*

The five kings who "have fallen" (died) are the Julio-Claudian emperors: Augustus (28 BCE–14 CE), Tiberius (14–37 CE), Gaius, or Caligula (37–41), Claudius (41–54), Nero (54–68). The next two—the "one [who] is living" and the one who will arise but "remain only a little while"—refer respectively to Vespasian (69–79) and his son Titus, who only ruled as emperor for two years

FIGURE 11.3

Colossal statue of Domitian from Temple of Flavian Sebastoi at Ephesus (89 CE). For the location of this temple, see Figure b in Box 8.5.

(79–81). Revelation 17:10 makes it explicit that the first five kings have "fallen" and the short-lived one has not yet "arisen"; therefore, the reference to the "one who is alive" is the ostensible date for the "now" of the text. In other words, the fictional setting for the delivery of the vision to John is during the reign of Vespasian. It is probably meant to be early in his reign just after the destruction of Jerusalem. Of course, the fact that the imperial cult was not established until 89 CE by Domitian tells us that the real setting is later, as is also shown by the portrayal of the next two emperors. Again, this temporal device is typical of apocalyptic literature, as it allows the unfolding images to "predict" future events up to the actual time of writing. From the perspective of the audience, however, the historical referents are quite clear.

The first Jewish revolt provides much of the backdrop to the dramatic imagery of Revelation. It must be remembered that the war began in 66 CE, under Nero, but that Nero killed himself rather than face assassination in 68 CE. Vespasian had been Nero's hand-picked general at the start of the war. When Nero died, Vespasian had to put the siege of Jerusalem on hold and eventually return to Rome to become emperor. His son Titus then finished the siege and destruction of Jerusalem and eventually succeeded his father as emperor. Thus, the same Flavian emperors who had destroyed Jerusalem only a few years earlier were now being worshiped as gods in the new imperial cult of Ephesus and throughout the cities of Asia.

It is the "eighth" beast noted in the text that now becomes most important, since he is "one of the seven." This refers to the emperor Domitian, the younger son of Vespasian, who would rule from 81 to 96 CE. The enigmatic statement that he "was, and is not" alludes to an earlier comment regarding the same seven-headed beast in which it says, "One of its heads seemed to have a mortal wound, but its mortal wound was healed, and the whole earth followed it in wonder" (Rev. 13:3). In Asia a rumor circulated, even among pagans, that the emperor Domitian was actually the evil emperor Nero come back to life. Indeed, Domitian, like Nero, was infamous for his brutality and megalomania. He even managed to get the Senate to confer the title *Dominus et Deus* ("Lord and God") on him during his lifetime. Such proclamations of the emperor's divinity were normally reserved for after death. The imperial cult would have been the sounding board for such a proclamation in major cities like Ephesus. Eventually, Domitian was assassinated, in 96; his images and symbols were permanently "damned," or blotted out from public display. Thus, the Beast from the Sea (Rev. 13:1), who has the power of Satan and who has "a blasphemous name upon his heads," is the self-proclaimed god Domitian, thought of as Nero come back to life.

The beast from the land (Rev. 13:11) must be understood as either the governor of Asia or the high priest of the Flavian Imperial cult, both of whom would have been based in Ephesus. They would have presided over the local imperial cult festivals and led people in worship of the "image of the beast" (13:14–15). In all probability, therefore, the enigmatic 666 is a numerological symbol for the name and title of Domitian as emperor (in Greek, *Kaiser* or *Sebastos*) as it would have appeared locally on coins or inscriptions.[34] Thus, the point of the polemic in Revelation is that to pay homage to the image of Domitian, the beast, is the same as worshiping Satan, because these are the very people who earlier made war on the saints and destroyed the holy city Jerusalem (cf. Rev. 13:5–7; 11:1–3). In turn, God will punish all those who worship this beast (14:9–11), when Babylon itself falls (14:8; 18:1).

Organization and Purpose

Following an epilogue in which the author narrates the occasion of his revelatory experience and the first vision, Revelation presents the text of letters to each of the seven churches mentioned (2:1–3:22). This is the first of a series of "sevens" that will serve as an important symbol as well as organizing principle in the text (see Box 11.6). In the second vision (4:1–11:19), John is shown the heavenly throne room and the enthroned King of Heaven holding a scroll with seven seals. The opening of each seal in turn (6:1–8:1) then provides the occasion for delivering each new segment of the vision pertaining to destructions that have been rained down on the earth. The opening of the seventh seal then turns out to be a series of seven trumpets (8:1–11:18). These interlocking sequences allow additional symbolic images to be described, as readers are drawn deeper and deeper into the mythic world of the text. As each of six trumpets is sounded, new trials and tribulations appear. Then there are seven thunders when an angel brings forth another "little scroll" (10:1–4), after which John is shown Jerusalem (11:1–8).

This is our first clue that the unfolding vision is in fact a reference to the war and the destruction of Jerusalem, which is now also associated with the crucifixion of Jesus and the persecution of two prophets. These are called the "woes" (11:9–13). Finally, then, the seventh angel blows his trumpet and there is a triumphal chant as the full heavenly panorama is opened for John to see (11:19).

The point of this second vision seems to be to describe the trials and tribulations that have come about as a result of the war. Other questions are left hanging: Why have these afflictions come about? How will God deliver the elect, and when? The triumphal blast of the seventh trumpet and the opening of the new scene of heaven now signal the inner vision that will answer these questions.

The most important part of Revelation is the vision in chapters 12–16, which explains how a cosmic conflict in heaven between God's archangels and Satan, the great red dragon, has in later times spilled over onto the earth (12:13–17). This is a classic motif of apocalyptic, but it has been tailored in such a way as to reflect the events surrounding the revolt and its aftermath. More specifically, it says that the age-old dragon, Satan, had appointed two beasts, one from the sea (13:1–10) and one from the land (13:11–18), to oversee its kingdom on earth. As we have already seen, the seven-headed Beast from the Sea is both the city of Rome and its emperors, as is made clear in a subsequent angelic interpretation (17:7–14). The seven-headed beast, then, is the agent of Satan who both subjugated the Jews and destroyed Jerusalem.

But the cosmic war is not yet over. Now the armies of the beasts are poised to confront the army of the Lamb at Zion for a final series of battles (14:1–16:21). Again we see how each set of visions opens upon itself. Rather than a series of linear signs that are to be interpreted sequentially or as consecutive historical events, they are interlocking elements of a mythic vision of the cosmic order that the text is attempting to explain. The fourth vision (Rev. 17:1–22:5) continues the story by returning to the heavenly scene opened earlier (in 11:19–12:1) to show what will be the outcome of its cosmic drama. One of the seven angels who had overseen the portents of the final battles (14:16) now presents a series of visions that predict the fall of Babylon, that is, Rome, another opening of heaven, and the vision of a new Jerusalem descending (21:9–22:5).

The main purpose of Revelation is to offer a cosmic vision both to explain why Jerusalem was destroyed, and by what evil force, and to offer hope that there will be a future reversal as God sends Christ as an angelic warrior. Thus too the death of Jesus is part of the evil actions of Rome, and yet mythically explains his heavenly role as avenging angel. Rome will be defeated and Jerusalem will be rebuilt. In all these elements Revelation reflects very traditional apocalyptic themes and interpretations. The destruction of Jerusalem is thus interpreted as but a preliminary skirmish to the final eschatological battle between God and Satan. The readers of Revelation were told from the beginning that what was being shown them was to take place soon: "Blessed is the one who reads aloud the words of the prophecy, and blessed are those who hear and who keep what is written in it; for the time is near" (Rev. 1:3). The eschaton and the fall of Rome were imminent, and the death of Domitian was doubtless the first signal that the final battle was about to begin. The same theme, then, that opens the book now returns in the final exhortation. The time is near.

> *"See, I am coming soon! Blessed is the one who keeps the words of the prophecy of this book." I, John, am the one who heard and saw these things. And when I heard and saw them, I fell down to worship at the feet of the angel who showed them to me; but he said to me, "You must not do that! I am a fellow servant with you and your comrades the prophets, and with those who keep the words of this book. Worship God!"*
>
> *And he said to me, "Do not seal up the words of the prophecy of this book, for the time is near. Let the evildoer still do evil, and the filthy still be filthy, and the righteous still do right, and the holy still be holy."*
>
> *"See, I am coming soon; my reward is with me, to repay according to everyone's work. I am the Alpha and the Omega, the first and the last, the beginning and the end." (Rev. 22:7–23:13)*

But there is a second and more important purpose to Revelation, as shown in these final verses. By linking the destruction of Jerusalem with the beasts of chapter 13 and the cosmic forces of Satan, it draws a line of demarcation for its readers, the Christians of Asia at the end of the first century. Here we must return again to the message of the letters to the seven churches, for each one calls on its members to remain steadfast or warns them about being lukewarm (3:15–16) or eating food offered to idols (2:14, 20). Public banquets were celebrations of the imperial cult in which Christians might participate. Rather than a situation in which persecution of Christians was a rampant problem, the dilemma faced by the author of Revelation was that Christians in Asia Minor were prepared to honor Emperor Domitian and accommodate to Roman imperial rule, just as letters from "Peter" and "Paul" had encouraged them to do. John's warning is dire for those who would do so:

> *Then another angel, a third, followed them, crying with a loud voice, "Those who worship the beast and its image, and receive a mark on their foreheads or on their hands, they will also drink the wine of God's wrath, poured unmixed into the cup of his anger, and they will be tormented with fire and sulfur in the presence of the holy angels and in the presence of the Lamb. And the smoke*

of their torment goes up forever and ever. There is no rest day or night for those who worship the beast and its image and for anyone who receives the mark of its name." (Rev. 14:9–11)

The author shows dramatically through visions and powerful dualistic symbols that to accommodate is the same as worshiping Satan himself and, in the spirit of traditional apocalyptic sectarianism, to put oneself on the losing side when God finally triumphs over Satan. The book of Revelation, then, should be seen in the context of the revival of Jewish apocalypticism in the 80s and 90s to deal with the destruction of Jerusalem, but its major concern is the "problem" of Christians in Roman culture.

PART FOUR

The Third Generation

From Sect to Church

CHAPTER TWELVE

Christology and Conflict

The Beginnings of Normative Self-Definition

By the beginning of the second century, the name "Christians" was becoming more recognizable in the large cities of the Roman Empire.[1] To some it must have still suggested a strange and dissident Jewish sect. To others it may have sounded like another foreign cult. But lines of demarcation were being drawn. The rift with Judaism had begun as a fissure in the aftermath of the first revolt, in part as a result of the cognitive shock in seeing Jerusalem destroyed and the subsequent vacuum of religious leadership. The period of reconstruction saw consternation, dislocation, and recrimination on all sides within Judaism. Gradually the Pharisaic movement emerged as the leading voice in the new "homeland" of the Galilee (see Chapter 9). The Gospel of Matthew shows that some followers of the Jesus movement retained their basic Jewish self-understanding all along; however, growing marginalization created new sectarian tensions (see Chapter 10). Their response was to lash out at the rabbis of their own day by placing the blame for Jesus's death on conspiracies by his Pharisaic contemporaries. Although this rhetorical strategy likely assuaged their situation and bolstered their group identity, it sharpened the lines of separation. Over time, as the Gospel of Matthew was read in new and very different social contexts, these polemics were taken to be historical fact rather than literary license. The rift grew wider and deeper. Even so, Jewish Christianity would last for centuries (see Chapter 15).

The Parting of the Ways

The growing separation between the Jesus movement and rabbinic Judaism un-doubtedly had numerous causes and facets. It proceeded at a different pace in different localities depending on the local makeup of emerging Christian groups. The process of reflection seen in Luke-Acts, Ephesians, and 1 Peter shows that their self-understanding was indeed changing, at least among the growing major-ity who were gentile by birth. Jewish self-understanding was also adjusting to new circumstances and a new outlook in both the homeland and the Diaspora. Other Jews were feeling the tensions too. Sectarian rivalry and separation do not occur on one side of the fence alone; there has to be pulling as well as push-ing from both. Thus, one component of the process of separation seen in Luke-Acts is the theme of rejection by Jews; Paul is portrayed as going first to the local synagogue in each locality, only to be rejected, and then turning outward toward non-Jews. At the end of Acts, even this rejection is interpreted on the basis of the Hebrew prophets. This picture hardly fits with Paul's own account and probably says more about the experience and reflection of later Christians near the turn of the second century.[2]

At least in the Jewish homeland these tensions became more pronounced in the early part of the second century with the growing consolidation of the rab-binic movement and the events surrounding the second Jewish revolt against Rome (132–35 CE). One of the remarkable developments of this period within Judaism was its change of orientation with regard to sectarianism. Virtually from the moment the first exiles had returned home from Babylon over six hundred years earlier, there had been disagreement and strife, more often than not centering on the Temple itself. Sectarianism thus proliferated, especially under the influence of apocalyptic, but was generally tolerated, as we have seen, throughout the Hasmonean period, down through the first revolt, and into the interwar period.[3]

By the end of the second revolt, however, there was a new sense that sectari-anism was also to blame for some of the ills.[4] Now "sects" would come increas-ingly to be viewed as "heresies." As noted above in Box 6.2, the Greek word *hairesis* (literally meaning "choice") is the term usually applied by Josephus, the author of Luke-Acts, and others to the different Jewish "sects"; however, it is also the root word from which we get "heresy." The difference is one of conno-tation or nuance reflecting a sense of social distance. If "sect" connotes a tolera-ble degree of dissidence and disagreement within a larger society, "heresy" connotes a normative judgment going beyond the society's limits of tolerance. The difference between the two senses is sometimes very small. Expanding and contracting the boundaries of normative self-definition often depends on other social factors in a particular context.

In the development of Judaism after the first revolt the rabbinic tradition became normative, in part because many of the other sects, such as the Essenes, had been wiped out. Rabbinic theology also offered a unifying cultural response to the loss of the Temple and to the questions of Jewish worship and piety. At the same time, the growing dominance and centrality of the rabbinic leadership meant that the Jesus sect, by taking its dissidence and polemics to greater extremes, moved increasingly beyond the limits of tolerance. Key points of disagreement—over scripture, Torah observance, and messianic identity—ultimately became the rhetorical battleground for the growing sense of separateness and animosity on both sides.

A story from the second Jewish revolt (132–35 CE) shows the rupture. Justin Martyr says that Christians in Judea were persecuted by the followers of Bar Kochba if they refused to join in the war.[5] Since Bar Kochba, whose name means "Son of the Star,"[6] was a self-proclaimed messiah, this posed a dilemma, especially for Jewish Christians. Jewish Christians were being forced to choose between believing in the messiahship of Jesus and their loyalty, both political and religious, to Israel. In some ways, this was the last straw for many of them. But the problems had been brewing for some years.

According to a commonly cited theory, the rabbis had already forced a sharper divide with Christians in the year 90 CE at what is known as the "Council of Yavneh." The theory is based on Jewish sources regarding the first generation of rabbinic leaders after Yohanan ben Zakkai established the academy in the coastal city of Yavneh (Jamnia, on the outskirts of modern Tel Aviv) following the destruction of Jerusalem in 70. At the time that Rabbi Eleazar ben Azariah was taking over the leadership of the academy, the assembly began to vote on certain matters of interpretation and ritual practice, according to the Mishnah.[7] One issue reflected in this section of the Mishnah is whether some of the writings of the Jewish scriptures, namely, Song of Songs and Ecclesiastes (or Qoheleth), "defile the hands" because they are holy.[8] It was proposed, therefore, that it was during this discussion that the rabbis finally settled their canon of the Hebrew scriptures in the form of the Torah, the Prophets (Nevi'im), and the Writings (Kethubim). From these three classifications comes the modern designation for the Jewish canon as Tanak. Left out of the canon were a number

of other writings (those later called the "Apocrypha") that had been read as
scripture in the Septuagint, some of which were very important to Christian
interpretation. Hebrew (and Aramaic) originals were given priority over those
composed or used primarily in Greek. The closing of the Hebrew canon thus
served as a cultural and linguistic dividing line.

In most regards, however, the theory of a "Council of Yavneh" is more symbolic than real. To be sure, the Jewish canon was finally closed along these lines;
however, both the notion of a formal "council" at Yavneh and the date of 90 CE
lack any historical grounding.[9] The actual closing of the Jewish canon occurred
somewhat later, perhaps in the 120s up to the mid-second century, but the lines
of debate must have begun earlier. Eventually, it did mark a decisive break with
Christians.

A further indication of the hardening divide arising from a Jewish sense of
normative self-understanding is reflected in rabbinic texts of the second century that exclude various kinds of "heretics"—those who do not believe in the
resurrection, those who do not think the Torah is from heaven, or those who
read heretical books.[10] A more pointed reference to Jewish Christians is seen in
a late addition to the Eighteen Benedictions (*Shemoneh esreh*) as a part of the
Standing Prayer (*'amidah*) in the synagogue service. Known as the "curse
against the heretics" (*birkat ha-minim*), its use in a liturgical context was intended to exclude those who could not pronounce the curse on themselves.

> *For the renegades let there be no hope, and may the arrogant kingdom [or gov-*
> *ernment] soon be rooted out in our days, and the **Nazarenes** and the **minim***
> *perish as in a moment and be blotted out from the book of life and with the*
> *righteous may they not be inscribed. Blessed art thou, O Lord, who humbles*
> *the arrogant. (*Benediction 12)

The word *minim* basically means "sectarians," derived from a root meaning "to
separate or apportion." It was applied generally in rabbinic writings to a variety
of dissenting groups or opinions among Jews. Here, however, by virtue of its
combination with "Nazarenes" it most likely does refer to Jewish Christians
who were still attending the synagogue. Recitation of this curse would have the
effect of excluding these "sectarians" from the synagogue service. On the other
hand, in Jewish tradition that is not the same as banning them from the Jewish
nation per se, but it did begin to force the issue at the level of normative self-
definition.

There is, in addition, a chronological problem. It has often been assumed
that this curse was imposed as a sanction against all Christians at a relatively

early date. Some have said as early as 70 CE; others, about 100. The historical evidence does not support these conclusions, however. For one thing, a later rabbinic legend places the introduction of the "curse" in the time of Rabbi Simeon, who died in about 80 CE, but such dates are often more symbolic than real, as we saw in the case of the Yavneh story.[11] The term "Nazarenes" seems to be an even later addition to the benediction found in only two Jewish manuscripts of medieval date from Egypt. If the reference to "arrogant kingdom" refers to Rome, then it could have arisen as a general curse against Rome and heretics in the period after the first revolt, or conceivably even after the second revolt. In this sense "sectarians" might refer to Zealot extremists or messianic claimants, such as Bar Kochba, as well as others. The subsequent addition of "Nazarenes" transforms this more general curse into a boundary marker against Jewish Christians. But the question remains: When and where was this done? It appears that this may have been a more limited or localized effort, perhaps to prevent Jewish Christians as precentors in Alexandrian synagogues, but a date prior to the middle of the second century is very unlikely.[12]

Rather than representing the final break between Judaism and Christianity, the *birkat ha-minim* reflects the slow and gradual process that was taking place throughout the second century and in different localities. The term *minim*, meaning either "sectarians" or "heretics," was not used in rabbinic sources to refer to gentile Christians, whose teachings are instead simply called "foreign."[13] In other words, there are two different lines of development that resulted in the parting of the ways: one was the gradual predominance of Gentiles in the wider Christian movement; the other, the tensions for Jewish Christians toward both the gentile form of the movement and their Jewish tradition. As we shall see later, these Jewish Christians continued in this tenuous middle ground for several more centuries. Still, it is possible to see how the widening chasm was being felt by local congregations of Jews and Christians especially during the early second century. Pronouncement of curses, as well as blessings, can be heard from time to time on both sides.

Other Gospel Trajectories

As Christianity became more and more separate from Judaism, polemical portrayals were used on both sides as vehicles for denunciation and self-definition. On the Christian side, Christological affirmations became a prominent mechanism of boundary definition for communities in conflict. Before examining the Gospel of John and Hebrews in greater detail, we shall here give a brief sketch of some other early trajectories of Gospel materials that were circulating by the early second century. Each one shows new aspects of Christological definition arising from an increasingly non-Jewish sense of identity.

The Gospel of Peter

According to the Christian historian Eusebius, an ancient Gospel attributed directly to Peter was known to Serapion, bishop of Antioch, in about 200 CE.[14] Eusebius preserves Serapion's report concerning the matter, in the form of a letter, in which he judges finally that the Gospel falsely bears the name of Peter because it was infused with false teachings by docetists (*docetae*). The term "docetists" derives from a Greek verb (*dokeo*) that means "to seem or appear to be something." As we shall see later in this chapter, it refers to the view that Jesus was divine, but only appeared to be a flesh-and-blood human. Serapion's discussion supposes that the *Gospel of Peter* was an earlier document that had been taken over and corrupted by docetic additions. Both components of this characterization deserve further consideration, since it points, on the one hand, to the idea of an early, and otherwise authentic, Gospel tradition circulating under the name of Peter, but, on the other hand, to its misappropriation by later Christian writers and interpreters. In other words, it represents an early "apostolic" source with a problematic trajectory of usage.

A Greek fragment of this *Gospel of Peter*, lost for centuries, was found in 1886–87 in the tomb of a Christian monk at Akhmim in Upper Egypt.[15] The manuscript is rather late, dating from the seventh to the ninth century CE, and was part of an early Christian book containing the *Apocalypse of Peter*, *1 Enoch*, and the *Martyrdom of Julian* (whose identity is otherwise unknown). Nearly a century later, in 1972, two more fragments were found among the Oxyrhynchus papyri that belong to an earlier Greek copy from a scroll datable to about the same time as Serapion's letter. Commencing with the trial of Jesus and ending with his appearance to the disciples at the Sea of Galilee, the text clearly claims to be Peter's first-person narration: "But I, Simon Peter, and Andrew, my brother, took our nets and went to the sea . . ."[16] (See Box 12.1.)

Clearly, many features of this text are later additions. It blames Herod[17] for Jesus's death in collusion with the Jewish priests. Among the canonical Gospels Herod plays no role in the trials of Jesus, except in Luke 23:6–16, where he sends Jesus back to Pilate. In the *Gospel of Peter*, in contrast, Herod presides over the trials and *orders* Pilate to carry out the death sentence. Pilate is thus completely exonerated and later confesses that Jesus must have been the "Son of God" (11.43–46). The anti-Jewish element has been intensified, as the elders and priests recognize their "evil" and lament, "Woe, because of our sins, the judgment and the end of Jerusalem is at hand" (7.25). It also contains the anti-Jewish legend of the guards at the tomb found otherwise only in Matthew 27:62–66 and 28:11–15.

The docetic elements noted in the letter of Serapion are not much in evidence in the preserved portion of the text but may be reflected in the fact that Jesus is said to "feel no pain" while hanging on the cross (4.10) and that at the moment of his death he was "taken up," rather than just dying (5.19). The most striking and unusual scene in the text is an actual description of the resurrection itself:

> *They [the soldiers] then saw three men exit the tomb, two supported the one, and a cross followed them. The heads of the two reached to heaven, but the one whom they supported with their hands stretched beyond the heavens. And they heard a voice from the heavens which said, "Have you preached to the ones who are asleep?" And they heard an answer from the cross, "Yes." (Gos. Pet. 10.39–42)*

Because this form of resurrection or epiphany scene is out of keeping with docetic assumptions, it has been suggested that it may go back to an earlier form of the text.[18] Because its only parallels in the Gospel tradition resemble the transfiguration story (but not the empty tomb scenes), it has been suggested that it may even reflect a form of the Passion narrative older than that in Mark. As a result, some scholars would date the earliest layer of this tradition to the mid-first century. From there it may have influenced the synoptic tradition through Mark but then traveled independently and was adapted and elaborated in later versions, probably first in Syria. During the second century, the text was given some colorations from the other canonical narratives (including John). The numerous anti-Jewish and docetic elements were added perhaps in more than one stage. In its final form, the *Gospel of Peter* has now become a boundary marker not only between Jews and Christians but also between docetists and other Christians.

The Preaching of Peter (Kerygma Petrou)

Also claiming the legacy and authority of Peter is a document known as the *Kerygma Petrou,* or *Preaching of Peter.*[19] Only portions of the text are preserved because they were quoted by the Christian philosopher Clement of Alexandria

BOX 12.1

The Gospel of Peter

DATE: Early layers: mid-first century CE (?); later layers: early to mid-second century

AUTHOR: Unknown

ATTRIBUTION: Peter

LOCATION: Syria

AUDIENCE AND OCCASION: An early source tradition regarding the Passion and resurrection of Jesus later reworked with synoptic elements, anti-Jewish polemics, and docetic elements as a Christological affirmation for an emerging Christian community. Later considered heretical. Condition of the text is fragmentary.

OUTLINE (The story opens in the middle of the trial scene.)

Herod (Antipas) takes charge of Jesus's trial and commands Pilate to carry out the execution (1.1–2).

Joseph (of Arimathea), a friend of Pilate, begs for the body (2.3–5).

Prior to crucifixion, on the day leading up to Passover, they enthrone and mock Jesus (3.6–9).

Jesus is crucified between two criminals (4.10–14).

Jesus dies on the cross (5.15–20).

Jesus's body is removed from the cross and buried (6.21–24).

The elders and priests lament over their evil deed; Peter and the disciples mourn (7.25–27).

---

writing in about the year 200 CE.[20] No ancient manuscript has yet been discovered. Its main interest is also the Passion of Jesus, but it is presented as "Peter's" preaching on the topic and thus has the quality of apologetic or missionary discourse. From his references to the work, it is clear that Clement considered it genuine. It was also used as a source by several Christian apologists of the latter half of the second century.[21] Consequently, it was probably in circulation by the early part of the second century. Since it seems to know Christological formulations from the Gospel of John, it must be slightly later than John; it probably circulated in the region of Asia Minor.

By the mid-third century, however, it came under suspicion because it was used by Gnostic writers. The limited content of the remains suggests that they were presented as "sermons" on individual topics, including a defense of monotheism, a denunciation of pagan idolatry, and a parallel denunciation of Judaism

The scribes and Pharisees approach Pilate to request that guards be put at the tomb beginning on the evening of the Sabbath (8.28–9.34).

The next evening, while the guards are watching the tomb, two heavenly figures descend, roll away the stone, and carry Jesus out, followed by the cross (9.35–10.42).

The guards, preparing to report what they have seen to Pilate, see "a man" descend from heaven and enter the tomb. They then run off to Pilate confessing that Jesus must have been the "Son of God." Pilate confesses the same, then commands them not to tell anyone (11.43–49).

The women come to the tomb planning to anoint the body and perform mourning rituals (12.50–54).

The women find the tomb open with a young man inside who announces that Jesus has arisen. The women flee, terrified (13.55–57).

On the last day of Passover, Peter, Andrew, and Levi, still mourning, take nets and go to the sea . . . (text breaks off; 14.50–60).

FURTHER READING

Crossan, J. D. *The Cross That Spoke*. San Francisco: HarperSanFrancisco, 1988.

Hennecke, E., and W. Schneemelcher. *New Testament Apocrypha*. 2 vols. Philadelphia: Westminster, 1964. 1:179–87. Text and introduction.

Koester, H. *Ancient Christian Gospels*. Philadelphia: Trinity Press International, 1990. Pp. 217–23.

———. *Introduction to the New Testament*. 2 vols. 2d ed. Berlin: DeGruyter, 2000. 2:167–69.

Mirecki, P. A. "Peter, Gospel of." *Anchor Bible Dictionary*. 5:278–81.

and Jewish worship. There are also some passages that seem to take texts from the Hebrew scriptures to elaborate on Christological themes. The work thus shows the growth of an apologetic defense on theological and Christological themes used to reinforce a Christian identity separate from both Jews and Gentiles (or pagans); Christians are instead a "third race."[22] This self-definition will become increasingly important in the apologetic literature of the later second century.[23]

The Gospel of Thomas

The *Gospel of Thomas* is a collection of 114 sayings (or *logia*) of Jesus originally composed in Greek. It is attributed to Didymus Judas Thomas, one of the original disciples of Jesus. The name Thomas appears in the lists of Jesus's disciples in the synoptic Gospels, but the fuller name Didymus (Judas) Thomas occurs only in the Gospel of John and the *Gospel of Thomas*.[24] The name is an important part of the later lore about this apostle, since Didymus and Thoma(s) both mean "twin," in Greek and Aramaic, respectively.[25] Among its sayings are a large number from Q,[26] as well as others that parallel Mark and unique material in Matthew and John.[27] It has been argued, therefore, that the sayings tradition used by the *Gospel of Thomas* seems to be independent of the synoptic tradition even though its date of composition may well be later.[28]

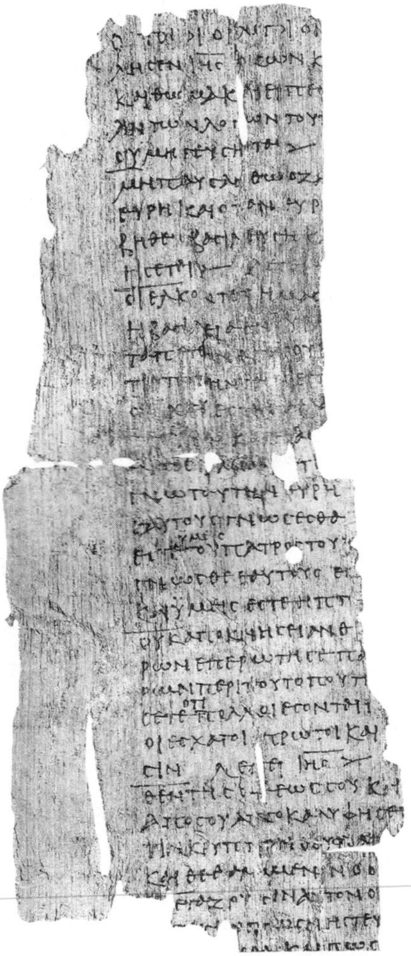

The fragment opens with: "These are the words [. . . which the] living Jesus spoke a[nd which Judas], also called Thomas, [wrote down]." (Lines 1–3).
The name Thomas (Greek ΘωΜΑ) appears as the second word in line 3.

FIGURE 12.1

A fragment of the *Gospel of Thomas* in Greek (P.Oxy 654; early third century); the text corresponds to the prologue and *Logia* 1–3. (From *The Oxyrhynchus Papyri*, ed. Grenfell and Hunt, vol. 4, Plate I; © Egypt Exploration Society, London)

The dates suggested for *Gospel of Thomas* range from as early as 60–70 to as late as about 140 CE. The work is not mentioned by other Christian writers until the end of the second century, when it was considered "heretical."[29] The earliest extant fragments of the text are three Greek papyri dating to the beginning and middle of the third century CE (see Fig. 12.1). The full text was preserved only in a Coptic version of the later fourth century discovered in 1945 among the Nag Hammadi Codices (II.2). Although an early date has recently become popular in some scholarly circles, caution is still warranted, in part because we cannot be sure that the version from Nag Hammadi represents the original form of the tradition.[30] It is likely that an original form of the text was later supplemented with elements from the canonical Gospels or other apocryphal Gospel materials. The original provenance of the work is usually thought to be Syria, and it may have some relation to the origins of the Gospel of John. (See Box 12.2.)

The theology of the *Gospel of Thomas* shows marked development to meet the needs of a new community situation. The eschatology is thoroughly spiritualized or "realized," and Jesus speaks as a heavenly figure—with the voice of Wisdom (Sophia)—giving instructions to those who are presently in the divine kingdom. These shifts are in some cases created by giving a slightly different emphasis or change of wording to some traditional sayings, often to give an antimaterial slant. They seem to be addressed to a particular community of believers with regard to membership and life within the community. Most striking is the fact that there is no reference to Jesus's death, burial, and resurrection. Instead, the figure of Jesus has docetic features that are symbolized in the idea of "twinship"—in which the human believer is symbolized by Thomas, the twin, and "the living Jesus" (*log.* 1) is an entirely spiritual image to be emulated (13). He is the inner spiritual light (24).

For the followers of this tradition, the ritual of baptism, also likened to a "bridal chamber," serves as an entry, not only into emulation of Jesus through inner knowledge, but also into a spiritual union with Jesus. The traditional baptismal symbol of disrobing now means a removal of the physical body (21, 37). In keeping with this, the ethics of the text invoke an ideal of ascetic renunciation of material life in terms of possessions and sexuality (11, 22, 23, 30, 49, 75, 106), and gender symbols are often used to embody these ideals (22, 114). Finally, the sayings in their present form are intentionally formulated to be esoteric, enigmatic, or mysterious. They require interpretation or instruction in order to be used as a means of entry into the community. Thus, the text served simultaneously as a community-defining book and a reflection on the person of Jesus, and these two senses reinforced one another, at least for insiders.

BOX 12.2

The Gospel of Thomas

DATE: Early layers: ca. 60–70 CE; later layers: late first or early second century

AUTHOR: Unknown

ATTRIBUTION: Didymus Judas Thomas

LOCATION: Syria

AUDIENCE AND OCCASION: An early source tradition that has been reworked for a new community situation. Stress on a docetic image of Jesus and asceticism. Thomas, "the twin," is symbolic of the esoteric teachings communicated in the text and for the relationship between the human community and the spiritual Jesus.

OUTLINE: The text in its present (later) form is made up of 114 sayings that do not have a clear sequential or thematic order. It is possible, however, to group them by key themes or topics that recur throughout. The numbers at the right refer to the standard numbering of the *logia*.

1. Secrecy	1, 2
2. Proper Understanding	3, 5, 6, 13, 15, 17, 19, 21, 56, 62, 108
3. Jesus (and Thomas)	Prologue, 10, 13, 15, 17, 18, 24, 28, 37, 38, 43, 59, 61, 62, 72, 77, 91, 108, 111, 113
4. Eating and Drinking	7, 11, 14, 27, 28, 60, 61, 63
5. Male and Female, the Body	21, 22, 37, 61, 87, 112, 114
6. Becoming One, Being Solitary	11, 22, 23, 48, 49, 61, 75, 79, 106
7. The Bridal Chamber	75, 104, 106
8. Discipleship, Election (vs. Materialism)	13, 18, 19, 23, 42, 49, 50, 55, 56, 64, 65, 75, 108, 111, 113
9. The Kingdom	3, 20, 22, 27, 46, 49, 54, 57, 76, 82, 96, 97, 98, 99, 107, 108, 113, 114

FURTHER READING

Cameron, R. "Thomas, Gospel of." *Anchor Bible Dictionary.* 6:535–40.

Hennecke, E., and W. Schneemelcher. *New Testament Apocrypha.* 2 vols. Philadelphia: Westminster, 1964. 1:511–22. Text and introduction.

Koester, H. *Ancient Christian Gospels.* Philadelphia: Trinity Press International, 1990. Pp. 75–127.

———. *Introduction to the New Testament.* 2d ed. 2 vols. Berlin: DeGruyter, 2000. 2:154–58.

Layton, B. *The Gnostic Scriptures: Ancient Wisdom for the New Age.* New York: Doubleday, 1987. Pp. 376–99. Text and introduction.

Pagels, E. *Beyond Belief: The Secret Gospel of Thomas.* New York: Random House, 2003.

Patterson, S. *The Gospel of Thomas and Jesus.* Sonoma, CA: Polebridge Press, 1993.

Riley, G. J. "The *Gospel of Thomas* in Recent Scholarship." *Current Research in Biblical Studies* 2 (1994): 227–52.

Valantasis, R. *The Gospel of Thomas.* London: Routledge, 1997.

The Dialogue of the Savior

Closely related to the *Gospel of Thomas* is another work discovered among the Nag Hammadi codices (III.5), where it carries the title *Dialogue of the Savior*. In its present form it is a series of dialogues between Jesus and some disciples, but it is probably a secondary compilation at least partly based on the *Gospel of Thomas* and the Gospel of John. It is therefore possible that it originated in Syria and that its earliest layers go back to the first part of the second century, if not earlier. Its final form has additions based on later canonical and noncanonical materials. The dialogues seem to be dependent on earlier forms of individual sayings like those in the *Gospel of Thomas*. They show a later reworking in keeping with a fully developed Gnostic theology and into a new genre known as the "Gnostic revelation dialogue." It may be an effort to synthesize several earlier Gospel sources, such as the Gospel of John and the *Gospel of Thomas*, into a more highly developed Gnostic theological system.

The Johannine Circle: The Gospel and 1 John

The Gospel of John shares some notable features with these early-second-century Christian texts. It shows awareness and adaptation of the synoptic tradition, reflects a much greater degree of separation from—and open hostility toward—Judaism, and looks on Jesus as a more heavenly or spiritual being. All these features point to a new social context, one no longer dominated by a Jewish worldview, but by a Hellenistic one instead. At the same time, the Gospel of John stands in some tension with these other, more docetic forms of Christology and thus hints at other lines of conflict at work in the early church of its day.

Authorship, Date, and Location

That the author was the apostle John, son of Zebedee, has been the "official" attribution at least since the time of Irenaeus in the later second century.[31] Even so, there were doubts and debates through the third and fourth centuries because the Gospel was so popular among Gnostic Christians.[32] Other allusions to the text are rare in the second century. The problem is that the name of the author and direct references to the apostle John are missing from the narrative. As with all of the Gospels, the titles were added later as the books were being compiled into formal collections.

A key to the authorship seems to be the intentional avoidance of discussing the figure of John, whose name never appears in the Gospel, even in general lists of the disciples.[33] Instead, an important, but somewhat enigmatic, figure known as the "beloved disciple" becomes prominent in the Passion narrative (beginning at 13:23).[34] Various suggestions have been made as to the identity of this character other than John, including Lazarus (11:1–44) and Nicodemus (3:1–15; 19:39). Absolute certainty is thus impossible; however, it seems clear that the audience of the Gospel was supposed to know the identity of this figure, especially in view of the testimonial about him in the closing verses of the Gospel (21:20–24). At the least, we can say that community members thought of him as the source of "their" Gospel, and, more than likely, as the founder of their community. The weight of the evidence, therefore, points in favor of "the beloved disciple" being the apostle John, son of Zebedee, as the later traditions also affirmed.

Even so, the final testimonial to the role of the "beloved disciple" raises other issues. The passage comes in conjunction with Jesus's last appearance to the disciples after the resurrection (21:1–14). What follows (21:15–19) is a discourse between Jesus and Peter that serves as a recapitulation of Peter's three denials (18:15–17; 25–27), as Jesus now asks Peter three times, "Simon, do you love me?" Then at the end of this discourse, Jesus predicts Peter's death, as is clearly reflected in the author's editorial comment: "He said this to indicate the kind of death by which he [Peter] would glorify God" (21:19).

What follows next is a similar authorial testimony regarding the "beloved disciple":

> Peter turned and saw the disciple whom Jesus loved following them; he was the one who had reclined next to Jesus at the supper and had said, "Lord, who is it that is going to betray you?" When Peter saw him, he said to Jesus, "Lord, what about him?" Jesus said to him, "If it is my will that he remain until I come, what is that to you? Follow me!" **So the rumor spread in the community that this disciple would not die. Yet Jesus did not say to him that he would not die**, but, "If it is my will that he remain until I come, what is that to you?"
>
> This is the disciple who is testifying to these things and has written them, and **we know that his testimony is true**. (John 21:20–24)

The author takes great pains here to make sure the audience knows who is being described by referring back to the story of the last supper at which this same disciple, "whom Jesus loved," reclined next to Jesus (13:23–25). Then in another editorial comment, similar to the one about Peter, the author explains that a "rumor spread in the community that *this disciple* would not die" (21:23); the author then goes on to show that the rumor was false, since it was based on a misunderstanding of what Jesus had meant. In other words, the author of the Gospel is having to account for the fact that the "beloved disciple" is now dead. ∨

This editorial comment tells us several things about the authorship of the Gospel. First, it shows that the Gospel as we now have it was completed after John's (or the "beloved disciple's") death. Several early legends held that John was the last of the original disciples to die, in about 95 CE.[35] The testimonial also shows that there were some Christians who thought John would not die before the return of Jesus, so the occasion of his death has caused chagrin, which the author is trying to allay. Since the rumor is attributed to a saying of Jesus himself, it may well derive from a variation on the statement reported in Mark 9:1: "Truly I tell you, there are some standing here who will not taste death until they see that the kingdom of God has come with power." John's death raised once again a traditional apocalyptic expectation that the author of the Gospel had to dispel. On the other hand, the testimonial finally says that this is indeed "John's" Gospel; however, it also adds an affirmation: "and *we* know his testimony is true" (21:24). Here we have evidence that others in the community, people who thought of themselves as disciples of the "beloved disciple," have carried on the process and completed the Gospel after his death.

Who, then, compiled John's Gospel? We do not really know. The most widely accepted theory is that what we call the Gospel of John is really the product of several distinct stages of transmission and editing, the earliest core of which was thought to be from John himself.[36] According to this theory, there were as many as five distinct stages of editing and composition, of which at least the last two or three occurred after the death of John. If John only died in about 95 CE,[37] this might push the date of final composition into the early 120s. Nonetheless, an early manuscript fragment of John 18 ($\mathfrak{P}^{52}$) is perhaps datable to the mid-second century.[38] (See Fig. 12.2.) So a reasonable date for the *final* stages of composition is between 95 and 120.

As to the place of composition, several legends placed John in Ephesus at the end of his life, and this has been the traditional assumption.[39] Good arguments have also been made that the Gospel—or at least some of its layers—reflects the situation of a Christian community in Syria.[40] It is possible that the trajectory of John's Gospel involves not only multiple layers of authorship but also several changes in social location. This may help to account for the complex nature of the Johannine composition (see Box 12.3 and Fig. 16.1).

Composition and Relation to the Synoptic Gospels

To anyone steeped in the synoptic tradition of Jesus's life the Gospel of John seems at once strange and yet familiar. So it was also in the second century. As early as 200 CE Clement of Alexandria referred to John as "the spiritual Gospel" as a way of accounting for the clear differences while still defending Johannine authorship.[41] Some key changes may be summarized as follows:

1. In the Synoptics, Jesus enters Jerusalem for the first time in the last week of his life (the "triumphal entry"). In John, Jesus goes back and forth to Jerusalem from the beginning of his public career. (See the outline in Box 12.3.)

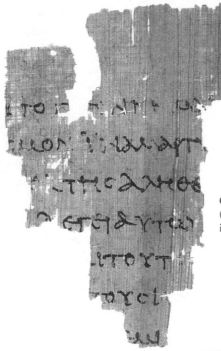

On the front is John 18:31–32; on the reverse (shown here) is John 18:37–38 (visible words are in bold):

> [*"For*] **this I was born**
> [*and I came into the*] **world to bear wit**
> [*ness to the truth. Everyone who is*] **of the truth**
> [*hears my voice."*] **Said to him**
> [*Pilate, "What is truth?"*] **And this**
> [*saying, he went out again to*] **the Je-**
> [*ws and said to them, "No*]**thing**
> [*of a crime do I find in him. But*]

FIGURE 12.2

Partial page from the Gospel of John; probably the earliest datable copy of any New Testament book, $\mathfrak{P}$52 (Rylands Papyrus 457, from Egypt ca. 150–200 CE). (Used by permission of the John Rylands University Library of Manchester)

2. In the Synoptics, the only Passover mentioned is the one on the night *before* the crucifixion. In John, three Passovers are mentioned (2:13; 6:3; 19:31), thus creating the "three-year" ministry of Jesus.

3. In the Synoptics, the cleansing of the Temple occurs just after the triumphal entry, and for Mark is the explicit reason for the plot to kill Jesus (see Box 9.2 for the sequence in Mark). In John, the cleansing of the Temple occurs on Jesus's first visit to Jerusalem (2:13), some two years earlier, and thus has no connection to his death. In John, the raising of Lazarus (11:45–54), who accompanies Jesus in the triumphal entry (12:9–11), is made the explicit basis for a plot by the high priest to kill both Jesus and Lazarus.

4. In the Synoptics, the last supper is the first seder of Passover. In John, the last supper is "before Passover" (13:1), and the crucifixion and burial both take place on the day leading up to the first seder of Passover, which is also the Sabbath (19:31).

The last of these is a well-known and irreconcilable difference between John's Passion narrative and that in the Synoptics (see Box 5.2 for a comparative chart). Yet it would appear that the author(s) of John have made this change quite intentionally in order to render the symbolism of the Passover lamb narratively as a way of interpreting, both theologically and dramatically, the significance of Jesus's death. This theme of the "lamb of God, who takes away the sins of the world" is woven into the narrative from the very beginning of the story when Jesus first comes to John the Baptist (John 1:29, 36). These differences are indeed stark, but they may well have been made intentionally and with full awareness of the synoptic tradition. Several features of the Johannine narrative seem to reflect such an awareness and use of the synoptic tradition, including direct verbal similarities with distinctive linguistic formulations or narrative elements in Mark[42] and Luke,[43] respectively. An awareness of the Synoptics would also help to explain the enigmatic way of portraying the apostle John as the author. It may well be the case that the Johannine author(s) assumed that the audience was aware of the synoptic outline and recognized the changes as a way of creating theological and thematic emphasis through the narrative.[44]

Two other distinctive features of John's narrative merit close attention. The first is its use of a unique collection of miracle stories not found in the synoptic tradition. Usually called the "signs source," these stories reflect an early collection of miracles in which the stories had already been enumerated: the "first

BOX 12.3
The Gospel of John

DATE: Final, ca. 95–120 CE

AUTHOR: Unknown

ATTRIBUTION: John, son of Zebedee (the "beloved disciple")

LOCATION: Syria and/or Ephesus

AUDIENCE AND OCCASION: Written for an early gentile Christian community that has now become fully separate from Judaism, although some tensions are still high. It also is facing some challenges from other Christians who espouse a docetic view of Jesus. The Gospel gives a portrayal of Jesus to support the community's self-understanding and ongoing church life.

OUTLINE

I. Prologue (1:1–18)

II. Beginning of Jesus's Ministry (1:19–51)
    A. Testimony of John the Baptist (1:19–34)
    B. Call of the first disciples (1:35–51)

III. The Ministry of Jesus: The Book of Signs and Discourses (2:1–12:50)
    A. From Cana to Jerusalem to Cana (2:1–4:54)
        1. "First miracle" at Cana (2:1–12)
        2. To Jerusalem for Passover: cleansing of the Temple (2:13–25)
        3. Discourse with Nicodemus (3:1–15) and editorial summary (3:16–21)
        4. John the Baptist's "decrease" and editorial summary (3:22–36)
        5. To Samaria: discourse with Samaritan woman (4:1–45)
        6. To Cana: "second miracle" at Cana (4:46–54)
    B. From Jerusalem to Galilee to Jerusalem (5:1–10:42)
        1. Miracles in Jerusalem at festival (5:1–30)
        2. Confrontation with Jewish leaders (5:31–47)
        3. Galilee (at Passover): feeding the five thousand and walking on water (6:1–21)
        4. Bread of Life discourse and confrontation with Jews (6:22–71)
        5. Jerusalem: feast of Succoth, controversy, and near arrest (7:1–52)
        6. Light of the World discourse and condemnation of Jews (8:12–59)
        7. Healing of the blind man (expulsion from synagogue; 9:1–41)
        8. Good Shepherd and Door discourses (10:1–21)
        9. Hanukkah: Jesus rejected and near arrest (10:22–42)

C. Final signs and confrontations in Jerusalem (11:1–12:50)
1. Bethany: raising of Lazarus and Resurrection discourse (11:1–44)
2. The high priest's plot to kill Jesus (11:45–54)
3. Approach of Passover: anointing at Bethany (11:55–12:8)
4. Plot to kill Jesus and Lazarus (12:9–11)
5. Triumphal entry and discourses in Temple (12:12–50)

IV. The Passion Narrative (13:1–20:31)
A. Before Passover: the last supper, betrayal plot, and discourse (13:1–14:31)
B. Discourses on the way to Gethsemane (15:1–17:26)
C. The betrayal and arrest (18:1–11)
D. Trial before high priest and Peter's three denials (18:12–27)
E. Trial before Pilate and sentencing (18:28–19:16)
F. The crucifixion, death, and burial (on the day leading up to Passover; 19:17–42)
G. The empty tomb and appearances in Jerusalem (20:1–29)
H. Summary (20:30–31)

V. Epilogue: Final Appearance in Galilee and Testimonial (21:1–25)

FURTHER READING

Brown, R. E. *The Community of the Beloved Disciple: The Life, Loves, and Hates of an Individual Church in New Testament Times.* London: Chapman, 1979.
———. *The Gospel According to John.* Anchor Bible. 2 vols. New York: Doubleday, 1985.
Culpepper, R. A. *Anatomy of the Fourth Gospel: A Study in Literary Design.* Philadelphia: Fortress, 1983.
———. *John, the Son of Zebedee: The Life of a Legend.* Columbia: University of South Carolina Press, 1994.
Koester, H. *Introduction to the New Testament.* 2d. ed. Berlin: DeGruyter, 2000. 2:182–83.
Kysar, R. D. "John, The Gospel of." *Anchor Bible Dictionary.* 3:912–31.
———. *John, the Maverick Gospel.* Atlanta: John Knox, 1976.
Martyn, J. L. *History and Theology in the Fourth Gospel.* 2d ed. Nashville, TN: Abingdon, 1979.
Meeks, W. A. "The Man from Heaven in Johannine Sectarianism." *Journal of Biblical Literature* 91 (1972): 44–72.
———. *The Prophet-King.* Leiden: Brill, 1967.
Schnelle, U. *Antidocetic Christology in the Gospel of John.* Minneapolis: Fortress, 1992.
Smith, D. M. *The Composition and Order of the Fourth Gospel.* New Haven, CT: Yale University Press, 1965.
———. *Johannine Christianity: Essays on Its Setting, Sources, and Theology.* Columbia: University of South Carolina Press, 1987.
———. *John Among the Gospels: The Relationship in Twentieth-Century Research.* Minneapolis: Fortress, 1992.

sign" (2:11), the "second sign" (4:54), and concluding with a summary (20:31–32). These miracle stories are unique to John, seem to have some allegorical symbolism regarding Jesus, and have been used as a narrative thread in the story.

The second feature is John's use of a peculiar form of self-disclosure discourse in which Jesus unfolds key elements of his identity to his followers. Called the "I am" discourses, these speeches employ a pronouncement formula regularly used in hymns or aretalogies of gods and heroes in Greco-Roman tradition. They also have affinities with the later genre known as the "Gnostic revelation dialogue."[45] The discovery in Egypt of an unknown gospel (Papyrus Egerton 2) shows that dialogues like this were in circulation in the early part of the second century and might have served as one of the sources for the Gospel of John.[46] In John, these "I am" discourses are also frequently paired with miracle stories in which Jesus exemplifies a particular theme or symbol. For example, the "Bread of Life" discourse (6:25–58) follows immediately upon the feeding of the five thousand (6:1–14); the "Light of the World" discourse (8:12–58) is followed immediately by the healing of a blind man (9:1–34); and the "Resurrection and Life" pronouncement (11:25–27) is contained within the raising of Lazarus story (11:1–44).

Jesus and the Jews in the Johannine Gospel

The discourse units in John are important devices in yet another way, for they also serve as occasions for controversy, especially where "the Jews" react negatively to Jesus's self-disclosure. At the same time, each discourse reveals new aspects of Jesus's heavenly nature, and these two features are mutually reinforcing. The basic structure is this: Jesus announces his "descent from the Father" in conjunction with a basic metaphor or symbol, the Jews react, and Jesus denounces them using some form of the same symbolism. Here is the pattern as reflected in two moments within the "Bread of Life" discourse, which plays on the symbolism of the manna from heaven in Exodus 16 (cf. John 6:31, 49).

*Jesus said to them, "**I am the bread of life**. Whoever comes to me will never be hungry, and whoever believes in me will never be thirsty. But I said to you that you have seen me and yet do not believe. Everything that the Father gives me will come to me, and anyone who comes to me I will never drive away; **for I have come down from heaven**, not to do my own will, but the will of him who sent me. And this is the will of him who sent me, that I should lose nothing of all that he has given me, but raise it up on the last day. This is indeed* *the will of my Father, that all who see the Son and believe in him may have eternal life; and I will raise them up on the last day."*

Then the Jews began to complain about him because he said, "I am the bread that came down from heaven." They were saying, "Is not this Jesus, the son of Joseph, whose father and mother we know? How can he now say, 'I have come down from heaven'?" (John 6:35–42)

"Your ancestors ate the manna in the wilderness, and they died. This is the bread that comes down from heaven, so that one may eat of it and not die. I am the living bread that came down from heaven. Whoever eats of this bread will live forever; and the bread that I will give for the life of the world is my flesh."

*The Jews then disputed among themselves, saying, "How can this man give us his flesh to eat?" So Jesus said to them, "Very truly, I tell you, **unless you eat the flesh of the Son of Man and drink his blood, you have no life in you. Those who eat my flesh and drink my blood have eternal life,** and I will raise them up on the last day; for my flesh is true food and my blood is true drink. **Those who eat my flesh and drink my blood abide in me, and I in them.** Just as the living Father sent me, and I live because of the Father, so **whoever eats me will live because of me." (John 6:49–57)***

One will quickly recognize that the discourse plays on eucharistic metaphors from the worship of the early church.[47] Its liturgical resonance also gives it confessional force for members of the Johannine community.

The "I am" discourses are, on the one hand, pivotal to the Johannine Gospel's Christology—Jesus as a heavenly figure—and, on the other, pivotal to its castigation of Jews. They function as boundary-defining mechanisms for the Johannine community. These controversies become increasingly more heated as the Johannine Jesus denounces the Jews in harsher terms:

"I know that you are descendants of Abraham; yet you look for an opportunity to kill me, because there is no place in you for my word. I declare what I have seen in the Father's presence; as for you, you should do what you have heard from the Father." . . .

They said to him, "We are not illegitimate children; we have one father, God himself." Jesus said to them, "If God were your Father, you would love me, for I came from God and now I am here. I did not come on my own, but he sent me. Why do you not understand what I say? It is because you cannot accept my word. You are from your father the devil, and you choose to do your father's desires." (John 8:37–44)

This passage comes at the end of the "Light of the World" discourse and bases the confession as well as the denunciation in retrospect of Jesus's crucifixion. These denunciations are symbolically very powerful, because they are paired with liturgical and confessional elements and thus make John's polemic some of the most inflammatory anti-Jewish rhetoric in the early Christian tradition.

The Gospel of John thus represents a social situation in which there is much greater separation between the Christian community and its Jewish neighbors. The theme of rejection of the message about Jesus has now been magnified into a total rejection of Jesus as the one sent from heaven by God. The community's own confessional statements about Jesus now function as strict boundary markers against Judaism per se.

At the same time, there are reflections of the ongoing tensions that must have led to this harsh turn in the polemics of separation. The miracle of the blind man (John 9:1–34), which follows the "Light of the World" discourse, exemplifies the dilemma. Jesus heals a man who has been blind from birth, but the Pharisees—anachronistically portrayed as religious authorities who oversee piety compliance—challenge the one who has been healed and his parents, seeking to denigrate Jesus's power. Finally, they threaten anyone who persists in *confessing* Jesus with expulsion from the synagogue (9:22); so when the blind man does so, they "cast him out" (9:34).

An anachronism for the days of Jesus, this story reflects the experience of some within the Johannine Christian community for whom confession of Jesus had meant expulsion from the Jewish community. Yet in John's social context this experience cannot have been the norm any longer, as the distance from Judaism has grown. The story thus serves as further rationale for the denunciation of Judaism, because *it* had rejected both Jesus and his followers. For the Johannine community, at least, the breach with Judaism had become irreparable. The Johannine Christology—Jesus, the man from heaven—is a nascent form of creedal confession that provides a correlative theological warrant for separateness.[48]

John, Thomas, and Docetism: The Evidence of 1 John

The "man from heaven" Christology grew in part out of the increasing separation from Judaism and in part from a Greco-Roman cultural matrix. It was nonetheless able to draw on traditional forms of Jewish and Jewish Christian theology, such as the Wisdom tradition and Q. The well-known use of the term *Logos* ("Word") in the prologue to the Gospel (John 1:1–18) relies on the speculative appropriation of the Wisdom tradition in Philo, where the *Logos* is the "heavenly *human*" created in the image of God. This *Logos* and "man from heaven" imagery is worked out, however, through the self-disclosure discourses of Jesus. The language of Jesus in these discourses comes from older forms of speculative Jewish theology that had already come into specifically Christian usage. Now Jesus speaks as a heavenly figure.[49]

By the early part of the second century, however, another question began to arise regarding the relationship of this new and powerful Christological symbolism to the traditional affirmation of Jesus as a crucified, and very human, suffering messiah. The Johannine Gospel seems to be intent on trying to hold these two rather different traditions together by asserting that Jesus is the Logos or man from heaven who "became flesh and lived among us, and we have seen his glory, glory as the father's only son" (John 1:14). John's Gospel, in sharp contrast to the *Gospel of Thomas,* is emphatic in preserving traditional synoptic elements, most notably the Passion narrative itself.

An additional clue to the social context for this kind of debate among Christians comes from another document of the Johannine circle, commonly called 1 John. Not a letter in form, 1 John does not have even superficial epistolary trappings, even though its authorial voice addresses the audience in the second person: "My little children, I am writing to you . . ." (1 John 2:1, 7, 18, 26, 28). There is a high degree of congruence between uniquely Johannine vocabulary and themes in the Gospel and those found in 1 John, as seen in its prologue:

> *What was from the beginning—what we have heard, what we have seen with our eyes, what we have looked at and **our own hands have touched**—concerning the Word of Life: this Life was made manifest, and we have seen it and testify to it, and declare it to you to be the eternal Life that was with the Father and was manifested to us. (1 John 1:1–2)*[50]

Even so, there are also some notable differences.[51] So it does not appear that 1 John and the Gospel were written by the same author(s), although they probably come from the same community of thought (see Box 12.4).

It has been argued that 1 John was written slightly before the Gospel, at least in its final form.[52] If so, 1 John would reflect a debate among Christians over docetic theology and a later form of the Gospel developed to settle the conflict in a normative fashion. Others have argued that 1 John was written a decade or so after the Gospel and thus reflects an effort to assert the orthodoxy of the Gospel over against those who saw it as too docetic. In fact, legends about John espousing a docetic theology still circulated in the middle to latter part of the second century in the apocryphal *Acts of John* (see Chapter 15).[53] That the

BOX 12.4
The First Letter of John

DATE: Either ca. 95–105 or ca. 120–130 CE, probably the latter

AUTHOR: Unknown

ATTRIBUTION: John, son of Zebedee (assumed but unspecified)

LOCATION: Syria and/or Ephesus

AUDIENCE AND OCCASION: Written for an early gentile Christian community that has now become fully separate from Judaism and is also facing some challenges from other Christians who espouse a docetic view of Jesus. Closely related to the Gospel of John in date, authorship, and situation; however, the precise relationship between the two and the sequence of composition is debated.

OUTLINE

   I. Prologue (1:1–4)

  II. Light and Darkness (1:5–2:11)

 III. The Believer and the World (2:12–17)

 IV. Truth and Lies (2:18–27)

  V. Children of God and Children of the Devil (2:28–3:10)

 VI. Love for One Another (3:11–18)

VII. Truth and Lies (3:19–24)

VIII. False Prophets (4:1–6)

 IX. Love for One Another (4:7–21)

  X. Testimonies of the Son (5:1–12)

 XI. Concluding Exhortation (5:13–21)

FURTHER READING

Brown, R. E. *The Community of the Beloved Disciple: The Life, Loves, and Hates of an Individual Church in New Testament Times.* London: Chapman, 1979.

———. *The Epistles of John.* Anchor Bible. New York: Doubleday, 1982.

Culpepper, R. A. *John, the Son of Zebedee: The Life of a Legend.* Columbia: University of South Carolina Press, 1994.

Houlden, J. L. *The Johannine Epistles.* Harper New Testament Commentary. New York: Harper & Row, 1973.

Kysar, R. D. "John, Epistles of." *Anchor Bible Dictionary.* 3:900–912.

Lieu, J. *The Theology of the Johannine Epistles.* Cambridge: Cambridge University Press, 1991.

Rensberger, D. *1 John, 2 John, 3 John.* Abingdon New Testament Commentary. Nashville, TN: Abingdon, 1997.

Schnelle, U. *Antidocetic Christology in the Gospel of John.* Minneapolis: Fortress, 1992.

Smith, D. M. *First, Second, and Third John.* Interpretation. Louisville, KY: John Knox, 1991.

———. *Johannine Christianity: Essays on Its Setting, Sources, and Theology.* Columbia: University of South Carolina Press, 1987.

Johannine circle was already at the center of such a Christological debate is also shown from 1 John's warning about "false prophets:"

*Beloved, do not believe every spirit, but test the spirits to see whether they are from God; for many false prophets have gone out into the world. By this you know the Spirit of God: every spirit that confesses that Jesus Christ has come in the flesh is from God, and every spirit that does not confess Jesus is not from God. And this is the spirit of the **antichrist**, of which you have heard that it is coming; and now it is already in the world. (1 John 4:1–3)*

The term "antichrist" only occurs in the Johannine letters, and, as here, it refers in each case to Christian prophets who profess a different Christology:[54] specifically, they do not confess that "Jesus came in the flesh" (cf. 2 John 7). In other words, the antichrist refers to docetic Christians, those who said that Jesus only appeared to be human but was really a divine apparition.

Docetism as a theological expression within Christian circles is not attested before the last years of the first century. Apart from the reflections we have already seen in the *Gospel of Thomas*, the *Gospel of Peter*, and 1 John, it began to be discussed as a problem by writers of the early second century.[55] Most notable are the comments of Ignatius, bishop of Antioch in Syria, who wrote letters while visiting in Asia Minor in about 110–13 CE. He thus represents the axis of intra-Christian relations also found in the Johannine and Thomas traditions, and he was most likely a close contemporary of the debates reflected there. (See Chapters 13 and 16.)

Although the Gospel of John in its final form seems fully in agreement with this antidocetic emphasis, it is also likely that some of these features were strengthened over time in the editorial process. As some forms of Christianity became more extreme in their use of the "man from heaven" Christology, it is possible that the Johannine community found it necessary to mediate the problem. One narrative adaptation in the story may let us in on this intra-Christian debate. Other than the Syrian Thomas tradition, out of which came the *Gospel of Thomas*, only the Gospel of John gives any serious attention to the figure (and name) of Thomas "the twin."[56] Yet through the characterization of the Johannine Gospel he comes to be more famous as "doubting Thomas." The crucial scene comes just after Jesus has appeared for the first time to the disciples (John 20:19–23):

But Thomas (who was called the Twin), one of the twelve, was not with them when Jesus came. So the other disciples told him, "We have seen the Lord."

But he said to them, "Unless I see the mark of the nails in his hands, and put
my finger in the mark of the nails and my hand in his side, I will not believe."
*   A week later his disciples were again in the house, and Thomas was with*
them. Although the doors were shut, Jesus came and stood among them and
said, "Peace be with you." Then he said to Thomas, "Put your finger here and
see my hands. Reach out your hand and put it in my side. Do not doubt but
believe." Thomas answered him, "My Lord and my God!" Jesus said to him,
"Have you believed because you have seen me? Blessed are those who have not
seen and yet have come to believe." (John 20:24–29)

The postresurrection scene in which Jesus and Thomas come face-to-face is
the climax of the Gospel. It is all the more telling, then, that Thomas is now
made the vehicle for touching the flesh of the crucified and risen Christ. Is this
a conscious and overt effort on the part of the Johannine author(s) to counteract the more extreme forms of docetic theology of the *Gospel of Thomas*? It may
well be.[57] If so, it means that the Johannine community is now facing self-
definition questions on two very distinct fronts. The "man from heaven" Christology has been a successful tool in ratifying the separation from Judaism, but
now some Christians have taken it too far. The older tradition of the Jesus
movement—with its Jewish messiah and emphasis on the death and resurrection—is in jeopardy of marginalization. The innovative solution of the Johannine community is its incarnation/Passion Christology.

The Letter to the Hebrews

Another effort to use innovative Christological reflection is seen in the so-called
letter to the Hebrews. Although this work was early on associated with Paul, it
nowhere bears Paul's name. Nor does it resemble a letter—and especially not a
Pauline letter—except at the very end. Instead, it seems to be a homily, a "word
of exhortation" (Heb. 13:22), seeking to bolster faith by giving Christological
exposition. It thus reflects another effort near the beginning of the second century to systematize hitherto disparate Christian teachings as a way of reinforcing communal identity.

Authorship, Date, and Location

The earliest manuscripts of Hebrews place it among the letters of Paul.[58] Even
though the final salutations (Heb. 13:22–25) look like a conscious effort to ape

Pauline names and formulas, its stylistic differences were recognized by the early Christian writers of the second through the fourth centuries. It was variously attributed to Barnabas (so Tertullian), to Luke (so Clement of Alexandria), and to Clement of Rome.[59] Even so, its high status as a book of the church is reflected in Origen's cautious view: "As to who wrote it, God alone knows."[60] A clearer sense of date and location is nonetheless possible. The date of Hebrews seems to be fixed by the fact that *1 Clement* quotes or paraphrases it on several occasions. The most important of these is *1 Clement* 36.2–6, which has a series of psalmic attestations to Christ drawn from the Septuagint, all in the same order as they appear in Hebrews 1:3–13. In one of these, Hebrews (1:7) and *1 Clement* (36.3) have the identical variant to the LXX wording of Psalm 104(103):4. It is usually assumed, therefore, that *1 Clement* is working from a copy of Hebrews.[61]

The traditional date of *1 Clement* is about 95–96, based on the legendary identification of the author, Clement of Rome, with a certain Flavius Clemens who was executed under Domitian.[62] In fact, there is no direct or known connection between Clement of Rome and the senatorial family of Flavius Clemens, who was a relative of Domitian. Consequently, *1 Clement* has been dated as late as 140, but a more reasonable date would be about 100–120 CE.[63] Hebrews must be still earlier but may date anywhere between 90 and 115 CE.[64]

The connection to Clement may well provide the best hint about a location for Hebrews in Rome. This view is further supported by the fact that Hebrews seems to have affinities with language and themes in 1 Peter, which was also from Rome (see Chapter 11), and there are final salutations from "the saints from Italy" (Heb. 13:24).

As to the identity and location of the audience of Hebrews, that too "God only knows." That they were Jewish Christians from the homeland seems unlikely, given the sophisticated nature of the Greek and the literary command with which the LXX is used. Instead, its retrospective outlook (2:3; 13:7) shows that the author and audience come from a later generation now looking back on the apostles as a past age.[65] It may well be that a later Roman Christian from roughly the time of Clement was consciously imitating and building on Pauline tradition, perhaps with a knowledge of some Pauline, and even deutero-Pauline, letters, and possibly even Luke-Acts.[66] If such is the case, some passages are meant to sound as though "Paul" is now going beyond his earlier instructions by giving a more mature theology (Heb. 6:1–2).[67] What little can be detected from other internal references suggests a Christian congregation facing some crisis of faith. Whether this is a real situation or a literary device to propel its exposition of the faith is difficult to say.[68] (See Box 12.5.)

BOX 12.5

The Letter to the Hebrews

DATE: ca. 90–115 CE

AUTHOR: Unknown

ATTRIBUTION: Paul? (indirectly)

LOCATION: Probably Rome

AUDIENCE AND OCCASION: The stated purpose is to present a "word of exhortation" (13:22) that will instill a more mature understanding of Christ beyond the elementary teachings that had already been learned (6:1–2). Constructed as an extended *midrash,* or exposition, on Christological themes built around several key passages from the Septuagint, especially Psalm 110:1–4, it exhorts the audience to hold to its faith in Christ, "the pioneer and perfecter" of salvation, who is now seated at the right hand of God (2:10; 5:9; 12:2).

OUTLINE

    I. Exordium: The Exalted Son (1:1–4)

   II. His Exaltation over the Angels After Humiliation (1:5–2:18)
      A. Christ superior to the angels (1:5–14)
      B. Exhortation (2:1–4)
      C. Midrash on Ps. 8:5–7 (2:5–18)

  III. His Exaltation over Moses and Joshua (3:1–5:10)
      A. Christ superior to Moses (3:1–6)
      B. Midrash on Ps. 95:7–11 (3:7–4:5)
      C. Exhortation (4:6–13)
      D. Christ the high priest (4:14–5:10)

Midrash as Christological Reflection

Hebrews represents a very different type of Christological reflection from that seen in the Gospel of John. Missing from Hebrews are the docetic tinges of John's (or Thomas's) "man from heaven" Christology and its polemical tone. Hebrews works, instead, from a more decidedly Jewish frame of reference based in the exposition of the scriptures, but exclusively in Greek from the Septuagint. Common in Jewish tradition, this kind of exposition, in which various passages of scripture are strung together by means of verbal or thematic similarities to create an intertextual signification, is called *midrash.* It also draws exten-

FURTHER READING

Attridge, H. W. *Hebrews*. Hermeneia. Philadelphia: Fortress, 1989.
———. "Hebrews, Epistle to the." *Anchor Bible Dictionary*. 3:97–105.
Filson, F. V. *"Yesterday": A Study of Hebrews in the Light of Chapter 13*. London: SCM, 1967.
Fuller, R. H. "Hebrews." In *Hebrews, James, 1–2 Peter, Jude, Revelation*. Proclamation Commentaries. Philadelphia: Fortress, 1977. Pp. 1–27.
Hay, D. M. *Glory at the Right Hand: Psalm 110 in Early Christianity*. Missoula, MT: Scholars Press, 1973.
Peterson, D. *Hebrews and Perfection*. Cambridge: Cambridge University Press, 1982.
Swetnam, J. *Jesus and Isaac: A Study of the Epistle to the Hebrews in the Light of the Aqedah*. Rome: Pontifical Biblical Institute, 1981.
Thompson, J. W. *The Beginning of Christian Philosophy*. Washington, DC: Catholic Biblical Association, 1982.
Williamson, R. *Philo and the Epistle to the Hebrews*. Leiden: Brill, 1970.

sively from the wisdom tradition (Sirach and Wisdom of Solomon) as well as other Jewish scriptures (*1 Enoch, Psalms of Solomon, Martyrdom of Isaiah,* 1, 2, and 4 Maccabees). Allusions are woven around and through passages from the Psalms, Genesis, Leviticus, and the prophets to create a tapestry of images and themes regarding the role of Christ in the divine scheme of salvation.

At the center of the Christological midrash in Hebrews are two themes. One concerns the idea that Jesus, the suffering messiah, was the preexistent son of God who was made human in order to die in a sacrificial manner and who was then exalted to heaven. This descent and ascent Christology has raw structural analogies to themes found in the Gospel of John but is nonetheless different in its

overall scheme. Its starting point is drawn, instead, from earlier Pauline formulations about the suffering and exalted messiah (e.g., Phil. 2:6–11) that had already been elaborated with wisdom traditions in the Pauline school (cf. Col.
1:15–20; Eph. 1:3–10, 20–23) and with sacrificial ideas of atonement in 1 Peter
(2:12–15; 3:16–18). Thus, Hebrews may reflect a distinctive effort to work out
these Christological themes within the churches at Rome.

The second central theme in Hebrews is the high-priesthood of Christ,
which provides both the culmination of his exaltation in heaven and the replacement for the earthly Temple of Israel. Here the midrash weaves together
passages and themes about sacrifice, the layout of the Temple, and the operations of the levitical priesthood that reflect an astounding fascination with early
Israelite cultic traditions from the scriptures. These themes then turn around
the key Christological image for Hebrews, namely, that through his sacrificial
death and exaltation Jesus becomes "a priest forever after the order of
Melchizedek" (Ps. 110:4; Heb. 5:6, 10; 6:20; 7:1–28). This elaborate image rests
on the enigmatic and legendary figure of Melchizedek, who was visited by
Abraham in Genesis 14:17–20 (Heb. 7:1–10). His name in Hebrew means "king
of righteousness" or "righteous king" (cf. Heb. 7:2); he is also identified as king
of Salem (i.e., Jerusalem), and thus "king of peace" (Heb. 7:3). This story from
Genesis is used to elaborate the sense of Psalm 110:

> *The Lord said to my lord, "Sit at my right hand until I make your enemies
> your footstool." The Lord sends out from Zion your mighty scepter. Rule in the
> midst of your enemies.* **With [by means of] you is the beginning in the day
> of your power, in the splendor of the holy ones, I bore you from the womb
> before the morning star.** *The Lord has sworn and will not change
> his mind, "You are a priest forever according to the order of Melchizedek."*
> *(Ps. 110 [109]:1–4, LXX)*[69]

Although the first verse of this psalm had been used by Paul (1 Cor. 15:27; Rom.
8:34), Luke-Acts (Acts 2:34–35), and the Pauline school (Eph. 1:20; Col. 3:1) to
validate the final exaltation of Christ through the resurrection, verses 3–4 (in
their distinctive LXX version) had not previously been used as a way of ex-
pounding the idea more fully. Thus Hebrews develops the Melchizedek imagery in conjunction with other messianic triumph themes in Psalm 2:7–8 and
Psalm 8:5–7 to show that the rule of the messiah-Christ in heaven as an eternal
priest is the ultimate plan of God from and for the ages.

The figure of Melchizedek was occasionally used in Judaism. References appear in the Dead Sea Scrolls to validate an eschatological messianic claim on the

Jerusalem Temple.[70] The mode of exposition in Hebrews, however, is a thoroughly Christian reinterpretation and results in a rhetoric showing Christ as the culmination of the tradition of Israel. In that sense, it is perhaps the first thoroughgoing effort to work out a Christian supersessionist theology, that is, that Christ—and thus Christianity—had superseded Moses, the law, the Temple, and so forth as a means of approach to God. The tight interplay of scriptures to effect this theological claim is indeed so sophisticated and powerful that it may be a prime example of why the Septuagint and the Greek apocryphal books were eventually rejected in the formation of the rabbinic canon. Similarly, the intertextual play with Pauline and deutero-Pauline traditions served as a new theological filter through which Paul's ideas about the Torah and Judaism were to be read. Especially when Hebrews was placed in the collection of Paul's letters immediately following Romans, it became more difficult for later Christians to read Paul's very Jewish theology on its own terms.

Finally, Hebrews punctuates its Christological midrash with alternating exhortations that stress the ultimacy of this confession. Since Christ is so far superior to all else in God's scheme of redemption as seen in the Hebrew scriptures, how can one turn away from this faith? The gauntlet is down; a clear line has been drawn. It is no longer only that some Jews might have rejected Jesus; rather, God had all along intended Jesus to replace Judaism. Although it retains a self-conscious and exclusive identity from Judaism, the Christology of Hebrews now becomes an absolute sanction that excludes all other modes of access to that same God of Israel. This is a new and distinctive mode of normative self-definition, at least for those who read and used Hebrews.

CHAPTER THIRTEEN

With the Voice of
an Apostle

A New Generation of Leaders

Now Polycarp was not only taught by apostles and hung out with many who had seen the Lord, but he was also appointed bishop by apostles in Asia in the church of Smyrna. We even saw him in our early years, for he lived a long time and passed from this life in extreme old age, an honored and illustrious martyr. He always taught those things which he had also learned from the apostles, which are the traditions of the church, those things which alone are true. (Irenaeus Against Heresies 3.3.4)

Although new works continued to be penned in the name of apostles into the early years of the second century, there was nonetheless a growing awareness that the old generation had passed on and a new one had dawned. It was an uneasy moment. The days of Peter, Paul, and James, who had died some fifty years earlier, were long past. It was only the legends about John and the tales and reminiscences of those who had actually known apostles that kept the tradition fresh. Now even they were passing away, and all one could do was preserve their memories by writing them down. The age of the "apostles" was gone.

The word "apostle" (*apostolos* in Greek) literally means "one sent out" or "an emissary." When Paul uses it, he usually just means a "missionary," that is, one sent out to spread the word about Jesus (Rom. 16:7; 1 Cor. 12:28; 15:7; 2 Cor. 12:11–12; Gal. 2:7–8; 1 Thess. 2:7). In some cases he uses it to refer to an "emissary," such as Epaphroditus, sent by one of his churches (2 Cor. 8:23; Phil. 2:25). It was not limited to the original disciples of Jesus, sometimes referred to simply as "the twelve," or to those who had seen Jesus after the resurrection (cf. 1 Cor. 15:5; Gal. 1:19). Already in Luke-Acts at the end of the first century there is a self-consciousness of coming from a later generation.[1] Now "the apostles" is beginning to mean the earliest followers of Jesus, the leaders of the first generation of the movement. By the time we get to Irenaeus in about 177 CE, the picture is complete. And yet another generation stood in between; it included others, such as Polycarp, who had known the apostles.

The term "apostolic fathers" is the name popularly ascribed since the seventeenth century to that group of authors or writings that seem to continue the apostolic legacy in the generation immediately following the apostles. They typically include Clement of Rome (*1–2 Clement*), Ignatius of Antioch, Polycarp of Smyrna, the *Shepherd* of Hermas, the *Epistle of Barnabas,* and the *Didache.* Other writers sometimes included in the list are Papias, Quadratus, and the anonymous work known as the *Epistle to Diognetus.*

In early modern scholarship all these writings were thought to be indisputably genuine and datable to the lifetime of Paul or shortly thereafter. In large measure, this view arose from the fact that the two letters ascribed to Clement of Rome were included in the New Testament of Codex Alexandrinus, one of the first discoveries of a complete Christian Bible that actually dated to the early church.[2] This view seems to continue an earlier Alexandrian Christian belief that *1–2 Clement*, the *Didache,* the *Epistle of Barnabas,* and sometimes the *Shepherd* of Hermas were inspired scriptures.[3] They were thus traditionally assumed to convey the "main stream" of orthodox Christian succession directly from Peter and Paul.[4]

The apostolic fathers represent a diverse picture of regional developments spanning from the third into the fourth generation of the Christian movement. They are contemporaneous with or, in some cases, even earlier than certain New Testament documents (to be discussed in Chapter 16). In general, their dates range from the beginning of the second century down to the mid-150s CE; therefore, we must deal with issues of dating, identity, and historical situation as we look at the individual writings of this group. One characteristic that does seem to run through all of them is a concern to give instruction, exhortation, or correction to existing Christian groups regarding the proper ordering of church life. Pivotal issues include the conduct of worship, emerging questions over belief or doctrine, and sources of authority or leadership in deciding such matters.

Syria: The *Epistle of Barnabas* and the *Didache*

The Epistle of Barnabas

The *Epistle of Barnabas* is actually an anonymous treatise that early on was ascribed to Barnabas, the one-time associate of Paul (see Box 13.1). The name Barnabas does not appear in the text, however. The work was considered genuine especially among Alexandrian Christians from the time of Clement of Alexandria (ca. 200 CE) and was included in the New Testament canon in Codex Sinaiticus (early fifth century).[5] Despite the title, the work is not really a letter, although it does have hortatory addresses to ostensible recipients at the beginning and the end (chaps. 1 and 21, respectively). It is better understood as a sermon of sorts that is rather clearly divided into two distinct parts: chapters 2–16 deal with the "correct" interpretation of the Jewish scriptures as they pre-

---

BOX 13.1

Barnabas in the New Testament and Tradition

In Paul's Letters

Barnabas was Paul's co-worker in Cilicia and Antioch in the period leading up to and immediately following the Jerusalem conference, but they had a falling out at the time of the "blowup" with Peter at Antioch (Gal. 2:1–13). Paul charged Barnabas, like Peter, with hypocrisy for refusing to eat with gentile converts. Paul gives no other information about Barnabas, although some later allusions (1 Cor. 9:4) might seem to suggest that they continued to interact, or at least that Paul's partnership with Barnabas was generally known. A passing reference in Colossians 4:10 (whose authorship by Paul is debated by scholars; see Box 11.1) would also make Mark the cousin of Barnabas and seems to have them still associated with Paul at a relatively late stage of Paul's career.

In Acts

Acts 13:1–15:41 portrays the relationship somewhat differently. A Jew (and Levite) originally from Cyprus, Barnabas had joined the movement in the early days after Pentecost (Acts 4:36), where he rose to early prominence. It was Barnabas who reportedly introduced Paul at Jerusalem shortly after his conversion (Acts 9:27, but cf. Gal. 1:17–23; see Chapter 7). Barnabas was later dispatched to Antioch by the Jerusalem church, at which time he recruited

figure and validate Christian beliefs, and chapters 18–20 give ethical instruction in a form known as "The Two Ways."[6] (See Box 13.2.)

The first external reference to the *Epistle of Barnabas* comes from Clement of Alexandria, and so the work was widely known and considered authentic by the end of the second century. The date of the work is uncertain but must come well after the destruction of Jerusalem in 70 CE, an event clearly mentioned in *Barnabas* 16.3. Since this reference is followed by an expectation that the Temple will soon be rebuilt (16.4), it has usually been suggested that it must date before the Bar Kochba revolt (132–35 CE). *Barnabas* 4.4–5 uses apocalyptic images of the beast with ten horns (from Dan. 7), and these images might suggest that the work derives from the period of resurgence of apocalyptic expectations between about 95 and 120 CE.[7] It seems to show a strong affinity for Jewish traditions, including pre-Mishnaic midrashim and the "Two Ways," but derived apparently from Greek sources. Because *Barnabas* 4.14 may be a quotation from

---

Paul to move from Tarsus to help him there (Acts 11:20–30). Barnabas and Paul traveled together in Cyprus, Cilicia, and Phrygia (Acts 13–14) prior to the Jerusalem conference (Acts 15:1–30) and returned to Antioch (15:31–35). Acts finally portrays a more amicable parting (Acts 15:36–41), occasioned because Barnabas wanted to take John Mark with them against the wishes of Paul.

In Later Christian Tradition

Based in some measure on the early value placed on the *Epistle of Barnabas,* later Christian legends grew up around Barnabas. Clement of Alexandria identified him as one of the seventy disciples of Jesus mentioned in Luke 10:1.[1] Tertullian credited him with writing Hebrews.[2] The Pseudo-Clementine tradition says that he went to Rome at an early stage and was the one who converted Clement of Rome[3] (see Chapter 15). According to a later Roman tradition (the *Decretum Gelasianum*), he was also the author of a Gospel, but no such work is now extant; however, a sixth-century *Acts of Barnabas,* attributed to John Mark, gives a fanciful account of his missionary work and martyrdom on Cyprus.[4]

---

[1] *Stromateis* 2.20.

[2] *On Modesty* 20.

[3] *Recognitions* 1.7–13.

[4] J. B. Daniels, "Barnabas (person)," *Anchor Bible Dictionary,* 1:610–11.

Matthew 22:14, it has been widely thought to come from an early branch of the Christian movement in Syria; however, a provenience in Alexandria is possible, especially given the work's later popularity there.[8]

The *Epistle of Barnabas* as an Early Catechism

The *Epistle of Barnabas* retains a strong eschatological expectation of Christ's imminent return, albeit recalibrated in the light of post-70 developments. In this way it is similar to some of the later Jewish apocalypses, such as 4 Ezra or 2 Baruch, with which it shares themes and traditions. The "Two Ways" section (chaps. 18–20) also retains a traditionally Jewish and very apocalyptic flavor similar to material in the *Rule of the Community* from the Dead Sea Scrolls. Given these overall affinities for Jewish (or Jewish Christian) background, then, the

---

BOX 13.2

The Epistle of Barnabas

DATE: ca. 100–120 CE

AUTHOR: Unknown

ATTRIBUTION: Barnabas

LOCATION: Syria or Alexandria

AUDIENCE AND OCCASION: Written for an early Jewish Christian community that has now become fully separate from and antithetical toward Judaism. The work gives an authoritative mode of interpreting the Jewish scriptures that "proves" basic elements of belief in Jesus and emerging Christian practice. The work also serves as a manual of Christian behavior by incorporation of an older section of Jewish moral instruction called the "Two Ways." This section of *Barnabas* has many similarities to the "Two Ways" section of the *Didache*, probably derived from a common source; however, the work as a whole makes no use of other New Testament writings, except perhaps the Gospel of Matthew.

OUTLINE

  I. Introductory Exhortation (1.1–6)

  II. First Main Section: On the Proper Interpretation of the Scriptures (2.1–17.2)

     A. An appeal for understanding and perseverance in the face of the coming eschatological crisis (2.1–3.6)

Christological affirmations of the first part of the text (chaps. 2–17) reflect the hardening lines of separation from Judaism. Jesus is called the preexistent "Lord of the World," who assisted God in creation (5.5) and who came in the flesh as "Son of God" to endure suffering "in order to sum up the completeness of sins against those who persecuted his prophets unto death" (*Barn.* 5.11). In contrast, Jesus's descent from the lineage of David—a traditionally Jewish feature of his messianic identity, especially in Matthew—is explicitly denied (12.10–12). Instead, Jesus now prepares the covenant for a new people: "that he should redeem *us* from darkness and prepare a new people for himself" to replace the sinful Israel that was not worthy of the covenant delivered through Moses (14.4–6).

In this way, *Barnabas* shows some similarities to the kind of "supersessionist" theology also found in Hebrews, and an elaborate patchwork of quotations

FURTHER READING

Barnard, L. W. "The Epistle of Barnabas in Its Jewish Setting." In *Studies in Church History and Patristics.* Thessaloniki: Patriarchon Hidryma Paterikon Meleton, 1978. Pp. 52–106.

Kraft, R. A. *The Apostolic Fathers.* Vol. 3, *The Didache and Barnabas.* New York: Thomas Nelson, 1965.

Lowy, S. "The Confutation of Judaism in the Epistle of Barnabas." *Journal of Jewish Studies* 11 (1960): 1–33.

Treat, J. C. "Barnabas, Epistle of." *Anchor Bible Dictionary.* 1:611–14.

from the Septuagint is likewise employed to validate the argument. For example, *Barnabas* 9.7–8 argues that the cross of Christ has replaced physical circumcision and was divinely prefigured in Genesis 17:23–27. Ironically, this is the very passage in which Abraham ratified his covenant with God by circumcising himself and all his male family members while swearing an oath that made circumcision a binding commandment for all his descendants. *Barnabas's* rather unusual argument is based on numerical symbolism found "hidden," according to the author, in the text of Genesis itself.

Here is how it works. According to Genesis 14:14, Abraham had 318 male servants in his household when he went out to fight the five kings (Gen. 14:1–16). In the Septuagint of Genesis 14:14, the number is written out in Greek as "three hundred, ten and eight." *Barnabas,* however, now quotes—or invents—a variant reading of Genesis 17:27 that includes the number 318, but following the word order in the Hebrew text of Genesis 14:14. The number of those circumcised is thus written out in Greek as "eighteen and three hundred." The author then explains how the number may also be rendered in Greek numerical notation as IHT (*iota-eta-tau*). The author of *Barnabas* argues that this number is really a prefiguring of Christ's death, since IH are the first two letters of the name Jesus in Greek (ΙΗΣΟΥΣ or *Iēsous*), while T represents the cross.[9] As a result, he concludes, the circumcision performed by Abraham was not meant to be literal at all, but a symbol for the coming of Christ.

Such elaborate interpretive machinations are thus meant to use scripture to "prove" ideas that are taken to be normatively Christian, at least in *Barnabas's* circle. The literal or historical meaning of such passages is largely ignored or repudiated outright. This method of interpretation, called "perfect *gnosis* (knowledge)" by the author (*Barn.* 1.5), forms a kind of code by which to understand the secrets of the Jewish scriptures, but now apart from Judaism and its practices. In fact, *Barnabas* 9.4 claims that literal interpretation of the Jewish scriptures was actually brought about by an evil angel who misled the people of Israel. Consequently, the author is able to "prove" that all aspects of Jewish observance (sacrifice, fasting, circumcision, kosher laws, Sabbath restrictions, and the Temple itself) were based on a demonic misunderstanding. Instead, Christians possess the "true" spiritual understanding of these practices as ordained by God through imparted *gnosis*.

On the other hand, the *Epistle of Barnabas* shows no awareness of other writings from the New Testament, except perhaps for the Gospel of Matthew.[10] Authority for Christian belief and practice is deduced exclusively from this "spiritual" meaning of the Jewish scriptures. *Barnabas* quotes or paraphrases numerous late or pseudepigraphic Jewish texts, including *1 Enoch* (at 4:3), 4 Ezra (at 12:1), and *2 Baruch* (at 11:9–10), but rarely are any of the sources, even of recognized passages from Torah, identified other than as "the scriptures."

Finally, the "Two Ways" section of the *Epistle of Barnabas* similarly claims a kind of revealed *gnosis* for Christian behavior and practice by counterposing those things ordained by God ("The Way of Light," *Barn.* 19) and those of Satan ("The Way of Darkness" or "The Way of the Black One," *Barn.* 20). The mode of opposition is typical of the radical dualism found in traditional Jewish apocalyptic. Much of this section is in the form of rigorous moral instruction, but the work also gives glimpses of emerging patterns of Christian community ethos and practice, including the importance of Sunday observance (15.8–9) and regular assemblies (4.10), baptism (11.1–11), public confession of sins (19.12), spiritual gifts (16.9–10), sharing of possessions (19.8), and the authority of teachers, those who are in superior positions (21.2), and those who, like the author himself, "proclaim the word of the Lord" (19.9).

The Didache

The work now commonly known as the *Didache* ("Teaching") was mentioned during the second to fourth centuries,[11] but the text was only rediscovered in 1873 in an eleventh-century Byzantine manuscript from Constantinople.[12] Its full title in Greek is given as either *The Teaching (Didache) of the Twelve Apostles* or *The Teaching of the Lord to the Gentiles Through the Twelve Apostles.* Recovery of the text has made it possible to see that the work was extremely influential in later centuries, especially as a source for liturgical and church-order manuals in Byzantine, Syriac, Coptic, Ethiopic, Latin, and even early Slavonic (Georgian) branches of Christianity. The work as we now know it was probably composed in the early to mid-second century (ca. 100–140 CE) in Syria; however, it may well incorporate an independent trajectory of earlier materials going back to the last part of the first century. Of the Gospels it seems to quote most directly from Matthew, and social ties to Matthean Christianity have been convincingly argued. If so, the *Didache* may reflect the development of an early form of Jewish Christianity in lower Syria distinct from the urban Christianity that developed in and around Antioch. Even so, other scholars have argued for a location in Egypt or Asia Minor, but these views remain a minority opinion today.

The Didache as Church-Order Literature

Even more than the *Epistle of Barnabas,* the *Didache* is presented as a series of instructions for ordering church life and practice. In this sense, it may be called the first example of "church-order literature" (see Box 13.3). The work opens with an elaborated version of the "Two Ways" tradition very similar to that found in *Barnabas;* however, this section is introduced by a catena of quotations or paraphrases of Jesus's words. These include the Great Commandment (cf. Matt. 22:37–39) and the Golden Rule (cf. Matt. 7:12). The "Two Ways" section, then, has taken on the form of "the word of the Lord" as an official catechetical instruction for the ordering of behavior and daily life among the members of the Christian community. The section ends with a warning against those who might try "to lead you astray from the way of this teaching" (*Did.*

BOX 13.3

The Didache
The Teaching of the Lord Through the Twelve Apostles

DATE: ca. 100–140 CE

AUTHOR: Unknown

ATTRIBUTION: Jesus and the apostles

LOCATION: Syria (or Alexandria?)

AUDIENCE AND OCCASION: One of the earliest pieces of "church-order literature," probably produced out of one stream of the Jewish Christian tradition. It became the source for many later church-order and liturgical handbooks in the third to the sixth centuries. Seems to show dependence primarily on the Matthean tradition and also on some older forms of material dating from the latter part of the first century CE, such as independent circulation of Jesus's sayings and the "Two Ways" tradition. Provides some of the earliest evidence for the formal development of the liturgy.

OUTLINE

    I. The "Two Ways" (1.1–6.3)

        A. Introduction (1.1)

        B. The way of life (1.2–4.14)

            1. Commands of the Lord (1.2–2.7)

            2. Further instructions (3.1–4.14)

6.1) Even so, it takes a restrained approach to ascetic and charismatic forms of piety: "If you can bear the whole yoke of the Lord, you will be perfect, but if you cannot, do what you can" (6.2).

The second half of the work contains a series of instructions on the practice of worship, including how to perform baptism (*Did.* 7), rules for fasting and personal prayers (8), and instructions on the Eucharist (9–10). The discussion of baptism now provides specific guidelines on the liturgical formula to be pronounced: "in the name of the Father, the Son, and the Holy Spirit" (*Did.* 7.1). It also gives specific guidelines on the type of water to be preferred (cool running water), along with a ranked list of alternatives.

Concerning the Eucharist (*Did.* 9–10), it provides model prayers and guidelines for the fellowship meals that formed part of the worship. Because this is the earliest example of such prescribed eucharistic prayers and because it

FURTHER READING

Draper, J. A. *The Didache in Modern Research.* Leiden: Brill, 1996.

Jefford, C. N. *The Didache in Context: Essays on Its Text, History, and Transmission.* Leiden: Brill, 1995.

———. *The Sayings of Jesus in the Teaching of the Twelve Apostles.* Leiden: Brill, 1989.

Kraft, R. A. *The Apostolic Fathers.* Vol. 3, *The Didache and Barnabas.* New York: Thomas Nelson, 1965.

———. "Didache." *Anchor Bible Dictionary.* 2:197–98.

Kloppenborg, J. S. "Didache 16:6–8 and the Special Matthean Tradition." *Zeitschrift für die neutestamentliche Wissenschaft* 70 (1979): 54–67.

Layton, B. "The Sources, Date, and Transmission of Didache 1:3b–2:1." *Harvard Theological Review* 61 (1968): 343–83.

Niederwimmer, K. *The Didache.* Hermeneia. Minneapolis: Fortress, 1998.

Vööbus, A. *Liturgical Traditions in the Didache.* Stockholm: ETSE, 1968.

employs the term "Eucharist" for these acts of worship, it is useful to quote the passage here:

> *Now concerning the Eucharist, give thanks in this way.*
>
> *First, concerning the Cup: "We give thanks to you, our Father, for the holy vine of David, your servant, which you made known to us through your servant Jesus. To you be the glory forever."*
>
> *And concerning the Bread: "We give thanks, our Father, for the life and knowledge which you made known to us through your servant Jesus. To you be the glory forever. Just as this broken bread was scattered upon the mountains and being gathered together became one, so let your church be gathered together from the ends of the earth into your kingdom. Because yours is the glory and the power through Jesus Christ for ever."*
>
> *But let no one eat or drink from your Eucharist, except those who have been baptized in the name of the Lord.* (Did. 9.1–5)

As this passage shows rather clearly, the name Eucharist (Greek *eucharistia*) is derived from the opening word in both prayers, which is *eucharistoumen* ("we give thanks"). This shows that the liturgical formalization has progressed in several ways. It should also be noted that the prayer for the cup precedes that for the bread, which is thus the reverse of other early forms of the Lord's Supper tradition (1 Cor. 11:23–26; cf. Mark 14:22–25). However, it is similar to aspects of Jewish Sabbath meal (kiddush) and Passover practice. Finally, the restriction on who can partake of the Eucharist is another "first" in the formal development of the liturgy.

Although the *Didache* thus shows an increasing degree of formalization and even innovation in liturgical practice, it nonetheless preserves a number of more traditional forms that clearly go back to the first century. For example, in the discussion of fasting, which it encourages, it specifies that it should be done on Wednesdays and Fridays instead of Mondays and Thursdays "like the hypocrites" (*Did.* 8.1). This innovation seems to be in direct response to the emerging practices of rabbinic Judaism. At the same time, it validates these innovations by summoning the tradition of Jesus's sayings, especially from the Gospel of Matthew (e.g., Matt. 6:8, 18) and even quotes in full the Lord's Prayer in its distinctive Matthean form (Matt. 6:9–13). Similarly, in the eucharistic prayers for the fellowship meal it includes a prescribed prayer on behalf of the church:

> *Remember, Lord, your church—to deliver it from all evil, to make it perfect in your love, and to gather it together from the four winds being made holy for*

your kingdom, which you have prepared for it; for yours is the power and the
glory forever. Let grace come and let this world pass away. Hosanna to the God
of David. If anyone is holy, let him come; if anyone is not holy, let him repent.
Marana tha. Amen. (Did. *10.5–6*)

Although this prayer is also innovative, it is clearly built on traditional elements, the most important of which is the old Aramaic eschatological invocation *Marana tha* ("Our Lord, come!"), which we also saw in Paul (1 Cor. 16:22). In this case, the liturgical traditions incorporated into the *Didache* can be seen to go back not just one generation (to the time of Matthew's Gospel), but two, that is, back to the first generation and even its generative Aramaic substratum (see Chapter 6).

The *Didache* also gives instructions on how to treat traveling Christian prophets and teachers and includes warnings if such prophets should stay too long or ask for money. Still, it grants those wandering prophets who appear to be true authority to perform their own eucharistic prayers (11). The existence of such prophets reflects a continuity with the wandering charismatic preachers of the earliest days of the Jesus movement, although there is now a heightened wariness about such people (13).[13] Similarly, hospitality is to be offered to other traveling Christians; however, there are cautions about false teachers and free-loaders (12). Finally, the work closes with instructions on the conduct of Sunday worship (14), the need to appoint church leaders (bishops and deacons), although explicit qualifications are not given (15), and a concluding exhortation to be watchful for the imminent eschatological return of Christ (16). The *Didache* is thus a reflection of a growing degree of formalization in liturgical matters and church offices.

Rome: Clement and Hermas

Clement of Rome

Clement of Rome is the traditional name of the author of a letter written from the churches in Rome to the churches in Corinth. Commonly known as *1 Clement*, the document was one of the earliest to be associated with the leadership of the church after the apostles. It was contained in the New Testament in Codex Alexandrinus (ca. 400 CE) and in other early Christian Bibles[14] and was retained in the Syriac New Testament through the Middle Ages. It was probably known to Polycarp, but apparently without awareness of the namesake of the author. Eusebius preserves a letter from Dionysius, bishop of Corinth (ca. 170 CE), written to Soter, the bishop of Rome, in which he says that "your letter sent to us through Clement" was still being read in their churches on a regular basis.[15] Accorded scriptural status by Clement of Alexandria (ca. 200),[16] it was widely used in worship down to the time of Eusebius (early fourth century).

The name Clement does not appear in the oldest manuscripts of the letter, whose only address is given in the greeting and the subscription: "Letter of the Romans to the Corinthians" (*1 Clem.* 65.2). Even so, the work was associated with the name of Clement at least by the 170s.[17] By the time of Origen (ca. 235),[18] it was typical to assume that this Clement was the same person mentioned in Paul's Philippian letter (4:3). Though erroneous, this equation was furthered by the assumption that the Philippian letter was written from Paul's final imprisonment in Rome. Hence, it was assumed that the author of *1 Clement* knew both Peter and Paul at Rome. By the end of the second century, the tradition had developed that this Clement was the third bishop of Rome after Peter, in the succession after Linus and Anacletus.[19] A rival tradition preserved by Tertullian says that Clement had been ordained bishop by Peter himself, while the Pseudo-Clementine tradition says that he was converted by Barnabas.[20] Local tradition at Rome held that Clement's house had been used as an early meeting place and was eventually transformed into the parish church (or *titulus*) of St. Clement, not far from the Colosseum.[21] Other legends associated the Domitilla catacomb at Rome with his family.

It is the fourth-century church historian Eusebius who finally consolidates these disparate pieces of tradition into a single legend by juxtaposing his comments about Clement, co-worker of Paul and author of a letter to the Corinthians, with a catalog of Domitian's persecutions, including members of the family of Titus Flavius Clemens, the emperor's cousin and his fellow consul for the year 95.[22] This further equation with a Roman senatorial family seems to rely on a patchwork of testimonies from Roman historians. Suetonius (early second century CE), for example, says that Flavius Clemens was executed on a slight charge, but gives the impression that Domitian feared he might rival his own young sons for the throne.[23] Dio Cassius (early third century CE) adds that Flavius Clemens was executed and his wife, Flavia Domitilla, was banished to Pandateria on the grounds that they practiced Jewish "atheism."[24] This last component probably led Eusebius (or his sources) to suppose that they were in fact Christians, but there may be other factors that led to the confusion.

This legend is further clouded by several aspects of Eusebius's own account. First, Eusebius mentions the exile of Flavia Domitilla (but to Pontia) in this connection, but identifies her as the niece of Flavius Clemens, not his wife.[25]

Second, he does not say that Flavius Clemens himself was killed.[26] Elsewhere Eusebius places the Christian Clement's death in the third year of the reign of Trajan (101/102 CE), after he had become bishop of Rome in the twelfth year of Domitian (92/93 CE).[27] There is, therefore, no known connection between the Christian Clement and the senatorial family of Flavius Clemens.[28]

All this leaves us in a bit of a quandary on the dating of *1 Clement,* since its traditional date was falsely predicated on the death of Flavius Clemens in 95/96, during a wave of persecution at Rome and elsewhere by Domitian.[29] If Flavius Clemens and Flavia Domitilla were not Christians, as now seems most likely, then there is no evidence of a persecution of Christians in the latter years of Domitian's reign.[30] Moreover, since the episcopal succession elaborated by Eusebius is also a later legend, his placement of the death of Clement in 101/102 is no more reliable. As a result, *1 Clement* has been dated by some scholars as late as 140, but a more reasonable date would be about 100–120 CE, and perhaps only slightly earlier than Hermas, Ignatius, and Polycarp.[31]

1 Clement: The Situation

Although its date and authorship remain far from clear, *1 Clement* is nonetheless quite informative for understanding developments in church organization in the early part of the second century (see Box 13.4). The situation is this: the church at Rome has become aware—how is not stated—that political strife over church leadership has broken out within the congregations at Corinth. Specifically, the letter says, it wishes to address a matter of dispute among them, namely, how "foreign and alien to the elect of God, a defiled and unholy sedition which a few rash and willful persons have inflamed to such madness so that your reputation, venerable, famous, and worthy of love, has been greatly slandered" (*1 Clem.* 1.1). The key term here is "sedition" (Greek *stasis*), which really means public or civic "discord"; it was widely discussed in the early second century as a particular problem in the Greek cities under Roman rule.[32] Their endangered reputation refers to Paul's Corinthian correspondence, especially 1 Corinthians, which is cited frequently in *1 Clement.*

The letter makes clear that the problem arose when a group of younger men within the Corinthian congregations had deposed the older leaders, or "elders" (Greek *presbyteroi*), of the church and taken over (*1 Clem.* 44.3–6; 46.9; 47.6). Consequently, the Roman church has sent the letter to intervene in the dispute and to restore the elders to their rightful position. It calls on the Corinthians to "bow the neck and become obedient" by restoring the proper "harmony and

---

BOX 13.4

Clement of Rome, *Letter to the Corinthians*
First Letter of Clement

DATE: ca. 100–120 CE

AUTHOR: Clement (unnamed in the letter)

ATTRIBUTION: Later legend names Clement as the third bishop of Rome

LOCATION: Rome

AUDIENCE AND OCCASION: A letter of advice and persuasion written by the
church at Rome to the church at Corinth. The situation: a group of
younger men in the church at Corinth have deposed the "elders" and
taken their place. The letter stresses themes of harmony and concord
over against sedition and "discord" and calls for the Corinthian Christians to be subject to the rightful elders in compliance with Rome's
request. The letter uses numerous themes and motifs from popular
discussions of "harmony and discord" among the orators and philosophers of the day.

OUTLINE

Salutation

I. The Situation (1.1–3.4)

II. The Virtues of the Christian Life (4.1–39.9)

    A. The vices of enmity and strife (4.1–6.4)

    B. The necessity of repentance (7.1–8.5)

---

concord" in the church (63.1–2). Carrying the letter were three emissaries from
the church at Rome, who were to help in the matter and report back on the response of the Corinthians. It is further indicative that these emissaries,
Claudius Ephebus, Valerius Vito, and Fortunatus (65:1), are described as "faithful and prudent men, who have been blameless among us while growing from
youth to old age" (63:3).

1 Clement: Its Main Themes

The primary theme of *1 Clement* is "harmony and concord" and it uses the
Septuagint as well as Paul's 1 Corinthians to legitimate its basic argument—
namely, that "discord" is against God's will, not only for the sake of the church,
but also for the sake of the whole cosmos. At the same time, this theme was a

C. The virtues of obedience, faith, and hospitality (9.1–12.8)
D. The cardinal virtue: humility (13.1–19.1)
E. God the source of order and peace (19.2–20.12)
F. Our response to God (21.1–22.8)
G. Eschatological warrant (23.1–28.4)
H. A call for holiness and blessedness (29.1–36.6)
I. Concluding exhortation (37.1–39.9)

III. Harmony and the Divine Order of the Cosmos (40.1–61.3)
A. The divine origins of order (40.1–44.6)
B. Opposition by the wicked (45.1–46.9)
C. The necessity of love and harmony (47.1–50.7)
D. Call for obedience, peace, and harmony (51.1–58.2)
E. Liturgical prayers (59.1–61.3)

IV. Call for Compliance and Concluding Exhortation (62.1–65.2)
Subscription

FURTHER READING

Bakke, O. M. *"Concord and Peace": A Rhetorical Analysis of the First Letter of Clement.* Tübingen: Mohr-Siebeck, 2001.

Bowe, B. *A Church in Crisis: Ecclesiology and Paraenesis in Clement of Rome.* Philadelphia: Fortress, 1981.

Grant, R. M., and H. H. Graham. *The Apostolic Fathers.* Vol. 2, *First and Second Clement.* New York: Thomas Nelson, 1965.

Hagnar, D. A. *The Use of the Old and New Testament in Clement of Rome.* Leiden: Brill, 1973.

Welborn, L. L. "Clement, First Epistle of." *Anchor Bible Dictionary.* 1:1055–61.

commonplace among Stoic moralists of the time.[33] It is thus an exercise in persuasion and exhortation and employs numerous motifs and metaphors from the popular rhetoric of "advice" or "counsel" (Greek *symboule*) of its day:

> *Accept our counsel (*symboule*), and there will be nothing for you to regret. For God lives and the Lord Jesus Christ lives, and the Holy Spirit also, the faith and hope of the elect, because the one who performs the righteous deeds and commandments given by God in ungrudging humility with earnest moderation shall be registered and reckoned in the number of those being saved through Jesus Christ. (*1 Clem. 58.2*)

Nothing is ever said about what caused the strife between the old leaders and the new, only that it was a "shameful report" (47.5–7). Nor does the corrective treat matters of false teaching. When basic aspects of Christian faith and teaching

are discussed, they are treated as matters on which everyone agrees. Even a thoroughly pagan tradition, such as the myth of the phoenix, can be used to validate belief in the resurrection, which everyone accepts (*1 Clem.* 24–26). Rather
than strictly theological matters, then, it seems that economic and social conditions are the more likely source of the problem. The letter simply calls for
compliance on the premise that the kind of concord described is its own self-
evident good and in complete agreement with divinely created order.

Finally, this mode of argumentation is all the more important in light of the
fact that *1 Clement* shows no awareness of the New Testament as a collection or
source of authority unto itself. The letters of Paul are cited as authority, but this
is done because Paul was an "apostle" and his apostolic authority was passed on
in the church by the appointment of bishops and deacons.[34] For *1 Clement*,
"scriptures" still refers to the Jewish scriptures, the Septuagint. Yet the author,
like the apostle Paul, also speaks and writes through the Holy Spirit (63.2). It
has also been shown that both the decision of the Roman church to dispense
such advice and the form in which it was presented are modeled on the prerog-
atives of the capital, specifically the Senate and the emperor of Rome, to manage the affairs of its provinces and cities.

Other Literature in the Name of Clement

So famous was the name of Clement, that by the third and fourth centuries
there began to grow up a body of pseudepigraphical literature around him.
One part of this later tradition, usually called the Pseudo-Clementine literature, will be discussed in Chapter 15. It is important because it summons the
name and authority of Clement as the transmitter of the "true" teachings of
Peter and James, over against certain heretics who would pervert them. In this
case, however, Clement's name is used to legitimate a strongly Jewish form of
Christianity.

Two other letters were contained in the Syriac New Testament under the
name of Clement. The epistolary address seems to be a conscious effort to emulate the tradition associated with Clement and other "apostolic" letter writers.
In reality, they form a single composition advocating asceticism and virginity as
the highest calling of the Christian life. They probably originated in Palestine
in the third century or later. The second letter refers to the practice of male and
female monastics living in communities together and inveighs against it. The
letters were cited under the name of Clement by fourth-century writers such as

Jerome and Epiphanius, and fragments were also preserved in Greek and Coptic. In the latter, however, the author is named as Athanasius.[35]

Also widely attributed to Clement of Rome, at least by the fourth century, was an anonymous sermon. As a result it is erroneously called *2 Clement*, a second letter of Clement to the Corinthians. This tradition was so prevalent that the text was regularly included right after *1 Clement* in many of the ancient manuscripts, including in the New Testament of Codex Alexandrinus. It dates from the latter part of the second century. One hypothesis concerning its confusion with the name of Clement suggests that it might have been the letter sent by Soter, bishop of Rome, to the church in Corinth in about 170 CE. This letter of Soter is mentioned in the letter of Dionysius, bishop of Corinth, which is also the earliest explicit reference to *1 Clement*.[36] This hypothesis falters, however, since the work contains no epistolary features and no direct references to either Rome or Corinth. It is, instead, a sermon on the church, ethics, and repentance, in large part based on an exegesis of Isaiah 54:1. At least one notable feature in its scattered theological exposition is that it affirms an antidocetic Christology in terms that are reminiscent of the Gospel of John. It may thus constitute one of the earliest allusions to the Gospel of John in later Christian literature.[37]

Hermas

A treatise called the *Shepherd* (or *Pastor*) was attributed in the early church to a certain Hermas, a member of the church at Rome. One tradition, as found in the Muratorian Canon,[38] held that Hermas wrote the work while his brother Pius was serving as the bishop of Rome; this legend would then place the writing in the period between 140 and 154 CE, and Hermas would thus be contemporary with Justin Martyr, Valentinus, and Marcion in the complex diversity of early Christianity at Rome. It must be noted, however, that the identification of Hermas in the Muratorian Canon serves to discredit the work as scripture, since it was "recent." In other Christian circles, notably in Alexandria, the *Shepherd* was considered part of the New Testament. So, for example, both Clement of Alexandria (ca. 200 CE) and Tertullian (ca. 210 CE) treat it as scripture, while Eusebius later admits that its authority is debated.[39] It was contained in the New Testament in Codex Sinaiticus (early fifth century) and early versions of the Latin Vulgate Bible; it was known as early as the time of Irenaeus (ca. 177 CE).[40] Other than the name of Hermas, little is known about the author; some references in the work suggest that he might have been contemporary with or at least knew the reputation of Clement of Rome (Herm. *Vis.* 2.4.3). As a result, it has long been thought that the work was probably composed by one or more authors before 140 CE, and perhaps over a period of time from about 100 or 110 to about 140 (see Box 13.5).

The Shepherd: Genre and Themes

On the surface, the *Shepherd* claims to be an apocalypse, a series of revelations from God received by the author, Hermas. Hermas claims to be a former slave who had been brought to Rome and sold to a woman named Rhoda. Having become a freedman, he later met her socially and fell in love with her (*Vis.* 1.1.1–2). It was at this time, he claims, that he had the first vision, while on a journey from Rome to Cumae; in his vision the woman Rhoda now accused him of sinful lusts. As the revelations progress, however, the "woman" turns out to be neither Rhoda nor the Sibyl, the famous oracle of Cumae (*Vis.* 2.4.1), but rather a vision of the church, personified as a woman who tries to lead him to a more pious life.

The structure of the work is built around a series of such visions that Hermas is said to have experienced in and around Rome; the work is thus divided into three main sections. The first is a series of *Visions* (1–4) by the woman, the personified Church.[41] Next comes a fifth *Vision* presented by a man described as a Shepherd, who will serve as principal revealer from here on (hence the title of the work). This new vision really serves to introduce the next section of the work, called the *Mandates,* a series of twelve injunctions on the content of the Christian faith. In some ways these *Mandates* resemble the confessional and ethical instructions found in the "Two Ways" sections of the *Didache* and the *Epistle of Barnabas.*[42]

The work purports to be an apocalypse, but it is more like a catechetical treatise, at least in its fully developed form. The last section of the work is a series of ten *Similitudes,* also delivered by the Shepherd, who turns out to be the "angel of repentance." This portion of the work tells parables, or similitudes, using florid descriptions and allegorical interpretations to give instructions on piety, sin, and repentance in the church. It advocates fasting (*Sim.* 5.2) and warns against the vice of luxury (*Sim.* 6.2). Both here and in the first visions (esp. *Vis.* 3), the genre of these descriptive allegories is very similar to pagan moralizing texts of the time in which the Virtues and Vices, personified as women, each vie for the devotion of a wayfarer who seeks guidance in choosing the right path.[43]

BOX 13.5

The Shepherd of Hermas

DATE: ca. 100/110–140 CE

AUTHOR: Hermas

ATTRIBUTION: Later legend makes Hermas the brother of Pius, bishop of Rome ca. 140–54

LOCATION: Rome

AUDIENCE AND OCCASION: Written in the form of an apocalypse, the work describes a series of visions received by Hermas in and around Rome. The first four visions are delivered by a woman, the personified "Church," while the remaining visions and instructions are delivered by the "Shepherd," who turns out to be the angel of repentance. The work reflects the use of apocalyptic genre to deliver moral exhortation and catechetical instruction to a settled Christian community of later generations. It advocates a rigorous piety and stresses that Christians are expected to live a sinless life after baptism. It is notable for its provision that only one repentance for sins can be offered after baptism.

OUTLINE

I. Introduction and *Visions* 1–4 (delivered by a woman, the "Church")

II. *Vision* 5 and *Mandates* 1–12 (delivered by the Shepherd)

III. The Ten *Similitudes* (delivered by the Shepherd and an angel)

IV. Concluding Exhortation (*Sim.* 10.4)

FURTHER READING

Aune, D. E. *Prophecy in Early Christianity and the Ancient Mediterranean.* Grand Rapids, MI: Eerdmans, 1983.

Osiek, C. *Rich and Poor in the Shepherd of Hermas.* Washington, DC: Catholic Biblical Association, 1983.

——. *The Shepherd of Hermas.* Hermeneia. Minneapolis: Fortress, 1999.

Pernveden, L. *The Concept of the Church in the Shepherd of Hermas.* Lund: Gleerup, 1966.

Snyder, G. F. *The Apostolic Fathers.* Vol. 4, *The Shepherd of Hermas.* New York: Thomas Nelson, 1968.

——. "Hermas' The Shepherd." *Anchor Bible Dictionary.* 3:148.

The main purpose of the work in its final form is to advocate a rigorous Christian ethic in regard to sexual practices, including asceticism, and other aspects of daily life. One of the features of this rigorous ethic is its claim that, after baptism, the Christian is expected to live a sinless life. Even so, it says that if one should sin after baptism, there is one, but only one, remaining opportunity to receive forgiveness through repentance in the church (*Vis.* 2.2.4–5;

Mand. 4.3.1; *Sim.* 7.4). Consequently, the work seeks to validate by means of revelatory authority this new ethos for living. On the one hand, this means that the *Shepherd* is appealing to earlier kinds of authority, like the "revelations" of old in the days of the apostles. On the other hand, the work is clearly aimed at a later generation of followers who have, in some cases at least, grown up in the church and for whom "becoming a Christian" has lost some of its earlier, more sectarian or conversionist qualities. There is not much evidence of threatening persecution,[44] nor are there warnings about "false" teaching. In contrast, "falling away" from the church is a concern (*Vis.* 3.8.3; 3.9.1), and tensions between rich and poor in the church are discussed (*Sim.* 2). The work thereby functions as catechetical instruction for a more settled or institutionalized stage of Christian church life at Rome in the first half of the second century.

Antioch and Asia Minor: Ignatius and Polycarp

Ignatius of Antioch

It appears that Ignatius was bishop of the church in Syrian Antioch during the first decades of the second century. We know nothing else about his life or earlier career before about 113–15,[45] when he was arrested in Antioch and then sent under guard to Rome for trial. En route he was allowed to visit with Christians in some of the cities of Asia Minor and Greece. He then wrote letters to these churches and to the church in Rome.

The route apparently took Ignatius overland at least for a portion of the journey through Roman Asia (western Turkey); consequently, the detachment of soldiers would have been forced to stop along the way in various cities. Apparently the word had been passed among Christian circles that Ignatius was being transported to Rome, and so Christians in some of the towns wanted to see him. By the time he had reached the western areas of Asia near the Aegean coast, his circumstances and his fame were already well known. It is also possible that he and others in the churches of Antioch had contacts in various other cities, and that they had written ahead asking that he be looked after along the way.

This is where the story picks up in the letters themselves. After a stop in Philadelphia, the entourage moved on to Smyrna, one of the most important cities of Roman Asia after Ephesus, the capital. While waiting in Smyrna, perhaps for sea passage to the next stop, Troas, Ignatius was allowed to visit with

Polycarp, the bishop of the church in Smyrna. It would appear that Ignatius and Polycarp already knew one another or at least had mutual friends within the Christian networks of the eastern Roman Empire. While Ignatius was staying with Polycarp, delegations of Christians came to visit him from the nearby cities of Ephesus, Magnesia, and Tralles. Afterward Ignatius wrote a letter to the churches in each of these cities. Also while he was in Smyrna, he wrote a letter ahead to the Christians in Rome in anticipation of his eventual arrival there. Specifically, he asked them not to use any political influence they might have to secure his release, for he was looking forward to a martyr's death.

Next, Ignatius and his guards moved on to Troas, a prominent Roman harbor on the coast of Asia; it served as the natural point of departure for a short sea voyage over to Greece, where he would pick up the Via Egnatia at Neapolis near Philippi (Ign. *Pol.* 8.1). This is the same route that Paul had taken more than half a century earlier (see 1 Thess. 2:1–3:6 and Chapter 8). This means that they intended to take Ignatius by way of the Via Egnatia across Macedonia to Apollonia on the Adriatic coast, where they would have caught a ship for Brundisium on the "boot heel" of Italy. From there they would have taken the main highway to Rome. While in Troas, Ignatius was joined by two more Christians, Philo, a deacon from Cilicia, and Rheus Agathopus from Antioch (Ign. *Phld.* 11.1). On arriving, they reported to Ignatius about matters in Philadelphia, where he had also visited before arriving in Smyrna. So now Ignatius wrote a letter to the Christians in Philadelphia. Finally, he wrote two more letters: one to the Christians in Smyrna and one to Polycarp himself.

The last we hear of Ignatius is from Polycarp, who later wrote to the Christians in Philippi. From Troas, Ignatius and the combined guard detachment had moved on. Their fate is assumed but not described. In any event, Ignatius's fame was secure, and Polycarp reports that he had made a collection of Ignatius's letters at the request of the Philippian Christians. Polycarp's letter served as the cover letter for the entire collection (Pol. *Phil.* 13.2).[46] It seems that the churches in Smyrna and Ephesus had jointly paid for the services of a scribe named Burrhus, a deacon from Ephesus, who was to assist Ignatius in writing to all the churches he had visited (Ign. *Eph.* 2.1; *Phld.* 11.2; *Smyrn.* 12.1); however, the process was interrupted when the entourage suddenly left Troas for Neapolis (Ign. *Pol.* 8.1).[47]

Only the seven genuine letters of Ignatius will be discussed here; by the fourth century they had been supplemented with several pseudepigraphic letters and a fictional account of his martyrdom in Rome (see Box 13.6). Pious legends from the fourth century also generated a fuller account of his life that is not historically reliable. Eusebius names him as the second bishop of Antioch succeeding a certain Euodius.[48] Elsewhere Eusebius places the beginning of his episcopate in about 69 CE and his martyrdom in 107.[49] These dates are considered very unlikely by modern scholars, some of whom would push his death into the reign of the emperor Hadrian (117–38 CE).[50]

The Letters of Ignatius

Taken together, the letters of Ignatius provide glimpses into a number of issues emerging in the second and third decades of the second century. Ignatius regularly gives advice on church affairs, presumably out of his own experiences and

---

BOX 13.6

The Letters of Ignatius of Antioch

DATE: ca. 113–17 or 117–38 CE

AUTHOR: Ignatius, bishop of Antioch

ATTRIBUTION: Penned by Ignatius, the letters were later collected by Polycarp, bishop of Smyrna

LOCATION: Smyrna and Troas

AUDIENCE AND OCCASION: Following his arrest, the bishop of Antioch was transported by a military detachment to Rome for trial. Along the way, he was allowed to visit with local Christians in some of the cities where they stopped. He then wrote letters to these churches. The letters reflect Ignatius's advice concerning local issues of church life as well as his recommendations on certain organizational issues, notably the role of the bishop and clergy as hierarchical, central authority in the churches. Ignatius apparently died a martyr's death in Rome and became one of the early heroes after the age of the apostles. His fame is reflected in the production of later pseudepigraphic letters in his name and a fictitious account of his martyrdom.

OUTLINE

The Seven Genuine Letters

LETTERS WRITTEN FROM SMYRNA

I. *To the Ephesians* (Ign. *Eph.*)

II. *To the Magnesians* (Ign. *Magn.*)

based on the organization of his church at Antioch. At the same time, we hear about numerous local issues. The churches in Antioch were some of the oldest and most renowned, going back to the days of Paul and Peter in the 40s (see Chapter 8). The author of Luke-Acts also seems to show some direct knowledge of the churches there and even provides the important historical note that the term "Christians" (*Christianoi*) was first used there (Acts 11:26; see Chapter 6).

When we come to Ignatius, however, we find that the "name" (i.e., Christian) is a commonplace (Ign. *Eph.* 7.1; *Rom.* 3.2) and is used positively to mean someone who "devotes himself to God" (*Pol.* 7.3). Moreover, it is in Ignatius (*Magn.* 10.1–3; *Phld.* 6.1) that we hear for the first time the term *Christianismos* (usually translated "Christianity," but literally "Christianism"), where it is directly

III. *To the Trallians* (Ign. *Trall.*)
IV. *To the Church in Rome* (Ign. *Rom.*)

LETTERS WRITTEN FROM TROAS

V. *To the Philadelphians* (Ign. *Phld.*)
VI. *To the Smyrneans* (Ign. *Smyrn.*)
VII. *To Polycarp, bishop of Smyrna* (Ign. *Pol.*)

Later Pseudepigraphic Literature (fourth century CE)

VIII. *Letters to and from Mary of Cassobola* (ostensibly written while still in Antioch)
IX. *To the Tarsians* (ostensibly written from Philippi)
X. *To the Antiochenes* (ostensibly written from Philippi)
XI. *To Hero, deacon of Antioch* (Ignatius's putative successor; ostensibly written from Philippi)
XII. *To the Philippians* (ostensibly written from Rome)
XIII. *The Martyrdom of Ignatius*

FURTHER READING

Grant, R. M. *The Apostolic Fathers*. Vol. 2, *Ignatius of Antioch*. New York: Thomas Nelson, 1966.
Lawson, J. *A Theological and Historical Introduction to the Apostolic Fathers*. New York: Macmillan, 1961. Pp. 101–52.
Schoedel, W. "Ignatius and the Reception of the Gospel of Matthew in Antioch." In *Social History of the Matthean Community*. Edited by D. Balch. Minneapolis: Fortress, 1991. Pp. 129–77.
———. "Ignatius, Epistles of." *Anchor Bible Dictionary*. 3:384–87.
———. *Ignatius of Antioch*. Hermeneia. Philadelphia: Fortress, 1986.
Trevett, C. *A Study of Ignatius of Antioch in Syria and Asia*. Lewiston: Edwin Mellen, 1992.

set over against *Judaismos* ("Judaism"). One must guess that this new term had also been coined in Antioch, perhaps only a few years earlier.

Two important issues show up in the letters. The first is a concern over false teaching or "heresy" within the churches. On the one hand, Ignatius warns against being deceived by certain Jewish teachings; he dismisses them as "false opinions [Greek *heterodoxia*] and ancient myths that are worthless" (Ign. *Magn.* 8.1). Here he seems to be most concerned with attitudes toward the Jewish scriptures and particularly whether the Jewish laws are still binding. Consequently, he sets "Christianism" in opposition to "Judaism" (*Magn.* 10.3), just as the observance of the Sabbath is opposed to the "Lord's Day" (*Magn.* 9.1). Even so, he does very little with the interpretation of the Hebrew scriptures as such. The real issue is whether or how one can find "proofs" in them regarding Jesus. Ignatius turns it the other way around: the scriptures are subordinated to Jesus as the true "archive" (*Phld.* 8.2), and he seems to be quite willing to resort to more exotic Jewish texts, such as the *Ascension of Isaiah,* as a source for interpreting the life of Jesus.[51]

Ignatius is far more concerned with Christians who hold the view that Jesus was divine but never a flesh-and-blood human. We saw this same problem, called docetism, reflected in the Johannine tradition at roughly the same time.[52] Specifically, Ignatius charges that such a person "blasphemes my Lord, since he does not agree that he was *flesh-bearing*" (Ign. *Smyrn.* 5.2). Elsewhere he spells out why this view is so dangerous, since it means that Jesus could not really suffer and die:

> But if, as some who are godless, that is, unfaithful, say, "His suffering was merely an appearance [dokein]"—it is they who are only an appearance— then why am I in bonds, and why do I pray also to fight the beasts? Then I am dying for no purpose. Indeed, then I am lying concerning the Lord. (Ign. Trall. *10.1*)

Where had Ignatius encountered this docetic Christology? One possibility is that it was already more of an issue in Syria, as we have already seen in the *Gospel of Thomas* (see Chapter 12). Irenaeus describes a teacher at about that time in Antioch named Satornilus (or Saturninus), who said, "The savior was without birth, without body, and without figure, but was supposedly a visible human being" (*Against Heresies* 1.24.2). It is also possible that some of these ideas had spread into western Asia by the second and third decades of the century, as we shall see below in Chapter 16.

A related issue arises from the fact that Ignatius shows little awareness of those writings from the New Testament that would have existed in his day. He shows some limited awareness of Paul and may paraphrase at times from 1 Corinthians, but does not seem to know the other letters. It is possible that he encountered these Pauline materials for the first time upon arriving in Smyrna.[53] Among the Gospels, he may have read Matthew (see Ign. *Smyrn.* 1.1), although it was not a central fixture of Antiochene Christianity.[54] The scriptures, for Ignatius, are the Jewish scriptures of the Septuagint. On the other hand, Ignatius does seem to know a wide range of early Christian traditions of vaguely recognizable character, as he shows regularly in his staccato annunciations of the "facts" about Jesus's life and death (as in Ign. *Trall.* 9.1–2, noted above). Some of these might have already crystallized around baptismal catechesis (as in *Eph.* 18.2–19.1).[55] That Ignatius did not seem to be dependent on "quoting" texts for his authority comes down finally to his claim that he himself had divine inspiration (*Phld.* 7.1–2) and embodied Christ through his own sufferings.[56]

A second key issue is the role of the bishop and clergy in a hierarchical structure for maintaining the authority and unity of the churches:

> *It is fitting that you should live in harmony with the will of the bishop, as indeed you do. For your justly renowned presbytery, worthy of God, is attuned to the bishop, as strings on a lyre. Therefore, by your concord and your harmonious love Jesus Christ is hymned. So, let each of you join in this chorus, so that being in harmony through concord, having received the chord in unison from God, and sing with one voice to the Father, through Jesus Christ. (Ign. Eph. 4.1–2)*

Here Ignatius employs an extended musical metaphor to stress the unity of the church under the bishop. In most of the letters he advocates a three-tiered hierarchical structure with the bishop (or "overseer," Greek *episkopos*) above a group of elders (*presbyteroi*) and deacons (*diakonoi*). This structure with a single bishop at the head is sometimes called the monarchical episcopate or monepiscopacy. Ignatius says that without the bishop there can be no assembly (Ign. *Eph.* 5.2–3; *Magn.* 7.1) and no Eucharist, baptism, or *agape* meal (*Smyrn.* 8.1–2; cf. *Phld.* 4); he further calls the Eucharist "the medicine of immortality" (*Eph.* 20.2). It seems that this innovative structure was advocated by Ignatius himself, partly out of his own experience at Antioch and partly to help defend against "false teachers." By the middle of the second century, such hierarchical organization was becoming more commonplace (see Chapter 14).

Polycarp of Smyrna

We have already been introduced to Polycarp through the preceding discussion of Ignatius. Polycarp was bishop (or elder)[57] of Smyrna and hosted Ignatius during his transport to Rome. In turn, Ignatius wrote letters both to the church in Smyrna and to Polycarp himself expressing thanks. The letter to Polycarp is the only personal rather than congregational letter among Ignatius's writings. Afterward, Polycarp wrote a letter to the church in Philippi describing what had happened to Ignatius and asking for further information, if they had any, since Ignatius had passed through Philippi on his way to Rome. The letter also served as a cover letter for a copy of Ignatius's letters requested by the Philippians. It was Polycarp who had assembled the collection of Ignatius's letters.

Like other figures of this transitional generation, Polycarp was the object of much legendary speculation from the end of the second century on. As a result, the real facts of his life are somewhat clouded. In part, the source for much of the later legend is the story of Polycarp's martyrdom, which took place in Smyrna in about 156 CE. The account of his death in the arena is thus one of the first pieces of martyrological literature.[58] Although the basic events surrounding the death of Polycarp are certainly historical, the hagiographical account known as the *Martyrdom of Polycarp* is highly elaborated and includes extensive use of conflated traditions from the Passion of Jesus overlaid with popular athletic imagery. As a result, there have been numerous theories regarding later interpolations in the text.[59]

The Martyrdom of Polycarp

The *Martyrdom* purports to be a letter written by a certain Marcion (not the heretic), who witnessed the events, and a scribe Evarestus (*Mart. Pol.* 20.1–2); it was sent to a neighboring church in Philomelium. A secondary subscription (*Mart. Pol.* 22), however, says that a certain Gaius copied the text from Irenaeus, bishop of Lyons in Roman Gaul (ca. 177–80 CE) and that this copy was transcribed by a certain Socrates in Corinth. Yet the same subscription continues with the testimonial of Pionius, a presbyter of Smyrna who died in the persecution of Decius in about 250 CE. Pionius says further that he had made the present copy, after searching diligently for the text, because Polycarp had appeared to him in a vision. The statement of Pionius gives the impression that until then the text was missing.

All this means that the present text of the *Martyrdom* is actually a mid-third century document, probably written during the early part of the Decian persecution (249–51 CE) to exhort other Christians to remain steadfast. Rediscovering the "original" text remains problematic. It is more likely that the text as we know it comes from a later period in which martyrdom was becoming something of a problem within Christian circles and when the martyrs were beginning to be revered as saints.[60] For example, the *Martyrdom of Polycarp* presupposes later practices such as commemoration of the martyrs with a meal on the date of death and a growing church calendar of such dates (*Mart. Pol.* 17.1–18.3).

Dates for Polycarp's Life and Death

The precise date of Polycarp's death is disputed by modern scholars. Eusebius knows the tradition but ascribes it to 167 CE during the reign of Marcus Aurelius.[61] Most scholars prefer a date in 155–56 based on other evidence, but certainty is impossible. The name of the proconsul of Asia, Statius Quadratus, who ostensibly presided at Polycarp's trial and execution (*Mart. Pol.* 21) is nowhere attested in the provincial records. All this uncertainty becomes important when we return to the earlier career of Polycarp, since the usual dates for his life are predicated on a statement in the *Martyrdom* during his cross-examination. When implored by the proconsul to "take the oath and renounce Christ," Polycarp is reported to have said, "For eighty-six years have I been his servant, and he has done me no wrong" (*Mart. Pol.* 9.3). On this basis it has been traditional to assume that Polycarp was born in about 70 CE to a Christian family. His appointment as bishop of Smyrna is sometimes dated as early as 95–100 in order to reconcile his career with an early dating for the death of Ignatius. This date is also predicated on the tradition from Irenaeus that Polycarp knew the apostle John and had been ordained bishop by "apostles in Asia."[62] At issue especially for Irenaeus, and later Eusebius, is the idea that there was a direct chain of orthodoxy that extended from the apostles to his own time. We shall return to this issue in the next chapter. In the final analysis, neither the date of his birth nor that of his ordination can be determined with any certainty.

Polycarp's *Letter to the Philippians*

We must turn, then, to Polycarp's *Letter to the Philippians* for the few bits of information that it can tell us about circumstances in Polycarp's own time (see

Box 13.7). The letter was apparently written sometime shortly after the death of Ignatius, which might be anywhere between 115 and 138 CE (see the discussion of Ignatius's own life above). According to Irenaeus, Polycarp wrote numerous letters to neighboring churches, but none of the others have survived.[63] Eusebius preserves a portion of the letter to Philippi that is missing in most of the Greek manuscripts.[64] The only full text of the letter is preserved in Latin and there are some internal contradictions.[65] Taken together, then, these factors have led some scholars to argue that what we now have as a single letter combines elements of two distinct letters:[66] an earlier letter (Pol. *Phil.* 13–14) written by Polycarp as the cover letter for his collection of the letters of Ignatius and a later letter (Pol. *Phil.* 1–12) to deal with other problems, including those prompted by the teachings of Marcion. Other scholars think the letter is a unitary composition as is.

Whether one letter or two, Polycarp's *Letter to the Philippians* reflects some key issues in the development of church order and authority. The letter is written at least in part as advice and exhortation. One problem seems to concern a presbyter named Valens whom he characterizes as "greedy" and calls on the congregation to discipline, but with an eye toward repentance and forgiveness (Pol. *Phil.* 11.1–4). He also gives a catalog of the proper character that presbyters ought to possess (6.1). This is the first such list of "qualifications" that we find in the early Christian literature.[67] Elsewhere, he warns strenuously against false teaching, especially docetism (7.1).

Polycarp's Use of Scripture

Perhaps the most notable feature is Polycarp's use of numerous pieces of earlier New Testament literature to validate his admonitions in a kind of patchwork of phrases and allusions. It is all the more striking in light of the fact that Ignatius seems to know or cite few of these same texts. Polycarp seems to know the Gospel of Matthew and there are at least hints of Luke-Acts (Pol. *Phil.* 1.2). He does not seem to know the Gospel of John. On the other hand, there appears to be fairly close similarity of wording between *Letter to the Philippians* 7.1 and 1 John 4:2 (the passage warning against docetic teachers, whom it labels "antichrist"). But this passage is typical of the problem, since the wording is not precise enough to classify as quotation, and Polycarp does not refer to a source. It is possible that both works are drawing from a common formulation in use in local churches at that time. It is also possible that 1 John was drawing on Polycarp.[68]

BOX 13.7

Polycarp's *Letter to the Philippians*

DATE: ca. 117 or 117–38 CE

AUTHOR: Polycarp, bishop of Smyrna

LOCATION: Smyrna

AUDIENCE AND OCCASION: Following the departure of Ignatius, the Philippians had apparently written to Polycarp asking for copies of Ignatius's letters. Polycarp replies with a letter of advice that also serves as a cover letter for the collection of Ignatius's seven letters.

OUTLINE

Greeting

I. Expression of Joy at the Faith of the Philippians (1.1–3)

II. General Exhortation: Scripture Catena (2.1–3)

III. Purpose of the Letter: Advice on Virtue (3.1–6.3)

   A. Exhortation (3.1–3)

   B. On greed (4.1)

   C. To wives and children (4.2)

   D. To widows (4.3)

   E. To deacons and younger men (5.1–3)

   F. To presbyters (6.1–3)

IV. Warning Against False Teaching (docetism; 7.1–2)

V. Call for Endurance (8.1–10.3)

VI. Call for Discipline of the Presbyter Valens (11.1–4)

VII. Concluding Exhortation (12.1–3)

VIII. Final Comments Regarding Letters to Antioch and the Collection of Ignatius's Letters (13.1–2)

IX. Concluding Salutation (14)

FURTHER READING

Harrison, P. N. *Polycarp's Two Epistles to the Philippians.* Cambridge: Cambridge University Press, 1936.

Koester, H. *Introduction to the New Testament.* 2d ed. 2 vols. Berlin: De Gruyter, 2000. 2:308–10.

Schoedel, W. *The Apostolic Fathers.* Vol. 5, *Polycarp, Martyrdom of Polycarp, Fragments of Papias.* New York: Thomas Nelson, 1967.

———. "Polycarp, Epistle of." *Anchor Bible Dictionary.* 5:390–92.

A similar problem occurs in some of Polycarp's use of Pauline materials, notably Romans and Galatians; however, he does make explicit reference to several of Paul's letters, notably 1 and 2 Corinthians and especially Philippians (Pol. *Phil.* 11.2–3). Consequently, it does seem likely that he possessed at least a partial collection of Paul's letters. He does not call them scripture, but he does assume that the teaching of Paul carried significant authority, especially for the Philippians. In other words, he knows not only the tradition of Paul's founding the church in Philippi, but also the letter in which Paul makes reference to it (e.g., Phil. 1:3–5; 4:15; see Pol. *Phil.* 3.2–3).

Polycarp may also know *1 Clement*,[69] 1 Peter,[70] and Ephesians,[71] but without naming them directly. When he once refers to the "scriptures," he has in mind the Jewish scriptures, specifically the Psalms.[72] Even in this passage, he demurs to the Philippians in "knowing the scriptures," and he shows little use of the Jewish scriptures on a broad basis. All of this points to a growing awareness of earlier Christian language and writings, particularly some of the letters of Paul, and may well reflect the kinds of collections that were beginning to circulate in both Asia Minor and Rome by the early part of the second century. Yet it also suggests that these Christian writings were not yet considered "scripture" in the same way as the Septuagint. In other words, there was not as yet an emerging sense of the "New Testament" as such.

CHAPTER FOURTEEN

Legitimacy and Order

A New Scrutiny

By the early years of the second century CE, Christian groups in many parts of the Roman world increasingly viewed themselves as somehow distinct from Judaism; fiery rhetoric on both sides fueled and sharpened the break. At the same time, the fact that the Christian "sect" came out from under the umbrella of Judaism brought important political consequences in the eyes of Roman authorities.

The historian Cornelius Tacitus gives one of the earliest notices of the Christian movement by a Roman author. Writing in about the year 117 CE, he describes Christians as Nero's scapegoats for the great fire of 64 CE:

> *Nero fastened the guilt and inflicted the most exquisite tortures on a class hated for their abominations, called **Christians** by the populace. **Christus**, from whom the name had its origin, suffered the extreme penalty during the reign of Tiberius at the hands of one of our procurators, Pontius Pilatus, and a most mischievous superstition thus checked for the moment, again broke out not only in Judea, the first source of the evil, but even in Rome, where all things hideous and shameful from every part of the world find their center and become popular. (Annals 15.44)*

The Legal Status of Christianity

As we have seen earlier, Tacitus's statement confirms basic, albeit scant, historical information about the death of Jesus and the origin of the name "Christian." Perhaps more important, it also gives some indication of how Christians were viewed, at least by his time. It is rather doubtful that the name Christian was in wide circulation by 64 and, even if it were, whether Nero and other Romans really understood it as a "new religion." There is no real reason why they would have thought that these Christians were separate from Judaism in Nero's day; certainly the followers of Jesus did not yet think so. Writing a full generation later, however, Tacitus likely reflects a new level of awareness of the story by virtue of his own experience.

In 93 CE Tacitus had returned from a provincial assignment to Rome to witness the deterioration of Domitian's reign—a series of assassination attempts followed by vicious reprisals and ultimately a posthumous condemnation by the Senate. Tacitus then served as suffect consul in Rome for the year following Domitian's death (97 CE) and thereby had a hand in the restoration of order during Nerva's short reign (96–98 CE). His rhetorical and historical writings evince his republican sympathies and distaste for abuses of imperial power. Hence, his comment regarding the Christians quoted above says more about his attitude toward Nero than anything else. His apparent dislike for foreigners and their unusual religious habits was not restricted to Christians alone. Elsewhere he betrays a similar ethnic prejudice against Jews more generally as well as other foreigners.[1]

By 117, however, Tacitus knew a bit more about the Christians, since he served as proconsul of Asia in 112–13 CE at about the same time that his friend, Pliny the Younger, was in Bithynia-Pontus.[2] It was about this same time that Ignatius, the Christian bishop of Antioch, also traveled through Asia and stayed with Polycarp on his way to a martyr's death in Rome (see Chapter 13). Thus, when Tacitus wrote his *Annals of Rome* after returning from his tour of duty in Asia, he saw Christians in a much clearer and more distinctive light. The letters of his friend Pliny, written only a few years earlier from nearby Bithynia, are our first witnesses to Roman prosecution of Christians on legal grounds.

Pliny the Younger

Caius Plinius Caecilius Secundus, better known as Pliny the Younger, was born at Comum in northern Italy in about 61 CE to a prominent equestrian family. His maternal uncle was the Roman naval commander and naturalist Pliny the Elder, who died aboard his ship while observing the eruption of Mt. Vesuvius in 79 CE. The elder Pliny left his fortune and his name to his nephew by virtue of testamentary adoption. From there the younger Pliny managed his wealth successfully and ascended to the senatorial order during the reign of Domitian

(81–96 CE). He became especially prominent during the reign of Trajan (98–117 CE), achieving the office of consul in the year 100 at the remarkably young age of thirty-nine. In the following years he pursued literary and social interests befitting a Roman aristocrat. From 100 to 109 Pliny meticulously edited and published his personal correspondence in nine books.[3]

In 109 or early 110 Trajan appointed Pliny to serve as imperial legate and corrector, a special administrator, for the province of Bithynia-Pontus, just to the north of Asia. The occasion arose when the Senate voted to change the status of Bithynia-Pontus from a senatorial, or "public," province to an imperial province. The reasons behind this change are complex but seem to stem from several cases of administrative corruption and numerous reports of political infighting in the major cities. When Trajan assumed direct control of the province, therefore, he delegated Pliny to serve as special legate to evaluate the situation and audit provincial and local civic accounts before appointing a regular governor. The tenth book of Pliny's letters represents his official correspondence with the emperor during this duty.[4]

Pliny's personal letters show him to be a thoughtful and well-educated member of the ruling aristocracy who viewed his wealth and status as a sacred trust. He was also politically well connected due to his favored position with Trajan. His social connections in Greece and Asia, as reflected especially in his letters, further attest to his intellectual and political acumen; he knew the philosopher-statesman Plutarch and the renowned orator Dio Chrysostom along with numerous other notables of the day.[5] Pliny died suddenly in about 113, perhaps before returning to Rome.

Pliny's Correspondence About the Christians

Pliny arrived in Bithynia in early September of the year 110[6] and began almost immediately to write reports of his actions and findings to the emperor. He spent the first year dealing with numerous issues in the capital, Nicomedia, and other large cities in the western part of the province. He found, for example, that public funds had been embezzled in the city of Prusa, Dio's hometown.[7] Following the emperor's instructions, he prohibited the proliferation of private clubs and other fraternal organizations that seemed to promote political discord. In light of this rule, therefore, Pliny at one point wrote to ask whether it would be all right to organize a new fire brigade in Nicomedia. Trajan wrote back warily, urging instead that it would be better if the locals simply banded together to fight fires when needed rather than risking political intrigue by forming yet another "club."[8] Finally, in the latter part of III, Pliny began a tour of some of the eastern cities of the province to deal with a variety of local matters. To address a water-supply problem in Sinope on the Black Sea, he commissioned a land survey so that a new aqueduct could be built.[9] Going farther east to Amisus, he once again encountered the matter of private clubs, but this time clubs with both a social and religious dimension.[10]

It was on the return portion of this same trip during the last months of III CE that Pliny apparently encountered the issue of Christians for the first time. The precise location is uncertain, but we do know that about this time there was a Christian community in Sinope, and probably others in nearby cities.[11] So when Pliny arrived at one of these cities he was met with complaints, probably from local merchants, that the presence of some Christians, whom they denounced by name, had created a stir.[12] Pliny's report to Trajan makes it clear that he had not previously had any dealings with these so-called Christians, nor had he ever been present when they came before a court.[13] Thus, his letter outlines the steps he had taken with those so charged:

> In the meantime, here is the procedure I have followed in the case of those brought before me on account of being Christians. I asked them whether they were Christians. If they confess to it, then I ask them a second and third time, while threatening punishment. If they persist, I order them to be led away [to execution]. For whether [or not] there be anything at all they should admit to [in the way of a crime], I have no doubt that at least stubbornness and inflexible obstinacy ought to be punished. There have been others, likewise mad, whom I listed for dispatch to Rome, since they were Roman citizens. (Epistles 10.96.2–4)

Pliny next details some of the other matters that had come up. Once it became known that he was hearing charges against Christians, other denunciations came in anonymously. Here he apparently questioned the persons so accused and released anyone who denied having been a Christian, which they were required to demonstrate by invoking the gods, offering wine and incense to the emperor's statue, and cursing Christ. He adds regarding these measures: "None of these things are said to be possible to compel them to do for those who are truly Christians."[14]

Finally, Pliny investigated some others who said that they had indeed been Christians but had ceased to be so a few years earlier—some said, as much as twenty. These were also required to perform the same demonstration, but from them Pliny learned more about the practices of the Christians:

*They insisted that the extent of their guilt or error was this: that it was their customary practice to assemble before daylight on a fixed day and by turns with one another to sing hymns to Christ as to a god, and to bind themselves with an oath, not for a crime, but rather that they should commit neither theft nor robbery nor adultery nor break a trust nor deny return on a deposit. After this, it was their custom to depart and to assemble again to partake of food, but food of an ordinary and harmless sort. But they declared that they had even ceased this practice after my edict, following your mandate, in which I had prohibited the existence of such clubs. In this matter I felt it necessary to examine under torture whether the claims were true from two female slaves who were called **ministers** [or **deaconesses**]. I discovered nothing more than a perverse and excessive superstition.*

*For this reason I took the recourse of putting off further trials in order to consult with you. For it seemed to me a matter worthy of consultation, especially because of the number of those at peril. Indeed, many people, of all ages, of all ranks, and both sexes, are being and will be summoned to trial. And not only those in the cities, but the contagion of this superstition has spread even to the villages and the countryside. Even so, it seems possible to halt and correct the situation. (*Epistles *10.96.7–9)*

Pliny's report thus shows that there were no real "crimes" as such with which the Christians could be charged, but that their meetings fell under the prohibition against "private clubs" that he had promulgated throughout the province at the emperor's direction. His use of the same terminology (*hetaeria*) for the Christian gatherings is perhaps indicative of the way the churches were viewed at that time by generally educated, but otherwise uninformed, pagans. Other than following an excessive "superstition" that Pliny found loathsome and the fact that, like other "clubs," they were potentially subversive, the Christians practiced strict moral rules. Their groups included people of high social rank as well as slaves, including women, some of whom held a sort of special priestly office. Aristocratic Romans had a hard time understanding some of these practices. It was probably the predawn rituals that had raised more than a little concern, since such clandestine activities had for centuries been associated in Rome with potentially subversive foreign cults such as the Dionysiac Bacchanalia.

What is most remarkable about Pliny's report is his sense of novelty in this superstitious private club. Everything he "knows" about them was a product of hearsay from local officials or things that admitted Christians—or former Christians—reported in the course of cross-examination. Although their obstinate behavior before a Roman imperial official was sufficient grounds for

summary execution, Pliny had begun to worry because of the sheer number of
people who were being charged. His custom of consulting the emperor offered
a useful interlude to the growing momentum of the judicial proceedings. Trajan wrote back affirming Pliny's basic procedure of using invocations and sacrifices as demonstrations of loyalty and repentance of any questionable conduct.
More significant, he instructed Pliny not to go out hunting for Christians or to
accept any anonymous denunciations.

The Later Persecutions

For the next 138 years the principles and procedures outlined in Trajan's *rescript*
(or reply) to Pliny governed the official Roman treatment of Christians. There
was no universal prohibition against Christianity as such, even though there
were faint suspicions. The precedent was ratified by a similar rescript of the emperor Hadrian:

> *To Minucius Fundanus. I received the letter written to me from Serennius
> Granianus, a most illustrious man and your predecessor. It does not seem to
> me, then, that the situation should remain unexamined, lest people be dis-
> turbed and an occasion for mischief be afforded to slanderers. Therefore, if the
> provincials are able to affirm due cause against the Christians, as might be
> judged before the tribunal, they may turn their decision on this alone, but not
> by mere opinions or outcries. For it is far more proper, if someone wishes to
> make an accusation, that he show you proof. Therefore, if someone makes an
> accusation and shows their actions to be contrary to the law, so render your de-
> cision according to the degree of the offense. But, by Hercules, if someone
> should bring a gratuitous charge for purposes of slander, consider this even
> more serious and render judgment as befits their crime.*[15]

The rescripts of Trajan and Hadrian were widely cited by Christians in Asia and
other parts of the empire during the second century.[16]

Other than these imperial rescripts, we have few Roman sources on the persecution of Christians in the second and early third centuries.[17] Most of our information comes from Christian sources, especially the burgeoning martyr
literature. The first empirewide action taken against Christians took place
under the emperor Decius (249–51 CE). We have more information regarding it
because all citizens were required to perform sacrifices as signs of loyalty and to
obtain an official petition (or *libellus*) that affirmed their compliance. Some of
these petitions have survived. What they show is that the basic precedent estab-

lished by Trajan was still operative, albeit turned by Decius into an aggressive measure. Even so, it does not appear that the Christians were Decius's main concern or that there was an attack on the church as institution. An all-out effort to suppress Christianity by arresting leaders, confiscating church property and books, or destroying church buildings did not occur until the so-called Great Persecution under the emperor Diocletian (303–13 CE), at the end of which the new emperor Constantine declared Christianity a legitimate religion of the empire.[18]

The *Acts* of the Martyrs

Prior to the time of Decius, then, when persecutions occurred, they tended to be prompted by local uprisings. Even then they remained sporadic. Moreover, they tended to focus on the more prominent members of the local churches, especially the bishops, elders, or other leading members, such as Ignatius or Polycarp. The total number of martyrs was quite small, but their stories loomed large in Christian tradition (see Box 14.1). The *Acts* of the martyrs, as they are often called, became much more popular in the third and fourth centuries, especially after the persecutions of Decius and Diocletian.[19]

The *Acts* of the martyrs as a genre of literature was primarily addressed to Christians as a way of encouraging faith and endurance during times of persecution. Some were written for additional theological purposes as well. Consequently, the lengthy speeches attributed to the martyrs in which they explicate aspects of Christian belief were really intended for pious Christian readers. It is doubtful that any Roman magistrate ever heard such a speech in court. For the most part the full spectrum of Christian beliefs and practices remained opaque to Roman officials and ordinary citizens alike for many more decades. What they saw instead was a growing number of Christians in the local population. Even so, Christians were a tiny minority, too small to pose any real threat. So the other source of Roman concern must have resulted from a growing awareness of the broad outlines of evolving church organization.

The Bar Kochba Revolt and Anti-Jewish Reprisals

One other political factor is sometimes overlooked in connection with the public perceptions and sporadic persecutions of Christians. It comes from the tensions in the eastern part of the empire (especially eastern Anatolia, Syria, Palestine, and Egypt) at the time of the Bar Kochba revolt (132–35 CE). The

BOX 14.1

Evidence of Local Persecutions During the Second Century CE

Date	Location	Emperor	Number of Victims	Source
111–12	Bithynia	Trajan	?	Pliny *Epistles* 10.96–97
115 (or later)	Antioch (but taken to Rome)	Trajan or Hadrian	3	Letters of Ignatius Polycarp *To the Philippians* Cf. Eusebius *C.H.* 3.36.3–4
124–25	Asia	Hadrian	?	*Rescript to Minicius Fundanus* (Justin *Apology* 2.68) Eusebius *C.H.* 4.9; cf. 3.32.1
ca. 138	Rome	Antoninus Pius	1	Eusebius *C.H.* 5.6.4
ca. 140–50	Rome	Antoninus Pius	2	*Martyrdom of Ptolemy and Lucius* in Justin *Apology* 2.2
156	Smyrna	Antoninus Pius	1	*Martyrdom of Polycarp* Eusebius *C.H.* 4.15.1–46
164	Rome	Marcus Aurelius	7	*Acts of Justin and His Associates* Eusebius *C.H.* 4.16.1–9
ca. 167?	Pergamon	Marcus Aurelius	3	*Martyrdom of Carpus, Papylus, and Agathonice*** Cf. Eusebius *C.H.* 4.15.48*
177	Lyons and Vienne (Gaul)	Marcus Aurelius	8	Irenaeus's letter re: *The Martyrs of Vienne and Lyons* in Eusebius *C.H.* 5.1.3–63
180	Scilli (North Africa)	Commodus	12	*Acts of the Scilitan Martyrs*
ca. 185?	Rome	Commodus	1	Eusebius *C.H.* 5.21* *Acts of Apollonius***
ca. 195?	Carthage	Septimius Severus	?	Tertullian *Apology* 5
202–3	Alexandria	Septimius Severus	2	Eusebius *C.H.* 6.2.12; 6.3.1–7
203	Carthage	Septimius Severus	3	*Passion of Perpetua and Felicitas*
206	Alexandria	Septimius Severus	4	Eusebius *C.H.* 6.4–5*
212	Carthage and Asia	Caracalla	?	Tertullian *To Scapula* 5

KEY: Items in bold type represent the earliest, authentic *Acts* of the martyrs. For text and discussion, see H. Musurillo, *The Acts of the Christian Martyrs* (Oxford: Clarendon, 1972). Items marked with a single asterisk (*) are likely spurious. Items marked with a double asterisk (**) are considered by most scholars to come from a later period, probably the persecution of Decius or later.

revolt broke out in the aftermath of Hadrian's state visit to the eastern empire in 130–32. The imperial entourage stopped in Caesarea and Jerusalem, among other cities, and gave imperial grants for numerous public-works projects. Caesarea, for example, got a new aqueduct, and in turn honored Hadrian as benefactor. (See Box 14.2.) After visiting Jerusalem Hadrian refounded the city as a Roman colony now to be named Aelia Capitolina, after his family name, Aelius. For most cities of the empire such a bequest would have been a singular honor. Not so in Jerusalem, at least for some. It was also rumored that he intended to build a temple to the Capitoline gods, Jupiter, Juno, and Minerva, on the site of the Jewish Temple, which still lay in ruins after the destruction of 70. This was the spark, or at least the excuse, that led to the outbreak of the new revolt.

In fact, there had been tensions brewing for some time prior to Hadrian's visit. In 115–17 there had been a minor rebellion by many of the Jewish communities living in Egypt and Cyrenaica. It was prompted in part by earlier incidents of local riots against Jews, but the situation generally deteriorated when the Roman administrators refused to intervene. When hostilities broke out, the result was a swift and violent Roman crackdown with arrests and confiscations of Jewish property in various localities. It should be noticed, then, that these tensions and reprisals occurred at just about the same time as Ignatius's arrest in Antioch. One wonders if some of the tensions in Antioch, and even within Ignatius's own churches, might have resulted from local sympathies for or against the Egyptian Jews. We do hear of local Jewish communities elsewhere sending aid and encouragement to the Jews of Egypt at this time. To be sure, Ignatius's letters show him to be more than ready to draw a sharp line between Jews and Christians.

In the aftermath of the Bar Kochba revolt, then, there were further repercussions in the deteriorating relationship between Jews and Christians. One came from the sheer fact that the southern region of Judea was even more ravaged than it had been after the first revolt. Roman efforts to root out Bar Kochba and his followers from their cave hideouts near the Dead Sea were uncompromising and vicious (see Box 14.2). So more of the Jewish population moved north to the Galilee, where the rabbinic movement was taking hold and becoming more institutionalized. When this development was paralleled by the growing institutionalization within Christianity, the gulf between rabbinic Judaism and Christianity was further widened. Another result was that Roman authorities and local citizenries of the eastern empire must have become more and more aware of these Christians and their curious, novel, and exclusivistic ways. At the same time, the specter of sedition hung over their heads.

BOX 14.2
The Bar Kochba Revolt (132–35 CE)

The emperor Hadrian conducted an official state visit to Syria, Arabia, and Judea in 130–32 CE en route to Egypt. As was typical on such visits, local Roman administrators and other leaders made special plans to honor the emperor on his arrival in hopes that he would then pronounce some special imperial gift. Hadrian announced a new aqueduct for Caesarea Maritima. At Jerusalem, he announced that he was going to refound the city as a Roman colony under his family name; it was to be called Aelia Capitolina. Some reports also suggest that Hadrian intended to transform Jerusalem into a more fully "pagan" city, which would have been appropriate for a Roman colony, and that this would have meant certain limitations on Jewish religious practice. Apparently it was these rumors that ultimately set off the spark for the second revolt.

The leader of the revolt was Simeon bar Kosibah. He took the name Bar Kochba as a messianic title after the famous Rabbi Akiba pronounced a wordplay on his name from the messianic language of Numbers 24:17, which says "a star (kochav) shall come forth from Judah." Akiba is also reported to have called him "the King Messiah." Both reports come from the Jerusalem Talmud (Ta'an. 68d). Based on the available evidence, Bar Kochba seems to have been a forceful leader, and some sources seem to indicate that he might have claimed Davidic lineage or to be a prince (nasi). Yet much remains uncertain. It appears that Bar Kochba's forces at some point captured Jerusalem and held it for a time. Several coins struck by the Jewish forces carry the legend "For the freedom of Jerusalem" or "In the first year of the freedom of Israel." Some seem to represent the Temple rebuilt (see Fig. b). So it appears that Bar Kochba intended to restore Jerusalem and even rebuild the Temple.

In the end, however, the Romans retook the city and forced Bar Kochba and his troops to flee to the Judean desert, not too far from Masada. There they held out in several large and elaborate caves. The Roman forces, under the command of C. Julius Severus, surrounded these caves and eventually starved the rebels out. In one cave, known as the Cave of Horrors, forty

a (left) Statue of Hadrian from Caesarea Maritima. (Collection of Israel Antiquities Authority; photo © Israel Museum, Jerusalem)

b (above) A Jewish coin of the Bar Kochba Revolt. The coin shows the Temple "restored" and carries the legend "Sim(e)on." On the reverse it carries the legend "Deliverance of Jerusalem." (Used by permission of the British Museum)

people died of starvation; another cave contained a cache of letters and other important artifacts, plus eighteen skeletons.

One of the most important discoveries in the Cave of Letters was a collection of fifteen letters either to or from Bar Kochba himself. Another nearby cave in Wadi Murabba'at contained six more letters. Together they give significant insight into the outlook of the insurgents, including preparations for celebrating the Jewish feast of Sukkoth.

FURTHER READING

Isaac, B., and A. Oppenheimer. "Bar Kochba." *Anchor Bible Dictionary.* 1:598–601.
Wise, M. O. "Bar Kochba Letters." *Anchor Bible Dictionary.* 1:601–6.
Yadin, Y. *Bar Kochba.* London: Weidenfield, 1971.

The Church Begins to Become an Institution

The notices of Pliny and Trajan show a clearer sense of Christians as a distinct religious group. They also show considerable uncertainty about what this might mean with regard to social organization and practices. Were Christians a "political faction," a "private club," an "aid society," a "foreign cult," or what? Now part of the fluid religious panorama of the Roman Empire, Christianity faced the dilemma of defining itself more clearly over against Judaism, over against paganism, and in other ways. Once again the changing social location of the movement and the diverse cultural traditions it encountered and embraced precipitated new modes of reflection, adaptation, and consolidation. Looking to the legacy of the apostles had supplied some of these needs in the past, but increasingly the new situations and the stresses they exerted on the social cohesion of small church groups summoned up questions of authority and organization.

It has long been noted that the kinds of issues that preoccupy the Christian writers of the early second century are quite typical of a movement that is in the process of becoming more institutionalized. Sects and cults, as we saw earlier, rely on the raw energy and dynamism of their founders. Passion and intensity are evidence enough of their faith, an unshakable confidence that their cause is right and true. This is especially so when their message is further substantiated by miraculous powers or visions and revelations. Such leaders possess a charismatic appeal for their followers. Hence, the sectarian quality of earlier forms of Jewish apocalypticism went hand in hand with its revelatory claims and imminent eschatological expectations. But as is so often the case, there is a fine line between charismatics and fanatics, especially as seen from the outside. So also for the followers of the early Jesus movement. Sects often tend to form around charismatic leaders, but as time passes and the first generations of founders and leaders pass away, a vacuum of authority appears. The sense of crisis can be exacerbated if the social location of the movement is also changing.

Typically, the crisis comes with the transition to a third generation. What we often see is that the transition from founders to the second generation is in some ways more stable because the "mantle of leadership" seems to be determined by the founders themselves. Thus, their charismatic authority is passed on, as it were, by selecting their successors. The challenge comes when the successors begin to die off and have to effect a similar transition, for now there are often more people who can claim to be in line for leadership. Sometimes, these new claimants will disagree on the source of their personal authority. For example, one might say that he is the "handpicked" successor of the immediate past leader, while a second might say that she serves as patron and host to the community. Still another might say that he is more in tune with the wishes or ideals of the original founders, while a fourth might say that she has charismatic authority equal to that of earlier leaders. All are making claims on the lines of authority by appealing to the charisma of earlier figures. The result is a conflict over authority and charisma.

Such power struggles within small informal groups, and especially among religious sects and cults, often give rise to a process of institutionalization of offices and authority structures. People do not merely "emerge" as authority figures by virtue of their own personal qualities or religious claims; instead, they are appointed to offices by the collective will of the group. The offices then receive definition and come to take the place of personal charisma. This is what is normally called the "routinization of charisma."[20] It is a fragile process, especially in key transitional moments when there may still be distinct legacies from the earlier generation.

We saw this kind of problem in the *Didache* (Chapter 13), where liturgical order is vested in local teachers but traveling prophets still have the right to perform their own prayers extemporaneously. The traveling prophets still possess the charismatic powers of an earlier generation, going back to the days of the earliest Jesus movement, whereas the local leaders are responsible for the ongoing life of a settled community. Thus, it is very telling that the *Didache* allows for prophets to exist while providing serious warnings against "false prophets" who might disrupt the settled community. As a piece of church-order literature, the *Didache* is designed to educate and validate these new lines of local authority and does so by claiming to come from Jesus and the apostles as the source of that authority.

Modes of Institutionalization

We may now summarize the key factors that converge in the third generation of the Jesus movement to stimulate its transformation into a more institutionalized religious organization, now becoming known as "Christianity" or, more literally, "Christianism" (*Christianismos*):[21]

1. The growing sense of separateness from Judaism results in the concomitant need for a distinctive sense of identity. This shift creates a new Christian self-definition apart from Judaism and paganism alike.

This general transformation of self-definition has four additional correlates:

    a. For some the tensions of separation from Judaism will not mean that their social location is entirely non-Jewish, while for others a more substantial separation will be required. As a result, the ethos of each different group may grow farther from the ethos of others, thus creating greater diversity and potential for internal tensions.

    b. Christological speculation is a prominent part of this process but can lead to further diversity among Christian groups.

    c. Having come out from under the umbrella of Judaism means that Christians are now more visible to the populace and susceptible to investigation by Roman authorities, simply on the grounds that they are novel and therefore potentially dangerous. Appeals to high ethical standards and support for the state serve as apologetic responses to such suspicions.

    d. The changing expectation of the place of Christians within the "plan" of God for Israel's future means also that traditional forms of eschatology must be reinterpreted accordingly.

2. There is a new stress on church order with regard to liturgical formalization and norms of practice and ethics.

3. Charismatic authority tends to be replaced by fixed offices such as bishops, elders, and deacons.

4. Concerns over theological diversity produce debates over "true beliefs" and warnings about "false teachers" that result in stricter definitions of orthodoxy and heresy.

5. The formation of a fixed canon of scripture serves to ratify these basic organizational structures, liturgical practices, and patterns of belief.

We have seen glimpses of all these items in the literature of the third generation already discussed (Chapters 12 and 13). Concerning the church-order tradition, compare the strict ethical catechesis in the *Epistle of Barnabas,* the *Didache,* and the *Shepherd* of Hermas. On the liturgy, notice the regulation of the performance of baptism and eucharistic prayers as well as the strictures on who can receive the Eucharist in the *Didache.* Ignatius adds other strictures by arguing that there can be no baptism or Eucharist without the bishop, or someone he delegates, present. Debates over heresy and orthodoxy and the formation of the canon will be taken up in later discussions (Chapters 16 and 17, respectively). For now, we focus on the emergence of church offices as a key element in the social organization of the movement in the early to mid-second century.

The Emergence of Church Offices

It is in Ignatius's letters that we have for the first time explicit directions on church offices in a fixed hierarchical structure. He advocates a three-tiered structure with the "bishop" (*episkopos,* literally "overseer") above a group of "elders" (*presbyteroi,* literally "older men"), and below them the "deacons" (*diakonoi,* literally "ministers" or "servants"). This structure is known as mon-episcopacy, meaning "single bishop." For Ignatius it is the church in unity under a single bishop that is able to withstand heresies and guard the truth. But the question is this: Was this already the norm in church organization? Ignatius seems to hint that it was, since he claims that there were bishops in every local-ity (Ign. *Eph.* 3.2). Or was this an innovation born of necessity with the rise of new and diverse teachings?

In a very influential study of this process Hans von Campenhausen[22] argues that the apostles and prophets of the first generation of the movement were the sole sources of authority. They derived their authority from Jesus himself and from spiritual powers or charismatic gifts. The most common term for such people in the early Jesus movement was "prophet,"[23] and even Jesus and John the Baptist were thought of in this way.[24] Von Campenhausen argues that as time passed these charismatic figures were replaced by fixed offices (elders or bishops) that were patterned, respectively, after Jewish or Greek models of so-cial organization.[25] This rigid dichotomy between charisma and social organi-zation is probably too strong and does not recognize that house-church patrons, both men and women, had considerable authority in Paul's day. In fact, Paul was often obligated to his patrons due to their financial support. Paul even speaks of their financial support, teaching, and hospitality as their "spiritual gifts" or "love" both for him and for the church (Rom. 12:4–13; cf. 1 Cor. 12:28–31; Philem. 5). He also uses the term *diakonia* ("ministry") of financial support (2 Cor. 8:4; 9:1, 12; Rom. 12:7; 15:31; 16:2). So the exercise of power was not a one-way street in Paul's day, as Von Campenhausen supposes. Paul calls for the congregations to be subject to the local house-church patrons, both men and women, who host, lead, admonish, and labor among them (1 Thess. 5:12; 1 Cor. 16:16). It may be argued, then, that the development of church offices grew in part out of the model of the house-church patrons as well as other patterns of social organization from the culture, such as collegial organizations and guilds or local Jewish communities.[26]

By the time of Luke-Acts at the end of the first century, we see some hints of the emergence of local leaders, usually called "elders" or "presbyters" (*presbyteroi*). In Acts Paul is said to have appointed local elders (Acts 14:23), and the practice is linked directly to models of Jewish organization from Jerusalem and Antioch (4:5; 11:30; 15:2). In one case (Acts 20:17, 28), the term seems to be used interchangeably with "bishops." As we saw in *1 Clement,* there seems to have been a group of elders in Corinth who had been displaced by another group of younger men. Here too it appears that the terms "elder" and "bishop" are interchangeable. *1 Clement* now expands on the tradition of apostolic succession or appointment to validate the position of the rightful elders at Corinth:

> *Our apostles also knew through our Lord Jesus Christ that there would be strife for the title of bishop. For this reason, therefore, since they received perfect foreknowledge, they appointed those who have already been mentioned [the elders], and afterwards added the codicil that should these fall asleep other approved men should succeed to their ministry. We consider therefore that it is not just to remove from their ministry those who were appointed by them, or later on [appointed] by other eminent men, with the consent of the whole church.* (1 Clem. 44.1–3)

Notice that the author clearly acknowledges the fact that the deposed elders belong to the third generation, since they were appointed by the successors of the apostles.

The monarchical episcopate and three-tiered hierarchy of bishops, elders, and deacons seem to be an innovation of Ignatius probably pioneered in his own churches at Antioch. He even refers to himself at one point as "the bishop of Syria," probably meaning that he was the bishop over all the churches in the city of Antioch and its immediate surroundings (Ign. *Rom.* 2.2). In turn, each congregation would have had its own elders and deacons. At one point he claims to have received this teaching by inspiration from God (Ign. *Phld.* 7.1–2). That it was not the universal norm is perhaps reflected by indications that the churches in Antioch had been experiencing strife under Ignatius's own leadership (Ign. *Phld.* 10.1–2; *Smyrn.* 11.2; *Pol.* 2.3; 7.1).[27] It may well be that Ignatius had advocated this more hierarchical structure and sought to extend it to the churches in Asia based on his own experience in Antioch. On the other hand, Ignatius did not seem to think his authority to impose such a structure could be extended over the church at Rome.

For Ignatius and those who followed him, monepiscopacy seemed a logical extension of their theology and went hand in hand with emerging patterns of liturgical order in the churches. Here is how Ignatius put it:

> *For when you are in subjection to the bishop, just as to Jesus Christ, it is clear to me that you are living not according to humans but according to Jesus Christ, who died on account of us, so that by believing in his death you may escape death. Therefore, it is necessary—as you also do—that you do nothing without the bishop, but be subject also to the presbytery, as to the apostles of Jesus Christ, our hope, for if we live in him we shall be found in him. . . . Likewise, let everyone respect the deacons as Jesus Christ; so also, as the bishop is a type of the Father, and the presbyters as the council of God and as the band of the apostles. Without them the church cannot be called church. (Ign.* Trall. *2.1–3.1)*

So the "heavenly" order of God, Christ, and apostles is replicated in the ecclesiastical order of bishop, presbyters, and deacons.

Elsewhere Ignatius says explicitly that without the bishop there should be no church assembly (Ign. *Eph.* 5.2–3; *Magn.* 7.1) and no Eucharist, baptism, or fellowship (*agape*) meal (*Smyrn.* 8.1–2; *Phld.* 4). When he also refers to the Eucharist as "the medicine of immortality" (*Eph.* 20.2), it means that the hierarchically ordered church has become an intermediary for salvation. Increasingly, this idea will be described as the church's "ministry" (*diakonia*). At the same time, this type of hierarchical structure restricts the free exercise of genuine charismatic gifts and limits the role of women in the church. Both of these issues will continue to be sources of tension throughout the third and fourth generations.

By the middle of the second century, we find the hierarchical definition of ministry becoming more widespread, due in large measure, one must guess, to the growth of "false teachers" and congregational factions.[28] In addition, a new aura of charismatic authority came from Ignatius's impending martyrdom. The later legends regarding Clement and Polycarp also reinforce episcopal authority with that of the martyr as a new type of charismatic or prophetic figure. By the third century, however, even these two sources of authority, martyrs and bishops, would run into conflict.

Regional Church Networks

The exercise of hospitality for traveling Christians and letter writing to churches had been the mainstays of Paul's missionary strategy. Undoubtedly, his innovative personal efforts served as a model for others, but there were no established links between churches. Even Paul's sending of Phoebe to Rome to spearhead the mission to Spain and his efforts to assemble a delegation of gentile converts to carry the contribution to Jerusalem came from his own peculiar theological self-understanding.

In contrast, Clement, Ignatius, and Polycarp advocate regular communication between churches and even the sending of emissaries and delegations to confer with and support one another. Thus, there is a growing network of ecclesial relations from city to city and within regions. From their correspondence we can see that several axes or vectors of political alliance had begun to consolidate. One such axis linked the churches in Antioch with those in eastern Turkey and western Asia Minor. Another, but to a large extent independent, axis linked the churches of Asia with those of Greece and Rome. One looked east; the other, west. Each axis constitutes its own functional network of contacts, affiliations, and loyalties. The networks naturally overlap, but they are not identical. They are rather like interlocking circles between which some figures, such as Polycarp himself, and perhaps whole churches, represent "gateways." There was another distinct network linking the Syro-Palestinian churches outside of Antioch, as reflected in the connections between the Gospel of Matthew, the *Didache,* and *Barnabas.* It might well have interacted with the Antiochene network, but probably in a different orbit. We may imagine these regional networks with a simple illustration (see Fig. 14.1).

One must also recognize that each network had its own literary and theological trajectory, as we saw in Rome's peculiar development of the apostolic literature associated with Paul (including the deutero-Pauline letters, Luke-Acts,

FIGURE 14.1

Regional church networks in the early second century.

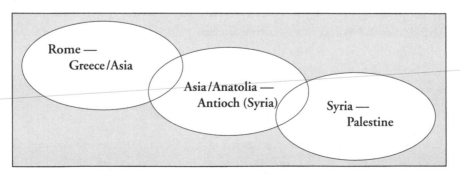

and Hebrews) as well as the tradition of Peter (1 Peter). In the Asia Minor network Paul had some force, but other literature, especially the Johannine letters and the apocryphal acts, became, if anything, even more important at times. Eventually, these conflicts had to be mediated too.

These early networks are still casual social structures; that is, they develop organically out of the personal ties and loyalties of individuals and smaller groups.[29] By nature, they are also temporary in that they rely on personal relations and goodwill rather than some sort of formal protocol. They are not imposed from the top down or perpetuated as if blanks in a preexisting organizational chart had to be filled. Nor are they like umbrella organizations, such as political parties, denominational conventions, or ecclesiastical councils. Permanent structures of the latter sort might well evolve out of these networks at a later date, but they tend to do so by reifying or idealizing what was earlier an implicit, organic, and dynamic social interaction. Here we see an interesting contrast between Clement and Ignatius. Ignatius has a much more formal and hierarchical form of internal organizational structure but refrains from imposing it, at least on Rome. The author of *1 Clement* has a less hierarchical internal structure but feels free to impose his will on other churches that are well beyond his own orbit. Each writer reflects an emerging but distinctive trend in the institutional ordering of power.

As we shall see in the next chapter, there were other networks, especially in Egypt. In light of the theological controversies that emerged by the latter half of the second century CE, these networks and their ability to interact become extremely important for the development of a normative consensus, or what usually gets called "orthodoxy." How churches managed these diverse lines of influence would become a pivotal concern both organizationally and theologically in subsequent generations.

An Inside View: The Apologists

One might easily get the impression that the second century saw the Christian movement growing more and more isolated from Roman culture even as it was growing more visible in Roman society. To be sure, that is how the martyr literature seems to portray things at times. On the whole, this view is the product of a later generation of Christian thinkers, such as Eusebius, who take a triumphalist orientation toward Rome. The picture in the middle of the second century is rather different, and we see this in particular with the rise of a new genre of Christian literature known as "apologies."

The Apologists

The term "apology" (Greek *apologia*) is the technical term in Greek law for a defense speech in court. Over time it developed into its own genre in both rhetoric and literature. The classic form is seen in the speeches of Demosthenes (ca. 385–322 BCE), while its literary appropriation may be seen in Plato's rendering of the *Apology of Socrates*.[30] Many works of literature, pagan, Jewish, and Christian, came to have similar apologetic intent, as seen in Philo's *Life of Moses* or Luke-Acts, but there also developed a special genre in the Roman period based on the form of petitions to the emperor or Senate, such as Philo's *Legation to Gaius*.[31] Another type of apologetic literature took the form of a dialogue with or polemic against a particular opponent, as in Philo's *Against Flaccus*. Addressed ostensibly to the proconsul of Egypt who had ruled against the Jews in the pogrom of 37, this document also served an apologetic function for Judaism. Apologetic and polemic literature are thus two sides of the same coin.

With the increase in local persecutions in the second century, these various forms of apologetic literature became a prominent and specialized mode of literary expression in defense of the Christian faith on both legal and intellectual grounds. Several were even addressed to the emperor, including Justin's *First Apology* (addressed to Antoninus Pius) and Athenagoras's *Supplication for the Christians* (addressed to Marcus Aurelius and Commodus). This literary device might well have been prompted by the rescript of Hadrian concerning the treatment of Christians published in Ephesus in 124–25 (see above). A number of the apologists cite this rescript, and it serves as a natural point of departure in discussing the alleged "crimes" of the Christians.

Even so, it was never the intent or expectation that these treatises would actually be read by the emperor; nor were they intended to be delivered to Roman officials. They were instead written for other Christians as a way of arming them with an outlook and arguments for dealing with criticisms and suspicions they might encounter in day-to-day life. In other words, they were written with an eye toward the encounter between Christians and their pagan or Jewish neighbors. As such they give us some of the most important glimpses of Christian life in its interaction with Greco-Roman culture. At the same time, they helped to forge and reinforce Christian identity and practice. This effect may also be related to the development of the "defense speech" as a common feature in the martyr literature.[32] The latter part of the second century and the early part of the third have sometimes been called the "age of the apologists," so prominent was this mode of literary expression in both Greek- and Latin-speaking Christianity. Some have seen in it the beginnings of more systematic efforts to work out a cohesive and consistent Christian theology.[33] (See Box 14.3.)

Some Key Themes

The kinds of issues treated by the Christian apologists arose from two distinct but related perspectives. One came from popular rumors and suspicions; the other from philosophical criticisms. The popular rumors seem to have derived from ill-informed ideas about what went on in Christian homes and assemblies. Such reports range from vague suspicions about sedition to rumors of more explicit "crimes." Some were prurient and salacious, including wild rumors about incest or other sexual activities and cannibalistic banquets.[34] It has often been suggested that such ideas might have come from pagan misunderstanding of ordinary Christian language, such as "loving brothers and sisters" or "eating the flesh and drinking the blood of Christ."

A more difficult challenge to Christian identity and self-understanding came from philosophical critiques, which also began to arise in the later second century. The most famous of these came from the philosopher Celsus (ca. 180), to whom Origen would write a lengthy reply in the mid-third century.[35] Among other things, Celsus took aim at the absurdity of certain Christian beliefs, such as the resurrection. Or he asked why a god would choose to become human. He also denigrated the Christians as poor, ignorant, and gullible; their teaching, he said, is nothing but superstitious drivel for women, children, and slaves.[36]

The different apologists responded to both sets of ideas in different ways. With razor wit, Tertullian lampooned the absurdity of such claims and the rashness of the pagan populace:

> *If the Tiber rises to the walls, if the Nile fails to rise to the fields, if the sky doesn't move or if the earth does, if there is famine, if there is plague, the cry goes up at once: "The Christians to the lion!" What, all those Christians to one lion? (Apology 40.2)*

Some of the more rational responses concern how Christians live within Roman society. Athenagoras picks up the idea of Christians as a "third race" (i.e., neither Jews nor Gentiles) from the earlier work called *The Preaching of Peter* (see Chapter 12). He uses it to describe their high moral character in terms that even the most educated pagan would find admirable, and in doing so invests Christianity with its own version of Stoic ethics. In some ways, these arguments are similar to the kind of popular Stoic philosophy used by Clement of

Rome in calling for harmony and concord on the model of the universe (see Chapter 13).

Another line of philosophical response is that from the anonymous apology *To Diognetus:*

> *For the distinction between Christians and other folk is neither in country nor language nor customs. For they do not dwell apart in cities of their own, nor do they use some strange deviation of dialect, nor do they practice a peculiar manner of life. . . . Yet while living in Greek and barbarian cities, as each one has been allotted, and following the local customs, both in clothing and food*

BOX 14.3

The Apologists of the Second Century

In the following chronological catalog of Christian apologetic literature concerning life in the Greco-Roman world, all of the works were originally written in Greek unless otherwise noted. (Not included in this catalog is Christian literature addressed to Jews, usually found in the form of polemics, often titled *Against the Jews,* or dialogues, such as Justin's *Dialogue with Trypho the Jew.*)

Quadratus, Asia Minor, ca. 120–38 CE
An apology (title lost) addressed to the emperor Hadrian. The work is lost, but fragments are preserved in Eusebius *Church History* 4.3.1–2.

Aristides, Athens, ca. 120–47 CE
Apology, addressed to the emperor Hadrian. The original Greek work is lost (notice in Eusebius *Church History* 4.3.3), but it was preserved in a Syriac manuscript discovered in 1891. In the Syriac manuscript, it was addressed to Antoninus Pius (hence ca. 138–47).

Justin Martyr, Rome, ca. 150
First and Second Apologies, addressed to the emperor Antoninus Pius.

Tatian, the Syrian (a student of Justin), Rome, ca. 170
Address to the Greeks (fragments preserved). Cf. Irenaeus *Against Heresies* 1.28; 3.23.8; Eusebius *Church History* 4.16.7; 5.13.8.

and the rest of life, they show forth the wonderful and admittedly strange character of their citizenship. They dwell in their native lands, but as sojourners. . . . They pass their time on earth, but their citizenship is in heaven. . . . In a word, what the soul is in the human body, so Christians are in the world.
(Epistle to Diognetus *5.1–10; 6.1*)

From a philosophical perspective, this is a fascinating statement of how Christians can be simultaneously at home and alien because it is based on a philosophical (Stoic and Platonic) discussion about the "world soul." What pagan who knew the story of Socrates could really disagree?

Melito, bishop of Sardis, ca. 175
> An apology (lost), addressed to the emperor Marcus Aurelius. Cf. Eusebius *Church History* 4.26.5–11.

Claudius Apollinaris, bishop of Hierapolis, ca. 175
> An apology (lost), addressed to the emperor Marcus Aurelius. Cf. Eusebius *Church History* 4.21; 4.27; 5.5.4; 5.16.1; 5.18.12–14.

Athenagoras, Athens, ca. 177
> *Supplication for the Christians,* addressed to the emperor Marcus Aurelius and his son Commodus.

Theophilus, bishop of Antioch, ca. 180
> *To Autolycus* (an attack on idolatry and defense of basic Christian beliefs).

Tertullian, Carthage, ca. 196–97
> (1) *To the Nations,* (2) *Apology* (Latin).

Minucius Felix, Ostia or North Africa, ca. 200
> *Octavius* (a dialogue between a Christian, Octavius, and a pagan friend, Caecilius; in Latin).

Anonymous, ca. 161–203
> *To Diognetus.* Perhaps addressed to the tutor of Marcus Aurelius (ca. 161–80) or an Alexandrian official of the same name (whose dates are ca. 197–203). The work is sometimes called the *Epistle to Diognetus,* but it is not really a letter.

FURTHER READING

Grant, R. M. *Greek Apologists of the Second Century.* Philadelphia: Westminster, 1988.

Justin Martyr

Perhaps the best known and most influential of the second-century apologists was the Christian teacher and philosopher called Justin Martyr. He tells us that he was born about 100 CE to a pagan family, "son of Priscus and grandson of Bacchus," from the Roman colony of Flavia Neapolis (modern Nablus) in Palestine.[37] He tells also of an intellectual pilgrimage from one philosophical school to another that took him to Athens and the great cities of the empire.[38] But he had witnessed Christians facing martyrdom and was taught Christianity as the only true philosophy by a wise old man. He says it kindled his soul.[39] Justin migrated to Rome by about 140 CE, during the reign of Antoninus Pius, to whom he would address his *Apologies* around 150 CE. Once in Rome Justin established his own school of philosophy, like so many others of the time, but his was a school of Christian philosophy. He describes his debates with other philosophers of the day as well as other Christian teachers, notably Valentinus and the followers of Marcion, and Jews.[40] Ultimately, he was brought up on charges before the urban prefect of Rome, Junius Rusticus (162–67 CE), and died a martyr in 164.

Justin wrote two apologies, but in many ways the shorter, second one is just a continuation of the first. In his *First Apology,* Justin makes a reasoned, philosophical defense of the Christian faith. Christian teaching about Jesus's death and resurrection is no different than pagan belief in the dying and rising gods, such as Asclepius, Dionysius, or Herakles:

> *In saying that the Logos, who is the first offspring of God, was born for us without sexual union, as Jesus Christ our teacher, and that he was crucified and died and after rising again ascended into heaven, we introduce nothing new beyond [what you say of] those whom you call sons of Zeus. You know how many sons of Zeus the writers whom you honor speak of—Hermes, the hermeneutic Logos and teacher of all; Asclepius, who was also a healer and after being struck by lightning ascended into heaven, as did Dionysius, who was torn in pieces; Herakles, who to escape his torments threw himself into the fire; the Dioscuri born of Leda; and Perseus [born] of Danaë; and Bellerophon who, though of human parentage, rode the horse Pegasus [to the heavens]. Need I mention Ariadne and those who, like her, are said to have been placed among the stars? And what about your deceased emperors, whom you regularly think worthy of being raised to immortality, summoning as witness one who swears to have seen the cremated Caesar ascending into heaven*

from the funeral pyre. . . . But the son of God who is called Jesus, even if only an ordinary human, is worthy to be called son of God because of his wisdom. And if we say, as we said before, that he, peculiarly in comparison to an ordinary birth, was born from God as the Logos of God, such should be ordinary to you who call Hermes the angelic [or premonitory] Logos proceeding from God. (Apology 1.21–22)

So, Justin retorts that charges of atheism against the Christians, just like those against Socrates, are at the instigation of demons, whereas the ancient Greek philosophers really foresaw the truth of Christian teaching.[41] Finally, Christ is the same Logos, the preexistent *spermatic logos,* that the Stoics describe as infiltrating the entire cosmos and all humans.[42]

According to the *Acts of Justin,* the record of his trial and execution, his Christian school and at least one of the congregations of Rome were still housed in rented apartments on the upper floors of a large urban bath complex.[43] This is indicative of Christian practice at Rome in the mid-second century before there were formal church buildings. In his *Apology,* then, Justin gives one of the most insightful pictures of Christian worship. He says:

I will explain the manner in which we have dedicated ourselves to God, having been renewed through Christ, so that we will not appear pernicious by leaving something out of the exposition. If any are persuaded and believe that what we teach and say is true, and if they promise that they can live accordingly, they are instructed to pray, and, while fasting, to beseech God for forgiveness. . . . Then they are led by us to a place where there is water, and they are reborn in the same manner of regeneration by which we ourselves have been reborn. . . .

After thus washing the one who has been persuaded and who has assented, then we lead him to those who are called brothers, in the place where they regularly assemble. . . . We finish our prayers and salute one another with a kiss. The bread and a cup containing water and wine are brought to the president of the brethren. And taking them, he offers praise and glory to the father of all through the name of the son and the holy spirit, and he gives thanks at length for being judged worthy of these things by him. . . . When the president has given thanks and the whole congregation has assented, those who are called deacons by us give to each one present a portion of the bread and water mixed with wine for which the thanksgiving has been made. Then they take it to those who were not present [at the assembly]. . . .

And on the day that is called the Day of the Sun there is a meeting together in one place of all who dwell in cities or the country. As long as time permits the memoirs of the apostles or the writings of the prophets are read. When the reader has finished, the president gives exhortation in a discourse and invitation to imitate these good things. Then we all rise up in unison and offer prayers, and, as we said before, when we have finished praying bread is brought and wine with water. The president offers prayers and thanksgiving in same manner, to the best of his ability, and the congregation assents by saying the Amen. (Apology 1.61, 65, 67).

Although most of the features of this description are entirely recognizable in later Christian practice—baptism, the Eucharist, and the Sunday assembly—the informality with which Justin describes them is still remarkably refreshing even near the end of the third generation.

PART FIVE

The Fourth Generation

Coming of Age in the Roman World

CHAPTER FIFTEEN

Networks of Faith

Literary Trajectories and Regional Trends

When Justin Martyr gives his insightful description of the Sunday gathering of Christians in Rome just on the cusp of the fourth generation, he says: "As long as time permits the *memoirs of the apostles* or the *writings of the prophets* are read. When the reader has finished, the president gives exhortation in a discourse and invitation to imitate these good things."[1] This is the first time that we hear of readings as a formal feature of Christian worship. Eventually, the "reader" will become an official position as well, since it took more than rudimentary literacy. Required was an ability to read in public from Greek manuscripts that were written without punctuation, without even breaks between words or sentences. It was not so simple to read these ancient texts extemporaneously. So began the tradition of the lectionary, the reading of scriptures followed by exposition in worship.

But what scriptures were they reading in Justin's congregation? For Justin, the "memoirs of the apostles" refers primarily to the Gospels of Matthew and Luke. He might have known Mark and certainly used some apocryphal materials, but it is most unlikely he knew John. By "writings of the prophets" Justin clearly means selections from the Septuagint, but not necessarily limited to those books now called "the prophets."[2] Likely other "scriptures" were read as well, and those will have varied from church to church and region to region. The scriptures—or more precisely, *which* scriptures—would become the principal battleground for Christian self-definition and orthodoxy in the fourth generation.

Scriptures and More Scriptures

For most people today the term "scriptures" connotes a set body of literature with a fixed order. Whether Jewish or Christian, Catholic or Protestant, there is a built-in expectation regarding a particular configuration of the canon that goes with each line of tradition. It has been this way for centuries, of course, so long, in fact, one would think it was always so. Yet it was not, for the actual body of writings that makes up the scriptures differs rather significantly for each of these main religious traditions that emerged out of the earlier generations of Judaism.

Moreover, in common parlance we are used to hearing "scripture" (derived from the Latin *scriptura*) as a distinctive term over against ordinary "writing" or literature. Hence "scripture" now connotes sacrality as well as a particular collection. But in Roman times *scriptura* referred to any sort of writing, from wills and contracts to philosophical treatises, religious books, poetry, and novels. The equivalent Greek term was *graphē*, which had an even wider range of meaning.[3] Only when combined with an adjective meaning "holy" or "sacred" did these terms signify what we commonly mean by "scripture" today; in Hellenistic Jewish and early Christian usage that is how the Septuagint was referred to.[4] Terms like "Old Testament" and "New Testament" would not arise until the very end of the second century, indeed as an outgrowth of the debate over the scriptures (see Chapter 17).

1 Enoch

In addition to the Septuagint there were other "scriptures." Fanciful elaborations on the Jewish scriptures, especially Genesis, had begun in earnest in the late third century BCE. Starting from six meager verses of Genesis, and disconnected ones at that (Gen. 5:23–24; 6:1–4), *1 Enoch* tells the story of what the obscure antediluvian patriarch Enoch saw when he was prematurely taken away to heaven.[5] The result is a thoroughly improbable story of angels, sex, giants, and all manner of evil (from magic to metallurgy and mascara), but, most of all, it is the story of Satan. He is only called Semyaz, and later Azaz'el, since the name Satan still meant other things at the time, but it is the same character, the angel who rebels against God. *1 Enoch* is the story of how a band of unruly angels under his leadership rebelled against the authority and order of God, raped human women, and were cast out of heaven. From this innovative story the adversary of God was known by many different names and became one of the mainstays of Jewish apocalyptic. Nowadays *1 Enoch* will be found in no one's Bible, and yet it is one of the most influential stories in early Judaism and had an even greater impact on Christian tradition.[6]

The story of the fallen angels was also known to pagans as a basic belief of Jews and Christians.[7] Celsus made use of it in his polemic against Jesus; he said:

> *Let us put aside the many arguments which refute what they say about their teacher [Jesus], and let us assume, instead, that he really was some sort of angel. Was he the first and only one to have come? Or were there also others before him? If they were to say that he is the only one, they would be convicted of telling lies and contradicting themselves. For they say that others also have come, and, in fact, sixty or seventy at once, who became evil, and were punished by being cast under the earth in chains. And they say that their tears are the cause of hot springs.*[8]

The reference is to the core story of *1 Enoch* contained in chapters 1–36 (called "The Book of the Watchers"), within which chapters 6–11 tell of the rebellion of the angels. This "book" and chapters 72–82 (called "The Astronomical Book" or "Book of the Heavenly Luminaries") are the two sections of the longer work that are reckoned to be the oldest parts of the Enoch literature, written in the latter part of the third century BCE. This early material was elaborated further in the second century BCE by the addition of two more sections of material (chaps. 91–107[8] and 83–90) that help weave the basic story into a larger and somewhat reinterpreted apocalyptic vision.[9] Later still, another section was added (chaps. 37–71 [and 108?]) containing a Book of Similitudes, or parables, attributed to Enoch. It is significant that only this portion of the larger work is not represented among the copies at Qumran, which has led to the suggestion by some scholars that it was added later by Christians who took over the entire work as a part of their scriptural heritage.[10] If correct, the full text of *1 Enoch* would testify to the ongoing elaboration of the Jewish scriptures by Christians of the second century as part of their own literary activity.[11] These traditions thus became available as "scriptural" sources for later forms of Christian interpretation, such as we shall see below in the Nag Hammadi and Pseudo-Clementine literature.[12]

The Life of Adam and Eve

We now have more direct evidence for such pseudepigraphic literary production by second-century Christians in a work known as the *Life of Adam and Eve*.[13] This work is known from several different manuscripts and versions (Greek, Latin, Slavonic, Armenian, and Georgian) that reflect its popular dissemination in Christian circles from the ancient to the medieval periods. A shorter Greek version was also known under the erroneous title *Apocalypse of Moses*. Because of its subject matter, it had traditionally been classed, since the mid-nineteenth century, with other Jewish pseudepigrapha. Even though no Hebrew version was known, it was generally assumed to go back to a Hebrew original dating somewhere between the second and first centuries BCE. Recent scholarship has shown, instead, that the *Life of Adam and Eve* is a thoroughly Christian composition in Greek dating to the early second century CE. Later, the story was further expanded, especially in the Latin versions.

The original story, as found in the shorter Greek version, is basically an expansion on Genesis 3, the temptation and fall. Like *1 Enoch,* it starts from the text of Genesis and fills in the gaps in order to render a new understanding or interpretation of what the story is really about. Hence the narrative focuses on what happened after Adam and Eve, referred to in Greek as the *protoplasts* (or "first formed"), were expelled from the garden. The core of the story is a "Testament of Eve" (chaps. 15–30), in which Eve tells Seth and her other children what happened in the garden. The occasion for her testament is the impending death of Adam (chaps. 1–14; 31–32). His burial (38:1–42:2) is followed shortly by Eve's own death and burial (42:3–43:4) to close the story.[14]

What gives the story its peculiar interpretive slant, and thus its Christian colorations, is the way it presents both Adam and Eve reflecting on their sin and telling how they were led astray. Adam shares in the guilt, but Eve accepts the heaviest blame because she, *like the serpent,* was deceived by Satan. Hence, the enmity between humans and animals results from God's punishment of both Eve and the serpent (based on Gen. 3:15) for disrupting God's order. Satan— who is not yet equated with the serpent!—is the archenemy of both the creator and the creatures. But the story does not end there. At his death Adam repents and is taken by the archangel Michael to be baptized in the lake of Hades before being taken away to heaven (chap. 37); at her death Eve joins him to await the last judgment (42–43). In other words, there is hope for salvation through repentance even for Adam and Eve. Thus, the work was produced by Christians to answer basic questions about human sinfulness and repentance in the light of their continued acceptance of the Jewish scriptures.[15] At the same time, it served as an exegetical filter for understanding these scriptures, including the pseudepigrapha, in the light of Christian faith. The importance of the *Life of Adam and Eve* can be seen in its influence on several discussions in the later second to fourth centuries, including those by Irenaeus, Theophilus of Antioch, Tertullian, Clement of Alexandria, and Eusebius.[16]

Other Christian Elaborations

In the early second century, rabbinic tradition began to close the Jewish canon, resulting in what is now called the Tanak (see Chapter 12). Among other things, the prevalent Christian use of the Septuagint as a rich source for "prophecies" relating to Jesus, as seen in Hebrews and *Epistle of Barnabas,* made it less palatable for Jewish use. One result was to revert only to those texts in Hebrew or Aramaic, rather than Greek, as seen in the Tanak. For diaspora Jews, however, who largely spoke only Greek, this was not a fully satisfactory solution. So the second century saw the rise of some new Greek translations of the Jewish scriptures as alternatives for the Septuagint. Known as the Aquila and Symmachus versions, these new translations tend to give more Semitic or "Hebraizing" renderings of the Greek as well as other local, more Jewish traditions.[17]

At times we can see how these different versions of the text became sources for ongoing debates between Jews and Christians. For example, in his *Dialogue with Trypho* 73, Justin Martyr reproaches Jews for using the scriptures inappropriately by quoting Psalm 95 (96, LXX):10, "The Lord reigns," but *erasing* the words "from the wood." The last words are apparently a variant form of the text used or invented by Christians as a proof-text; that is, it was effectively taken to mean "The Lord reigns from the *cross.*"[18] Similarly, in the preceding paragraphs (71–72) Justin argues that Jews ignore the "true" meaning of the scriptures when they reject some of the words of Jeremiah and Ezra. What he means are the longer Greek versions of Jeremiah and 2 Esdras (= 4 Ezra) that only occur in the Septuagint. Thus, the battle lines over the scriptures and their interpretation had already been drawn in the proof-texting debates between Christians and Jews that heated up in the early to mid-second century. Now too they would become the battleground among diverse Christian groups.

Writings from the Jewish pseudepigrapha that show signs of Christian appropriation and further literary elaboration include 4 Ezra (along with the later 5 and 6 Ezra), the *Martyrdom and Ascension of Isaiah, 3 Baruch,* and the *Testaments of the Twelve Patriarchs.* In each of these cases there is clear evidence of an earlier form of the work from more strictly Jewish contexts. Several of these (4 Ezra, *3 Baruch, Martyrdom and Ascension of Isaiah*) are rather late, that is, date to the end of the first century CE, even in their original Jewish form.[19] Christian appropriation of these works began as early as the second century and continued into late antiquity. Although the *Testaments of the Twelve Patriarchs* represents a much older Jewish tradition, as evidenced by its presence at Qumran and in its influence on Paul, it was similarly appropriated and reworked by Christians beginning in the second century CE.[20]

In addition, there are other works like the *Life of Adam and Eve* that show Christians creating their own form of pseudepigraphic expansions. Another was the *Odes of Solomon*. Continuing a line of Jewish pseudepigraphic tradition (e.g., *Psalms of Solomon* and Wisdom of Solomon), the *Odes of Solomon* was produced by Christians near the end of the first century CE in some proximity to the Gospel of John and *Gospel of Thomas* (see Chapter 12 and below).

One of the most influential of these was the Christian form (or sections) of the *Sibylline Oracles*. The Sibyl was an ancient oracle located at Cumae (near Naples, Italy) who was associated with the founding legends of Rome. Books of her "oracles" served as important sources for the ritual calendar of pagan Rome, but the traditions about her oracular powers (similar to those of the Delphic oracle in Greece) were important to Roman legend and imperial ideology.[21] Books 3, 4, 5, and 11 of the *Sibylline Oracles* were Jewish compositions, ranging in date from the second century BCE to the late first century CE. Books 6 and 7 (and part of 12), on the other hand, were entirely Christian compositions dating to the second and third centuries CE.[22] Throughout the Middle Ages, the Christian *Sibyllines* were some of the most influential apocalyptic traditions in Latin Christianity.[23]

Finally, the *Apocalypse of Elijah* seems to have originated as a Greek document in second-century Christian circles but was further elaborated and revised into several different forms by later Christian groups, especially within Coptic-speaking monasticism in Egypt.[24] Thus, although such Christian elaboration of the pseudepigraphic tradition was widespread from the second century onward, it should also be noted that the interpretive tendencies represented divergent regional trajectories.[25]

If, as we have just seen, the "writings of the prophets" were continuing to be edited or written by Christians in the second century and later, so also were "the memoirs of apostles" (for these two terms see the beginning of this chapter). These too tended to follow regional trajectories and thus bear witness to the growing diversity within the Christian movement. In the remainder of this chapter we shall survey several of these types of literature and regional developments.

Syria: The Traditions of Thomas and Thaddaeus

The Roman province of Syria covered a wide and very diverse region on the eastern edges of the empire. It was largely formed on the lands of the Seleucid dynasty conquered by Pompey the Great in 63 BCE. After conquest, the thoroughly hellenized areas of the coast, from Antioch southward toward Phoenicia and Judea, became the center of Roman Syria; its capital was Antioch. Outlying areas, such as Palmyra, Adiabene, and the Hauran retained more of their local cultural heritage, even though they too were both hellenized and Romanized as time went on. Rome also expanded its power in the region in the early second century under Trajan and Hadrian (116–18) and then again under Marcus Aurelius (165–66); it finally incorporated the region of Mesopotamia all the way to the Persian Gulf.

There was extensive contact and cross-fertilization between these cultural subregions, but differences persisted. We have already seen this in part by noticing the different networks operative in Antioch over against the more Jewish Christian trajectory associated with southern Syria and the Galilee. The *Gospel of Thomas* and the later Thomas tradition were particularly associated with the northern areas of Syria in the upper Euphrates Valley, the region called the Osrhoëne, where local client kings continued to rule until 243 CE. The chief cities of this area were the capital, Edessa, Nisibis, and Mosul, all of which lay on the old Silk Road to Bactria, India, and China.[26] (See Fig. 15.1.)

It is generally assumed that Christianity radiated out to this region from Antioch by the end of the first century CE. A Jewish community was also present, and the pathway from Antioch likely followed Greek-speaking Jewish networks, just as it did elsewhere. It does not appear, however, that these were primarily Jewish Christians, at least not in the same sense as one finds in lower Syria. Eventually, the Osrhoëne would give rise to a distinctively Syriac-speaking Christianity that came to be associated with names such as Bar Daysan (d. ca. 222), Aphraates (fl. 336–45), and Ephrem (d. 373). The transmission and preservation of the New Testament text and many other pieces of early Christian literature owe much to the Syriac manuscript copyists.[27] Many of the earliest pieces of literature, however, remain anonymous and were

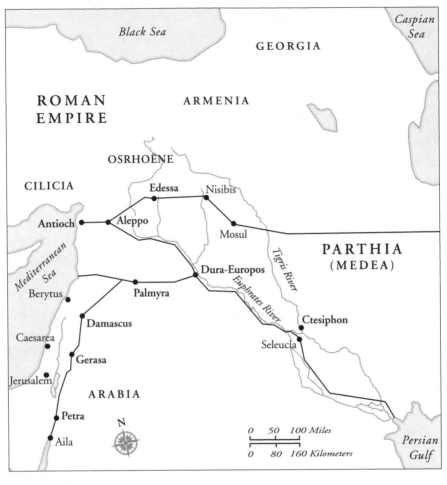

FIGURE 15.1

Map of Roman Syria.

preserved in both Greek and Syriac. In some cases it is not clear which was the
original version. The *Gospel of Thomas* was probably born out of this cultural
matrix near the beginning of the second century CE (see Chapter 12 and Box
12.2). Some scholars think that the Gospel of John, or at least some of its early
layers, also originated in Syria, perhaps closer to Antioch, as a reaction against
the docetic tendencies found in *Gospel of Thomas*.[28] Scholars have also argued
that the *Odes of Solomon* was produced by Christians in this region, dating
sometime between the end of the first and the early third century CE.[29]

The earliest Syrian Christian author known by name is Tatian (ca. 130–

200 CE). He traveled to Antioch and finally to Rome, where he studied under Justin Martyr. He returned to Syria in the 170s and there wrote his *Address to the Greeks,* an apology in Greek (see Box 14.3). He also compiled a version of the four Gospels harmonized into one narrative; known as the *Diatessaron* ("through the four"), it was probably composed in Greek and Syriac.[30] It has also been suggested that Tatian's mode of quotation from the Gospels is related to that found in the *Gospel of Thomas.* Tatian was also a proponent of asceticism. Later, ascetic Christians came to be called the Encratites, from the Greek word *enkrateia,* meaning "continence" or "self-control"; Eusebius names Tatian as the founder.[31] The Syrian monastic tradition remained strong throughout later antiquity.

The Thomas Literature

Later forms of the Thomas tradition in Syria continued to promote ascetic piety by blending together elements of the legend of the apostle Thomas with the ascetic theology of Tatian. This tradition is exemplified in the apocryphal *Acts of Thomas,* which was composed in Edessa, perhaps in Syriac and Greek, near the beginning of the third century CE.[32] The *Acts of Thomas* tells the story of how Jesus came to send the apostle Thomas, his twin brother, off to India to spread the gospel. An example of the novelistic genre, it recounts his journey, preaching, and conversions in various localities.[33] Most of it is quite fanciful, of course, and even the setting in India is a fiction, no doubt prompted by the romantic intrigue of localities at the other end of the Silk Road. In the end, Thomas dies heroically as a martyr in a faraway land. Other local legends referred to his burial place in Edessa itself.[34]

In addition to its ascetic teaching, the *Acts of Thomas* is also noteworthy for its incorporation of early forms of liturgical prayers and hymns that probably come from the late second century. They reflect a distinctive orientation to worship and theology that may also be called "proto-Gnostic." One of these is a bridal song (*Acts Thom.* 6–7); two more are liturgical hymns addressed to "the compassionate mother" (Sophia), who is also called the "holy name of Christ" (*Acts Thom.* 27–28). Finally, there is the "Hymn of the Pearl" (*Acts Thom.* 108–113), an allegorical poem about the soul's awakening and quest for union with God. Another portion of the *Acts of Thomas* appears to be a version of the same tradition found in the Nag Hammadi library under the title *Book of Thomas* (NHC II.7, sometimes called the *Book of Thomas the Contender*); Thomas shows how to "contend" or struggle with the body's lusts and passions.[35] Like the *Gospel of Thomas,* these other traditions associated with the apostle migrated sometime in the second or third century to Egypt, where they circulated in Greek and later in Coptic. Our only complete copy of *Gospel of Thomas* is the Coptic version found in the same volume of the Nag Hammadi library (NHC II.2).

The *Gospel of Thomas, Acts of Thomas,* and *Book of Thomas* thus reflect the growth of an independent "Thomas tradition" beginning in Syria but continuing in Egypt as well. Also preserved was an *Infancy Gospel of Thomas,* which tells of Jesus's early years growing up in Nazareth, between birth and age twelve.[36] The fabulous tales of his miraculous powers derive from a second-century source, but the surviving form of the text is considerably later.[37] Given the stress on Jesus's superhuman nature, it may well be that the work originated in the same docetic circles as the other Thomas literature but was later adjusted to a more orthodox form.

The Legend of Thaddaeus (Addai)

If the Thomas trajectory reflects a divergent stream or network of Christianity in northern Syria, its latent power as a local tradition may be seen both in its survival and in subsequent efforts to tame it for emerging orthodoxy. The latter process is best seen in another cluster of Syrian traditions associated with the apostle Thaddaeus, one of the more obscure names in the Gospel lists of Jesus's disciples.[38] Later legend held that Thaddaeus had been sent by Thomas to Edessa, presumably while Thomas went on to India. According to this legend, then, Thaddaeus, better known as Addai, became the founder of the church there.

The basic legend resulted by the later third century in the production of another work of pseudepigraphic literature, an exchange of letters between Jesus and King Abgar of Edessa.[39] The king, having heard reports of Jesus's miraculous healing powers, wrote to ask him to come to Edessa and give medical assistance. Jesus replied that he would not be able to since he was going to be with his father, but he offered instead to send one of his disciples. After Jesus's departure, therefore, Thomas sent Addai to Edessa. So famous was this literary creation that it was even rendered as lengthy inscriptions and set up, like public billboards, in cities such as Ankyra, Ephesus, and Philippi by the early fifth century.[40]

The *Teachings of Addai* is an apocryphal "acts" of Addai's preaching to King Abgar of Edessa and his eventual death there. The document was produced (fourth century) to reflect a more "orthodox" form of Christianity in Syria, where strong affinities with Jewish tradition were still maintained.[41] All of this suggests that the earliest forms of Christianity in Edessa might have been docetic, as reflected in the Thomas literature, but that there was a later effort to

rewrite the founding legends of the church there to make it seem more orthodox. As we shall see in the following discussion, legends about apostles as
founders and patrons of these far-flung regions became a prominent feature of
each local tradition.

Egypt: Gnostic Currents and the Nag Hammadi Library

According to a later legend preserved by Eusebius, Christianity was brought to
Egypt by the Gospel writer Mark, who was dispatched from Rome by Peter
himself.[42] Eusebius also says that Philo had met with Peter while on his delegation to Rome and that the austere and saintly Jewish sect known as the Thera-
peutai, made famous by Philo's glowing description, was really made up of Jewish
Christians.[43] Eusebius also places the death of Mark in 62 CE, when he was succeeded as "bishop" of Alexandria by a certain Annianus.[44] Of course, this account is entirely fanciful. It would place Peter in Rome by about 37–41 CE, at
the latest, and implies that after writing his Gospel, Mark had already left for
Egypt prior to Philo's visit in 40.[45] Even so, the legend that Mark went to Egypt
seems to go back to the second century. It is reflected in a letter attributed to
Clement of Alexandria (ca. 200 CE), in which he discusses a document called
the *Secret Gospel of Mark*. Only partially preserved through Clement's excerpts,
the *Secret Gospel* was ostensibly written by Mark after arriving in Alexandria
as an alternative form of his own Gospel for more "spiritual" Christians.[46]
Another legend held that Apollos, a protégé of Paul in Corinth and Ephesus,
was already a Christian when he came from his native Alexandria.[47]

Shadowy Beginnings

Precisely when and how the Jesus movement first spread to Egypt is not known.
Given the strong ties between the large Jewish communities in Alexandria and
Judea, it is most likely that the Jesus movement originated in Egypt within Jewish circles, just as it had in the homeland. Christians began to emerge with a
distinctive identity only in the early second century, probably around the time
of the Jewish revolts in Egypt and Cyrenaica in 115–17.[48]

It may well be that Hellenistic Judaism in Alexandria, with its long history
of philosophical influences culminating in Philo, set the tone and provided
the resources for the vibrant interpretive climate of second-century Egyptian

Christianity. The earliest Christian writings that can be confidently assigned to Alexandria are Gospel texts: *Secret Mark* (mentioned above), the *Gospel of the Hebrews,* and the *Gospel of the Egyptians.* All three seem to come from the mid-second century and are partially preserved through the citations in Clement of Alexandria.

As its name suggests, the *Gospel of the Hebrews* has a strongly Jewish flavor and looks to the authority of James, the brother of Jesus. It also shares some unique sayings found in the *Gospel of Thomas.*[49] The *Gospel of the Egyptians* seems to have been written primarily for Greek-speaking Egyptians of Alexandria who had a strong ascetic bent. It, too, shares some material with *Gospel of Thomas.*[50] It is only at the end of the second century with the leadership of the bishop Demetrius and the establishment of a school under Clement of Alexandria that a more mainstream form of Christianity started to develop.

"Gnostic" Currents

The distinctive character of early Egyptian Christianity is seen most clearly in what is usually called Gnosticism. From the Greek word *gnosis* (meaning "knowledge"), "Gnosticism" is a modern term coined to describe various types of early Christianity that came to be viewed as heretical by the end of the second century. The traditional view, as reflected in the writings of Irenaeus and others, was that certain teachers brought these ideas into Christianity and thus distorted it. The "founder" of heresy, and Gnosticism in particular, according to this view, was Simon Magus ("the Magician").[51] The story of his conversion and subsequent rebuke by Peter (Acts 8:9–24) later became a widely used cipher for expressing the opposition between Christian groups; Simon Magus becomes the prototypical opponent of truth.[52]

Following this traditional view, it was once typical in scholarship to describe Gnosticism as a non-Christian (and non-Jewish) religious phenomenon that gradually crept into Christianity in the first or second century, especially in Egypt. Two figures were closely associated by Irenaeus with this process: Basilides (ca. 120–60 CE) and Valentinus (ca. 130–75). It may well be that Valentinus was a student of Basilides. Basilides' teaching is only known indirectly from the comments of others but seems to be an eclectic blend of popular Greek philosophy, Jewish ideas, and Christian ideas of redemption. In this way he was probably not that far theologically from Clement of Alexandria.[53] Valentinus, on the other hand, seems to have been a more original thinker, a reformer of earlier gnosticizing currents. He moved to Rome in about 140 and became a popular teacher in the church there alongside Justin Martyr. At least one of his authentic writings, the *Gospel of Truth,* has been preserved among the Nag Hammadi codices (NHC I.3; XII.2).[54]

The Nag Hammadi Library

Our understanding of the nature and development of Egyptian Christianity and Gnosticism has changed dramatically since the discovery and publication of the Nag Hammadi library. Originally found in 1945 buried in a large clay jar (*pithos*), the cache comprised thirteen papyrus books (codices) bound in leather (see Figs. 15.2 and 15.3). These volumes contain a total of fifty-two works (forty-six different tractates) written in Coptic. Based on papyrus scraps used in the covers, it is possible to conclude that the books were copied sometime in the late fourth century and probably buried by the early fifth century. It may well be that the collection was indeed part of the library of a nearby Coptic monastery at Chenoboskion; it seems it was buried after an edict by the bishop of Alexandria called for the suppression of "heretical" books. The collection represents a wide array of Christian and non-Christian philosophical texts, but many have a decidedly "Gnostic" character.[55] A list of all the works contained in the collection may be found in Box 15.1.

FIGURE 15.2

The Nag Hammadi library, a collection of thirteen leather-bound papyrus codices written in Coptic, discovered in 1945 at the modern village of Nag Hammadi, Egypt. (Used by permission of the Institute for Antiquity and Christianity, Claremont, CA)

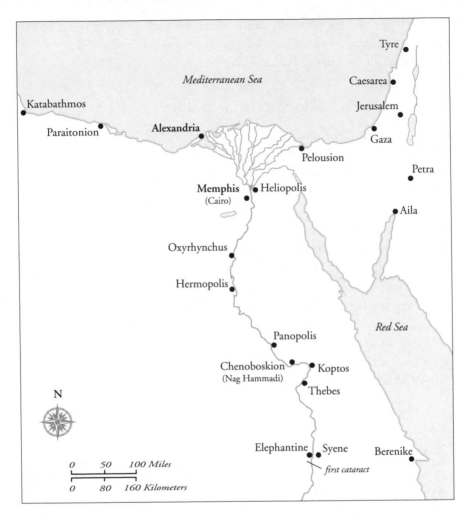

Mediterranean Sea

Tyre

Caesarea

Jerusalem

Katabathmos

Paraitonion

Alexandria

Gaza

Pelousion

Petra

Memphis
(Cairo)

Heliopolis

Aila

Oxyrhynchus

Hermopolis

Red Sea

Panopolis

Chenoboskion
(Nag Hammadi)

Koptos

Thebes

N

Elephantine

Syene

Berenike

first cataract

0   50   100 Miles

0   80   160 Kilometers

FIGURE 15.3

Map of Roman Egypt.

BOX 15.1

The Nag Hammadi Library

Contents by Codex

CODEX I
- I.1 *Prayer of the Apostle Paul*
- I.2 *Apocryphon of James*
- I.3 *Gospel of Truth*
- I.4 *Treatise on the Resurrection*
- I.5 *Tripartite Tractate*

CODEX II
- II.1 *Apocryphon of John*
- II.2 *Gospel of Thomas*
- II.3 *Gospel of Philip*
- II.4 *Hypostasis of the Archons*
- II.5 *On the Origin of the World*
- II.6 *The Exegesis of the Soul*
- II.7 *Book of Thomas the Contender*

CODEX III
- III.1 *Apocryphon of John*
- III.2 *Gospel of the Egyptians*
- III.3 *Eugnostos the Blessed*
- III.4 *The Sophia of Jesus Christ*
- III.5 *The Dialogue of the Savior*

CODEX IV
- IV.1 *Apocryphon of John*
- IV.2 *Gospel of the Egyptians*

CODEX V
- V.1 *Eugnostos the Blessed*
- V.2 *Apocalypse of Paul*
- V.3 *First Apocalypse of James*
- V.4 *Second Apocalypse of James*
- V.5 *Apocalypse of Adam*

CODEX VI
- VI.1 *Acts of Peter and the Twelve Apostles*
- VI.2 *Thunder: Perfect Mind*
- VI.3 *Apocalypse of Peter*

- VI.4 *The Concept of Our Great Power*
- VI.5 *Plato,* Republic 588b–589b
- VI.6 *Discourse on the Eighth and Ninth*
- VI.7 *Prayer of Thanksgiving*
- VI.8 *Asclepius 21–29*

CODEX VII
- VII.1 *The Paraphrase of Shem*
- VII.2 *Second Treatise of the Great Seth*
- VII.3 *Apocalypse of Peter*
- VII.4 *The Teachings of Silvanus*
- VII.5 *The Three Steles of Seth*

CODEX VIII
- VIII.1 *Zostrianos*
- VIII.2 *The Letter of Peter to Philip*

CODEX IX
- IX.1 *Melchizedek*
- IX.2 *The Thought of Norea*
- IX.3 *The Testimony of Truth*

CODEX X
- X.1 *Marsanes*

CODEX XI
- XI.1 *The Interpretation of Knowledge*
- XI.2 *A Valentinian Exposition*
- XI.3 *Allogenes*
- XI.4 *Hypsiphrone*

CODEX XII
- XII.1 *The Sentences of Sextus*
- XII.2 *Gospel of Truth*
- XII.3 *Fragments*

CODEX XIII
- XIII.1 *Trimorphic Protennoia*
- XIII.2 *On the Origin of the World*

A number of the Nag Hammadi treatises represent later forms of theological exploration, but at least some preserve important foundational documents from the second century, such as *Gospel of Thomas* and *Book of Thomas*. These works from the Syrian Thomas tradition are not "Gnostic" in the fullest, technical sense, but their presence in the library suggests that docetic and ascetic elements of Syrian Christian tradition were likely important influences on the development of Egyptian "Gnosticism." Among the other foundational documents are the *Apocryphon of John* (NHC II.1; III.1); the *Hypostasis of the Archons* (NHC II.4); the *Apocalypse of Adam* (NHC V.5); and the *First and Second Apocalypse of James* (NHC V.3–4).

Of these, the *Apocryphon* ("Hidden Teaching") *of John* presupposes the same basic mythological scheme as that of Valentinus. Its underlying premise is a cosmological explanation for the body-soul relationship in humans and a model for redemption or salvation based on releasing the soul from its physical "prison" (the body) in order to be reunited with the divine spirit. Yet this idea assumes a basic dichotomy, drawn in part from Greek philosophy, between a lower *Demiurge* (or creator God) and the *Good God,* who is the origin of the soul. Although elements of this basic idea are found in a number of earlier forms of Greek and Jewish thought, it is probably best now to view "Gnosticism" as a Christian philosophical development of these ideas, rather than as a separate or foreign religious movement. In other words, "Gnosticism" operated as a kind of elitist and secretive spirituality movement within Christian circles.[56] Rather than bizarre rituals or libertine sexual mores, as described with prurient interest by Irenaeus and others, it was probably spiritual elitism and overt philosophical speculation about the biblical story of creation that caused "Gnosticism" finally to be labeled as "heretical."

Local Heroes: The Apostolic Novels

The Nag Hammadi library represents a complex philosophical form of Christian literature, but it surely was not for everyone. A more popular type of literature began to develop in the later second century in the form of novels about the travels, miracles, preaching, and deaths of individual apostles. Because they were modeled to some extent on Luke-Acts, and specifically the travels of Paul (Acts 13–28), they have traditionally been called "the apocryphal acts." In genre and style, however, they were much more like Hellenistic novels (or romances, as they are sometimes called). These pagan novels proliferated in the second and third centuries CE and typically were structured around a long and often dangerous journey. Tales of lost love and miraculous events are also common themes. Like *The Golden Ass* of Apuleius, they often functioned simultaneously as entertainment and religious propaganda.[57]

There were also some notable Jewish novels, including Tobit and Judith in the Septuagint (both from the Hellenistic period) and *Joseph and Aseneth* (from Roman Egypt). They too were filled with fabulous journeys and tales of magic that could serve as models. According to Eusebius, when Thaddaeus was sent to Edessa by Thomas at the behest of Jesus, he stayed in the house of Tobias son of Tobias. This allusion links the Addai legend to the Septuagint novel about Tobit. Never mind that the story of Tobit was set more than eight hundred years earlier; intertextual allusions of this sort provided the Christian novels, like their pagan and Jewish models, with an ability to telescope across time and space.[58]

One of the most fabulous and extensive of the apostolic novels was the *Acts of Andrew*. It has Peter's brother, Andrew, travel to the Black Sea area and northward into the wild regions of Scythia (southern Russia) and Thrace.[59] The combination of the fabulous journeys of the apostle and his noble death will become the common pattern for all the later apocryphal acts. Part of its popularity stems from the fact that the *Acts of Andrew* seems to emulate some of the more famous episodes from Homer's *Odyssey*. One of the more notable is when Andrew is sent to rescue Matthias, who has been captured by giant cannibals similar to the Cyclops in Homer.[60] Thus, whereas Luke-Acts employed novelistic elements in service to its historiographical interests,[61] these individual spin-offs—for that is what they were—carried the genre in new directions narratively, geographically, and, as we shall see, theologically. Each one produced a local hero and patron apostle for a particular stream of Christianity, and sometimes they were at odds with one another.

The Acts of John

Legends about the apostle John flourished in the second century. As noted earlier, he was by all accounts the last of the original disciples of Jesus to die; still, we do not know a precise date. Most of the later legends placed him in Ephesus, where he lived to an advanced age and died in about 95/96 CE. In the latter part of the second century, Irenaeus could still boast that he knew Polycarp, who had actually known John. He reports, for example, that Polycarp told a story of how John once fled naked from the baths in Ephesus when the notorious heretic Cerinthus showed up.[62] In a similar vein, Clement of Alexandria preserves a story of how John once encountered a famous bandit chieftain who then re-pented of his evil ways.[63]

Sometime in the mid-second century such colorful legends began to coa-lesce into an edifying narrative and hero tale eventually known as the *Acts of John*.[64] Even so, no widespread knowledge of the story is attested prior to the time of Eusebius (ca. 310 CE).[65] It appears that there may have been some older layers of the evolving novel that were later taken over and sanitized or supple-mented because they were theologically suspect. The earliest layers (especially chaps. 87–105) seem to be dominated by docetic and ascetic ideas. For example, when the earthly ministry of Jesus is described, the *Acts of John* stresses that he frequently changes shapes or seems to be of vastly different ages. When he walks he leaves no footprints, and even on the cross he speaks as a heavenly re-vealer (chaps. 87–93). Instead of a last supper, Jesus leads the disciples in a joy-ous dance to an antiphonal hymn of otherworldly expectation (chaps. 94–96). This Jesus stands in sharp contrast to the Logos who "became *flesh*" of the Gospel of John, showing why the Johannine tradition remained popular among Gnostic Christians.[66] The *Acts of John* served as an interpretive filter for just this purpose. The later versions of the story shift the emphasis to John him-self. Anticipating later hagiographical literature (the lives of the saints genre), it portrays John as a powerful but charming miracle worker—even bedbugs duti-fully obey him (chaps. 60–61)—who leads an exemplary life.

The Legends of Peter and Paul

There is some debate among scholars over which came first, the *Acts of Peter* or the *Acts of Paul*. The reason is that there seems to be a close connection between the two works, as though one were borrowing from the other. One major com-ponent of both is the journey to Rome, and it seems that the story of Paul in Acts, further elaborated in the second century, may well be the base legend. The *Acts of Peter* opens with Peter's travel to Rome after Paul's departure for Spain. On the other hand, another key component is Peter's conflict with Simon Magus, based on Acts 8:9–24, which evolves into a running battle—God's champion versus Satan's—as Peter follows Simon to Rome. The climax of the *Acts of Peter* is a miraculous showdown between Peter and Simon. Simon demonstrates his supernatural power by ascending from the earth and flying around. Peter calls on Jesus to bring him down. When he falls and breaks his leg, the crowds stone him to death.

So it may well be that each of these basic story lines had already begun to evolve as popular legend in the mid-second century. It is usually suggested that both stories originated in Asia Minor, but the *Acts of Peter* in its final form bears marks of Roman tradition. So it may be that the legends grew and developed local colorations as the stories were passed along. Justin Martyr reported in about 150 CE that Simon had a cult following in Rome, where he was called "the first god" by native Samaritans.[67] Slightly later, Irenaeus attributed the origins of the Gnostic "heresy" to the teachings of Simon Magus, while Eusebius, following Irenaeus, makes him the virtual founder of all the heresies that came to plague Christianity.[68] He thus became a cipher for numerous enemies (see the last section of this chapter). The *Acts of Peter* was written in part to consolidate disparate legends regarding Peter's place at Rome and the tradition of "orthodoxy" that was attached to him.

The *Acts of Peter* and the *Acts of Paul* are just one part of a broad array of legendary literature in the name of these apostles (see Box 15.2). By the end of the century they would each influence the story of the other, with the *Acts of Paul* coming perhaps slightly later than the *Acts of Peter* in its final form.[69] Popular legend held that both Peter and Paul were martyred in Rome in 64 at the hands of Nero; Peter was crucified upside down, while Paul was beheaded. Both legends were crystallized in the final portions of the respective *Acts,* which recount the apostles' martyrdom. The stories of their martyrdoms also circulated independently in the third century and later, like other pieces of the growing martyr literature.

The Acts of Paul and Thecla

One distinctive component of the *Acts of Paul* in its fullest form concerns the heroic trials and tribulations of a co-worker, an attractive young woman named Thecla. Recent scholarship has shown that the Thecla cycle was part of the original work that was later removed because of its positive portrayal of women and sexual renunciation.[70] Thecla clearly becomes the hero in this portion of the story. It opens during Paul's stay in Iconium (cf. Acts 14:1–6), where Paul preaches in the house of a certain Onesiphorus:

> *While Paul was preaching . . . a virgin named Thecla—her mother was Theocleia—who was betrothed to a man named Thamyris, sat at a nearby window and listened night and day to the word of the virgin life as it was spoken by*

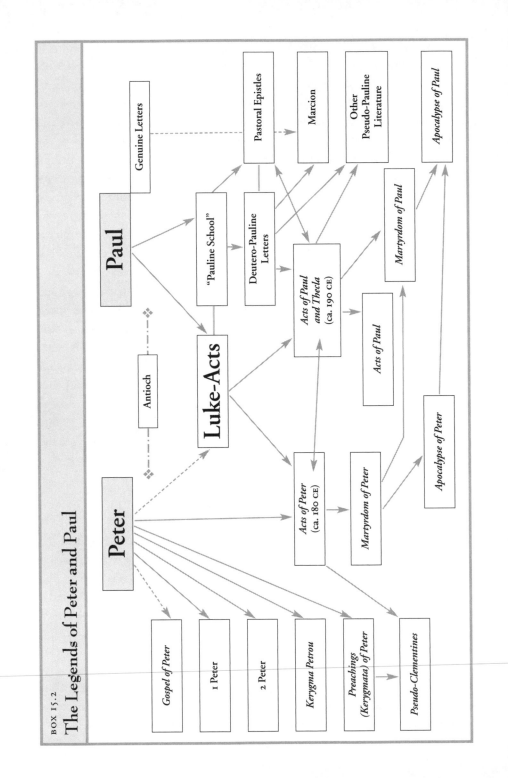

BOX 15.2
The Legends of Peter and Paul

Peter

Paul

Genuine Letters

Antioch

Luke-Acts

"Pauline School"

Deutero-Pauline Letters

Pastoral Epistles

Marcion

Other Pseudo-Pauline Literature

Acts of Paul and Thecla (ca. 190 CE)

Acts of Paul

Martyrdom of Paul

Apocalypse of Paul

Acts of Peter (ca. 180 CE)

Martyrdom of Peter

Apocalypse of Peter

Gospel of Peter

1 Peter

2 Peter

Kerygma Petrou

Preachings (Kerygmata) of Peter

Pseudo-Clementines

Paul; and she did not turn away from the window, but pressed on in the faith
rejoicing exceedingly. Moreover, when she saw many women and virgins going
in to Paul she desired to be counted worthy herself to stand in Paul's presence
and hear the word of Christ; for she had not yet seen Paul in person, but only
heard his word. Since she did not move from the window, her mother sent to
Thamyris. He came in great joy as if he were already taking her in marriage.
So Thamyris said to Theocleia, "Where is my Thecla, that I may see her?" But
Theocleia said, "I have a new tale to tell you, Thamyris. . . . This man is up-
setting the city of the Iconians, and your Thecla in addition; for all the women
and young people go in to him and are taught by him: 'You must fear one sin-
gle God and live in chastity.'" (Acts of Paul and Thecla 3.7–9)[71]

Thamyris's angry response is predictable, as his future wife is being denied him
by Paul's preaching. As a leading man of the city, therefore, Thamyris has Paul
and his co-workers brought before the magistrates; Paul was arrested, flogged,
and eventually forced into hiding with other Christians.

Thecla continued to follow Paul even when she was threatened by the governor with being burned at the stake for refusing to marry Thamyris. When they
tried, however, the fire was extinguished by a torrential rain. Finally, Paul and
Onesiphorus took Thecla with them, left the region, and came to Antioch.
Again Thecla's beauty attracted unwanted attention, this time from a Syrian
named Alexander. Once again she was threatened with martyrdom for refusing
to yield to his advances, but when she was thrown into the arena with a raven-
ous lioness, the beast only licked her feet. Amazed, the other women in the
crowd began to call on her to perform miracles, especially for their sick and
dying children. Finally, at the end of the story Thecla moves on, following in
the footsteps of Paul. She preaches as she goes and even cuts her hair short and
wears men's clothing. In short, she has become a missionary apostle like Paul
himself.

The story of Thecla thus reflects a rigorously ascetic brand of Pauline Christianity that flourished somewhere in Asia Minor or eastern Anatolia in the later
second century. Although the letters of Paul are not mentioned, this ascetic
"Paulinism" could surely have found ample support for its ideals in Paul's own
instructions and personal example (esp. 1 Cor. 7:1–9). From the perspective of
the members of this group, at least, they were continuing the authentic tradition
of Paul. In fact, Thecla continued to be an important symbol of faith and martyrdom for centuries (see Fig. 15.4). Yet such strict forms of asceticism would
eventually produce reactions within other Pauline circles (see Chapter 16).

FIGURE 15.4

Thecla as ascetic hero and martyr; a
plate from North Africa from the time
of St. Augustine (ca. 350–430) showing
Thecla between two lions. The inscription plaque to her left reads "Lady, the
victory [is yours]." (Used by permission
of Annewies van den Hoek)

A Jewish Christian Novel:
The Pseudo-Clementines

Naturally, the people who wrote and read such novelistic literature never
thought of themselves as "heretics." Yet they might point the finger at others, as
seen most clearly in the Pseudo-Clementine literature.[72] The name *Pseudo-
Clementines* comes from the fact that this body of traditions circulated with
three pseudepigraphic covering letters—one from Peter to James, brother of
Jesus, followed by James's attestation of Peter's instruction, and the third from
Clement of Rome to the same James. It is the last that forms the basic fiction
around which the story revolves, as Clement narrates his life story. Part of the
story concerns his rediscovery of long-lost family members. Called the *Recognitions* from the recurring motif of a joyous reunion, this part of the story is
probably later (perhaps fourth century) in its present form. Clement also tells
how he traveled to Judea after hearing that the Son of God had appeared there;
he came to meet Peter, was converted by Barnabas, and was finally appointed
bishop by Peter himself. He then tells the truths he learned from Peter's preaching. This portion of the story, called the *Homilies,* represents the earlier form of
the same basic novel, probably based on second-century legends. It is this layer
of the Pseudo-Clementine tradition that concerns us here.

By the later second century, it should be remembered, *1 Clement* was considered part of the New Testament scriptures. The legends about Peter thus create

a natural triangle of relations between Peter and Clement, on the one hand, and between Peter and James, leader of the church in Jerusalem, on the other. The cover letters crystallize these putative relations by having Peter commission James to guard the "book of his preachings," as imparted also to Clement.[73] The story is also built upon the contest between Peter and Simon Magus, derived from the *Acts of Peter*.[74] It also contains a homily with distinctively Jewish Christian theology.[75] The *Pseudo-Clementine* novels weave these components together to stress the basically Jewish message and identity of Jesus, as preserved authentically by Peter, James, and Clement. Over against this "true" message stand the perversions fostered by "Simon," whose real identity will become clear shortly.

These traditions come from a group of strict Jewish Christians known as Ebionites.[76] The origin of the name Ebionites is obscure, but the most likely case is that it derives from a Greek transliteration of an Aramaic word meaning "poor."[77] The term became the honorific self-designation for certain Jewish Christian groups that traced their lineage to the old Jerusalem church of James.[78] The earliest description of them comes from Irenaeus (ca. 177 CE):

> *Those who are called Ebionites agree that the world was made by God, but their opinions with respect to the Lord are similar to those of Cerinthus and Carpocrates. They only use the Gospel according to Matthew, and repudiate the apostle Paul, maintaining that he was an apostate from the Law. As to the prophetic writings, they endeavor to expound them in a somewhat peculiar manner; they practice circumcision, persevere in the observance of customs that are enjoined by the Law, and in their Judaic manner of life they also venerate Jerusalem as if it were the house of God.* (Against Heresies 1.26.2)

Origen adds that they continued to observe the Jewish feasts, such as Passover, and that some Ebionites accepted the virgin birth of Jesus, while others did not, claiming that Jesus was the natural child of Joseph.[79] According to all the early accounts a key point was their view that Paul was a heretic.[80]

It is the last issue that comes out most clearly in the *Pseudo-Clementines*, since Simon Magus, the archenemy of Peter, has now become a cipher for Paul. Peter warns:

> . . . *anyone can understand to whom **Simon** belongs, who first went to the Gentiles, before me; and to whom I [Peter] belong, who came after him, appearing as light after darkness, as knowledge after ignorance, as healing after sickness. . . .*

> *Therefore remember above all not to receive any apostle or prophet or teacher who has not first presented his gospel to James. Otherwise the wicked one [Satan] will send against you a herald, as now he has sent **Simon** against us, preaching under pretext of truth, in the name of the Lord, but actually sowing error.* (Hom. *II.17.3–4; XI.35.4–5*)[81]

Elsewhere Peter challenges Simon's (i.e., Paul's) claims to authority based upon his revelatory experiences (*Hom.* XVII.18–10) and generally warns that anyone who preaches a gospel that denies the abiding validity of Torah is not an apostle from God, but Satan (*Peter to James* 2.3–4).[82]

It is very likely that the name "Ebionites" as used by Irenaeus (and later Epiphanius, ca. 373 CE) was but one way of referring to a broad stream of Jewish Christianity that resisted the general abandonment of Jewish observance and tradition by other, typically gentile, forms of the Christian movement. Sometimes they were called "Nazoreans." The *Pseudo-Clementines* do not use any such term to refer to their group; they are, after all, the true church, the church of the Hebrews. They look back to the original form of the Jesus movement and decry any subsequent changes that seem to distort the original message. Paul was the archenemy. Ironically, however, in the long run this type of Jewish Christianity came to be labeled as heretical by the emerging mainstream of the Christian movement because they insisted on Torah observance and claimed that Jesus was human-born and only adopted as God's son, the messiah, at his baptism, in accordance with the scriptures. *In accordance with the scriptures.*

CHAPTER SIXTEEN

The Dilemma of Diversity

Delineating Heresy and Orthodoxy

If some Jewish Christians of the later second century had begun to cast a suspicious eye on Paul—or more precisely certain forms of Pauline Christianity—as archenemy of the true faith, wary looks were also shooting in the other direction. There was, in fact, a growing rift between Jewish and gentile streams within the Christian movement. It was to be expected, perhaps, as the split with Judaism itself had further polarized the rhetoric on both sides. The movement itself was becoming predominantly gentile in background and looked increasingly to its cultural affinities with Greco-Roman culture.

For example, by the 160s there arose a considerable debate over the observance of Christ's "Passion" (or the *Pascha*, as it was called in Greek). Should it be at Passover (*Pesach* in Hebrew), following the Jewish calendar, that is, on the fourteenth day of Nisan? Many Christian leaders of Asia Minor and Syria insisted on the traditional date in keeping with the last supper in the synoptic Gospels. Others, however, including Christian leaders at Rome, favored moving the observance to the following Sunday so as to coincide with the traditional day of Christian worship and to emphasize the resurrection.[1] Gradually, the latter position won out, at least in churches aligned with Rome. It also suggested new symbolic correlations, such as celebrations of the spring equinox, that eventuated in what is now called Easter.

Jewish Christians were increasingly caught in the middle. They could still look back to the figure of Jesus and to the role of the prophets in their own understanding of him. Certain continuities were still there. But now there were more fissures, as some forms of gentile Christianity seemed to be even farther removed from the Jewish roots of the movement. Perhaps more than any other Christian thinker of the second century, one person would push this issue to its limits—and with it several others. His name was Marcion.

Pushing the Limits: Marcion

Marcion came from Sinope on the southern coast of the Black Sea in the Roman province of Pontus. This was the area visited by the Roman senator Pliny the Younger in 111–12 CE when he first encountered Christians (see Chapter 14). Precisely when Marcion was born is uncertain, probably sometime in the last decades of the first century CE. At least one report (that of Hippolytus in the early third century) held that he was the son of the Christian bishop of Sinope. Although this tradition is rather suspicious, it does seem likely that Marcion was raised as a Christian.[2] Another report says that Marcion, and presumably his father as well, was a wealthy shipowner operating out of this prominent port city.[3] Certainly, his wealth is attested in various reports. It appears that Marcion moved to Ephesus by around the 120s, and there he began to study the letters of Paul. They would be a pivotal influence on his later thinking. Marcion wanted to be accepted in the churches of Asia as a teacher, but he was rebuffed, perhaps by Polycarp himself. The story told by Irenaeus of his own reminiscences of Polycarp included an encounter (either in Smyrna or in Rome) in which the revered bishop of Smyrna reportedly called Marcion "the firstborn of Satan."[4]

Finally, Marcion moved to Rome in the 130s. He was initially welcomed, since he made a benefaction to the church of some two hundred thousand sesterces (or roughly the minimum fortune of a Roman senator). He then set up his own school in Rome and began to teach and write about his theological ideas. He was thus a contemporary of Justin Martyr, Valentinus, and Tatian in the Christian intellectual and catechetical circles of the capital. Writing about 150, Justin acknowledged his presence but decried his teachings about "some other god greater than the creator."[5] He presented his books of teachings to the elders and leaders of the church at Rome, and they were roundly rejected. Or so the story goes. In fact, it appears that Marcion had already attracted a substantial following both at Rome and elsewhere. He was eventually expelled in about 144.[6] Tertullian emphatically notes, however, that they gave back the money.

Marcion died sometime later, perhaps in the mid-150s, but his movement continued on.[7]

Marcion's Teaching

Five main components of Marcion's teaching proved troublesome for the church at Rome:

1. Marcion argued that the creator God of Genesis was a different and inferior God to the Father of Jesus Christ. Although this was not an unheard-of idea, Marcion seems to have radicalized it in a way similar to that of some Gnostics. Even so, Marcion was not a Gnostic.

2. He argued that all the Jewish scriptures were therefore meaningless as revelations about Christ and should be entirely discarded by Christians. Here he avoided the contrived and convoluted interpretations of the Septuagint found in Hebrews or the *Epistle of Barnabas* as well as Gnostic mythological elaborations on creation found in the *Apocryphon of John*. Nonetheless, Marcion went farther by denying altogether that Christianity was the fulfillment or culmination of the traditions of Israel.

3. Marcion maintained that Jesus was not born as actual flesh and blood. Like some other docetists, he thought that Christ was an entirely spiritual being who had inhabited a human body temporarily and then departed at the moment of the crucifixion.

4. He argued that Paul alone had understood the true message that brought freedom from the laws of the creator God. To this end he could make good use of Paul's own powerful affirmation that there is only "one gospel," the one he preached (cf. Gal. 1:6–9).

5. Finally, on this basis Marcion formed his own collection of authoritative scriptures containing only an expurgated form of the Gospel of Luke and ten letters of Paul.[8] He referred to them as the Gospel and the *Apostolicon,* meaning "Apostolic Witness" or just "Apostle."[9]

To this collection Marcion appended one of his own writings, a treatise called the *Antitheses.* Largely an arrangement of paired quotations, it set passages from the Jewish scriptures in opposition to passages from his twofold canon; these were then followed by a systematic treatise. Unfortunately, the *Antitheses* is now lost, but we are able to reconstruct some of its basic formulations from later comments by disciples as well as opponents. Here are several examples out of the thirty known antithetical pairs:[10]

> *1. The Creator was known to Adam and to the following generations, but the Father of Christ is unknown, just as Christ himself said of him in these words: "No one has known the Father except the Son" [Luke 10:22].*
>
> *2. The Creator did not even know where Adam was, so he cried, "Where are you?" [Gen. 3:9], but Christ knew even the thoughts of men [cf. Luke 5:22; 6:8; 9:47].*
>
> *8. In the Law it is said: "An eye for an eye, a tooth for a tooth" [Exod. 21:24; Deut. 19:21], but the Lord, being good, says in the Gospel: "If anyone strikes you on the cheek, offer him the other as well" [Luke 6:29].*
>
> *25. The Creator established the Sabbath [Gen. 2:3; Exod. 20:11]; Christ abolishes it [Luke 6:5].*

Marcion's "point of departure," as Adolf von Harnack called it, lay in the Pauline opposition of law and gospel, and he came to the realization—perhaps he thought it a revelation—that the gospel presented by Christ and Paul "proclaimed an entirely new God."[11] His arrangement of the *Antitheses* was thus intended to dramatize this fundamental opposition. In so doing, however, he effectively created an anti-scripture in replacement of the Septuagint. His "Bible" now contained three main components: the *Antitheses,* the *Gospel* (Luke), and the *Apostle* (Paul's letters).

Marcion's Impact

Even excommunication did not quash Marcion's influence. In effect he established his own churches as a sectarian offshoot of Christianity, and they were successful competitors. Of course, he and his followers considered it the only true church. One still hears of Marcionite churches in various parts of the eastern Roman Empire through the fourth and fifth centuries.[12] During the latter half of the second and into the third century, debates about and refutations of his teaching raged, thus provoking some important developments in notions of heresy and orthodoxy. His impact may be seen in four issues that he brought to the fore.

1. The emphasis on Pauline theology as the only norm for "true" Christianity.

2. The complete rejection of the Jewish scriptures and Judaism.

3. The delimitation of a "canon" of authoritative scriptures.

4. Emphasis on the proper (or original) wording of these scriptures.

Marcion viewed himself as a reformer out to restore Christianity to its true center, the teachings of Jesus as understood correctly by Paul alone. He thought that these basic truths had been perverted by other Christians, especially those with "Judaizing" intentions. One might argue, therefore, that Marcion was one of the first to develop the idea of "heresy" as perversion of the pure message. In effect, he hung the heresy label on any Christian who read the Septuagint.

Many scholars would argue that Marcion's greatest impact arose from his twofold effort at defining the Christian scriptures—rejecting the Septuagint outright and insisting on only the Gospel of Luke and Paul's letters.[13] Until this time, as we have already seen in the preceding chapter, Christians were quite content to consider a wide array of writings as scripture, with no set limits on which ones were or were not authoritative. Some Christians might have used more scriptures, others less; it varied from community to community and region to region. By setting such restrictive limits in regard to both the Jewish scriptures and other "apostolic" writings, such as the Gospels of Matthew and John, Marcion forced the issue. In order to refute Marcion, other Christians at Rome and elsewhere had to come to some clearer definition about their own ideas of scripture, specifically, the value of the Jewish scriptures as found in the Septuagint and a role for more than one of the Gospels.

New Revelations: Prophecy or Peril?

The Apocalypse of Peter

New apocalypses continued to appear into the mid-second century. There were, in fact, two distinct documents known as the *Apocalypse of Peter*. One is a Gnostic revelation dialogue preserved in Coptic in the Nag Hammadi library (NHC VII.3); however, it dates to the third or early fourth century.[14] The other work that goes under the title *Apocalypse of Peter* was mentioned by Clement of Alexandria as an authentic writing of the apostle (see Box 16.1). It is a Greek apocalypse of a more traditional sort and was considered scripture in the churches of Alexandria at that time (ca. 200 CE).[15] Even though the work is only fully known from an Ethiopic translation, roughly half the work is preserved in Greek fragments from Egypt.[16] The original work probably dates to the time after the Bar Kochba revolt (132–35 CE) and may come from Jewish Christian circles in Syria-Palestine.[17]

BOX 16.1

The Apocalypse of Peter

DATE: ca. 135 CE or slightly later

AUTHOR: Unknown

ATTRIBUTION: Jesus speaking to Peter

LOCATION: Syria-Palestine

AUDIENCE AND OCCASION: This work follows the basic form of an apocalypse in that it has Jesus "reveal" to Peter what will happen in the latter days to the righteous (the martyrs) and the wicked (those who persecute them) when the day of the Lord finally arrives. It is based on the so-called synoptic apocalypse (Mark 13; Matt. 24) but extends the discussion to make predictions about what will happen when false messiahs arise. It seems to be a reaction to the Bar Kochba revolt, when Jewish revolutionaries attempted to coerce Jewish Christians into joining their cause. This work then set the stage for the fuller development of the "pictures of hell" that became very popular in the literature and preaching of the Middle Ages.

OUTLINE

I. Jesus and Peter on the Mount of Olives (chaps. 1–2)

II. Jesus Shows Peter the Souls of All Humans in the Palm of His Hand (chap. 3)

III. The Day of Judgment Described (chaps. 4–5)

    A. The righteous join the angels in a shining cloud (chap. 6)

    B. A tour of the place of torment for the wicked (chaps. 7–12)

    C. The angels bring the righteous to God (chaps. 13–14)

IV. Jesus Takes the Disciples onto the Mount of Transfiguration, Where They See Him with Moses and Elijah (chaps. 15–17)

FURTHER READING

Bauckham, R. *The Fate of the Dead: Studies on the Jewish and Christian Apocalypses.* Leiden: Brill, 1998.
———. "Jews and Jewish Christians in the Land of Israel at the Time of the Bar Kochba War, with Special Reference to the Apocalypse of Peter." In *Tolerance and Intolerance in Early Judaism and Christianity.* Edited by G. N. Stanton and G. G. Stroumsa. Cambridge: Cambridge University Press, 1998. Pp. 228–38.
Bernstein, A. E. *The Formation of Hell: Death and Retribution in the Ancient and Early Christian Worlds.* Ithaca, NY: Cornell University Press, 1993. Esp. pp. 271–301.
Hennecke, E., and W. Scheemelcher. *New Testament Apocrypha.* 2 vols. Philadelphia: Westminster, 1965. 2:663–83. Text and an extensive introduction.

The *Apocalypse of Peter* seems to depend on several recognizable sources. Its point of departure is the "synoptic apocalypse" (Matt. 24:4–36; Mark 13:5–37; Luke 21:8–36), in which Jesus predicts events surrounding the destruction of Jerusalem. Now "Jesus" gives fuller information and instruction on what will happen at his second coming, the "end of the world." The work culminates in a tour of Hades to show the rewards of the righteous (partly lost?) and the punishments of the damned.[18]

Finally, the *Apocalypse of Peter* seems to depend on the Christian version of 4 Ezra (after ca. 100 CE) and used it to interpret events surrounding the second revolt as "false prophecies" about the coming of Jesus.[19] The *Apocalypse of Peter* was very influential in the Greek East and was one of the major sources for the *Apocalypse of Paul.* Together they popularized elaborate descriptions of Hades and the "last judgment" that circulated widely in medieval Latin Christianity and served as a principal source of Dante's *Inferno.*

Montanus and the "New Prophecy"

According to Eusebius, Montanus was a newly baptized Christian in Ardabav in southern Phrygia who suddenly burst into ecstatic prophesying.[20] The date is difficult to pin down, but most scholars place it near 170 CE. Eusebius also says that Montanism spread to Rome by 177, where it was condemned by the bishop Eleutherus. Even so, a date in the third quarter of the second century seems secure.

The idea of charismatic gifts or prophesying "in the Spirit" was not in itself a problem, even at that relatively late date. Rather, Montanus claimed to speak as the voice of God. Soon he was joined by two women prophets named Maximilla and Priscilla.[21] Together they claimed to be a direct conduit for divine words uncorrupted by the will or intellect of the medium, in a way similar to the modern notion of "trance channeling."[22] In most respects Montanus and his followers did not differ on key Christian ideas, but problems arose when they asserted prophetic knowledge of the meaning of certain scriptures, or what has been called "charismatic exegesis." As a result, they seem to have developed even more rigorous forms of piety, including more frequent fasts, greater restrictions on remarriage, and a high regard for martyrdom.

These austere practices only seem to have made the Montanists more popular within Christian circles in Phrygia, Rome, and eventually North Africa.[23] One feature of their teaching that quickly provoked controversy was their view that Jesus would return soon. In other words, they understood themselves to be fulfilling signs from the Apocalypse of John (Revelation), and they named the city of Pepuza in Phrygia as the "New Jerusalem" where Christ would descend.[24] Hence, for a variety of reasons, the claims of "new prophecy" were increasingly deemed suspicious by some Christian leaders.[25]

False Prophets and Apostolic Warnings: The Johannine School

As we see, claims to prophetic powers were still dynamic forces among many Christian groups in the second century. At the same time, we begin to hear more frequent warnings about "false prophets," schismatics, and other false teachers, as we have seen already in the *Pseudo-Clementines*. In this section we shall profile several writings that address these issues, all of which were eventually considered part of the New Testament.

2 and 3 John

The relationship of 2 and 3 John to the Johannine corpus (meaning the Gospel of John and 1 John; see Chapter 12) is based on traditional attribution alone, for the name John does not appear in any of them. Although some literary relationship is demonstrable between 1 John and the Gospel of John, based in large measure on phrasing and vocabulary, such ties cannot be so clearly established between them and 2 and 3 John. It is very unlikely that 2 and 3 John belong to the same author, and neither of these sets of writings comes from the same author who wrote Revelation. Only later did these quite distinct literary units agglomerate to the namesake of a single author named John. Yet the theories regarding the relationships between these "Johannine" writings remain numerous and complex. (See Box 16.2.)

Both 2 and 3 John were written by a single author who identifies himself simply as "the Elder" in the opening address of each letter. He is someone like Polycarp or Papias. That these works later became associated with the name of John led Eusebius, based on traditions from Papias, to insist that there were two different Johns at Ephesus, one of whom was called "John the Elder."[26] The two letters represent the efforts of this unnamed local elder to deal with matters of Christians traveling among the churches of the region. In the process, problems have arisen: in one case, authorized emissaries have been unduly rejected (3 John); in the other, "false prophets" have been admitted to the hospitality of the church (2 John). Both cases are instructive for what they tell us about the development of church organization and the growing concern over "heretical" teachings.

The letter 2 John is addressed by the Elder to an unspecified Christian congregation or, more likely, a group of congregations. He calls them symbolically "the *elect lady* and her children" (2 John 1). It can hardly be read as anything but a reference to the feminine noun *ekklesia* ("church") used in an abstract or institutional sense. The closing formula, "the children of your *elect sister* greet you" (v. 13), reinforces the idea that the "children" are the members of several congregations in another city or district. The main warning in the letter concerns the fact that "many deceivers have gone out into the world, those who do not confess that Jesus Christ has come in the flesh; any such person is the deceiver and the antichrist! Be on your guard, so that you do not lose what you have worked for, but may receive a full reward" (2 John 7–8). The problem addressed is clearly some form of docetism. The author is exhorting local churches to be on the watch for it.

What follows is all the more interesting for what it says about church organization in light of the older ideals of hospitality. It says that if anyone comes to the congregation and does not bring the proper doctrine—namely, that Christ came *in the flesh*—they are not to "receive him into the house or welcome" him (v. 10); that is, he should not be given any kind of hospitable reception into the fellowship of the house church. Then it adds an additional sanction by warning that anyone who dares to offer such hospitality to a docetist "participates in his evil deeds" (v. 11). So it should be noticed that the offering of hospitality, the "right hand of fellowship," on entry into the place of worship has now become the testing ground for proper belief.

The letter 3 John shows even more clearly that matters of hospitality in the church fellowship have reached a critical moment in institutional development. In this case, the letter is addressed to a certain Gaius, presumably a local house-church patron who has shown appropriate loyalty to the Elder by accepting his emissaries (3 John 1–3).[27] This greeting is followed by a more general exhortation on the exercise of this same sort of hospitality for traveling Christians by welcoming them and "sending them on" their way (vv. 5–8). Just as in earlier usage by Paul (cf. Rom. 15:24), these formulas refer not only to lodging guests but also to paying for the next leg of their journey. Near the end of the letter (v. 12) the author refers to a certain Demetrius, probably another local church leader. Taken together, it suggests that the primary concern of the letter is the authority of the Elder within his network of local congregations.

BOX 16.2

The Second and Third Letters of John

DATE: ca. 120s–130s CE

AUTHOR: The Elder

ATTRIBUTION: John the apostle (or John the Elder?)

LOCATION: Ephesus or Asia Minor

AUDIENCE AND OCCASION: These two letters represent the ecclesiastical instructions and exhortations of a local presbyter (perhaps an early monarchical bishop) written to two different congregations in his orbit of influence. 2 John was written to deal with matters relating to traveling docetic Christians. 3 John was written to deal with interrelations between several local congregations, particularly the case in which one local house-church patron had refused to accept emissaries from the Elder.

Both letters show the growth of organizational procedures for guarding the purity of the congregation but reflect certain tensions in the emergence of institutional authority. Although these letters have been grouped in the New Testament with the Gospel of John and 1 John, they are not by the same author(s).

OUTLINE

2 John

   I. Epistolary Address (vv. 1–3)

   II. Thanksgiving (vv. 4–6)

This fact is borne out by the central part of the letter in which the author complains to Gaius, the recipient, about another house-church patron named Diotrephes, who has refused to accept the Elder's authority in some matter. The issue had come to a head when Diotrephes refused hospitality to "the brothers" (v. 10a). This undoubtedly refers to traveling Christians who came from another of the Elder's churches, probably bearing letters of recommendation and instruction from the Elder. In addition, it says that Diotrephes even "prevents those who want to [welcome them] and puts them out of the church" (v. 10b).[28]

It should be noticed that the actions taken by Diotrephes are precisely those advocated by the Elder himself in 2 John for dealing with docetists. Even the expelling of those who dare welcome them is the same. So the procedure itself

III. Warning About False Teachers (vv. 7–10)

IV. Final Greetings (vv. 11–13)

3 John

I. Epistolary Address (v. 1)

II. Prayer on Behalf of the Recipients (vv. 2–4)

III. Exhortation to Harmony Among the Churches (vv. 5–8)

IV. Warnings About the Inhospitality of Diotrephes (vv. 9–10)

V. Appeal to Side with the Elder (vv. 11–12)

VI. Final Greetings (vv. 13–15)

FURTHER READING

Brown, R. E. *The Community of the Beloved Disciple.* New York: Doubleday, 1979.

————. *The Epistles of John.* Anchor Bible 30. New York: Doubleday, 1982.

Houlden, J. L. *The Johannine Epistles.* Harper's New Testament Commentary. New York: Harper & Row, 1973.

Kysar, R. "John, Epistles of." *Anchor Bible Dictionary.* 3:900–912.

Lieu, J. *The Second and Third Epistles of John.* Edinburgh: Clark, 1986.

Malherbe, A. J. "Hospitality and Inhospitality in the Church." In *Social Aspects of Early Christianity.* 2d ed. Philadelphia: Fortress, 1983. Pp. 92–112.

Rensberger, D. *1 John, 2 John, and 3 John.* Abingdon New Testament Commentary. Nashville, TN: Abingdon, 1997.

Smith, D. M. *First, Second, and Third John.* Interpretation. Louisville, KY: John Knox, 1991.

Strecker, G. *The Johannine Letters.* Hermeneia. Minneapolis: Fortress, 1996.

is not the problem; rather, it is by whose authority these fellowship networks are established and maintained. Thus, the control of hospitality has become a tool for unifying local churches in light of the emerging threat of heresy.

Moreover, the procedures involved in giving or refusing hospitality are important in their own right, since this is the first time that we have seen the physical space of the church assembly serving as the boundary of the community. Admission to fellowship and expelling from the church are both defined in terms of "the house" where the church meets. Entry into the house marks the threshold of church membership and fellowship in worship.[29] Now too we see a creedal test (2 John) and acceptance of letters of recommendation (3 John) as mechanisms for crossing into this more tightly guarded arena of religious fellowship.

Consolidation of the Johannine School

The practical issues addressed by 2 and 3 John also shed more light on the situation that must be envisioned behind the writing of 1 John, especially in its concern over traveling docetic teachers. In particular, 1 John 4:1–3 constitutes an instruction to administer the creedal test "that Jesus Christ has come in the flesh" to anyone who comes to the door of the church; it uses the term "antichrist" (1 John 4:3; cf. 2:18) of docetic Christians in exactly the same way as 2 John 7. Hence, even though the Johannine letters may come from different authors, they probably do relate to a growing consolidation of antidocetic networks in the area of Asia Minor in the 120s–130s. The problem, as noted earlier, is how to understand the relationship between these various nodes of the so-called Johannine school.

Some scholars have seen the Gospel of John as the earliest component, with the letters coming after it in more or less their canonical order.[30] Others have seen the three letters as the product of a single author, a "successor" to John, who used the Gospel as a source.[31] Still others have seen 3 John and 2 John as the earliest pieces, from one author, with 1 John, and perhaps the Gospel, coming later from different authors.[32] In keeping with this last view, it is possible to see 1 John as an effort to pull the whole "Johannine tradition" together. It has thus been likened to the effort by the author(s) of the Pastoral Epistles in relation to the Pauline tradition (which will be discussed in the next section of this chapter).

Often overlooked in this regard is the fact that Polycarp seems to be wrestling with similar issues at about this same time. He even offers instructions to the Philippians that sound very much like those in 1 John 4:1–3 and 2 John 7 (Pol. *Phil.* 7.1; see Chapter 13). Based on the wording, it is not possible to say with any certainty that Polycarp is quoting from either of these Johannine letters. It is more likely that Polycarp is articulating some of the same concerns. They may all be drawing on a common rhetoric that had developed in the region. The "antichrist" label and the creedal test seem to be distinctive local forms of polemic that evolved in the debate. Or it is just possible that Polycarp himself was the source, having already heard a similar warning against docetic teachers from Ignatius (Ign. *Smyrn.* 5.2; *Trall.* 10.1; see Chapter 13). This may help to account for how and why the Gospel of John was imported into mainstream church use in Asia Minor at about this time. In this light, we may see 1 John as the culmination of the process of consolidation of the Johannine school in Asia Minor (see Fig. 16.1).

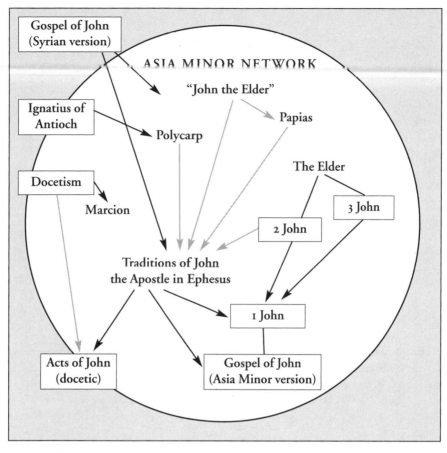

FIGURE 16.1

Development of the Johannine school.

Scoffers and Sophists:
The Letters of Jude and 2 Peter

Because 2 Peter uses Jude as a source, even to the point of taking over whole sections of material,[33] we may appropriately treat them as another literary ensemble. The warnings are quite explicit, as are the similarities (italics indicate identical or nearly identical words in the Greek, even though the NRSV translations differ slightly):

Jude 4–6, 17–19	*2 Peter 2:1–4; 3:2–3*
For certain intruders have stolen in among you, people who long ago were designated for this condemnation as ungodly, who pervert the grace of our God into *licentiousness* and *deny our only Master* and Lord, Jesus Christ. Now I desire to remind you, though you are fully informed, that the Lord, who once for all saved a people out of the land of Egypt, afterward destroyed those who did not believe. And *the angels* who did not keep their own position, but left their proper dwelling, *he has kept in eternal chains in deepest darkness for the judgment* of the great Day.	But false prophets also arose among the people, just as there will be false teachers among you, who will secretly bring in destructive opinions [*haireseis*]. *They will even deny the Master* who bought them— bringing swift destruction on themselves. Even so, many will follow their *licentious* ways, and because of these teachers the way of truth will be maligned. And in their greed they will exploit you with deceptive words. Their condemnation, pronounced against them long ago, has not been idle, and their destruction is not asleep. For if God did not spare *the angels* when they sinned, but cast them into hell and *committed them to chains of deepest darkness to be kept until the judgment* . . .
But *you*, beloved, *must remember the predictions of the apostles of our Lord* Jesus Christ; for they said to you, *"In the last time there will be scoffers, indulging their own ungodly lusts."* It is these worldly people, devoid of the Spirit, who are causing divisions.	*You should remember the words* spoken in the past by the holy prophets, and the commandment *of the Lord* and Savior *spoken through your apostles.* First of all you must understand this, that *in the last days scoffers will come,* scoffing and *indulging their own lusts* . . .

These interrelated texts reflect a trajectory of growing alarm over matters of false teaching. Both use the story of God's punishment of the rebellious angels from *1 Enoch* as a warning *from scripture* of the impending punishment for "scoffers." Of Jude's scant twenty-five verses, nineteen are at least partially replicated in 2 Peter (sixty-one verses total). Thus, although it was once thought that 2 Peter came before Jude, the predominant view now is that Jude came first and 2 Peter constructed a longer and more detailed warning and exhortation around it.

The Letter of Jude

The letter of Jude is attributed to "Judas, a servant of Jesus Christ and brother of James" (v. 1).[34] Since a Judas is named alongside James as one of Jesus's brothers in Mark 6:3 and Matthew 13:55, it is usually assumed that this is the person meant. According to Hegesippus, writing in the 170s, this Judas, "who is brother, according to the flesh, of the savior," had grandsons living in Jerusalem who were persecuted by Domitian (ca. 95 CE) but continued as leaders in the churches of their day down through the time of Trajan (98–117 CE).[35]

Apparently there were other legends too. Luke 6:16 and Acts 1:13 list a "Judas *of James*" among the disciples of Jesus; the usual translation of such Greek constructions would be *"son of James."* Because Luke-Acts omits the name Thaddaeus from the list, but includes the name of Thomas in its usual position, it has often been assumed that Thaddaeus and this "third" Judas must be one and the same. This might also be the equation intended in the apocryphal Abgar correspondence, where Judas Thomas is reported as sending Thaddaeus, "who was one of the seventy," to Edessa.[36] Why would Jesus's brother, Thomas, have this authority? This designation presupposes the listing of the disciples in Luke-Acts, since Thaddaeus is not one of the Twelve, but it makes him one of the "seventy disciples" sent out by Jesus in Luke 10:1–16.[37] Of course, this number also evokes the tradition of the "seventy elders" who translated the Septuagint, and hence its name.

In later tradition this group, usually just called "the seventy," became an important symbol for notions of "apostolic succession" and thus for authoritative teaching. For example, in the *Pseudo-Clementines* Peter instructs James to guard the "books of his preachings" from anyone who is not approved, namely gentile Christians like Paul, and he uses the "seventy who succeeded to Moses's chair" as a model for this notion of authoritative succession "of the brethren among us."[38] Similarly, Eusebius shows knowledge of the "seventy apostles," which included Thaddaeus, along with Matthias, Barnabas, and James the brother of Jesus.[39] Eusebius says that no list of the seventy existed in his day, but he clearly knew a number of other names from a legend he inherited from Clement of Alexandria; these included Paul's co-worker Sosthenes and the "Cephas" whom Paul denounced in Antioch.[40]

At least one such catalog of "the seventy apostles" is known from a fragmentary work entitled *On the Twelve Apostles* attributed to Hippolytus at Rome (ca. 170–236 CE). It lists Thaddaeus along with Sosthenes, Barnabas, and sixty-seven others, most of whom are identified as the bishop of a particular city. Although considerably later, this list would seem to be a form of the legend also known by Clement and Eusebius. It may well have been a basis for Hegesippus's (ca. 110–80) efforts to establish lists of the earliest "orthodox" bishops, which in turn was used extensively by Eusebius.[41] Another fragment of Hippolytus's treatise says: "Jude, who is also called Lebbaeus [Thaddaeus], preached to the people of Edessa, and to all Mesopotamia, and fell asleep at Berytus, and was buried there."[42] It seems, then, that later Christians read the name Judas in Luke 6:16 and Acts 1:13 as *"brother of James"* by conflation with Judas, brother of Jesus, and they equated him with Thaddaeus. He thus became the namesake for an "orthodox" alternative to the apostolic founding legends in the Thomas tradition and/or the *Pseudo-Clementines.*[43]

This legend is quite far-fetched, of course, but it does show the growing fascination of later Christians with members of Jesus's own family. Although a few scholars still argue that the letter of Jude might have been written by the actual brother of Jesus and James sometime in the 50s or 60s, nothing in the text suggests such an early date.[44] Even Eusebius says that its authenticity was debated down to his day.[45] On the contrary, the attribution to "Judas, brother of James" bears the marks of later tradition, since it avoids calling him the brother of Jesus. It also assumes a later conflation of traditions about James of Jerusalem and may show a dependence on the letter of James as well as Matthew and Luke-Acts. The date of this pseudepigraphic work is better situated sometime near the end of the first century, or in the first decades of the second century (see Box 16.3).

The letter of Jude uses a litany of examples from the Jewish scriptures dealing with groups or individuals who rebelled against God. These include Satan and the fallen angels (from *1 Enoch* and the *Assumption of Moses*). These examples of God's punishment for rebellion are finally summed up by returning to an "ancient" warning from *1 Enoch* that is said to refer to people in the audience's own day (vv. 14–15). What follows is a condemnation of all "grumblers and malcontents" (v. 16), which then leads into the main warning (vv. 17–19, quoted above). In this the author looks back to the "predictions of the apostles" regarding scoffers who will come in the last days and cause schisms. The author then calls on the members of the group to remain steadfast and resist these "scoffers" (vv. 20–23).

Little more can be said about the precise situation, but the age of "the apostles" is clearly in the distant past. Our conclusions regarding the location of 2 Peter may shed further light on the location of Jude.

2 Peter

The letter 2 Peter expands these warnings and thus gives more clues about the situation created by people called "false prophets" or "false teachers," who "bring in destructive opinions [lit., heresies]" (2:1); their teaching is trivialized as "cleverly devised [lit., sophistic] myths" (1:16) and private interpretations of

BOX 16.3
The Letter of Jude

DATE: ca. 90–110 CE

AUTHOR: Unknown

ATTRIBUTION: Judas brother of James, one of the brothers of Jesus

LOCATION: Rome ?

AUDIENCE AND OCCASION: Jude bears the semblance of a letter, but it is really an exhortation concerning the spread of false teachers in the church, whom the author denounces as licentious and disorderly.

OUTLINE

I. Opening (vv. 1–4)

    A. Address (vv. 1–2)

    B. Appeal to contend for the faith once received (vv. 3–4)

II. Main Argument: God's Punishment for Those Who Rebel (vv. 5–23)

    A. Three ancient examples of rebellion against God (vv. 5–7)

        1. Korah's rebellion (v. 5)

        2. The fallen angels (*1 Enoch;* v. 6)

        3. Sodom and Gomorrah (v. 7)

    B. The rebellion of the false teachers (vv. 8–13)

    C. Enoch's "prophecies" regarding such people (vv. 14–16)

    D. Prediction of the apostles regarding these same people "in the last days" (vv. 17–19)

    E. Exhortation to remain faithful (vv. 20–23)

III. Closing Doxology (vv. 24–25)

FURTHER READING

Bauckham, R. *Jude and the Relatives of Jesus in the Early Church.* Edinburgh: Clark, 1990.

————. "Jude, Epistle of." *Anchor Bible Dictionary.* 3:1098–1103.

————. *Jude, 2 Peter.* Word Biblical Commentary 50. Dallas: Word, 1983.

Krodel, G. "The Letter of Jude." In *Hebrews, James, 1 and 2 Peter, Jude, Revelation.* Proclamation Commentaries. Philadelphia: Fortress, 1977. Pp. 92–98.

Neyrey, J. H. *2 Peter and Jude.* Anchor Bible 37C. New York: Doubleday, 1993.

the scriptures (1:20). We can also see more evidence of earlier sources assumed by the author and audience to give authority to the text. It claims to be by the apostle Peter, of course, and makes reference to an earlier letter, presumably 1 Peter (2 Pet. 3:1). As we have already seen, it incorporates a good bit of material from the letter of Jude, which has been rearranged and expanded with additional biblical examples.[46] There is also an allusion to Jesus's prediction about the death of Peter from John 21:18–19 (2 Pet. 1:14). Finally, it refers to "our beloved brother Paul" and a collection of "all his letters"; however, these are part of the warning, since "there are some things in them hard to understand, which the ignorant and unstable twist to their own destruction, as they do the other scriptures" (3:15–16).

The work is in the form of a letter, but the tone and language suggest a conscious effort to use the authority of Peter in later generations. This fact is further supported by the repeated use of motifs regarding prediction and reminder (2:1–3; 3:1–4) that emulate testamentary literature. In other words, 2 Peter is meant to function as "Peter's" last will and testament, and specifically as a warning about the false teachers who would arise in later times. Of course, the real author and the audience are living in these later times or "last days" (3:3), as is betrayed when the author reminds them that this was a prediction *"of the past"* through the prophets and apostles (3:2). From these indicators, taken together with the multiple lines of literary dependence seen above, one must guess a fairly cosmopolitan environment in which a number of New Testament writings (Jude, 1 Peter, the Gospel of John, and Paul's letters) were available. If 1 Peter was written from Rome, it is very likely that 2 Peter was also (see Chapter 11).[47] It has a number of affinities with the *Shepherd* of Hermas as well as *1 Clement* and even *2 Clement.*[48] In turn, 2 Peter seems to have been used by the author of the *Apocalypse of Peter* in the period after the Bar Kochba revolt. It probably dates to the 120s or 130s CE and is thus one of the latest documents in the New Testament (see Box 16.4).

We also see more clearly the nature of the false teaching that is stirring up such trouble. It has to do with "scoffers" who are now questioning when—or *if*—Jesus will return (3:1–7). They seem to be pagan converts (1:4; 2:20) who deny some of the traditional apocalyptic expectations of the movement. Its retort is famous: "With the Lord one day is like a thousand years and a thousand years are like one day"; that is to say, one cannot count the delay of Jesus's return as slowness in God's time (2 Pet. 3:8–9). Yet the similarities to Hermas, *2 Clement,* and the *Apocalypse of Peter* show that this was not an unusual concern of the time; even *2 Baruch* (on the Jewish side), Cerinthus, and Justin Martyr reflect various expectations of an imminent eschaton or return of Jesus.[49]

It is also quite significant that 2 Peter warns about those who "twist" Paul's letters, which might refer to any number of nascent varieties within Pauline Christianity in the latter years of the third generation. As a "testament," then, 2 Peter seeks to control and normalize these divergent teachings. If Jude and 2 Peter both came from Rome, they reflect growing concerns over "false teachers,"

BOX 16.4

The Second Letter of Peter

DATE: ca. 120s–130s CE

AUTHOR: Unknown

ATTRIBUTION: The apostle Peter

LOCATION: Rome

AUDIENCE AND OCCASION: The opening verses take the form of a civic decree honoring an individual, but it is here turned to honor the Lord Jesus Christ. The rest of the work is largely an exhortation to live in accordance with the truths that have come from being called into his kingdom, but set forth as "Peter's" last will and testament (1:15). The primary concern is false teaching, which is largely based on a reworking of the letter of Jude (see Box 16.3). The special problem addressed in this case is the delay of Jesus's return.

OUTLINE

  I. Opening (1:1–21)
   A. Epistolary address (1:1–2)
   B. The decree honoring Jesus (1:3–11)
   C. Peter's testament (1:12–15)
   D. Warnings about clever myths and private interpretations (1:16–21)

  II. Warning About False Prophets and False Teachers (2:1–22)
   A. The warnings of the apostles in times past (2:1–3)
   B. Examples of those who rebelled against God (2:4–16)
   C. The deplorable character of the false teachers (2:17–22)

  III. Instructions About the Delay of Jesus's Coming (or *Parousia;* 3:1–13)

  IV. Final Exhortation (3:14–18)

FURTHER READING

Bauckham, R. *Jude, 2 Peter.* Word Biblical Commentary 50. Dallas: Word, 1983.

Danker, F. W. "2 Peter." In *Hebrews, James, 1 and 2 Peter, Jude, Revelation.* Proclamation Commentaries. Philadelphia: Fortress, 1977. Pp. 99–120.

Elliott, J. H. "Peter, Second Epistle of." *Anchor Bible Dictionary.* 5:282–87.

Farkasfalvy, D. "The Ecclesial Setting and Pseudepigraphy in Second Peter and Its Role in the Formation of the Canon." *The Second Century* 5 (1985–86): 3–29.

Fornberg, T. *An Early Church in a Pluralistic Society: A Study of 2 Peter.* Lund: Almqvist, 1977.

Neyrey, J. H. *2 Peter and Jude.* Anchor Bible 37C. New York: Doubleday, 1993.

Smith, T. V. *Petrine Controversies in Early Christianity: Attitudes Toward Peter in Christian Writings of the First Two Centuries.* Tübingen: Mohr-Siebeck, 1983.

probably meaning the kinds one finds developing in the Thomas tradition or
Marcion. Consequently, it would appear that Jude and 2 Peter represent a re-
sponsive effort to consolidate the "orthodox" tradition around Peter, James,
and Paul, bolstered now by yet another "brother" of Jesus.

Domesticating Paul: The Pastoral Epistles

In the Pauline tradition, 1 and 2 Timothy and Titus, also known as the Pastoral
Epistles, originated out of a similar need to rein in diverse and schismatic interpretations that had developed in the name of Paul or were based on his letters.
Thus, the letters offer "Paul's" own testament as refutation of inappropriate
teachings in his name. In their final form, at least, they too were produced as a
literary ensemble, perhaps by a single author or group of authors. Some have
argued that they were written by a member of Paul's circle and close to Paul's
own time, but the weight of evidence from their language and glimpses of their
internal situation points to a much later date, perhaps in the 120s to 140s. A
date as late as the 170s has been proposed, but it is not widely accepted. It has
also been argued that Polycarp himself wrote the Pastorals.

Authorship

The name "Pastoral Epistles" is a modern designation stemming from the fact
that they were addressed not to churches but to individuals. Unlike Philemon,
however, they were addressed to those who would "shepherd" the church after
Paul's departure. Hence, in early Protestant theology the ostensible recipients
were likened to pastors in local churches. At the same time, such a differential
classification for these three letters also captures something of their ambiguous
position in the early church. They do not appear at all in the earliest copy of
Paul's collected letters ($\mathfrak{P}^{46}$), which dates to about 200 (to be discussed further
in Chapter 17).[50] Moreover, Marcion (ca. 130s to 140s) did not include them in
his canon or mention them in his known treatises.[51] Given their dominantly
Hellenistic language and character, it is doubtful that he would have rejected
them as being too Jewish if he had known of their existence. The earliest quotation of the Pastorals comes from Irenaeus (ca. 180 CE), who calls them letters of
Paul.[52] The earliest known copy of the Pastorals is a third-century fragment of
Titus (1:11–15 + 2:3–8) that seems to come from a small separate codex just for
these letters (John Rylands Papyrus 5 or $\mathfrak{P}^{32}$). Their authenticity was debated
in Alexandria during the third century, with the result that Titus might have
been more widely accepted than 1 and 2 Timothy.[53] Finally, in some of the

earliest canon lists, they appear as an appendix at the very end of the New Testament, and in one of these, the Muratorian Canon, Titus comes before 1 and 2 Timothy.

For the past two centuries or more, virtually since the beginning of modern New Testament scholarship, the authorship of the Pastorals has been questioned based on a number of other internal features. First, although the letters are addressed to well-known members of Paul's missionary entourage, the way these people are characterized is somewhat at odds with Paul's own references. Most notable in this regard is the portrayal of Timothy, who was clearly considered a mature and trustworthy representative in the genuine letters (cf. 1 Cor. 4:17; Phil. 2:19–24). In the Pastorals Timothy is portrayed as still immature (1 Tim. 4:12), lacking in strength (2 Tim. 2:3–6), and prone to youthful lusts (1 Tim. 5:2; 2 Tim. 2:22). These features are doubtless intended to facilitate the general ethical exhortation that is so central to the Pastorals, but they do not fit the historical situation of Paul's day.

Second, a related problem is "Paul's" circumstances as envisioned in the Pastorals. In Romans, the latest of Paul's genuine letters, Paul was on his way to Jerusalem before journeying to Rome and on to Spain. The legends hold that while in Jerusalem Paul was arrested and eventually taken to Rome as a prisoner, where he would eventually die a martyr. Acts 21–28 reconstructs at least part of this story in novelistic fashion but ends with Paul under house arrest in Rome; however, the final outcome is not given. In 2 Timothy 4:6–10 Paul is in prison and facing imminent death, and the names of those with him in 2 Timothy 4:21 (Pudens, Linus, and Claudia) seem to reflect Rome.[54] In contrast, 1 Timothy and Titus place Paul in Macedonia and Nicopolis, on the western coast of Greece (1 Tim. 1:3; Titus 3:12), where he will spend the winter. Although it is possible to imagine this itinerary as Paul's transport to Rome under arrest, similar to the route supposed by Polycarp for Ignatius (see Chapter 13), it does not match the sea route described by Acts 27. Consequently, it has often been assumed that the Pastorals have Paul released from imprisonment in Rome, only to be arrested again later and finally executed.[55] This way of aligning the Pastorals with Acts goes back at least to the time of Eusebius but is a forced harmonization at best.[56]

Moreover, the travels and locations of Timothy, Titus, and others as reflected in the Pastorals are somewhat jumbled. In Titus and 1 Timothy, Timothy is in Ephesus, Titus is on Crete, and Tychicus is en route to Crete, while in 2 Timothy, Tychicus is going to Ephesus, Timothy is elsewhere in Asia Minor (probably Iconium or Lystra), and Titus has gone to Dalmatia. Such travels are hard to reconcile with any movements of Paul or the others in the genuine letters or

Acts and have far more affinities with the travels described in the *Acts of Paul and Thecla.*[57]

Third, the language, tone, and style of the Pastorals is noticeably different from those in the genuine letters. Some earlier scholars still defending Pauline authorship attributed such differences to Paul's use of a secretary (or amanuensis), especially if he were "in chains."[58] But this argument does not solve the problem, since it is clear now that Paul employed trained scribes as secretaries for most, if not all, of his genuine letters (cf. Rom. 16:22). Thus, the differences remain stark.

In regard to the vocabulary, for example, of the 848 total words contained in the Pastorals (excluding proper names), 306 (or about 36 percent) do not occur anywhere else in the genuine letters or even in the debated letters (Colossians, Ephesians, 2 Thessalonians). Out of these 306 words, 175 do not occur elsewhere in the New Testament, while 211 appear regularly among mainstream Christian writers of the second century, notably the apostolic fathers. In contrast, the vocabulary within the Pastorals is quite consistent across all three letters. Certain terms, such as "piety" (Greek *eusebeia*), "sound doctrine," "heretical," "Jewish," "widows," or "the Savior" as a regular epithet of Jesus, do not occur at all in Paul and are generally more reflective of second-century developments in Christian theology and church organization. Finally, in tone and style the Pastorals are, if anything, *less* personal—despite being addressed to individuals—and more hieratic than the known genuine letters. Much of the exhortation seems to reflect set pieces of moral instruction, like catechetical lectures or philosophical commonplaces.[59]

Fourth, the situation addressed, especially in matters concerning heresy, church order, and authority structures, seems to fit better with the developments of the second century than with anything during Paul's own life time.

Thus, although some have defended Pauline authorship into fairly recent times,[60] the prevailing view has long been that these three letters were written sometime later to deal with new situations that had arisen within Pauline church circles after Paul's death. That they are intended to maintain a strong sense of Pauline tradition is not in doubt. The question is: How much later and what new situations? (See Box 16.5.)

Composition and Situation

The general view now is that the Pastorals were composed all together as a literary package by a single author or group of authors working together. One early hypothesis proposed that, though clearly secondary in their present form, they were based on an early core that came from Paul himself.[61] This core was understood to be Paul's farewell letter to his co-workers, which was later taken over and reworked to form the present three-letter ensemble.[62] Some scholars have linked this literary effort to the author of Luke-Acts, but the discrepancies in the putative situation of Paul weigh against this view.[63]

An alternative view holds that the three letters were composed as a kind of "last will and testament" meant both to consolidate Pauline theology and to defend Paul against criticisms arising from the use of his letters by numerous "heretical" groups. In this way, they were meant to "domesticate" the more radical implications of Pauline thought and to bring him into the mainstream in the areas of both theology and church order. It is noteworthy, therefore, that the dominant fiction of the letters has "Paul" addressing the situation of his churches in Asia and Greece before his departure and death. The key forms of Pauline Christianity that had become troublesome—including Marcionism, the rigorous asceticism of the *Acts of Paul and Thecla,* and some elements associated with Gnostic Christianity—had all originated in Asia Minor or elsewhere. This way of presenting the problem would accord well with the loftier view of Paul in Rome, where there was an early collection of his letters. It would also correlate directly with warnings about those who would "twist" Paul's letters in 2 Peter 3:15–17, which may also come from Rome.

A good example is the following "instruction" rejecting ascetical practices in marriage and diet, which may be contrasted with Paul's own teaching in 1 Corinthians 7:1–9:

> *Now the Spirit expressly says that in later times some will renounce the faith by paying attention to deceitful spirits and teachings of demons, through the hypocrisy of liars whose consciences are seared with a hot iron. They forbid marriage and demand abstinence from foods, which God created to be received with thanksgiving by those who believe and know the truth. For everything created by God is good, and nothing is to be rejected, provided it is received with thanksgiving. (1 Tim. 4:1–4)*

So we notice the theme of apostolic warnings about false teachings that will arise "in later times," seen earlier in Jude, 2 Peter, and the Johannine letters. These false teachings are variously characterized as "myths and endless genealogies" (1 Tim. 1:4) or "godless and silly myths" (1 Tim. 4:7; cf. 2 Tim. 4:4; Titus 3:9).[64] They have often been equated with early forms of Gnostic teaching, such as that brought to Rome by Valentinus.

BOX 16.5

The Pastoral Epistles
First and Second Letters of Timothy, Letter of Titus

DATE: ca. 120s–130s CE
AUTHOR: Unknown
ATTRIBUTION: Paul
LOCATION: Ephesus or Rome
AUDIENCE AND OCCASION: The Pastoral Epistles were composed in their present form as a literary ensemble to consolidate Pauline teaching toward a more orthodox center in light of divergent uses of the Pauline materials in the late first and early second centuries. They are concerned with false teaching, guarding the "deposit" of the faith, and hierarchical institutional organization in the churches. Posed as Paul's "farewell" letters to his trusted co-workers Timothy and Titus, the letters are intended to represent Paul's final instructions for ordering his churches. Timothy and Titus are to pass these instructions along to the next generation of leaders.

OUTLINE

Titus

   I. Greeting (1:1–4)

   II. The Commission of Titus to Appoint Elders (1:5–16)
     A. Qualifications of leaders (1:5–9)
     B. Warnings about heresy (1:10–16)

   III. The Commission of Titus to Teach Sound Doctrine (2:1–3:11)
     A. The household duty code (2:1–9)
     B. Exhortation (2:10–15)
     C. Honor governing authorities (3:1–7)
     D. Exhortation (3:8–11)

   IV. Farewell and Closing (3:12–15)

1 Timothy

   I. Greeting (1:1–2)

   II. Commission to Timothy to Beware of False Teachers (1:3–20)

   III. Sound Teaching Delivered to Timothy (2:1–3:16)
     A. Honor the authorities (2:1–7)
     B. Decorum in the assembly (2:8–15)
     C. Qualifications of bishops (3:1–7)
     D. Qualifications of deacons (3:8–13)
     E. Exhortation and confession (3:14–16)

IV. False Teachings of Asceticism and Sexual Renunciation
(4:1–10)

V. Exhortation to Teach and Minister: Church Order and
Leadership (4:11–6:19)
- A. Preaching, teaching, and exhorting (4:11–16)
- B. On rebuke: honor for older men and widows (5:1–8)
- C. Enrolling of widows and instructions for women (5:9–16)
- D. Honors for elders (5:17–22)
- E. Individual instructions (5:23–6:2)
- F. Ethical exhortation (6:3–10)
- G. Concluding exhortation to "fight the good fight" (6:11–19)

VI. Farewell and Blessing (6:20–21)

2 Timothy

I. Greeting (1:1–2)

II. Thanksgiving and Blessing of Timothy (1:3–14)

III. Paul's Farewell Instructions to Timothy (1:15–3:9)
- A. Asia has abandoned Paul's teaching (1:15–18)
- B. Encouragement to be strong in the face of such trials (2:1–13)
- C. Warning to avoid disputes (2:14–26)
- D. Warnings about the last times (3:1–9)

IV. Final Charges to Timothy (3:10–4:18)
- A. Teaching (3:10–17)
- B. Preaching and suffering (4:1–5)
- C. Paul's "departure" (4:6–8)
- D. Personal instructions (4:9–18)

V. Final Greetings, Farewell, and Blessing (4:19–22)

FURTHER READING

Collins, R. F. *Letters That Paul Did Not Write*. Wilmington, DE: Michael Glazier, 1988.
Harrison, P. N. *The Problem of the Pastoral Epistles*. London: Oxford University Press, 1921.
Kelly, J. N. D. *A Commentary on the Pastoral Epistles: I Timothy, II Timothy, and Titus*. Harper New Testament Commentary. New York: Harper & Row, 1963.
Knight, G. W. *The Faithful Sayings in the Pastoral Epistles*. Grand Rapids, MI: Baker, 1968; repr. 1979.
MacDonald, D. R. *The Legend and the Apostle: The Battle for Paul in Story and Canon*. Philadelphia: Westminster, 1983.
Quinn, J. D. *The Epistle to Titus (with Introduction to Titus, I and II Timothy)*. Anchor Bible 35. New York: Doubleday, 1990.
———. "Timothy and Titus, Epistles to." *Anchor Bible Dictionary*. 6:560–71.
Verner, D. *The Household of God: The Social World of the Pastoral Epistles*. Chico, CA: Scholars Press, 1983.
Wilson, S. G. *Luke and the Pastoral Epistles*. London: SPCK, 1979.

The ostensible recipients, Timothy and Titus, are now instructed on how to defend against these "false teachings" by installing proper safeguards, including ethical instruction:

> But as for you, teach what is consistent with sound doctrine. Tell the older men to be temperate, serious, prudent, and sound in faith, in love, and in endurance. Likewise, tell the older women to be reverent in behavior, not to be slanderers or slaves to drink; they are to teach what is good, so that they may encourage the young women to love their husbands, to love their children, to be self-controlled, chaste, good managers of the household, kind, being submissive to their husbands, so that the word of God may not be discredited. Likewise, urge the younger men to be self-controlled. Show yourself in all respects a model of good works, and in your teaching show integrity, gravity, and sound speech that cannot be censured; then any opponent will be put to shame, having nothing evil to say of us. Tell slaves to be submissive to their masters . . . (Titus 2:1–9)

Here we see a further elaboration on the household duty code (found earlier in Ephesians, Colossians, and 1 Peter) along with the ordering of church life according to the model of the ideal Roman household. Finally, the hierarchical church offices of bishops (1 Tim. 3:1–7) and deacons (1 Tim. 3:8–13) are modeled after the head of the family (1 Tim. 3:4–5, 12). In turn, these male offices are paralleled by a subordinate order for women (widows, older women, and younger women) that is meant to ensure that the proper teachings will be followed (1 Tim. 2:8–15). This is a far cry from the free flow of charismatic expression and the leadership of women as house-church patrons that one sees in the genuine letters of Paul. The kind of tradition reflected in the *Acts of Paul and Thecla* might well stand behind the restrictions now being imposed both in matters of ascetic piety and in the active leadership by women.

Finally, the Pastorals present a view of Christian doctrine that is emerging as a more tightly bounded body of beliefs. The Greek word *paratheke* (usually translated "entrusted") is used frequently in the Pastorals (1 Tim. 6:20; 2 Tim. 1:12, 14) but occurs nowhere else in the New Testament. The word really means a "deposit" or something "given in trust," and implies the "deposit of the faith" that is the truth that had been handed down from Paul and the other apostles of the first generation. These affirmations go along with a number of "faithful sayings" that appear throughout the letters in the form of quasi-hymnic repetitive formulas (e.g., 1 Tim. 3:16; 2 Tim. 2:11–13; Titus 3:4–7). They seem to replicate what must have been well-known units of catechetical instruction from the time. The "pastors," Timothy and Titus, are those "ordained" by Paul (1 Tim. 1:18; 2 Tim. 1:6; 4:14) who are supposed to hand the teaching on to "faithful men" (2 Tim. 2:1–2). Thus, the Pastorals establish a mechanism for the authoritative succession of leadership in subsequent generations. They are thus part of the evolving church-order literature, but couched in terms of apostolic testaments.

Sound Teaching:
Defining Heresy and Orthodoxy

By the latter half of the second century, or the fourth generation, it was becoming common for Christians to think of themselves as a "third race," distinct from Jews and Gentiles. Even so, there is no evidence that they used the term "Christian" as a polemical tool in dealing with those holding divergent beliefs or practices. They might call such people false prophets, apostates, or heretics, from the Greek word *hairesis*, meaning "a sect or school of thought." But they were still Christians.[65] The problem had already arisen in the latter years of the third generation. In the Pastoral Epistles "sound" or "healthy" teaching (1 Tim. 1:10; 2 Tim. 1:13; 4:3; 6:3; Titus 1:9, 13; 2:1–2; cf. 3 John 2) stands in sharp contrast to "silly myths." We can well imagine the litany of diverse opinions that might come under this heading: docetism, Marcionism, Jewish Christianity, asceticism, and Gnosticism. All were increasingly understood to be human inventions or heresies (Titus 3:10; 2 Pet. 2:1), or, worse yet, demonic forgeries (1 Tim. 4:1).[66]

The Origins of Heresy

Where did heresy come from? Was it an external force that crept in to pollute and pervert the original teachings of Jesus and the apostles? Or was it somehow intrinsic to the development of the early movement due to its changing social horizons and cultural contexts? It is an old question.

The traditional view that emerged in third and fourth generations was that the teaching of Jesus and the apostles had represented a uniform and undiluted stream of tradition—or "deposit of faith" (2 Tim. 1:14)—until it was disturbed by foreign doctrines introduced by heretics like Simon Magus. This is exactly how Irenaeus understood Simon to be the originator of all heresy:

This Simon, then, who feigned faith, supposing that the apostles themselves performed their cures by the art of magic, and not by the power of God. . . .

He, then, not putting faith in God a whit the more, set himself eagerly to con-
tend against the apostles, in order that he himself might seem to be a wonder-
ful being, and applied himself with still greater zeal to the study of the whole
magic art, that he might the better bewilder and overpower multitudes of
men. Now this Simon of Samaria, from whom all sorts of heresies derive their
*origin, formed his sect [*hairesis*] . . . (Against Heresies 1.23.1–2)*[67]

Of course, that is essentially what the Jewish Christians (or Ebionites) said about
Paul, and what Marcion said about everybody else. Pointing the finger at heresy
was becoming a frequent exercise; however, it was a matter of perspective and
the interpretation of scripture.

Hence, Irenaeus opened his treatise *Against Heresies,* written about 180, with
these words:

Inasmuch as certain men have set the truth aside, and bring in lying words
*and vain genealogies, which, as the apostle says, "**minister questions rather***
***than godly edifying which is in faith**" [1 Tim. 1:4] and by means of their*
craftily constructed plausibilities draw away the minds of the inexperienced
and take them captive. [I have felt constrained, my dear friend, to compose
the following treatise in order to expose and counteract their machinations.]
These men falsify the oracles of God, and prove themselves evil interpreters of
the good word of revelation. (1.1)[68]

It is worth noting that Irenaeus supports his contention by quoting from
1 Timothy, the first clear reference to the so-called Pastoral Epistles by later
Christians. They too were now part of the battle over heresy in the interpretation of Paul. Orthodoxy was to be identified with the teachings handed down
from the apostles alone, preserved in their authentic writings and protected by
those whom they appointed. The guardians of orthodoxy could say that they
spoke "in accordance with the whole church," as opposed to the peculiar or
idiosyncratic opinions of sects (*haireseis*). Here we remember the warnings
about "private interpretation" of the scriptures (2 Pet. 1:20). In Greek "according to the whole" is *katholikos,* from which we get "catholic."[69]

Writing only two decades later (ca. 200 CE) in Carthage was Tertullian, the
first prominent Latin author in early Christianity. Although Greek was still the
principal language of Christians in the East and even in Rome and Gaul, Latin
first became the common language of Christians in the Roman province of Africa
(modern-day Libya and Tunisia). Thus, Tertullian often provides an important
window into developments of his day as he translates and disseminates matters

of debate for North African Christians. Harking to the notion of "healthy teaching" as seen in the Pastorals, Tertullian likens heresy to a disease that infects the body. In other words, heresy is an external force that creeps in and disrupts the health of the body. It must be expunged either by drugs or surgery if the body is to return to proper health:

> *Taking the similar case of fever, which is appointed a place amongst all other deadly and excruciating issues (of life) for destroying man: we are not surprised either that it exists, for there it is, or that it consumes man, for that is the purpose of its existence. In like manner, with respect to heresies, which are produced for the weakening and the extinction of faith, since we feel a dread because they have this power, we should first dread the fact of their existence; for as long as they exist, they have their power; and as long as they have their power, they have their existence. But still fever, as being an evil both in its cause and in its power, as all know, we rather loathe than wonder at, and to the best of our power guard against, not having its extirpation in our power. Some men prefer wondering at heresies, however, which bring with them eternal death and the heat of a stronger fire, for possessing this power, instead of avoiding their power when they have the means of escape: but heresies would have no power, if (men) would cease to wonder that they have such power. . . . It would no doubt be a wonderful thing that evil should have any force of its own, were it not that heresies are strong in those persons who are not strong in faith. In a combat of boxers and gladiators, generally speaking, it is not because a man is strong that he gains the victory, or loses it because he is not strong, but because he who is vanquished was a man of no strength; and indeed this very conqueror, when afterwards matched against a really powerful man, actually retires crest-fallen from the contest. In precisely the same way, heresies derive such strength as they have from the infirmities of individuals who have no strength whenever they encounter a really powerful faith. (*Prescription of Heretics 2)*[70]

Ironically, only a few years later Tertullian himself would be classed as a heretic—a Montanist—because of his dissenting views on some key theological issues. Tertullian was much stricter in his interpretation of certain scriptures than were others within the orthodox church.

Which Came First?

Despite the traditional way of understanding the development of heresy and orthodoxy, the picture is more complex. In a now famous study, the German scholar Walter Bauer argued that in certain localities or regions the earliest documented form of Christianity was what later came to be labeled as heresy.[71] His principal examples were Edessene Christianity and Egyptian Gnosticism. He then proposed an overall hypothesis that "heresy" usually preceded "orthodoxy" in the development. He also argued that it was the gradual domination of "catholic Christianity" from Rome that suppressed these earlier and more original forms of local Christianity. Thus, legendary elements, such as Eusebius's long lists of bishops in each major city, were mere fabrications of the Roman tradition to assert an original "purity" that eventually triumphed over the threat of Gnosticism or some other heresy.

Contemporary scholarship no longer accepts the Bauer thesis, as it is usually called, in its original form. For one thing, Bauer's view assumes that the "heretics" somehow knew that they were heretics and that their form of Christianity was different from others. As we have seen, that is hardly the case. Every form of early Christian heresy seems to have begun with the idea that it, and it alone, had preserved a kernel of true teaching inherited from Jesus and the original disciples. The "heretics" could cite the scriptures with equal force, and sometimes with greater insight into their original meaning. Their mutual discovery that other Christians had different beliefs was a surprise to one and all. Hence, some modern scholars have favored a view that there was a basic set of common propositions that was treated with some degree of flexibility down into the late second century. Others have seen diversity as the basic dynamic of development from the very beginning.[72] Some might even say that it was an inevitable consequence of the sectarian origins of the Jesus movement. John Gager puts it this way:

> *One unfortunate consequence [of some modern discussions of heresy and orthodoxy] has been a tendency to regard the phenomenon of heresy as a detour that deflected the churches' energies from more important matters. But if we examine it in the broader context of social conflict and institutional development, we may learn to appreciate it in a rather different light. Quite apart from the commonsense assumption that some amount of conflict is inevitable in any form of social existence, it is now possible to argue that conflict serves a positive function in solidifying social groups and in shaping the complex symbolic and institutional apparatus needed to sustain them.* **Put in its strongest terms, this means that if the church had not encountered heretics, it would have created them.**[73]

In other words, debates over heresy and orthodoxy were a necessary by-product of diversity and the growing consolidation of the movement in both social and theological terms.

It must be remembered that Judaism in the period before 70 CE was rife with sectarian division, but in the aftermath of the failed revolt there was greater tendency to limit sectarianism as a means of restoring ethnic and religious identity. Sects became unwelcome threats to an already threatened existence. It was in this period of rabbinic consolidation (ca. 90–150 CE) that followers of the Jesus movement began to find themselves more and more marginalized. Yet sects always stress tensions with their parent culture and use religious ideas and symbols as markers of true and false teaching. Being ostracized by dominant authorities can easily be reinterpreted by sectarians to show all the more that they are right.

The gradual transformation of the earliest Jesus movement from a Jewish sect into an established religion of the Roman world projected these same arguments onto a larger cultural stage. After generations of development in some isolation from one another, however, further differences became inescapable. To take just one of several diametrically opposed pairs of views that had evolved by the latter part of the second century, it was no longer possible to reconcile such extremes as Marcion's theology and the Jewish Christianity of the *Pseudo-Clementines.* Both sides claimed scripture and truth, and yet both raised serious questions about how to understand the relationship with Jewish tradition and what to do with Paul's letters and his thought. Thus the real problem was diversity.

The fourth generation witnessed the sharper delineation of orthodoxy and heresy among Christians. At stake were strong and well-defined patterns of belief and practice that had developed in distinct and different cultural contexts. The battleground was the scriptures—which ones to read and how to interpret them. The ammunition was a growing battery of labels for "us" and "them," or what is sometimes called "othering" language. To some extent, the mind-set had always been there in the Jesus movement, as it was intrinsic to the sectarian dynamics and rhetoric of apocalyptic Judaism. But for the most part, discussions over who should be "in" and "out" of the church in the first and second generations had focused on ethical behavior rather than on doctrine as such.[74] This trend continued even into the third generation with the "Two Ways" tradition (see Chapter 13). Yet in the third generation, with the process of institutionalization, matters of "false teaching" were becoming increasingly important. Now false teaching could be labeled "heresy"; its opposite was "orthodoxy," which literally means "right thinking or opinion." By the fourth generation "catholic" and "orthodox" could be used synonymously, and this was increasingly the rhetorical position of the church at Rome and other church networks that were beginning to align with it.

FIGURE 17.1

La Donna Velata ("The Veiled Lady"); a Christian *orans,* or "praying" figure, from the catacomb of Priscilla, Rome (late third century). (Used by permission of Scala/Art Resource, New York)

CHAPTER SEVENTEEN

Closing Ranks

The New Testament Takes Shape

Women and men should **go to church** *decently attired, with natural step, clinging to silence, possessing genuine love, being pure in body and pure in heart, and fit to offer prayers to God. All the more, a woman should observe the following: let her be completely veiled, unless she happens to be at home. . . . For the Logos [Christ] wishes this, seeing that it is fitting for her to pray veiled. . . . Those dedicated to Christ ought to present and shape themselves throughout life in the same manner as they fashion themselves with propriety in the churches. They ought thus to be—and not just seem to be—gentle, pious, and loving. And yet I know how they change their dress and manners with their location, just like an octopus. . . . Indeed after their departure thence [from the church], laying aside the inspiration of the assembly, these people become just like the masses with whom they associate. (Paedagogue 3.11)*

Going to Church

Writing just prior to the year 200 CE Clement of Alexandria gives these telling, though perhaps subconscious, insights into evolving Christian social practices and worship. It is the first documented use of the phrase "going to church" and clearly presupposes a regular place of assembly. Patterns of dress and behavior are also in evidence, such as the requirement that women wear veils (or shawls) while praying (cf. 1 Cor. 11:2–26). (See Fig. 17.1.) Nonetheless, Clement's complaints betray a familiar concern over "secular" influences. Once again, the passing of another generation shows through.

Clement (ca. 160–215 CE) originally came from Greece or Asia Minor. Having received an education in philosophy, he eventually migrated to Alexandria, where he became the protégé of a local Christian philosopher. Eusebius says that his teacher was Pantaenus, the head of the newly created catechetical school of the church there, and that Clement succeeded him in this official capacity.[1] Eusebius may overemphasize the ecclesiastical organization and succession of teachers. There is no evidence that Pantaenus was Clement's teacher or that Clement was Origen's teacher. It is more likely that Clement established his own private "school" of philosophy and rhetoric similar to those of the Stoic Epictetus at Nicopolis and the rhetorician Flavius Damianus at Ephesus. Giving lessons in moral philosophy and theology, he cultivated an elite clientele within Alexandria's aristocratic circles and became the voice of a lively, acculturated expression of Christian philosophy. In 203 he was forced to flee in the face of new persecutions. His departure made way for a new intellectual leader, a young philosopher named Origen (ca. 185–258 CE). It is to Clement, however, that we owe much of our understanding of the latter years of the second century and our sense of the growing institutionalization of Christianity at the end of the fourth generation.

From House Churches to Church Buildings

One of the key shifts is the beginning of more formal church buildings.[2] Until the latter part of the second century, Christians continued to meet in the homes of individual members. Commencing in the days of Paul, these house churches had no particular adaptation for assembly or worship and the gatherings probably centered in the dining room of the house. As late as 164 Justin Martyr said that his congregation still met in some rented apartments "above the baths."[3] Two things began to change. One was the size of the groups and the other was the need for a more permanent space for meeting. As a result, Christian congregations, especially those in the larger cities, began to regularize their meeting place and to make more permanent alterations for specific worship use. This might have begun by setting aside one room of a house just for Christian use. Gradually, they would make more specific modifications to the space and expand into other areas of the house, until finally the whole house was effectively being used for church purposes, rather than as a family residence. At this point additional renovations might be undertaken to make the space fit the specific needs of church use. These might be minimal at first and become more extensive over time, as the congregation grew or as more money was available.

At least one clear archaeological example of this process can be seen from the discovery of a synagogue and a Christian building at Dura-Europos in Roman Syria (see Box 17.1). Here an ordinary house was given over to church use (Fig. a in Box 17.1). On one side of a central court a suite of rooms was combined to form a large hall of assembly. On the other side, a small room was outfitted with a baptismal font (Fig. b). No longer used for domestic purposes, the house had become a *domus ecclesiae* ("house of the church"), that is, a church building. Even so, there was still no set architecture for church buildings and renovation of existing structures would carry on throughout the third century. The fact that the synagogue edifice (Box 17.1, Fig. c) and the Christian edifice go through similar processes of renovation and development shows that it was somewhat ordinary for new religious groups to grow this way.

We can also detect elements of the shift in the Christian literature of the period, as in the quotation above from Clement of Alexandria. Whereas "church," like "synagogue," originally just meant the assembly itself, Clement shows that it has now become more or less identified with the regular place of meeting. In other comments, however, Clement discusses the fact that the "sacrality" of the place of meeting comes from the assembled "church."[4] Even so, one can see the gradual change of attitude that emerged, as in 2 and 3 John, where admission to the "house" has begun to mark an important boundary of congregational identity (see Chapter 16).

Clement gives some other clues as well. For example, it seems that the growing size of congregations began to make a regular meal setting impractical as the locus of worship. Clement also gives us the first evidence for this process and the way it altered the shape of the worship setting by showing that the Eucharist has now become fully separated from the fellowship meal, or *agape* ("love feast").[5] Now the dining room or other domestic space could be enlarged as a hall just for congregational assembly, as we see at Dura-Europos. Now too the acts of worship, or liturgy, became more standardized, as they were removed from the distinctive social rituals associated with dining.

Reading the Scriptures

We know that the reading of scriptures had been an important part of the worship for some years, but it is not the case that most people had copies for their own personal use. The scriptures were heard in worship. A few people, such as Clement and other scholars, would have had copies for study. Bibles, at least as we now think of them, did not yet exist. Beginning in the second half of the second century, the copying of manuscripts proliferated with the growth of a more formal practice of reading the scriptures in the liturgy.

BOX 17.1

Discoveries at Dura-Europos

Dura-Europos was a Roman garrison town on the Euphrates River near the border between modern-day Syria and Iraq (see Fig. 15.1). During excavations there in the 1930s two important discoveries were made on the same street. One was a house converted into a Christian church building in about 241 CE

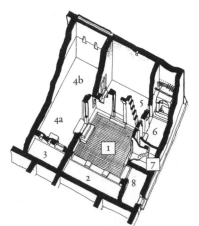

(see Figs. a–b). The other was a house that had been converted into a synagogue in two separate stages (see Figs. c–d). Because the city was destroyed and partially buried in 256 by an invading Sassanian Persian army, these buildings were remarkably well preserved.

a (left) The Dura-Europos Christian building; isometric after renovation (ca. 241–56 CE).

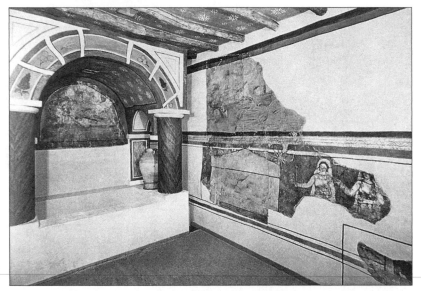

b The baptistery of the Dura-Europos Christian building (room 6); the lower register on the right-hand wall shows "five women" coming to the tomb of Jesus, apparently based on the *Diatessaron,* a copy of which was found nearby. (*HarperCollins Concise Atlas of the Bible*)

The Dura Christian building is the earliest known archaeological evidence ever discovered for a church edifice. That it was renovated from a private house shows continuities from the earlier generations of the Christian movement, when worship was held in the homes of individual members. This practice continued until the latter part of the second century, until the partial and then full renovation of these places resulted in creation of a permanent meeting place.

From the street, one entered the house through a vestibule (Fig. a) to an open courtyard (1). Room 4 became the assembly hall after a partition wall was removed between the earlier dining room (4a) and an adjacent chamber (4b). In room 6 a baptismal font was installed, the first documented indoor baptistery, and the walls were painted with scenes from the Gospels (see Fig. b).

The synagogue at Dura (Fig. c, left) was also renovated from an ordinary private house, with a plan similar to that of the house that became the church building. The entry vestibule from the street (3) led to a central courtyard (1). Room 4 is a typical dining room, while rooms 5 and 6 seem to have been used for some domestic functions. Room 2 was probably created by combining two smaller rooms to make the assembly hall for the Jewish congregation. There were benches around the walls, and a small niche was cut into the

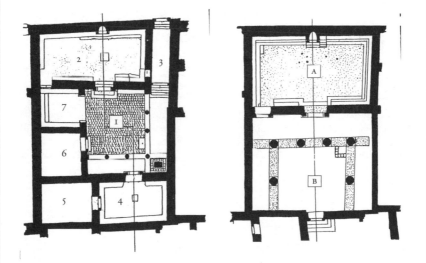

c Left: The early synagogue at Dura-Europos (ca. 175 CE). Right: The later synagogue at Dura-Europos (ca. 244–56 CE).

western wall to house the Torah scrolls. Room 7 also seems to have been used for some purpose in conjunction with worship.

It appears that the Jewish congregation outgrew the accommodations of the synagogue building after a number of years and decided to enlarge it (Fig. c, right). Now its members undertook a more extensive renovation that involved knocking down all the interior walls and one or more of the exterior walls. They then erected thicker load-bearing walls to form a larger hall of assembly (A) and a forecourt (B) with a colonnaded portico in the space that had been the earlier house. They also annexed the adjacent house to the east so that the access to the forecourt was mediated through a series of entry rooms. The total area of the synagogue complex was more than doubled. Both the property acquisition and the construction suggest a rather expensive project, a fact further indicated by the elaborate decorative program in the hall of assembly (see Fig. d).

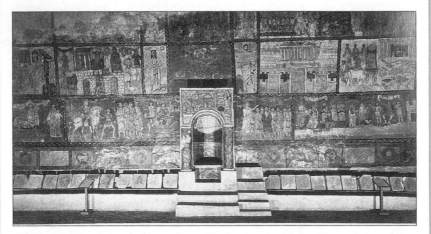

d Wall of the later synagogue's hall of assembly showing the elaborate decorative program; a central Torah niche is on an elevated step surrounded by frescoes depicting biblical scenes. The steps to the right of the Torah niche were where the reader stood, mirrored by the painted figure of Moses reading the Torah scroll just above (see also Fig. 17.2 for detail). (*HarperCollins Concise Atlas of the Bible*)

We can also see such provisions for liturgical reading of scripture in the archaeological evidence from Dura-Europos (Box 17.1, Fig. a). At one end of the Christian assembly hall (Room 4), a raised dais or platform stood as the focal point of the room. It was likely used by the person who spoke and read. The baptistery room was decorated with scenes from the Gospels (Fig. b in Box 17.1). They are among the earliest datable examples of Christian art. But given the out-of-the-way location of Dura-Europos, they are not likely the first. They were probably patterned after art that had developed a little earlier in larger cities such as Antioch or Alexandria at about the same time that Clement was writing.

Perhaps more significant is the fact that, even as late as the mid-third century, these paintings still reflect the harmonized version of Jesus's life in Tatian's *Diatessaron* instead of the versions in the canonical Gospels. Indeed, the lone surviving manuscript of the *Diatessaron* is a Greek fragment discovered at Dura-Europos not too far from the Christian building. The Dura synagogue also shows artistic representations of biblical stories reflecting a parallel use of "their" scriptures by the local Jewish congregation (Box 17.1, Fig. d). The Torah as symbolic center, both physically and liturgically, was already a prominent part of worship (see Fig. 17.2). On the Christian side, Clement once again provides an important insight, since he is one of the earliest authors we know of to use the terms "Old Testament" and "New Testament" in reference to the emerging shape of the Christian scriptures: "For God is the cause of all good things, of which some are primary, such as the Old Testament and the New Testament, while others are secondary consequences, such as philosophy."[6]

Assembling the Scriptures

Together with the debates over heresy and orthodoxy, these changes in the setting and practice of worship undoubtedly had a role in shaping the development of the Christian canon. Writing at the same time as Clement was Tertullian (ca. 197 CE), the Latin apologist and theologian from Carthage (see Chapter 16). Regarding the use of the scriptures, he said:

> *We come therefore to (the gist of) our position . . . so that we may now join issue on the contention to which our adversaries challenge us. They put forward the Scriptures, and by this insolence of theirs they at once influence some. In the encounter itself, however, they weary the strong, they catch the*

weak, and send those wavering on their way with doubt. Accordingly, we op-
pose to them this step above all others, of not admitting them to any discussion
*of the Scriptures. (*Prescription of Heretics *15)*[7]

As we saw in the previous chapters, debates about the scriptures had begun
in the middle of the second century even as there was an explosion of writing
new scriptures, both Jewish and Christian. As a result, controversies over Christian practice and belief gradually came to use these scriptures in debate. Similarly, the routinization of charisma that began to occur in the third generation
required a shift away from direct "revelation" as a source of authority. For example, at the beginning of the century Clement of Rome had argued against

FIGURE 17.2

Moses reading the law in the form of a
Torah scroll, on the western wall of the
later Dura-Europos synagogue. (Yale
University Art Gallery)

the schismatics in Corinth from his own authority as well as that of Paul, while Ignatius claimed the office of bishop as the guardian against heresies such as docetism. For the latter, citing scriptures was still secondary. In contrast, Justin Martyr, writing about 150 CE, had debated with Jews over wording and interpretation of the Septuagint,[8] while the author of 2 Peter warned against those who "twist" the letters of Paul.[9] Perhaps he had Marcion in mind, but there were surely others as well.

The problem is that the term "scriptures" still had a broad meaning. From early times, whether used by Jews or Christians, it typically meant the "Jewish scriptures," and specifically the Septuagint. Beyond the five books of Torah and the earlier prophetic works, however, there was no universal agreement as to which books were included. Nor was it much debated, at least not at first. By the 130s, however, things had begun to change. The tensions that arose with the gradual split of Judaism and Christianity had first led to the consolidation and delimitation of the Jewish scriptures within the emergent rabbinic movement. Even so, in diaspora circles newer writings, such as the Wisdom of Solomon and 4 Ezra, were added, and the still flexible Septuagint collection continued to be the primary scriptures for Christians. Some groups included more writings, such as *1 Enoch* or the *Life of Adam and Eve*. The numerous Christian works that went under the names of apostles (*Gospel of Thomas* or *Apocryphon of John*) were clearly accorded scriptural status, at least in some Christian circles, while "apostolic writings" such as *1 Clement* and the *Epistle of Barnabas* were considered scripture even in orthodox circles down to the fifth century.

The problem is that we have no direct information on when the Christians first began according any of their own writings the status of scripture alongside the Septuagint. Well into the second century, as the testimony of Papias makes clear, Christians had a strong preference for oral tradition as the primary source of authority.[10] Even the passage from 2 Timothy 3:16, "Every scripture inspired by God is also profitable for teaching, for reproof, for correction, and for training in righteousness,"[11] does not clearly indicate *which* scriptures are meant. Had it actually been written by Paul, it could have only meant the Septuagint. That it was written in the second century and in reaction to "false teachings" may mean that it looks to the authentic letters of Paul as scripture. Ironically, if that is the intent, then it vitiates the Pastorals' claim to Pauline authorship. The roughly contemporaneous comment regarding Paul's letters in 2 Peter is more explicit:

> *So also our beloved brother Paul wrote to you according to the wisdom given him, speaking of this as he does in **all his letters**. There are some things in*

*them hard to understand, which the ignorant and unstable twist to their own destruction, as they do **the other scriptures.** (2 Pet. 3:15–16)*

Most likely written from Rome in the 120s or 130s, this statement presupposes some collection of Paul's letters as well as debates over their interpretation. What was included in the collection is unfortunately not given, a point to which we shall return in the next section. The final comment, however, seems to classify this Pauline letter collection with "the other scriptures."

It is really not until the middle of the second century that we start to hear Christians using citation formulas that emulate those used to refer to the Septuagint and other Jewish scriptures—such as, "the scripture says" or "it is written"—regarding Paul or the Gospels. It happened gradually, beginning with specific sayings of Jesus, as in *2 Clement* 2.4 (ca. 140s CE), which introduces a quotation of Jesus (Mark 2:17; Matt. 9:13b) with the formula "another scripture says." Also at Rome at roughly the same time Justin Martyr used the formula "In the Gospel, it is written" to introduce a quotation of Matthew 11:27.[12] He also called the Gospels the "memoirs of the apostles" that were read alongside the prophets in the worship.[13]

It is generally recognized now that Marcion was probably the single most important stimulus to Christian efforts to assemble the scriptures into a fixed canon, or at least the beginnings of one. It was a process of selection. The term "canon" is a Greek word meaning "a straight edge" and thus "a measuring stick." It thus came to be used of various kinds of rules or tables, ranging from tax rosters and astronomical tables to rules of grammar or mathematics. Hence "canonical" meant something "straight" or "by the rules"; the Latin equivalent was *regula* ("rule").

By selecting, editing, and arranging those scriptures he deemed to be both authentic and authoritative, Marcion himself formed the first Christian canon around 140 CE. Yet it created problems because he excluded all the Jewish scriptures, all the Gospels except Luke, and every other known Christian writing of the time except the known letters of Paul. Even these were expurgated of passages that Marcion viewed as objectionable, on the assumption that they had been inserted later by "Judaizing" Christians. What was left was his heavily edited three-part work, the *Antitheses,* the *Gospel* (Luke), and the *Apostle* (Paul). In terms of the later form of the Christian canon, these three components correspond to the Jewish scriptures, the Gospels, and the Apostolic Witness (meaning Acts, the letters of Paul, and the general letters), respectively. Naturally, Marcion's very limited canon made it much easier for him to prove his theological ideas from the scriptures. After all, having many scriptures from diverse backgrounds makes "proof-texting" debates like playing tic-tac-toe.

The Letters of Paul

Marcion's canon contained ten letters of Paul: Galatians, 1 and 2 Corinthians, Romans, 1 and 2 Thessalonians, Laodiceans (= Ephesians), Colossians, Philemon, and Philippians.[14] The order was based on what he considered to be their chronological sequence; however, there were theological considerations that caused him to place Galatians at the head of the list. He apparently did not know of the Pastoral Epistles, if they existed in his day. Marcion's collection presupposes an earlier collection of Paul's letters. It is widely thought that the process of collecting the letters began sometime around the end of the first century, but the precise sequence of events and the concerns that led to it remain unclear. For example, a few scholars would argue that the author of Luke-Acts knew at least a partial collection of the letters, from which some basic facts about Paul's life were drawn. It may have been the effort to write Luke-Acts that led the author, who was from the Pauline tradition, to seek out some of the letters.

Another impulse to collect Paul's letters might have come from the first efforts to write later letters in his name, notably Ephesians and Colossians. It has sometimes been proposed, for example, that Ephesians was intended to serve as a kind of cover letter for such a collection. It is clear, however, that some form of collection existed by the time *1 Clement* was written (ca. 100–120). Ignatius (ca. 113) seems to know of at least some of the letters, although just how many or how well is debated, while Polycarp clearly knows of Philippians and other letters. So it would appear that by about 120–130 CE a basic collection had already developed both in Asia Minor and in Rome, and it was supplemented by the deutero-Pauline letters Ephesians, Colossians, and 2 Thessalonians.

The Roman form of this collection seems to have been known and used by both Valentinus and Justin Martyr, but with some selectivity in both cases. This edition of the letters seems to have been organized by length, as was typical in the composition of scrolls. The order was 1 and 2 Corinthians, Romans, Ephesians, 1 and 2 Thessalonians, Galatians, Philippians, Colossians, and Philemon. It may well be the earliest form of the Pauline corpus.[15] In this collection it had already become normal to group letters to the same location together. At some point it seems they were thought of as "letters to seven churches."[16] Thus, it has also been suggested that the collection of Paul's letters might have been one of the stimuli for Christians to begin using the codex form of the book rather than the traditional scroll (see Box 17.2).

The earliest known manuscripts of Paul's letters date to the end of the second century. One of the most important of these is known as $\mathpzc{P}^{46}$ (the Chester Beatty II Papyrus and Michigan Papyrus 6238; see Fig. 17.3). It is a single-quire codex of 208 pages containing only the letters of Paul. The letters appear in a modified order by length but with one significant addition, namely, Hebrews. The order is: Romans, Hebrews, 1 and 2 Corinthians, Ephesians, Galatians, Philippians, Colossians, 1 Thessalonians. Unfortunately the first few pages of Romans are missing, and the manuscript breaks off after 1 Thessalonians, the last chapter of which is fragmentary.

Even so, the construction of the codex provides further information. Because they were formed by folding the sheets of papyrus into a quire, such codices always contained an even number of pages. In the case of $\mathpzc{P}^{46}$ the pages were numbered, and the number of lines was calculated at the end of each letter (see Fig. 17.3). The first surviving page begins at Romans 5:17 and is numbered as page 14. Based on this fact, then, it is possible to calculate the same number of pages missing at the end, thus allowing just enough space for 2 Thessalonians (and probably Philemon). The Pastoral Epistles were clearly omitted.

The inclusion of Hebrews is significant, of course, as it suggests ties to Rome, even though the manuscript clearly came from the Alexandrian tradition. Later tradition continued to debate whether Paul wrote Hebrews, but its inclusion here may well have arisen from the effort to counter Marcion and to domesticate Paul. So read, Hebrews provided a much-needed affirmation that Paul both used and valued the Jewish scriptures as pointing ultimately to Christ.

How Many Gospels?

The "words of the Lord Jesus" were perhaps the earliest elements of the Christian tradition to receive a special status.[17] In Paul's day and later they were still known only through malleable oral tradition,[18] and the free-flowing use of oral tradition continued to give rise to new Gospels throughout the second century. Because all the early Gospels, including those now in the canon, were written and used by particular communities, they did not initially have a universal status. Local or regional forms of emergent Christianity tended to look to one Gospel as the primary source for their knowledge of Jesus's life and teachings. It was only when mutual awareness of "other" Gospels began to arise, in the early to middle part of the second century, among these local groups that comparison began. In view of the differences among the Gospels, conflict invariably ensued.

Perhaps the earliest effort to consolidate the accounts of several early Gospels may be seen in the Gospel of John, at least in its later stages of development in the first decade of so of the second century. In this later form, it seems that the Gospel of John presupposes knowledge of the earlier Gospels of Mark and Luke, from the synoptic line of tradition, as well as the docetic tradition associated with the *Gospel of Thomas*.[19] If so, then there was a more or less conscious effort to harmonize some aspects of the various accounts while simultaneously modifying or correcting others. The explicit refutation of docetic elements seems clearly intended. It might thus be argued that the Gospel of John was written with an eye toward promoting the reading, or at least the knowledge, of

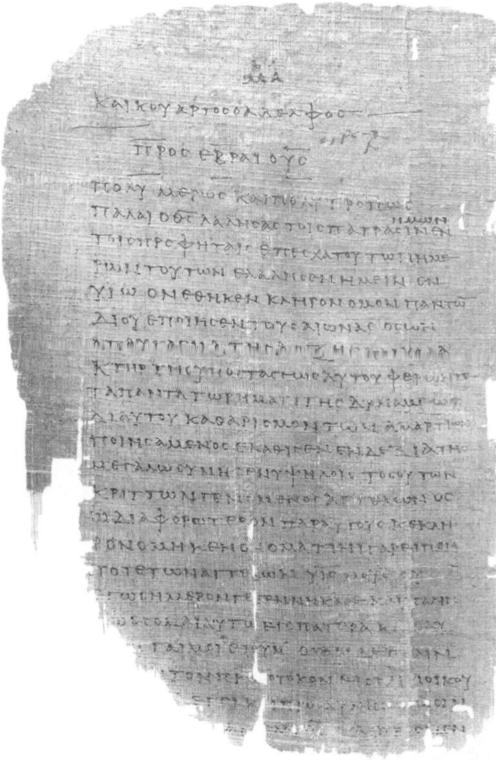

The first line gives the page number in Greek numerical notation: MA = 41.

The second line gives the ending of the letter to the Romans, but at 16:23, instead of 16:27. It reads: *"and Quartus the brother."*

The third line gives a scribal notation for the number of lines up to this point: 1,000 (or perhaps 900).

The fourth line gives the title of the next document: *"To Hebrews."*

The fifth line gives the opening words of Heb. 1:1: *"In many and varied . . ."*

The page breaks off at the bottom after the beginning of Heb. 1:7: *"And to the [angels he . . ."*

Notice the scribal correction in the sixth line. The word "our" (*hēmon*) was added later above the line. The handwriting is clearly different, and this word is omitted from many manuscripts.

FIGURE 17.3

The first page of Hebrews from 𝔓⁴⁶ (Michigan Papyrus 6238, leaf 21 recto). (Used by permission of the Papyrology Collection, Graduate Library, The University of Michigan)

BOX 17.2

From Scroll to Codex
The Shape of Christian Books

For most of ancient literature, Jewish or Greco-Roman, the scroll was the preferred form of book. *Biblios* is the Greek word for "scroll"; the Latin equivalent is *volumen,* meaning "rolled," from which we get "volume." We may
probably guess that Paul's original letters were in scroll form, as were the
other individual books written by early Christians (see Fig. 7.3). When Christians began to collect these works together to form what would eventually become the New Testament, however, the traditional scroll form became less
practical. Accommodating all Paul's letters in one collection would have required a very large scroll, if it were possible at all. The longest known scrolls
from Roman times measured some thirty to forty feet (twelve to thirteen meters) in total.[1] Even allowing for very compressed writing, it would have been
difficult to get all ten letters in one manageable scroll, and then it would have
been very hard to read in a public context. Texts intended for regular public
reading tended to use slightly larger letters and less condensed writing.

A *codex* is a sheaf of pages stitched or bound along one edge (see Fig. 15.2).
It is the beginning of what we typically think of as the "bound book," which
became the norm in western European culture in large measure because of its
popularity among Christians. Typically, a codex was formed by taking a stack
of folios, or larger papyrus sheets, and folding them in half. This is called a

several Gospels. Conversely, it might mean that the Gospel of John was intended to replace them outright, especially in view of various forms of docetic
Christianity. Yet the first commentary we know of on the Gospel of John comes
from the Alexandrian Gnostic Herakleon in about 170 CE. Apart from its use in
Asia Minor (where debates over docetism were strong) and among Egyptian
Gnostics (who used it in exactly the opposite way), the Gospel of John does not
seem to have enjoyed much widespread use in other areas of Christianity until
the later part of the second century.[20] It was too particular, or perhaps too unusual, for most Christians of that time. Even Clement of Alexandria was forced
to call it "the spiritual Gospel" as a way of accounting for the sharp differences.[21]

Consequently, it appears that the early part of the second century saw the
rise of two competing tendencies in the use of a growing number of written
Gospels: one, the desire to collect as many traditions as possible about Jesus for

quire. The quire was then stitched at the fold and could be bound in a leather cover if desired. Eventually, larger books were formed by placing several quires in a single binding. The great Bibles of the fifth century, such as Codex Sinaiticus and Codex Alexandrinus, were formed this way. In the beginning, however, the single-quire codex was more typical. One of the advantages of the codex was the ability to write on both sides of each leaf. Although Christian writing and reading habits did not invent the codex form, it seems to have become the most popular form among Christians beginning in the second century. It was more practical, since it could contain more material, and it facilitated the process of "searching the scriptures," that is, looking back and forth between different biblical books.

FURTHER READING

Gamble, H. Y. *Books and Readers in the Early Christian World.* New Haven, CT: Yale University Press, 1995.

Gigante, M. *Philodemus in Italy: The Books from Herculaneum.* Ann Arbor: University of Michigan Press, 1995. Pp. 15–48.

Reynolds, L. D., and N. G. Wilson. *Scribes and Scholars: A Guide to the Transmission of Greek and Latin Literature.* 2d ed. Oxford: Clarendon, 1974.

White, L. M. "A Measure of Parrhesia: The State of the Manuscript of *PHerc.* 1471." In *Philodemus and the New Testament.* Edited by J. T. Fitzgerald, D. Obbink, and G. S. Holland. Leiden: Brill, 2004. Pp. 103–32.

---

[1]This is longer than is sometimes stated, but it is based on the growing body of research from the Herculaneum papyri. See H. Y. Gamble, *Books and Readers,* 62–63; and White, "A Measure of Parrhesia," 115–18, in suggestions for further reading.

the sake of comprehensiveness; the other, the desire for a single self-contained and consistent account.[22] Such impulses also affected the text of the individual Gospels. For example, the so-called shorter ending of the Gospel of Mark at 16:8—immediately after the women discover the empty tomb—is widely attested in the earliest manuscripts as the original form; however, the fact that it stops before recounting the appearances of Jesus came to be viewed as a problem. At some point, then, an addendum, comprised of Mark 16:9–20 (and its variant forms), was tacked on to the end of Mark to make it more compatible with the Gospels of Matthew and Luke.

Once again, it seems that Marcion provided an impetus to the collection by his denial of all the Gospels but one, the Gospel of Luke. Just a few years later came Justin Martyr (ca. 150), the first Christian writer to show a use of multiple written Gospels, as in his reference to "the memoirs of the apostles" read during worship at Rome.[23] Even so, it does not appear that he knew the Gospel of John, and he sometimes cites oral traditions about Jesus that are not attested in known Gospels. In other words, even though he used the three synoptic Gospels, he did not seem to restrict authority to them alone.

The first effort to integrate the Gospel of John into the standard Roman cycle of Matthew, Mark, and Luke came from a student of Justin, Tatian, who had originally come from Syria. Known as the *Diatessaron* (ca. 170 CE), Tatian's harmony of the four Gospels seems to have been very popular at the time, because it was possible to read a single narrative and it resolved many discrepancies. For example, any reading of the different accounts of the women at the empty tomb of Jesus will readily show that the names vary for the two women who accompany Mary Magdalene. Rather than try to account for the differences by using nicknames or husbands' names, Tatian's account simply names five different women.[24] This is the scene depicted on the wall of the baptistery room of the Dura-Europos Christian building, where there are five women approaching the tomb of Jesus (see Box 17.1, Fig. b). At other times, however, Tatian resorted to "correcting" the texts in order to make them fit together in just the right way, and this did not always sit well.

Irenaeus and the "Catholic" Canon

A basic list of ten (or eleven, with Hebrews) letters of Paul had been settled on by the middle part of the second century, but the debate over the number of Gospels lasted until nearly the end of the century. Although popular, Tatian's solution was no more acceptable than Marcion's; after all, most of the "heretical" groups scored heavily in debates by stressing "their" particular Gospel over the others. Thus, one Gospel was too little; any more seemed too much. There had to be other criteria, and Irenaeus agreed.

Irenaeus was bishop of Lyons in Roman Gaul (southern France) in about 177–90 CE. Born about 120 (or later) in Roman Asia, he claims to have known Polycarp during his youth, before moving to Rome. He then migrated to Gaul, where there were strong commercial ties to Rome, and he eventually became a presbyter in the church at Lyons in the lush wine region of the Rhône Valley. By the mid-170s he was sent to Rome to consult on the matter of Montanism in Gaul. In about 177 he witnessed the martyrdom of Christians from Viennes and Lyons and was delegated to write the letter describing the events to fellow Christians in other cities. About this time he became the bishop of Lyons. His two known writings are *Proof of the Apostolic Preaching* and the treatise *Against Heresies,* written sometime in the 180s.

Many scholars see Irenaeus as a watershed in the transition away from appeals to tradition alone to a "new age of canonical standardization"; thus he is often called the first "catholic theologian."[25] He was convinced that there was a universal (*katholikos*) truth to be found in the Christian message. Although the proper use of the scriptures was a safeguard against heretical distortion, the truth of the message was the "measuring stick" (*canon*) by which to judge the validity of the scriptures:

> *The church, though dispersed throughout the whole world, even to the ends of the earth, has received from the apostles and their disciples this faith: It believes in one God, the Father almighty, maker of heaven and earth and the sea and all things that are in them; and in one Christ Jesus, the Son of God, who became incarnate for our salvation; and in the Holy Spirit, who proclaimed through the prophets the dispensations of God, the advents, the birth from a virgin, the passion, the resurrection from the dead, and the ascension into heaven in the flesh of the beloved Christ Jesus, our Lord. (Against Heresies 1.10.1)[26]*

This series of statements anticipates the more fully developed form of the creed and probably reflects some basic confessions already at work in the practice of baptism.[27] Thus, for Irenaeus, the *canon* was first and foremost the "rule of faith" (in Latin, *regula fidei*) inherited from the apostles and summarized in the basic creedal affirmation of the church.[28] In this context, he also began to use the terms "Old Testament" and "New Testament," not generally as a reference to the canons of scripture as such, but rather to the successive covenants by which God interacted with humans.[29] Nonetheless, these covenants are properly reflected in the respective scriptures.[30] Finally, he argues that the proper understanding of the scriptures was guarded from "private interpretations" by the succession of bishops from the days of the apostles to his own time.[31]

On this basis, then, Irenaeus advocated specific writings that accorded with his understanding of the canonical faith of the church universal (*katholikos*). Perhaps most important is his effort to defend the fourfold Gospel, meaning Matthew, Mark, Luke, and John:

> *But it is not possible that the Gospels can be either more or fewer in number than they are. For since there are four zones of the world in which we live, and four principal winds, while the church has been scattered throughout the*

*world, and since the "pillar and ground" of the church is the Gospel and the spirit of life, it is fitting that she should have four pillars, breathing incorruption on every side, and vivifying humans afresh. From this fact, it is evident that the **Logos**, the fashioner [demiourgos] of all, he that sits on the cherubim and holds all things together, when he was manifested to humanity, gave us the gospel under four forms but bound together by one spirit. (*Against Heresies 3.11.8)*[32]

What may appear to us a kind of "grasping at straws" was for Irenaeus an argument from the harmony of the universe created by the same God that gave the scriptures.

In the continuation of this famous passage, Irenaeus goes on to describe each of the Gospels using a symbolic creature. These four symbols—a lion (Mark), a calf (Luke), an eagle (John), and a man (Matthew)—became common in later Christian iconography of the Gospels. Drawn from the Psalms, such symbols were also prominent features in the apocalyptic description of the heavenly throne room, alluded to above by mention of the cherubim. Circular as these arguments may seem, for Irenaeus the *canon* of faith and the *canon* of scriptures constituted mutual ratification for each other. In addition to the Gospels, he included the Acts of the Apostles, the letters of Paul (probably meaning the Roman list of ten plus Hebrews), 1 Peter, 1 and 2 John, the Apocalypse of John (Revelation), and the *Shepherd* of Hermas. He is the first to include the Pastoral Epistles as well, and he frequently cites *1 Clement* in such a way as to indicate its status as scripture. Given his concern over heresy, especially Marcionism, Montanism, and Gnosticism, one can well understand why he adds some of these extra works to his list. Even so, his canon list was not yet fully "closed."

Closing the Book

By the end of the second century, there was an emerging view of those Christian writings that were clearly considered scripture over against those that were clearly the product of heresy. Yet there was no single list, or any lists of an authoritative sort, for that matter, and some works remained in the shadows. They were long shadows at that, for the Western canon would not be finalized until the very end of the fourth century at the Council of Carthage (394), which produced the list that came down in the medieval Latin Vulgate. Even then the Eastern, or Greek, canon remained different, containing *1 Clement,*

Barnabas, and the *Shepherd* of Hermas, but omitting Revelation. Closing the canon was no easy task and was further influenced by subsequent theological controversies of the third to fifth century.

Part of the story must come from the nature of the books themselves. There was no single Bible "book" containing Old and New Testaments until about 400 CE, as seen most decisively in the grand works known as Codex Sinaiticus and Codex Alexandrinus. Even they contained additional works in the New Testament, notably *1 Clement,* the *Shepherd* of Hermas, the *Epistle of Barnabas,* and the *Apocalypse of Peter.* At the end of the second century, however, no such comprehensive collection could be imagined. The codex books were not yet capable of accommodating all the material. Consequently, following the earlier patterns of use of the Jewish scriptures, there were usually several smaller collections, each of which made up its own book. For example, even in early Septuagint collections, the Torah seems to have comprised its own "book," as did the "book of the twelve" (i.e., the so-called minor prophets).

So too the New Testament was initially a collection of several smaller codices. As we have already seen in the case of P^{46}, the ten (or eleven) letters of Paul might easily fit one such codex, but hardly anything more. Another example of about the same date (ca. 200 CE) is P^{75} (the Bodmer Papyrus 14–15), a single-quire codex of 144 pages also from Alexandria; it contained only the Gospels of Luke and John. In fact, the end of Luke is on the same page as the beginning of John (leaf 47 recto, or page 94). This shows that, in view of the debates with Marcion, the four-Gospel canon had indeed taken root, but with the resultant effect that Luke and Acts were permanently separated in the later literary tradition. Acts was often consigned to another codex containing the so-called general letters (i.e., the letters of Peter, James, John, and Jude). The configuration of P^{75} also seems to presuppose that Matthew and Mark were placed together in their own separate codex. Thus, assuming that such separate, smaller codices were intended to form the lectionary of an early Alexandrian church, one must imagine that it contained at least four, and probably more, total volumes, written in such a way as to be read easily in public worship. By the third century it became desirable to keep all the Gospels together in one book. The Chester Beatty I Papyrus (P^{45}) contained all four Gospels plus Acts in a codex of approximately 225 pages.

Tertullian gives one of the earliest discussions that suggests that a list might be forming in the last years of the second century. He was also instrumental in translating the scriptures into Latin. He differentiates the Gospels of John and Matthew, who were both "apostles" of Jesus, from those of Mark and Luke, who were merely "apostolic men" who came afterward. The distinction was intended to discredit Marcion's sole reliance on Luke.[33] Tertullian's "New Testament" apparently consisted of the four Gospels, perhaps in the order given above, thirteen letters of Paul (including the Pastorals, but not Hebrews), Acts, 1 John, 1 Peter, Jude, Revelation, and the *Shepherd* of Hermas.[34]

Contemporaneous with Tertullian, Clement gives the clearest picture for the Greek East. He uses the terms "Old Testament" and "New Testament" with a somewhat clearer sense of application to the scriptures. His "New Testament" included the four Gospels, probably in the order Matthew, Luke, Mark, John,[35] fourteen letters of Paul (including Hebrews and the Pastorals), 1 and 2 John, 1 Peter, Jude, and Revelation. He left out 2 Peter and 3 John but included *1 Clement,* the *Epistle of Barnabas,* the *Shepherd* of Hermas, the *Preaching of Peter,* the *Sibylline Oracles,* and the *Didache.* According to Eusebius's account of a lost work of Clement, the *Hypotyposes* ("Outlines of Theology"), the latter also discussed the fact that some books among the "testamented scriptures" (notably the letter of Jude and the *Apocalypse of Peter*) were "disputed."[36] He also knew and discussed other "apocryphal" Gospels that he did not condemn as heretical. In other words, although a core of writings (the four Gospels and letters of Paul) that were considered the New Testament scriptures was reaching some degree of consensus, there was much left undecided, and so it would remain for several centuries more. Yet even the disputed works were clearly an important part of the story that had given rise to the Christian movement and the "New Testament" that tells its story. *And the rest,* as they say, *is history.*

Chapter 2

1. Josephus *Antiquities* 18.26: "in the 37th year after Caesar's defeat of Antony at Actium." The battle of Actium occurred in 31 BCE and made it possible for Octavian to assume the title Caesar Augustus as first emperor of Rome in 29 BCE.

2. Josephus *Antiquities* 18.1–3; quoted in Box 2.5.

3. Josephus *Jewish War* 2.117–18; *Antiquities* 18.23–25.

4. See Wayne A. Meeks, *The Moral World of the First Christians* (Philadelphia: Westminster, 1986), 11–17; Robert Doran, *Birth of a Worldview* (Boulder, CO: Westview, 1986).

5. Alan Segal, *Rebecca's Children: Judaism and Christianity in the Roman World* (Cambridge, MA: Harvard University Press, 1986), 1–3; Shaye J. D. Cohen, *From the Maccabees to the Mishnah* (Philadelphia: Westminster, 1987), 24–26.

6. See Peter Ackroyd, *Exile and Restoration* (Philadelphia: Westminster, 1968).

7. See especially the discussion of Cohen, *From the Maccabees to the Mishnah*, 124–42, 159–71, 224–27. See also M. Simon, *Jewish Sects at the Time of Jesus* (Philadelphia: Fortress, 1980); and M. Smith, *Palestinian Parties and Politics That Shaped the Old Testament* (2d ed.; London: SCM, 1987).

8. See Cohen, *From the Maccabees to the Mishnah*, 177–203.

9. These terms have come over the years to refer to a specific body of "deuterocanonical" and "noncanonical" writings from Jewish tradition. More recent attempts to study and classify this literature have made significant strides but are beyond the scope of the present book. James H. Charlesworth, ed., *The Old Testament Pseudepigrapha*, 2 vols. (Garden City, NY: Doubleday, 1983–85). For an introduction to this literature, see G. W. E. Nickelsburg, *Jewish Literature Between the Bible and the Mishnah* (Philadelphia: Fortress, 1981); M. E. Stone, *Jewish Writings in the Second Temple Period* (Minneapolis: Fortress, 1987); and numerous studies on the individual documents.

10. For Philip and Antipas, see especially the story in Mark 6:14–29; however, this account seems to have some confusion about the facts, since Herodias was never married to Philip, although her daughter Salome was. So see Josephus *Antiquities* 18.109–19. It is also this Antipas before whom Jesus was tried in the unique account of Luke 23:6–16.

11. For the circumstances leading up to his removal, see Josephus *Antiquities* 18.1–100, which explicitly says that Quirinius, the governor of Syria, conducted a census of Judea at this same time.

12. Agrippa I is also called Herod in Acts 12. His father was Herod's son Aristobulus (who was executed by Herod in 7 BCE). Aristobulus's mother was Herod's wife Mariamne, a Hasmonean princess and granddaughter of the last Hasmonean king, Hyrcanus II. On Agrippa I, see Josephus *Antiquities* 19.330–50. Contrast the assessment given in Acts 12:19–23.

13. *Antiquities* 17.355; 18.1–2, 26.

14. See Josephus *Antiquities* 17.355. On the problems of the dating, see B. Reicke, *The New Testament Era* (Philadelphia: Fortress, 1968), 106, 136; R. E. Brown, *The Birth of the Messiah* (New York: Doubleday, 1977), 547–56; J. Fitzmyer, *The Gospel According to Luke*, Anchor Bible (New York: Doubleday, 1981), 1:399–405; and D. Potter, "Quirinius," *Anchor Bible Dictionary*, 5:588–89.

15. See also Philo *Embassy to Gaius* 302, which characterizes his administration by "his veniality, his violence, his thefts, his assaults, his abusive behavior, his frequent executions of prisoners without trial, and his endless savagery" against the Jews; cf. *Against Flaccus* 105.

16. Josephus *Jewish War* 2.169–77.

17. Josephus *Antiquities* 18.85–89.

18. Josephus *Jewish War* 2.232–36; cf. *Antiquities* 20.117–21. The outbreak of the conflict between the Samaritans and the Galileans occurred when some Galilean Jews were passing through Samaria on their way to Jerusalem for Passover. One of the Galileans was murdered by a Samaritan, and a number of Galileans then descended on the Samaritans, bent on revenge. Cumanus then rounded up the Galileans, and a number were executed at Caesarea. These three cases together provide some of the same elements noted by Luke 13:1 and also show why there might have been some confusion.

19. See Josephus *Antiquities* 18.4; note the allusion also in Acts 5:37. See also Box 2.6.

20. See Martin Goodman, *The Ruling Class of Judea: The Origins of the Jewish Revolt Against Rome A.D. 66–70* (Cambridge: Cambridge University Press, 1987).

21. Richard Horsley and John Hanson, *Bandits, Prophets, and Messiahs: Popular Movements at the Time of Jesus* (Minneapolis: Fortress, 1985). For relations to Jesus and the Gospels, see also R. Horsely, *Jesus and the Spiral of Violence: Popular Jewish Resistance in Roman Palestine* (Minneapolis: Fortress, 1993).

Chapter 3

1. Arthur Darby Nock, *Conversion: The Old and the New in Religion from Alexander the Great to Augustine of Hippo* (London: Oxford University Press, 1933), 48–76.

2. *Annals* 15.44; see also later in the chapter.

3. Ramsay MacMullen, *Roman Social Relations* (New Haven, CT: Yale University Press, 1974), 77–104.

4. Karl Galinsky, *Augustan Culture* (Princeton, NJ: Princeton University Press, 1996), 164–79; Ramsay MacMullen, *Romanization in the Age of Augustus* (New Haven, CT: Yale University Press, 2000), 124–37.

5. Many of Herod's inscriptions proclaim him "Friend of Caesar" and "Friend of the Romans." In addition to the imperial cult temple he dedicated to Augustus at Caesarea Maritima, he built two more temples to Roma and Augustus: one at Sebaste (the ancient city of Samaria) and the other at Panias (later renamed Caesarea Philippi); cf. Matt. 16.13; Mark 8.27.

6. Paul Zanker, *The Power of Images in the Age of Augustus* (Ann Arbor: University of Michigan Press, 1990), 98–100.

7. See Galinsky, *Augustan Culture*, 91–93.

8. Glenn W. Bowersock, *Hellenism in Late Antiquity* (Ann Arbor: University of Michigan Press, 1990).

9. *Annals* 15.44, quoted earlier in the chapter.

10. A good example is the famous Rosetta Stone, an inscription found in Egypt with the same text carved in Egyptian hieroglyphs, Egyptian demotic script, and Greek. Dating from 196 BCE, the text is a series of divine honors paid to the king Ptolemy V Epiphanes; his very name means "God manifest." It should also be remembered that the epithet used by the infamous Seleucid king Antiochus IV (who in 167 BCE desecrated the Jewish Temple and touched off the Maccabean revolt) was also Epiphanes ("God manifest").

11. Among the best examples of the Stoic argument from the first century CE is the anonymous tractate known as *The Tabula of Cebes*. Similar descriptions may be found in Dio Chrysostom and Plutarch.

12. See Nock, *Conversion*, 164–86. *The Tabula of Cebes* as conversion literature is discussed on 180. Nock (171) calls Epicurean preaching "evangelical fervor." See also Martha Nussbaum, *The Therapy of Desire: Theory and Practice in Hellenistic Ethics* (Princeton, NJ: Princeton University Press).

13. It was once common to draw a sharp distinction between magic and religion, but such a distinction is not really valid. Recent studies have shown that the two were much more thoroughly integrated. See Fritz Graf, *Magic in the Ancient World* (Cambridge, MA: Harvard University Press, 1997), 13–19; Howard Clark Kee, *Miracle in the Early Christian World: A Study in Sociohistorical Method* (New Haven, CT: Yale University Press, 1983), 1–41; John G. Gager, *Curse Tablets and Binding Spells from the Ancient World* (New York: Oxford University Press, 1992), 24–25.

14. In some ancient discussions, astrology was categorized as one of the types of "natural divination," and such would be appropriate. But because of its popularity (both in ancient times and today) and its specialized nature, we have chosen to list it separately.

15. Note that in Virgil's *Fourth Eclogue* (quoted earlier in the chapter), the paean to the new "golden age" begins with a reference to a "prediction" by the Sibyl (line 5: "Cumae's song").

16. New "Sibylline Oracles" were created by both Jews and Christians in order to link these ancient "prophecies" to the biblical tradition. See Chapter 15.

17. Later Christian tradition, adopting terms from Jewish apocalyptic, created a distinction by calling only the bad type "demons" and the good type "angels." Greek and Roman pagans would not generally have recognized this distinction.

18. Gager (*Curse Tablets and Binding Spells*) provides a taxonomy of uses and formulas, including Jewish and Christian examples.

19. Gager, *Curse Tablets and Binding Spells*, 23–24; Ramsay MacMullen, *Enemies of the Roman Order* (Cambridge, MA: Harvard University Press, 1966, 1992), 95–127. We shall encounter additional legends about this Simon Magus in some second-century Christian novels; see Chapter 15.

20. The complete text may be found in Hans Dieter Betz, *The Greek Magical Papyri in Translation,* 2d ed. (Chicago: University of Chicago Press, 1992).

21. *PGM* 4.3007–86 (translation adapted from Betz, *Greek Magical Papyri,* 96–97; italics added).

22. The myth is also found in a Latin version in Ovid's *Metamorphoses,* where the names of the deities are translated as Ceres and Proserpina.

23. Plutarch *On Isis and Osiris* 357B–E, 361E.

Chapter 4

1. Shaye J. D. Cohen, *From the Maccabees to the Mishnah* (Philadelphia: Westminster, 1987), 138–39.

2. Cohen (*From the Maccabees to the Mishnah,* 137) calls this "proto-sectarianism," but the point is the same.

3. Paul D. Hanson, *The Dawn of Apocalyptic,* 2d ed. (Philadelphia: Fortress, 1979).

4. Cohen, *From the Maccabees to the Mishnah,* 140–41.

5. Cohen, *From the Maccabees to the Mishnah,* 139.

6. George W. E. Nickelsburg, *Jewish Literature Between the Bible and the Mishnah* (Philadelphia: Fortress, 1981), 71–100.

7. For the older biblical passages reflecting this kind of creation myth, see Ps. 74:12–17; Isa. 51:9–11. Both texts date from the postexilic period and summon hearers to take consolation and strength from the knowledge that their God—the same God who created the earth by destroying the sea dragon called Leviathan or Rahab—will deliver them from present trials and tribulations. For other reflections, see Isa. 27:1; 30:7; Job 9:13; 26:12–13; Ps. 89:9–10. This expectation of deliverance by trusting in the power of God, the Creator of all, may well be one of the earlier Jewish sources of proto-apocalyptic thinking.

8. See John J. Collins, *The Apocalyptic Imagination: An Introduction to Jewish Apocalyptic Literature,* 2d ed. (Grand Rapids, MI: Wm. B. Eerdmans, 1998), 1–32.

9. Michael E. Stone, *Scriptures, Sects, and Visions* (Philadelphia: Fortress, 1976), 27–47; George W. E. Nickelsburg, "Enoch, First Book of," *Anchor Bible Dictionary,* 2:508–16. Chapters 72–82 may derive from an earlier source.

10. Stone, *Scriptures, Sects, and Visions*, 34–35; Collins, *Apocalyptic Imagination*, 33–42.

11. Collins, *Apocalyptic Imagination*, 41.

12. Norman Perrin, *The New Testament: An Introduction* (New York: Harcourt Brace, 1974), 65.

13. It should be noted here that for the Greeks "world" is *kosmos* and refers to the entire universe as they understood it, not to the earth alone.

14. For sociological definition of sectarianism with further bibliography, see L. Michael White, "Christianity, Early Social Life and Organization," *Anchor Bible Dictionary*, 1:927–28; and Box 6.2.

15. The text is sometimes called the *Testament of Moses*. By the later Hellenistic period, the legend had been widely accepted that Moses did not die before entering the promised land (as reported in Deut. 34); instead, God took him away to heaven. This tradition is reflected in Philo's *Life of Moses* as well as in the Gospel tradition that has Moses come from heaven with Elijah to visit Jesus at the Transfiguration (Matt. 17:1–8; Mark 9:2–8; Luke 9:28–36).

16. *Antiquities* 18.11–25.

17. See George W. Ramsay, "Zadok," *Anchor Bible Dictionary* 6:1034–36; and James Vanderkam, *From Joshua to Caiaphas: High Priests after the Exile* (Minneapolis: Fortress, 2004).

18. Josephus *Antiquities* 20.199, which also links him to the death of James the brother of Jesus.

19. Wayne A. Meeks, *The First Urban Christians: The Social World of the Apostle Paul* (New Haven, CT: Yale University Press, 1983), 152.

20. On the different types of "rebels" that get lumped together under the name Zealots, see Richard Horsely and John Hanson, *Bandits, Prophets, and Messiahs: Popular Movements at the Time of Jesus* (Minneapolis: Fortress, 1985).

21. *Antiquities* 18.65–84.

22. Suetonius *Claudius* 25.

23. Emphasis in quotations from the Bible and classical authors is added by the author.

24. Wisd. of Sol. 7:22. One of these, here translated "unique," is the Greek word *monogenes*, which occurs in John's Gospel (1:14; 3:16) as an attribute of Jesus as God's Logos.

25. E. R. Goodenough, *An Introduction to Philo Judaeus* (Oxford: Oxford University Press, 1962), 139–52.

26. L. M. White, *The Social Origins of Christian Architecture*, 2 vols., Harvard Theological Studies 42 (Harrisburg, PA: Trinity Press International, 1996–97), 1:60–101. This fact will become important when we look at how Paul formed "house churches" (Chapter 8). See also Box 17.1.

Chapter 5

1. For Tacitus's attitude toward Jews, see his *Histories* 5.5.

2. This brief resumé of the polemics is based on a summary of Mishnaic and Talmudic extracts by R. T. Hereford, *Christianity in Talmud and Midrash* (London: Williams & Norgate, 1903), 348–49.

3. See Howard Clark Kee, *Jesus in History: An Approach to the Study of the Gospels*, 3d ed. (Orlando, FL: Harcourt Brace, 1996), 47–52.

4. Louis H. Feldman, "Josephus," *Anchor Bible Dictionary*, 3:990–92; Everett Ferguson, *Backgrounds of Early Christianity*, 2d ed. (Grand Rapids, MI: Wm. B. Eerdmans, 1993), 457–60.

5. Origen *Commentary on Matthew* 10.17; *Against Celsus* 1.47.

6. *Antiquities* 20.200.

7. Feldman, "Josephus," 3:991. For example, to say "people who accept the *unusual* with pleasure" is actually a way of calling someone rash or gullible. Josephus in fact uses the term "pleasure" this way several other times in this section of the *Antiquities*. Also many readers of Josephus have not noticed that the word "truth" (in place of "unusual") does not actually occur in the original manuscripts of Josephus.

8. Plutarch *Alexander* 2.1–3.2.

9. Suetonius *Augustus* 2.94.1–7.

10. *The Jefferson Bible*, with an introduction by F. Forrester Church (Boston: Beacon Press, 1989). A facsimile of the original handwritten title page appears on p. 32.

11. Letter to John Adams, 13 October 1813. Quoted from *The Jefferson Bible*, 17.

12. The original German title was actually *From Reimarus to Wrede*.

13. See the discussion in Chapter 2 and Box 2.5. In general on the birth narratives, see Raymond E. Brown, *The Birth of the Messiah* (New York: Doubleday, 1977). A further note on bibliography: in each of these topics, I have given only one or two references. There are, of course, many other books and articles one could cite for each one. Those I have listed here give, in my view, a balanced, scholarly treatment of the historical issues while also surveying other views. They will also provide ample bibliography for those who wish to pursue each issue further.

14. Brown, *Birth of the Messiah*, 513–17.

15. John P. Meier, *A Marginal Jew: Rethinking the Historical Jesus*, 3 vols. (New York: Doubleday, 1991–98), 1:253–314; John Dominic Crossan and Jonathan L. Reed, *Excavating Jesus* (San Francisco: HarperSanFrancisco, 2001).

16. Josephus *Jewish War* 1.3.

17. E. M. Meyers and J. F. Strange, *Archaeology, the Rabbis, and Early Christianity* (Nashville, TN: Abingdon, 1981), 62–91.

18. Paul W. Hollenbach, "John the Baptist," *Anchor Bible Dictionary*, 3:887–99.

19. Howard Clark Kee, *Medicine, Miracle, and Magic in New Testament Times* (Cambridge: Cambridge University Press, 1986), 67–94.

20. Norman Perrin, *Rediscovering the Teachings of Jesus* (New York: Harper & Row, 1976).

21. Raymond E. Brown, *The Death of the Messiah*, 2 vols. (New York: Doubleday, 1994), 2:1350–78. See also Box 5.2 below.

22. Ellis Rivkin, *What Crucified Jesus: The Political Execution of a Charismatic* (Nashville, TN: Abingdon, 1984); Paul Winter, *On the Trial of Jesus* (2d ed.; New York: DeGruyter, 1974); E. P. Sanders, *The Historical Figure of Jesus* (London: Allen Lane, The Penguin Press, 1993), 249–75.

23. Sanders, *Historical Figure of Jesus*, 276–83.

24. In the three synoptic Gospels there are a total of thirty-two individual miracle stories, *not* counting the duplicates or parallels where the same basic story occurs in either two or all three (e.g., the Gadarene/Gerasene Demoniac: Matt. 8:28–34; Mark 5:1–20; Luke 8:26–39). Of these, eleven occur in all three Synoptics, while eight more occur in two out of the three. There are ten different exorcism stories in the three Synoptics, *not* counting the duplicates or parallels.

25. More recently, a few scholars have proposed that there might be earlier and later strata, or layers, in the Q material found in Matthew and Luke, but this view is not the majority opinion. Those who hold it point to the *Gospel of Thomas*, an apocryphal "sayings gospel" from the late first or early second century, as further literary evidence of this Q tradition. We shall discuss the *Gospel of Thomas* in Chapter 12.

Chapter 6

1. Matt. 26:26–29; Mark 14:22–25; Luke 22:15–20. Notice that Luke has an extra cup *before* the bread and there are some additional comments of Jesus (Luke 22:16–17).

2. The Greek word often translated "betrayed" literally means "to hand over" or "deliver up [to death]." Paul uses it frequently in reference to Jesus's death, just as here, but where there is no sense of "betrayal." Compare Rom. 8:32, where God is the one who delivers him to death, and Gal. 2:20, where Christ delivers himself to death. In other words, Paul is not referring to the "betrayal" by Judas. See William Klassen, "Judas Iscariot," *Anchor Bible Dictionary* 3:1092.

3. The word "handed on" in Greek is a verb form of the word "tradition" (*paradosis*).

4. Some scholars have argued that the Pentecost miracle of the tongues (Acts 2:1–4) is a later variation of the appearance to five hundred, but if this were the case, it would constitute a rather radical change in the story.

5. Cf. Matt. 28:16 (11); Luke 24:13–32 (only 2); 24:33 (11); Acts 1:26 (11); 2:14 (11); John 20:19–25 (only 10); 20:26–29 (11); 21:1–3 (only 7).

6. The source here is Ignatius, the Christian bishop of Antioch, who wrote letters to churches in Asia Minor and Rome while en route to a martyr's death in Rome. For his use of the term *Christianismos,* see Ign. *Magn.* 10.1–3, where it is specifically set alongside of "Judaism" (*Ioudaismos*). We shall discuss Ignatius and his letters more fully in Chapter 13.

7. Notably in Acts 24:5, 14; 28:22, while Acts 5:17 and 15:5 use the term *hairesis* to refer to the "sects" of the Sadducees and Pharisees, respectively (cf. Acts 26:5). Josephus uses the same term to refer to the Pharisees, Sadducees, and Essenes in *Antiquities* 13.171–73 and in *Jewish War* 2.119–66.

8. *Antiquities* 14.15.

9. His book *The Sociology of Early Palestinian Christianity* (Philadelphia: Fortress, 1978) originally carried the German title *Die Sociologie des Jesusbewegungs* (Munich: Kaiser Verlag, 1977). The term *Bewegung* ("movement") in German is often used in compounds of this sort to signify social, religious, and political currents, groups, or uprisings.

10. The fragments of Papias's work are only preserved by the fourth-century Christian historian Eusebius of Caesarea (*Church History* 3.29.16; written ca. 310–20 CE). Papias most likely means Aramaic here, but the statement remains problematic, since the Gospel of Matthew was written in Greek.

11. Matthew Black, *An Aramaic Approach to the Gospels and Acts* (Oxford: Clarendon, 1946), 206. Black attempted to demonstrate that the so-called Synoptic Sayings Source (or Q; see Chapter 5) was originally in Aramaic. More recent scholars have shown less confidence in this position. See the final section of this chapter.

12. The word has sometimes erroneously been thought to be a diminutive form representing the childlike evocation "Daddy." This familiar sense is very unlikely, and efforts to base a reconstruction of Jesus's self-understanding and theology on this sense of familiarity are misguided. See Geza Vermes, *The Religion of Jesus the Jew* (Minneapolis: Fortress, 1993), 180–83.

13. Because the phrase is transliterated, it is less clear precisely which form of the Aramaic lay behind it. It is usually thought to come from *marana tha* ("Our Lord, come!"), but might also be rendered as *maran atha,* which would then be translated either "Our Lord has come" or "Our Lord is coming." The majority understanding is the first form given, with its imperative call for the coming Lord.

14. John Gager, *Kingdom and Community: The Social World of the Early Christians* (Englewood Cliffs, NJ: Prentice Hall, 1975), 16–49.

15. L. Michael White, "Christianity: Early Social Life and Organization," *Anchor Bible Dictionary,* 1:927–29.

16. The same geographical "jump" shows up in Acts 15:3, when Paul returns for the Jerusalem conference.

17. See L. E. Elliott-Binns, *Galilean Christianity,* Studies in Biblical Theology 16 (Chicago: Allenson, 1956), 43–53.

18. Josephus *Antiquities* 20.200.

19. How many sayings Paul knew and by what source is debated, since there are often variations in the wording. It is striking, however, that Paul never mentions any miracle performed by Jesus. The key "sayings" include 1 Cor. 7:10–11; 9:14; 11:23–24 (the Lord's Supper); and 1 Thess. 4:16–17. Less direct allusions (or "echoes") might also be found in verses such as Rom. 12:14, 17 and 1 Thess. 5:2. See Box 6.3. Helmut Koester, *Ancient Christian Gospels* (Harrisburg, PA: Trinity Press International, 1990), 52–54; Calvin Roetzel, *The Letters of Paul: Conversations in Context* (Atlanta: John Knox, 1982), 45–46; David L. Dungan, *The Sayings of Jesus in the Churches of Paul* (Philadelphia: Fortress, 1971).

20. Koester, *Ancient Christian Gospels,* 133; and J. Kloppenborg, *The Formation of Q: Trajectories in Ancient Wisdom Collections* (Philadelphia: Fortress, 1987), 219–26.

21. There are forty-eight passages in all that are parallel between Q and the *Gospel of Thomas*. For a listing, see Box 6.3. For full discussion of the *Gospel of Thomas,* see Chapter 12.

22. See J. S. Kloppenborg, ed., *The Shape of Q: Signal Essays on the Sayings Gospel* (Minneapolis: Fortress, 1994), 51–58 (the influential 1964 essay on genre by James M. Robinson), and 138–55 (Kloppenborg on instructional features).

23. Cf. Wisd. of Sol. 6:12–23; 10:15–11:1; Sir. 4:11; 24:23–29.

24. Kloppenborg (*The Shape of Q,* 148–50) lists the following Q units in this connection: S8–14, which contain the original elements of the Sermon on the Mount/Plain (Luke 6:20b–49); S21–26 (Luke 9:57–62 and 10:2–16, 21–24); S35–39 (Luke 12:2–12); and S41–42 + 44 (Luke 12:22b–34, 39–40).

25. *Gos. Thom.* 10: "I have cast fire on the world, and behold I am guarding it until it is ablaze"; *Gos. Thom.* 16: "Perhaps people think I have come to cast peace upon the world. They do not know that I have come to cast conflict upon the earth: fire, sword, war. For there will be five in the house: there will be three against two and two against three, father against son and son against father, and they will stand alone."

26. Cf. S56a (Luke 14:26; Matt. 10:37); cf. *Gos. Thom.* 55; 101.

27. The wedding garment parable has a parallel in rabbinic sources, where it is taken to mean "Be ready, for you do not know when you will die." See the tractate *Shabbat* (153a) in the Babylonian Talmud. My own view is that Matthew also takes this parable from a more rudimentary version also found in Q; see S43 (Luke 12:35–38). A second and even more elaborated version of this idea is found in Matthew's eschatological parable of the wise and foolish maidens (Matt. 25:1–13).

Chapter 7

1. Adolf Harnack, *What Is Christianity?* (1902; repr., New York: Harper Torchbooks, 1957), 176, 180, 182, 190.

2. See John Knox, *Chapters in a Life of Paul* (Nashville, TN: Abingdon, 1950); Robert Jewett, *A Chronology of Paul's Life* (Philadelphia: Fortress, 1979).

3. The inscription is published by W. Dittenberger, *Sylloge Inscriptionum Graecarum,* 3d ed. (Leipzig: S. Hirtzelium, 1915–24), no. 801D. Important discussions of the text and its date may be found in F. J. Foakes Jackson and K. Lake, *The Beginnings of Christianity,* Part I: *The Acts of the Apostles,* 5 vols. (London: Macmillan, 1920–33), 5:460–64; Adolf Deismann, *Paul: A Study in Social and Religious History,* 2d ed. (New York: Harper, 1927; repr. Harper Torchbooks, 1957), 261–86; and C. K. Barrett, *The New Testament Background,* rev. ed. (San Francisco: HarperSanFrancisco, 1989), 51–52.

4. It is possible that he could have arrived as early as the very end of the year 50, but no earlier, and he might well have arrived in the latter part of 51.

5. Based on ancient ways of describing time, the phrase "after three years" might easily mean "something over two years." Also, it is not clear whether "after fourteen years" (Gal. 2:1) is meant to be in addition to or to include the "three years" (Gal. 1:18). It is usually assumed that the three years is included in the fourteen, and thus that the date is slightly later.

6. On the problem, see W. C. van Unnik, *Tarsus or Jerusalem: The City of Paul's Youth* (London: Epworth, 1962); Hans Dieter Betz, "Paul," *Anchor Bible Dictionary,* 5:187.

7. The intention of Acts is clear, even though the terminology is somewhat less so. See A. N. Sherwin-White, *Roman Law and Roman Society in the New Testament* (Oxford: Oxford University Press, 1963), 144–62. The technical term for "citizenship" (*politeia*) is used only once in Acts 22:28, and that is in reference to the centurion who arrests Paul. All the references to Paul's status are implied (as in his reply to the centurion in Acts 22:28) or use a different term simply meaning "Roman" (*Romaios*) without always indicating actual citizenship (cf. Acts 2:10; 25:16; 28:17). For a more skeptical assessment see Helmut Koester, *Introduction to the New Testament,* vol. 2: *History and Literature of Early Christianity,* 2d ed. (New York and Berlin: DeGruyter, 2000), 107; Betz, "Paul," 5:187.

8. The same term is used this way in the LXX version of Judges 13:3, an angelic appearance; cf. Num 14:3, 15. In 2 Cor. 12:1 Paul uses these same two words in combination; see below.

9. J. D. Tabor, *Things Unutterable: Paul's Ascent to Paradise in Its Greco-Roman, Judaic, and Early Christian Contexts* (Lanham, MD: University Press of America, 1986); M. Himmelfarb, *Ascent to Heaven in Jewish and Christian Apocalypses* (New York: Oxford University Press, 1993), 107–10. See also Chapter 4. Because Paul prefaces this report by saying "fourteen years ago," people have wrongly identified this vision with his "conversion" experience. Rather, they seem to be two entirely different events.

10. The passage from Jeremiah points more directly to the prophet's self-understanding as a result of a "call" experience. The passage from Isaiah, however, comes from one of the so-called suffering servant songs. In these the "servant" has been interpreted as the prophet himself, as the king of Israel (as symbol for the chosen people), or as the nation itself, as a kind of "prophetic peoplehood" whose role is to proclaim their allegiance to God as a summons to the rest of the peoples of earth. Only much later were these same suffering servant songs reinterpreted to fit the figure of Jesus as suffering messiah.

11. This is now a widespread understanding; see Koester, *History and Literature of Early Christianity,* 108.

12. Alan F. Segal, *Rebecca's Children* (Cambridge, MA: Harvard University Press, 1986), 104; see also his *Paul the Convert: The Apostolate and Apostasy of Saul the Pharisee* (New Haven, CT: Yale University Press, 1990).

13. Many elements of Paul's dealings with his gentile converts depend first on this basic change of understanding to Jewish monotheism. This can be seen in some of the Jewish slogans that crop up in his letters, e.g., 1 Cor. 8:4: "For we know that *'an idol has no real existence'* and that *'there is no God but one.'*"

14. Col. 1:15–20 is also thought by many scholars to be an early hymn, even though the Pauline authorship of the Colossian letter itself is debated.

15. Most of these are clearly classed as letters; however, even the book of Revelation, in genre an apocalypse, contains seven letters to churches (chaps. 2–3) as part of its preamble.

16. As reflected in a gift tag composed by Martial (*Epigrams* 14.188) dating to the early 80s CE.

17. The fact that Seneca was imprisoned under Emperor Nero at about the same time as the legends regarding Paul's martyrdom contributed in later centuries to the production of an apocryphal correspondence between Paul and Seneca, in which Paul seems to win his fellow prisoner over to Christian views (see Box 7.1).

18. Pliny *Epistles* 10.96–97, dated ca. 110–13 CE, when Pliny was serving as imperial corrector for the province of Bithynia. We shall discuss these letters in Chapter 14, since they present some of the earliest evidence for Roman attitudes toward Christians and the beginnings of legal procedures against them.

19. See Stanley K. Stowers, *Letter Writing in Greco-Roman Antiquity* (Philadelphia: Westminster, 1986), 17–26.

20. There has been some recent debate over the extent of literacy in the ancient world. Notably, William V. Harris, in *Ancient Literacy* (Cambridge, MA: Harvard University Press, 1989), argues that there was far less literacy than had been supposed in older studies of the Greek and Roman world; however, the question finally comes down to what we mean by "literacy." A cautious view would still allow for the fact that far more people in the Roman world had some minimal functional literacy than in previous or subsequent periods of Western culture up until modern times, even though many of these people were still not able to read or write *literature* in the stricter sense.

21. L. D. Reynolds and N. G. Wilson, *Scribes and Scholars: A Guide to the Transmission of Greek and Latin Literature* (Oxford: Clarendon, 1974); Marcello Gigante, *Philodemus in Italy: The Books from Herculaneum* (Ann Arbor: University of Michigan Press, 1995), 1–48; H. Y. Gamble, *Books and Readers in the Early Church: A History of Early Christian Texts* (New Haven, CT: Yale University Press, 1995), 1–41.

22. For example, the emperor Augustus invited the aspiring poet Horace to serve as his secretary; see Suetonius, *Life of Horace,* quoting a letter from Augustus, who complains that his official duties make it impossible for him to keep up with his correspondence with friends. On letter writing in the educational program, see Stowers, *Letter Writing in Greco-Roman Antiquity,* 32–35.

23. For the last, see the Gallio inscription (discussed above), a letter from the emperor Claudius to the city of Delphi.

24. See Pliny the Elder *Natural History* 13.68–83 (in Barrett, *The New Testament Background,* 24–28).

25. For discussion of the handbooks, see Stowers, *Letter Writing in Greco-Roman Antiquity,* 51–57, and W. G. Doty, *Letters in Primitive Christianity* (Philadelphia: Fortress, 1973), 8–11.

26. From the handbook of Pseudo-Demetrius, *Epistolary Types* 2, translated by L. M. White.

27. The letter is Oxyrhynchus Papyrus 292, translated by L. M. White.

28. *Eucharisto* is also the word from which we get the term "Eucharist" for the Lord's Supper or Mass. It derives from some early liturgical prayers that began "We give thanks" (see *Did.* 9–10 and my Chapter 13). In modern Greek *parakalo* and *eucharisto* (pronounced *efcharisto*) remain common expressions meaning "Please" and "Thank you," respectively.

Chapter 8

1. Cf. Acts 15:36–41, which has Paul part ways with Barnabas over the helper named John Mark, who had been associated earlier with Peter and James in Jerusalem (Acts 12:12–17). See Box 13.1.

2. See the analysis of the episode in connection with the Acts accounts by W. A. Meeks and R. L. Wilken, *Jews and Christians in Antioch in the First Four Centuries of the Common Era* (Missoula, MT: Scholars Press, 1978), 13–17; and J. H. Schütz, *Paul and the Anatomy of Apostolic Authority* (Cambridge: Cambridge University Press, 1975), 138–40, 171–72.

3. See the cryptic comment in Gal. 5:11.

4. In Paul's usage "apostle" (from the Greek *apostellein,* "to send out") simply means "one sent" as an emissary or on a mission, hence our translation "missionary."

5. Paul's movements correspond roughly to those described in Acts 16, but the facts remain uncertain. According to Acts, after leaving Antioch Paul took the southern route directly to Derbe and Lystra, where he met up with the young Jewish follower of Jesus named Timothy for the first time (Acts 16:1–4). From there they were prevented "by the Holy Spirit" from going westward toward Ephesus, and so turned north into Phrygia and Galatia and then westward through Mysia to Alexandria Troas (Acts 16:6–8). From there he sailed to Neapolis and moved on to Philippi (Acts 16:11–12).

6. Further information is provided by his comments in the later letter to the community at Philippi (Phil. 1:5; 4:15–16): his first converts in Philippi helped him financially when he moved on to Thessalonica.

7. Acts 17:1–9 describes the problems in Thessalonica as a disturbance among the Jews; however, there is no real evidence for Jewish factions of this sort in either Philippi or Thessalonica. Acts 16:16–34 has Paul preaching and making a few converts in Athens, but makes no mention of his sending Timothy back to Thessalonica. Instead, Acts 17:14–15 says that Paul left Silas and Timothy in Beroea (just south of Thessalonica) when he moved on to Athens, and that they then joined up with him later in Corinth (18:5).

8. See especially the works of A. J. Malherbe noted in Box 8.2.

9. In other words, Paul could have argued, "Yes, I still require 'circumcision' [meaning baptism] for those Gentiles who join us"; however, more traditional Jewish followers of the Jesus movement would have replied, "Not good enough!"

10. Since Colossians is one of the "debated" letters of Paul, it will be discussed in Chapter 11; however, the language of these verses is widely recognized to be very early in character.

11. W. A. Meeks, *The First Urban Christians: The Social World of the Apostle Paul* (New Haven: Yale University Press, 1983), 150–57.

12. My translation. That this was a liturgical formula is suggested by the repetition of pairs of opposites: Jew/Greek, slave/free, male/female. At least two of these three pairs occur in similar order in each of the three cases in which the formula is repeated (Gal. 3:28; Col. 3:11; 1 Cor. 12:13), and in each case there is a universalizing phrase at the end.

13. See L. M. White, *The Social Origins of Christian Architecture*, 2 vols., Harvard Theological Studies (Harrisburg, PA: Trinity, 1996–97).

14. For Jerusalem: 2:46; 5:42; 12:12; for Paul: 16:15, 34; 17:7; 18:7; 20:7.

15. For further reading: L. M. White, "Christianity, Early Social Life and Organization," *Anchor Bible Dictionary,* 1:927–33; *Social Origins of Christian Architecture* (see n. 16); A. J. Malherbe, *Social Aspects of Early Christianity,* 2d ed. (Philadelphia: Fortress, 1983), 60–91; Meeks, *The First Urban Christians,* 74–83; R. S. Ascough, *What Are They Saying About the Formation of Pauline Churches?* (New York: Paulist Press, 1998); C. Osiek and D. L. Balch, *Families in the New Testament World: Households and House Churches* (Louisville, KY: Westminster–John Knox, 1997); K. J. Torjesen, *When Women Were Priests* (San Francisco: HarperSanFrancisco, 1993), 9–110.

16. See the text notes in the RSV and NRSV.

17. P. R. C. Weaver, *Familia Caesaris: A Social Study of the Emperor's Freedmen and Slaves* (Cambridge: Cambridge University Press, 1972); J. F. Hall, "Caesar's Household," *Anchor Bible Dictionary,* 1:798.

18. See J. T. Fitzgerald, "Philippians, Epistle to the," *Anchor Bible Dictionary,* 5:322–23, for discussion of the options and references.

19. Acts 16:18–28 tells of an overnight stay in jail because he had exorcised the mantic spirit of a young girl with oracular powers; however, the story in Acts 16 does not mesh well with the historical record in Philippi. For example, neither of the converts mentioned in Acts 16 (Lydia, the purple dealer, and the jailer) show up in Paul's references or greetings in the letter. See L. M. White, "Visualizing the 'Real' World of Acts 16: Towards Construction of a Social Index," in *The Social World of the First Christians: Essays in Honor of Wayne A. Meeks,* ed. L. M. White and O. L. Yarbrough (Minneapolis: Fortress, 1995), 234–61.

20. That he visited again is suggested by the sequence of movement reflected in 2 Corinthians, to be discussed below. At least a portion of 2 Corinthians was written from Philippi.

21. Cf. 1 Cor. 10:16, where the same word is translated "communion" (KJV), "participation" (RSV, NAB), "sharing" (NRSV), or Gal. 2:9, where it is rendered "right hand of fellowship."

22. The Greek phrase translated "concern" in the NRSV is in the one rendered "having the same mind" elsewhere in the letter.

23. It is possible that this earlier letter contained exhortations similar to those in 3:2–4:1, which Paul chose to repeat on the later occasion. See Box 8.7.

24. Timothy must have been the bearer of several of these letters, especially the second "note" regarding Epaphroditus's illness; cf. Phil. 2:19–23.

25. This traditional view is still reflected in some commentaries, such as P. T. O'Brien, *Colossians and Philemon,* Word Biblical Commentary 44 (Waco, TX: Word Books, 1982), 266–67; N. R. Petersen, *Rediscovering Paul: Philemon and the Sociology of Paul's Narrative World* (Philadelphia: Fortress, 1985), 264.

26. This view was proposed by Peter Lampe, "Keine 'Sklavenflucht' des Onesimus," *Zeitschrift für die neutestamentliche Wissenschaft* 76 (1985): 135–37, and has been followed recently by S. Scott Bartchy, "Philemon," *Anchor Bible Dictionary,* 5:307–8; J. D. G. Dunn, *The Epistles to the Colossians and Philemon,* New International Greek Testament Commentary (Grand Rapids, MI: Eerdmans, 1996), 301–4; and Osiek and Balch, *Families in the New Testament World,* 174–77.

27. As proposed by S. C. Winter, "Methodological Observations on a New Interpretation of Paul's Letter to Philemon," *Union Seminary Quarterly Review* 39 (1984): 203–12; and "Paul's Letter to Philemon," *Novum Testamentum Supplement* 33 (1987): 1–15.

28. Also, if "Epaphras" mentioned in Philem. 23 as Paul's "fellow prisoner" were a shortened or

familiar form of Epaphroditus, then it might mean that Philemon was written just slightly before Philippians. This is a possibility suggested by J. R. Harris, "Epaphroditus, Scribe and Courier," *Expositor* 8 (1898): 101–10. According to Col. 4:12, Epaphras was from Colossae instead; however, there is the question of the authenticity of Colossians.

29. R. F. Hock argues that it was to be Paul's helper in his old age. "A Support for His Old Age: Paul's Plea on Behalf of Onesimus," in White and Yarbrough, eds., *The Social World of the First Christians,* 67–81.

30. See L. M. White, "Paul and *Pater Familias*" in *Paul in the Greco-Roman World,* ed. P. Sampley (Harrisburg, PA: Trinity, 2003), 753–55.

31. Cf. the opposite conclusions reached by S. Mitchell, "Galatia," *Anchor Bible Dictionary,* 5:871 (who accepts the southern hypothesis), and H. D. Betz, "Galatians, Epistle to the," *Anchor Bible Dictionary,* 5:872 (who accepts the northern hypothesis). Even so, the northern hypothesis is presently the majority position. Among current commentaries, only that of F. F. Bruce (*The Epistle to the Galatians,* New International Greek Testament Commentary [Grand Rapids, MI: Eerdmans, 1982, repr. 1998], 14–18, 55–56) argues for the southern hypothesis; he places the letter before 1 Thessalonians and even proposes a date *before* the Jerusalem conference.

32. Composition in Ephesus is adopted by most commentators who assume the northern hypothesis, e.g., Betz, "Galatians," 5:872, and *Galatians: A Commentary,* Hermeneia (Philadelphia: Fortress, 1979), 9–12; J. L. Martyn, *Galatians,* Anchor Bible 33A (New York: Anchor/Doubleday, 1997), 19–20; J. D. G. Dunn, *The Epistle to the Galatians,* Black's New Testament Commentaries (Peabody, MA: Hendriksen, 1995), 19–20; P. F. Esler, *Galatians* (London: Routledge, 1998), 32–36; cf. R. Jewett, *A Chronology of Paul's Life* (Philadelphia: Fortress, 1979), 103; and H. Koester, *Introduction to the New Testament,* 2d ed., 2 vols. (Berlin: DeGruyter, 2000), 2:123–26.

33. W. G. Kümmel, *Introduction to the New Testament,* rev. ed. (Nashville, TN: Abingdon, 1975), 296–97, 303 (after the imprisonment before going to Macedonia); N. Perrin and D. Duling, *The New Testament: An Introduction,* 2d ed. (New York: Harcourt Brace, 1982), 182–83 (after the imprisonment but from Macedonia); J. P. Sampley, "Paul's Frank Speech in Galatians and Corinthians," in *Philodemus and the New Testament,* ed. J. T. Fitzgerald, G. Holland, and D. Obbink (Leiden: Brill, 2004), 295–321.

34. I do not view 6:14–7:1 as an interpolation or as a fragment of the lost Letter A. It is integral to the argument in 2 Cor. 1–7.

35. It is also possible, but less likely in my view, that Letter E was drafted as a parallel letter, assuming that it was carried by Titus, who went elsewhere first to finish the collection, while Timothy went directly to Corinth carrying Letter D, and then they all met up in Corinth.

36. See especially G. Theissen, *The Social Context of Pauline Christianity: Essays on Corinth* (Philadelphia: Fortress, 1982), 21–67.

37. Patronage and hospitality are very important to the social organization of Paul's house churches. In addition to discussion of this issue in earlier letters, see also P. Marshall, *Enmity in Corinth: Social Conventions in Paul's Relations with the Corinthians* (Tübingen: Mohr-Siebeck, 1987). Also, it must be remembered that hospitality and support were an issue in the missionary instructions of the early Jesus movement as reflected in the Q source (see Chapter 6).

38. According to Acts 18:1–4, Prisca and Aquila had moved to Corinth from Rome following the expulsion of the Jews by Claudius in 49 CE. This account indicates that they were Jewish by birth but were possibly already followers of the Jesus movement—still considered a sect of Judaism—while in Rome.

39. Some scholars think that Rom. 16 did not originally belong to the letter and was added on later, when a copy of the letter was sent to Ephesus, the last known residence of Prisca and Aquila (1 Cor. 16:19). See Koester, *Introduction to the New Testament,* 2:143. Other scholars have argued convincingly, however, that chapter 16 belongs with the letter as it was sent to Rome. See C. D. Myers, "Romans, Epistle to the," *Anchor Bible Dictionary,* 5:818–21 (with additional references).

40. This outline is adapted from Wayne Meeks.

41. See N. A. Dahl, "The Atonement—an Adequate Reward for the Akedah?" in *The Crucified Messiah and Other Essays* (Minneapolis: Augsburg, 1974), 146–60.

42. S. K. Stowers, *A Rereading of Romans: Justice, Jews, and Gentiles* (New Haven, CT: Yale University Press, 1994); H. Räisänen, "Paul, God, and Israel: Romans 9–11 in Recent Research," in *The Social World of Formative Christianity and Judaism,* ed. J. Neusner et al. (Philadelphia: Fortress, 1988), 178–206.

43. J. G. Gager, *The Origins of Anti-Semitism: Attitudes Toward Judaism in Pagan and Christian Antiquity* (New York: Oxford University Press, 1985), 197–264; and *Reinventing Paul* (New York: Oxford University Press, 2002).

Chapter 9

1. This is a translation of the passage from the Septuagint, as it would have been read by Paul. He makes an allusion to this section of Isaiah in Rom. 10:20–21, where he also talks about the occasion for the Gentiles turning to the Lord. There are some important differences in the Greek version, which I have put in bold: it explicitly adds the Greeks to the catalog of gentile nations. Tarshish was a traditional Semitic name for Spain, while Lud (Lydia), Tubal (Cappadocia), and Mosoch (Pontus) were regions of Asia Minor. Paul could thus have read this passage as applying very literally to his gentile mission.

2. See Josephus *Antiquities* 20.168–72; *Jewish War* 2.261–65, also discussed in Chapter 2, above. The Egyptian seems to have been active in Judea in 54–55 CE. Josephus places these events under the procurator Felix (52–60 CE). Acts has this same Felix take charge of Paul's first trial (23:23–24:27). Since Acts 24:27 has Paul held in custody for two years under Felix, that would place the date of the arrest sometime in 58 or early 59, but the chronology is complicated by the dates of Festus, the successor to Felix. See J. B. Green, "Festus, Porcius," *Anchor Bible Dictionary,* 2:795.

3. Josephus *Jewish War* 2.272–77.

4. Josephus *Jewish War* 2.258. These conditions also exist under Felix; in the next breath Josephus recounts the episode of the Egyptian.

5. *Jewish War* 2.254–56; *Antiquities* 20.186–88, 208–10. In another passage, Josephus implicates the procurator Felix in the assassination of the high priest Jonathan (*Antiquities* 20.162).

6. *Antiquities* 20.185. The situation deteriorated further when the procurator Albinus released other criminals from custody to prey on the populace (20.215).

7. *Antiquities* 18.9–10.

8. *Jewish War* 6.301–6. Cf. the similar wording of the oracle attributed to the other Jesus in Luke 7:29 (cf. Matt. 8:11–12).

9. *Antiquities* 20.200–201.

10. *Jewish War* 2.280–92.

11. *Jewish War* 2.293–96.

12. *Jewish War* 2.305–8. Florus even dared to crucify Jews who held Roman citizenship and equestrian rank.

13. *Jewish War* 2.540–56.

14. *Jewish War* 2.307–15.

15. This was the title of one of the Essenes' works, now better known as the *War Scroll*, an apocalyptic battle plan for the final conflict between the angelic forces of God and the Satanic armies of Rome.

16. *Jewish War* 4.399–409.

17. *Jewish War* 4.491–93; cf. Suetonius *Nero* 47–48.

18. The governor of Egypt who assisted him was no less than Tiberius Julius Alexander, the nephew of Philo, now ascended to the ranks of Roman aristocracy.

19. *Jewish War* 4.654–63.

20. *Jewish War* 5.1–21. Josephus (5.248–51) reports the size of the Jewish armies as follows: John of Gischala had 6,000 men; Eleazar, 2,400; and Simon bar Giora, 10,000, with 5,000 more Idumeans outside the city.

21. *Jewish War* 5.302–48.

22. *Jewish War* 5.362–412.

23. *Jewish War* 5.429–38, 512–18.

24. *Jewish War* 6.164–68.

25. This double event is memorialized in Jewish tradition as the Ninth of Ab (roughly August 30). Cf. *Jewish War* 6.249–51.

26. *Jewish War* 6.271–80.

27. *Jewish War* 6.316–18.

28. *Jewish War* 6.403–10.

29. For Josephus's description of the procession, including description of the spoils and the execution of Simon, see *Jewish War* 7.132–62.

30. The Flavian dynasty included Emperor Vespasian (69–79 CE) and his two sons, Titus (79–81 CE) and Domitian (81–96 CE). See Chapter 11.

31. *Jewish War* 6.420. As in most ancient histories, these numbers tend to be exaggerated, but the ultimate toll was devastating.

32. The poignant account is found in *Jewish War* 7.252–406. Eleazar son of Jairus was a relative (either cousin or nephew) of Menahem, the leader of the *sicarii,* who had earlier captured Masada. This Menahem was also a son of Judas the Galilean, the so-called founder of the Zealot movement in 6 CE. His group had held part of the Temple in the early stages of the siege of Jerusalem. See *Jewish War* 2.433–47.

33. *Jewish War* 7.162.

34. *Jewish War* 7.406.

35. S. J. D. Cohen, "Literary Tradition, Archeological Remains, and the Credibility of Josephus," *Journal of Jewish Studies* 33 (1982): 385–405.

36. *Jewish War* 7.336 (the end of Eleazar's first speech).

37. From the second speech, *Jewish War* 7.378–87.

38. For historical and literary discussion of these texts, see G. W. E. Nickelsburg, *Jewish Literature Between the Bible and the Mishnah* (Philadelphia: Fortress, 1981), 280–303.

39. He tells the story in *Jewish War* 3.340–408, but he also alludes to it in his *Life,* one of the earliest examples of the literary genre of autobiography to come down to us from antiquity.

40. The similarities to the story of Masada have long been noticed.

41. For a similar use of lots to allow God to direct the course of human events, compare the selection of Matthias as Judas's replacement after the death of Jesus (Acts 1:23–26).

42. *Jewish War* 3.351–55.

43. For the legend in later rabbinic sources and discussion of the historical issues, see G. G. Porton, "Yohanan ben Zakkai," *Anchor Bible Dictionary,* 6:1024–26. The similarity to the story of Josephus has long been noted, but Josephus's version is far earlier. There are notable anachronisms in the legend of Yohanan, one of which is that Vespasian was not present at the final siege of Jerusalem.

44. This view is reflected in the title of Jacob Neusner's book about Yohanan, *First-Century Judaism in Crisis: Yohanan ben Zakkai and the Renaissance of Torah* (Nashville, TN: Abingdon, 1975).

45. See A. F. Segal, *Rebecca's Children: Judaism and Christianity in the Roman World* (Cambridge, MA: Harvard University Press, 1986), 117–41; J. Neusner, *From Politics to Piety: The Emergence of Pharisaic Judaism,* 2d ed. (New York: KTAV, 1979).

46. From *The Fathers According to Rabbi Nathan* 6. I follow the version in Neusner, *First-Century Judaism in Crisis,* 169; cf. Segal, *Rebecca's Children,* 131.

47. Eusebius *Church History* 3.39.14–15. Elsewhere, Eusebius dates the writing of Mark before 40 CE (*Church History* 2.24; cf. Chapter 15 below for full discussion).

48. Josephus *Jewish War* 7.23–42. In fact, any of the other cities of Syria, such as Berytus or Tyre, might be considered possible locations.

49. The later Christian writer Clement of Alexandria (ca. 200 CE) discusses another version of Mark, known as the *Secret Gospel of Mark,* and says that Mark brought it from Rome to Alexandria. See M. W. Meyer, "Mark, Secret Gospel of," *Anchor Bible Dictionary,* 4:558–59 and Chapter 15 below.

Chapter 10

1. The Gospel of Matthew is alone among the New Testament Gospels in identifying the disciple Matthew as a "tax collector," which it does on two occasions: 9:9–13 and 10:3. By contrast, in Mark the tax collector is named Levi, son of Alphaeus (Mark 2:13–17). Since there is also a disciple named James son of Alphaeus, it would appear that the story in Mark refers to this person rather than Matthew. For discussion of the problem, see D. C. Duling, "Matthew [Disciple]," *Anchor Bible Dictionary,* 4:618–22.

2. Preserved in Eusebius *Church History* 3.39.16. This is the passage immediately following Papias's comment regarding the tradition of Mark (discussed in Chapter 9).

3. For these arguments based on a location in Antioch, see J. P. Meier, "Matthew, Gospel of," *Anchor Bible Dictionary,* 4:623–26.

4. E. M. Meyers and J. F. Strange, *Archaeology, the Rabbis, and Early Christianity* (Nashville, TN: Abingdon, 1981), 31–47; D. R. Edwards and C. T. McCollough, *Archaeology and the Galilee* (Atlanta: Scholars Press, 1997); S. Freyne, *Galilee, Jesus, and the Gospels* (Philadelphia: Fortress, 1988); and Freyne, "Galilee, Hellenistic-Roman," *Anchor Bible Dictionary,* 2:895–98.

5. This is the view now taken by Overman, Harrington, and Saldarini. See Box 10.2 for references. See also A. Segal, "Matthew's Jewish Voice," in *Social History of the Matthean Community,* ed. D. L. Balch (Minneapolis: Fortress, 1991), 3–37; and L. M. White, "Crisis Management and Boundary Maintenance: The Social Location of the Matthean Community," in *Social History of the Matthean Community,* 211–47.

6. My translation of the literal Greek.

7. Cf. Gen. 5:1; 6:9; 10:1, 32; 11:10, 27. In Genesis this formula serves as a structural device to bring the story down to Abraham (Gen. 12:1), so it is significant that Matthew's genealogy of Jesus starts with Abraham.

8. See especially the work of K. Stendahl, *The School of St. Matthew* (Philadelphia: Fortress, 1968).

9. Matt. 4:23 (= Mark 1:39 and Luke 4:44), but cf. Matt. 9:35; 10:17; 12:9; and 13:54, where the word "their" is added in each case.

10. The very next passage in Matt. 24:1 continues by integrating the apocalyptic discourse on the destruction of Jerusalem into this same sermon.

11. A person named Luke is mentioned only once (Philem. 24), and there without further description, in the genuine letters of Paul. He is called "Luke the physician" only in Col. 4:14, one of the debated letters. He is also mentioned in 2 Tim. 4:11. He is identified as the author of both the Gospel and Acts in the early list of the New Testament known as the Muratorian Canon.

12. According to the more fully developed form of the legend as found in the apocryphal *Acts of Paul* 11.1 (late second century), Luke returned from a mission to Gaul to meet Paul and Titus in Rome, and he remained with Paul until Paul's execution. On the *Acts of Paul,* see also Chapter 15.

13. See L. T. Johnson, "Luke-Acts, Book of," *Anchor Bible Dictionary,* 4:403–20. That the author was the "historical" Luke is still accepted by Johnson, Hengel, and Marshall. Those who do not think the author was the actual traveling companion of Paul include Fitzmyer, Esler, and Pervo (see Box 10.3 for references).

14. For this later dating, see Esler and Pervo (Box 10.3) plus H. Conzelmann, "Luke's Place in the Development of Early Christianity," in *Studies in Luke-Acts,* ed. L. E. Keck and J. L. Martyn (Nashville, TN: Abingdon, 1966), 298–316, and W. G. Kümmel, *Introduction to the New Testament* (Nashville, TN: Abingdon, 1965), 186. Conzelmann argues for a range of 90–110.

15. Even though this episode in Luke uses the same Q material as that in Matt. 10:5–42, the adaptation is quite different, since Matthew explicitly says not to preach to Gentiles.

16. The quotation is taken from Isa. 61:1–2 in the Septuagint version; however, it omits one phrase from v. 1 ("to heal the brokenhearted") and adds a phrase ("to let the oppressed go free") at the end of the verse. The addition comes instead from Isa. 58:6. Both changes seem to be an effort of the Lukan author to make the passage fit more precisely the apocalyptic meaning.

17. The phrase in Greek is *eschatais hemerais*, a typical way of referring to the eschaton, which is from the same root. The bulk of the quotation is from Joel 3:1–5 in the Septuagint version; however, there are several changes. Among others, the words "in the last days God declares" are an insertion and do not occur in the Septuagint or Hebrew version of this passage. It seems that the Lukan author has added the phrase to make the eschatological connections of the prophecy more explicit.

18. This line of interpretation was first proposed by H. Conzelmann in *The Theology of St. Luke* (New York: Harper & Row, 1961), 16–17, but has been modified in more recent work. See the references in Box 10.4.

19. On the apologetic intent, see P. F. Esler, *Community and Gospel in Luke-Acts: The Social and Political Motivations of Lucan Theology* (Cambridge: Cambridge University Press, 1987), 205–10.

Chapter 11

1. So Irenaeus *Against Heresies* 3.14.1, written ca. 180 CE.

2. In Philemon, Onesimus is indeed returning home carrying the letter, but he has only recently been baptized by Paul in Ephesus (Philem. 10). For discussion of the situation of the letter to Philemon, see Chapter 8.

3. E. Best, "Who Used Whom? The Relationship of Ephesians and Colossians," *New Testament Studies* 43 (1997): 72–96.

4. I have rendered the Greek here as literally as possible to reflect the identical wording; only those words printed in italics are different between the two passages.

5. This is the view taken by Mitton, Furnish, Lincoln, Sampley, and Taylor. The only contemporary commentary arguing for authorship by Paul is Barth. See Box 11.2 for references.

6. This is the view suggested by Dahl in his later work and that of Gnilka. See Box 11.2 for references.

7. Tertullian *Against Marcion* 5.11.17. Marcion seems to have given it the title "from Laodicea" or "from the Laodiceans" based on Col. 4:16. For more on Marcion, see Chapter 16.

8. The first to note these differences and question Pauline authorship was Erasmus (1469–1536).

9. See E. Käsemann, "Ephesians and Acts," in *Studies in Luke-Acts*, ed. L. E. Keck and J. L. Martyn (Nashville, TN: Abingdon, 1966), 288–97.

10. Including Best, Jewett, Marshall, and Malherbe. See Box 11.3 for references.

11. Including Bailey, Collins, Hughes, Holland, Krentz, Krodel, and others. See Box 11.3.

12. Other than this reference, in the New Testament only Revelation uses "Babylon" to mean Rome in this way (cf. Rev. 14:8; 16:19; 17:5; 18:2, 10, 20). As we shall discuss below, there may be at least an indirect connection between them.

13. Cf. *2 Baruch* 11:1; 67:7; *4 Ezra* 3:1–2, 28; *Sibylline Oracles* 5:143.

14. Cf. 1 Pet. 5:1 to Rom. 8:17; also 1 Pet. 1:14 to Rom. 1:22–25; 12:2; 1 Pet. 2:5 to Rom. 12:1.

15. Eusebius *Church History* 3.4.2.

16. See especially *Politics* 1.1253b.1–14; *Magna Moralia* 1.1194b.5–28.

17. Philo *Apology for the Jews* (*Hypothetica*) 7.14; Josephus *Against Apion* 2.190–219.

18. For further reading, see D. L. Balch, *Let Wives Be Submissive: The Domestic Code in 1 Peter* (Chico, CA: Scholars Press, 1981); D. L. Balch, "Household Codes," *Anchor Bible Dictionary*, 3:318–20; C. Osiek and D. L. Balch, *Families in the New Testament World: Households and House Churches* (Louisville, KY: Westminster–John Knox, 1997), 118–21; E. Schüssler Fiorenza, *In Memory of Her: A Feminist Theological Reconstruction of Christian Origins* (New York: Crossroad, 1983), 251–68.

19. In the household code of Ephesians the injunction to wives and husbands is supplemented by a reference to Gen. 2:24: "and the two shall become one flesh" (Eph. 3:31), which is also assumed in the background of the baptismal reunification formula.

20. *Antiquities* 20.200. See Chapter 9.

21. See D. A. Hagner, "James," *Anchor Bible Dictionary,* 3:616–18; F. M. Gillman, "James, Brother of Jesus," *Anchor Bible Dictionary,* 3:620–21.

22. The earliest is Origen *Commentary on John* frag. 124. Eusebius of Caesarea (*Church History* 3.25.3; 2.23.24–25) attributes it to the brother of Jesus but also indicates that not all Christians of the time considered it scripture.

23. Cf. 1 Clem. 10 to James 2:23; 1 Clem. 12 to James 2:25; Herm. *Mand.* 3.1 to James 4:5.

24. See *2 Baruch* 11:1; 67:7; 4 Ezra 3:1–2, 28; *Sibylline Oracles* 5:143, and Chapter 9.

25. See 1 Pet. 5:13; Rev. 14:8; 16:19; 17:5; 18:2, 10, 20.

26. It was not considered canonical in the Greek Orthodox Church until the twelfth century and is still not included in the Syrian Orthodox canon.

27. Irenaeus *Against Heresies* 5.30.3. For Gaius and Dionysius, see Eusebius *Church History* 3.28.

28. Eusebius *Church History* 24.

29. See Justin Martyr *Dialogue with Trypho* 81; cf. Irenaeus *Against Heresies* 5.28–36 and Tertullian *Against Marcion* 3.13, 24.

30. They are Ephesus, Smyrna, Pergamum, Thyatira, Sardis, Philadelphia, and Laodicea. There is an individual letter addressed to each city in Rev. 2–3.

31. It has also been argued, however, that Irenaeus's date for the vision (ca. 96) might be earlier than the actual date of the writing, which would place it sometime in the reign of Trajan (98–117 CE). See A. Farrar in Box 11.6.

32. In general on the imperial cult in Roman Asia, see S. R. F. Price, *Rituals and Power: The Roman Imperial Cult in Asia Minor* (Cambridge: Cambridge University Press, 1984).

33. This term is also found in Acts 19:35 in relation to the career of Paul, but the usage there is anachronistic. On the cult of the Flavian Sebastoi at Ephesus, see S. J. Friesen, *Twice Neokoros Ephesus: Ephesus, Asia, and the Cult of the Flavian Emperors* (Leiden: Brill, 1993).

34. A numerical cryptogram of this sort in Hebrew referring to Nero was found among the Dead Sea Scrolls. The symbolism worked by taking the numerical values of each letter in a name or title and totaling them. For example, the Greek *Domitia. Kais.* is an abbreviation for "Domitian Caesar," the sort of abbreviation one might typically find on a coin legend or in a public inscription. An earlier coin of Domitian from Rome (73 CE) has this type of legend, but in Latin: *Caes. Avg. F. Domit. Cos. II* (meaning "Caesar Augustus Flavius Domitianus, consul for the second time"). Using the standard numerical values for the Greek alphabet, the letters *Domitia. Kais.* total 666. Of course, we should not assume that this is the exact form of the symbol in Rev. 13:17, but it shows how such calculations were made. In some early manuscripts of Revelation the number is 616 instead.

Chapter 12

1. We shall return to the legal implications of this recognition from a Roman perspective in Chapter 14.

2. J. G. Gager, *The Origins of Anti-Semitism: Attitudes Toward Judaism in Pagan and Christian Antiquity* (New York: Oxford University Press, 1983), 149–51.

3. S. J. D. Cohen, *From the Maccabees to the Mishnah* (Philadelphia: Westminster, 1987), 124–37.

4. L. H. Schiffman, "At the Crossroads: Tannaitic Perspectives on the Jewish-Christian Schism," in *Jewish and Christian Self-Definition,* vol. 2, *Aspects of Judaism in the Greco-Roman Period,* ed. E. P. Sanders, A. I. Baumgarten, and A. Mendelsohn (Philadelphia: Fortress, 1981), 115–56.

5. *Apology* 1.31.

6. His real name was Simeon bar Cosibah. Bar Kochba was a made-up name to signal his messianic identity by allusion to the kingly expectation in Num. 24:17: "a star shall arise in Judah." (See Chapter 14, below.)

7. *Yadaim* 4:1.

8. *Yadaim* 3:5.

9. S. J. D. Cohen, "The Significance of Yavneh: Pharisees, Rabbis, and the End of Jewish Sectarianism," *Hebrew Union College Annual* 55 (1986); 17–53; J. P. Lewis, "Jamnia (Jabneh), Council of," *Anchor Bible Dictionary,* 3:634–37.

10. Mishnah *Sanhedrin* 10:1.

11. The legend regarding Rabbi Simeon comes from a very late source in the Babylonian Talmud, *Berakoth* 28b–29a, dating to the fifth or sixth century CE.

12. J. T. Sanders, *Schismatics, Sectarians, Dissidents, Deviants: The First One Hundred Years of Jewish-Christian Relations* (Valley Forge, PA: Trinity Press International, 1993), 58–61; W. Horbury, *Jews and Christians in Contact and Controversy* (Edinburgh: Clark, 1998), 8–14.

13. R. Kimelman, "*Birkat Ha-Minim* and the Lack of Evidence for an Anti-Christian Jewish Prayer in Later Antiquity," Sanders et al., eds., in *Jewish and Christian Self-Definition,* 2:226–44.

14. Eusebius *Church History* 6.12.2–6.

15. For the discovery and analysis of the text, see P. A. Mirecki, "Peter, Gospel of," *Anchor Bible Dictionary,* 5:278–81. For the text and additional references, see Box 12.1.

16. *Gos. Pet.* 14.60 (the quotation is the next to the last line before the text breaks off); earlier in 7.26 Peter's lament as Jesus was buried is given in first person.

17. This presumably means Herod Antipas, son of Herod the Great, and tetrarch of the Galilee 4 BCE–38 CE. He shows up in connection with the trials and death of Jesus only in the Gospel of Luke. On the other hand, the text is sufficiently vague and the characterization of Herod is particularly negative, so that it almost appears to be an anachronistic use of the Matthean characterization of Herod the Great

18. This is the view of H. Koester and J. D. Crossan.

19. There is another work known as the *Preachings of Peter* (*Kerygmata Petrou*), which should not be confused with this one, although the two titles may derive from a similar ideal of Petrine tradition. We shall discuss the *Kerygmata Petrou* below in Chapter 15 in conjunction with the Pseudo-Clementine literature.

20. The extracts are quoted in Clement's *Stromateis* 1.29.182; 2.15.68; 6.5.39–41, 43, 48; 6.7.58; and 6.15.128. They are collected and discussed in E. Hennecke and W. Schneemelcher, eds., *New Testament Apocrypha,* 2 vols. (Philadelphia: Westminster, 1964), 2:94–102.

21. Especially Aristides, Athenagoras, and Theophilus, who will be discussed in Chapter 14 below.

22. *Stromateis* 6.5.39–41.

23. See K. E. Corley, "Peter, Preaching of," *Anchor Bible Dictionary,* 5:282; H. Koester, *Introduction to the New Testament,* 2d ed., 2 vols. (Berlin: DeGruyter, 2000), 168.

24. For the simple name Thomas, see Mark 6:18; Matt. 10:3; Luke 9:15; and Acts 1:13; it is usually listed in close proximity to Matthew. For Didymus Thomas, see John 11:16; 20:24; and 21:2, 6. Other than in the *Gospel of Thomas,* the full name Didymus Judas Thomas only occurs in a Syriac manuscript of John (at 14:22).

25. For the later literature associated with the Thomas tradition, see Chapter 15.

26. There are forty-eight passages in all that are parallel between Q and the *Gospel of Thomas.* For a listing, see Box 6.3.

27. A total of sixty-eight sayings have some affinity for one of the canonical Gospels, including John. For a complete catalogue of these relationships, see Koester, *Ancient Christian Gospels* (Harrisburg: Trinity Press International, 1990), 86–128.

28. H. Koester, *Ancient Christian Gospels,* 132.

29. Hippolytus *Against All Heresies* 5.7.20.

30. R. Valantasis (12–17) and B. Layton (377–379) argue for a date ca. 100–110 CE. S. Patterson (113–18) argues for a date in the mid–first century CE. H. Koester (*Introduction,* 157) accepts an early date for the earliest layers of the text only, but argues for later reworkings. See Box 12.2 for references.

31. *Against Heresies* 3.1.2. See also E. Pagels, *The Johannine Gospel in Gnostic Exegesis* (Missoula, MT: Scholars Press, 1972).

32. A fact already noted by Irenaeus (*Against Heresies* 3.2.12). Cf. Origen's *Commentary on John,* which was directed as a counter to an earlier commentary by a Gnostic interpreter named Heracleon (ca. 170 CE).

33. There is only one oblique reference to "the sons of Zebedee" in John 21:2. If one assumes a knowledge of the synoptic lists of the disciples or stories such as that in Mark 10:35–40, then this clearly points to John. Even so, John as a character is never mentioned by name.

34. The other references to "the beloved disciple" are 19:26–27; 20:1–8; 21:7; and 21:20–24. The last of these refers directly to the passage in 13:23 and will thus become important. In two other passages (18:15–16; 19:35) an unnamed disciple has been thought to be the same as "the beloved disciple," but it is not certain.

35. This tradition was also related to the date and authorship of Revelation. See Chapter 11.

36. This is the widely accepted view of R. Brown. See Box 12.3 for references.

37. Mark 10:35–40 has been taken by some to indicate that both of the sons of Zebedee had died before or during the first revolt, as Acts 12:1–4 confirms for James.

38. Some have argued that $\mathfrak{P}^{52}$ (John Rylands Papyrus 457) can be dated as early as 125, thus making a date for the Gospel as late as 120 impossible; however, the merits of this dating for $\mathfrak{P}^{52}$ are very questionable on papyrological grounds. It should be dated between 150 and 200 CE. See now B. Nongbri, "The Use and Abuse of $\mathfrak{P}^{52}$: Papyrological Pitfalls in the Dating of the Fourth Gospel," *Harvard Theological Review* (forthcoming).

39. The situation of 2 and 3 John reflect this tradition. See Chapter 16 and Fig. 16.1. For the later legends see Irenaeus *Against Heresies* 2.22.3; 3.1.2; 3.4; Justin Martyr *Dialogue with Trypho* 81.4; Clement of Alexandria *Who Is the Rich Man?* 42; Eusebius *Church History* 3.18.1; 23.3–4; 39.3–4; 4:18.6–8; 5.8.4; 18.14; 20.6. An apocryphal *Acts of John* that circulated in Asia Minor in the latter half of the second century also placed John in Ephesus. See Chapter 15.

40. This is the view of Koester and others. See Box 12.3 for references.

41. Eusebius *Church History* 6.14.7.

42. John 5:8–9 / Mark 2:11–12; John 6:7 / Mark 6:37; John 12:3, 5 / Mark 14:3, 5; John 12:25 / Mark 8:35 (et par.); John 13:20 / Mark 9:37 (et par.); John 14:31 / Mark 14:42; John 18:18 / Mark 14:54; John 18:39 / Mark 15:9.

43. John 12:3 / Luke 7:38; John 12:2–8 / Luke 10:38–42; John 13:2, 26 / Luke 22:3; John 13:38 / Luke 22:34; John 18:10 / Luke 22:50; John 18:13, 24 / Luke 3:2 + Acts 4:6.

44. This is the view of D. M. Smith, *John Among the Gospels.* See Box 12.3 for reference.

45. As reflected in *The Dialogue of the Savior* (see above) along with other texts from Nag Hammadi.

46. These two "unknown gospels" are extant only in fragmentary form; therefore, title and attributions are not preserved. Neither one matches any passage or event in the canonical Gospels or other known apocryphal Gospels. One of these (Oxyrhynchus Papyrus 840) has affinities with the Synoptics, but in the form of a controversy dialogue about "living water" (compare John 4:10). The other (Egerton Papyrus 2) contains several unique dialogues similar to those in the Gospel of John. For text and introduction, see Hennecke and Schneemelcher, *New Testament Apocrypha,* 1:92–97.

47. John also presupposes a recognition of eucharistic ritual patterns in the feeding miracle based on the use of the key terms "take," "give thanks," and "give out" (6:11).

48. See the works of Meeks and Martyn. References in Box 12.3.

49. It has often been compared to the *Odes of Solomon.* For an introduction and the text, see J. H. Charlesworth, ed. *Old Testament Pseudepigrapha,* 2 vols. (Garden City: Doubleday, 1985), 2:725–71; see also J. H. Charlesworth, "Solomon, Odes of," *Anchor Bible Dictionary,* 6:114–15.

50. I have given here a more literal rendering of the Greek to show the similarities of language to the prologue of the Gospel of John. The *touching* with "our own hands" is highly reminiscent of the "doubting Thomas" episode in John 20:24–29, to be discussed below.

51. For example, 1 John 2:18 and 4:17 reflect an imminent eschatological expectation not found in the Gospel, which assumes more of a realized eschatology typical of docetism.

52. This is the view most recently of U. Schnelle. See Box 12.4 for references.

53. See also Koester, *Introduction to the New Testament*, 2:202–4.

54. The term "antichrist" is used only in 1 John 2:18, 22; 4:3; and 2 John 7. It is not used in, nor does it have any connection to, Revelation.

55. The actual term "docetists" (Greek *dokētai*), as seen in the letter of Serapion regarding the *Gospel of Peter*, was coined by Christian writers of the late second century and after, for whom it is associated with "heretical" teachings: Clement *Stromateis* 7.17 (ca. 200 CE); Hippolytus *Against Heresies* 8.2, 8, 11; 10.16 (ca. 220 CE).

56. The name "Didymus Thomas" is given at John 11:16; 14:5; 20:4, 26–28; and 21:2. A Syriac manuscript of John 14:22 (where for the only time in John a disciple named Judas other than Judas Iscariot is mentioned) gives the name "Judas Thomas."

57. This is the view of U. Schnelle, *Antidocetic Christology in the Gospel of John*, 139–44, who also argues that the Gospel in its final form is subsequent to 1 John (53–63). See Box 12.3 for reference.

58. In 𝔓⁴⁶, one of the earliest manuscripts of the Pauline letters (ca. 200 CE), Hebrews comes immediately after Romans. For further discussion of the formation of these early books of scripture, see Chapter 17 and Fig. 17.3.

59. Tertullian *On Modesty* 20; for Clement, see Eusebius *Church History* 6.14.2; 6.25.14. Various other names have been proposed by modern scholars, including Prisca and Apollos, but none have gained substantial support.

60. Eusebius *Church History* 6.25.14.

61. It is not impossible that the relationship goes the other way, i.e., that *1 Clement* originated this catena of scripture quotations and that the author of Hebrews seized upon it as a thematic compositional device; however, this is not the majority opinion.

62. This identification was first made explicit in the fourth century by Eusebius (*Church History* 3.16–18).

63. For more on *1 Clement* and the question of dating, see Chapter 13.

64. This is the widely accepted view of H. W. Attridge, *Hebrews*, Hermeneia (Philadelphia: Fortress, 1989), 7–8; some older arguments for an early dating of Hebrews (ca. 60–80 CE) are no longer considered likely by the majority of scholars.

65. R. Fuller ("Hebrews," 1–3) compares the tone and perspective both to Luke 1:1–4 and to the prologue to the Gospel of John. See Box 12.6 for references.

66. *1 Clement* clearly presupposes a knowledge of at least some of Paul's letters, especially Romans and 1 Corinthians. The same might well be true for the author of Hebrews. So notice Heb. 2:6–9, an exposition of Ps. 8:5–7, which is both based on earlier allusions to Ps. 110:1 (Heb 1:3, 13) and anticipates the distinctive, central exposition on Ps. 110:1–4 (Heb. 5:11–10:25). Among earlier writings only 1 Cor. 15:25–27 explicitly uses this passage from Ps. 8 to explicate Ps. 110:1 in reference to the death and exaltation of Christ. This kind of exposition is perhaps also anticipated in Eph. 1:20–22, which in turn is an expansion on the "Christ hymn" of Col. 1:15–20 (but see also *1 Clem.* 36.2–6).

67. As noted by Attridge (*Hebrews*, 155, 163), the earliest known manuscript of Heb. 6:1–2 (𝔓⁴⁶), in which Hebrews follows immediately after Romans, puts "instruction" at the beginning of v. 2 in apposition to "foundation" in v. 1. The NRSV thus translates it correctly as follows: "Therefore let us go on toward perfection, leaving behind the basic teaching about Christ, and not laying again the foundation: repentance from dead works and faith toward God, instruction about baptisms, as well as laying on of hands, resurrection of the dead, and eternal judgment." In other words, the "foundational teachings" that the community is moving beyond includes this entire list of items that sounds like a summary of early Pauline themes from the genuine letters and/or from Acts.

68. For the various, and largely inconclusive, theories regarding the situation of the addressees, see the commentary by Attridge, *Hebrews*, 9–13.

69. I have given here a translation of the Septuagint version because it has a slightly different wording of v. 3 from that found in the Hebrew: "Your people will offer themselves willingly on the

day you lead your forces on the holy mountains. From the womb of the morning, like dew, your youth will come to you" (Ps. 110:3, MT). The difference of the wording in v. 3 allows the Septuagint to be read as a reference to the preexistence of Christ as well as his eternal priesthood after the order of Melchizedek.

70. A scroll from Cave 11 at Qumran is called "Melchizedek" because it explores the subject.

Chapter 13

1. Note especially the prologue in Luke 1:2: "delivered to us by those who were eyewitnesses and servants of the word."

2. The manuscript of Codex Alexandrinus was written ca. 400 CE. The Greek Orthodox patriarch of Constantinople, Cyril Lucar, who had previously been patriarch of Alexandria, sent it as a gift to King James I of England (namesake of the King James Version of the Bible). It arrived in 1627 and in 1757 was deposited in the British Museum, where it still resides.

3. As seen in Clement of Alexandria (ca. 200 CE) and Origen (ca. 220–54 CE). For further discussion, see Chapter 17.

4. This assumption was based on a convergence of elements. The name Clement occurs in Paul's letter to the Philippians (4:3), traditionally assumed to have been written from Rome (see Chapter 8). The most widespread legends held that Paul and Peter died in Rome at the hands of Nero in 64 CE. Hence later Christian tradition from at least the mid-third century identified Clement of Rome with the Clement of Philippians; see Eusebius *Church History* 3.4.9. Eusebius (*Church History* 3.3.3, citing the second-century bishop Irenaeus) further identified this same Clement as the third bishop of Rome after Peter, while Tertullian says that Clement was consecrated directly by Peter himself (*On the Prescription of Heretics* 32).

5. See J. C. Treat, "Barnabas, Epistle of," *Anchor Bible Dictionary*, 1:611–14.

6. Some scholars have proposed that chaps. 2–16 constitute an earlier edition that was reworked when the "Two Ways" material was added.

7. Cf. 4 Ezra (see Chapter 9) and Revelation 13 (Chapter 11).

8. R. Kraft, *Barnabas and the Didache*, vol. 3 of *The Apostolic Fathers* (New York: Thomas Nelson, 1965), 45–56. Asia Minor has also been proposed, but this seems rather unlikely.

9. The author of *Barnabas* is rather emphatic on the order of the letters, which may suggest that he is well aware of the different wording in the LXX passages of Genesis.

10. H. Koester (*Introduction to the New Testament*, 2d ed., 2 vols. [Berlin: DeGruyter, 2000], 2:282), followed by Kraft (*Barnabas and the Didache*, 20), argues that the *Epistle of Barnabas* does not use any New Testament document, including the Gospels, but that it shows knowledge of a general oral tradition of Jesus that is, if anything, presynoptic. Its method of scriptural interpretation is similar to Hebrews and is exemplary of the mode of "searching the prophets" for material that might be applied to Jesus.

11. The earliest possible references come from a fragmentary text attributed to Irenaeus (ca. 180 CE) and from allusions in Clement of Alexandria (ca. 200 CE). In both cases it seems to be given "scriptural" authority, but it is not certain whether they refer to the text in the form now known. From the fourth century, see Eusebius *Church History* 3.25.4, where it is labeled as "illegitimate" for inclusion in the New Testament; however, Eusebius's statement might refer to a different work with a similar title, "The Teachings [plural!] of the Apostles."

12. The manuscript, known as Codex Hierosolymitanus, also contained a copy of the *Epistle of Barnabas*, *1–2 Clement*, the *Letters* of Ignatius (longer version), a work on the Old Testament by John Chrysostom, and some other, hitherto unknown documents. In 1922 a fragmentary copy from a miniature papyrus codex (P. Oxyrhynchus 1782) was found in Egypt, and scholars were thus able to confirm the basic form of the text.

13. See Chapter 6, and cf. Matt. 10:5–23, but note also the warning about "false prophets" in Matt. 7:15–20.

14. Notably it occurs in a fifth-century Coptic codex Bible as well as in Codex Hierosolymitanus, the eleventh-century codex containing the text of the *Didache*.

15. Eusebius *Church History* 4.23.11.

16. *Miscellanies* 5.12.; Eusebius *Church History* 3.16.

17. The letter of Dionysius of Corinth (noted above) would be the earliest direct reference to its authorship by Clement; the notice of Irenaeus (*Against Heresies* 3.3.3, ca. 177–180 CE), discussed below, is the next oldest.

18. Origen *Commentary on John* 6.36.

19. Irenaeus *Against Heresies* 3.3.3.

20. Tertullian *Prescription of Heretics* 32; Pseudo-Clement *Recognitions* 1.7–13.

21. For discussion and bibliography, see L. M. White, *The Social Origins of Christian Architecture*, 2 vols. (Harrisburg, PA: Trinity Press International, 1996–97), 1:114; 2:1–5, 219–28.

22. Eusebius *Church History* 3.15–18.

23. Suetonius *Domitian* 15. He does not mention the wife but does add that as consul Flavius Clemens was "most contemptibly lazy."

24. Dio Cassius *History of Rome* 67.14.

25. Here he is most certainly wrong, for she is actually the granddaughter of Vespasian and thus a niece of Domitian himself. Flavius Clemens is a relative as well as her husband but cannot be her uncle.

26. Eusebius *Church History* 3.18.

27. *Church History* 3.34, 3.15.

28. The hypothesis of J. S. Jeffers (*Conflict at Rome: Social Hierarchy in Early Christianity* [Minneapolis: Fortress, 1991], 50–62) that the Christian Clement was a freedman of the family of Flavius Clemens and that Flavia Domitilla had bequeathed a tomb for the Christian members of her household is an ingenious solution to the problem; however, Jeffers's argument is entirely unconvincing, particularly on the archaeological evidence from the catacomb inscriptions and that of San Clemente itself.

29. Eusebius *Church History* 3.17, where he makes it a continuation of the "campaign" of evil inaugurated by Nero.

30. The point is still debated among scholars, but the weight of the evidence indicates that the opening sentence of *1 Clement*, which refers to "the sudden and repeated misfortunes and hardships that have befallen us" (1.1), does not refer to a persecution at Rome. See L. L. Welborn, "Clement, First Epistle of," *Anchor Bible Dictionary*, 1:1060, and the fuller discussion in O. M. Bakke, *"Concord and Peace": A Rhetorical Analysis of the First Letter of Clement* (Tübingen: Mohr-Siebeck, 2001), 8–11.

31. The reference to Clement in the *Shepherd* of Hermas suggests a connection and a slightly later period for Clement's activities. In a vision Hermas was told to give his book to Clement, "who will send it to cities abroad, for he had been entrusted with that task" (Herm. *Vis.* 2.4.3). It is hard not to think that this is a reference to Clement as letter writer for the church at Rome, and thus to his association with *1 Clement*. For Hermas, Ignatius, and Polycarp, see the discussions below.

32. See especially G. W. Bowersock, *Greek Sophists in the Roman Empire* (Oxford: Clarendon, 1969), 68. Bowersock stresses that this is a particular issue in the early to middle part of the second century, or what is usually called the "Second Sophistic." Among many other examples we may cite the public speech of Dio Chrysostom (*Oration* 38) delivered to the people of Nicomedia in Bithynia in 101 CE, in which he refers to the prevailing opinion at Rome that civic discord (*stasis*) is a peculiarly "Greek failing" (*Oration* 38.38). The opposite of *stasis* is "concord" or "harmony," as used by both by Dio Chrysostom and *1 Clement*.

33. See C. Breytenbach, "Civic Concord and Cosmic Harmony: Sources of Metaphoric Mapping in *1 Clement* 20.3," in *Early Christianity and Classical Culture: Comparative Studies*, ed. J. T. Fitzgerald, T. H. Olbricht, and L. M. White (Leiden: Brill, 2003), 259–73.

34. *1 Clem.* 42.4; 44.1–6; 47.1, 6. We shall return to this issue in the next chapter.

35. Athanasius was the bishop of Alexandria at the time of the Council of Nicea (325 CE). For discussion, see J. Quasten, *Patrology*, 3 vols. (Washington, DC: Newman Press, 1962), 1:58–59.

36. Eusebius *Church History* 4.23.9–11 (discussed above).

37. For further reading, see R. M. Grant and H. H. Graham, *The Apostolic Fathers*, vol. 2, *First and Second Clement* (New York: Thomas Nelson, 1965); R. M. Grant, "Clement, Second Epistle of," *Anchor Bible Dictionary*, 1:1061; Quasten, *Patrology*, 1:53–58; and K. P. Donfried, *The Setting of Second Clement in Early Christianity* (Leiden: Brill, 1974).

38. A third- to fourth-century list of the books accepted as scripture.

39. Clement *Miscellanies* 1.29; Tertullian *On Modesty* 10; Eusebius *Church History* 3.4.6; 3.25.4.

40. *Against Heresies* 4.20.

41. Some scholars have argued that this is the earliest layer of the work and was composed independently of the rest.

42. For example, *Mandate* 1 is an admonition to believe in the one God, creator of the world; cf. the opening of the "Two Ways" in *Did.* 1.2.

43. Cf. *The Tabula of Cebes*, a first-century CE moral allegory from the Stoic tradition. For discussion of possible relationships with Hermas, see J. T. Fitzgerald and L. M. White, *The Tabula of Cebes: Text and Translation with Introduction and Notes* (Chico, CA: Scholars Press, 1983), 16–20. See also C. Osiek, *The Shepherd of Hermas*, Hermeneia (Minneapolis: Fortress, 1999), 25.

44. Some have seen the reference to persecution in Herm. *Vis.* 2.2.7 as a more pressing issue, but the comment seems rather isolated.

45. These are the most frequently cited dates for the letters, but we shall discuss the matter further below.

46. The main Greek manuscript of the letters puts them in a different order, thus: *Smyrneans, Polycarp, Ephesians, Magnesians, Philadelphians, Trallians, Romans*. It has been suggested that this was the order in which Polycarp had placed them in his collection. Although this premise is possible, owing to the relative importance of the cities, at least from Polycarp's vantage point, it is difficult to be sure. Of all the letters, those to Ephesus and Magnesia are the longest. The first to work out the chronological sequence based on Ignatius's location (as described above) was Eusebius (*Church History* 3.36.5–10).

47. Cf. Ign. *Eph.* 20.1, where Ignatius promises to write "a second petition"; however, no such document exists even among the spurious writings.

48. *Church History* 3.22.

49. *Church History* 3.36.2; *Chronicon* 2.158, 162. John Malalas, an early Byzantine chronographer from Antioch (sixth century CE), dates his appointment to 44 CE, i.e., near the time that Peter was assumed to have departed from Antioch. Such a date and situation are purely fictional. Even so, it is Malalas who dates the arrest of Ignatius under Trajan at the time of a great earthquake in Antioch. The earthquake would place the arrest (and the persecution of Christians) after December 115 CE. See G. Downey, *Ancient Antioch* (Princeton, NJ: Princeton University Press, 1963), 131–33.

50. According to the hypothesis of R. Joly, the entire corpus of Ignatius's letters was a fictional compilation of ca. 160–170 CE. For discussion, see W. Schoedel, *Ignatius of Antioch*, Hermeneia (Philadelphia: Fortress, 1985), 6–7. Also for discussion of the problems of dating and the authenticity of the letters, see C. Trevett, *A Study of Ignatius of Antioch in Syria and Asia* (Lewiston, NY: Edwin Mellen, 1992), 6–15. For example, Irenaeus (*Against Heresies* 5.28.4) quotes a passage from Ignatius, Ign. *Rom.* 4.1, and attributes it simply to "a certain man . . . when he was condemned to the wild beasts." The reference, if to Ignatius, is remarkable, since one would have thought his name would have been more famous. It is also striking that Theophilus, bishop of Antioch ca. 169–180, who wrote a defense of Christians (*To Autolycus*), makes no reference whatsoever to Ignatius or his letters.

51. Notice his "mythological" reading of the origins of the heavenly Christ as a star that was worshiped by a heavenly chorus of the sun, moon, and other stars (Ign. *Eph.* 19). The passage is reminiscent of the dream of Joseph (Gen. 37:9–11). The elaborate mythological tradition in the *Ascension of Isaiah*, which also contains "Isaiah's" vision of the angelic worship of God, contains a second entity

called "the angel of the Holy Spirit" (*Ascen. Isa.* 9.33–36). This Jewish text dates originally from the second to first century BCE but shows numerous effects from later reworking, especially by Christians. So, note in particular *Ascen. Isa.* 10–11, which has strong similarities to that in Ign. *Eph.* 19.

52. See Chapter 12, and note that a similar axis of influences between Syria and Asia Minor seems to be at work.

53. See Ign. *Eph.* 9.2 ("the last of them and an untimely birth"), where he seems to allude to Paul's phrase regarding his own call vision in 1 Cor. 15:8. It is not a quotation, however, only an allusion. There are also some reverberations of the deutero-Pauline Ephesian letter (see Chapter 11), but direct knowledge of the text is not certain. It is possible that Ignatius had only heard bits of Paul's language from scattered sources, including Polycarp himself. Polycarp certainly did know at least some collection of the letters of Paul. See below.

54. On this point, see W. Schoedel, "Ignatius and the Reception of the Gospel of Matthew in Antioch," in *Social History of the Matthean Community,* ed. D. Balch (Minneapolis: Fortress, 1991), 129–77.

55. See W. Schoedel, "Ignatius, Epistles of," *Anchor Bible Dictionary,* 3:386.

56. Schoedel, "Ignatius," 3:385.

57. Ignatius clearly calls him bishop (Ign. *Pol.* address), as does Irenaeus (*Against Heresies* 3.3.4); however, Polycarp seems to use only the term elder (*presbyteros,* Pol. *Phil.* 5.3, 6.1, and the address).

58. For the martyr literature in relation to the early persecutions, see the next chapter and Box 14.1.

59. W. Schoedel, "Polycarp, Martyrdom of," *Anchor Bible Dictionary,* 5:392–93.

60. Schoedel, "Polycarp," 395.

61. Eusebius *Church History* 4.15.1–46, which quotes extensively from the *Martyrdom* in the form known from Pionius. The exact date is provided by Eusebius's *Chronicon.*

62. Irenaeus *Against Heresies* 3.3.4; Eusebius *Church History* 4.14.

63. Irenaeus's statements are preserved in Eusebius *Church History* 5.20.8.

64. *Church History* 3.36.13–15.

65. Most notably, in Pol. *Phil.* 9, Polycarp refers to Ignatius's death as a past event, while in Pol. *Phil.* 13 he asks if the Philippians know any more about what happened to Ignatius.

66. This is the hypothesis first proposed by P. N. Harrison, *Polycarp's Two Epistles to the Philippians* (Cambridge: Cambridge University Press, 1936); see W. Schoedel, "Polycarp, Epistle of," *Anchor Bible Dictionary,* 5:390–92.

67. The qualifications for bishops and deacons in the Pastoral Epistles are later. See Chapter 16.

68. It is just possible that the source for this discussion comes from the letters 2 and 3 John (see esp. 2 John 7). The author of these letters is simply called "the Elder," and it is thus tempting to think that they might represent some of the lost letters of Polycarp mentioned by Irenaeus or at least someone close to his orbit of influence. See Chapter 16.

69. Cf. Pol. *Phil.* 2.3 with *1 Clem.* 13.2.

70. Cf. Pol. *Phil.* 8.1 with 1 Pet. 2:22–24. Given that this is a catena of references to the death of Jesus, which in turn are based on passages from Isaiah, it is not possible to be certain that 1 Peter is the source. Both could be working from a common tradition.

71. Cf. Pol. *Phil.* 12.1 with Eph. 4:26.

72. Pol. *Phil.* 12.1, which combines a quote from Ps. 4:5 with the allusion to Eph. 4:26 noted above.

Chapter 14

1. See *Histories* 5.5.

2. Pliny's *Epistles* 4.13 is addressed to Tacitus (in 104 CE) and shows their close friendship. Also, in *Epistles* 4.15 Pliny refers to Tacitus's friendship. There are a total of eleven letters from Pliny to Tacitus, most dating to the period between 100 and 109; cf. *Epistles* 1.6.

3. On Pliny's career and letters, see A. N. Sherwin-White, *The Letters of Pliny: A Historical and Social Commentary* (Oxford: Clarendon, 1966), 69–82.

4. For Book 10, see Sherwin-White, *Letters of Pliny,* 523–54; W. Williams, *Pliny: Correspondence with Trajan from Bithynia (Epistles X)* (Warminster: Aris & Phillips, 1990).

5. For a list of Pliny's friends and acquaintances, see Sherwin-White, *The Letters of Pliny,* 738–62.

6. R. L. Wilken, *The Christians as the Romans Saw Them* (New Haven, CT: Yale University Press, 1984), 1–30. Wilken assumes the traditional date of 17 Sept. 111 for his arrival; however, Sherwin-White dates the mission earlier, beginning in 109–111 (*Letters of Pliny,* 81). Most recently, Williams's analysis of the letters has yielded the date 17 Sept. 110 for Pliny's arrival, and his dates will be followed here.

7. Book 10, *Epistles* 17–24 (fall 110).

8. Book 10, *Epistles* 33–34 (Nov. 110–Jan. 111).

9. Book 10, *Epistles* 90–91 (Sept.–Oct. 111).

10. Book 10, *Epistles* 92–93 (fall 111).

11. The "heretic" Marcion (who died in ca. 154) had been born in Sinope, where his father was reportedly a prosperous shipowner and also the local Christian bishop. Marcion himself moved from Sinope to Ephesus by ca. 120. Hence, the presence of a Christian community earlier in Sinope comes very close to the time of Pliny's visit, if not some years earlier. The next identifiable location in Pliny's letters, Amastris (*Epistles* 98), is also a possibility. On Marcion, see also Chapter 16 below.

12. Pliny's report is Book 10, *Epistles* 96. Trajan's reply is *Epistles* 97.

13. *Epistles* 96.1. This is a telling comment since Pliny began his public career as a lawyer specializing in inheritance cases, and his official career at Rome would have included serving as public magistrate to adjudicate certain kinds of civil proceedings.

14. *Epistles* 10.96.5.

15. His full name is Caius Minicius Fundanus. The form Minucius is most likely from rendering the Latin into Greek. He served as proconsul of Asia in 124–25 CE. The text is preserved in Eusebius (*Church History* 4.9), who says Justin Martyr included a Latin copy of the letter in his writings; however, no such copy of the edict is preserved in any manuscripts of Justin. The text is in Greek and is said to be Eusebius's own translation from the Latin in Justin. While serving as suffect consul in Rome in 107 CE, Minicius Fundanus also received several letters from Pliny the Younger, notably *Epistles* 1.9, 4.15, 5.16, and 6.6.

16. Alluded to by Justin Martyr (*Apology* 1.68; 2.68; ca. 140–60); by Hegesippus (ca. 160s), as preserved in Eusebius (*Church History* 3.32.1); and by Melito, bishop of Sardis (ca. 170–80), as preserved in Eusebius (*Church History* 4.26).

17. Eusebius (*Church History* 4.13.1–7) also records another rescript regarding the Christians addressed to the Council of Asia by Marcus Aurelius (160–80 CE); however, many scholars consider it spurious or at least heavily reworked by Christian writers.

18. W. H. C. Frend, *Martyrdom and Persecution in the Early Church* (Oxford: Blackwell, 1965).

19. For collections and discussion, see H. Musurillo, *The Acts of the Christian Martyrs* (Oxford: Clarendon, 1972); G. Bisbee, *Pre-Decian Acts of Martyrs and Commentarii* (Philadelphia: Fortress, 1988); T. D. Barnes, "Pre-Decian *Acta Martyrum,*" *Journal of Theological Studies* 19 (1968): 509–31; and E. Ferguson, "Martyrs, Martyrdom," *Encyclopedia of Early Christianity,* 2d ed., 2 vols. (New York: Garland, 1997), 2:724–28.

20. See J. Gager, *Kingdom and Community: The Social World of Early Christianity* (Englewood Cliffs, NJ: Prentice Hall, 1975), 66–92.

21. As noted in Chapter 13, Ignatius is the first to use the term: Ign. *Magn.* 10.1, 3; *Rom* 3.3; *Phld.* 6.1.

22. H. von Campenhausen, *Ecclesiastical Authority and Spiritual Power in the Early Church* (Stanford, CA: Stanford University Press, 1969).

23. Paul: Rom. 12:6; 12:10; 14:6, 22; 29–32; Acts 13:1; 15:32; 21:9–10; cf. Eph. 4:11.

24. Matt. 11:9; 13:57; 14:5; Mark 6:4; Luke 7:26, 36; 24:19.

25. Von Campenhausen's notion of *charisma* is based on that of Max Weber. See also Gager, *Kingdom and Community*, 68–69.

26. L. M. White, "Paul and *Pater Familias*," in *Paul in the Greco-Roman World: A Handbook*, ed. J. P. Sampley (Harrisburg, PA: Trinity Press International, 2003), 457–87; P. Lampe, "Paul, Patrons and Clients," in Sampley, *Paul in the Greco-Roman World*, 488–523. Specifically on Von Campenhausen's thesis in light of Eph. 4, see L. M. White, "Social Authority in the House Church Setting and Ephesians 4:1–16," *Restoration Quarterly* 29 (1987): 209–28.

27. This is the view well articulated by P. N. Harrison, *Polycarp's Two Epistles to the Philippians* (Cambridge: Cambridge University Press, 1936), 79–106.

28. *Against Heresies* 3.3.4 (quoted at the beginning of Chapter 13).

29. Network theory is an analytical method of group interactions in sociology. For theoretical definitions and historical application, see L. M. White, *Social Networks in the Early Christian Environment: Issues and Methods for Social History*, Semeia 56 (Atlanta: Scholars Press, 1991).

30. Socrates was allowed to commit suicide in 399 BCE after losing the case. Plato's account of the trial and Socrates's defense was not written until ten or twenty years later and was intended to serve as a defense of Socrates as teacher in the way that he was idealized within Plato's own school.

31. This was the formal petition delivered by the Jewish delegation led by Philo in the aftermath of the pogrom in Alexandria of 37 CE. It was addressed to the emperor Gaius (Caligula), who died in that same year, and was eventually received by Claudius, who acted in favor of the Jews.

32. A variant of this same goal may be seen in the martyr literature when the Christian who is on trial delivers a speech in defense of his or her faith. In real life lengthy speeches of this sort were most unlikely in the Roman court context, as is illustrated in the court-style records in the *Acts* of the martyrs literature (see Box 14.1). The exchanges in these court scenes are usually very clipped and brief. Hence when lengthy defense speeches appear in the martyr literature, they are probably being influenced by the genre of the apology and, similarly, were written primarily for Christians.

33. R. M. Grant, *Greek Apologists of the Second Century* (Philadelphia: Westminster, 1988); E. F. Osborn, "The Apologists," in *The Early Christian World*, ed. P. F. Esler, 2 vols. (London: Routledge, 2000), 1:525–51; E. F. Osborn, *The Emergence of Christian Theology* (Cambridge: Cambridge University Press, 1993).

34. Athenagoras *Supplication for the Christians* 3.

35. R. J. Hoffmann, *Celsus on the True Doctrine: A Discourse Against the Christians* (New York: Oxford University Press, 1987), 5–45.

36. Celsus, *True Discourse*, as preserved in Origen *Against Celsus* 3.49.

37. *Apology* 1.1.

38. *Dialogue with Trypho* 2–8.

39. *Dialogue with Trypho* 8.1; *Apology* 12.1.

40. *Apology* 2.3.1; 1.26.8; *Dialogue with Trypho*.

41. *Apology* 1.5–6; 1.46.

42. *Apology* 2.6, 13; cf. Athenagoras *Supplication* 10.2–5. Apparently, Justin does not know the Gospel of John.

43. *Acts of Justin* 3.1–4. See the discussion in L. M. White, *Social Origins of Christian Architecture*, 2 vols. (Harrisburg, PA: Trinity Press International, 1996–97), 2:42–43.

Chapter 15

1. *Apology* 1.67, dating to ca. 150 CE (quoted in full at the end of the previous chapter).

2. H. Koester, *Ancient Christian Gospels: Their History and Development* (Philadelphia: Trinity Press International, 1990), 37–42.

3. The Greek term can also mean lines, drawings, paintings, or other representations.

4. Cf. Rom. 1:2; *1 Clem.* 45.2; 53.1. Other adjectives (such as "of the prophets") might also be used, as in the passage quoted above from Justin (cf. Matt. 26:54). Interestingly enough, the term (with or without the adjective) does not occur in the letters of Ignatius or Polycarp.

5. For the text, see *The Old Testament Pseudepigrapha*, ed. J. H. Charlesworth, 2 vols. (Garden City, NY: Doubleday, 1983), 1:5–90; M. E. Stone, *Scripture, Sects, and Visions* (Philadelphia: Fortress, 1980), 37–56.

6. Several different copies of *1 Enoch* were found among the Dead Sea Scrolls (Cave 4). For early allusions to the story in which it is simply taken for granted that it belongs to the "scriptural" tradition, see Luke 10:17–18; 1 Pet. 3:19–20; 2 Pet. 2:4; Jude 6, 14–15; *Barn.* 4.3; 16.5; Justin *Apology* 2.5; Athenagoras *Supplication* 24–25; and Irenaeus *Against Heresies* 4.16.2. For further discussion, see W. Adler and J. C. VanderKam, *The Jewish Apocalyptic Heritage in Early Christianity* (Minneapolis: Fortress, 1996), 33–101.

7. A reference to the God "who burned up the stubborn giants" was incorporated in the Paris Magical Papyrus as part of an exorcism spell, *PGM* IV. 3007–86, quoted in Chapter 3.

8. Quoted in Origen *Against Celsus* 5.52 (as translated by H. Chadwick, *Origen, Contra Celsum* [Cambridge: Cambridge University Press, 1965], 305); the translation has been adapted by the author.

9. J. C. VanderKam, *Enoch and the Growth of an Apocalyptic Tradition* (Washington, DC: Catholic Biblical Association, 1984), 76–178.

10. This is the view of J. T. Milik, *The Books of Enoch: Aramaic Fragments from Qumran Cave 4* (Oxford: Clarendon, 1976), 89–98; but see G. W. E. Nickelsburg, *Jewish Literature Between the Bible and the Mishnah* (Philadelphia: Fortress, 1981), 221–23, for other possible dates and sources (including a later Jewish polemic against Christians) ranging from the last decades of the first century BCE to the second century CE.

11. There was also a *2 Enoch* (late first century CE) and *3 Enoch* (fifth–sixth century CE). The latter is certainly Christian, while the former may well be anti-Christian.

12. See Adler and VanderKam, *Jewish Apocalyptic Heritage*, 70–80.

13. The text is most accessible in *The Old Testament Pseudepigrapha*, ed. Charlesworth, 2:249–96; however, a new edition is being developed in light of the recent scholarship.

14. J. R. Levison, "Adam and Eve, Life of," *Anchor Bible Dictionary*, 1:64–66.

15. M. de Jonge, "The Christian Origin of the Life of Adam and Eve," in *Pseudepigrapha of the Old Testament as Part of Christian Literature: The Case of the Testaments of the XII Patriarchs and the Greek Life of Adam and Eve* (Leiden: Brill, 2003), 184–87, 198–200.

16. De Jonge, "The Christian Origin of the Life of Adam and Eve," 187–98; see also M. de Jonge and L. M. White, "The Washing of Adam in the Acherusian Lake (Greek *Life of Adam and Eve* 37.3) in the Context of Early Christian Notions of the Afterlife," in *Pseudepigrapha of the Old Testament as Part of Christian Literature*, 201–27.

17. See de Jonge, *Pseudepigrapha of the Old Testament as Part of Christian Literature*, 21, 24–28.

18. This is how Justin quotes and interprets the passage in *Apology* 1.41.1–4. In this case, it looks as though the words were added to the text by Christians, rather than being removed by Jews, as Justin alleges.

19. M. de Jonge, "The Christian Transmission of Pseudepigrapha: Some Cases," in *Pseudepigrapha of the Old Testament as Part of Christian Literature*, 39–68; T. A. Bergren, "Christian Influence on the Transmission History of 4, 5, and 6 Ezra," in *Jewish Apocalyptic Heritage*, 102–28.

20. M. de Jonge, "*The Testament of the Twelve Patriarchs* as a Document Transmitted by Christians," in *Pseudepigrapha of the Old Testament as Part of Christian Literature*, 84–106.

21. Notice that Virgil's *Eclogue* 4 (sometimes referred to as Roman "messianism") opens with a reference to "Cumae's song." See the quotation and discussion in Chapter 3.

22. J. J. Collins, "Sibylline Oracles," *Anchor Bible Dictionary*, 6:2–6.

23. The tradition is reflected in later Christian art, as seen in the strong presence of the Sibyl and the Delphic oracle in Michelangelo's composition in the Sistine Chapel.

24. O. Wintermute, "Elijah, Apocalypse of," *Anchor Bible Dictionary,* 2:466–69; D. Frankfurter, *Elijah in Upper Egypt: The Apocalypse of Elijah and Early Egyptian Christianity* (Minneapolis: Fortress, 1993).

25. D. Frankfurter, "The Legacy of Jewish Apocalypses in Early Christianity: Regional Trajectories," in *Jewish Apocalyptic Heritage,* 129–200.

26. Edessa is modern Urfa in eastern Turkey, while Nisibis is modern Nusaybin on the border between Turkey and Syria, and Mosul is in northwest Iraq.

27. The Syriac *Peshitta* preserves the most important lines of this tradition for the development of the biblical canon and is generally thought to have originated in Edessa and/or Adiabene. In the New Testament it seems to depend in part on an older Syriac version (called the *Vetus Syra*) that was in turn based on older materials such as Tatian's *Diatessaron* (see below).

28. See Chapter 12. This is the view of H. Koester, *Introduction to the New Testament,* 2d ed., 2 vols. (Berlin: De Gruyter, 2000), 2:190, also discussed in Chapter 12.

29. J. H. Charlesworth, "Solomon, Odes of," *Anchor Bible Dictionary,* 6:114–15. A relationship between *Odes of Solomon* and the Gospel of John is widely accepted, but the lines of dependency are debated. See Chapter 12.

30. H. J. W. Drijvers, "Syrian Christianity and Judaism," in *History and Religion in Late Antique Syria* (Aldershot: Variorum, 1994), 129–30. Though the *Diatessaron* is mentioned by several ancient authors, only one Greek fragment of it has been found at Dura Europos (see Box 17.1). Its effort at harmonizing the Gospels will be discussed further in Chapter 17.

31. Eusebius *Church History* 4.29.6; however, Irenaeus attributes it to Saturninus (Satornilus), a younger contemporary of Ignatius at Antioch (*Against Heresies* 1.28). Of course, neither legend is certain, and it is possible that both have an element of history, insofar as this radical form of Christian asceticism seems to have originated in Syria.

32. H. W. Attridge, "Thomas, Acts of," *Anchor Bible Dictionary,* 6:531–34.

33. The *Acts of Thomas* was probably patterned after one or more of the second-century apocryphal acts. For more on the genre in Christianity, see below.

34. John Chrysostom *Homilies on Hebrews* 26.2 (which dates from sometime between 381 and 404 CE).

35. J. D. Turner, "Thomas the Contender, Book of," *Anchor Bible Dictionary,* 6:529–30.

36. P. A. Mirecki, "Thomas, Infancy Gospel of," *Anchor Bible Dictionary,* 6:540–44.

37. See Irenaeus *Against Heresies* 1.20.1.

38. Mark 3:18; Matt. 10:3; the parallel name in Luke's list is Judas, son of James (Luke 6:16; Acts 1:13); some scholars take the reference to Judas in John 14:22 to be to Thaddaeus instead of Thomas.

39. The legend is preserved in various places, including Eusebius *Church History* 1.13.

40. The text of "letters" as reported by Eusebius (*Church History* 1.13.6–10) is slightly different from that in the two identical inscriptions found at Ephesus and Philippi, thus indicating that the legends circulated independently from the version in Eusebius. See K. E. McVey, "Abgar, Epistle of Christ to," *Anchor Bible Dictionary,* 1:12–13; and L. M. White, "Urban Development and Social Change in Imperial Ephesos," in *Ephesos, Metropolis of Asia,* ed. H. Koester (Harrisburg, PA: Trinity Press International, 1995), 38–39.

41. H. J. W. Drijvers, "Jews and Christians in Edessa," in *History and Religion in Late Antique Syria,* 90–96.

42. *Church History* 2.15.

43. *Church History* 2.16–17. Philo's description, which shows some affinities to the Essenes, is found in his treatise *On the Contemplative Life.*

44. *Church History* 2.24.

45. There are numerous discrepancies connected with Eusebius's account. In his *Chronicon,* Eusebius places Mark's departure for Alexandria in the third year of Claudius, i.e., 43–44 CE. In contrast, Paul's account of the Jerusalem conference (Gal. 2:1–10) would place Peter, James, and John still in Jerusalem through the late 40s.

46. M. Meyer, "Mark, Secret Gospel of," *Anchor Bible Dictionary,* 4:558–59. There is still considerable controversy over this letter of Clement discovered in 1958 by M. Smith, but a number of scholars think it is genuine and reflects an authentic component in the literary trajectory of the Markan Gospel.

47. Paul refers to him in 1 Cor. 1:12; 3:4–6; 4:6; 16:12, but never mentions anything about his background. The legend that he was already a Christian is based on a variant reading found in one manuscript of Acts 18:24–25; Codex D (Bezae, fifth century) adds "he had been instructed in his homeland in the word of the Lord."

48. B. A. Pearson, "Christianity in Egypt," *Anchor Bible Dictionary,* 1:954–60; B. A. Pearson and J. E. Goehring, *The Roots of Egyptian Christianity* (Philadelphia: Fortress, 1986), 132–59; C. H. Roberts, *Manuscript, Society, and Belief in Early Christian Egypt* (London: Oxford University Press, 1979).

49. R. Cameron, "Hebrews, Gospel of the," *Anchor Bible Dictionary,* 3:105–6. Note that the *Gospel of the Hebrews* tells of a postresurrection appearance of Jesus to his brother James. This episode is reflected in the earliest oral tradition (1 Cor. 15:7) but is otherwise omitted in most Gospel traditions.

50. There is a Coptic *Gospel of the Egyptians* in the Nag Hammadi library (NHC III.2 and IV.2), but it is an entirely unrelated work.

51. Irenaeus *Against Heresies* 1.23–27.

52. We shall see this motif in the last two sections of this chapter.

53. P. A. Mirecki, "Basilides," *Anchor Bible Dictionary,* 1:624–25; K. Rudolf, *Gnosis: The Nature and History of Gnosticism* (San Francisco: Harper & Row, 1984), 309–12; B. Layton, *The Gnostic Scriptures* (New York: Doubleday, 1987), 417–44.

54. P. A. Mirecki, "Valentinus," *Anchor Bible Dictionary,* 6:783–84; Layton, *The Gnostic Scriptures,* 267–353.

55. B. Pearson, "Nag Hammadi Codices," *Anchor Bible Dictionary,* 4:984–92; J. M. Robinson and R. Smith, *The Nag Hammadi Library in English,* 3d ed. (San Francisco: HarperSanFrancisco, 1988).

56. B. Layton, "Prolegomena to the Study of Ancient Gnosticism," in *The Social World of the First Christians,* ed. L. M. White and O. L. Yarbrough (Minneapolis: Fortress, 1995), 334–50; M. A. Williams, *Rethinking "Gnosticism": An Argument for Dismantling a Dubious Category* (Princeton, NJ: Princeton University Press, 1996); K. L. King, *What Is Gnosticism?* (Cambridge, MA: Harvard University Press, Belknap Press, 2003).

57. Apuleius is the principal example in Latin. Other examples in Greek include Chariton's *Chaereas and Callirhoe* (second century); Achilles Tatius's *Leucippe and Clitophon* (ca. 200); Longus's *Daphnis and Chloe* (early third century); Heliodorus's *The Ethopian Tale* (or *Theagenes and Charicleia,* ca. 220); and Xenephon of Ephesus's *An Ephesian Tale* (or *Anthia and Habrocomes,* ca. 260). For texts with introductions, see B. P. Reardon, *Collected Ancient Greek Novels* (Berkeley: University of California Press, 1989); for the genre, see T. Hägg, *The Novel in Antiquity* (Berkeley: University of California Press, 1983).

58. See R. F. Stoops, *The Apocryphal Acts of the Apostles in Intertextual Perspectives,* Semeia 80 (Atlanta: Scholars Press, 1997).

59. For text and introduction, see E. Hennecke and W. Schneemelcher, eds., *New Testament Apocrypha,* 2 vols. (Philadelphia: Westminster, 1964), 2:390–425.

60. See D. R. MacDonald, *The Apocryphal Acts of Apostles,* Semeia 38 (Atlanta: Scholars Press, 1986); *Christianizing Homer: The Odyssey, Plato and the Acts of Andrew* (New York: Oxford University Press, 1990).

61. R. Pervo, *Profit with Delight: The Literary Genre of the Acts of the Apostles* (Minneapolis: Fortress, 1987).

62. Irenaeus *Against Heresies* 3.3.4; cf. Eusebius *Church History* 4.14; 5.20.4–8.

63. *Who Is the Rich Man That Will Be Saved?* 42; cf. Eusebius *Church History* 3.39.3–4.

64. For text and introduction, see Hennecke and Schneemelcher, eds., *New Testament Apocrypha*, 2:188–258. See also J. N. Bremmer, *The Apocryphal Acts of John* (Kampen: Pharos, 1995).

65. *Church History* 3.25.6.

66. E. Pagels, *The Johannine Gospel in Gnostic Exegesis* (Nashville, TN: Abingdon, 1973).

67. *Apology* 1.26.1–3.

68. Irenaeus *Against Heresies* 1.23.2; Eusebius *Church History* 2.13.1–5.

69. For text and introduction, see Hennecke and Schneemelcher, eds., *New Testament Apocrypha*, 2:259–322 (Peter), 322–90 (Paul). See also R. F. Stoops, "Peter, Acts of," *Anchor Bible Dictionary*, 5:267–68.

70. P. Sellew, "Paul, Acts of," *Anchor Bible Dictionary*, 5:202–3; D. MacDonald, *The Legend and the Apostle: The Battle for Paul in Story and Canon* (Philadelphia: Westminster, 1983); V. Burrus, *Chastity as Autonomy: Women in the Stories of the Apocryphal Acts* (Lewiston: Edwin Mellen, 1987). See also A. van den Hoek and J. Herrmann, "Thecla the Beast Fighter," *Studia Philonica Annual* 13 (2001), 212–49; and J. Herrmann and A. van den Hoek, *Light from the Age of Augustine: Late Antique Ceramics from North Africa* (2d ed.; ISAC; Austin: The University of Texas, 2003), 59–60.

71. Schneemelcher's translation, adapted by the author.

72. F. S. Jones, "Clementines, Pseudo-," *Anchor Bible Dictionary*, 1:1061–62. For a partial text, see Hennecke and Schneemelcher, eds., *New Testament Apocrypha*, 2:532–70.

73. The *Homilies* are thus meant to represent the preaching of Peter, and it has thus been argued that one of the sources for the work was a collection called the *Kerygmata Petrou*, dating to sometime before 200 CE. It is possible, however, that the *Kerygmata Petrou* was just the designation for these core teachings that James (and Clement) were to guard carefully as alluded to in the cover letter of Peter to James.

74. References to Simon (Magus) are scattered throughout the *Homilies* (e.g., II.15–17; II.22–26; II.35; III.38–43; XI.35; XVII.13–19).

75. Found in *Recognitions* 1.27–71. See F. S. Jones, *An Ancient Jewish Christian Source on the History of Christianity: Pseudo-Clementine Recognitions 1.27–71* (Atlanta: Scholars Press, 1995); R. Bauckham, "The Origin of the Ebionites," in *The Image of the Judaeo-Christians in Ancient Jewish and Christian Literature*, ed. P. Tomson and D. Lambers-Petry (Tübingen: Mohr Siebeck, 2003).

76. Irenaeus *Against Heresies* 1.26.2; 3.21.1; 5.1.3; Epiphanius *Panarion* 30.16.6–9. Cf. W. L. Peterson, "Ebionites, Gospel of the," *Anchor Bible Dictionary*, 2:261–62. This work might have been known by other titles in the second and third centuries.

77. It may go back to Jesus blessing the "poor": Matt. 5:3; Luke 6:20 (from the Beatitudes, an important unit of material from the Q tradition). Compare Rom. 15:26 (in reference to Paul's collection for the "poor among the saints at Jerusalem"); cf. Gal. 2:10.

78. Origen was aware of this derivation (*Against Celsus* 2.1; *On First Principals* 4.3.8).

79. *Against Celsus* 5.61; cf. Eusebius *Church History* 3.27.2–3.

80. Cf. Epiphanius *Panarion* 28.5.1–3.

81. As translated by W. Meeks and adapted by the author.

82. Perhaps based on Gal. 1:8–9, 15–17, but more likely as filtered through the account of Acts 9. They seem to have interpreted the "blinding light" as Satan's descent from heaven.

Chapter 16

1. It was known as the Quartodeciman (or "fourteenth") controversy. See Eusebius *Church History* 3.31.3; 5.23–25 (esp. 5.24.1–8); S. G. Hall, "The Origins of Easter," *Studia Patristica* 15 (1984): 554–67; T. Talley, *The Origins of the Liturgical Year* (New York: Pueblo, 1986).

2. J. J. Clabeaux, "Marcion," *Anchor Bible Dictionary*, 4:514–16. Reasons for doubt arise from the excessive polemical tone of Hippolytus's account, since he also says that Marcion's own father had excommunicated him for seducing a virgin. Cf. Epiphanius *Panarion* 42.

3. Tertullian *Prescription of Heretics* 30; cf. *Against Marcion* 1.1.

4. Irenaeus *Against Heresies* 3.3.4.

5. *Apology* 1.26.

6. Tertullian *Against Marcion* 1.19.

7. A conflicting reference by Tertullian (*Prescription of Heretics* 30) places his excommunication at Rome in the mid-170s or later, but this seems very doubtful even as a date for his death.

8. The collection of letters included Romans, 1 and 2 Corinthians, Galatians, Ephesians (which he called Laodiceans, based on Col. 4:16), Philippians, Colossians, 1 and 2 Thessalonians, and Philemon. Marcion seems to have placed the letters in a more or less chronological order, at least as he understood it, with Galatians and 1 and 2 Corinthians at the beginning, Laodiceans (Ephesians) and Colossians together, and Romans, Philippians, and Philemon near the end. He did not accept Hebrews and probably did not have knowledge of the Pastoral Epistles, if they existed at the time. The letters were also expurgated of elements he thought were added by "Judaizing" Christians.

9. On the contents of Marcion's *Gospel,* see J. J. Clabeaux, "Marcion, Gospel of," *Anchor Bible Dictionary,* 4:516–20.

10. They were restored (and numbered) by Adolf von Harnack in *Marcion: The Gospel of the Alien God,* trans. J. E. Steely and L. D. Bierma (1924; Durham: Labyrinth Press, 1990), 60–63; the translation here follows that of W. A. Meeks, *The Writings of St. Paul* (New York: Norton, 1972), 188–90.

11. Von Harnack, *Marcion,* 21.

12. Note the warning given by the bishop Cyril of Jerusalem (ca. 350 CE, in his *Catechetical Lectures* 4.4) that "orthodox" Christians need to be careful when traveling so that they do not wander into a Marcionite church by mistake; cf. Theodoret of Cyprus (ca. 450 CE) *Compendium of Heretical Myths* 25.

13. J. Knox, *Marcion and the New Testament* (Chicago: University of Chicago Press, 1942); E. C. Blackman, *Marcion and His Influence* (London: Williams & Norgate, 1948). We shall return to this issue in the next chapter.

14. F. Wisse, "Peter, Apocalypse of (NHC VII.3)," *Anchor Bible Dictionary,* 5:268–69.

15. Eusebius *Church History* 6.14.1.

16. For text and introduction, see E. Hennecke and W. Schneemelcher, eds., *New Testament Apocrypha,* 2 vols. (Philadelphia: Westminster, 1964), 2:663–83.

17. This is the view argued by R. Bauckham in several articles; see the summary and additional bibliography in R. Bauckham, "The Origin of the Ebionites," in *The Images of the Judaeo-Christians in Ancient Jewish and Christian Literature,* ed. P. J. Tomson and D. Lambers-Petry (Tübingen: Mohr Siebeck, 2003), 162–81, esp. 173.

18. This seems to be modeled in part on the parable of Luke 16:19–31, but expanded with Greco-Roman elements.

19. R. Bauckham (see note above) has argued that the *Apocalypse of Peter* was dependent on canonical 2 Peter, a document from the Roman church; however, it is also possible that the relationship goes the other way. We shall return to this issue in a later section of this chapter.

20. *Church History* 5.16.7–10; 5.17.2–3; cf. Hippolytus *Refutation of All Heresies* 8.19.1–3.

21. Eusebius *Church History* 5.16.13.

22. Epiphanius *Panarion* 48.

23. Tertullian became a Montanist in ca. 210 CE, and the *Martyrdom of Perpetua and Felicitas,* which describes an event in 203, bears strong Montanist colorings regarding Perpetua's visionary powers. The rigorous piety of Montanism seems to have remained a strong influence in North African Christianity.

24. Eusebius *Church History* 5.16.8; 5.18.2; Epiphanius *Panarion* 48.2.4; 49.1. The actual site of Pepuza has only recently been discovered; see http://www.theologie.uni-hd.de/wts/lampe/pepouza.html.

25. For further reading, see R. E. Heine, "Montanus, Montanism," *Anchor Bible Dictionary,* 4:898–902; D. E. Aune, *Prophecy in Early Christianity and the Ancient Mediterranean World* (Grand Rapids, MI: Eerdmans, 1983); W. Tabbernee, *Montanist Inscriptions and Testimonia: Epigraphic*

Sources (Macon, GA: Mercer University Press, 1996); R. E. Heine, *The Montanist Oracles and Testimonia* (Macon, GA: Mercer University Press, 1989).

26. No such title or identification is found in either the Gospel of John or 1 John. The putative connection to Johannine tradition may simply derive from later confusion of names and identities: (1) John was reportedly very old when he died, and (2) there are reports generally ascribed to Papias, bishop of Hierapolis, about a leader at Ephesus named John the Elder. According to Eusebius (*Church History* 3.39.3–8; 15–16) this John the Elder was the author of Revelation, instead of John the Apostle, son of Zebedee. Although there may have been a John the Presbyter at Ephesus who was entirely distinct from John the Apostle, the author of 2 and 3 John is probably different from both.

27. This Gaius is unidentifiable; however, it is worth noting that there is a listing for "Gaius, bishop of Ephesus" (presumably one of the earliest) in the catalog of "the seventy apostles" attributed to Hippolytus (A. Roberts and J. Donaldson, eds., *Ante-Nicene Fathers,* vol. 5 [Grand Rapids: Wm. B. Eerdman, 1971], 5:256). Ignatius, however, names Onesimus as the bishop of Ephesus at the time of his visit to Asia Minor (Ign. *Eph.* 1.3). On the "seventy," see also below.

28. A. J. Malherbe, *Social Aspects of Early Christianity,* 2d ed. (Philadelphia: Fortress, 1983), 92–112.

29. L. M. White, *The Social Origins of Christian Architecture,* 2 vols. (Harrisburg, PA: Trinity Press International, 1996–97), 1:110; see also Chapter 17.

30. R. E. Brown, *The Epistles of John,* Anchor Bible 30 (New York: Doubleday, 1982).

31. D. Rensberger, *1 John, 2 John, and 3 John,* Abingdon New Testament Commentary (Nashville, TN: Abingdon, 1997); D. M. Smith, *First, Second, and Third John,* Interpretation (Louisville, KY: John Knox, 1991); T. F. Johnson, *1, 2, and 3 John,* New International Biblical Commentary (Peabody, MA: Hendriksen, 1993).

32. J. L. Houlden, *The Johannine Epistles,* Harper's New Testament Commentary (New York: Harper & Row, 1973).

33. J. H. Elliot, "Peter, Second Epistle of," *Anchor Bible Dictionary,* 5:282–87.

34. Although the name in Greek and Latin is clearly Judas, English translations have traditionally rendered the name as Jude in order to distinguish the author from Judas Iscariot.

35. This legend is preserved in Eusebius *Church History* 3.19.1–20.5.

36. Eusebius *Church History* 1.13.4, 11. *Acts of Thomas* 1 uses the Lukan form of the list of disciples, including "Judas of James."

37. In some manuscripts of Luke, as in several of the other legends, a variant of the number is given as seventy-two, undoubtedly because it is a multiple of twelve.

38. From the *Epistle of Peter to James* (or *Kerygmata Petrou*) 1–3; cf. 4.1; cf. *Recognitions* 1.40.4; 1.34.2.

39. Eusebius *Church History* 1.12.1–5; cf. 1.10.7; 1.12.1–5; 1.13.5, 11; 2.1.2–5.

40. *Church History* 1.12.1–2; in other words, this "Cephas" has been taken by Clement and Eusebius to be different from the apostle Peter, whose name was also Cephas and who is the real referent in Gal. 2:11.

41. Eusebius *Church History* 2.23; 3.11–12, 16, 19–20, 32; 4.7–8, 11, 21–22.

42. Text in *Ante-Nicene Fathers,* 5:254–55. A number of ancient manuscripts of the New Testament also give Lebbaeus as a variant reading for Thaddaeus, or in some cases "Lebbaeus, who is called Thaddaeus," in the apostle list of Matt. 10:3 (and at Mark 3:18 in Codex D [Bezae]).

43. Cf. John 14:22: "Judas, not Iscariot," who is often equated with Thaddaeus. Although this person cannot be the author of the letter of Jude, it is not impossible that the second-century traditions made this equation. R. D. Miller, "Judas [7]," *Anchor Bible Dictionary,* 3:1090.

44. This is the view of R. Bauckham, *Jude and the Relatives of Jesus in the Early Church* (Edinburgh: Clark, 1990); and "Jude, Epistle of," *Anchor Bible Dictionary,* 3:1098–1103. It has not persuaded the majority of scholars.

45. *Church History* 2.23.25.

46. For example, the story of Noah and Lot (2 Pet. 2:4–10). J. H. Elliott, "Peter, Second Epistle of," *Anchor Bible Dictionary,* 5:282–87, esp. 284.

47. Although the Petrine tradition was equally strong in Asia Minor, as noted by Elliott ("Peter, Second Epistle of," 5:287).

48. R. Bauckham, *Jude and 2 Peter*, Word Biblical Commentary (Dallas, TX: Word, 1983), esp. 148–62.

49. Eusebius *Church History* 3.28.2; Justin *Dialogue with Trypho* 80.

50. This collection contained the ten letters attributed to Paul plus Hebrews. The manuscript breaks off at 1 Thess. 5:28, but calculations show that there are only enough pages left in the codex at this point to accommodate 2 Thessalonians and Philemon, but not the Pastoral Epistles.

51. Tertullian (*Against Marcion* 5.21) says that Marcion rejected them even though he accepted Philemon. What this really means, however, is that they do not appear at what was becoming their "normal" place in the canon list by Tertullian's time (early third century).

52. *Against Heresies* 1.1; 1.16.3; 2.14.7; 3.14.1.

53. Clement of Alexandria *Miscellanies* 2.11; Jerome reports that Origen wrote a commentary on Titus, but none on 1 and 2 Timothy.

54. It may well be that this Linus was supposed to be the same person who succeeded Peter as bishop of Rome and who died in ca. 80 CE (Irenaeus *Against Heresies* 3.3.3; Eusebius *Church History* 3.2.1; 3.4.8; 3.13.1; 3.21.1). It is not clear, however, which came first, the legend of Linus or 2 Timothy.

55. The *Acts of Peter* 1 has Paul departing Rome, but for Spain. Nonetheless, this shows something of the later legends that circulated about Paul's subsequent travels.

56. *Church History* 2.22.2.

57. It should be remembered that an abridged version, called just the *Acts of Paul*, developed later and was very popular in orthodox circles. One might guess that the Pastorals represent part of the impulse and the mechanism for generating the "normative" legends about Paul.

58. E. Richards, *The Secretary and the Letters of Paul* (Tübingen: Mohr-Siebeck, 1991).

59. J. D. Quinn, "Timothy and Titus, Epistles to," *Anchor Bible Dictionary,* 6:560–71.

60. J. N. D. Kelly, *A Commentary on the Pastoral Epistles: I Timothy, II Timothy, and Titus* (New York: Harper & Row, 1963), following J. Jeremias.

61. Key passages include 2 Tim. 3:12–15 and others in a similar vein.

62. P. N. Harrison, *The Problem of the Pastoral Epistles* (London: Oxford University Press, 1921).

63. Quinn, "Timothy and Titus, Epistles to," 6:569; J. D. Quinn, *The Letters to Titus and Timothy,* Anchor Bible (New York: Doubleday, 1995); R. H. Fuller, "The Pastoral Epistles," in *Ephesians, Colossians, 2 Thessalonians, and the Pastoral Epistles,* ed. G. Krodel (Philadelphia: Fortress, 1978), 97–121.

64. Here the rendering of the RSV is much closer to the Greek.

65. So notice the comment of Hegesippus preserved by Eusebius: "All those who begin from them [the heretics, such as Marcion] as we said, are called Christians just as the name of philosophy is common to philosophers though their doctrines are not held in common" (*Church History* 4.11.9).

66. The claim is made more explicit by Justin Martyr (*Apology* 1.58; cf. *Dialogue with Trypho* 69–70).

67. A. Roberts and J. Donaldson, trans., *The Ante-Nicene Fathers,* vol. 1 (repr. Grand Rapids, MI: Eerdmans, 1973), 347–48.

68. Roberts and Donaldson, *Ante-Nicene Fathers,* 1:315.

69. This idea is the basis for what came to be known as the "rule of faith" in Irenaeus (*Against Heresies* 1.10.1; 3.42) and Tertullian (*Prescription of Heretics* 13).

70. Roberts and Donaldson, *Ante-Nicene Fathers,* 3:243.

71. W. Bauer, *Orthodoxy and Heresy in the Early Church* (1934; Eng. trans.: Philadelphia: Fortress, 1972).

72. The last is the view of J. M. Robinson and H. Koester, *Trajectories Through Early Christianity* (Philadelphia: Fortress, 1971). The various views are nicely surveyed in A. Hultgren, *The Rise of Normative Christianity* (Minneapolis: Fortress, 1994), 7–18. See also J. D. G. Dunn, *Unity and Diversity*

in the New Testament: An Inquiry into the Character of Earliest Christianity (2d. ed.; London: SCM, 1990).

73. J. G. Gager, *Kingdom and Community: The Social World of Early Christianity* (Englewood Cliffs, NJ: Prentice Hall, 1975), 79 (emphasis added).

74. So of. 1 Cor. 5:9–13; Matt. 18.15–20. With the latter one can also make direct comparisons with the procedures for exclusion from the Qumran community in *The Rule of the Community* (also called *The Manual of Discipline*) from the Dead Sea Scrolls.

Chapter 17

1. Cf. *Church History* 6.6; 6.11; 6.13–14.

2. L. M. White, *The Social Origins of Christian Architecture*, 2 vols. (Harrisburg, PA: Trinity Press International, 1996–97), 1:107–23; 2:1–32.

3. *Martyrdom of Justin and His Associates* 3; White, *Social Origins* 2:42–43.

4. *Miscellanies* 7.5.

5. Clement *Paedagogue* 1; see also Jude 12 and *Did.* 9–10.

6. *Miscellanies* 1.5.

7. A. Roberts and J. Donaldson, eds., *Ante-Nicene Fathers* (repr. Grand Rapids: Wm. B. Eerdmans, 1971), 3:250–51 (adapted by the author).

8. *Dialogue with Trypho* 73; see Chapter 15.

9. 2 Pet. 3:15–17; see Chapter 16.

10. Eusebius *Church History* 3.39.4; H. Y. Gamble, "The Pauline Corpus and the Early Christian Book," in *Paul and the Legacies of Paul*, ed. W. S. Babcock (Dallas, TX: Southern Methodist University Press, 1990), 271.

11. Not the traditional translation of the verse, this rendering of the Greek is given as an alternative in the RSV and NRSV and is thought by many scholars to reflect the original sense more accurately.

12. *Dialogue with Trypho* 100.1.

13. *Apology* 1.66–67.

14. J. J. Clabeaux, *A Lost Edition of Paul's Letters: A Reassessment of the Text of the Pauline Corpus Attested by Marcion* (Washington, DC: Catholic Biblical Association, 1989).

15. Gamble, "Pauline Corpus," 272.

16. The ten-letter corpus was referred to in this manner in the Muratorian Canon (ca. third to fourth century); Gamble, "Pauline Corpus," 272.

17. As in *1 Clem.* 13.2, 4.

18. 1 Cor. 7:10–11, possibly a citation of a "teaching of Jesus" (cf. Mark 10:11–12). The earliest compilation of such teachings probably dates to roughly the same period (the 50s and 60s CE), when the Q tradition began to consolidate. See Chapter 6.

19. D. M. Smith, *John Among the Gospels* (Minneapolis: Fortress, 1997); see Chapter 12.

20. H. Y. Gamble, "Canon, New Testament," *Anchor Bible Dictionary*, 1:855.

21. Eusebius *Church History* 6.14.7.

22. H. Y. Gamble, "Canon, New Testament," 1:854.

23. *Apology* 1.66–67.

24. Matt. 27:56; 28:1 (Mary Magdalene, Mary the mother of James and Joseph, and the mother of the sons of Zebedee); Mark 15:47 (Mary Magdalene and Mary the mother of Joses); Mark 16:1 (Mary Magdalene, Mary the mother of James, and Salome); Luke 24:10 (Mary Magdalene, Joanna, Mary the mother of James). Tatian apparently resolves this list into five: Mary Magdalene, Mary the mother of James and Joseph/Joses (cf. Mark 15:40), Salome, Joanna, and the mother of the sons of Zebedee.

25. H. von Campenhausen, *The Formation of the Christian Bible* (Philadelphia: Fortress, 1972), 182.

26. A. Roberts and J. Donaldson, *Ante-Nicene Fathers,* 1:330.

27. Cf. *The Epistle of the Apostles*, a baptismal catechism from ca. 180, and a text found in Hippolytus *Apostolic Tradition* 21.12–18 describing the baptismal confession practiced in Rome at the beginning of the third century; and *The Old Roman Baptismal Symbol* (or Confession), which is preserved in a late-fourth-century text but represents an early liturgical from Rome. J. N. D. Kelly, *Early Christian Creeds* (London: Longmans, 1960), 88–91; 114–15.

28. L. M. McDonald, *The Formation of the Christian Biblical Canon* (Nashville, TN: Abingdon, 1988), 93.

29. Irenaeus *Against Heresies* 4.28.1.

30. *Against Heresies* 4.15.2.

31. *Against Heresies* 3.3.3–4; 3.4.1.

32. Roberts and Donaldson, *Ante-Nicene Fathers,* 1:428.

33. Tertullian *Against Marcion* 4.2.2–5.

34. See *Against Praxeas* 15. Tertullian prefers the Latin term *instrumentum* rather than *testamentum,* so it is difficult to say that he meant the same thing. Cf. Von Campenhausen, *Formation of the Christian Bible,* 267–68.

35. Eusebius *Church History* 6.14.5–7.

36. *Church History* 6.14.2–3.